HAMILTON FISH

THE INNER HISTORY
OF THE GRANT ADMINISTRATION

HAMILTON FISH IN LATER LIFE

AMERICAN CLASSICS

HAMILTON FISH

The Inner History
of the Grant Administration

By
ALLAN NEVINS

With an Introduction by
JOHN BASSETT MOORE

VOLUME II
Illustrated

REVISED EDITION

FREDERICK UNGAR PUBLISHING CO.
NEW YORK

CONTENTS

Volume I

Volume II

CONTENTS

ILLUSTRATIONS

Volume I

ILLUSTRATIONS

Volume II

AT the very moment when Fish, De Grey, and the other members of the Joint Commission buckled down to the labors which resulted in the Treaty of Washington, the quarrel between the Administration and Sumner came to its bitter climax. The Massachusetts autocrat still enjoyed a greater prestige than any other Senator, still exercised a potent sway over his old Abolitionist and Radical following. But Grant was of too military a temper to endure insubordination long. He and the hard-fisted politicians about him resolved that Sumner should be shorn of the chairmanship of the Foreign Relations Committee; and immediately after the new Congress opened on March 4, 1871, they brought the question before the Republican caucus. In a sense, it was a battle between the old Republican order and the new; between the last great representative of the Vindictives of the period of sectional upheaval— for Thad Stevens, Ben Wade, Stanton were all gone—and the rising new school of Stalwarts who based their political power upon the strength of special interests and of well-geared machines.

Sober friends of both Grant and Sumner had hoped that their conflict, bitter indeed when Sumner defeated the Santo Domingo treaty and the President asked for Motley's resignation, might end at that point. Each had dealt the other a heavy blow. The Santo Domingo treaty had deserved defeat; Motley had deserved dismissal. Why not let the quarrel end there? But such hopes took little account of the temperament of two born fighters. Neither Sumner, fierce in his prejudices, fiery in his oratory, adept in stinging epithets, nor Grant, the grim exponent of relentless slugging warfare, was a man whose blood cooled quickly. A vindictive spirit rowelled them both. Lurid newspaper stories and mendacious gossip added to their resentment. The battle had to be fought to the grim end, and that end might easily be predicted— for Grant was armed with the greater power, and determined to halt at nothing to vanquish the haughty Bostonian.[1]

I

It must be counted against Sumner that he took the aggressive and rushed upon his fate. It was he who kept the Motley controversy alive

[1] Cf. Schouler, *United States*, VII, 167.

throughout the fall of 1870; it was he who reopened the Santo Domingo quarrel in December by the gratuitous invective of his "Naboth's Vineyard" speech. He was probably the most intolerant man that American history has ever known; and as it is written that they who take the sword shall perish by the sword, so also it might be written that those who resort to intolerance shall perish—yea, and their good fame after them shall perish too—by the intolerance they create.

In private conversation during the latter part of 1870, Sumner unquestionably referred to Grant in highly opprobrious terms. The evidence is overwhelming. Bancroft Davis testifies that the Senator "spoke publicly, abusively, and insultingly of the President" even before Motley's recall.[2] The historian Schouler, then a young lawyer in Washington, heard that he stigmatized Grant as "a colossus of ignorance" and Fish as "a gentleman in aspect with the heart of a lackey." [3] Sumner's biographer admits that "there was doubtless free talk at the Senator's house." [4] On a lecture tour in the autumn of 1870 he spoke with great bitterness of Grant to a Chicago reporter, and a highly offensive version of his statements (which he called garbled) was telegraphed throughout the nation. In December, 1870, Boutwell told Fish at the White House that within a week Sumner had mentioned to him charges against the President so outrageous that he was unwilling to repeat them. "Sumner," he added, "forgets what he says." "Yes," rejoined Fish, "Sumner is crazy—a monomaniac—upon all matters relating to his own importance and his relations with the President." They discussed his charge that Grant had been intoxicated at their famous initial conversation upon Santo Domingo. "I was there," said Boutwell. "He was no more drunk or excited than when we left him upstairs five minutes ago —no more so than Sumner himself." [5]

Conkling, spending a Sunday evening in January with Fish, likewise expressed himself warmly upon Sumner's vituperative tongue. "I don't like to think the man a deliberate liar, but he certainly makes extraordinary statements and then denies them." Lyman Trumbull had remarked one day in the Senate: "Conkling, you annoy Sumner very much. He doesn't mind what I say to him; I call him a liar and prove it, and he is quite indifferent to that. But you argue him into a perfect fury." Fish again said that he believed—like Richard H. Dana, Jr.,

[2] Davis, *Mr. Fish and the Alabama Claims,* 56.
[3] Schouler, *op. cit.,* 168.
[4] Pierce, *Sumner,* IV, 454.
[5] Diary, December 23, 1870.

Tenterden   Sir Stafford Northcote   De Grey   Bernard
                    Macdonald   Thornton

THE BRITISH HIGH COMMISSIONERS, 1871

and others—that Sumner was no longer wholly sane. "Upon a certain class of questions, and whenever his own importance and influence are concerned, or upon anything relating to himself or his views past or present or his ambition, he loses the power of logical reasoning, and becomes contradictory and violent. This is mental derangement." [6]

Though during the autumn Fish and Sumner had maintained the outward forms of courtesy, their relations showed a steadily increasing tension. The Secretary felt hurt because Motley had made no reply to his letter of personal regret at the time of Grant's abrupt demand for a resignation. The Boston *Advertiser* and a few other New England journals seized every opportunity to assail him in cutting terms. After one bitter attack by the *Advertiser* which bore an inspired look, he sent a pained letter to Sumner. Referring to his protracted efforts to protect the Minister, he wrote: "If Mr. Motley be, as I suppose him to be, a just man and a grateful one, if *he knows the truth* he would blister his tongue and tear out his heart before he would turn upon me." Instead of a reasonable reply, Sumner poured forth a long letter of reproach.[7] He denied that Motley had ever spoken abusively of Fish (Sumner always had a peculiar definition of abuse when uttered on his own side). He accused Fish of being a party to the removal. He controverted in offensive language a number of incidental statements that Fish had made. And he concluded in these peevish terms:

Allow me to ask you, in all candor, if during these latter weeks you have spoken to me of Motley with any friendliness? Did you not even give support to the President's first allegation that he was not enough American? Do you not still adhere to the theory that he volunteered to write his instructions? Do you not disparage his magnificent Memoir, which while precisely coincident with the September dispatch states the American case with at least equal force? Did you not even menace a McCracken exposure, being a letter or communication last December as to private conversation, without, as in the other McCracken case, giving him an opportunity of reply? These things do not seem to me very consistent with that "generosity" which lays him under such perpetual obligation.

But why go into these details? The removal was a mistake and a wrong. So it will be considered historically—the most grievous personal wrong ever done in the Department of State, and from the character of the victim not to be forgotten. This is at least my judgment. Sincerely and unfeignedly, and with the friendship of years stirring in me, I regret your participation in it. But you may ask, "What could I do!" Let me give the remark which I hear con-

---

[6] Diary, January 8, 1871.   [7] Fish Papers.

stantly: "Mr. Fish, is a gentleman; why did he not resign?" Had you done this, there would have been no question as to your position—no question as to your sense of justice or friendship for Motley. Instead of this you vindicate the act. . . .

P. S. An elaborate article in the *Independent* of September 8th, in many respects excellent and just to Motley and regretful for the Administration, has another curious allegation, that Motley had given offence by correspondence with Mr. Sumner! Now, I have not received a line from Motley which you have not seen, and for months before his recall I had not written him one word on any political question—nor anything but a note of introduction. The newspaper allegation seems sustained by a letter just received from a distinguished Senator, giving what the President said to the Senator—that he wished the Minister to represent him. This is a new stone to hurl.

In speaking of Motley's removal as the most grievous *personal wrong* in the history of the Department of State, and destined to be so chronicled hereafter, I did not remark on its absolute eccentricity. It is unique—a paragon—a "none-such." Never before has the Department of State played the part of King Pyrrhus' elephant and trampled down its own friends—trampled down an illustrious citizen abroad—also the Senators and Representatives of a Republican State, and still more the people of this faithful State, and the sentiments of scholars and gentlemen throughout the country.

To the last, despite Motley's sullen behaviour, Fish strove to shield his proud spirit from further humiliation. For example, we find in the diary:

October 21, 1870.— . . . While speaking of the British Mission, the President proposed to recall Motley at once. I advised against doing so. It certainly is very indelicate in Motley to remain under the circumstances. A sensitive man, with high and generous instincts of self-respect, would not remain; but one who would refuse to resign a position of confidence held at the pleasure of the party who requests his resignation will do things that cannot be expected from one of high honor or of nice instincts. Nevertheless, I urge the President not to recall him until his successor reaches there. It would make a clamor, and his friends would call it persecution. As it is, he must be losing the respect of those who reflect on the subject. For the present, the President acquiesces; how long he will remain quiescent, I know not. He is apt to hold on to an idea of the kind which has once made a lodgment.

But the temperamental historian, ignorant of Fish's course, bore him nothing but ill-will. On November 10, at Grant's direction, the Secretary transmitted a formal notice of his recall. Motley immediately sat down and penned a contentious defense entitled "End of Mission," covering more than sixty pages of manuscript, which he mailed to Fish on December 7, 1870.[8] In it he maintained that he had done his duty faithfully and had always shown "scrupulous and minute fidelity to instructions"; he declared that after condemning Motley's first interview with Lord Clarendon, Fish had then expressed precisely the same statements in his September note; he loftily asserted that his resignation had been demanded "for no reason whatever"; and he devoted three paragraphs to the theory that Grant had dismissed him in order to obtain revenge upon Sumner. Obviously he gave this theory full credence. He ironically noted as "an historical fact" that the Senate had rejected the Santo Domingo treaty June 30, and that the request for his resignation had been dated July 1.

Motley's needlessly quarrelsome paper reached Washington at the same time that Sumner rose in the Senate, December 21, to deliver his needlessly abusive speech entitled "Naboth's Vineyard." This erudite philippic, pronounced with intense passion, was ludicrously disproportioned to its occasion.[9] Grant had asked in his annual message for a commission to negotiate a treaty with the Dominican Government for the annexation of that country. Knowing the Senate would never consent, Morton and other Administration leaders introduced a resolution for a mere commission of inquiry. This was essentially a face-saving proposal; it might furnish valuable information, and would commit the United States to nothing. The treaty idea was dead. But Sumner prepared an invective which recalled his fiercest utterances against slavery. He charged that the resolution committed Congress to a "dance of blood," and went further by declaring that it marked "another stage in a drama of blood"—although not a drop had yet been shed. He asserted that Grant's use of the navy in Haitian waters had been a usurpation of powers, involving acts of violence and war in violation of the Constitution. He accused the President of greedy designs upon Haiti. In caustic passages he likened him to Franklin Pierce and James Buchanan, asserting that his policies recalled the Kansas-Nebraska Act and Pierce's measures in behalf of that law—recalled the Lecompton Constitution and Buchanan's efforts to force it upon

[8] Published in Senate Exec. Doc. 11, 41st Congress, 3rd Session, p. 27 ff.

[9] Published in Sumner's Works, XIV, 89–131. Sumner was shooting a dead raccoon. To be sure, Grant had written Baez, October 17, 1870: "My interest in extending the authority of the United States over the territory and people of San Domingo is unabated. My thorough conviction of the mutual benefits to both peoples by the union of the two nations is unchanged. On the assembling of Congress I shall make such recommendations as may then seem proper for the accomplishment of this object." Grant's Letterbooks. But the scheme was now politically impossible.

Kansas. He even urged Vice-President Colfax to counsel Grant, before it was too late, to shun all approach to the ignominious example of these men and of Andrew Johnson.

In the night-long debate which ensued the whole host of Administration Senators descended upon Sumner.[10] His arrogance, intolerance, and assumption of moral superiority had made enemies on every side. Morton and Harlan kept their tempers, but Chandler and Conkling flung acrid personalities at him. The sharpest thrusts of all came from Edmunds of Vermont, who declared that Sumner had once more demonstrated "that the worst enemy he has in North America today is himself." As dawn broke on December 22, Morton's resolution was carried, 32 to 9.[11] All the wounds of the previous spring had been torn open again; Sumner's intemperate speech was a fresh declaration of war upon the President. Against his and Motley's attack, some defense seemed imperative.

With good reason, Fish felt outraged by Motley's final paper. It took the form of an official dispatch, although Motley had ceased to hold office, and was professedly written from the legation, though that legation was no longer in his charge. Moreover, Motley sent a copy to Sumner, who promptly began talking about it. Propriety requires that any Minister who wishes to place his views in the legation archives must ask permission, but Motley had assumed his right to do so. The Secretary might have thrown the paper into the fire, but he preferred to answer it. "Questioning the taste and denying the right of his assumption, I nevertheless allow a place in the diplomatic records of the country to Mr. Motley's history of the end of his mission." In a letter of December 30 to Moran, he demolished all the really important arguments that Motley had advanced.[12]

It is unnecessary to rehearse Fish's telling summary in detail. He showed how grossly the Minister had disobeyed his instructions in his first interview with Lord Clarendon, and explained that only kindness had then saved him from immediate dismissal. He pointed out that Motley's initial offense was, however, less serious than the second—his omission to state that he had submitted the report of his interview with Clarendon in writing to that gentleman before sending it to Fish:

[10] *Congressional Globe*, 41st Cong., 3rd Sess., p. 51 ff., December 20, 21, 1870.
[11] Thirty Senators absent; Pierce, *Sumner*, IV, 459.
[12] Published in Senate Exec. Doc. 11, 41st Congress, 3rd Sess., 27 ff.

Had that submission been known at the date of my acknowledgment, on the 28th of June, of his statement, it cannot be doubted that a very different reply would have been made. . . .

When the President was informed that Mr. Motley had withheld this important fact until after he had obtained the acknowledgment and the reply of the Department to a dispatch which had already drawn to the utmost upon his kindness and forbearance, it may be imagined that his confidence and his respect for his Minister did not remain as they had been. From that time it was impossible that he should remain as the representative of the Government longer than the exigencies of the public service, as to the other matters specially committed to his charge, might require.

So far as Motley's conduct went, the "Moran letter" was conclusive. Unfortunately, in its rebuttal of the accusation regarding Grant's motives it broke down, for Fish attempted to defend the indefensible. Grant *had* acted, in part, to revenge himself upon Sumner; full evidence of this lay in Fish's own diary. In his loyalty to his chief, in his consciousness that the President possessed good reasons for asking Motley's resignation, Fish went beyond the facts. He declared that the suggestion that Grant "would visit upon a third party resentments caused by real or imagined indignation against another, is unworthy of Mr. Motley." Ironically comparing Motley's arguments with Sairey Gamp's in *Martin Chuzzlewit,* he explained the date of Grant's demand by referring to the death of Lord Clarendon:

To some minds *post hoc, propter hoc* is conclusive of cause and effect. . . . It were useless to attempt to refute such logic. But Mr. Motley and the world know that the hospitality and opposition of the Senator in question to the San Domingo Treaty had accomplished all that they could accomplish toward its rejection many months before he was invited to resign. The treaty was admitted to be practically dead, and was waiting only the formal action of the Senate, for weeks and months before the decease of the illustrious statesman of Great Britain. This event, which took place on the 27th of June, determined the time for inviting Mr. Motley to make place for a successor who might be entrusted with the negotiations in case a disposition should be shown on the part of the successor of Lord Clarendon to enter upon the discussion and adjustment of the "Alabama claims."

Of course Lord Clarendon had never entered Grant's head on the day he demanded Motley's dismissal. Fish must be severely censured for this paragraph, which was uncandid if, as human responses to attack go, quite explicable. Perhaps the kindliest explanation is that in his just resentment of Motley's conduct, his zeal to defend the President, he confused the motives which he himself would have felt in demanding the resignation with those which Grant actually did feel.

With this exchange, Motley now stepped from the political stage, for which he was so ill fitted, forever. The very qualities which made him eminent as a writer had disabled him for diplomacy. Imagination, poetry, the irritability of the artist, moods of intense nervous exaltation followed by intense depression, the fervent pride of a natural aristocrat—all these were assets to a historian writing in the grand manner; but they had no place in the hard, cautious business of a legation. It is pleasant to record that his pen was soon again busy in the historic house of The Hague from which the brothers De Witt had gone forth to be torn in pieces by the mob; that his good spirits and creative capacity came back with undiminished force. When he died in 1877 in England, the Duke of Bedford inscribed over his grave the words, "John Lothrop Motley, Minister of the United States, Historian of the Dutch Republic." Of the host that admire him as an historian, how few know that he was ever Minister, or care a fig whether he made a good or bad one! After all, it was not Grant, who had taken him out of diplomacy, who did him a disservice, but Sumner, who had placed him in it.

II

The section in Fish's letter to Moran which most aroused Sumner's ire was neither the scathing indictment of Motley nor the misleading defence of Grant, but what the Senator called "Fish's insult" to himself.[13] In his letter Fish stated that the slur upon Grant's motives had originated in a source bitterly, personally, and vindictively hostile to the President.[14] Pointing out that many Senators who opposed the treaty in a generous spirit had continued to enjoy Grant's undiminished friendship, and declaring that he was singularly tolerant of honest differences of opinion, he asserted that no man living "is more sensitive to a betrayal of confidence, or would look with more scorn and contempt upon one who uses the words and the assurances of friendship to cover a secret and determined purpose of hostility." This plainly referred to Sumner; we cannot dismiss the reference as dubious, as Bancroft Davis tried to

---

[13] Pierce, *Sumner*, IV, 465.
[14] Sumner had certainly spread the slur amain; he had written Longfellow the previous summer that he would soon "tell you of this story of—Revenge!" *Ibid.*, IV, 448.

do,[15] by saying that Sumner had no right to take offense "unless the coat fitted." The Secretary had read his letter to Conkling and to Bancroft Davis, who both approved it. At the White House he had read it to the President and Vice-President; Schuyler Colfax protested against this passage, but Grant said, "I do not want a word changed." [16] The charge of hypocrisy was deliberately made.

Of course Sumner was one of the most sincere men alive—even fanatically sincere—and the charge was not justified in the sense in which he took it to his bosom. In another sense, the sense that Sumner had deceived himself and had indulged in certain pretences, it had a very real measure of justification. Fish was referring to three different facts: first, to the way in which Sumner had pretended during the spring of 1870 to have an open mind upon Santo Domingo long after it was really closed; second, to his request of certain documents from the State Department without disclosing that he meant to use them against Grant; and above all, to a more recent discrepancy between his words and acts. On December 20 he had stood up in the Senate and asserted that he had never spoken of Grant save in respect and kindness; yet all Washington knew what harsh epithets he had been applying to the President. It was Sumner's way to deny that he ever uttered personalities, and then to fill his discourse with them; and he made these lofty denials in the very speech in which he accused Grant of violating the Constitution and warned him of Andrew Johnson's fate. Fish felt that for months Sumner, whether self-deceived or not, had pursued a devious course, and he characterized it in blunt terms. But while we can understand his impulse, while we can agree that a stern rebuke was needed, his most judicious friends must have wished that these sentences, like others in his letter, had been more soberly phrased.

III

Motley's "End of Mission" and Fish's reply, with their previous correspondence, were made public January 9, 1871. Fish wrote Schenck that day that the step was necessary to satisfy a public curiosity aroused by enemies of the Administration.[17] "Mr. Motley's letter was heralded in advance of its receipt at this Department, and it was announced that an eminent Senator, 'which his name is Sumner,' had a

---

[15] Davis, *Mr. Fish and the Alabama Claims*, 59.   [16] Diary, January 2, 8, 1871.
[17] Letterbooks.

copy. . . . The President is well. Nothing especially new. The sharp debate in the Senate a fortnight ago has done no harm; it may serve to draw lines and define positions, but open hostilities are far better than those that are secret."

The reception of Fish's reply was all that he could have wished. The press almost unanimously accepted it as clearing the Administration and discrediting Motley. Senator Howe wrote Fish [18] that it was "a triumphant vindication." Thurlow Weed was delighted.[19] "I had long hoped for it, and while I did not doubt that the government had acted wisely, I had not dared hope that the evidence of its wisdom would be so conclusive—so triumphant. . . . This petted and spoiled diplomatist has been 'discharged, cured.' " English journals were also impressed; Thornton had asked the Foreign Office to see that they said nothing to imperil the pending negotiations, and their editorials pleased Fish. Badeau, now consul-general in London, wrote that he had never known a more complete demolition than that of Motley.[20] "The exposition your letter affords of the views and policy of the Administration is eminently clear and amazes the English, who thought rather that Mr. Motley was mollifying the President's animosity! This comes in the nick of time for Schenck, and will make the English Government more than well disposed to listen to him. Several members of the Cabinet have told me so."

But from this moment it was war à l'outrance between Sumner and Fish. The Senator told Schenck, even before he read the reply to Motley, that its publication released him from all obligations of confidence in regard to Fish's communications, and that he could use one in particular in a highly damaging way. "What he refers to I cannot imagine," commented Fish.[21] "Poor fellow! He is crazy." A little episode in January, 1871, augmented Fish's doubts upon Sumner's sanity. The Senator dictated and signed a letter to Fish. Then, deciding not to send it, he took it from its envelope and destroyed the *envelope*. His clerk found it and mailed it. "A sane man," writes Fish,[22] "would have destroyed *the letter*." Boutwell agreed, according to the diary, that Sumner suffered from egotistical delusions:

[18] Howe to Fish, January 10, 1871; Fish Papers.
[19] Weed to Fish, January 12, 1871; Fish Papers.
[20] January 26, 1871; Fish Papers. For Thornton's "secret and confidential" message asking that the *Times* be restrained from comment on the Fish-Motley correspondence, see PRO, FO 5, 1214, Thornton to Granville, January 17, 1871.
[21] Diary, January 20, 1871.   [22] Diary, January 21, 1871.

Boutwell tells me that Sumner claimed to him having originated and moved the amendment to the Army Appropriation Bill, prohibiting the ordering of the General of the Army away from Washington and directing that all orders be transmitted through him, etc., etc.; said he had drawn and offered it. Boutwell told him he was mistaken and gives me the history of that amendment, viz.: That Stanton sent for him, and told him his apprehensions of the designs of Andrew Johnson to send Grant away and to make use of the Army for his purposes; that he (Boutwell) drew the amendment and took it to Thaddeus Stevens, who incorporated in the printed bill an amendment from the Committee on Appropriations, etc. . . . Roscoe Conkling once told me of a similar appropriation by Sumner of the origination of a proposition or resolution in caucus for the successive adjournments of Congress during the recess of a long vacation in Johnson's time.

On January 20, 1871, Schenck gave a dinner which included Sumner, Bancroft Davis, and Fish. Sumner's biographer states that he refused to recognize Fish. Actually he was guilty of no such affront to his host. The Secretary's diary says merely that he was "cold and distant, evidently not wishing to converse with either Davis or me."

IV

From the moment of Sumner's preposterous demand for "hemispheric withdrawal" by Britain, Fish ignored him in his arrangements for the Joint High Commission. Whenever the Secretary communicated with the Foreign Relations Committee, he wrote to Senator Cameron. More and more it seemed to him and others that Sumner's obstructive position unfitted him for the chairmanship. If he had not committed himself in advance against the forthcoming treaty, he had almost done so. It was highly unfortunate at this critical moment to have a chairman who was abusive of the President, bitterly hostile to the Secretary of State, and full of preconceptions on the English settlement.

Justin S. Morrill had already warned the Senator that he was imperilling his place. Soon after Congress met in December a movement to drop him took shape. Sumner charged in the Dominican debate that Grant was engineering it but durst not proceed—that leaders had warned him that it would be unpopular, and that Schurz's displacement would alienate the German vote. Chandler and Conkling hotly called for proofs, and denied that Grant had proposed a change.[23] But on his

[23] *Congressional* Globe, December 21, 1871.

own account, Conkling threateningly remarked that the time had come when "the Republican majority here owes it to itself to see that the Committee on Foreign Relations is reorganized, and no longer led by a Senator who has launched against the Administration an assault more bitter than has proceeded from any Democratic member of this body." Chandler took the same view. The *Herald* of December 24, 1870, reported that he was "going around calling for blood," and that the movement to remove Sumner "is more strong and determined than was at first supposed." Fish was approached, but did his utmost to discourage the movement. As yet he saw no sufficient reason for it.

After the Christmas recess the movement revived. Senators Howe, Carpenter, Nye, and Edmunds, joined hands with Chandler and Conkling. Doubtless Grant inspired this group. He must keenly have resented Sumner's vigorous opposition early in February to the confirmation of his brother-in-law M. J. Cramer as Minister to Denmark. And on receiving Sumner's hostile "hemispheric withdrawal" letter, and hearing of his other threats against a settlement—not before—Fish abruptly changed front. At the critical moment he threw his whole weight into the scale, for he feared that Sumner would wreak the treaty—if not by open opposition, at least by offering drastic amendments. There being 74 members in the Senate, 24 votes would suffice to kill or mutilate the instrument; 14 Democrats might yield to the temptation to humiliate the Administration, and Sumner and Schurz need gain only 8 other Republican Senators. To leave Sumner in a position of power seemed to the Secretary perilous, and he moved to have him dropped.

"Sumner is malicious," Fish wrote Thurlow Weed.[24] "He has, I am told, declared that no settlement with Great Britain, and no determination on the foreign affairs of the country, shall be made by Grant's Administration. He cannot control, and wishes to defeat. With him it is 'Sumner Omnipotent' or 'nothing to be done.' The country may suffer unless Sumner resigns. Clay and Benton were both said to be arrogant and overbearing; the two together were not as arrogant as Sumner. But he is, I think, crazy, really a monomaniac; his vanity and conceit have overturned his judgment, which never was of the best." To Elihu Washburne he unbosomed himself more fully: [25]

---

[24] February 4, 1871; Letterbooks. For Grant's hatred of Sumner, see George Frisbie Hoar, *Autobiography*, I, 210 ff.; W. L. Stewart, *Reminiscences*.
[25] February 20, 1871; Letterbooks.

. . . We have made an advance in our negotiations with Great Britain, and toward the end of the week we expect the arrival of the British Commissioners to meet five appointed on our side to discuss and settle the Canadian questions and the *Alabama* question. I have strong hopes that some satisfactory conclusion will be reached. I may say (in strict confidence) that Great Britain was advised not to make her first proposal (of course the whole thing was discussed before the formal notes were passed) unless she was prepared to make "very large concessions" as to the *Alabama,* etc., beyond what she had hitherto expressed a willingness to do. She declared a willingness to "express regret" and was told emphatically that that would not be sufficient; how far she will go remains to be seen. I think she finds her own precedents are inconvenient, especially in view of possible European complications.

Sumner is bitterly vindictive and hostile; he is determined to oppose and if possible defeat everything that the President proposes or wishes or does. He is at work in advance, endeavoring to prevent any settlement of the English questions. I am convinced that he is crazy; vanity, conceit, ambition have disturbed the equilibrium of his mind; he is irrational and illogical, and raves and rants. No mad bull ever dashed more violently at a red rag than he does at anything that he thinks the President is interested in. He exhibits what I believe is a very common incident to insanity, and an equally unfailing sign of it, a constant apprehension of designs to inflict personal violence on him.

Some time since he called upon his colleague Wilson, and told him the President had threatened him with personal violence; shortly after he had the same alarm as to General Babcock. Wilson called upon the President and on Babcock, not crediting the cause of alarm, but to assure Sumner. Again, a few days since Sumner returned to his fears and told Wilson and others that Babcock was again about to assault him, and on Saturday it was given out that he was suffering from the maladies that he experienced after Brooks's assault upon him. His friends should subject him to "treatment." That, I think, is the term they use in connection with the insane. . . .

When the new Congress opened in March, Chairman Anthony of the Republican caucus appointed a committee on committees. Two members, Morrill of Vermont and Sherman of Ohio, favored keeping Sumner at the head of the Foreign Relations Committee; two, Nye of Nevada, and Pool of North Carolina, were against him. The fifth and deciding member, Howe of Wisconsin, wavered. On March 6 the question was presented to Fish, who writes: [26]

Before going to the office (on the way) I met Robeson, who suggested that I had better see Howe on the subject of a change in the chairmanship of the Committee on Foreign Relations. I call on the Senator. He thinks it ought to

[26] Diary, March 6, 1871.

be done, but as Sumner has foregone making his speech [a proposed second speech on Santo Domingo], he thinks perhaps it may be regarded as a proscription and excite some sympathy in his behalf. I reply that he could well afford to suspend the delivery of his assault on the Administration for a week or two to have the renewed confidence and approval of the Senate, and to be able to make the assault from a position of influence and of prominence. If reappointed on the Committee he will hold it for two years, and thus through the whole of Grant's Administration the chairman of the Foreign Relations Committee will be a person who has publicly assailed and vilified the President, and openly announced that he held no relations with him.

Howe proposed adding two members to the Committee, to which I objected. It would leave Sumner the official representative of the Committee, made such by the Senate.

He agrees that the change must be made.

Thenceforth Howe stood firm against Sumner,[27] and by a vote of three to two, the committee nominated Simon Cameron as chairman. When the issue came before the caucus on March 9th, Sumner called upon his great associates now in the grave—Douglas, Collamer, Fessenden—to testify whether during his ten years as chairman he had ever failed in any duty. He disdainfully rejected a lesser chairmanship; his friends, including Schurz, Trumbull, John Sherman, and Henry Wilson, protested in impassioned words. But by a vote of 26 to 21, including two distinguished New Englanders, Hannibal Hamlin and George F. Edmunds, the caucus was inexorable. On March 10th the Massachusetts Senator was shorn of his proudest dignity.

v

When Sumner was thus deposed Fish was busy night and day with the High Commission, now holding protracted sessions. He took little notice of the newspaper comment, most of which pronounced the deposition a political blunder. He took even less notice of Sumner's angry harangues to the Washington correspondents, reiterating that Fish had offered him "a vile and gross personal indignity," that he had "grossly misrepresented me," and that his pettiness and meanness were "absolutely despicable." For a time Sumner threatened to deliver another of his invectives against the Secretary, saying acridly: "I excuse Grant for his ignorance, but Fish is the Mephistopheles who entrapped and led him astray." Oliver P. Morton suggested that Fish write an article

27 Pierce, *Sumner*, IV, 470.

for the *Atlantic* presenting the true story of Sumner's attitude toward the Administration, but the Secretary rightly opposed any prolongation of the discussion. "Sumner's failure to be reappointed chairman," he wrote Washburne,[28] "has been seized upon to try and raise a little tempest, but I do not think that the teapot is going to boil over in consequence; although Sumner does."

He was satisfied that the Administration had done right, and that history would approve its action. It was true that Cameron was badly equipped for the place—that his horizon was bounded by Pennsylvania. It was true that Sumner was the only Senator who possessed a really expert knowledge of foreign affairs. But to argue on this ground was quite fallacious. Under the Constitution, the conduct of foreign affairs is entrusted to the President. To the Executive—that is, the President and Secretary of State—falls all the spade-work. It is not the function of the Chairman of the Senate Committee to talk with diplomats or negotiate treaties. His duty is to discuss with the President and Secretary such treaties as are negotiated, transmit their explanations to the Senate, and guide the Committee in making reports on treaties. It is therefore of cardinal importance that he be a sound organ of communication between Executive and Senate. Good relations with the Executive are so indispensable to constructive work that E. L. Godkin thought Sumner should have voluntarily resigned when he found himself in bitter hostility to Grant. Moreover, Fish genuinely feared for the treaty if Sumner remained. Legislatively, as Bryce says, the chairman is almost a second foreign secretary, wielding great powers. By a few fiery speeches, Sumner might easily have excited public opinion again; by adroit amendments, he might have played the rôle that Lodge played with reservations in 1919. From this point of view, the displacement of Sumner was the Administration's practical answer to the "hemispheric withdrawal" letter of January 17—of which the public as yet knew nothing. It was not an unprecedented step. Stephen A. Douglas had been similarly dropped from the chairmanship of the Committee on Territories under Buchanan, and though he had better reason to feel aggrieved, had smothered his resentment. John P. Hale had once been dropped as chairman of the Naval Affairs Committee because he had needlessly and abusively assailed the Secretary of the Navy.

The episode had its deepest significance in restoring the Foreign

[28] March 21, 1871; Letterbooks.

Relations Committee to its proper position in our governmental system. Perley Poore was correct in writing Senator Anthony that Seward had humored Sumner in the assumption of powers never given by law to a committee of Congress. Henry Adams was correct in writing in his autobiography that Sumner had created, side by side with the State Department, a Department of Foreign Relations, over which he ruled with arrogant sceptre at the Capitol. That dangerous and extra-constitutional department was now abolished—until Lodge and Borah recreated it in 1918.

Sumner's fall was greeted with especial pleasure in England. Disraeli, who had sneered at his "rowdy rhetoric . . . addressed to irresponsible millions," wrote Northcote on March 10 [29] to express delight over his "expulsion . . . from the seat of his ceaseless mischief and malice." We have seen that Granville felt the same way. At a later date Lord Houghton told Fish that he had betrayed and falsified every friendship, profession, and promise. Thornton wrote the Foreign Office that the action might make more enemies than friends for the treaty, and do the negotiations more harm than good.[30] But the event proved that it made no Senate enemies at all. Instead, it demonstrated that the Administration was now a unit behind Fish's efforts. Even if there were a small risk of continued intransigence on Sumner's part—and nobody, least of all Sumner himself, could say—all possible risks were to be avoided. Historians have disagreed as to the justifiability of the act. Charles Francis Adams, Jr., commends it; James Ford Rhodes condemns it, though with emphasis on Sumner's ill-temper and unreasonableness. But it was a natural precaution, and the best evidence of its propriety is that two and a half months later the Treaty of Washington passed the Senate without delay and with little opposition. Sumner then accepted what he could no longer prevent.

Subsequently, Fish added to the counts against Sumner the charge that he had made an inefficient chairman, and had delayed action on important treaties. Sumner's biographers have denied this charge. The fact is, as Senate records show, that when Sumner was dropped, six treaties, one protocol, and two naturalization conventions were in the

[29] Monypenny and Buckle, V, 139.

[30] For Houghton's attitude, see Fish's Diary, September 17, 1875. Thornton wrote Granville March 13, 1871, of a "general feeling" that "the step may have been expedient and even necessary." PRO, FO 5, 1215.

hands of the Foreign Relations Committee; all but one had been there for three months; and Cameron obtained favorable action upon eight within three weeks after taking his chair. Nevertheless, this accusation of negligence was both petty and needless, and Fish should never have made it. The fundamental justification of the deposition lay in Sumner's long hostility toward a reasonable settlement with England, his excitable temper, and his personal breach with the treaty-making arm of the government.

VI

Taken alone, Sumner's humiliation might have aroused little public indignation; but it occurred just after another sudden Cabinet decapitation. Jacob D. Cox's head had rolled to join those of Rockwood Hoar, Motley, Moses H. Grinnell, and David A. Wells. The circumstances of his dismissal were singularly shabby. He was hated by the spoilsmen, for he had gallantly resisted their demands in the Patent Office, Indian Bureau, and Census Bureau, and had protected his clerks against political tax-collectors. During the Congressional campaign of 1870 he published a letter sternly attacking political assessments, which angered the Republican Chairman, Zach Chandler. But the immediate causes of his undoing were his defense of the Indian Service from a new assault in the summer of 1870, and the opposition which he offered to the McGarrahan Claim, a fraudulent bit of land-grabbing.

As for the Indian Service, Cox wrote later that he had heard that a systematic effort would be made before Congress met again "to force a change in the policy we have been pursuing." As for the McGarrahan Claim, it was based upon a pretended Mexican land grant for which no documentary evidence existed, covering three leagues of California land, rich in minerals; Federal officers had repeatedly ruled against it; it had encountered adverse court decisions; but it still possessed vitality.[31] Passing to one McGarrahan as representative of a stock company, it was now being pushed in Congress by Ben Butler. According to the press, Cox denounced the claim as a transparent fraud; Grant faced him with the astonishing assertion that although it had to do with public lands under the Interior Department, Congress (in which Ben

[31] N. Y. *Tribune* articles, February 18–22, 1871.

Butler could of course act effectively) should be permitted to determine it; and in this rupture lay the secret of Cox's downfall.

Fish's diary shows that this cynical newspaper explanation was substantially true. On September 25, 1870, Chandler came to his house full of complaints regarding Cox's letter against political assessments. A few days later Grant returned from Long Branch, and Cabinet meetings were resumed. At the first, on October 4, Cox was absent:

Boutwell . . . mentioning an opinion published in the papers by Judge Parchal, said that the McGarrahan Claim was at the bottom of that opinion, as he heard that the Secretary of the Interior had issued a patent to the New Idria Company. The President, with much animation, and more feeling than I almost ever saw him exhibit, enquired if that were so. Boutwell replied that "he believed so—had heard so." The President instantly answered, "If it be so, I shall have a new Secretary of the Interior within an hour after knowing the fact."

He then mentioned having expressed his wish many months [ago], and having told Governor Cox at a Cabinet meeting, that he did not wish any patent issued to either party—that Congress had taken the subject in their hands, and he intended to let them decide it. That after hearing that argument had been heard before the Secretary of the Interior, he wrote him desiring that no patent should be issued, and had received while at Long Branch a letter from Governor Cox which had not pleased him. That after speaking very severely of the counsel in the case, he [Cox] concluded by saying, "that he had labored to administer his Department honestly, and to keep it free from fraud and corruption, and that if his efforts in that direction were not sustained by the President, he would desire to be relieved fom his office."

The President said he was fond of Cox and appreciated his thorough integrity, and that his Department had been better administered by him than ever before, but this remark had "cut him severely." He had shown the letter to Robeson at Long Branch. While speaking of it he took a bundle of letters from his drawer, and selected this letter of Cox and read the passage which I have given above from memory. He evidently has been much disturbed.

Fish easily conjectured what had happened. Grant had fallen under the influence of designing men who wished to capture the mineral lands and who had persuaded him that the Executive should keep his hands off; Cox was anxious to put a decisive end to the ill-founded claim. While various men had prejudiced Grant against Cox, the latter had acted tactlessly. Fish was prepared for the inevitable result, but too discreet to trust much information to his diary:

October 5, 1870.—Robeson, at my house this evening, says that Cox has resigned the Interior and that Delano is to be his successor. General Porter is Robeson's informant.

October 12, 1870.—Cox and Robeson dine with me. After dinner Cox explains the circumstances of his resignation, etc.

Cox's letter of resignation to Grant contained a sarcastic sentence: "The removal of the Indian Service from the sphere of ordinary political patronage has been peculiarly distasteful to many influential gentlemen in both houses; and in order to enable you to carry out your purposes successfully, I am satisfied that you ought not to be embarrassed by any other causes of irritation in the same department." [32]

His place was taken by a dry, baldish, clerical-looking man, with a sly, contriving air—Columbus Delano, oldtime Ohio criminal lawyer, who had gotten into Congress and had then become head in 1869, of that tainted department, the Bureau of Internal Revenue. His appointment marked a sad step in the deliquescence of the Administration, and Fish mourned it.

A few months later Grant wrote the new Secretary of the Interior, who was all pliability, on an application from McGarrahan's attorney for restoring to his client the record of his claim as it was, and for issuing a patent of title. The attorney had brought this application to the President himself! "Please examine the case at your leisure," wrote Grant,[33] "and give me your judgment as to the course that should be pursued, or whether as heretofore decided upon, the whole matter should be left with Congress, where the Administration found it." McGarrahan thus entrenched himself, and the controversy dragged on.

The elections of November, 1870, were disastrous to the Administration. The Democrats swept New York. Factional troubles there between Fenton and the imperious Conkling, who believed that the people liked a statesman with a "gamey flavor," had cost the party dear. Conkling, after inducing Grant to place Tom Murphy—a very gamey

[32] Cox wrote Garfield on October 24, 1874, that the pack had long been after him. During his vacation Chandler came to his department boasting that he was to be ousted, and the President, without consulting him, had peremptorily revoked his order in regard to clerical absences, "besides doing some other things which looked like giving way." He resolved to endure such contumely no longer. Garfield Papers. The combination of Chandler and Ben Butler, one interested in spoils and the other in the McGarrahan lands, was too much for him.

[33] May 31, 1871; Grant's Letterbooks.

man indeed—in charge of the Custom House, had seen to it that Murphy got rid of Fentonites and appointed Conkling men instead. The Democrats carried Indiana; in alliance with the Liberal Republicans, they elected B. Gratz Brown governor of Missouri; and they showed increased strength in other States. For the first time since 1864, the Republicans lost their two-thirds control of the House of Representatives. The political skies were darkening fast.

Against this gloomy background the breach between Grant and Sumner took deeper meaning. It was now as fierce as any other intra-party quarrel in our history; as that between Adams and Hamilton, between Jackson and Calhoun, between Roosevelt and Taft, between Smith and Franklin D. Roosevelt. Late in 1871 Grant told Fish that he had just received a visit from Morrill of Maine and Senator Harry Wilson, who wished a reconciliation between him and Sumner. "I told them," he said passionately, "that whenever Sumner should retract and apologize for the slanders he had uttered against me, in the Senate, in his own house, in street-cars and other public conveyances, at dinners and other public entertainments and elsewhere, as publicly, openly, and in the same manner in which he has uttered these slanders, I will listen to proposals for a reconciliation. Even then, I said that I would have no confidence in the man, or any faith that he would not repeat the performance." The Senators bowed to this outburst. "Morrill told me," Grant concluded, "that I was quite right in requiring such retraction and apology." For his part Sumner, as his letters to Gerrit Smith show, was denouncing Grant as a stupid and brutal autocrat, "without moral sense, without ideas, without knowledge"—"the lowest President, whether intellectually or morally, we have ever had."

In itself, Sumner's defection would have meant little. The American people knew his querulous ways; they knew how vehemently he had quarrelled with Lincoln, with Johnson, with every other President. But after all, he and Motley represented an intellectual, cultivated, and idealistic element in the sordid politics of the day; while their case gained strength as seeming to stand with that of such preëminently able and honest men as Hoar, Wells, and Cox. Many knew how close Fish himself had come to resigning. Grant seemed driving the fittest men from his side. In private correspondence Garfield was scoring "the surrender on the part of the President to the political vermin which infest the government." And all the while the reactionary policy of the

President in the South disgusted increasing numbers of Americans. "Let us have peace," he had said; and instead the nation read of continued bayonet rule, race riots, outrages, and a dictatorial Ku Klux Act that passed Congress early in 1871 with stern Presidential pressure behind it.

The outlook for Republican unity was dark, and the Administration sorely needed whatever popular prestige it could obtain. Happily, Fish was about to give the Grant régime its first great victory, and the proudest of all its achievements.

THE Joint High Commission set to work at the State Department on Monday, February 27, 1871.[1] The library had been cleared for the sessions; a large table was brought in; and Fish and de Grey faced each other at its two extremities, with the remaining commissioners disposed along the sides. From the start the atmosphere was business-like. De Grey courteously proposed that Fish preside, but the Secretary remarked that no chairman was needed. The two secretaries, Bancroft Davis and Lord Tenterden, were deputed to act as "protocolists" and keep a brief daily record of proceedings. Replying to Fish's questions, de Grey announced that his Commission—which he pointed out was not a British but an Imperial body, Canada being represented by Prime Minister Macdonald—was fully empowered to sign a treaty. Thereafter, beginning the next Saturday, the Joint Commission met almost daily.

Not all the omens were hopeful, for much suspicion lingered in both nations. Many Britons still credited Grant with an ingrained hostility toward their country. They were irritated when he received at the White House the fiery O'Donovan Rossa and other Irish Fenians who, recently liberated by the British Government, reached New York in January.[2] They knew of his close relations with Ben Butler, who had just said that a rupture with England would be the best means of re-invigorating the Republican Party for 1872. The London *Times,* an independent journal which had been a Palmerstonian organ and was now becoming hostile to Gladstone and Granville, hoped for the best but rather loudly feared the worst. It inclined to the view that the High Commission would lead to the ultimate worsting of England, for Grant's fear of the Irish and German vote would not permit a fair settlement. The Tory organ, the *Standard,* voiced still louder misgivings; and Disraeli seized upon the departure of the Commissioners for a speech proclaiming that it must be clearly understood "that England cannot be insulted or injured with impunity."

[1] Diary, February 27, 1871; Protocols. A full set of these Protocols is in the Fish Papers.
[2] London *Times,* April 20, 1871. Note that Thornton wrote to Granville, February 27, 1871 (PRO, FO 115, 524) that in receiving the High Commissioners Grant "was most cordial and friendly in his manner to Lord de Grey, and conversed with him for nearly an hour."

In the United States most journals greeted the British envoys with great cordiality. The *Tribune* declared that the American demands "will be pressed in a spirit that may make it easy to yield to them." The *Herald* predicted that the word Alabama would now revert to its aboriginal meaning, "Here we rest." *Harper's Weekly* thought that the Joint Commission offered a "simple and satisfactory" road to peace; the *Nation* called it "a triumph of civilization"; the *World,* relying upon "the firmness, moderation, patriotism, and sound judgment of Mr. Fish," hoped to see the question out of the way before the Presidential election. But there were dissenting voices. New England remained resentful toward Great Britain, and the Springfield *Republican* expressed morose apprehensions of a new rupture. The Irish bristled, the Germans grumbled. Dana of the *Sun* polished new epithets.

Fish himself confessed certain qualms. He felt deeply disappointed when Sir John Rose refused Gladstone's offer of the Canadian seat on the Commission, which fortunately went instead to Macdonald. Rose had excellent reasons; married to a Southern woman, a business partner of Levi P. Morton, possessing a host of American friends, he would have been open to Tory charges of bias. But his abstention, wrote Fish, "takes away much of my confidence in the future." Nor did Fish relish the appointment of Mountague Bernard to the Commission, or Lord Tenterden's position as secretary. These were unhappy choices, he told Thornton.[3] "Bernard wrote a very bad book about the Alabama Claims, and Lord Tenterden was the author of the once-famous *Notes* on them." Thornton reassured him. "Ah, that will make no difference; Lord Tenterden is only secretary, and as for Bernard, we shall persuade him." Actually Bernard's *Neutrality of Great Britain during the American Civil War,* published in 1870, contained much good law and calm reason, while Tenterden had been one of the warmest English advocates of a settlement. As for the selection of the Canadian Prime Minister, it was a master-stroke to win acceptance of the Treaty in the Dominion.

While still suspicious, Fish wrote Sickles of his doubts concerning the Joint Commission.[4] "What may come of it remains to be seen; they promise fair, but we are dealing with 'perfidious Albion.' Old Father Ritchie used to say, 'nous verrons,' which according to his Latin meant,

---

[3] Diary, February 9, 1871.
[4] February 14, 1871; Letterbooks. Gladstone had written that he wanted men "strong and sharp enough for Jonathan." Knaplund, *Gladstone and Imperial Policy,* 124.

'The best trump will take the trick.' A fair and liberal settlement is more to their interest just now than to ours. I have thought therefore that we should accept their proposal and try them."

But the atmosphere surrounding the Joint Commission rapidly improved. In England Fish's reply to Motley—the "Moran letter"—had a favorable effect, for it showed that he had labored against Sumner's opposition to effect a just settlement. As Smalley, London correspondent of the *Tribune,* informed the Secretary: [5] "Motley . . . had been regarded as the friend of England, the one American par excellence who was really in favour of peace, and that if he was resolute or harsh, or at all pressing and unkindly and imperative, he was goaded on by the bloodthirsty President behind him. When your letter demonstrated the contrary, that the President meant peace and courtesy, and fair, kindly dealing, and that Motley really acted against your wishes, the effect was instant." The United States suffered for lack of a Minister to influence London society. But John Russell Young, abroad on a mission for the Treasury, did effective work, and a letter of his in the *Times* evoked a friendly leading editorial.[6] The *Spectator* stood up manfully for the United States, while an article by Lord Salisbury in the *Quarterly Review* on the lessons of the Franco-Prussian War emphasized the isolated position of Great Britain.

In the United States the tact of the envoys accomplished much. "The British Commissioners have made a very favorable impression with all our people, officially and socially," Fish shortly testified.[7] They were a distinguished group. De Grey, who united two earldoms—he took the name of the second, Ripon, this year—had entered Parliament in 1853 as a radical, influenced by Charles Kingsley and Thomas Hughes. He still clung to progressive views; service as Secretary of War, Secretary for India, and Lord President of the Council had merely moderated his temper without lessening his liberalism. Short, heavy, pouter-breasted, with high forehead and flowing beard, immaculately dressed in frock coat, pearl waistcoat, and silk hat, using a monocle, he precisely suited the American idea of a nobleman. Mentally he was much like Fish. He was not brilliant or showy; he hated the limelight; he was neither a ready speaker nor a good writer. But he was industrious, painstaking,

---

[5] John Russell Young to Fish, March 7, 1871, quoting Smalley; Fish Papers.
[6] April 20, 21, 1871.   [7] Fish to Moran, April 17, 1871; Letterbooks.

honest, and shrewd; he was mild, genial, and a friend of compromise. Sir Stafford Northcote, tall, full-bearded, quicker of mind and movement than his chief, was the son of a baronet, an Oxford man, with twenty years of varied public service, beginning as Gladstone's secretary and culminating with the India Office, behind him. Though a Conservative, he was interested in civil service and other reforms; he had made his mark as a financial expert; and he knew something of Canada—he had been governor of the Hudson's Bay Company. Montague Bernard had occupied since 1859 the first chair of international law established at Oxford. He was a man of tact, laborious, impartial, and conscientious; a little over-finical, but with much common sense. Lord Tenterden, connected with the Foreign Office since 1854, and holder of an important place in London society, was witty and affable.[8]

Fish soon admitted that his apprehensions regarding Tenterden and Bernard were groundless. He had feared that they would play a pushing, aggressive rôle and take up contentious positions; instead, they showed perfect subordination to de Grey and scrupulous courtesy to the Americans. In discussion, the British delegation proved both frank and conciliatory. "We are on the best of terms with our colleagues," wrote Northcote,[9] "who are on their mettle and evidently anxious to do the work in a gentlemanly way and go straight to the point." Privately the Britons enlivened Washington society. De Grey took a house for his delegation and entertained lavishly. A round of dinners and balls was given in return. President Grant, as Thornton wrote home, showed a cordial liking for the earl. American Masonic leaders, knowing Tenterden's high rank in the English order, tendered a glittering reception to the Englishmen. A spring fox-hunt was even arranged in Virginia. At times it seemed that the treaty, like Lord Elgin's, would float through on a sea of champagne. One of Fish's dinners to the Commissioners gave him long-remembered chagrin when a newspaper reporter bribed a hired waiter to conceal him under the table, where he took notes on the conversation! [10]

[8] There is no life of Lord Tenterden; but see *Dictionary of National Biography*. On Northcote see Andrew Lang, *Sir Stafford Northcote, First Earl of Iddesleigh*, Chs. 4–11. Lucien Wolf's *Lord Ripon*, I, 240–271, is invaluable for the work of Treaty-making.

[9] The unpublished correspondence between the British High Commission and the Foreign Office is contained in nine volumes, "Conference at Washington," PRO, FO 5, 1296–1304.

[10] Mrs. Richard Aldrich, who had this story from friends of Mr. Fish, to author, November 18, 1935.

I

Usually the Joint Commission met at noon and sat until three, four, or even later. From time to time one or both sides retired for separate consultations, while each held frequent morning sessions to decide upon its course. Though the deliberations sometimes had to wait for replies to the long cablegrams which the British Commissioners sent to London, most of the delays were brief. On the American side Fish of course kept in constant communication with Grant; he would call at the White House, or the President, cigar in hand, would stroll across Lafayette Square to see him. But the Cabinet gave little attention to the negotiations. Not until the Joint Commission had labored almost a month did Fish make a statement covering the principal points at issue, and then the members offered little comment. Nor for the first month did he consult any Senators.[11] Only when definite results were being attained did he discuss certain questions with the Administration group, Conkling, Morton, Chandler, Cameron, and Edmunds.

The most vital part of the work was done by Fish and de Grey outside the meetings of the High Commission. Considering the complexity of the issues and the heat which they had recently aroused, the negotiation proceeded with remarkable smoothness. In two months, roughly-speaking, with a total of thirty-seven sittings, the complicated task was finished. This rapidity was due in part to long hours of labor, but above all to the confidential coöperation of the two chiefs. Fish's diary shows that they met privately and informally almost as often as in the High Commission. De Grey was always ringing Fish's doorbell; Fish was always drawing de Grey into his own room at the State Department. They made proposals "off the record," told each other what their Commissions could or could not accept, compromised on difficult points. Where eight men and two secretaries would debate for hours and come to a deadlock, these two moderate leaders sometimes found a way out in a few minutes. Fish was the freer agent, for Grant now trusted him in almost everything, while de Grey was sorely hampered by his home government. Northcote wrote of his chief: [12]

---

[11] Throughout his career as Secretary he frequently and cordially saw two Democrats, Senators Bayard and Thurman; to the former he was distantly related.
[12] Life, Letters, and Diaries, II, 13.

THE AMERICAN HIGH COMMISSIONERS

Schenck   Hoar   Fish   Williams   Nelson   Bancroft Davis

The U. S. Commissioners give him some trouble;
He don't blame them for *that*—it's their duty, you know;
And his Cabinet colleagues, they give almost double,—
They do it from love, and he likes it—so, so!

The two questions of cardinal importance were of course the *Alabama* Claims and the inshore fishery rights in Canadian waters. All the others—the San Juan boundary, coasting trade, transit of bonded goods across the Canadian boundary, St. Lawrence navigation, Fenian claims—were subordinate. At the outset the Commission determined to deal with each subject in the order in which it had been mentioned in the previous correspondence between Fish and Thornton; to pursue it until it had been settled or until some difficulty made further instructions necessary; and then turn to another, and so on until all were determined. This brought up the fisheries question—which the Canadian Government regarded as by all odds the most important, the real cause and crux of the negotiation—first. The very day after this decision, March 5, de Grey paid his first informal call. He broke the Sabbath afternoon by appearing at Fish's door, and before a fire in the study the two made a private arrangement. "I tell him," wrote Fish in his diary,[13] "that it seems unnecessary to discuss abstract questions or the irritation that has arisen. The point in question is the exclusion of American fishermen from the inshore fisheries. We wish to obtain this right and of course must make some compensation for it. I ask whether we had not better direct the inquiry and discussion tomorrow directly to this point, to which he assents." Next day the matter was taken up in regular session. Fish's diary states: [14]

Lord de Grey remarks that he understands that we want to obtain the right of the inshore fisheries: of course we must be prepared to give something for the right; we enjoyed it under the Reciprocity Treaty, and gave therefor the right of free trade in certain enumerated articles; they want to have the reciprocal free trade restored, and have looked to that as an equivalent.

The American Commissioners urge the difficulty of obtaining any legislation to that extent; that the people are opposed to this reciprocity of trade and are especially opposed to regulating tariff and custom regulations by treaty. That possibly some one or two articles that are especially connected with the Fisheries, etc., might be provided for exemption from duty, but any long list, would excite a general debate on the tariff and prevent any arrangement.

[13] March 5, 1871.   [14] March 6, 1871.

Retiring for consultation, the American Commissioners agree to propose the free entry of "fish, salt, coal, and fire wood," and to remark that many of the articles included in the Reciprocity Treaty now are either "free," or admitted at reduced duties. Should this proposal be rejected, the American Commissioners are to suggest the payment of a gross sum of money for the enjoyment in perpetuity of the right of inshore fishing. Returning to the conference room, the first proposal is made, and the British Commissioners reply that it is not sufficient, and cannot be entertained; the second proposition is made, (a money consideration) which is entertained "ad referendum," the British Commissioners declaring that it was not contemplated, or included in their instructions, and that they must consult their Government, which they will do by telegraph.

They are asked what other articles they more especially desire to have included in the free list. Sir John Macdonald replies, cereals of all kinds, and root crops, animals, lumber, products of the mines, copper ore, etc., etc.

It is suggested that possibly the basis of the equivalent for the inshore fisheries may be mixed; partly money and partly trade facilities.

Sir John Macdonald urges the admission of the British to the coasting trade, which I tell him at once cannot be entertained; he says the great bulk of shipping on the lakes is American, and a reciprocal admission to the coasting trade would give the Americans great advantages on the lakes.

The estimated value of the fisheries (inshore) is talked of. Adjourned unto Wednesday at noon.

For long weeks the wrangle over the fisheries question continued. The Canadian Cabinet at first refused to consider a sale of the fishing-rights for even a short term,[15] instructing Macdonald that this would be "equal to parting with a portion of the territory of the Dominion." But it soon manifested a certain readiness to compromise. On March 22 Sir Charles Tupper instructed Macdonald that the Government might agree to sell the fishery-rights for $500,000 a year, fish, coal, lumber, and salt to be admitted to the United States duty free. Fish had meanwhile offered $1,000,000 for the rights in perpetuity! Macdonald was outraged by this; he had figures to show that the American catch had been worth $6,000,000 a year, and told Judge Hoar that the terms would mean "giving up our Alsace and Lorraine" for a trifle. De Grey also thought the sum utterly inadequate. But as the Canadians tried to insist on coasting privileges and large tariff concessions, the British members grew impatient. In the end the fisheries question outlasted

---

[15] The Macdonald Papers in the Canadian Archives contain the "Treaty of Washington Correspondence" in six volumes. A good account of Canada's attitude is to be found in Goldwin Smith, *The Treaty of Washington*, MS, Ch. 4. See also Joseph Pope, *Correspondence of Sir John A. Macdonald*, and *Memoirs of Sir John A. Macdonald*.

all others; the sessions devoted to Canadian questions were 17, to the claims against England 10, and to the San Juan boundary 4. During April the willingness of Lord de Grey to make concessions generated angry feeling between Macdonald and the Englishmen. "They seem to have only one idea in their minds, to go home to England with a Treaty in their pockets, settling everything, no matter at what cost to Canada" —so Macdonald wrote.

Other entries in Fish's diary show how the negotiations progressed:

April 12, 1871.—I tell him [Lord de Grey] that I am rather glad that they are not willing to accept our proposals for the settlement of the fisheries, as I find the universal impression that we have proposed to give too much, and that the concessions offered would probably jeopardize the ratification of any treaty. He asks if we would substitute a moneyed equivalent, and is told that although our proposal in that direction had been refused, we might not object yet, to entertain such a proposal from them, but that our estimates (on the two sides) of the values of the right to the inshore fisheries were so different that I thought it would be quite useless to discuss it, and moreover that it would be impossible now to obtain an appropriation; it might have been done, when in the early days of the Commission it was proposed; now Congress was about to adjourn, and had determined to confine its legislation to two or three subjects; no appropriation could be obtained before next winter, and it would be very difficult then, in a Congress preceding a Presidential election to get such an appropriation through.

As a sudden thought to which I was not willing to commit myself, and had no right to commit anyone else, I asked how it would strike him to refer to arbitration the valuation of the right to the inshore fisheries; that if it struck him favorably he might see how it appeared to his associates; he said that it was "an idea worth considering."

In reply to a further question whether I could not suggest any mode of settling all the Canadian questions, I express inability, but say that if the *Alabama,* the fisheries, and the navigation of the St. Lawrence, could be settled upon terms somewhat reasonable, I would individually be disposed to consider the question of arbitration on the San Juan; but that Canada was so exacting, Great Britain sustained her in her high demands, so that I thought there was no inducement to consider the possibility of submitting San Juan to arbitration. He wished me to consider it further, and to see if some arrangement may not be made on that basis.

April 13, 1871.—Called upon the President. . . . I ask his opinion as to the purchase of the right of the inshore fisheries, at a price to be named by arbitrators without any trade privileges; he thinks favorably of it, provided the St. Lawrence navigation be settled satisfactorily, and as a last resort will consent to arbitration of San Juan in a separate treaty. I tell him the English Commissioners have insisted that all the questions be united in one treaty;

he then advises me to consult with my associate Commissioners, and with some leading Senators. He had given up his California trip for this spring: hopes to go in August or September; assigns as a reason for not going now, in addition to the uncertainty of having the British negotiation disposed of, that the absence of himself and cabinet, and of the General of the army, immediately after the enactment of the "Ku-Klux" Bill, would not be proper.

I call upon Senator Chandler; show him the British expression of regret for the Alabama, which he says is all that could be asked. He approves the purchase of the right of inshore fisheries at a price to be determined by arbitrators, and will consent to arbitration of San Juan if nothing better can be had; but suggests that Bancroft's letter and "protest" (as he calls it) should form part of the submission. He promises any aid he can render to help through the House and Senate any legislation that may be required.

April 19, 1871.—Lord de Grey says that they have not yet received an official answer from the Government on the subject of the fisheries, but tells me confidentially that he has received a private despatch by cable, stating that the British Cabinet would accept the plan of settlement proposed by the American Commissioners, of free fish and a moneyed payment, to be determined by arbitration, as the equivalent for the "inshore fisheries." He says that he does not wish this communicated to his own colleagues, until he receives the official reply; but mentions to me that we may be justified in proceeding to the discussion of the remaining questions, and asks if, under the circumstances, we will consider the San Juan this morning, to which I assent. This conversation took place at his house.

April 21, 1871.—Earl de Grey calls about 4 P. M.; had received the assent of his government to the negotiation of the fisheries question on the basis last proposed, viz: valuation of privileges of "free fish" into the United States and of the inshore fisheries; also of reference of the San Juan arbitration to either the Emperor of Germany or of Brazil, and of the submission of the question between the Haro and the Rosario Channels, without intermediate or any companion channel.

He says they have trouble with the Canadian questions, and fears the question of the Canals may make difficulty; wishes us to be "as easy as we can" in the language, etc., of the "fisheries" articles. Thinks we may be able to conclude all questions tomorrow, so that nothing but the phraseology will remain to be settled, and that if either of the American Commissioners wish to go home for a few days, he thinks they may be able to do so.

Not until the end of April did Macdonald resentfully give way. He had threatened on April 21 to resign from the Commission; he still threatened to refuse to sign the treaty. It took immense pressure, including a masterly letter of argument, suggestion, and reprimand from Northcote, to bring him around.[16] The final agreement was that for

[16] April 15, 1871; in Macdonald Papers, "Treaty of Washington Correspondence," I, 422 ff.

ten years American fishermen should hold the right to inshore fishing along the eastern coast of the Dominion, including Prince Edward Island; that Canadian fishermen should have equal rights during that period on the American coast; that each country should ship fish and fish-oil free of duty to the other; and that since the Americans received the greater advantages, an international commission should determine what sum ought to be paid by the United States as additional compensation.[17] Gladstone had succeeded in his desire to "sweeten" the *Alabama* question for the United States by bringing in Canada.

Yet this final agreement on the fisheries was fair. It caused intense though shortlived discontent in the Dominion, where Macdonald was assailed for giving them away for nothing; but this rested upon a misapprehension. The Canadians had exaggerated their trading-value. Protection was now too firmly rooted in the United States to permit the exchange of a reciprocity agreement for the fishing rights. Had Fish been free to act alone, he would gladly have arranged reciprocity, but he had to think of Congress at every step. Even when he made the modest suggestion of a free entry of coal, salt, and firewood he heard grumblings in Washington, and when Macdonald proposed a longer list, vehement protests reached the Secretary.[18] Zach Chandler, representing Michigan's interests, said that he would fight to the last ditch any treaty which permitted the free entry of Canadian salt and lumber. The British Commissioners sympathized with Fish's unwillingness to risk Senate votes. Moreover, reference of the question of compensation to three men, one American, one Imperial, and one neutral, sufficiently protected Canada. It protected her so well, in fact, that Congress later rebelled against the Halifax Award to the Dominion, and refused to accept it as the basis of a permanent fisheries settlement. The Canadian fisheries were still an infant industry. What they needed above everything else for their growth was the free American market. As Sir Stafford Northcote wrote Macdonald, the Dominion might have found it wise to trade the inshore rights for this market "even if you got nothing to boot."

Other Canadian questions were fairly compromised. It would have been absurd for the two countries to growl, like mastiffs with a bone, over their great common system of waterways. The St. Lawrence was thrown open in perpetuity to the Americans, while the same principle

[17] For the Canadian position, see Appendix II.   [18] Diary, April 8, 1871.

was applied in Canada's favor to rivers which flowed through Alaska to the sea. Various small border issues were equitably arranged. When the claims for Fenian damages were dropped by the British Commissioners on the ground that they had not been included in the agenda, and were merely constructive and inferential, many Canadians expressed indignation. But de Grey had told Macdonald on April 16, on the strength of private assurances from Granville, that Great Britain would indemnify Canada if the United States refused to do so. Gladstone justly believed that England, through her indefensible Irish policy, was primarily responsible for these raids. In the end, the Treaty clauses on Canadian questions were not unsatisfactory to the Dominion interests concerned or to far-sighted Dominion leaders. Macdonald was gratified to find that the people of the Maritime Provinces, at first uneasy, soon manifested anxiety for the adoption of the treaty. They saw that the removal of the American tariff on fish was all-important—it would offer a real market for their highest-priced catch. Moreover, many Canadians perceived that the primary need of their new state was a period of tranquillity and harmony, during which its resources might be developed and its national spirit strengthened. The political storm which the Ministry had feared died away after a few months of mild rumbling by Liberal newspapers and agricultural interests.

The final Canadian question of importance, the San Juan boundary, was left to William I of the newly-united German Empire for a decision.[19] Though the disputed islands were neither large nor valuable, the question had excited so much feeling on the Pacific coast that Fish moved carefully. Some Americans asserted, to the astonishment of the English, that the ambiguous clauses in the Treaty of 1846 on the boundary had been a trick, and that the Hudson's Bay Company had then prodded the British Government into an unfair stand. Actually, the negotiators under Aberdeen and Polk in 1846 had used ambiguous language simply because they were ignorant of Western geography. Settlers in Washington Territory also feared that England would fortify San Juan Island against the Americans. For some weeks Fish opposed anything less than an outright cession. In this connection he made his last bid for Canadian territory. At least twice he urged de Grey to agree to a new boundary, ceding all or part of British Columbia, for which the United States would pay an equivalent in money or otherwise.[20]

[19] See Articles XXXIV–XLII, Treaty of Washington.   [20] Diary, March 16, 18, 1871.

As de Grey could not discuss shutting Canada off from the Pacific, Fish reluctantly consented to arbitration.

II

But to the world in general the *Alabama* Claims were the paramount object of interest. They were first taken up on Wednesday, March 8. The previous day the American group had discussed the presentation of their case at length, and Fish had drawn up a careful statement. At noon on the 8th he read it to the High Commission.[21]

In this document he said nothing about the Queen's proclamation of neutrality, but confined himself to the damage wrought by the cruisers. After describing the injury they had done, he declared that Great Britain, failing to observe her duties as a neutral, had become liable for them "upon principles of International Law which we shall submit." He went on to say that the claims for property destruction thus far presented reached about $14,000,000, without interest, and that more would doubtless be offered; that the cost of destroying the cruisers was easily ascertainable; and that indirect claims also existed for the transfer of much of the American merchant marine to the British flag, costs of insurance, and "the addition of large sums to the cost of the suppression of the rebellion." Finally, after asking for an expression of regret by the British Government, he spoke of modes of settling the claims. The easiest and most practical, he said, would be for the British to empower the Joint High Commission to fix a sum for their nation to pay; a sum covering all claims, including the costs of pursuit, with interest.

Was this sum to cover the national or war-prolongation claims? In the course of his paper, Fish made an interesting statement upon this. He declared that "in the hope of an amicable settlement, we present no estimate of the indirect losses, but without prejudice to the right to indemnification on their account. . . ."

The British Commissioners of course denied that their government had failed to discharge its duties under international law or was liable for the losses from the cruisers. This reply was no hollow form. Englishmen were still almost unanimous in holding that their country had never violated international law. They would admit only that, through

[21] Protocols; Diary.

governmental negligence, their own neutrality statutes had not been enforced with proper strictness; and for this, as Rose had indicated, they were ready to express regret. The Commissioners asserted that while England had always disavowed responsibility for the cruisers, she was willing to submit the question of liability and damages to arbitration.

Arbitration was of course the golden portal through which the two nations were intended to pass to an amicable future. But a curious diplomatic colloquy ensued. The American Commissioners, obviously prepared, said in effect that arbitration might be acceptable if the principles of neutrality to govern the tribunal in weighing the facts could first be agreed upon. The British, equally prepared, replied that they had no authority to consent to this, but were willing to discuss what principles of neutrality should be adopted for observance *in the future*. Fish rejoined that his group would gladly consider future principles, with the understanding that when agreed upon they "should be held to be applicable to the facts in respect to the *Alabama* Claims." And de Grey answered that he would consult his government upon this.

Fish's statement indicated that the United States was at last reducing its contentions to a fairly realistic level. No statements about our alleged grievance in the Queen's proclamation; no hints about Canada; an implication in the sentence quoted above that the huge claims for prolongation of the war *might* eventually be given up—all this was hopeful. The vague sentimental trappings which had been added to our hard legal grievances were being shorn away.

III

But at one point the United States still obviously asked a good deal. For consenting to arbitration, Fish and his colleagues demanded that the High Commission define the duties of neutrals with respect to the outfitting of belligerent ships, and require the arbitrators to apply these principles to the *Alabama* Claims. New rules were to be drawn up and virtually made retroactive. Fish had talked with Thornton the previous autumn about a special convention upon maritime neutrality, and had shown him a rough minute "made hastily one evening, written in pencil"; he had thought upon the subject since. Now he and his colleagues, after prolonged discussion on March 7, 1871, drafted four rules of neutrality, and next day presented them to de Grey.[22]

The first rule asserted that any great maritime Power was bound to use active diligence in order to prevent the construction, fitting out, equipping, or augmentation in force, of any vessel to be employed against a Power with which it was at peace. The second rule stipulated that if such a vessel escaped, the Power was bound to use like diligence to arrest and detain her if she again came within its jurisdiction. Under the third rule, the delinquent Power was also bound to instruct its naval forces to arrest such a vessel wherever found upon the high seas. Finally, according to the fourth rule, any Power failing to observe this code was to be held responsible for the damage wrought by the escaped vessel.

The significance of these rules is indicated by Fish's statement in his diary that they were presented as "the foundation of the American claims called the *Alabama* Claims." In form, the United States was yielding to England by permitting the arbitration of the question of British liability. In actuality, it was stipulating that the arbitration should be based upon principles which bound the judges to accept in advance a great part of the American case. Fish was reaching by a circuitous path the very settlement he had originally proposed, under which the liability of the British Government was assumed, and only the amount of damages was arbitrated.

Technically, the essence of the dispute had always been the question, What were the recognized principles of international law in 1861? Now the United States was insisting that the arbitrators be told that the principles were precisely what America had understood them to be, and what Great Britain had denied them to be! Naturally London would regard this as unreasonable. But it was evident that Great Britain would have to make some concessions. For several days the High Commission debated the subject. Fish consented to minor modifications in the four rules. Then, seeing that they could gain no more, de Grey and his colleagues on March 14 cabled the Gladstone Ministry recommending that it accept them as instructions to the Tribunal.

This telegram resulted in two stormy sessions of the British Cabinet. The pill was hard to swallow. Granville, who was eager for an agreement, wrote de Grey that there was "a tremendous row." He, William E. Forster, Lord Kimberley (the Colonial Secretary), and four other

[22] Diary; see also Bancroft Davis, *Mr. Fish and the Alabama Claims*, 74, 149–154.

members stood staunchly by the recommendation. The Duke of Argyll criticized it, but was for conciliation. A minority of three raged violently against it, even using the word "dishonour." Gladstone himself agreed with the recommendation, though reluctantly.[23]

But the Cabinet, while finally assenting, did not accept a flat agreement that the rules should be admitted to have been in force in 1861. Instead, it sent word that Great Britain would accept them as binding for the future; and that it would also agree "that in deciding the questions between the two countries arising out of those claims, the arbitrators should assume that Her Majesty's Government had undertaken to act upon the principles set forth in these rules." This was a distinction without much difference. It was of course perfectly acceptable to the Americans. On March 18 de Grey came to Fish and made a final effort to obtain a *quid pro quo* for the British agreement to the four rules.[24] He said that while he did not know that they would be rejected in Westminster, he did feel sure that they would be swallowed at once "if we would agree either to arbitrate the San Juan boundary or to accept an intermediate channel." Fish of course refused to listen to this effort to connect two diverse questions. The process by which the British finally came around to an almost complete surrender on the four rules is amusingly depicted in Fish's diary:

Friday, March 24, 1871.—Joint High Commission was to have met at two P. M.; at that hour Lord de Grey calls, and says they are not prepared to proceed today with the other Canadian matters. He handed me the British modification of the propositions of public law for submission with the *Alabama* question, and hoped that we would make as few alterations as possible. He now refers to it, and hopes we may give him an answer this afternoon to be telegraphed to London for consideration by the Cabinet tomorrow. The American Commissioners proceed to consider it, and make some alterations which I take to him in the afternoon. In the evening while at dinner he calls and reads me an alteration which he desires to make to the fourth clause; he says they wish to avoid certain expressions which may expose them to attacks in Parliament, and assures me that the object of their amendment is not to vary the meaning of our article but only for the purpose mentioned. I tell him that I cannot speak for the other American Commissioners, who are anxious to have no changes, but for myself I will endeavor to meet his views, and to use the language he proposes, but some change must be made. He made some alterations on my suggestion. This interview did not last five minutes. Subsequently, late in the evening, he sent me a note enclosing the proposed altera-

[23] Foreign Office Papers; "Conference at Washington."   [24] Diary.

tion. On reading it, I find it will not answer.

Saturday, March 25, 1871;—. . . . The fisheries are discussed. After adjournment Earl de Grey, taking me aside again, begs that we consider their position with Parliament; their work will be severely criticized, and they think they have already yielded very much. He again assures me that the object of their last amendment is not to lessen or limit liability; that they understand under it that the liability incurred by the original criminality of a vessel continues after her receiving a commission, and after her entrance thus commissioned into another port of the neutral.

Tuesday, March 28, 1871.—Joint Commission visited Mount Vernon. On the passage Earl de Grey tells me that he has an answer from his government to the proposed articles on international duties in connection with the *Alabama* Claims, and hands me a copy which I am not able to read on board the boat. It amends the *first* article, accepts the second and third, and proposes a substitute for the fourth.

Thursday, March 30, 1871.— . . . An informal conversation had with Lord de Grey about the Alabama propositions. A meeting of the American Commissioners was held to consider a substitute proposed by the British Commissioners for the fourth article. I subsequently leave with de Grey the agreement reached by the American Commissioners.

Sunday, April 2, 1871.—Earl de Grey brings me in the afternoon a copy of the alterations by the British Cabinet in the last proposed articles on neutrality, for submission in case of an agreement to arbitrate. They are not satisfactory. He says the British Government will consent to omit the fourth article entirely.

Tuesday, April 4, 1871.—In the evening received a note from Earl de Grey that the British Government had agreed to the articles on neutrality, as prepared by the American Commissioners, to be submitted to the articles in connection with the *Alabama* Claims.

Thus an agreement was at last reached and ratified at the joint meeting of April 6. The articles on neutrality—reduced to three—were of far-reaching importance, for they would not only determine the extent of British liability, but bind both governments in the future.[25] Their essence, in final form, was that a neutral government was bound to "use due diligence" to prevent the outfitting or arming of any vessel which it had "reasonable ground" to believe was intended to make war against another nation, and to prevent the departure of any such vessel. Second, it was bound to prevent any belligerent from making use of its ports or waters as a base of naval operations, or for procuring military supplies, arms, or recruits. Third, it must exercise "due diligence" in its ports and waters and over all persons within its jurisdiction to pre-

25 Cf. S. F. Bemis, ed., *American Secretaries of State*, VII, 168.

vent any violation of these obligations.[26]

Grant was a little uneasy about the effect of the new rules on the proposers! Fish read them to the Cabinet on March 31. "President and Boutwell," he writes, "seem to think that these articles are possibly more stringent than the United States would like to have them in the future."

IV

In this fashion, with important concessions on both sides, but with the Americans the principal victors, the *Alabama* question—as all hoped —was at last disposed of. The High Commission had done its work well. But at one point, as men learned later, it had unfortunately failed to remove a tremendous obstacle. In one sense, the most important single issue before it might be thus formulated: Was the United States really entitled to ask compensation for the indirect or *national* damages inflicted by the Confederate cruisers in prolongation of the war and other costs? That question should have been definitely (though not necessarily publicly) cleared away. It was not, and the penalty was paid later in months of controversy, resentment, and anxiety.

The ideal solution would have been for the Joint Commission to agree upon a clear "No." But Fish felt unable to do this. The American position, clearly outlined by Seward, violently stated by Sumner, and cautiously restated in Cushing's note, had held the indirect claims to be thoroughly valid. If Fish and his colleagues had now surrendered them, a storm would have burst upon their heads. Perhaps they exaggerated this danger; there is no way of telling—we cannot explore the might-have-beens of history. We can only say that the Senate has often dealt very harshly with treaties; that but 24 votes were needed to bring about a defeat; and that an alliance of the Sumner-Schurz group with the Democrats would have been formidable. It was best for Fish to take no chances. On the other hand, it was equally impossible for the British Commissioners to agree that the indirect claims *would* go before the arbitrators; for Parliament would have rebelled against a possible bill for war-prolongation. It seemed necessary to be imprecise on this subject—so far as written records went. Mr. Harold Nicolson tells us in his book *Peacemaking* that imprecision is the greatest peril that can beset any diplomatic negotiation. In this instance the imprecision

[26] Article VI, Treaty of Washington.

was deliberate and was also probably correct. Both sides agreed upon a courteous vagueness as to the admissibility of the indirect claims.

As a matter of fact, what was needed was a *tacit* dropping of the war-prolongation claims. But this tacit exclusion should have been clearly understood by both sides, and it was not. The British Commissioners thought they had obtained it, but the Americans never for a moment thought they had given it—and thence sprang a world of trouble.

A little more courage on both sides might have settled the matter. De Grey should have gone to Fish and said, "My dear sir, it really must be understood (though not a word goes on paper) that the indirect claims will quietly disappear from your case." Thus cornered, Fish could and probably would have consented to make only *pro forma* use of such claims. He had some ground to think that such use would probably satisfy the Senate. When he had first discussed the proposals of Sir John Rose with Senator Morton, as he records in his diary for January 15, 1870, the latter had been very conciliatory on the indirect claims. He thought that if Great Britain paid the expenses of running down the *Alabama* that "would be regarded as 'consequential' damage and would satisfy the public expectation on that point." Some quiet agreement should have been possible. But it was not reached. Instead, on two occasions de Grey and Fish politely and timidly skirted the issue.

The first occasion was on March 8, the day work on the *Alabama* question really began. Fish read his statement of American grievances.[27] After reviewing the direct claims, he declared that the British-equipped cruisers had also caused indirect losses, including the prolongation of the rebellion and the addition of large sums to the cost of its suppression. He went on, as already noted: "At the present, and in the hope of an amicable settlement, we present no estimate of the indirect losses, but without prejudices to the right of indemnification on their account. To yield them would be a very large concession." This statement was later included in the Protocol attached to the Treaty. The British thought it meant that if an amicable settlement, i. e., a treaty, were made, the indirect claims would be permanently dropped. The Americans thought it meant that their discussion was *temporarily* dropped to facilitate the drafting of a treaty. That accomplished, the claims, explicitly left "unprejudiced," might be reviewed.

[27] Protocols.

The second occasion was on April 8, when the Joint Commission took up the formal drafting of the Treaty.[28] They first dealt with what de Grey called the "enacting parts" or preliminary sections. Fish proposed a sentence stating that the two nations agreed that "all the differences between the two governments" growing out of the acts of the British-built cruisers should be submitted to five arbitrators. De Grey at once objected to the phrase "all the differences" as too wide and vague. Then ensued the sort of word-chopping so characteristic of diplomatic parleys. Fish argued at some length for the use of a broad term, asserting that "a partial submission will probably produce dissatisfaction in both countries, certainly in this country." After long debate, de Grey proposed another formula. It was a statement that the two nations "think it desirable that all the differences, etc., shall be settled, and agree to submit the claims, etc." Fish partly assented, saying that something of the sort might do, and agreed to bring a modified sentence to the next meeting. He also asked if there were any other points objected to. A great part of the American draft of a treaty was then read aloud. In the course of the reading Fish interrupted to say that he understood there was to be some expression of regret on the part of the British Government. De Grey agreed to this, and the British Commissioners promised to draft the apology while Fish redrafted the "enacting part."

De Grey and his colleagues thought that this was a bargain. They inferred from the close of the discussion that they should offer England's regrets, and in return the Americans would limit the arbitration to the direct and private claims. But it is evident from Bancroft Davis' Journal that the Americans thought nothing of the kind. They had insisted all along upon an expression of regret. Fish had mentioned it to Sir John Rose months earlier; had mentioned it again in opening the discussion of the *Alabama* Claims. They saw no reason to give a *quid pro quo*. And the "enacting part" agreed upon at the next meeting contained nothing whatever about omitting the indirect claims. On the contrary, it provided that "to remove and adjust all complaints and claims on the part of the United States," the two nations would submit *"all* the said claims, growing out of acts committed by the aforesaid vessels and generically known as the 'Alabama Claims.' " to a tribunal of arbitration.

[28] *Ibid.*

Finally, at the meeting of the Joint Commission on April 13 [29] a new dispute arose over this enacting clause. The subject under discussion was the Tenth Article, providing that if the Tribunal found Great Britain liable for damages, but did not award a gross sum, a Board of Assessors should be set up to fix the amount. The question was raised whether this permitted the United States to claim reimbursement for the costs of pursuing the cruisers. As debate continued, feeling for the first and last time became angry.

De Grey snapped out that the British would never let the tenth article be construed as enlarging the enacting clause of the first article; they would go home first. He rose and resolutely locked his box. Fish hurriedly calmed him. He and the other Americans then withdrew to consult. In their own room they manifested much difference of opinion as to the effect of the enacting words, but Fish dominated the council. He returned and told the British that the Americans would leave the terms of the first and tenth articles untouched; but "we assent to the language used because we consider it sufficient to include all claims of the government which the arbitrators may find just." De Grey, mollified, said that this was satisfactory. Once more, the British thought Fish had yielded, while the Americans thought he had stood firm. Had he not spoken of "all claims?"—a phrase that also went into the Protocol. Thus to the very end the British failed to obtain a *precise* understanding about the tacit abandonment of the claims.

It was not merely unfortunate; it was destined to prove almost tragic. But meanwhile the final touches were put to the treaty in an atmosphere of the blandest courtesy. It was agreed that the Arbitral Tribunal should consist of five men, named by President Grant, Queen Victoria, the King of Italy, the President of the Swiss Confederation, and the Emperor of Brazil; and that they should meet in Geneva at the earliest convenient day. The Treaty in final form contained clauses granting equal rights of navigating the St. Lawrence, the Yukon, Lake Michigan, and the Welland and other Dominion canals to Americans and Canadians. It also contained a British expression of regret "for the escape, under whatever circumstances, of the *Alabama* and other vessels from British ports, and for the depredations committed by those vessels."

[29] *Ibid.;* April 13, 1871; Bancroft Davis states (*Mr. Fish and the Alabama Claims,* 77) that Fish privately told his colleagues that "he supposed it was pretty well agreed that there were some claims which would not be allowed by the Arbitrators, but he thought it best to have them passed upon."

By the beginning of May the work was practically completed. Fish on the 2nd read important sections of the Treaty to the Cabinet; on the 5th he discussed it with Senators Cameron, Morton, and Howe, and asked Caleb Cushing to prepare explanatory articles for newspaper publication.[30] On Saturday, May 6, all was finished except the signing of the instrument. It was read through by the Commissioners to save time on Monday—for several wished to catch the noonday train and reach New York for dinner—and sealed. The final scene on May 8, a brilliant spring day, was the proudest in Fish's life, and cannot better be described than in his own words: [31]

The treaty with Great Britain is signed at the Department of State, the last signature being affixed at twelve minutes past eleven A. M.; the attaches of the British High Commission, the under-secretaries of the British legation, and most of the clerks of the State Department being present to witness the signatures.

At the conclusion of the signing, Lord de Grey took my hand and with much emotion said: "This is the proudest day of my life. I congratulate you, and myself, and my two countries, and I thank you most cordially for what you have done. Without your efforts no treaty could have been agreed to." Thornton also was much moved, and holding my hand, said: "This is a great result. You and I have worked hard for this, and have done what these gentlemen do not know to bring it about; we have worked for two years."

When Sir John Macdonald was about to sign, while having the pen in his hand, he said to me (in a half-whisper), "Well, here go the fisheries." To my reply, "You get a good equivalent for them," he said, "No, we give them away—here goes the signature"; and thereupon signed his name, and rising from the table, said, "They are gone." Northcote was calm, but expressed himself much gratified with the treaty, that it was fair and honorable, that Great Britain had conceded very much, much more than he thought she would be induced to do, and very much more than she could have done two years ago. Bernard expressed himself to the same effect.

The exchange of photographs and autographs was general, and the members parted in great good spirits and with cordial handshaking and leavetaking.

Several Senators, Morton, Hamlin, Frelinghuysen, and Patterson, called during the day to inquire as to the provisions of the treaty.

After the departure of the Commissioners, and [while] giving directions for the clearing up of the room which had been occupied by them, etc., I experience very much the same sensation that I used to have when in college after a laborious preparation for examination, when striving for the honors of the college and having passed the examination, and waiting to know the result and the standing of the class. A feeling of want of something to do,

[30] Diary, May 2, 3, 5, 1871.   [31] Diary, May 8, 1871.

and of the absence of the excitement under which the labor had been sustained.

And while the idea of having nothing to do is upon me, in spite of myself, I have nearly a hundred dispatches and letters upon my table requiring examination.

Sir Stafford Northcote burst into poetry with an Ode to the Fourth Article; everybody took a piece of red-and-blue ribbon as a souvenir; autographs and photographs were exchanged; and amid a mass of flowers sent by Washington ladies, they all sat down to strawberries and ice-cream! [32]

V

The task of obtaining ratification loomed immediately ahead, for Grant had summoned the Senate to meet in special session on May 10. Fish was in favor of prompt publication of the treaty, but before officially released, the text leaked out in slightly incorrect form to the *Tribune* and *World*. There seemed little doubt of favorable action. Of the numerous Senators who came to the Department to read the treaty and hear Fish explain it, only two or three withheld their approval. Howe of Wisconsin was at first dubious about several points, particularly the articles defining neutral duties; Carl Schurz was non-committal. "Poor Patterson," wrote Fish on May 9th, "belongs to somebody; yesterday he was in favor of the treaty; he passed some time last evening with Sumner; today he don't know where he is, or to whom he belongs; he higgles, he wants to support it but does not know whether he will be allowed to do so." But Simon Cameron and a majority of the Foreign Relations Committee could be counted upon, while Hannibal Hamlin, Frederick T. Frelinghuysen, and several others showed enthusiasm.[33]

The most interesting question was as to Sumner's attitude. Though he had been ignored by Grant and Fish, the British Commissioners had paid assiduous attentions to him, and Rockwood Hoar had kept him informed of every conclusion reached. He still spoke in harsh terms of Fish. On April 18, pointing to a roll of manuscript on his Senate desk, he told Oliver P. Morton that it was an attack upon the Secretary which he intended to make before adjournment. After uttering some

[32] Lang, *Sir Stafford Northcote, First Earl of Iddesleigh,* Ch. XII.
[33] Diary, May 7, 9 ff., 1871.

words so harsh that Morton would not repeat them, he added bitterly that Fish's children had been brought up on his knees. "For several years," Fish commented in his diary, "he was in the habit of getting his dinner two, three, even four times a week at my table, and at this time he was not admitted into more than two or three houses in Washington. Having thus for years enjoyed the hospitality of my house he now assumes that it was he who was the benefactor. Bosh! Crazy!" Sumner still talked of damaging disclosures. We read in the diary:

April 21, 1871.—General Butler reads to me a copy of a letter which he says he wrote to Charles Sumner on the 16th inst., dissuading him from his threatened intent to make public some private letters which Sumner claims that I had written to him.

I told Butler that while probably I have written in the careless freedom of my long intimacy with Sumner many letters which may be very foolish, and which were never intended for the public eye, I am not aware of anything which if *truthfully* copied would affect me, or in any way enable Sumner to sustain any complaint against me. I tell him that for a couple of years at least I have regarded Sumner as insane upon a class of questions, and that I may have used expressions in writing, as I have done in conversation, intended to soothe and avoid exciting him, but that he can produce nothing of mine that can without distortion or misrepresentation injure me. However, I express to Butler my appreciation of the kindness of his effort; for the great breach of ordinary and decent propriety and confidence which Sumner had contemplated would have involved an unpleasant controversy and probably have compelled me to produce the real letters written by me, in full, and also many of Sumner's.

But confronting the treaty, Sumner could not deny that it was fair, that it contained none of the flaws which he had criticized in the Johnson-Clarendon Convention, and that American sentiment was strongly in favor of accepting it.

Most of the press, indeed, was enthusiastic. The New York *World* found that "nearly all the concessions were made on the British side." The *Times* and *Tribune* applauded vigorously. The Springfield *Republican* was all approval, though it wished that the treaty might have taken "an initial step at least towards the removal of the British flag." Most Boston newspapers attacked Ben Butler's effort to arouse the Massachusetts fishermen against the treaty. Beecher's *Christian Union* rejoiced in a victory for justice and humanity, and the *Independent* in "a long step towards the general principle of a Congress of Nations."

The *Nation* concluded that the United States had obtained all that a self-respecting nation could ask, or a self-respecting nation could give. Altogether, Goldwin Smith could write Gladstone that the effect of the treaty in America had been "as good as possible."

In the end Sumner took a sportsmanlike course. The Sunday after the treaty was signed, Rockwood Hoar called on Fish after a long talk with the Senator. He brought word that all was well—Sumner would shortly announce his approval. John V. L. Pruyn came later that afternoon with additional information; Sumner criticized certain points in the treaty and would offer amendments. He did propose amendments broadening the statements upon international law, but refrained from pressing them lest he endanger a compact which, he generously said,[34] would "be hailed with joy by the thinking men of Great Britain and the United States." On May 24 Fish was able to place in his diary the triumphant entry:

"Treaty with Great Britain ratified by a vote of 50 to 12."

All of the Republican Senators voted aye save Sprague of Rhode Island, Hamilton of Texas, West of Louisiana, and Blair of Missouri; while two Democrats, Bayard of Delaware and Hamilton of Maryland, broke from their party to support it.[35] In England the only important opponent was Earl Russell, and his speech to the Lords condemning the "British surrender" met a chilling response.

The date of the Senate's approval was Queen Victoria's birthday. Ratifications were formally exchanged in London on Bunker Hill day, June 17. President Grant proclaimed the treaty in full effect on July 4. The notice taken of these coincidences illustrated the feeling on both sides of the Atlantic that the treaty was an event of cardinal importance in the history of the relations of the two English-speaking Powers.

[34] Pierce, *Sumner*, IV, 489.

[35] Thornton wrote Granville of the ratification (PRO, FO 115, 525; May 29, 1871) saying that other Democratic Senators had expressed high approval of the treaty, but the caucus on May 23 had decided it would be to the party interest to oppose it! This was party folly. The diary of that good Democrat and friend of Fish, John V. L. Pruyn, shows that he lobbied hard for the treaty.

The fishery articles did not come into really final effect until Canada passed the necessary legislation. The House at Ottawa voted approval in May, 1872, by a wide margin—121 to 55.

As Fish replied to a shower of congratulatory letters during the last weeks of May, 1871, he felt that he had achieved the principal objects which had induced him to remain at the State Department beyond the few months originally intended. Indeed, he had achieved much more. He had not merely ensured a peaceful settlement with Great Britain, but had helped erect an imposing new precedent in international arbitration. "I trust it will not be considered vain," he wrote a friend,[1] "to give expression to the belief that the treaty inaugurates a new era in the relations of the two governments, and possibly (even beyond that) in the mode of settlement of grave questions between great Powers. I do not believe that wars are to cease forever because of the treaty; but I believe that many will be avoided which would otherwise occur." American relations with Spain, unless some unforeseen explosion occurred, now seemed proof against warlike alarums. The misadventure in Santo Domingo was being abandoned. In every direction the outlook was peaceful.

While he and de Grey still toiled long hours daily, he had hinted to friends that soon after the Treaty was ratified he would quit his post. He had suffered heavy financial losses through inability to watch his railway investments;[2] he disliked the social burdens of Washington; and above all, he missed his family. A deeply affectionate man, he had always delighted to have his eight children near him. "God grant," he wrote a younger friend,[3] "that you may never know what it is, after having been thus surrounded, to find yourself, as you began your married life, sitting down meal after meal, the same pair that you began, but without the *hope* that cheered that beginning, without the future that then beckoned you on." He meant to help Grant select the American Arbitrator and counsel, and to assist in preparing the legal case, but he hoped that by autumn his hands would be free.

In April the leaders of Congress learned with consternation of his plans. They at once attempted to dissuade him on general grounds, and in particular by the dire prospect that Oliver P. Morton would be the

---

[1] To Truman Smith, May 27, 1871; Letterbooks.
[2] To Samuel Welsh, May 18, 1871; Letterbooks.
[3] To George F. Edmunds, June 10, 1871; Letterbooks.

next Secretary and undo half his work. No one doubted Morton's ability, both executive and parliamentary. As war governor of Indiana, indefatigable in raising troops and stamping out the Knights of the Golden Circle, he had done the Union great service. Though a paralytic stroke made him a cripple, unable to stand long without support, he had entered the Senate in 1867 and proved one of Grant's ablest lieutenants. He spoke frequently and incisively and helped shape many measures. But he had taken the wrong side more often than the right; he had been a Radical upon Southern Reconstruction, a leader in Johnson's impeachment, an opponent of civil service reform, an advocate of greenback inflation, a warm supporter of Dominican annexation.[4] He liked to advertise his influence over Grant, informed the press of every conference with the President, and spread reports that he was soon to enter the Cabinet.[5] He had his eye upon the Presidency in 1877 and would gladly accept the State Department as a stepping-stone. Alarmed Republicans, eager to head him off, pleaded with Fish to stay.

Blaine, nursing Presidential ambitions of his own, was the first to call. "He expresses great apprehension of Senator Morton being my successor and of his influence over the President," writes Fish on April 22, 1871. "Expresses great mistrust of him; thinks him a demagogue, extremely ambitious and selfish, and does not accord to him much principle, either political or moral; mentions the statement made to him by a 'lady of Indiana, a discreet matron,' etc., that 'no lady in Indianapolis having any regard for her reputation would be seen walking or riding alone in company with him,' also other remarks affecting his character in other respects. Blaine says that a very general mistrust of Morton exists among the Republicans in the House of Representatives." Zach Chandler next day was even more scathing. "Damn it," he exclaimed, "Morton wants the public to think that he owns and runs Grant. And God damn him, he is making them believe it, and nothing could be more injurious to Grant and to the Republican Party." He accused Morton of being on both sides of all the great public questions at once, and of maintaining an intimacy with Schurz and Sumner while he wriggled into the confidence of Grant. "He is putting himself

[4] Schouler, *United States,* VII, 205. It should be noted that shrewd newspapermen deplored Morton's sway over Grant. The Chicago *Tribune* in 1872 called him the "evil genius" and "ruling spirit" of the Administration; the New York *World* "its master"; and the Louisville *Courier-Journal* "the ablest and most depraved" of all Administration Senators. W. D. Foulke, *Oliver P. Morton,* II, 263–265.

[5] Diary, April 23, 1871.

into a position to go with whichever may seem the strongest." His recent speech on the redemption of the public debt had cost the party 10,000 votes in Indiana. "If Morton succeeds you or otherwise goes into the Cabinet," Chandler said, "it will be impossible for the Republican Party to carry the next Presidential election, for nobody has any confidence in him." He was not a safe adviser, he "equivocated," and lacked principle. Senator Carpenter sent word to Fish that he held the same view—that the Secretary must not resign.[6]

Conkling came next, declaring that Morton as Secretary of State would be disastrous to any hope of future Republican success. "No one can tell from anything he has said or done at the Capitol whether he means to go with Sumner, Schurz, and Tipton, or with the President. He has neither moral nor social fitness for a Cabinet position."

But Fish was unmoved, for he was confident that the President had no intention of appointing Morton. He deferred notifying Grant of his decision until a week after the Treaty had been ratified. On May 29, at the close of a long conference on other matters, he said that he would like to quit office about August 1. Grant was shocked and grieved. He expostulated anxiously, saying that he could not replace Fish and would far rather spare any other member of his Cabinet. The conversation was interrupted by the entry of Secretary Delano, Cox's successor in the Interior Department, and General Parker. But Delano had heard enough to gather its character, and following Fish into the hall, pleaded with him not to resign. The sterling Wisconsin Senator, Timothy O. Howe, also spent half an hour trying to dissuade Fish. A fortnight later Fish again spoke of the matter, and once more Grant protested in urgent terms. He insisted that the Secretary remain till the close of his term, and finally induced Fish to promise to stay until November.

"I do not know whom I can name," exclaimed the President. They discussed Edwards Pierrepont, Edwin D. Morgan, and Isaac H. Bailey, and agreed that none would do. Morton was not even mentioned. "Have you ever thought of transferring some member of the Cabinet?" inquired Fish. "Yes, I have," said Grant. "It has occurred to me that Delano might do." He knew nothing of Delano's real character, and had not yet had time even to gauge his abilities! Fish was shocked. "I would rather suggest Robeson," he rejoined. But Grant correctly felt that

[6] Diary, April 22–26, 1871.

Robeson would be unacceptable to the public.[7]

Thus the matter was left for five months, until winter was at hand. "Well, we will talk it over another time," Grant had observed. But he took pains not to talk it over, and clearly wished to postpone the evil day. In a long summer, busy with many loose ends of foreign policy, Fish made no further allusion to resignation.

I

Santo Domingo, one of these loose ends, was important only in its relation to the growing revolt against Grant. The investigative commission authorized by Congress and appointed by the President sailed in January, 1871. Fish was pleased by the three members chosen: old Ben Wade of Ohio, a Radical Republican attached to all Negro causes; Andrew D. White, head of Cornell University, a publicist of exceptional literary power; and Samuel G. Howe of Massachusetts, lifelong reformer and close friend of Sumner. The Commission had a secretary in Frederick Douglass, the Negro leader, who believed in the possibility of colonizing his race in Santo Domingo, and a military adviser in General Franz Sigel, influential among the Germans swayed by Schurz. Besides geologists, mineralogists, and other scientists, ten newspaper correspondents were aboard. The party was talkative and merry. Howe had fought with Byron in Greece forty years earlier; another had been in the Crimea; a third had participated in half a dozen Latin-American revolutions; a number had served in the Civil War. At night in the cabin they listened to Ben Wade upon his quarrel with Toombs, or his anecdotes of Lincoln and Stanton; they heard Dr. Howe upon Boston men of letters, or Sigel upon his Missouri campaign; and Douglass told of his twenty years of bondage. On January 24, under a sun which burned the deck, they ran into the blue bay of Samaná, where the green hills, cocoanut groves, and thatched villages enchanted them. "Mr. Fabens, Judge O'Sullivan, and some others spend a great deal of time here, but can hardly be called inhabitants," wrote the *Tribune* correspondent.[8]

The party remained in Santo Domingo or the neighboring waters

[7] Diary, May 29, June 13, 1871.
[8] On the visit of this Commission, see A. D. White, *Autobiography,* I, 486 ff.; Laura E. Richards, *Samuel Gridley Howe;* letter of S. G. Howe in N. Y. *Tribune,* August 23, 1871; and above all, the Commission's report.

for five weeks. While it worked conscientiously, the time did not permit an adequate investigation; and though Fabens and Cazneau were absent, the geologist Gabb adroitly took the Commission in hand. He wrote Fabens that he had acted with great effect.[9] Wade had said that he thought the devil must have gotten into Brother Sumner. "They express themselves satisfied, thanks to my endeavors, that there is no underhand work or improper jobbery in our survey and we will get the biggest kind of a puff from them on the score of good faith. My annual reports to the government, which were very guardedly written with a view to the present contingency, will be quoted at length and endorsed as reliable. And—!! The Commissioners are all three 'down on' their own geologist!! For the news—with a dozen reporters here, there's nothing left for me to say—I've manufactured a good four-fifths of all the public opinion that will be formed by them and in this I consider that the Co. owes me at least 3 or 4 months extra salary." The Commission found most of the inhabitants strongly for annexation, and submitted a report favorable to that step. Wade, a Manifest Destiny man, and Howe, carried away by humanitarian zeal for the Caribbean, were quite uncritical, but White compelled them to include some scientific data in the report.[10]

Obviously it was too late for such a document to have any real effect. Public opinion had long since crystallized, and Grant's best friends had warned him that it would be impossible to annex the republic by joint resolution or any other means. He realized that the only utility of the report would lie in furnishing a partial justification of his original policy.

When the Cabinet took it up on March 31, 1871, Fish was relieved by his attitude. "President reads draft of proposed message communicating report, to which some amendments and alterations are suggested," states the diary. "In the main it is right; he submits the whole question to Congress and the people. Asks no action, recounts his action with regard to it, and claims that the report justifies his views and expressions." This quiet message, merely requesting publication of the findings, went at once to Congress. There was much dignity in the passage with which Grant closed it. Rejection of the treaty, he wrote,

9 February 11, 1871; Fabens Papers.
10 The correspondent of the N. Y. *Tribune* was H. J. Ramsdell; for his hostile reports see the issues of February 24 and March 17, 18, 1871, in particular. Cf. White, *Autobiography*, I, 487, 488.

had been accompanied by charges of "corruption on the part of the President or those employed by him." This had made an investigation imperative. The Commission had completely vindicated the purity of all those who conducted the negotiations for annexation. "And now my task is finished, and with it ends all personal solicitude upon the subject." [11]

But Sumner was not the man to forego the opportunity for a new attack upon the President. Anticipating the report by more than a week, he delivered from printed slips a speech of three and a half hours, full of eloquence and power.[12] Speaking not upon annexation, for that was dead, but upon the methods used to promote it, he harshly scored Babcock, Cazneau, and Fabens. But his principal target was Grant, whom he once more assailed as a violator of international law and a usurper of unconstitutional war powers; a leader who had used the navy to bully Haiti, and to interfere belligerently in Dominican affairs. Sensational rumors that he would castigate Grant for his nepotism and tolerance of corruption drew a throng to the galleries. But Sumner shrewdly reserved this part of his fire for the winter session. His most intemperate paragraphs were those which accused Grant of neglecting "fearful outrages" at home. Had he "been so inspired as to bestow upon the protection of the Southern Unionists, white and black, one half, nay, sir, one quarter of the time, money, zeal, will, personal effort, and personal intercession which he has bestowed on his attempt to obtain half an island in the Caribbean, our Southern Ku Klux would have existed in name only." This was doubly unjust; it was never one of Grant's faults that he was too lenient with the conquered South. But Boutwell soon returned from a New England trip reporting that the speech had produced not the slightest impression in Sumner's own section.

Now that the commission's report had been published, friends of the Administration hoped that Santo Domingo might be completely forgotten. Fish labored manfully to thrust the subject into the background. On June 16, 1871, the President showed the Cabinet [13] a pleading letter which Baez had written him on April 10—Fish having also had one from Secretary Gautier. They saw themselves on the brink

[11] Richardson, *Messages and Papers*, VII, 128–131.
[12] *Congressional Globe*, March 27, 1871. Two days later Carl Schurz made an extremely effective speech on Santo Domingo.
[13] Diary.

of ruin, and Dr. Howe, sympathizing with them, had urged Grant to renew the Samaná Bay lease and continue his protection of the Baez Government. Robeson remarked that the orders under which the navy was to repel any interloping nation had never yet been revoked. But Fish at once seized his opportunity. "Mr. President, all obligation of protection is at an end, and those orders ought to be annulled forthwith," he said. When Robeson and Boutwell spoke of the desirability of furnishing Baez some funds, he was equally emphatic: "I have none at the disposal of my department." Even if renewal of the Samana lease were wise, he went on, it would not justify continued naval protection of the Baez Government. Grant approved of a renewal of the lease, remarking that it would at least give Baez moral support. But Fish objected that nobody in Washington was empowered to negotiate for Santo Domingo. "Fabens is here," said Grant. But Fabens had been completely discredited, and Fish replied shortly: "It will not answer to negotiate with Fabens."

As a matter of fact, the treaty authorizing the lease had expired. Though an agreement authorizing its extension had been drawn up in July, 1870, just before Congress adjourned, Grant had mislaid it and forgotten all about it: "I rather think it was left in this room," he said, gazing about his office. Actually he had dropped it on the floor of his room in the Capitol, where it was temporarily lost. Fish felt no regrets over this, nor was he very sympathetic when sundry friends of the Baez Government told him of its desperate financial extremities. Its geologist, W. M. Gabb, reported to the Secretary that it had only about $4,000 in the treasury; [14] but Fish said in effect that Baez's plight was no affair of the United States. Boutwell, in a long talk with the Secretary on June 17, agreed that renewal of the lease or the protectorate would injure the Administration, and that the existing naval orders ought to be revoked.

When in October, 1871, Fabens turned up at the State Department and gaily announced that he desired a renewal of the lease, he met a peremptory refusal. "I will not negotiate any treaty with Santo Domingo except in the most formal diplomatic manner," said Fish. "Nor will I recognize you, Mr. Fabens—an American citizen—as the representative of Santo Domingo." Fabens defiantly said that the Dominican Government would not sign a lease unless protection were con-

[14] Diary, June 19, 1871.

tinued. "Continued!" exclaimed Fish. "The protection ceased long ago. It was intended to last only through the plebiscite on annexation. It lapsed as soon as that was over." He tells us that he spoke "with much emphasis." The unhappy Fabens stuttered something about an extension of both lease and protection. Fish rejoined that the extension had never been sent to the Senate. "I will not negotiate with you under any circumstances," he reiterated.[15] "My opinion is that the whole subject should be dropped for at least a year."

A fortnight later Fish read the Cabinet a formal request by Gautier for renewal of the lease without protection and without submission to the Senate. "I will not be a party," he said, "to any such arrangement." Grant was resigned: "We will drop the matter, and leave the whole question for Congress and the people." "Thus," comments Fish with evident relish,[16] "a troublesome, vexatious, and unnecessary question is, as I trust, finally got rid of." As a matter of fact, an unhappy sequel of it was later to haunt him. The first year's rent of Samaná had very improperly been paid by Grant out of secret service funds. A second year's rent was paid, purely as a speculation, by Spofford, Tileston & Co., with the less selfish aid of Jay and Henry D. Cooke. Before long they were asking for repayment from the government—and Grant was most unwisely abetting them! Yet the general question *was* dropped.

With the Presidential election looming ahead, it was dismissed in the nick of time; but great was the feeling it left behind. Grant never forgot the subject, and in his last annual message recurred to it with pain. Schurz, Sumner, and Trumbull were preparing to use the issue to help disrupt the Republican Party. And yet, unhappy as it seemed, the Dominican adventure had served two great purposes. But for it, Grant would never have been deflected so easily from Cuban intervention. But for the wedge it drove between Grant and Sumner, Fish's prompt, moderate, and pacific settlement with England might never have been possible.

II

The difficulties with Spain, which kept simmering up toward the boiling point, were lessened by the establishment on February 12, 1871, of an arbitral board to pass upon American claims for damage in Cuba.

---

[15] Diary, October 11, 1871.   [16] Diary, October 27, 1871.

Sickles had ably conducted the negotiations.[17] Consisting of one American, William T. Otto, one Spaniard, Don Luis de Potestad, and an umpire selected by both, the board served throughout the remainder of the Ten Years War in Cuba. Caleb Cushing acted as American counsel.[18] On emancipation and other reforms Spanish dilatoriness remained irritating in the extreme. Yet Fish and Don Lopez Roberts now often adopted a bantering tone. Roberts complained one day, for example, of the Cuban privateer *Hornet* as a "pirate," and Fish sharply reminded him that if Spain molested an American vessel on the high seas, it would be an act of war. But both then assumed a good-natured attitude: [19]

He thinks we have a bad record with respect to the vessels which have been fitted out against Cuba, to go before the tribunal at Geneva, and that it would be to our interest to settle with Spain before the trial. I laughingly say, "We have behaved well to Spain. What is there to settle?" He asks if I wish him to give me a memorandum on the subject. I reply, "Of course I will receive anything on the subject you give, but I do not invite any such memorandum." He says he does not propose to make any official or formal communication, but if it will not be inconvenient (and he thinks it will be convenient to have it), he will hand me a memorandum privately and unofficially. I answer that I am always glad to receive suggestions, and will receive his memorandum as an informal and unofficial suggestion.

An evil fate haunted the French Legation. In March, 1871, the new Minister, M. Treillard, went insane; he had been greatly depressed by the crushing national defeat and by the corruption of his consul-general in New York, who defrauded the French Government on arms bought in the United States.[20] "Besides this," Fish wrote Washburne, "he had lost largely by the destruction and carrying away of his property by the enemy in France." Meanwhile Baron Gerolt, Prussian representative since Polk's time, had fallen into difficulties with his government and been recalled. He blamed George Bancroft in Berlin for his misfortune. While Bismarck had certainly been displeased by some of Gerolt's statements as to the German objects in the Franco-Prussian War, no evidence existed that Bancroft had been a tale-bearer. But Gerolt came repeatedly to the State Department to pour out impassioned complaints. Fish sympathized with the old gentleman, his long

---

[17] Diary, February 12, 1871.
[19] Diary.

[18] See *Foreign Relations*, 1871, 697–773.
[20] Diary, March 12, 1871.

career ending amid dark clouds, and said many kind things; yet at times he lost patience. When Bancroft was commissioned Minister to the new German Empire, Gerolt burst in one evening to express a most unreasonable indignation. "Poor old Baron," wrote Fish.[21] "He has outlived his memory, his good temper, and his discretion. Pity!"

But the principal thorn in Fish's side was the perverse, mendacious, and treacherous Russian Minister, Count Constantin de Catacazy. This slippery diplomatist, a native Russian of part-Greek descent, had been sent over by Prince Gortschakoff in 1869. The count had always been a stormy petrel. When a handsome young secretary of legation in Rio de Janeiro he had caused an international scandal by running away with the wife of the aged Neapolitan Minister to Brazil. In 1848 he had turned up in Washington as First Secretary, and rented a cottage for his paramour in Blandensburg. His audacious wit had attracted Daniel Webster and others.[22] Now, regularly married, he was received by the best Washington society, and might have had an honorable career there. But he was never happy except in some intrigue; loving the atmosphere of plots, cabals, and stratagems, he should have been born in the age of Richelieu. Moreover, he was dishonest. A newspaperman gave Fish some confidential information on June 12: [23]

Frank Turk at my house this evening. Says Catacazy has defrauded his government; that the Government sent an amount of money for the purchase of land for a Greek Church in New York. That Catacazy purchased the lots for $17,000 greenbacks, and charged the Russian Government $20,000 gold; that he (Turk) investigated the title, and at Catacazy's instance induced the seller, very reluctantly, to insert $20,000 as the consideration in the deed, when only $17,000 were paid, and that Catacazy agreed to pay the United States revenue stamps on the additional $3,000 before the seller would consent, and did pay them; that the seller was some person from Long Island, and that he (Turk) had great difficulty in inducing him to insert in the deed a different consideration from that really paid. . . .

As long as Fish heard nothing worse of Catacazy than this he showed a chilly tolerance. The man was full of talent and very entertaining. But the so-called Perkins Claim—perhaps the most malodorous of the many claims upon which lobbyists, shysters, and political harpies fed

[21] Diary, June 1, 1871.
[22] The author has profited greatly from a paper on "The Catacazy Affair" by Mr. Reinhard H. Luthin. The State Department archives contain two volumes of briefs and affidavits entitled *Claim of Benjamin W. Perkins* and *Claim of Anna B. Perkins.*
[23] Diary. Cf. the article on Mme. Catacazy in *Every Saturday,* November 18, 1871.

during the Gilded Age—complicated their relations. Captain Benjamin W. Perkins, a figure worthy of E. Phillips Oppenheim, was a sea-rover of Worcester, Massachusetts, who during the Crimean War had allegedly entered into a contract with Captain Otto Lilienfeldt, Russian agent in New York, to place 35,000 arms in Sebastopol. Perkins also declared that he had a verbal agreement with Baron Stoeckl, the Russian Minister, to supply gunpowder. When the Russians repudiated both contracts, Perkins hurried to a lawyer. Ultimately his claim fell into the hands of a Washington lawyer and wirepuller, Joseph B. Stewart.[24] This man, able, unscrupulous, a reckless gambler in gold and stocks, was for years "the big boss of the lobby." He had much to do with corrupt "jobs" in connection with the Union Pacific Railroad and Credit Mobilier. Stewart and others induced Lewis Cass, Buchanan's Secretary of State, to ask the Russian Government for arbitration of the claim, which was indignantly refused. Then in the Lincoln Administration powerful men were enlisted—William M. Evarts, Caleb Cushing, and Thaddeus Stevens. A brief was prepared by Evarts and Cushing. The Perkins Claim was probably quite fraudulent. But by 1861 it had a powerful backing among politicians, lobbyists, and legal luminaries, and Secretary Seward demanded action in St. Petersburg. Gortschakoff flushed with anger and told the American Minister, "We will go to war before we pay a kopeck!" [25]

So the claim stood when Fish took office. Unlike Seward, he regarded it with deep distrust. But the acts of his predecessors constituted a precedent for asking arbitration. Moreover, the claim had entered into the complicated bargaining and corruption which accompanied the purchase of Alaska. House obstructionists interested in it had held up this purchase until they exacted certain promises from Seward and Stoeckl; the details are vague, but it is certain that the two men engaged to have it arbitrated as soon as the House passed the appropriation for Alaska. No wonder that Stoeckl, worn out, implored the Imperial Government: "Send me where I may breathe a purer air than that of Washington!" Fish found in 1869 that Stewart was still

[24] For matter on Stewart, see Rollin H. Kirk, *Many Secrets Revealed, or Ten Years Behind the Scenes in Washington City;* C. de Catacazy, *Un Incident Diplomatique;* and a mass of material in newspapers of the day. Some letters from him are in the Thaddeus Stevens Papers in the Library of Congress.

[25] *Cassius Marcellus Clay: Memoirs, Writings, Speeches,* 406. Cassius M. Clay had been Minister to Russia at the time.

pressing it, that N. P. Banks was still interested, and that Congress threatened action. Ben Butler was said to have bought a share in it.[26] Moreover, Stewart hastened to employ Frederick T. Dent and Judge Louis Dent, brothers-in-law of the President. Grant soon evinced a naïvely belligerent interest in the claim.

We may pass briefly over the preposterous events which followed. Grant took a stiff stand. Fish writes under January 28, 1870: "Cabinet; all present. President speaks of the Perkins Claim with remarkable earnestness; has read Seward's letter on the Claim, and is urgent that a settlement be made." While mildly urging arbitration on the Russian Minister, Fish acted cautiously.[27] He showed a frank resentment of the meddling by Grant's relatives. Thus under April 22, 1870, he writes again: "I . . . state [to the Cabinet], having Judge Dent in view, and indicating but not naming him, that when it was found necessary to employ a new agent or attorney, the amount of the Claims increased by the amount necessary to give him." Catacazy not only stood adamant, but brought up a counter-claim—one for interest on the purchase-money for Alaska, which had not been paid over until three months after the stipulated date!

And a newspaper war soon commenced. Stewart and the Dents inspired a flaming five-column article in the Washington *National Republican,* an "Administration organ" of disreputable tone edited by W. J. Murtagh, of whom we shall hear more.[28] Catacazy responded by a violent publication (in the form of letters to and from Cassius M. Clay) in the Washington *Morning Chronicle* of March 11, 1870. This irritated Secretary Fish. It was outrageous for a foreign Minister to engage the press under his own name upon an official question, and he sent a sharp note expressing his surprise. "You will oblige me by in-

[26] Butler had introduced a resolution to withhold $500,000 of the sum appropriated to buy Alaska in order to meet the claims of "American citizens" against Russia. *Cong. Globe,* Vol. 40, Pt. 2, pp. 4052–4053. Baron Stoeckl declared that Butler had a $30,000 share in the Perkins Claim; Frank A. Golder, "Purchase of Alaska," *American Historical Review,* XXV, 411–425.

[27] Fish wrote the chargé at the Russian Legation, Bodisco, asking for action on the claim, and Bodisco replied by sending a copy of a note Gortschakoff had written March 10, 1869, asking for authentic copies of the alleged Perkins contracts. When Fish called on Stewart for copies, the latter replied that the contracts had been verbal; Stewart to Fish, March 29, 1869. Fish was suspicious from the outset. But as he wrote Minister Curtin, "We cannot well let it drop. Were we inclined to do so Congress would not let it rest." April 22, 1870; Letterbooks.

[28] *National Republican,* April 22, 1870. Catacazy told Fish that Murtagh had a financial interest in the Perkins Claim, which is more than plausible; Diary, December 22, 1870.

forming me if that correspondence is genuine, and whether it was published with your sanction and at your instance." [29] Catacazy defiantly replied that he had had "the honor" to cause the publication. Thereupon Fish sent an indignant comment to Minister Curtin in St. Petersburg. The publication, he wrote,[30] "has been the subject of very severe criticism and comment among the diplomatic corps here. Many of them have taken occasion to speak to me about it, condemning it as most unwise, impolitic, and indecorous."

In February, 1870, reports reached Washington that Chancellor Gortschakoff had been succeeded by Ignatieff. On March 3 Grant summoned Fish to the White House. He read the Secretary two letters which Stewart and Dent declared they had obtained: One a dispatch from Ignatieff severely censuring Catacazy for his stand upon the Perkins Claim, and one Catacazy's answer, in which Grant and Fish were assailed and traduced. Fish called in Catacazy, who seemed furious. He denounced the letters as forgeries, which they proved to be. As a matter of fact, Gortschakoff had never been displaced by Ignatieff at all! Just who wrote these two clumsy forgeries may never be known. It was possibly one of Stewart's agents, though some observers, including Fish and Bancroft Davis, later believed it had been Catacazy himself![31] For Catacazy at once proceeded to make capital out of the incident. Though Fish wished to drop it and avoid "public scandal," the exuberant Minister chattered about the forgeries all over Washington. At dinner parties and receptions he used them to heap ridicule and denunciation upon the Perkins Claim. Fish noted with disgust that even at state dinners Catacazy dragged in the Claim; and he soon heard that the Minister was spreading slanderous tales about him and the President.

[29] Fish to Catacazy, March 12, 1870; State Department MSS, Notes to Russian Legation.

[30] April 22, 1870; Letterbooks.

[31] See Fish's *Diary*, March 3, 13, 14, 16, etc., 1870. See also Bancroft Davis's Diary, October 25, 1871, reporting a conversation with M. Chambrun. "I asked him if he knew the history of those papers. Said that he believed he did—that the papers were prepared, as he understood, by Catacazy, were given to Dolgourouski, who took them to Tasistro [another Russian adventurer]. Tasistro took them in French to Stewart, pretending that he had got them from Waldemar Bodisco, and offered them to Stewart, who took them in good faith. I said that tallied with what Mr. Fish had told me, except that in addition Tasistro had, to deceive Stewart, arranged that he, Tasistro, should go into Welches' Restaurant, and that Waldemar Bodisco should be made to follow him, and thus give an appearance of reality to the intrigue. I said that Mr. Fish was morally certain that Catacazy was the originator of the fraud." Verily, the tale even surpasses E. Phillips Oppenheim.

Although he observed a formal courtesy, and invited Catacazy to the diplomatic dinner and official receptions, relations between the two men rapidly grew strained. Catacazy was constantly trying to disturb Anglo-American relations. We have mentioned his manoeuvres when the Franco-Prussian War broke out. In November, 1870, following Russia's abrogation of the Black Sea convention, the Minister sent home two dispatches of the most brazen mendacity. He knew that Gortschakoff would be pleased by any evidence of American support. He therefore wrote that he had talked with Fish; and Fish had given him to understand that, if an Anglo-Russian War began, the Czar might contract an armed alliance with the United States, and that America would even be willing to send a squadron to the Black Sea to aid Russia! In his second dispatch he stated that Fish had asked for Russian support in the demands on England in the *Alabama* negotiations, and had again spoken of the feasibility of sending an American fleet to the Black Sea! These Munchausen tales were coldly received by Gortschakoff. But he mentioned them to Minister Curtin, and Curtin wrote about them to Fish. The Secretary was stunned. After he had regained his composure, he sat down and (January 9, 1871) answered Curtin:

I read to the President your letter of 18 Dec. He was quite indignant and says he has never held any conversation with Mr. C[atacazy] on the probable or possible course of the Government in the event of war between Great Britain and Russia; never intimated to him, or to anyone else the possibility or intention of sending a fleet to the Mediterranean or Constantinople. . . . I know that the Cabinet has never given a single moment to the consideration of an alliance, offensive or defensive, with Russia.

Fish would have been justified in asking for Catacazy's recall. But in the delicate state of relations with Great Britain and Spain, he was anxious not to impair Russian cordiality. His resentment rose, however, when it became plain that Catacazy was plotting to defeat the work of the Anglo-American High Commission. The British envoys no sooner arrived than he began to make slurring remarks; he aired his doubts of a settlement; he buttonholed men on each side and tried to excite their prejudices. To these meddling activities he added a personal affront to Fish. He gave a dinner to the Joint High Commission, invited every member except the Secretary, and then wrote a letter in which he boasted to a New York journalist: "You see, we did not invite Mr. and Mrs. Fish." This letter was shown to Fish's friends. Finally the Secretary discussed Catacazy's machinations with Grant, and the result was a sharp warning. He called at Fish's office about some routine matter: [32]

He was about to leave, and I request him to remain a moment, remarking that little birds are flying about and singing little stories into people's ears. He replies, "Ah, yes, those little birds!" I add that "the little bird says you have been making yourself unnecessarily occupied with the affairs between this country and Great Britain in connection with the Commission about to assemble, and the owl says that 'perhaps it may be well to observe a little more caution.' " He protests that he has spoken with only two persons on the subject; one of these was Thornton yesterday; the other Sumner on Saturday. (He forgets that he talked with me and I have heard of a number of others to whom he has spoken; it was on Saturday Thornton told me he was talking all about town.) I replied that prior to Saturday I had been told of his frequent conversations on the subject in the streets, in salons, and elsewhere, and the account of these remarks had reached the President prior to Saturday and caused him some disquietude; and I deemed it advisable to suggest to him that a little more caution and reticence might be prudent.

He says that Wendell Phillips was present with Sumner during his interview and claims that he told Sumner that it was not becoming a man of his calibre to resist a negotiation merely from personal hostility to the Administration. He says, "It is true I told him that I feared the negotiation would not result as successfully as I hoped it might." (He told me, "Oh, you will have everything you want. Lord de Grey comes out with Canada in his pocket to ask you to accept it.")

I suggest to him that Sumner and Phillips are two of the most bitter enemies of the President. . . . He is told that there can be no objection to his visiting whom he pleases, but what I desired was to intimate to him that the President was disturbed by the rumors which reach him of his interference and conversations about the relations of this government with Great Britain, and of the coming convention, and that it may be prudent to observe a little more caution.

Any man of prudence would have profited by this monition, but Catacazy could cease to plot as easily as he ceased to breathe. Within a week Fish learned that he had supplied the Washington correspondent of the Cincinnati *Commercial* with a venomous article under the heading: [33] "Reported Trouble Between President Grant and the Russian Minister." In this Catacazy informed the world that some of

[32] Diary, February 20, 1871.   [33] Diary, February 26, 1871.

Grant's entourage, notably Louis Dent, had a financial interest in pushing the Perkins Claim, and that he was valiantly defending his country against it. The Secretary called him in to ask about the article. "When I began reading it, he said, 'Oh, yes.' When I finished reading it, he protested that he had never seen it and knew nothing of it." But lying never troubled the "pestilent, intriguing, meddlesome" Catacazy, as Fish called him in a letter to Washburne. He was now inspiring publications in the *World* and other newspapers as part of a veritable campaign against Grant. At the same time he tried clumsily to cover his tracks, as another entry shows:

April 29, 1871.—. . . Dining at the President's [a dinner to the diplomatic corps]; Catacazy tells me that a Mr. E. A. Portois or some such name had recently called on him, and representing himself as connected with some newspaper, said he wished to learn what there was about the connection of persons high in the government with the Perkins Claims and their interest in the claim, and that he, Catacazy, disclaimed any knowledge and refused to converse with him. That when he was in New York lately the same person called upon Baron Osten Sacken . . . [and] said that Peshine Smith [former counsel to the State Department] had been given an interest in the claim, etc. The upshot of the story is, as Catacazy wants me to believe and he asserts, that this man is employed by Stewart and Tasistro to endeavor to entrap him into a conversation for the purpose of making charges against him, of criminating parties connected with the government and thus involving him in difficulties. This looks to me like a very shallow cover of another of Catacazy's movements.

Fish quietly gathered affidavits upon Catacazy's authorship of articles abusing the President. He paid the Marquis de Chambrun, of the French Legation, for procuring testimony with regard to dispatches from St. Petersburg forged by Catacazy. Grant, with characteristic abruptness, told the Cabinet on June 16, 1871, that he wished to dismiss the Minister at once. But Fish pointed out that this would offend the Russian Government, and that the proper course was to ask St. Petersburg to withdraw him. Already he had written Curtin that both governments would profit if Russia replaced Catacazy, and on June 19 he sent a more explicit request. But the Minister exhausted every means to hang on to his post. Among the dispatches which he forged were some from his government approving his diplomatic conduct, which he brazenly showed to other members of the diplomatic corps! He still invented Munchausen conversations with Grant:

October 9, 1871.—. . . . I read to the President Curtin's No. 120, September 10, St. Petersburg. When I read the passage giving Catacazy's dispatch detailing his visit to the President at Long Branch after his interview with me on 16th August, the President interrupted my reading, saying, "That is a lie from beginning to end, every word of it." When I had finished reading the dispatch, he expressed a regret that he had not dismissed Catacazy "immediately without asking his recall."

There seemed few limits to his impudence. Once in talking with Fish he had the effrontery to say, "I fear I do not possess the confidence or respect of the Secretary." Fish was significantly silent.[34]

In the end Catacazy had to go. The Grand Duke Alexis of Russia arrived in the fall of 1871 for a tour of our principal cities and a buffalo hunt in the Far West. Grant and Fish made it plain that while Catacazy was still nominally Minister, he was tolerated only for the purpose of attending the Grand Duke, and was not to receive diplomatic honors. Army and Navy officers were instructed to offer him no salutes except in company with the Grand Duke. Moreover, Fish informed the legation that if he used the Western tour to renew his intrigues he would be dismissed. The Russian Government grasped the situation, and Catacazy was overtaken in St. Louis by peremptory orders to return home. The Secretary's last communication to him was word that he had better get out as peaceably and quietly as possible. This was in an interview with the Russian chargé, Valerien de Schirkov, which throws an interesting light upon Fish's firmness of temper when once aroused: [35]

I add that information has reached me that Catacazy has threatened legal proceedings against Mr. Adams [the *World* correspondent] and has been annoying him by interrogatories, and has employed a lawyer (W. E. Chandler) who has advised Adams to engage counsel, etc., etc. . . . That if Catacazy resorts to the courts, or threatens citizens of the United States with legal proceedings, it will be a waiver of his diplomatic privilege of extraterritoriality, and I shall be forced to consider whether I shall not immediately terminate his immunities and allow any citizens who have been aggrieved by him, or who have claims against him, to bring him before the courts before he may leave the country.

He says he thinks there is some mistake and that Catacazy has no idea of instituting a suit; that he wishes to obtain evidence for his justification in St. Petersburg; that after his return there he may institute proceedings; and that then those who have claims against him may sue him there where he

[34] Diary.   [35] Diary, January 5, 1872.

will have no immunities.

I reply that that will not do; if he has any such intention, the suits by American citizens must be brought here. I will not have it understood that he is to begin a suit against one of our citizens and force those who have claims against him to go to Russia for their remedy. . . . I desire therefore to be informed either by note or orally, but officially, if Catacazy intends to bring any suits in this country or is preparing to bring one after his return to Russia, against any American citizen in this country. . . . I desire a reply today.

Later in the day (2 P. M.) Schirkov again calls. Says the whole thing is a misapprehension; that Catacazy has had no intention of instituting any legal proceedings either now or after his return to Russia.

III

Another of Fish's summer tasks was to help the President choose the American Arbitrator at Geneva, and the Agent or manager of the American case. The latter was easily found. Fish suggested Bancroft Davis, and Grant immediately assented. But the selection of an Arbitrator proved highly troublesome. Fish proposed Charles Francis Adams, but Grant demurred. A number of other names were then discussed in Cabinet and rejected for various reasons: William Cullen Bryant, because he was too old and politically opposed to the President; William Beach Lawrence (Fish's former law partner), because a Democrat; Edwards Pierrepont, because he did not speak French and knew little international law; William M. Evarts, because Grant disliked him; and Caleb Cushing, because busy elsewhere. Fish emphasized the importance of a fully equipped representative. Long study and training in international law were required; England, Italy, Switzerland and Brazil would send their ablest experts; few Americans save Adams or Lawrence had given careful study to such questions as would arise. After listening to these injunctions, Grant expressed willingness to name Morton McMichael—a Philadelphia journalist who knew practically no law of any kind! [36]

Fish's preference was strongly for Charles Francis Adams, but the independent New Englander met hostility from Grant and warm opposition from Boutwell and Creswell. In their second discussion of the question the President thought that Schenck would do, though he also knew no international law whatever. Creswell chimed in. "Yes, why go

[36] Diary, June–September, 1871.

out of the Commission?" But Fish pointed out that Schenck still had a
legal connection with Jay Cooke's Northern Pacific Railroad which
might interrupt his work, while it would be improper for him or Hoar
to take a position which they had helped create. William M. Meredith,
a Pennsylvania attorney who had been Secretary of the Treasury under
Zachary Taylor, was suggested; but he was seventy-two, and it was
learned that his health would not permit. At the third discussion,
June 15, 1871, Grant made a horrifying suggestion. Fish writes: [37]

President returned this morning from Long Branch. Creswell with him
when I went in. Referring to the Arbitrator . . . he asked what information
I obtained as to Mr. Meredith, and was told what Mr. Boker had told me;
also what he had subsequently written. President remarks that he thinks he
is too old, that he has a man who he thinks has most of the qualifications
needed, and names O. P. Morton, to which I object most strenuously, saying that I do not think he is in any way competent for the place. Subsequently,
after Creswell had left the room, I spoke more strongly; referred to his unpopularity with his colleagues in the Senate and their want of confidence
in him; mentioned what Chandler, Carpenter, Conkling, and Frelinghuysen
had said; alluded to his reputation for looseness of morals, and that the public
had no confidence in him, many persons did not believe him honest; that he
does not speak French, and would be entirely without influence on the Board.
That the President has much dependent on this Board, as his treaty would be
judged in a large degree by its decision, and that we needed the ablest and
most efficient man in the country, one who had both national and foreign
reputation, and therefore it was that I was willing to disregard all questions
of politics and appoint Charles Francis Adams; he objects decidedly to Adams,
would rather appoint an out-and-out Democrat. Richard H. Dana's name
being mentioned, he says he would much prefer him.

He says that Senator Harlan had suggested W. B. Allison as Agent under
the Twelfth Article (Claims) of the British Treaty. Harlan thinks he will be
reëlected to the Senate without much trouble, but that Allison is the only man
likely to be in his way.

Persistently Fish returned to the name of Adams, and finally Grant
gave way. The nomination was received with enthusiasm. Adams, who
had just refused the presidency of Harvard, had reputation, experience,
learning, energy—everything. He knew the history of the cruisers at
first hand; a friend of Argyll, Gladstone, Forster, Bright, he knew
how to deal with Englishmen; direct, judicious, he knew when to be
firm and when moderate. At the crisis of the Geneva Arbitration, he

[37] Diary.

was destined to save it from disaster. As James Ford Rhodes has observed, he was the hero of the Tribunal, and in insisting upon him when Creswell declared that even Thomas A. Hendricks would be preferable, Fish again showed his acute judgment of men.

During the summer Bancroft Davis, with some aid from Fish, prepared the American Case, and in November left the State Department to sail for Geneva. Meanwhile the counsel had been chosen. The first man to be selected was Caleb Cushing. Grant said on September 1st that he would "under no circumstances" appoint William M. Evarts, and asked Fish to offer the second place to William M. Meredith. The latter at first accepted, but soon quailed at the prospect of a voyage to Europe, and on October 17 resigned; whereupon Fish induced the President to invite both Benjamin R. Curtis and Evarts to serve. Curtis declined; but Evarts gladly took the appointment.

Unfortunately, he signalized this acceptance by a piece of gross carelessness. "He goes to see the President," ruefully chronicles the Secretary,[38] "and on the way drops in the street the printed copy of the Case which I had handed to him." Search was in vain; for the finder took it to the British Legation and there sold it for a round price. Evarts was later rallied as "the counsel who lost his case before he opened it!"[39] A third counsel was not necessary, but Davis wanted one. Secretary Delano therefore proposed to the Cabinet a fellow-Ohioan of whom the others had never heard—"a Mr. Waite of Toledo, who, he says, is the equal of any man in the country as a lawyer." Thus we find the next Chief Justice of the United States mentioned in Fish's diary! A few days later Grant asked Fish to offer Waite the post. On the British side, Lord Tenterden was to be Agent, and Sir Roundell Palmer and Mountague Bernard counsel.

IV

With the preliminaries of the arbitration complete, with the United States represented by five men of preëminent ability—Adams, Bancroft Davis, Cushing, Waite, and Evarts—and with our foreign affairs in a thoroughly happy state, the Secretary could resign without a qualm. On November 14, 1871, the President again urged him to remain until March 4, 1873. Fish replied that he wished to retire soon after the be-

---

[38] Diary.   [39] Hackett, *Reminiscences of the Geneva Tribunal,* 105.

ginning of December.⁴⁰ He wrote the section on foreign affairs for the President's annual message, which Grant promised to use with few if any changes. He drafted instructions to the counsel at Geneva, which the Cabinet approved without modification. He cleared his desk. Then, as the Cabinet meeting of December 5 closed, he handed Grant his written resignation.

The result was such a demonstration of protest as has seldom occurred in the history of the Cabinet. Grant expressed the deepest sorrow. As Secretary Fish walked out of the room, Robeson, who had guessed at the contents of the paper, intercepted him, crying: "Are you going to leave us?" Fish said he was. "Well," ejaculated Robeson, "all I have to say is it is a crime. I repeat, it is a crime." ⁴¹ The evening before, Roscoe Conkling had come to Fish and urgently remonstrated. He deprecated any change in the Cabinet, and feared especially that Edwards Pierrepont would be chosen; a fear which Fish shared, for in resigning he requested Grant not to appoint Pierrepont. The day after his resignation, the Secretary received a paper signed by the Vice-President and forty-four Senators of the United States: ⁴²

Senate Chamber
Dec. 6, 1871.

Hon. Hamilton Fish,
Sec'y of State.

The rumor which now assumes probability, that you contemplate laying aside your important official relations to the Government, causes us much regret, and includes us as friends of both yourself and the Administration and as those who at all times should look after the welfare of the country, to express the earnest wish, which we know the President also entertains, that you will not resign the Secretaryship of State.

We are aware that there may be personal and domestic reasons why you desire to retire to private life—but the eminent success which has attended the foreign relations of the country under your administration, the threatening complications which have been avoided but may again be renewed, the unfinished condition of most important measures which you have shared in inaugurating and with the spirit and details which you are entirely familiar, the harmony that exists between both the legislative and executive branches of the Government and yourself, and the peril that comes to the party with which we believe the best interests of the nation are identified by so important a change at this time in the cabinet, are considerations that lead us to deprecate your resignation and to urge your retaining the post. We know that one having no over-weening egotism, may, by the belief that others can as well perform

⁴⁰ Diary, November 14, 1871.   ⁴¹ Diary, December 5, 1871.   ⁴² Copy in Fish Papers.

Charles Francis Adams

the service, avoid what would otherwise be recognized as the claim of duty,—permit us to suggest that we, while sharing your interest in the welfare of the country, are much more impartial in our estimate of the importance of your retaining, if not at too great a sacrifice, your present position.

Knowing that whatever may be your conclusion you will appreciate our motives in thus addressing you, we are,

With much respect,
Your friends.

On that day, too, President Grant made a final plea to the Secretary to remain. Fish had business which carried him to the White House, and Grant referred sorrowfully to his resignation. He said that he knew he had promised not to urge the Secretary's continuance; that he had meant to adhere to his pledge, but he found himself heavily stricken by the loss, and did not know where to turn. He spoke in the highest terms of Fish's work, and referred feelingly to the completeness with which he had gained the confidence of both branches of Congress and of the American people.[43]

Fish was manifestly moved. He had made all his domestic arrangements for departure, he said, and he did not see how he could now alter them. But Grant saw that he was shaken, and followed up his plea by saying that he could arrange any changes in the Department, any improvements, any additions to the staff, which Fish desired; for Senators had told him that Congress would do anything the Secretary wished. That evening Schurz called at Fish's house. Though he was not one of the forty-four signers of the Senatorial paper, he said that he had now come to make a personal and fervent plea that Fish remain.[44]

Day after day this pressure was maintained. Cabinet members, Senators, Representatives, and Ministers urged the Secretary to reconsider, while letters poured in upon him. It was too much for a man of Fish's strong sense of public duty. He was especially impressed by the arguments that an essential part of his work remained unfinished, and that his resignation would weaken the Administration in the next election. The Liberal Republican revolt was gaining strength; executive committees for the new party had been formed in Ohio and Missouri, while important newspapers—Greeley's *Tribune,* Horace White's Chicago *Tribune,* Samuel Bowles' Springfield *Republican,* Bryant's *Evening Post,* Murat Halstead's Cincinnati *Commercial*—were applauding the

[43] Diary, December 7, 1871.   [44] *Ibid.*

movement. He knew also that while the Administration had begun the year 1871 sunk in discredit, it was closing it with heightened reputation, and that this due entirely to his own success in the British negotiation. If he resigned, how much strength would the Administration retain in liberal eyes? And after all, he had grown to enjoy the work of his office.

By December 20, 1871, he had resolved to stay with Grant until the end of his first term. The President called that day. "I tell him," writes Fish in his diary, "that in view of the urgent requests made to remain in office, and his own warmly expressed wish that I do so, I have determined to continue in the Department of State." Grant's gratitude was touching. "I cannot express to you what a gratification this affords," he exclaimed. "I simply could not fill your place." He spoke again of the brilliant success of Fish's policies and the importance of their continuance. "You have afforded me a great relief," he concluded, "and I am sure that every member of the Cabinet and of your friends in Congress and the country will be delighted with your decision."

These words were echoed by the press. Fish felt a pang as he gave up the hope of returning to his bright fireside in New York, where his children might be constantly beside him. But he was deeply gratified as he read the tributes which came from all parts of the country. He had labored unweariedly in his two and a half years in the old Orphan Asylum, and had endured much misunderstanding and abuse; but at last the country was recognizing his qualities.

The Chicago *Tribune* was one of the harshest critics of the Administration. But it remarked editorially that Fish had achieved a place with the greatest of his predecessors—with John Quincy Adams, Daniel Webster, and William H. Seward. "It is to his statesmanship, principally," it declared, "that we are indebted for the practical settlement of the *Alabama* Claims against Great Britain and the counterclaims of that power against us, as well as of the supplementary question of the fisheries, through the medium of the Washington Treaty, questions which more than once have come near involving the two countries in war. His diplomacy has been a protecting shield to American citizens in Cuba during the revolution against Spain, and whatever troubles have arisen between the two countries have grown out of the fact that some Spaniards became American citizens simply to claim the protection of the American flag—a trouble which could not have been avoided under the existing circumstances, and the almost utter confusion and anarchy which have prevailed and still prevail in that island. Under all circumstances which have required political sagacity, skilful diplomacy, and broad, comprehensive statesmanship, Secretary Fish has always been equal to the emergency, and, whether he shall resign his post or not, has deserved well of his country."

IN bitterly cold weather Bancroft Davis travelled from Paris to the initial meeting of the five Arbitrators in Geneva on December 15, 1871, where the Agents were to distribute copies of the Cases of America and Great Britain, with the evidence. He occupied a compartment with one of the Arbitrators, Baron d'Itajuba, the Brazilian Minister to France. Long afterward he remembered how they shivered together, and how at the stations the little tropic-loving Brazilian, in fur coat and fur-lined leggings, paced rapidly up and down the platform to get warm.

The cordial meeting of the Arbitrators and Agents offered a hopeful augury of the future. Count Sclopis of Italy seemed to surpass his colleagues in learning and in reputation as jurist and author; his books, especially the *History of Italian Legislation,* and *On the Judicial Power,* were authoritative. Tall, broadshouldered, courteous, and decisive, he sustained in personal intercourse, though well past seventy, the leadership his writings and offices had given him.[1] According to precedent, M. Jacques Staempfli, representing the country in which the arbitrators met, should have been presiding officer; but Count Sclopis' fame and his knowledge of English made him the unanimous choice. After the exchange of documents, protocols were drawn up by the secretaries. As the group sat waiting, Sir Alexander Cockburn launched into a history of the Tichborne Claimant, whose lawsuit had just been defeated. He had a gift for picturesque narrative, and, his mother having been a Frenchwoman, spoke French to perfection. His hearers sat entranced while the sun sank and twilight thickened, awakening to find it dark. Before the sittings broke up, Cockburn and Bancroft Davis gave a joint dinner to the arbitrators. They all parted in amity, and with golden hopes;[2] the Tribunal having decided that the Counter-Cases should be submitted on or before April 15, 1872, and that it should sit again on June 15.

But within six weeks these golden hopes had come to wreck upon

[1] Bancroft Davis, *Fish and the Alabama Claims,* 84, 85. Sir Alexander Cockburn probably had more legal learning and a quicker mind than the other Arbitrators. Now almost seventy, he had been Solicitor-General, Attorney-General, and Lord Chief Justice of England. Charles Francis Adams was his peer in stubborn ability. Staempfli and d'Itajuba were the weakest of the five Arbitrators.
[2] *Ibid.,* 89.

the grim promontory which had so long vexed Anglo-American relations, the indirect claims. The American Case, 480 pages long, was sent to the Foreign Office for study. As prepared by Bancroft Davis, it was far from a statesmanlike document; at points its tone was litigious rather than legal, and went beyond sound pleading to special pleading. Charles Francis Adams, Jr., later wrote [3] that its arguments "were advanced with an aggressiveness of tone and attorney-like smartness more appropriate to the wranglings of a quarter-sessions court than to pleadings before a great international tribunal"; Sir Roundell Palmer, the British attorney, that "its tone was acrimonious, totally wanting in international courtesy." Brusque contentiousness was especially evident in the first chapter, "The Unfriendly Course Pursued by Great Britain," which contained much that was inaccurate and more that was irrelevant. It boldly revived the discussion of the proclamation of neutrality, declaring that the British Government "was actuated at that time by a conscious unfriendly purpose toward the United States." Historians have proved that no unfriendly intent existed, and that the proclamation was to the advantage of the United States.

But the unhappiest feature of the Case appeared at its close.[4] Here, under the heading, "The Tribunal Should Award a Sum in Gross to the United States," Davis enumerated the national or indirect claims in four divisions. They were for the pursuit and destruction of the cruisers; insurance costs; losses in the transfer of tonnage to the British flag; and "the prolongation of the war, and the addition of a large sum to the cost of the war and the suppression of the rebellion." Under this last claim, the Case placed on Great Britain all the costs of the war after the battle of Gettysburg, and asked the Tribunal to decide whether she ought not to pay them with 7 per cent interest! In principle, this followed a line taken by the American Government in three successive Administrations. But Bancroft Davis now out-Sumnered Sumner by translating the general principle into wildly exaggerated estimates, addressed not to an American audience but to a grave international tribunal.

This was both needless and unfortunate. Whatever we may say of the first three classes of indirect claims, those for pursuit, insurance, and transfer of tonnage, the fourth, that for prolongation of the war,

---

[3] C. F. Adams, Jr., *Lee at Appomattox.*
[4] *Case of the United States Before the Geneva Tribunal.*

should have been included only in cursory terms and as a general make-weight. Care was the more necessary because de Grey had explicitly told Fish that he was not authorized to discuss the indirect claims, and that British opinion would not tolerate them. Both Davis and Fish knew that the "prolongation" claim had become a mere shadow. Its only real utility now was in impressing England with the American conviction that the wrong done the North went far beyond the destruction of a little maritime property. It should have been mentioned (and merely mentioned) not because of any true belief in the legality of such a tremendous demand, but first, simply as indicating the scope of American resentment, and second, in order to get rid of it once and for all. Care in statement would have been necessary, but diplomatists are supposed to be skilled in phrasing. By its mention, the criticisms of the Sumners and Ben Butlers would have been forestalled; while its definite rejection by the Tribunal would serve as an estoppel against similar claims in connection with any future war anywhere in the world. If the issue were left unsettled, it would haunt any nation which played the rôle of imperfect neutral in future conflicts, and the United States was usually a neutral in Old World quarrels. But to make an emphatic claim for all the costs of the war from Gettysburg to Appomattox, with 7 per cent interest, was absurd. It was worse—in view of British sentiment, it was dangerous to the arbitration.

Why was it done? Bancroft Davis, writing under intense pressure for time, prepared the last pages of the Case hurriedly. Although William Beach Lawrence and President Woolsey of Yale read the first five chapters, they did not see the last. Haste of composition and inadequate reflection upon possible consequences may have been partially responsible for the inclusion. Yet the action was deliberate. At a later date Thornton had a confidential statement from Fish on the matter.[5] Fish told him that as Davis drew up the Case, he had seen it page by page, frequently making alterations and additions. When they came to the indirect claims, Davis had expressed doubt whether they should be inserted. They discussed the question, and finally decided they could not be omitted. If omitted, "there would have been an outcry from the people of the United States and from the majority of the Senators and Representatives, and . . . it would have been impossible to have passed the laws necessary to carry into effect the provisions of the

[5] PRO, FO 115, 539 ff. Thornton to Granville, confidential, No. 96; February 7, 1872.

treaty." Fear of the Senate—there lay the main reason. Public sentiment is not merely a great fact in international negotiations; it is the basic and all-important fact. Davis and Fish believed that too much national sentiment was bound up in this "prolongation" claim to permit its relinquishment.

Yet Fish pointed out to Thornton that in asking the Tribunal to award the final war costs, the United States placed this demand (see the close of the Case) upon grounds of "equity" alone. "I myself," he said,[6] "wrote that passage and inserted the words *in equity* to show that I did not consider that there was any right *in law* to make such claims." The Secretary also confessed that Evarts had come to him and said he did not know how to deal with the indirect claims, inasmuch as they could not be supported before a court of law. Fish had told Evarts that he was aware the claims had no legal basis, and he need not say much about them; but added as a joke that Evarts might use them in his peroration "as bars on which the spread eagle might perch." No doubt Fish sincerely believed that British acts had prolonged the war, but he never believed that money could be collected on that account. If he and Davis had but phrased these pages more moderately and adroitly—if they had but made it clear that the indirect claims went in for the peroration and the spread eagle alone, much worry might have been saved. True, there was always the vigilant and tyrannical Senate; but could not bold tact have found a way?

I

How would the British take this revival of the indirect claims? The answer was not long in coming.

On December 15, 1871, a messenger left Geneva carrying the American Case posthaste to London. It was soon reprinted there, while additional copies arrived from America. Cabinet Ministers and editors had an early opportunity to study it.

The result was two waves of protest. The first was rather casual. On December 28 the Whig *Morning Post* carried an angry comment: "The extravagant nature of the demands is the best evidence that the Arbitrators . . . will refuse to entertain them." The *Daily Telegraph,* a Government organ, discounted the claims as "irrelevant matter,"

[6] *Ibid.*

saying that Grant's Administration would not really fall back upon Sumnerism. The *Daily News* also scouted the claims as included for American electioneering purposes, and certain not to be taken seriously by the Tribunal. The essence of this first wave of protest was that the indirect claims were an outrage, but that England would arbitrate none the less.

Not so with the second wave. Its essence was that the claims were such an utter outrage that England must think twice before arbitrating. The second movement was initiated by an editorial in the London *Times* of January 2, treating their inclusion far more seriously. The Leading Journal pointed out that the object of the American Case was to make England responsible first for the direct losses, and next for the indirect losses. Assuming that the United States did not intend to press the latter claims literally, and try to exact an indemnity "almost rivalling in amount that which Prince Bismarck extorted from the French," still England could not risk a judgment by default. "The safest, as well as the most dignified course," the *Times* argued, "is therefore to stand upon what we conceive to be sound legal principles, and to demur to any such claim for indirect damage . . . and to refuse to recognize liability for any such indirect and remote consequences."

The Foreign Office, scenting danger to the arbitration, immediately tried to pacify the *Times*. It sent the editor, Delane, the only copy of the British Case given to the press. On January 4 another editorial took more moderate ground; it declared that "there is no solid ground for the anticipations of disaster which have been abroad for the last day or two." But the damage had been done. The spark from the *Times* caught the mass of tinder existing in the widespread British dislike and resentment (especially among the upper classes) of the Treaty.

The *Morning Advertiser* of January 4, 1872, demanded whether it were really true that "imbeciles and fools" had so mismanaged the negotiations as to put it in the Tribunal's power "even by possibility to award our national degradation and financial ruin." Other journals, led by opposition papers, swelled the outcry to an excited clamor. The *Times* soon returned to the attack. As a whole, the press expressed as much surprise as indignation. Englishmen had been assured by their leaders that the indirect claims had been abandoned. Yet a close examination showed that neither the Treaty nor the Protocols absolutely ruled them out. These documents appeared capable of bearing the American interpretation. As a result, Britain might ultimately find herself faced with an award which she simply could not pay. The *Pall Mall Gazette* on January 29, noting the public excitement, predicted that unless the Government cut off these claims immediately, England would cut off the Government. The *Standard* argued that Great Britain should never submit the claims at Geneva, for this would admit a liability which was unanimously denied. The *Daily News* was also against admitting claims which Englishmen would certainly repudiate. The Manchester *Guardian* declared that such unjustifiable tactics as the United States was employing would discredit the whole principle of arbitration.

And what of the Ministry? Most of its members were taken by surprise. Gladstone himself was one. When Lord Tenterden came back from Geneva he had sent the Prime Minister a copy of the American Case, with a warning notation that the claims, "swelled in every possible way," resulted in a *prima facie* claim for four and a half millions sterling. Gladstone apparently never read the Case. He marked it "keep for use," and leaving it in his Downing Street office, departed for Christmas at Hawarden. Parliament did not open till February. During January he spent much of the month at Hawarden; Granville, crippled with gout, was secluded at Walmer. For at least part of the month Forster was the only Minister in London to answer a summons from the Queen.[7] Until all but too late, Gladstone simply did not awaken to the situation.

The Ministry seems to have hoped that the disturbance might soon die down and public opinion direct itself toward some less explosive topic. But instead of subsiding it increased and found more weighty spokesmen. Lord Westbury wrote Granville on January 7, urging him to refuse to treat the indirect claims as open for discussion at Geneva.[8] Sir Roundell Palmer partially endorsed this opinion in an indignant though cautious letter to Granville on the 10th. Few Englishmen, he declared, would ever have consented to arbitration had such pretensions been foreseen. It was utterly unreasonable to ask Great Britain to submit claims aggregating perhaps "several hundred millions of sterling"

[7] Morley's *Gladstone;* Reid's *Life of Forster;* cf. Gladstone's statement in Parliament February 6, 1872, Hansard CCIX, 84 ff.
[8] Roundell Palmer, Earl of Selborne, *Memorials Personal and Political,* II, 230 ff.; Henry Reeve, *Memoirs,* II, 294 ff.; Nash, *Life of Lord Westbury.*

to the decision of "a Swiss, a Brazilian, and an Italian lawyer—if lawyers even they be." The Americans were trying to found "enormous and intolerable" demands upon what seemed an improper broadening of the treaty's terms. He thought that the Ministry should ask the Law Officers for an opinion.

In the last few days before Parliament met at the beginning of February, 1872, a veritable wave of national hysteria broke upon Westminster.[9] Business interests, editors, politicians, and finally members of the Ministry itself joined in the indignant outcry. If Fish and Bancroft Davis had put in the indirect claims *pro forma,* as lawyers usually overstate any writ for damages or claim for insurance, why had they not made this clear? Many Englishmen believed that the Americans seriously wished to collect all the costs of the war after Gettysburg. Lord Granville himself shortly computed [10] that with 7 per cent interest the sum might reach $4,500,000,000—"an incredible demand." Prussia's recent exaction of a billion-dollar indemnity from France had made a painful impression upon all Europe; and the British public, when told that America was trying to submit to a panel of foreigners a claim which might prove absolutely ruinous to the nation, felt outraged. After the Cabinet meeting on January 30, Gladstone wrote the Queen that the American Case, along with a mass of "irrelevant and exasperating" matter, presented claims and pretensions "such as it is wholly incompatible with national honour to admit or to plead to before a Tribunal of Arbitration." Victoria replied [11] that she could well understand "that the Commissioners thought they were treating with gentlemen actuated by honourable feelings, and did not suspect that a trap was being laid for them."

II

To Grant and Fish, the British panic seemed totally artificial and unjustifiable.[12] The outburst fell upon them as a complete surprise, for they had supposed that nothing could disturb the fair understanding

---

[9] Disraeli wrote Lord Cairns on January 27, 1872: "Affairs are most critical and anxious. All is absorbed in the *Alabama* question. Hayward told Exmouth yesterday that unless they withdraw from the arbitration, the Cabinet must break up. Would that they could withdraw. But can they? After having advised their Sovereign to ratify—and in such haste!" Buckle's *Disraeli,* V, 178.

[10] Granville to Schenck, March 30, 1872; copy in Fish Papers.

[11] Buckle, *Letters of Queen Victoria,* 2d Series, II, 187, 188.

[12] Cf. Cushing's caustic comments on the contrast between the initial British silence and the subsequent uproar; *Treaty of Washington,* 42, 43.

embodied in the Treaty.[13] Fish's correspondence with de Grey had manifested the most cordial friendliness; for example, he had written just after New Year's: [14]

My Christmas dinner (which I enjoyed in New York) was graced with a kind token from Studley Royal for which I should sooner have returned my thanks. The birds were magnificent and in fine order, and as they came on the table with head and tail erect, looked as though they were about to crow A-la-ba-ma. . . .

Schenck occasionally gives me word of you. You and your genial and generous hospitality are much missed. Friends constantly inquire after you and Sir Stafford. . . .

Davis telegraphs that he and Lord Tenterden have exchanged their Cases and are at work on the same "old story." I have just now received a copy of the British Case, but have not had time to examine it carefully; if size and bulk determine the question, you will beat us, but we shall accept and abide by the result, be it what it may.

The Secretary's first warning that the Treaty was in grave danger arrived on February 3. On entering his office that Saturday morning, he was handed a cablegram from Schenck. It notified him that British indignation was increasing, that the Ministry did not consider the indirect claims within the intent of the treaty, and that the press was urging the government to withdraw from the arbitration if they were not given up. Fish cabled Schenck a firm answer: [15] "There must be no withdrawal of any part of the claims presented. Counsel will argue the Case as prepared unless they show to this government reason for a change. The alarm you speak of does not reach us. We are perfectly calm and intend to await the award, and do not anticipate repudiation of the Treaty by the other side." That afternoon Thornton called in great anxiety. Lord Granville had instructed him to inform Fish that the Ministry—as it had told Schenck in a friendly note—regarded the indirect claims as quite outside the terms of the Treaty.

"Well," said Fish, indignantly,[16] "then is all our work of last year to go for nothing?" Thornton replied that he hoped not. "At any rate," declared Fish, with great emphasis, "we can never withdraw any part of the claims. We are content to let the Tribunal pass upon the in-

---

[13] New York *Nation*, January 25, February 8, shows that the American press did not grasp the sudden British outburst until the latter date.
[14] Fish to Ripon, January 6, 1872; Fish Papers.
[15] Fish to Schenck, February 3, 1872; Letterbooks.
[16] Fish Diary, February 3, 1872.

direct claims and if it rejects them we shall make no complaint; but we will never allow Great Britain or any other Power to dictate what form our Case shall take or what claims we shall advance."

But Fish's firmness met an ironclad British determination. It was now a truly national feeling; there was doubtless some party politics in it (Disraeli had disliked the Treaty, though Sir Stafford Northcote's part in writing it prevented him from attacking it) but not much. It was a Whig, Earl Russell, who assailed Gladstone most vehemently and announced a resolution for British withdrawal at Geneva. Many of the strongest attacks came from the Liberals themselves. Disraeli does not seem to have wished to turn Gladstone out, and Delane, the editor of the *Times,* wrote: "I suppose the Ministry must stay until the *Alabama* Claims are settled." The British refusal to submit to the indirect claims gained confidence from the fact that the Franco-Prussian War and Black Sea question were now disposed of; it gained strength from the fact that the treaty had never really been popular in England. While Englishmen had accepted the treaty as a mode of escape from a very difficult position, they had never deemed it a pleasant escape. But at bottom the attack on the Case represented a genuine national alarm, and it enlisted some of the finest figures in British public life. At first three members of the Cabinet, Granville, de Grey, and W. E. Forster, were for protesting but nevertheless letting all the claims go to arbitration. But Goschen, Hartington, Halifax, Howe, and Cardwell were all for breaking off and taking a stern attitude—an attitude which would please public sentiment and add to the political strength of the Ministry.[17]

Gladstone, who had the deciding vote, was at first for going on with the arbitration. He wrote Granville from Hawarden on January 14 [18] that "I very decidedly agree with you that we ought not to go out of the line of proceeding laid down in the *Alabama* Code"; that Bancroft Davis's "bunkum and . . . trash might be handled in some degree as 'Americanism' due to want of knowledge of the world of European manners." But as he appreciated the boiling British indignation he quickly changed his course. His letter to the Queen on January 30 indicated that he was more and more disinclined to proceed at Geneva. A few days later he let off steam even more violently. He wrote the

[17] Reid's *Forster;* Morley's *Gladstone;* Reeve, *Memoirs,* etc.
[18] Gladstone Papers; copy supplied the author by Mrs. H. W. Wells.

Queen: "Even bearing in mind the proceeding of Prince Gortschakoff in the autumn of 1870, Mr. Gladstone is constrained to say that the conduct of the American Government in this affair is the most ·disreputable he has ever known in his recollection of diplomacy." By that date he had made up his mind against the view of Granville and Forster. On February 2 he swayed the Cabinet to approve a note of the sternest protest to the American Government—a note that Fish was soon reading with indignation: [19]

Her Majesty's Government hold that it is not within the province of the Tribunal of Arbitration at Geneva to decide upon the claims for indirect losses and injuries put forward in the Case of the United States, including the loss in the transfer of the American commercial marine to the British flag, the enhanced payments of insurance, and the prolongation of the war, and the addition of a large sum to the cost of the war and suppression of the rebellion.

The Prime Minister was soon declaring to the House that it was almost "insanity to suppose that any negotiations could intend to admit, in a peaceful arbitration . . . claims which not even the last extremities of war and the lowest depths of misfortune would force a people with a spark of spirit . . . to submit to at the point of death." He estimated that the "war prolongation claim" might come to $8,000,-000,000! A united nation supported the words which the Ministry put into the Queen's Speech at the opening of Parliament on February 6, 1872: "In the Case so submitted on behalf of the United States, large claims have been included, which are understood on my part not to be within the province of the Arbitrators."

Yet to Fish the British position seemed ridiculously untenable.[20] Was there anything in the Treaty that excluded the indirect claims? Not a word; on the contrary, it stated that the Arbitrators should "examine and decide all questions that shall be laid before them" by the two governments. Had any agreement been reached by the High Commission to exclude them? Fish, Hoar, Schenck, Williams, and Nelson all united in saying no.[21] They held that the Treaty gave the United States liberty to obtain as much as possible from the Arbitrators, and that it was fair to submit anything that might have weight in assessing damages. They deemed this a matter of elementary political necessity:

[19] Copy in Fish Papers.　　　　　　[20] Fish Diary, February 4, 5, 6, 7, 1872.
[21] Hoar's view of the indirect claims is stated fully in a letter to Fish, June 7, 1872. Fish Papers.

Fish had never believed that a compact which excluded the indirect claims could pass the Senate. Ben Butler was even now fighting tooth and nail in the House against appropriations to carry the Treaty into effect, while Sumner was searching for weapons to encompass the defeat of Grant in 1872. At the same time, our government did not desire a dollar from the indirect claims. Its principal motive for including them was succinctly described by Fish in a letter of April 5 to Bellamy Storer: [22]

I may say to *you*, that I never believed that the Tribunal would award a cent for the "indirect claims"; it is not the interest of the United States, who are habitually neutrals, to have it decided that a neutral is liable for the indirect injuries consequent upon an act of negligence. We have too large an extent of coast and too small a police, and too much of the spirit of bold speculation and adventure, to make the doctrine a safe one for our future. The "indirect claims" had been advanced and had (mainly owing to Great Britain herself) been too prominent in the history of the *Alabama* Claims to be unnoticed. They were therefore presented to the Joint Commission in the opening of the conference, and the British Commissioners never uttered the first word against them; they were set forth in the Protocol, and stand unchallenged as part of the American grievance and are not eliminated by the Treaty.

To have omitted them from the Case would not have been fair to either party; it would have been to not submit a part of the complaint, while the Treaty professed and designed to remove all causes of difference. They would have remained to be brought up at some future day when ill-temper or some momentary excitement might be in search of causes of irritation between the two governments.

It is in the interest of both governments that they be passed upon by the Tribunal, and in the interest of both that the Tribunal decide that a neutral is not liable to pecuniary damages for the indirect consequences of a breach of its neutral obligations resulting not from intentional wrong, but from accident or negligence.

III

At the root of this unhappy controversy, as we have said, lay a misunderstanding which illustrates the dangers of good-natured vagueness in diplomatic negotiations.[23] British members of the High Commission thought that they had disposed of the indirect claims by an expression of regret and an agreement to give *ex post facto* operation to the three

[22] Fish to Bellamy Storer, April 5, 1872; Fish Papers.
[23] Nicolson, *Peacemaking*, 207–210.

rules of neutrality. American members believed that the apology was merely an expression of proper contrition, and that neither it nor the three rules touched the claims at all. Neither view could have been given precise expression on paper; public opinion on both sides the Atlantic was too irritable for that. But an *unwritten understanding* could have been put in precise terms. Both groups of negotiators mismanaged their work: the Britons in not obtaining an express understanding upon exclusion of the claims, the Americans in not obtaining the opposite understanding. But manifestly the British were in the worse position, for in the absence of anything to the contrary inclusion would be implied. Granville himself held that the Treaty and Protocols, studied line by line, did not rule out the American claims; so did Lord Westbury; while Lord Coleridge, the Attorney-General, was doubtful. The British press so far agreed as to hold that de Grey had blundered shockingly, and berated the Ministry nearly as ferociously as it did the Americans.[24]

At first each nation refused to budge; the British press spoke bitterly of trickery, the American press scornfully of bad faith. A debate in Parliament on February 6 brought from Lord Derby a declaration that if the Treaty were abandoned as intolerably ambiguous, the country would give undivided support to the Ministry. Disraeli stated that the Americans were asking for the "tribute of a conquered people"; and Gladstone, so often indiscreet in the heat of debate that his followers trembled to see him rise, even challenged the honesty of the American Government. He rashly asserted the British construction of the Treaty "to be the true and unambiguous meaning of the words, and therefore to be the only meaning admissible, whether tried by grammar, by reason, by policy, or by any other standard." It is not strange that Fish resentfully wrote the owner of the New York *Times* that the Prime Minister had been violent and intemperate.[25] Even men friendliest to the North during the war now came out in sharp opposition to the American position; men like John Bright, Thomas Hughes, W. E. Forster, and J. R. Seeley.[26]

A shrewd letter that Bright sent to Granville soon found its way, through Schenck, to Fish's desk.[27] "The whole indirect claim," he

---

[24] See Godkin's excellent analysis, *Nation*, February 8, 1872.
[25] Fish to George Jones, February 14, 1872; Fish Papers.
[26] Schenck to Fish, March 14, 1872.
[27] Bright to Granville, Rochdale, February 14, 1872; Fish Papers.

wrote, "is absurd, because it is not capable of proof. I don't believe the pirate fleet prolonged the war for a day. I think it rather injured the rebel cause, as it exhausted their funds for fighting on a field where it was impossible for them to do anything." He suggested a sensible compromise. The United States should retain the indirect claims in its Case, as historic evidence of the magnitude of its sense of grievance, but should loftily refrain from submitting them to the Tribunal as a ground for an award in mere dollars and cents. Such utterances were the more worth heeding because journals usually cordial to America, like the London *Daily News* and *Spectator,* aligned themselves staunchly with the Government.

But Fish, suspecting the motives of Gladstone and Granville, began to show strong irritation. "The British Ministry," he wrote Schenck,[28] "appear to me to have got themselves embarrassed by their disingenuous efforts to operate through their press, upon the press and the public sentiment of the Continent, in order to bring an influence to bear upon the Arbitrators, and now that they are about to face Parliament, they find that they have raised a whirlwind and cannot control the storm." This was a misapprehension of events in England, where the press was prodding the Ministry, not the Ministry the press. But it was a natural misunderstanding, for the sudden English storm did have an artificial look. And Fish pointed argumentatively to the Mixed Claims Commission sitting in Washington. It had been allowed to pass (of course adversely) upon British claims based upon the cotton loan of the Confederacy; moreover, it had received British claims for indirect damages —one from a holder of railroad bonds who complained that under the Legal Tender Act he was paid in greenbacks, and several for property destroyed by Confederate troops. In view of this, Fish thought the British effort to limit the American claims at Geneva poor sportsmanship.

When the Cabinet met at the White House on February 6, every member was against withdrawal of the claims.[29] Granville's note of February 3 to Schenck was received by cable while the session continued. Grant, angry, was for a mere curt acknowledgment. When Fish said that would not do, he seized a sheet of paper and wrote a defiant statement: "Lord Granville's note of the 3rd inst. to you received. This

[28] Fish to Schenck, Private, February 3, 1872; Fish Papers.
[29] Diary, February 6, 1872.

JOHN BULL AND THE INDIRECT CLAIMS

Lion. "You may now, perchance, both quake and tremble here,
    When Lion rough in wildest rage doth roar."
                                        Midsummer Night's Dream.

(Nast in *Harper's Weekly*)

Government sees no reason for a change of its presentation of claims against the British Government. It is for the Geneva Commissioners to decide what claims are valid under the Treaty and to determine amount of awards." That, he said, "is about the substance of what I would send." That night the anxious Thornton called at 11:30 on Fish. In the course of a conversation which lasted until one, Fish showed him a tentative dispatch to Schenck:

An independent party to a submission submits its case and its claims in its own way, and in its own interest. It is the sole judge on that point. Its claims, its arguments, may be controverted by facts, by reason, by arguments. The selected tribunal must judge between the parties and their respective arguments.

There can be no withdrawal of any claim, or any argument advanced by either of two sovereign Powers to a submission to arbitration. We ask none, we can make none.

You may state this in form or in substance, at your discretion, but in a friendly way. We mean to abide by the reference to which we have agreed, but must control the management of our own case.

A few days later the Cabinet again discussed the question. "We must go on," said Grant. He thought the Ministers to Switzerland, Italy, and Brazil should be instructed to urge these governments to keep their Arbitrators at Geneva even if England withdrew hers. "I want you, Mr. Fish," he said, "to instruct Mr. Adams to remain and to sign the award *alone* if all the others withdraw!" This was Grant all over. Fish pointed out to him that the Treaty required a majority of the Arbitrators to sign any award.

The American and British members of the High Commission were immediately brought to the verge of a painful issue of veracity. Sir Edward Thornton said in a speech in New York late in April: [30] "No one supposes that the British Commissioners ever had an idea that claims for indirect damages were included in the treaty." Sir Stafford Northcote declared at Exeter on May 17 that the British Commissioners "were distinctly responsible for having represented to the Government that we understood a promise to be given that these claims were not to be put forward." De Grey more explicitly stated that he and his associates, supposing on March 8, 1871, that the Americans waived the indirect claims, had so notified their government. English-

[30] New York *Tribune, Times,* April, 1872.

men pointed out that Lord Granville, in explaining the Treaty to the House of Lords on June 12, 1871, had said that its great advantage over the Johnson-Clarendon Convention was that the claims for indirect damages entirely disappeared, owing to the "more limited reference." Northcote, moreover, had made a similar statement in the House of Commons.[31]

Fish did not question the good faith of the British Commissioners in these statements as to their impressions. But he was convinced that they rested upon a misapprehension, which he outlined to Schenck: [32]

The suggestion that we are to take notice of Sir Stafford Northcote, or any other gentleman's remarks made in either house of Parliament, even though our Minister may have been present, is too absurd even for a newspaper paragraph. No Parliamentary Government allows other Powers to question the debates of its Parliament; *a fortiori,* cannot expect a foreign Power to "take notice" of anything there said. While Northcote may have said that he did not understand the *"indirect claims"* to be within the intent of the negotiators, the late Lord Chancellor and the late Secretary for Foreign Affairs said they were in the submission.

The meaning of the Treaty is within its four corners.

I enclose herewith an extract from the Diary kept by Davis of the proceedings on 13th April last. We had then completed the general terms on which the Alabama questions were to be settled, and had a printed draft (the revise of 12th April) of the Articles before us. No doubt you remember the scene, when de Grey locked his box, and it looked as though we were going to break up; there was some temper on both sides. Although the immediate question was upon the claim for the expenses of pursuit and capture (which they now admit), they were given notice that we regarded the language of the Treaty (which they would not consent should be "altered, enlarged, or opened") as sufficient to include *all* claims of the Government *which the Arbitrators may find just,* and they agreed that the Article be passed subject to the arrangement at a future meeting of a Protocol, in which the claims of the United States should be set forth. That Protocol was approved on 4th May, and set forth the "indirect claims." The extract may refresh your memory.

I have very carefully gone through the Diary, and fail to find the first exception taken by the British Commissioners, directly and in terms, to the "indirect claims"; unless on 6th April, when, discussing the allowance of a

[31] *Nation,* February 22, 1872.

[32] Fish to Schenck, February 29, 1872; Fish Papers. The Government Printing Office issued a pamphlet, "The American Commissioners and the Statement of Sir Stafford Northcote at Exeter" (1872), with explicit denials by Hoar, Nelson, Schenck, and Williams that the indirect claims had been excluded. Hoar put the matter sensibly. Though the claims were too large for compensation, he always expected to see them put in as reason why the United States should be awarded a generous gross sum for the direct claims, without haggling over details.

gross sum, De Grey said he "thought the reference should not be made so wide as to allow the Arbitrator to take a claim which had been put forward in the correspondence, though he supposed not seriously, for compensation for the expenses to which the United States had been put by the prolongation of the war"; he added that he had no authority to refer such a claim. You remember, however, they never had authority for anything; had to get their authority daily as questions arose; and four weeks later enumerated this among the claims.

Although Fish did not impugn the sincerity of de Grey, he clung to his acid suspicion that the Ministry's sudden bolt was primarily the result of political cowardice and newspaper clamor. We have seen that he was wrong; but the important fact is that he honestly believed this. He wrote John Sherman that he had scrutinized the genesis of the English protests with care.[33] For seven weeks after copies of the American Case had been freely distributed in London and criticized by the press, no important statesman or jurist had objected to inclusion of the indirect claims. Opponents had called them extravagant, but had tacitly admitted them to be within the province of the Tribunal. But just before Parliament met, certain journals had begun a campaign of panic which Opposition elements took up. The Ministry, "with the fear of an adverse vote, abdicated to the press," and Mr. Gladstone made a speech full of "intemperate and unsustained statements." De Grey and the other Commissioners, eager to defend themselves and support Gladstone, had presented their opinions of the controversial exchanges in Washington as if they were proved facts. John Bull had then planted his boots obstinately and refused to budge. The whole threatened debacle, Fish bitterly commented, was based not upon the Treaty, but upon what the *Times, News, Standard,* and *Saturday Review* had forced Gladstone to say about the Treaty.

Nevertheless, Fish wrote Schenck in a mood of patient hopefulness: [34]

If the tone of the British Press be taken as the expression of the opinion and interest of the British Government, our Treaty may be regarded as ended. I am not yet willing to believe this, but when Mr. Bright and other gentlemen of calm judgment occupy themselves in endeavoring to "construct bridges for the American Government to retreat upon," instead of examining first the Treaty, and next the real object and meaning of our "Case" and its presenta-

[33] Fish to Sherman, "Personal," March 19, 1872, Fish Papers.
[34] Fish to Schenck, March 18, 1872; Fish Papers.

tion of the claims for "indirect losses," what are you to expect? Do these gentlemen wish this class of claims which have been so prominent, *especially in the British presentation* to their public, to be kept for future presentation? These claims were about all of Sumner's speech that the British press allowed the British public to know about. If not disposed of now they must remain for settlement at some future period. *If they be deferred (with the British estimate of their magnitude)* they may become disturbing at a critical moment. We wish them disposed of. I do not find the first man who expects or wishes to obtain a farthing for them. I supposed that Sumner might attach importance to them, but meeting Mr. J. S. Pike, night before last, he told me that in a conversation with Sumner, quite recently, the latter told him that he does not regard them subjects of computation for pecuniary indemnification, and that he had intended to present them in his speech as makeweights to enforce the validity of the direct claims.

Sir Stafford Northcote and Lord Ripon say they *thought* they were excluded from the Treaty; their declaration is conclusive that they *so thought;* but they fail to indicate when, where, or how they were eliminated. On our part we think they were not excluded, and our declaration on that point ought also to be accepted. We wish to get rid of them; we do not claim a pecuniary award on their account. In fact, it would accord more with our wishes and general views that the Tribunal should determine that they are within its province, but that a nation cannot be held liable for the indirect, remote, or consequential injuries resulting even from an act of negligence, rather than that the Tribunal decide that they have no jurisdiction over them.

Why does it not occur to Mr. Bright and some other of our neighbors on that side of the water to try their hand at building a bridge for the *British* Government to retreat upon?

IV

Fortunately, as soon as the threat to the Treaty grew serious (with a nasty undertone of war-talk on both sides) friends of peace leaped to the rescue. The American Legation in London, where Schenck worked into the small hours to try to save the situation, was filled with anxious visitors. One day a distinguished figure in a long cloak, with intellectual face and flowing hair, appeared. He had some ideas upon the preservation of peace. It was Tennyson. George W. Smalley lent a helpful shoulder with the press; Lord Granville spared no effort; Sir Roundell Palmer searched for a way out. The Opposition in Parliament showed patience, and Lord Derby ignored obvious opportunities to upset the Ministry.

Naturally Sir John Rose was early in the field.[35] On February 3 he cabled his partner Levi P. Morton that a settlement was impossible without abandonment of the indirect claims; that British sentiment was absolutely united; and that Morton should make an immediate effort to sound the Grant Administration. Morton caught the night train to Washington. On February 4th and 5th he notified Rose that our government still took a determined position, but might revert, upon request, to its original proposal that Great Britain settle the whole claims question by payment of a gross sum. Fish had said that he would favor such a solution if Great Britain made the offer, and Morton had gained the impression that four or five million pounds would suffice. As a matter of fact, however, Grant—as the next Cabinet meeting showed—was strongly opposed to a lump-sum payment. So also was the British Cabinet. Rose shortly cabled from London: [36] "No chance whatever gross sum nor any solution except modification claims. There is a sharp panic in stocks."

Indeed, financial interests on both sides of the Atlantic suffered heavily during the first fortnight of February. American stocks went down with a rush on European bourses. German holders began selling them at sacrifice prices; British and French investors followed. For some weeks the European market for American securities was practically paralyzed. Naturally, American business men who needed foreign capital were soon besieging the Administration to adjust the dispute. "This misunderstanding," Morton ruefully informed Fish two months after it began,[37] "is costing this country almost daily more than any amount we could possibly expect to receive, even if England would agree to refer the question of incidental damages." Another international financier, Cyrus W. Field, landed in New York asserting that, having travelled throughout Europe, he had found all the leading statesmen convinced that we were in the wrong. This statement did not harmonize with George Bancroft's report to the Secretary from Berlin: [38] "Bismarck thinks England must go on with the court at Geneva. He expressed the opinion to me as strongly as a man could." But with the post-war boom still on, with the Northern Pacific Railroad and other new enterprises hungry for European capital, financial circles

---

[35] Morton-Rose Cablegrams, February 3–8, 1872; Morton Papers.
[36] Rose to Morton; copy in Fish Papers.   [37] Morton to Fish, March 28, 1872.
[38] Bancroft to Fish, February 16; Fish Papers.

in the United States were aghast at the breach and urgent for a settlement.

Almost all the American press had applauded the American Case. At first most of it had been vigorously behind the Administration in defending the indirect claims. But February and March found many editors anxious for an adjustment by mutual concessions. The sharp newspaper censure of Granville and de Grey in England was soon matched by American animadversions upon Fish. The New York *Times* published editorials so hostile that the Secretary wrote a pained letter to the English-born proprietor, George Jones. The *Evening Post* printed Washington correspondence which he thought highly unfair, and which drew from him two more letters of protest.[39] The New York *Mail* presented with editorial commendation [40] a letter from John Bright to Cyrus W. Field, declaring that the American Case contained "too much of what we call 'attorneyship' and too little of statesmanship." The *Nation*, at first heartily blaming both sides, finally concluded that Fish was the more in the wrong.[41] *Harper's Weekly* declared that the United States should give way. This pressure of important editors for concessions had a salutary effect.

Secretary Fish was willing to do all that he reasonably could to attain a settlement. His first serious proposal, after failure of the lump-sum plan, was that the United States give up the indirect claims while Great Britain gave up her San Juan claim. George Bancroft had laid before the Kaiser a well-buttressed argument on the San Juan boundary, which he soon followed by a rejoinder to the British argument; both presented in German, whereas the British offered theirs in English and bad French.[42] The United States had insisted that the issue be restricted to a choice between Haro and Rosario Straits, ruling out a middle channel. Bancroft felt sure of the decision, and the British privately admitted that our case was the stronger. This being so, Fish felt that he asked them to surrender little. But in view of Canadian sentiment, Granville was unwilling even to talk of the proposal. "The fact is," Schenck reported,[43] "that Mr. Gladstone so committed himself at the opening of Parliament to an extreme position . . . that every step

---

[39] Fish to Charlton Lewis, February 8, 11, 1872.
[40] N. Y. *Evening Mail*, March 27, 1872.   [41] *Nation*, May 16, 1872.
[42] Bancroft to Fish, February 16, 1872.
[43] Schenck to Fish, March 20, 1872; Fish Papers. Cf. Howay and Scholefield, *British Columbia*, II, Ch. 18.

towards accommodation since has been, to a degree, if not entirely, arrested by the obstacle he then threw in the way."

V

As March closed, Fish still hoped that the British would put in their Counter Case on April 15. Granville would not—he surely could not—bring about a rupture. If only England would proceed at Geneva, he wrote Schenck,[44] "the mere passing of cautious and friendly notes reiterating adherence to opinions once expressed will not hurt anyone, however wearisome and profitless." But would they? Schenck, who had warned the British that to obstruct the arbitration would mean tearing up the Treaty, did not know. If they did destroy the Treaty, Fish was sure that England would suffer more than the United States. "You would be surprised at the utter indifference of the people here whether Great Britain repudiates the Treaty or not. I do not share it, but hear half a dozen times a day the remark, 'If they can stand it, we can.' "

When Granville's next note, dated March 20, 1872, arrived, Fish thought it unduly sharp, and was resentful. But it did not close the door, and news soon came that the British would submit their Counter Case. This, he wrote Schenck, was an important point gained.[45] "We advance another step, which will make it more difficult for England to back out and repudiate." He would be in no hurry, he added, to reply to Granville's "prevaricating, contradictory, and unfair note," accompanied as it was by memoranda in which he believed he saw Tenterden's "cunning and trickery." He thought that American courtesy had gone far enough when it was met with such "uncandid pettifogging." Gladstone's loss of his head on February 6 had made Granville's position difficult, but that did not excuse his unfair note. Yet Fish added next day:[46]

Keep John Bull in good humor about the Counter Case. I think it not unlikely that the decision may be against us on the "indirect claims." Perhaps it is to our interest that it should be so—*provided* the Tribunal *will take jurisdiction* and so award. To us, who are generally neutral, with an extended line of coast, a small navy, *no* police, and a very adventurous population, it

---

[44] Fish to Schenck, March 29, 1872; Fish Papers.
[45] Fish to Schenck, April 11, 1872; Fish Papers.
[46] Fish to Schenck, April 12, 1872; Fish Papers.

would not be unfavorable to our future interests should the Tribunal decide that a neutral is not liable in pecuniary damages for the indirect consequences of an accidental or unintentional breach of its neutral obligations.

A long Cabinet discussion on April 19 made it clear that the members all shared Fish's desire to save the Treaty.[47] They agreed that the indirect claims could not be withdrawn, and that it was to the interest of the United States that the Tribunal pronounce an explicit judgment against them. The Cabinet was anxious to prevent Congress, where an anti-British resolution was pending, from meddling with the situation. Creswell suggested that the State Department might inform Great Britain that while we wished the Tribunal to decide the issue, we would leave the *amount* of the damages to be arranged later by the two governments. This represented progress, but Grant made a more practical proposal.

Charles Francis Adams was about to sail for Europe again, and the President suggested that if Fish called him to Washington and gave him the opinions of the Administration, he could then drop reassuring hints in London. The Cabinet heartily approved this happy idea. But it was not necessary to summon Adams to the capital. Boutwell was going to Boston, and at Fish's request he conveyed the Administration's views to Adams. Adams at once told Boutwell that he also had decided that it was important to neutral nations, and especially to the United States, that the indirect claims be formally declared untenable.[48] He would be glad, as Fish suggested, to tell the British authorities that he thought so. They ought to feel greatly relieved when they learned that the American Arbitrator would join the British Arbitrator in opposing any award whatever for prolongation of the war.

Hopeful that he had loosed the Gordian knot, Fish on April 23 wrote an optimistic letter to Schenck.[49] He commended Disraeli for saying in a recent speech at Manchester that it had been impossible for the United States to withdraw the indirect claims, and went on:

> I think that we were bound to present them to the Arbitrators; not to have done so, would have been not to act in good faith either to ourselves, our people, or to Great Britain.

The pressure here comes (I think) from the bankers and the commercial

[47] Fish, Diary, April 19, 1872.   [48] Boutwell to Fish, April 22, 1872; Fish Papers.
[49] Letterbooks.

interest on both sides of the ocean, and the amateur diplomatists who always "know too much for one, and not enough for two," and are busybodies by intuition. Nevertheless, their activity with the press and otherwise is producing a public sentiment which will justify, or make easy, what otherwise it might be difficult to do.

I think that Adams' assurance of his opinion, and of the decision which he will be inclined to render, must relieve the British Government of the apprehension of any award of damages for the "indirect claims," and the efforts making to drive this government into a withdrawal will have prepared the public mind with us for a decision which will really be in the interest of both nations. . . .

I was glad to receive your telegram yesterday, stating the possibility of the overthrow of the Ministry on the Dublin University Bill; not that I am particularly anxious that the present Ministry be voted out, but that some other question than the Treaty is being made the object of assault. If a new Ministry comes in, I suppose they may find it easy if they think proper to go on with the Arbitration, throwing the responsibility of any errors upon their predecessors; they cannot fail to be assured that there is no danger of being burdened with a heavier obligation than was "imposed by Germany upon France."

If the matters involved in these questions were not of vast importance, one would be inclined to look upon the course of the British Ministry as a sort of harlequin's exhibition.

If we can only succeed in getting safely through with the Arbitration, I shall feel quite disposed to leave John Bull severely alone for a long time, and should it ever be my lot again to take part in negotiating a treaty with him, I feel now that I should be inclined to insist upon security that he will earnestly carry it out.

And on April 25th Fish took still another step toward an accommodation. He and Thornton had a long talk.[50] The British Minister assured him that his government had no intention of repudiating the Treaty, and when Fish complained that no constructive offer had come from London, asked if any new solution had occurred to him.

"I am hardly prepared to say that it has," observed Fish. "But a crude idea has come into my mind which may be elaborated into something practical. You have noticed that in none of my instructions have I demanded any compensation for the indirect claims. You also know that I have gone very far toward expressing the belief that nothing will be awarded for them. Now here is a possible way out. If Lord Granville should comment upon these points, and draw the conclusion

[50] Fish Diary, April 25, 1872.

that the American Government wishes to protect itself against the future; if he will state that Great Britain never has advanced claims for similar losses, and never will, whatever the future relations between England and the United States as belligerent and neutral; and if he will add that, in order to elicit a clear decision from the Tribunal, Great Britain will join the United States in submitting the abstract question of liability for such claims—on this formula we could probably come to an agreement."

"Very good," said Thornton, "I will telegraph Lord Granville at once."

Next day Fish formally presented his suggestion to the Cabinet, which approved it.[51] The President authorized him to inform Thornton that if Great Britain would pledge herself never to advance claims for similar losses against the United States, we would ask no damages for the indirect claims as they now went before the Tribunal. Thornton telegraphed this more explicit offer to Granville. That same day, April 26, Levi P. Morton arrived from New York, dined with the President, dashed later to the British Legation, and then came to Fish's residence. He had written a telegram imploring Rose to support the American offer, which Fish approved. All the prospects seemed hopeful.

VI

But agonizing days of worry and doubt lay just ahead. Gladstone's Ministry, like Grant's Administration, was laboring under heavy public pressure. Lord Russell's motion for suspending all proceedings on behalf of Her Majesty's Government until the indirect claims were "definitely withdrawn" had with difficulty been postponed from week to week. A majority of the House of Lords sympathized with it; so also did the Cabinet. Had the Opposition desired—which it did not—it could probably have passed a vote of censure against the Ministry at any time after April 15. Only Gladstone's active support of Granville's efforts kept the Treaty alive, and Gladstone had to pick his steps carefully.

Fish anxiously awaited the reply to the American proposal. At

[51] Fish Diary, April 26, 1872.

Thornton's request, he sent specific instructions to Schenck on April 27: [52]

> . . . The British Government may make a proposal to you to the effect that . . . in the future, should Great Britain be a belligerent and this country neutral and should there be any failure on the part of the United States to observe their neutral obligations, Great Britain will make or advance no complaints or claims against the United States by reason or on account of any indirect, remote or consequential results of such failure, and that in consideration of such stipulation the United States shall not press for a pecuniary award before the Geneva Tribunal on account of the [indirect] claims. . . . Should a proposal to this effect be made by the British Government the President will assent to it, it being understood that there is no withdrawal of any part of the American case, but an agreement not to demand damages on account of the claims referred to; leaving the Tribunal to make such expression of opinion as it may think proper. . . .

Alas, the reply which came May 2 was unsatisfactory! The Ministry proposed that the original British thesis of the non-arbitrability of the indirect claims be accepted at once, thus precluding any expression of opinion by the Tribunal. This was in flat disagreement with Fish's plan. It offered to lay this thesis down as the British principle of action in the future, if reciprocal assurance were given by the United States. But here also the reply was inadequate, for it limited the agreement by the British Government to a stipulation not to advance claims of that nature in similar cases and like circumstances—though two cases are seldom similar, and no circumstances could ever be like those of the Civil War.

"That practically means your withdrawal," Fish angrily exclaimed to Thornton when the latter called. He wrote in his diary, *"Under no circumstances* can the United States agree," and underlined the first three words savagely.[53] When next day Schenck confirmed the stubborn British demands, he wrote a rejection [54] and took it to Grant.

The treaty that day, May 3, hung on the verge of destruction. Grant smote his desk as he said that the United States had gone to the utmost limit in concessions, and must propose nothing more. He suggested that, to make sure of a united national front, both the Senate and House committees on foreign affairs be called immediately to

[52] State Department MSS, Diplomatic Drafts, 1872, Great Britain.
[53] Fish Diary, May 2, 1872.   [54] In Fish Papers.

listen to the recent correspondence, including Fish's new draft-reply. Babcock at once sent out invitations.

At ten o'clock on Saturday, May 4, a line of carriages drove up to the State Department. Grant, looking stern, descended from one. Others discharged four Senators, Harlan, Morton, Hamlin and Patterson, and five Representatives, Banks, Meyers, Willard, Ambler, Packard, and Buell. Frock coats and silk hats filled Fish's small office. The Secretary read the recent correspondence with Schenck. Morton and Banks, both aggressive men, thought the American offer of the 27th too generous and the United States well out of it; they wanted it now withdrawn. Others approved the instruction of the 27th, but shared the general resentment over England's reply. Grant directed that Fish's draft-dispatch be sent, with an addition of the character proposed by Banks to indicate that the offer of the 27th was no longer open. That same day Fish telegraphed Schenck that the British proposals were wholly unacceptable. But he did not withdraw the previous offer.

Tension in London and Washington was now acute. In London, Schenck came home after a sleepless night, and exclaimed as he threw his hat down, "It is all over. This is the end of the treaty." "Very well, sir," replied his young secretary Woodhull, "we shall fight Great Britain, and thank God, we are ready for it!" [55] In America the opinion of men who knew the critical posture of affairs was much divided. On May 6th Fish received two letters, one imploring him to yield, the other to stand firm: [56]

(Levi P. Morton to Fish, New York, May 4, 1872)

I have today received the following cable dispatch from Sir John Rose: "Important. Strictly Confidential. Pray use every influence to induce the government to accept the English modification. It is certain that the English Government have gone to the extreme length that the country would sanction and that your rejection would be fatal to the arrangement." It would seem a worldwide calamity if on the grounds of the presentation of the abstract question, or any technical point, this great Treaty should fall to the ground.

(James G. Blaine to Fish, Washington, May 5, 1872)

I have read the papers—and ventured to allow my wife and Miss Dodge to do the same. Their publication will do you immense credit. Your statements and arguments are irrefragably strong, and in comparison with Granville's replies have the strength of a giant. I do not think that any one of the many

---

[55] Hackett, *Reminiscences of the Geneva Tribunal*, 202.   [56] In Fish Papers.

meritorious acts of your public life will do you more credit than this correspondence.

I pray that you will not from pressure suffer yourself to lower the standard an inch. It is of immense consequence to our national prestige that we now stand firm, and is of surpassing importance to your reputation as a statesman that you maintain with positive firmness the position you have assumed with right and fortified with unanswerable arguments.

Fish and Thornton were deeply dejected. The handiwork on which they had spent months of anxious labor seemed lost. Both realized with grave apprehension that the question would go into the imminent Presidential campaign. Thornton had warned his Government in February that the Administration could and would make most effective use of British withdrawal in appealing to the voters.

But the day was not yet lost. Fish's reply no sooner went on the wires than Thornton, Rose, and most manfully of all, Schenck, besieged the British Ministry with pleas for conciliatory action. They assured Granville that Fish would have an almost solid nation behind him—that the British must yield something more.

The result was a new move by England. Inquiries were made through Schenck whether the two nations could not agree forthwith upon a rule defining the extent of liability for indirect damages resulting from a failure to observe neutral obligations; the United States meanwhile making no financial claim with respect to the indirect losses at Geneva. A Cabinet meeting at the White House on the 7th viewed this favorably. Fish writes: [57]

The present state of the Alabama question was considered. I read telegrams to Schenck of 4th and 6th and his to me of 5th and 6th; a long discussion ensues; Creswell expresses himself warmly in favor of maintaining the treaty. It is agreed by all that the proposition in Schenck's telegram of yesterday cannot be accepted; that no arrangement to bind the future action of the Government can be made except by treaty. The President at one time seemed inclined not to reply to this last proposal, but on the suggestion that it would throw upon this Government the responsibility of breaking the treaty, he immediately acquiesced, and on my saying that we might reply to the effect that the President, without the assent of Congress, cannot enter into an engagement to bind the future action of the Government; that in that view the suggestion in my telegram of the 27th April had been made; that he had gone to the verge of concession, but in his desire to save the treaty will consider any proposal for a new arrangement, and if he can approve will submit

[57] Fish Diary, May 7, 1872.

it to the Senate. Robeson says it is very easy to frame a dispatch in that view, whereupon I hand him a sheet of paper and request him to draft one. He does so and reads it. The President says it strikes him favorably, and successively asks the opinion of each member present, each answering approvingly. Bristow, however, intimates a doubt whether the President has the Constitutional right to say that he will not ask for pecuniary compensations for the indirect losses. Each one present having separately approved, the President authorizes an instruction to Schenck in the "spirit and general sense" of Robeson's paper.

At last a way out had opened! On May 10 Lord Granville handed Schenck the draft of a proposed additional article to the Treaty. "He grinned from ear to ear," Granville wrote Gladstone.[58] "I said, 'I suppose you have now what you want.' 'O, I can give no opinion . . . but I think it certainly opens the way.' " Under the new article each nation bound itself never in future to prefer a claim for consequential damages against the other, and in consideration of this the United States at once dropped its indirect claims. This was nearly all that Fish wanted. The ideal solution would be a formal decision by the Tribunal that *no* nation could be granted payment for indirect losses; next to this, we would be fairly well protected by a solemn treaty agreement that neither Great Britain nor the United States would ever ask for such payment.

On the night of the 11th, by Presidential summons, a distinguished assemblage met at the White House.[59] Three Cabinet members, Fish, Boutwell, and Robeson, were present. They shook hands with Speaker Blaine. A dozen of the weightiest Senators, including Edmunds, Hamlin, Frelinghuysen, Logan, Howe, and Oliver P. Morton, attended. President Grant dwelt upon his desire to save the treaty, and expressed a belief that the proposal just received might offer a means of doing so. Secretary Fish read the latest correspondence, and made what explanations were necessary. A general discussion ensued. Though there was "a tolerably free interchange of opinion," no effort was made to commit any Senator. Edmunds privately informed the Secretary that he thought it best to send the article to the Senate for advice rather than immediate ratification; it would then receive more votes, while a defeat would not be so humiliating.

Seeing that this course was wise, Grant and Fish on May 13 sent

[58] May 10, 1872; Gladstone Papers. Copy supplied by Mrs. H. W. Wells.
[59] Fish Diary, May 11, 1872.

the article to the Senate "for an expression of their disposition." Morton and Zach Chandler at once declared themselves in favor of it. But Sumner and Sprague made speeches in an effort to shelve it. Chandler, much worried, came to the Cabinet meeting on the 14th and advised that the Administration seek to rally its supporters behind the article. Fish immediately penned a telegram to Levi P. Morton, and other members sent duplicates to their friends in all parts of the country. Next day, through a leak in the *Herald,* the article became public.

But despite Chandler's fears, the Senate lost no time in passing a resolution of approval. Even Sumner finally voted aye, though he did not lose the opportunity of attacking both the American and British Commissioners. The result stood 42 to 9. But the Senate indulged in a clarification of the article by stating in the preamble that both nations adopted for the future "the principle that claims for remote or indirect losses should not be admitted as the result of the failure to observe neutral obligations, so far as to declare that it will hereafter guide the conduct of both" toward each other. "It is now for Great Britain to decide," wrote Fish to Levi P. Morton.[60] "If she is sincere, she cannot hesitate to accept the amendments. The article as proposed was uncertain and ambiguous." The last days of May were spent in anxious suspense. Then came word that Gladstone's Ministry—despite a plea from the Queen herself for acceptance—would not assent to the modifications.

It would not agree because it believed that the Senate had unwarrantably broadened the article. The amendment, it held, would prevent any future claim for indirect losses even when the breach of neutrality had been deliberate and malicious. As a matter of fact, the phrasing *had* been broadened, with a view to possible future offences by Americans against Canada. Fish told Thornton that, "As framed by the Senate, the Article prevents claims against us on account of the Fenian Raids, while the British draft would exclude only claims of a similar nature arising from acts of vessels, etc., etc., under circumstances which may probably never occur again." The Senate had done only what it thought fair. But the British Government might well doubt whether release from reparation for offences during the Civil War might not be bought too dearly by conceding to the United States

[60] Fish to Morton, May 26, 1872; Fish Papers.

an unlimited exemption from responsibility for similar wrongs which might be inflicted in all future time upon Great Britain by Americans! Even Granville and Forster were against the Senate's terms, and the Ministry acted unanimously.

VII

For the moment all seemed over and the Treaty lost. The Administration needed only to give the signal for a vigorous expression of national anger. Grant was eager to act. In high indignation, he wrote Fish on June 1: [61]

In view of the probable failure of the Washington Treaty, I suggest whether it is not advisable to have prepared for transmittal to the Senate, on Monday next, all the correspondence on the subject. It should be accompanied by a short message setting forth the concessions made by this government to secure the benefits of a treaty equally honorable and advantageous to the two countries directly interested in the treaty, and, as an example, to the civilized world. I would also suggest in the message that at the next session of Congress means should be provided for settlement with American citizens who suffered by the acts of vessels illegally fitted out in English waters.

But miraculously the treaty was saved at the last moment, not in Washington, not in London, but in Geneva itself. June 15 was the date set for beginning the arbitration. On the 13th Cushing, Evarts, and Waite set out from Paris, all firmly expecting to be back in the city within a few days. Cushing's secretary hardly thought it worth while to go along. When they reached Geneva they found that the five Arbitrators and the English party were already there. Roundell Palmer and Cockburn also expected to return home immediately.

At noon on Saturday the 15th, in a hall of the Hôtel de Ville, Count Sclopis impressively called the session to order. On the dais sat the five Arbitrators, with Charles Francis Adams at the extreme right, Lord Cockburn at the extreme left, and Sclopis in the centre. In front were the secretaries, the two Agents, and the counsel. With great dignity, Bancroft Davis arose and presented each Arbitrator with English and French copies of an argument. All eyes then turned to Lord Tenterden, who but for the still-unsettled dispute would have

[61] Fish Papers.

delivered in like fashion the British argument. Instead, he submitted a note, asking that in view of the differences remaining between the two governments, the Tribunal adjourn for a sufficient period to permit them to agree upon a supplementary convention.

By presenting its argument, the United States was placed, in Fish's opinion, in a position to invoke the judgment of the Tribunal whether Great Britain appeared before it or not. Charles Francis Adams had told W. E. Forster in London that if England withdrew, "I shall urge the other Arbitrators to go on." For this reason, among others, the British Government was asking for delay instead of withdrawing.

No one was more eager to prevent a break than Bancroft Davis. During the preceding three months he had given intense thought to the deadlock for which he was so largely responsible. He had sent Fish several letters discussing the possibility of getting rid of the indirect claims by an advance agreement of counsel upon points of law which would not be contested on either side, the rules for the measurement of damages to be included among them. Now he inquired how long an adjournment the British proposed. Lord Tenterden named eight months. Already Thornton had intimated to Fish that this would be the period requested by England. The Secretary had protested that this was too long; that it would postpone the question to so late a date that the next Congress could not pass legislation carrying into effect the Treaty provisions regarding the fisheries, the assessment board, and other practical matters. Fish had instructed Bancroft Davis that an adjournment should not run later than January 1, 1872. "Telegraph results immediately," he added.[62] But Davis did not debate the question before the Tribunal. Saying that he would have to learn the views of his government, he asked for another session on the 17th. The request was granted, and two days gained.

In these two days Charles Francis Adams, ably supported by Davis and Lord Tenterden, saved the battle. Apparently it occurred to both Davis and Adams simultaneously that the Tribunal, waving aside British objections, and acting summarily and rapidly, might at its very next meeting take up the indirect claims, reject them, and thus cut through all difficulties! They talked this over on Saturday afternoon. "It would be a way most unpalatable to England," said Adams,

[62] Fish to Davis, June 12, 1872; Letterbooks.

"but if there is pluck enough in the Tribunal, it might be done." "I don't believe there is pluck enough," said Davis.[63]

Adams suggested that Davis talk with Lord Tenterden on the subject. Davis, after some demur (for he believed that it would be better for Evarts to see Sir Roundell Palmer), therefore called at Tenterden's rooms at the Hotel des Bergues. The English Agent at first declared that nothing could be done. "I may as well tell you frankly that my instructions are positive and limited," he said. "They are to secure the adjournment we have asked for, or retire."

But as they talked, Tenterden began to see a light—indeed, a larger and brighter light than either of the Americans. It was a happy fact that the two Agents were gentlemen who trusted each other and could talk confidentially. Davis has described how, during their conference, the germinal idea of the final settlement blossomed: [64]

A conversation ensued, in which I ascertained that he thought it probable that the neutral Arbitrators would be willing to say that Great Britain could not be held responsible for the indirect claims, and he thought that the manifestation of such an opinion would probably induce the United States to instruct their Agent to say that they did not desire to have these claims further considered by the Tribunal. He added that there was a strong feeling in England that the United States expected that the Arbitrators would, while rejecting these classes of claims specifically, let them have weight when considering the other classes, and that they would desire some instructions to answer that objection, however unreasonable.

When I was fully possessed of his idea, I saw Mr. Waite and Mr. Evarts (Mr. Cushing had by this time retired), and told them what had taken place.

Late that night and all next day, Sunday the 16th, the conferences continued. Sir Roundell Palmer made objections; they were answered; the plan took fuller and better shape. On Sunday afternoon Adams handed to Davis a paper which went much further than any American proposal previously made. He wrote that it was "needless for the Arbitrators to do more than declare that they must decline to assume any jurisdiction over a question which is not fully recognized by both parties as legitimately within the powers conferred upon them by the terms of the Treaty." If more reasons were wanting to decide the

[63] Bancroft Davis, MS. Journal (a full copy is in the Fish Papers); Hackett, *Geneva Tribunal.*

[64] On Tenterden's capable activities, see Tenterden to Foreign Office, Nos. 7, 15, 16, 17, FO 1402, State Papers LXII, 192; Tenterden to Granville, Private, June 15, 16, 1872; in F. O. 5, 1417; Tenterden to Granville, "most confidential," June 17, 1872, No. 32, FO 5, 1417.

point, the Arbitrators could say that if such claims were pressed by the American Government, then the Tribunal would be "constrained in deference to what it holds the recognized rules of international law applicable to such cases to decide that Great Britain could not in their opinion be made responsible in damages therefor."

Both Davis and Cushing objected to part of this. They did not wish the Arbitrators wholly to decline jurisdiction; they did wish them to make an explicit assertion that application of the recognized rules of international law would at once dispose of the claims. Early on the 17th Cushing, Evarts, and Waite therefore agreed upon a substitute paper. Under its terms, the Arbitrators were to make a *declaration,* not a decision. It was to state that the American claims for indirect damages (including transfer of the American commercial marine, enhanced costs of insurance, and prolongation of the war), did not constitute in public law a valid foundation for a money award, and that the Tribunal was compelled, in deference to international law, to decide that Great Britain could not be made responsible in damages for them. The Tribunal was to offer this opinion not "as a present exercise of jurisdiction over the subject," but merely "as an expression of the views they have formed upon the question of public law involved."

Thus at last a satisfactory formula was decided upon. For this final suggestion, with some modifications, proved satisfactory to all. The Tribunal was in effect to give an "advisory" opinion. While declining to take up the question of its competence to decide the indirect claims, it stated that *if it were* competent it would find that they offered no basis in international law for an award! At the close of a formal session of the board on the 17th, the five Arbitrators remained for consultation. Adams in fluent French argued with them; he brought the reluctant Cockburn to agree that an *extra*-judicial opinion might be given; and he declared that he was ready to offer the proposal "not as an Arbitrator representing my country, but as representing all nations."

On June 19, with Lord Cockburn absent, the Tribunal met to make the agreed statement. Count Sclopis read it. After referring to the conflict of opinion over the right of the United States to submit the indirect claims, he went on: "the Arbitrators think it right to state that . . . they have arrived, individually and collectively, at the conclusion that these claims do not constitute, upon the principles of international law applicable to such cases, good foundation for an award of compensation or computation of damages between nations." [65] Fish then instructed the American counsel to announce that they accepted this statement. The British counsel withdrew their motion for adjournment, and on June 27th presented their argument. The arbitration had begun.

VIII

Thus, after years of vexatious discussion, the whole cloud of vague but portentous grievances called the indirect claims, like some fearsome Oriental afreet recalled to his urn, was exorcised by a few magic words. It would have been better by far had they never been raised to darken Anglo-American relations. Their history reveals no little bungling on both sides; but it also shows that, after the first step was taken, the whole imbroglio had a certain inevitable quality. Seward adumbrated the indirect claims. Sumner impressed them deeply upon the American consciousness. Once this had been done, no treaty of peace could extinguish the ill-feeling between the two nations which did not cover them —which did not deal with *all* the causes of ill-feeling. The American Commissioners knew that they could not debar them without arousing the resentment of the Senate and people. The British Commissioners, *per contra,* knew that they could not explicitly include them without arousing Parliament. The Joint Commission tacitly decided that the Treaty must neither exclude nor include them in explicit terms. Compromises are always dangerous when two irritable publics have to be satisfied, and vague compromises are the most dangerous of all because they are open to varying interpretations.

The opposing interpretations precipitated all the troubles. The British felt that under the compromise, the Americans were bound to say no more about the indirect claims. The Americans recognized no such obligation and saw three good reasons for mentioning them. First, they would strengthen our demands for a generous rather than niggardly estimate of direct damages. Second, they would strengthen the Treaty, still in danger of a failure of appropriations in the House. Third, for the good of all future neutrals, such claims should be decisively knocked

[65] Caleb Cushing, *Treaty of Washington,* 70.

in the head. In some European war, the United States herself might let a few cruisers escape to aid one belligerent; if the other were victorious, it might later demand half the costs of the conflict. Fish and Bancroft Davis were therefore correct in including the indirect claims. But we cannot avoid the conclusion that they were censurable for the manner in which they did it. They should have made it clear that the inclusion was merely *pro forma,* and that the United States disclaimed a monetary award on account of the prolongation of the war. This would have required ingenuity in wording the text. It would also have required courage in facing the American electorate; but courage is precisely the quality we expect from statesmen.

As we have said, haste in drafting the latter part of the Case was doubtless partly responsible. Ratifications of the Treaty were not exchanged until June, 1871; the Case had to be delivered in Geneva on December 15; in the brief interim Bancroft Davis, shaking off his burden at the State Department, had to write an elaborate historico-legal treatise of nearly 500 pages, see it through the press, and send it abroad. It is not strange that the last pages were hastily composed and read without due thought of their effect. Omission of the unfortunate sentence about costs of the war "after the battle of Gettysburg" would alone have wrought a vast improvement. But it must be said that after the outcry began in England, Secretary Fish labored with vigor and wisdom to reassure the British Government. First he made it clear that he would not push for any award under the indirect claims. Then, as the British clamor continued, he stated that he fully expected to see the claims rejected. Finally, he declared that the United States presented them for the explicit purpose of having them rejected and a sensible rule of international law established. But by this time the British public was in arms, and the Gladstone Ministry possessed too little freedom of action. The whole affair offered a memorable lesson to both governments upon the importance—nay, the necessity—of the utmost care and the closest scrutiny of future consequences in each step of a diplomatic negotiation.

BANCROFT DAVIS' telegram to Fish on June 27, 1872, is historic: "British argument filed. Arbitration goes on." The President and Secretary of State that afternoon were in Boston. When Fish had glanced at the telegram he handed it to Grant, who for a moment stood silent, tears of relief moistening his eyes. In England the heads of the Government felt the same emotion.[1] On the fateful 15th the Cabinet had sat in something like permanent session, Forster and Granville playing chess.[2] That night Gladstone waited anxiously with Granville at the Foreign Office. When just before midnight the telegraph brought details of the day's conciliatory proceedings, the Prime Minister rose in elated relief. "Thank God," he exclaimed, "that up to a certain point the indications on this great controversy are favorable."

From the end of June all went smoothly.[3] Throughout July, throughout August, during the first fortnight of September, the Tribunal labored in the beautiful city of Geneva. The scene of its sessions remained the small but adequate Salle des Conférences in the Hôtel de Ville—now known as the Salle de l'Alabama. The public was excluded, but since counsel on both sides employed a number of solicitors, translators, and secretaries, the room was well filled. Count Sclopis, large of frame, courteous and dignified in manner, presided with uninterrupted vigor. On one side Jacques Staempfli, stout, swarthy, plain-featured, was the picture of an independent Swiss burgher. On the other d'Itajuba of

[1] The British Cabinet held a long session on June 12 (the day the Arbitrator, Counsel, and Agent left for Geneva) and discussed whether the Government should proceed according to the Treaty provisions, or let it fall to the ground. The Cabinet reached no decision. "But the best spirit prevails and Mr. Gladstone will do his best to bring the Treaty to a conclusion," the Prime Minister wrote the Queen. Gladstone Papers; copy through Mrs. H. W. Wells. Cf. *Letters to Queen Victoria, Second Series,* II, 213. On June 14 Gladstone explained the position to the House, and on the 15th wrote his wife: "I got as far as to have pretty effectual preparations made for the worst that can happen." Gladstone Papers.

[2] Forster's diary describes the events of the day with humor and vividness; Wemyss Reid, *Forster,* II, 31 ff.

[3] News of the Tribunal's action on the indirect claims reached London June 19, 1872. "Hip, hip, hip, hooray," Forster wrote his wife. "My dearest, the final settlement of the indirect claims came during questions today, and Gladstone announced it amid great cheers on our side and the disgust of the Tories. This is a good year now, whatever happens." Reid, *Forster,* II, 33. When Fish heard the news, according to Thornton, he grumbled that he would have preferred to have the Tribunal assume jurisdiction. PRO, FO 5, 1403, Thornton to Granville, June 24, 1872, No. 441.

Brazil, small, frail, and refined, looked with his gold-bowed glasses like a college professor. But the most striking figures were Charles Francis Adams and Sir Alexander Cockburn. The former, short, bald, and ruddy, a fringe of white whiskers under his chin, might almost have sat for a portrait of his father, John Quincy Adams. His manner showed all the cold rigidity of the Adamses. In contrast, Cockburn's vivacity and excitability betrayed his Anglo-French descent. Short, bullet-headed, ruddy-cheeked, he had the eye of an eagle, while his hands, shoulders, and features were never still. A secretary wrote long after that this electric figure, alert at the end of the dignified row of Arbitrators, frequently bursting into explosive speech, seemed in memory to dominate the whole scene.[4]

Bancroft Davis, intensely suspicious of the British, eager to score for America in every possible way, had been busy for months influencing the press, working upon European opinion, and flattering the Arbitrators. His first act on reaching Paris the previous December had been to call with Elihu Washburne upon d'Itajuba. "I took care to say to him," he wrote Fish, "that we had read with pleasure and profit the Brazilian rules for the preservation of neutrality, and had incorporated a translation of them into the evidence to be submitted to the Tribunal."[5]

His second act was to make sure that the Americans got the French translation of their Case to the foreign Arbitrators before the British did. "This gives us an enormous advantage," he wrote Fish from Geneva on December 17.[6] "Staempfli and d'Itajuba don't understand one single word of English, either spoken or printed. Count Sclopis reads it with fluency, but speaks but little. We therefore have the field to ourselves for the present, and must inevitably get our side of the story into the heads of the neutral Arbitrators before the British." Thus early he had appraised Staempfli as a solid man of obstinate character. "The Baron d'Itajuba evidently approaches the subject with an impression that we have suffered wrongs. He has a great deal to say about the Brazilian orders and regulations, which we have reprinted at length in our sixth volume. The British, I observe, in their Case give prominence to the

---

[4] Hackett, *Reminiscences of the Geneva Tribunal, passim;* see also Roundell Palmer, Earl of Selborne, *Memorials Personal and Political,* I, 250 ff.

[5] The Fish Papers contain nearly all Davis' letters; see also the Bancroft Davis Papers.

[6] Bancroft Davis Papers. Davis was pleased by the attention his Case aroused. George Bancroft arranged a German edition at Leipzig, and Davis wrote Fish that it was "the most notable political book of the day in Europe."

seizure of the *Florida* at Bahia. On our side we shall make the most out of the Rules." Davis had a keen eye for personal foibles:

Count Sclopis . . . was made President nominally because Italy was the first neutral Power named in the Treaty, but really because he is the fittest for the place, and is the only man who has any knowledge of English. It so happened that the room was arranged with three seats and desks on a raised dais, with the central one one step higher than the other. Count Sclopis naturally took the central seat. Staempfli sat at his right, and Itajuba at his left. Mr. Adams and Sir Alexander Cockburn sat in chairs on the level of the floor in front of them. We thought the arrangement admirable. The next morning I was at the Bergues Hotel on my way to see Tenterden. In the hall I met the secretary, a friend and appointee of Staempfli. He wanted to know if I were going to Lord Tenterden's. I said yes. He said he should follow, as he wished to "address us." This formidable notice was followed by his coming into Tenterden's room. Standing before us, he said that he had come to make a reclamation on the part of Mr. Staempfli; that Mr. Staempfli thought the Powers in the Tribunal were on an equality, but that the Italian Arbitrator had been put in a higher chair, which implied superiority in Italy over Switzerland. We answered that that was an affair which the Arbitrators must regulate for themselves; that we had taken the room as furnished by the Swiss Government, and were not responsible for the inequalities in the level of the floor, and we added that we did not suppose that Mr. Adams and Mr. Cockburn by sitting in a lower seat than Mr. Staempfli and Baron d'Itajuba, intended to imply that America and Great Britain were inferior to Switzerland and Brazil. The matter was smoothed over, and at the second conference the Arbitrators all sat on the same level, much to their and our inconvenience. The manifestation was undoubtedly caused by disappointment. Mr. Staempfli expected to be named as the presiding officer. In that case he would probably have found no fault with the raised seat.

In January, 1872, Davis began a highly practical campaign to control the Continental newspapers. Schenck had told him that one reason the British press exploded so angrily was because the strength of the American Case worried it. "They are so evidently trying to forestall the effect of our Case and get possession of the public opinion of Europe," wrote Davis, "that I have written to Bancroft, Marsh, Rublee, and Jay confidentially, to see how the press is disposed at their different posts, and I have arranged to have Laugel sounded to see if he will write for the *Deux Mondes* a fair statement of our argument and proof. . . . If this should cost a little money, it will be money well spent." He thought the English were trying to affect Staempfli through the German press, and d'Itajuba thought the diplomatic corps in Paris. Several

THE LAST
SCENE OF THE
WILLIAM TELL
TRAGEDY.

COUNTER
CLAIMS

The Geneva Arbitration

(Nast in *Harper's Weekly*)

Ministers proved helpful; Davis wrote on January 31 that George Bancroft and Horace Rublee were laboring amain with the German and Swiss press, and Marsh he hoped with the Italian. But others were disappointments. He sent Fish another bulletin early in February: [7]

The general tone is against us in Paris. I am sorry to say that the Consul-General [John Meredith Read of Pennsylvania] does nothing to help us. He is so overcome with the grandeur of his English friends that he has little heart to say anything against them and for his country. Washburne is outspoken and strong—full of pluck—Jay [at Vienna] is weak as dishwater—needs a strong plaster put to his back every other day. I send with my dispatch today a copy of the last plaster I gave him. It is lamentable to have to use such tools in this work, but I suppose we must take Americans as we find them, and not quarrel with those who love the taste of an English Lord's backsides.

Fortunately for Davis, the French press has always been venal. Congress had appropriated $250,000 for expenses of the Arbitration, and Davis at once drew upon the fund: [8]

After consultation with Waite and Washburne [he wrote February 6], I have decided to close an arrangement by which we shut up at least some of the organs which England is trying to control. I enclose articles from the *Constitutionnel* and the *Soir*. I have already sent you the *Memorial Diplomatique*. I shall have the *Courier Diplomatique* in the same train, and shall have the support of the *Moniteur*, the *Patrie*, the *Presse*, and *Bien Public*. This list includes all the important political papers except the *Debats* and the *France*, and the *Journal de Paris*. The first two are bought by England; the latter I don't know about. All this costs money, but I shall take the responsibility, under Washburne's advice, of spending it. The article in the *Memorial Diplomatique* has been extensively copied and commented on, and has had a good effect in stiffening up public opinion here. The articles which are following are also doing good. The attacks from England were so steady and so persistent in misrepresentation that public opinion was beginning to set in strongly against us. It is now decidedly turning.

The British, Bancroft Davis wrote from Berlin, were spending money heavily on the German press, but with little result; partly because the government was against them.[9] "I saw Bismarck last night. He approves our position thoroughly (on the indirect claims); tells us that England

[7] Fish Papers; Bancroft Davis Papers.
[8] *Ibid*. Davis found the purchase of the French press cheaper than Mussolini, who was reported (1935–36) to have spent a half-million dollars to buy its support in his aggression upon Ethiopia.
[9] Fish Papers; Bancroft Davis Papers.

has nothing to do but go forward under the treaty, and abide the result of the Arbitration." Davis was urging J. Russell Jones in Belgium to secure the support of *L'Independence Belge*. He retained a German publicist named Brentano to write for the *Allgemeine Zeitung* and Frankfort and Zurich journals. By February 27 he was certain that "the Continental press is generally with us." Meanwhile, he arranged the preparation of two effective pamphlets by French authorities upon international law; one upon the general *Alabama* question, the other upon the indirect claims. The writings of the Belgian authority M. Rollin Jacquemyns and the Swiss German savant Bluntschli on the American side had indubitable influence throughout Europe.

At the same time that he was bribing or otherwise influencing European publicists, Bancroft Davis had been supervising the preparation of the American Counter-Case, a work decidedly longer (with its many documents) than the original Case. Caleb Cushing and Evarts both gave poor Davis much trouble. The former insisted upon including many old controversial papers going back to his Attorney-Generalship, and showed the petulance of age. The latter, who had little patience with the indirect claims, sometimes took positions which Davis thought likely to weaken the Counter-Case. Once when the Agent frankly told Evarts that he did not like something he had written, "he was in a pet, like a spoiled child." At times twelve clerks and eight or ten translators were employed. By this arduous labor, the Americans were ready with an impressive volume of rebuttal on April 15.

Work on the Argument did not begin until a month later, for Evarts had announced that he would make no argument unless there was to be a court. But it also was elaborate, embodying a well-considered reply to the British Counter-Case. The English were caught napping. Apparently convinced that the Arbitration would be postponed, they did little work, and their Argument presented on June 27th bore evidence of hasty preparation.[10] It was called a "Summary," and fell far short of the closely-reasoned paper expected. In a letter to Evarts on June 17, Sir Roundell Palmer confessed that nothing adequate was ready by asking for a postponement to September to enable him to prepare one; a request which the Tribunal summarily denied.

[10] The British Argument included a report by the Board of Trade on individual American demands for damages. It rejected the claims on the ground of increased insurance, and arrived at a sum of $8,600,000 for the proper American claims.

I

As the Americans made the better preparations, so they had the better of the arguments before the Tribunal. Actual courtroom work began July 15. Sir Alexander Cockburn suggested that the Arbitrators deal first with general principles of law involved, and that the counsel assist them "so that arguments scattered over a mass of documents may be presented in a concentrated and appreciable form." This would have meant needless delay and confusion, for the abstract points of law were already fully discussed in the Cases and Arguments. Staempfli at once objected. The proper course, he said, was to take up specific allegations of unneutral conduct, scrutinize the facts, and then discuss and apply the law to each. Sclopis, d'Itajuba, and Adams supported him, and this course was followed. The Tribunal began by examining the case of the *Florida,* the first cruiser to escape. After discussing it, four of the Arbitrators, Cockburn dissenting, at once held Great Britain responsible for the damage she had done, though they reserved judgment upon a minor point.

So the hearings went on. Other cruisers were taken up *seriatim.* Unquestionably several members of the Tribunal had preconceptions favorable to America. D'Itajuba was influenced by the strict neutrality regulations of the Brazilian Empire, while he told the British counsel, "You are rich—very rich." Staempfli felt the sympathy of a citizen of a federated republic for a government like his own. Even Count Sclopis may have been affected by the strong judgment which the Italian jurist Pierantoni (whether "reached" by Bancroft Davis or not) had just published in favor of the United States. At various points the excitable Cockburn, gesticulating and pouring forth a torrent of words, supported Sir Roundell Palmer in asking the Tribunal to hear arguments upon abstract questions of law. The first was upon the meaning of the words "due diligence"; the second upon the legal effect of a commission. In all, half a dozen such hearings were granted. The Americans objected. But they soon realized that Evarts and Cushing were getting much the better of these encounters. Bancroft Davis wrote Fish on August 6: [11]

[11] Fish Papers; Bancroft Davis Papers.

You will see that Roundell Palmer has had his way in making an argument. It was decidedly for the best that it should be so. The course which
the English pursued to obtain it gained them nothing but ill-will from the
other Arbitrators. The argument when in is weak, because he had no case to
go upon. Our counsel are answering it with great power. The English went
way beyond the permission of the court. We took no exception to it, as it
opened up to us the full range of discussion, and enabled us to say some things
which our counsel wanted to say. Evarts' speech of yesterday pressed them
very hard. Roundell Palmer and Mountague Bernard sat before the Arbitrators
making constant gestures of dissent, and the peppery old Chief Justice kept
interrupting, but the more he interrupted, the harder Evarts bore down. Unfortunately the neutrals couldn't take it in. Itajuba read the newspapers,
Sclopis went to sleep, and Staempfli alone paid close attention. However, we
shall get it all in French, interruptions and all.

As the hearings proceeded, Cockburn greatly offended his fellow-
Arbitrators. Extenuating circumstances may no doubt be cited for his
rude and overbearing demeanour. He was overworked.[12] Before he came
to Geneva his duties as Chief Justice had prevented study of the voluminous papers, and he had to shut himself in his rooms, giving no
time to exercise, society, or recreation. According to Palmer, he was
"conscious of intellectual superiority" to his colleagues. Assuredly he
had no reason to feel superior to Charles Francis Adams, but he chafed
over weaknesses in others which he scathingly described to Lord Granville. "We could not have had a worse man than Staempfli or next to
him the President [Sclopis]. The first a furious Republican, hating
monarchical governments, and Ministries in which men of rank take
part, ignorant as a horse, and obstinate as a mule. The second vapid,
and all anxiety to give a decision which shall produce an effect in the
world, and to make speeches about 'civilization,' 'humanity,' etc., etc.,
in short *un vrai phrasier*. Baron Itajuba is of a far better stamp, but
not sufficiently informed and very indolent; and apt by reason of the
latter defect to catch hold of some salient point without going to the
bottom of things. . . ." As the tide went against Cockburn, his temper
became worse.

His excitement, anger, and rudeness became painful. His face flushed
and eyes moistened as his bitter eloquence rolled forth; he gesticulated
and pounded his desk until he upset the stationery of Count Sclopis

[12] See Caleb Cushing, *The Treaty of Washington;* Hackett, *Reminiscences of the
Geneva Tribunal*, 214 ff., Roundell Palmer, Earl of Selborne, *Memorials Personal and
Political*, I, 242–280, on Cockburn.

eight or ten feet distant. He spoke like a man unjustly treated by the Tribunal. He threw out reflections upon his colleagues— "There are men here not educated in the law, who are now examining questions about the great laws common to nations, for the first time." They plainly evinced their resentment. More than once Adams offered rebuke and protest. Staempfli, seeing that Cockburn regarded him as stupid and prejudiced, felt especially hurt. On August 1 Lord Tenterden wrote frankly to Granville of Cockburn's behavior: "The effect thus far is very damaging to our cause." In contrast, Adams was a model of austere self-restraint.

The American counsel, Evarts, Cushing, and Waite, were not abler than Sir Roundell Palmer (leader of the English bar) and Mountague Bernard, but they had better arguments. They worked in close harmony. "We have consulted freely and we have discussed largely in advance everything which had to be said or done by us," Cushing informed Fish [13] as the Arbitration neared its close. "In writing, of course, we have needed to accommodate ourselves to one another's peculiarities in order to produce joint work which should receive all our signatures. I took care at the start to relieve the subject of all questions of seniority and precedence either in the distribution of work or in personal action before the Tribunal. In fine, as we have prosecuted the work in mutual confidence and goodwill, so we have arrived at the conclusion. . . ." Socially, the British and American counsel got on admirably. They fraternized at dinners, balls, and receptions. Between Evarts and Sir Roundell Palmer a positive affection sprang up, and in his memoirs the Englishman pays high tribute to the lanky New Englander as "a man of whom any country might be proud."

"I try to run along day by day with your proceedings," Fish wrote Bancroft Davis on August 6,[14] "and imagine the Chief Justice mad and beating about, with Adams calm and cool, Cushing wary and watchful, Evarts self-possessed and dignified, Waite earnest and laborious, and you overworked as usual and holding all in hand." This fairly sums up his lengthy reports from Davis. The day of this letter Cushing delivered a remarkable "Reply Argument" to the main British defense, which surpassed even Evarts' best efforts. His secretary tells us that the compact, weighty, and eloquent paper was dictated in French almost word for word as later printed.

[13] Cushing to Fish, Geneva, September 5, 1872; Fish Papers.　　　[14] Letterbooks.

II

By mid-August it was certain the Tribunal would make an award in favor of the United States. Under the Treaty, it could order Great Britain to pay a sum in gross, or could set up a Board of Assessors to decide under its general findings which claims should be paid. Fish had instructed the American counsel the previous December to obtain, if possible, a gross award. Bancroft Davis concluded in August that the English counsel were determined to have a board created; and Schenck wrote him on September 1 that he believed this was likewise the wish of Downing Street.[15] "They have been forced to conclude that they are to have some award made against them at Geneva; and they not only want to reduce the amount, by every captious objection, to the lowest possible sum, but they are sore and ill-natured at the thought of having anything to pay at all. I believe that they would rather give us (much as they love money) $20,000,000 in a secret way, though, to square accounts, than to have $1,000,000 publicly adjudged to be due and be compelled to pay it. Only think what a very bitter pill it must be to Great Britain, after being so long accustomed to extort satisfaction from other nations, to find a government that first makes her own her wrong in a Treaty, and then pay up." But this was conjecture, and we know now that Cockburn believed it desirable to get rid of the dispute at one sweep by awarding a lump sum.

But how much? The Tribunal requested both parties to prepare estimates. A battle of figures ensued. Details are obscure, and we do not know how the final total was reached, though Bancroft Davis states that it was by mutual concession, and Lord Tenterden that it was a compromise between rival figures of $8,000,000 and $14,000,000, plus interest. Almost every figure seems to have been mentioned! Cockburn thought that $8,000,000 would measure the damage; d'Itajuba mentioned $14,000,000 as suitable; and Adams supported a proposal for $18,999,000 made by Staempfli. It was Staempfli, who enjoyed sifting statistics, who had most to do with the final computation.[16]

This battle of figures brought one dangerous explosion. When the American Agent and Counsel presented detailed estimates of damage,

---

[15] Bancroft Davis Papers.
[16] See Tenterden's dispatches to Granville, August 30, September 2, 1872; PRO, FO 5, 1407, 1408. Also Hackett, *Geneva Tribunal;* Cushing, *Treaty of Washington.*

Lord Tenterden attacked some of them with resentment. He was seconded by Cockburn, who in his overbearing manner virtually charged the American representatives with offering fictitious bills. One of his sentences, hastily rapped out, perhaps sounded more harshly than he intended. In a flash Charles Francis Adams had risen at the other end of the dais, and turning to face Cockburn, exclaimed in a voice that trembled with emotion, "I will not sit here on this Tribunal, and hear my country traduced!" He moved to leave the room. But Sclopis also leaped to his feet, extending his arms, and spoke a few calm but authoritative words. Cockburn, who realized that he was in the wrong, uttered a manful apology, and Adams resumed his seat. The incident thus ended as quickly as it had begun.[17]

The final session of the Tribunal on September 14, 1872, offered a dramatic scene. It met at half-past twelve of a refulgent day. The hall was crowded. Swiss officials, representatives of the European and American press, and the leading citizens of Geneva jostled for seats. For some unknown reason, Lord Tenterden and Sir Alexander Cockburn were late, until impatience turned into apprehension. Finally they arrived, and the protocol of the preceding meeting was approved. Then amid a breathless hush, the Secretary, M. Favrot, read in a firm voice the English text of the Award, a brief document of about 2,500 words.

It found Great Britain responsible for the damage wrought by the *Alabama, Florida,* and *Shenandoah* (after leaving Melbourne), and granted the United States a gross indemnity of $15,500,000; the Tribunal being unanimous as to the *Alabama,* four to one on the *Florida,* and three to two on the *Shenandoah.* Duplicate originals of the Award were then signed by four of the Arbitrators, and copies delivered to the two Agents. Cockburn, who had scowled darkly during the proceedings, refused to sign. Instead, he arose and presented a statement of reasons for not assenting, which the Tribunal ordered to be received and recorded—a statement soon published in both England and America. Finally, with appropriate words, Count Sclopis declared the labors of the Arbitrators finished and the Tribunal dissolved. Applause rang through the hall; it was echoed outside by cheers and a salute of artillery, while Geneva, already decorated, broke forth in the national colors of Switzerland, Great Britain, and the United States.[18] The thrill of that moment was felt throughout Europe, and has been given fine

[17] Hackett, *Geneva Tribunal,* 322.   [18] Cushing, *Treaty of Washington,* 128.

literary expression by no less a pen than that of August Strindberg.[19]

But meanwhile a strange scene had taken place within. "The instant that Count Sclopis closed," writes Cushing, "and before the sound of his last words had died on the ear, Sir Alexander Cockburn snatched up his hat, and, without participating in the exchange of leave-takings around him, without a word or sign of courteous recognition for any of his colleagues, rushed to the door and disappeared. . . ."

III

The verdict gave Fish the utmost satisfaction.[20] It is true that he had grumbled to Thornton in June that he wished the Tribunal had assumed jurisdiction over the indirect claims. He also thought that other vessels ought to have been included. When he first received confidential information that the *Georgia* had been ruled out, with Charles Francis Adams agreeing that England was not liable for her acts, he wrote Grant in deep disappointment.[21] "The depredations committed by the *Georgia* were less extensive than those of either of the cruisers fitted out in England. Her career was comparatively short, but she did a large amount of damage, and I cannot understand the ground on which Mr. Adams has given the opinion in favor of England in the *Georgia*. I thought it as bad as any." But Grant took the news with equanimity.[22] "I received your note reciting a paragraph from a private letter from Bancroft Davis. I was not much surprised—would not wonder if the whole case, except the *Alabama*, went against us. Would we not be better off if it did? We do not want to be bound by too strict rules as neutrals." Fish also regretted the relinquishment of the costs of pursuit. But they would have been hard to separate from the other expenses of the war; and had they been allowed, the precedent might have enabled some future belligerent to saddle a neutral from whose ports a hostile cruiser escaped with the upkeep of a large fleet.

On the whole, the United States received as much as it could justly expect. Its counsel, as Cushing admitted, had never felt real hope of winning damages for the *Sumter, Tallahassee, Nashville,* and *Chickamauga,* and were not "seriously disappointed" by failing with the

---

[19] *The German Lieutenant, and Other Stories.*
[20] For the verdict and award, see *Geneva Arbitration,* IV, 49 ff.; John Bassett Moore, *International Arbitrations,* I, 653–659.
[21] Garrison, August 19, 1872; Letterbooks.
[22] Grant to Fish, Long Branch, August 24, 1872; Fish Papers.

FINAL SESSION OF THE GENEVA TRIBUNAL: COCKBURN'S EXIT

Left to right, *Rear:* Waite, Evarts, Cushing, Davis, Adams, Staempfli, Sclopis, d'Itajuba, Cockburn. *In front:* Tenterden, Palmer, Bernard.

Georgia.[23] The American claim for "prospective earnings and freight" was too flimsy to sustain. No court, municipal or international, admits prospective profits as an element of damages. Nor was the cash award ungenerous. The claims filed by American citizens for the losses caused by the *Alabama, Florida, Shenandoah,* and *Georgia* had amounted to $12,838,000; add interest from 1865, and the total would come to about $20,000,000. But this estimate was that of claimants themselves, and claimants always exaggerate. Deduction of one-fourth for this exaggeration would bring the total to $15,000,000. More important than the precise sum were the findings of the court as to "due diligence." They were exactly what discreet Americans desired; for while they censured Great Britain for three instances of culpable and flagrant negligence, by rejecting the dubious instances they refused to create a precedent which might later embarrass the United States above all other nations.

The Tribunal, required by the Treaty "to be governed by the Three Rules therein specified," naturally gave its interpretation to these Rules. The construction which it placed upon them was that which Cushing, Evarts, and Waite vehemently advocated, and which the British counsel opposed; and Cushing soon afterward wrote of the American victory as a great triumph. But some American observers were not so sure. They believed that the adoption and interpretation of the new Rules might yet be found to place a very undesirable burden upon the United States as a future neutral. For the Tribunal clearly set forth three propositions as springing from the Rules. First, it declared, a neutral has absolute international duties, quite apart from the provisions of its own national laws; second, its own municipal law is in no sense or degree a criterion of these duties; and third, "due diligence" is a variable matter, to be exercised in exact proportion to the risks which either belligerent runs from a failure of neutrality. A commentator in the *Nation* [24] urged that since hereafter this construction and its practical consequences must weigh heavily against the United States—for in recurrent European wars America would be the greatest of neutrals—our government should drop the Three Rules. Many Englishmen were anxious to do so; and it was shortly moved in Parliament that in bringing them to the notice of foreign Powers, as required by the Treaty, the government should express dissent from the Geneva interpretation. Of Fish's attitude we shall say more later.

[23] Cushing to Fish, Geneva, September 5, 1872; Fish Papers.   [24] May 1, 1873.

"We are quite content with the Geneva Award," Fish wrote to Elihu Washburne.[25] "It decides that 'Great Britain was culpable.' That is the great point on which our people had any feeling. The *amount* awarded has been of secondary consideration with the people. The Administration strove to make it larger, but I shall not be surprised to find it sufficient to indemnify every actual loss sustained at the hands of the inculpated cruisers. Claimants are very expert in making out the figures of their claims." He added some appreciative words upon Bancroft Davis. "Working as few men can work, both laboriously and intelligently, he has been overwhelmed with bucketsful of sheer blackguardism and falsehood. He will, however, find his reward in time and in the justice of the public mind, if in nothing else." To Davis he sent the warm gratitude of the Administration, with assurances the President intended at an early date to give him some suitable reward.[26]

Inevitably, the decision brought its controversies. Annoyed by inaccurate newspaper criticism of the State Department, Fish had Adam Badeau write a review of the events leading up to and following the Treaty of Washington. It proved an expert, lucid, and at points penetrating history of the Treaty and the subsequent dispute over the indirect claims. Grant and Fish read it, and Fish sent it to George William Curtis, who inserted it in *Harper's Magazine* for November, 1872— unsigned. But one section gave offense. Badeau stated that "occasional articles in the American press, written by Englishmen who happened to have control of a newspaper published in the United States, or access to its columns, were paraded as evidence of what the better sort of Americans thought of the claims." This shaft was aimed at George Jones of the *Times,* and Jones bristled angrily.[27] Meanwhile friends of the Administration were irritated by a speech which Evarts made in New York on December 23. Responding to a toast to the Geneva Tribunal, he passed over Grant, Fish, and his own colleagues without a word, and declared that it had been the great Secretary Seward who "was able without war . . . to establish the principle of arbitration between England and us." [28] Could anything, demanded Bancroft Davis, be more cold, selfish, and malicious? [29]

[25] Washington, October 7, 1872; Letterbooks.   [26] October 31, 1872; Letterbooks.
[27] Fish to John C. Hamilton, December 22, 1872; Letterbooks.
[28] N. Y. *Times, Tribune,* December 24, 1872.
[29] Davis to Fish, New York, December 24, 1872; Fish Papers. But Evarts meant no disrespect to Fish. He sent the Secretary an inkstand bought in London "which dates from the time when the two nations, whose great litigation you have brought to so

But the worst storm was excited by Caleb Cushing's indiscreet book *The Treaty of Washington*. The principal object of this 250-page philippic was to retaliate upon Sir Alexander Cockburn for his provocative conduct at Geneva. The Americans had deeply resented Cockburn's cutting remarks during the sessions.[30] The "Reasons" which he delivered at the close were not a calm judicial document but a heated partisan argument, embodying allusions to the American counsel, their use of fact, and their arguments, which were insulting in the highest degree. He deserved castigation; but unfortunately Cushing supplied it with personal abuse and not a calm, severe analysis of his official labors. He called this most rigid, honest, and independent of Britons a Dugald Dalgetty, made other misleading charges, and in the end actually put American reviewers in the position of defending Cockburn.[31] The *Times* pronounced the book "execrable"; the *Evening Post* called it a "libellous assault"; the *Tribune* editorially described it as "inopportune, indecorous, and in every way inexpedient." [32] The best to be said for it was that it expressed the irritation of many Americans, and showed Englishmen how badly Cockburn had behaved.

Schenck wrote to Fish from London in the spring of 1873 that he had just met Motley at the Foreign Office dinner on the Queen's birthday.[33] "Have I ever told you how like a fool, with his puerile resentment, my predecessor has behaved? He has been here a number of times last year and this, but never comes near me or my family or the Legation— neither he nor any of his!" At the dinner the Ohio General stalked up to the historian with a bluff greeting. "He was confused—tried to stammer out explanations—was quite cordial;—but has never called on me; and it is now a week since." Schenck concluded: "Can't great men be small ones sometimes?" In reply, Fish alluded to the continued evidence of British resentment over the *Alabama* affair.[34] Since the distribution of Bancroft Davis' report on the Arbitration, "John's tail is straight up in the air and he dashes about, rushing at red rags in every direction." Fish had announced that he would pigeonhole Cockburn's "Reasons"

---

prosperous an end, were comprehended in one and lived under one King"; asking Fish to accept it "as a token of the respect and esteem, in this as in all things, of . . . William M. Evarts." November 2, 1872; Fish Papers.

[30] For Cockburn's voluminous opinion, see *Geneva Arbitration*, IV, 230 ff. See Davis to Fish, *ibid.*, 12, 13; Hackett, *Geneva Tribunal*, 356 ff.; Moore, *International Arbitrations*, I, 659 ff. Fish called the opinion "an extraordinary document;" *Geneva Arbitration*, IV, 546 ff.

[31] *Nation*, May 1, 1873.   [32] Fuess, *Caleb Cushing*, II, 351, 352.
[33] May 31, 1873; Fish Papers.   [34] June 15, 1873; Letterbooks.

for reference in future disputes with England, and the London *Times* had called this monstrous. "The future," commented Fish, "will lead them to think that it was something else than monstrous, viz: That it was 'troublesome' there and 'useful' here." The Secretary remarked that the discussion in the House of Commons on the Three Rules and the indirect claims showed much slipperiness and dishonesty. "I question if the biggest scalawags in our Congress could teach these fellows much in the way of sitting astride a fence, of riding two horses at once, or of open barefaced impudence and downright lying." He concluded:

Is Cockburn about to reply to Cushing? The latter's book was very sharp; possibly it might have been as effective with some passages suppressed and some expressions omitted, but it puts forth some facts in unmistakable language, more direct perhaps than polite. Cushing professes to desire a reply from Cockburn, to justify a replication. He says that his heaviest shots are still in the locker.

IV

It is fitting to record here the quiet scene which finally closed the Geneva Arbitration. Early on September 9, 1873, Fish arrived in Washington from Garrison.[35] A little later Sir Edward Thornton and Edward M. Archibald, the British consul-general in New York, called at the Department. Thornton sat down, remarking: "I believe my government owes the United States a sum of money, which it is my purpose to pay today." Taking out a pocketbook of Russia leather, and asking for a pen, he added, "I will soon settle this little outstanding indebtedness." He then produced a certificate of deposit with the Treasurer of the United States of $15,500,000, and a receipt. Fish signed the receipt and the certificate was handed to him. When the Englishmen departed, Fish and Davis personally took the certificate to the Treasury Department; where, in accordance with law, the money it represented was invested in five per cent government bonds to be held subject to the disposition of Congress. The receipt still hangs framed on the walls of Downing Street, both a grim reminder to British Governments of the penalties of carelessness in enforcing the rules of neutrality, and a priceless memento of the victories of peace.

[35] Diary, September 9, 1873.

A WEEK after Grant's inauguration realists had begun to suspect that he would not prove the greatest President since Washington. A year after, many were convinced that he was not even the greatest since Lincoln. Charles A. Dana became sulphurously denunciatory in the spring of 1869. That fall Henry Adams, Boston cambric to nose as he investigated the Black Friday stench, wavered between incredulity and despair. By the following spring Horace Greeley was growing peevish, and his bright young men were penning satirical paragraphs; only Grant's early conversion to total amnesty could placate the *Tribune*—and he remained unconverted. Then came Grant's worst fortnight since Cold Harbor: the fortnight of the Santo Domingo defeat, Hoar's and Motley's dismissal, Fish's temporary decision to leave. After that crisis, desertions became a steady stream. Editors like Samuel Bowles, Horace White, E. L. Godkin, William Cullen Bryant, gathered in clubs, Republican ink still on their fingers, to ask if seven years more of Grant were really a necessity. In a little while they began to ask if they were even a probability. What if the plain man found out the President?

There was small danger. The plain man had not elected Grant; he had elected an indestructible legend, a folk-hero. At its heart was Grant the reality; but the only change easily comprehended in the reality was that he wore a glossy silk hat instead of a black felt campaigner. Mention that monosyllabic name, and the prosaic laborer, farmer, clerk, or business man for once in his life saw a vision. It was a vision of four years of terror and glory. Painted on the clouds above his farm or shop, he saw the torrent of muddied blue uniforms rallying on the bluffs of Shiloh; he saw the butternut rush dissolving against a smoke-wreathed line at Champion's Hill; he saw the night torn by shell and rocket as gunboats spouting fire raced past Vicksburg; he saw the lines at Lookout Mountain waver, reform, and go on up; he saw two armies wait as Lee walked into the parlor at Appomattox. He heard the crackle of flames mingle with the roar of musketry in the Wilderness; the camp-fire chorus of "John Brown's Body"; the steady clapping as Sherman's army rolled down Pennsylvania Avenue. Clay from Illinois had saved the nation. The part of it called Lincoln was now clay indeed; the part called Grant had proved itself the will incarnate of the nation, and was rightfully in the White House. No conceivable error of Grant's could destroy these visions. Charles Sumner in revolt spoke of the gratitude due his own services to the nation. *His* services! There was one man whose services were really worth remembrance through thick and thin, through good and evil report, to whom endless gratitude was due. There was only one.

This man, so ignorant, so clumsy, so docile in his honest way to the most dishonest influences, to the deeper view so pathetic; this legend, so stirring, so impressive, so eminently one of the glories of the nation and the race—their incongruity pained and alarmed observers like Fish. For the legend was clearly an enormous force, an engine fit for a Titan. Properly used, it might remould America nearer to the heart's desire. Perverted, it might bring injury on tens of millions yet unborn. And the creator and wielder of this Titanic engine was at once weak and strong, naïve and inscrutable, reckless and plodding; a bundle of perilous contradictions. The levers of the engine were gripped by a stubborn boy. At times Fish believed that from the wreck of past hopes some splendid achievement could yet be built. He had kept Behemoth, so destructive of other men's dreams, from trampling his own handiwork; he had even used the legend to awe Congress into keeping peace with Spain, to win acquiescence when he settled with England for a few millions instead of half a continent. But there were dark moments when the legend seemed a force as cataclysmic as it was vast, a Mississippi on the rampage. Hoar, ejected from office and pleading with Fish to remain, declared solemnly: "You are the bulwark now standing between the country and its destruction." Was there any sure bulwark? Fish thought that it was not to be found in himself—a stiff, conservative, elderly gentleman, an ante-belium Whig dragooned into Republicanism, an aristocrat, a man without any political following whatever. But then where? In Sumner and Schurz? He would have laughed.

I

Washington was a microcosm of America; in it were reflected all of the forces playing upon Grant. And Washington, robust, rollicking, aggressive, corrupt, was a centre which can scarcely be drawn as it was without seeming a caricature. Small compared with the capital of today, it was large enough to be several cities in one. Fish knew best the Washington of politics. "You can't use tact with a Congressman," Henry Adams reports a Cabinet officer saying. "A Congressman is a hog! You must take a stick and hit him on the snout!" [1] While that sounds like Rockwood Hoar, it may have been Fish. But the image of the swine-pen is too gross. It was rather an auction room, a gallery where men interspersed patriotic platitudes with bids for sectional advantage, class advantage, above all the advantage of special interests.

Look at them! Simon Cameron, a shrewd, high-bred face, the austere look of a Covenanter, the high forehead of Sir Walter Scott—and behind that forehead the schemes of the Pennsylvania Railroad and the Monongahela ironmasters. Carpenter, dark, ponderous, buttoned tightly as if he held himself in with difficulty, an organ voice; deemed in Wisconsin a second Daniel Webster, but a Webster who thought only of tariffs, subsidies, and votes. Conkling, glossy auburn curl, Apollo-torso, fashion-plate clothes, ambition personified—but all his ambition directed to machines, wires, and spoils. Stewart of Nevada, blonde, burly, with a ruddy outdoor look as if the Sierra winds still played with his locks; actually a pocket-borough man at home in the offices of mining corporations and the Pacific railroads. Morton of Indiana, able to give even Blaine of Maine lessons in matador-waves of the bloody shirt, while springing gracefully aside for another thrust at the bleeding carcass of Jeffersonian and Lincolnian democracy. Banks, his small head crowned by rich masses of brown hair; Logan with his dark, sombre countenance and Indian-like mane; the elegant Fernando Wood, looking as if he belonged in the French Chamber; Bingham with his sharp-cut Roman face—all shrewd, adroit, empty, and on the make. Garfield, so versatile, brilliant, and full of the platform grace of a former preacher, that one forgot his quicksilver traits. And the salt that leavened the whole lump: honest Lyman Trumbull of Illinois, honest Timothy Howe of Wisconsin, honest Bayard of Delaware, honest William A. Buckingham of Connecticut, honest, fanatical Parson Brownlow of Tennessee.

Most of these men were Senators. We were nearing the ideal of government of the people, by the people, for the Senate, attained in Nelson W. Aldrich's time. The most exclusive club in the world was already taking on a millionaire flush. Few members approached the wealth of Sprague of Rhode Island, but even Simon Cameron paid $1,000 a month

[1] *Education of Henry Adams,* 261.

for his quarters at the Arlington. Everywhere in the capital money talked. Grant's White House dinners for thirty-six, with wines, cost $1,500, even $2,000; Secretary Fish (who could afford it and whose diplomatic entertainments demanded it) spent far more than his salary; [2] lesser figures lived profusely. Every winter until 1873 representatives of the Eastern press spilled adjectives over the "brilliant" social season; dilating on "the stately Mrs. Thornton," "the accomplished Mme. Gerolt and her fascinating daughters," and "the ravishing Kate Chase Sprague," they gave half a column to Mrs. Grant in full-flowing pink grenadine, flounced satin overskirt, japonica hair-adornments, diamond necklace, and gold fan. But if money talked brilliantly, little else in Washington did. Most of the conversation flowed to politics, power, and pelf. The atmosphere hardly favored intellectual honesty. When Senator Ratcliffe attacked the evolutionary theory, Mrs. Lightfoot Lee asked him not to be too hard on the monkeys: [3] "They are not in public life; they are not even voters; if they were, you would be enthusiastic about their intelligence and virtue."

Like America, Washington was half-built, war-littered, the scene of appalling contrasts; full of ambition, slovenliness, greed, and idealism, with touches of elegance and distinction. Shining carriages laden with sealskins and diamonds stuck in the mudholes of unpaved streets. Mansions resplendent with crystal chandeliers, mahogany, and silver stood beside Negro shacks. Livestock shared the streets with the new horse-cars; a Civil War hero, returning from church, found a steer asleep in his vestibule. Washington Monument was half-finished, a derrick pendant from its top. Reminders of the war were strewn everywhere: the ring of decaying forts around the city; lines of unpainted sheds built for army mules; colored uncles freed from the plow to hawk sassafras, crabs, and hot hominy about the Centre Street market below Capitol Hill. While George Dewey, Henry Adams, and Moorfield Storey waltzed with the belles, less fortunate young men—Lester F. Ward, John Burroughs, A. F. Bandelier—toiled in government offices for a pittance. [4]

Lafayette Square was society. In a little circle about it were Fish's house (Fifteenth and I); those of Robeson, Creswell, Sir Edward

---

[2] Account-books are preserved in the Fish Papers.   [3] Henry Adams, *Democracy.*
[4] See G. A. Townsend, *Events at the National Capital;* E. W. Martin, *Behind the Scenes in Washington;* M. C. Ames, *Ten Years in Washington;* David Macrae, *The Americans at Home,* I, 92 ff.; Helen Nicolay, *Our Capital on the Potomac;* W. B. Bryan, *History of the National Capital,* II.

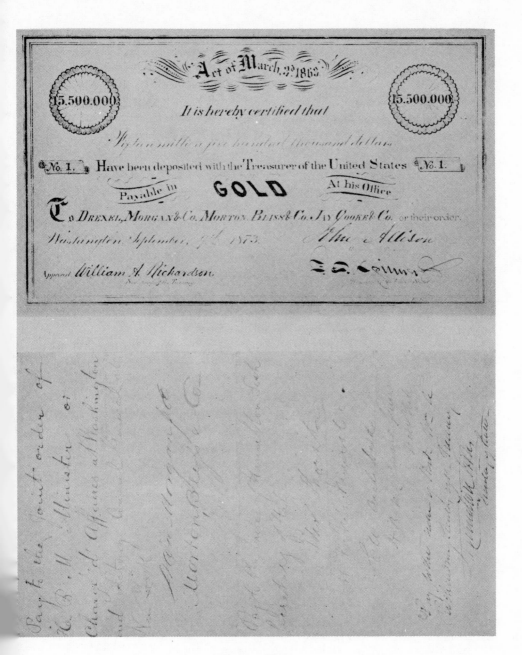

PAID IN FULL

Thornton, General Sherman, Colfax, and other luminaries; the four-story mansion Sumner built for the bride who deserted him. Out in Georgetown dwelt the Antiques, select families chiefly Southern, often of historic names, who respected Banker Corcoran but looked down on Cabinet members. On Capitol Hill a few stubborn Congressional leaders clung to the red-brick houses; bachelors even maintained two or three oldtime messes. These were all recognized centres of the city, pivots of social intercourse. Another precipitant in the Washington ferment was offered by the hotels. At Willard's, which had grown from a steward's business on the Hudson steamboats, at the New National, where Clay died, at the shining new Ebbitt House, generals, Supreme Court justices, and Senators were gaped at. The Wormley and Arlington were more exclusive; wealthy New Yorkers, titled foreigners, and rich lobbyists shut out most politicians. On Fourteenth just off Pennsylvania Avenue was Newspaper Row. Here in the summer heat chairs stood under the trees; darkies came running with juleps and sherry cobblers; rhetorical prestidigitators—Dana, Murat Halstead, Watterson, G. A. Townsend—got down to the hardpan of politics with Congressmen.

But some less savory parts of town were equally important. The lobbyists had a capital of their own. Old as the republic, the corporation era was making them unprecedentedly rich and impudent. They had called dashing young women, the Laura Hawkinses of the Gilded Age, to their aid. They boasted men of mark and power. Cornelius Wendell had won fairer treatment for the whiskey industry. Henry D. Cooke represented his brother Jay Cooke and other railway barons. John L. Hayes, with skill acquired before the war as agent for iron interests, influenced tariffs for the benefit of the wool interests. Agents of Collis P. Huntington poured out a Pactolian stream, and discreetly made no accounting. A Congressman who knew one or two of these men might go home much the richer.[5]

But the king of the lobby was Sam Ward, brother of Julia Ward Howe, wit and *bon vivant*, who had come to Washington long ago as agent of the Barings and had stayed to serve others. He really did something for American civilization; at his quarters on E Street Plaza dining was an art. Like Webster, he went marketing for his own terra-

[5] E. P. Herring, *Group Representation Before Congress*, gives a modern view of the lobby.

pin and canvasback; he imported his own China tea and blended his own coffee; he discussed wines with the best European Ministers. Sometimes with a shudder, he studied the gustatory tastes of committee chairman. To House investigators he once quoted Talleyrand,[6] "Diplomacy is assisted by good dinners." With the help of an expert chef, he said, a man could ask a civil question and get a civil answer. "We keep up a certain circle of friends, and once in a while an opportunity comes of getting something that is of real service, and for which compensation is due and proper. But the entertainments are proportioned to the business of the season. When business is good, so are the entertainments." Ward's political friends usually saw to it that business was good.

Goals may be achieved in various ways. At John Chamberlain's sumptuous restaurant—first near Willard's, but after 1873 in the former British legation at Seventeenth and I—guests could retire to small upper rooms with black walnut panelling and English hunting prints; waiters deposited cards, cigars, and Bourbon.[7] Here, strange to say, practised lobbyists often lost large sums to green Congressmen. Other gambling-houses were frank and unashamed. They clung to the region of the hotels and Newspaper Row. Over soft rugs, past oil paintings, marched politicians, financiers, and plain citizens. Everybody knew the story of Thad Stevens pausing in front of one to hand his night's winnings to a Negro deacon collecting money for a church, and ejaculating: "God moves in a mysterious way his wonders to perform." The chief of police reported on July 1, 1869, that in three months he had broken up fifteen gaming-places, but that since Congress had adjourned thirty had closed voluntarily; good evidence that Charles James Fox still had his followers. A long war on the gamblers during Grant's first years achieved something, and the depression after 1873 did more. But not even the depression materially injured business in one part of town—the "Division," part of the triangular area between the Mall, the E Street Plaza, and Pennsylvania Avenue, given over to groggeries and houses of ill-fame. Good Washingtonians ignored the Division, and history has emulated them. But it was no insignificant fact of post-bellum life in America that a generous strip of the national capital, planted squarely between the halls of Congress and

---

[6] House Committee Report 268, 43rd Congress., 2nd sess., 408–410.
[7] See N. Y. *World*, January 18, 1876, for a description.

the White House, was given up to protected vice.

Yet on the whole, more of sweetness and light was found in Washington than readers of *Democracy* and *The Gilded Age* would suppose. When there gathered about Fish's mahogany tree such men as General Sherman, Hannibal Hamlin, Rockwood Hoar, and the sparkling Evarts or urbane Caleb Cushing, the talk reached a rare level of sense and wit. The plain solid people in the plain solid houses on F and G Streets—the Middle Ground Aristocracy, Mark Twain called them [8]— deserved high respect. There were some true intellectuals; the Literary Society which John G. Nicolay, Lincoln's private secretary, had founded, and of which Garfield was president during part of the Grant period, drew distinguished visitors—George W. Curtis, Bayard Taylor, Oliver Wendell Holmes. So did the Saturday evening salon of Cornelius King on H Street. The scientists had a sphere of their own, centring in the Smithsonian Institution, though Dr. Henry, Clarence King, and F. V. Hayden went everywhere. A Congress which numbered the philosophical Lamar, the adventurous Schurz, the courageous Lyman Trumbull, the scholarly George Frisbie Hoar, to name but a few, could not be dismissed with a sneer. The hundred members of the diplomatic corps lent a cosmopolitan touch. Laxity of moral tone? In good society the tone was severely Victorian. Outside it, some of the laxity could be forgiven a youthful republic which had just emerged from one of the most terrible ordeals, one of the fiercest exertions, a nation has ever faced. There are times when peoples, like individuals, recover from intolerable tension by going on a spree.

But the dominant note in Washington was not laxity; the two strongest notes were vitality and heterogeneity. The *nouveaux riches;* the military strutters; the grotesques like Sumner, Ben Butler, and Conkling, more incredible than characters in Dickens; the lobbyists; the prostitutes, bummers, gamblers; the $600 a year clerks; the hungry, shivering Negroes; diplomatic eccentrics like the hot-tempered Mme. Catacazy, or the niece of Dictator Rosas who wrote a French yellowback called *Love in the Pampas,* or the querulous Baron Gerolt—these made up a picturesque and vivid world. It might be uncomfortable to ride to a costly banquet past the open sewer of the "Tiber" canal; it might be disconcerting to view contrasts like that between Zach Chan-

---

[8] Mark Twain and Charles Dudley Warner, *The Gilded Age,* 295 ff. See Gail Hamilton, "The Display of Washington Society," *The Galaxy,* June, 1876.

dler and his wife—he rough, loud-voiced, vulgar, she a woman of fashion, icy in reserve, with Worth gowns; later it might be sad to think how Washington honored bribe-takers like Colfax and Belknap while ignoring a truly great Southern leader like Benjamin H. Hill. But the capital had one merit—it was interesting. Correa da Serra had called it the city of magnificent distances; Dickens, the city of magnificent intentions. After the war it evinced a certain maturity, and under Boss Shepherd was soon on the way toward realizing some of the intentions. Long an overgrown Southern village, then briefly a great military camp, at last it really mirrored the spirit of the ambitious, fast-growing republic. For the dominant notes in the life of the republic were also heterogeneity and vitality.[9]

II

The White House was inevitably the centre of Washington social life—a restored centre, for the long feud between President Johnson and Congress had temporarily isolated it.[10] The code of etiquette which President Washington, after consulting with such friends as Hamilton, Adams, and Jay, had drawn up in 1789, and which had been somewhat modified by Presidents Jefferson and Madison, still governed the social observances of the Administration. The reception on New Year's day, when the diplomatic corps presented themselves in court costume and the army and navy officers in full uniform, opened the season. The President held other receptions, roughly one each week, for stated groups of guests—usually first the Cabinet officers, then the diplomatic corps, then the justices of the Supreme Court, then the Senators and Representatives, and finally the principal army and navy officers. Guests filed through the Red Room, the Blue Room, where the President and his wife greeted them, and on through the Green Room into the East Room, where they chatted. If the reception were large, it imposed a heavy strain on the hosts. Henry Adams, describing one in his novel *Democracy,* tells how his heroine Madeleine, taking her place in an interminable line, finally "found herself before two seemingly mechanical figures . . . both their faces stripped of every sign

[9] William Saunders, *Through the Light Continent,* 88 ff.; G. M. Towle, *American Society,* I, 23 ff., 78 ff.
[10] See W. H. Crook, *Through Five Administrations,* 155–222, for the White House under Grant; and Anon, "Life at the National Capital," *Lippincott's Magazine,* December, 1873.

of intelligence, while the right hands of both extended themselves to the columns of visitors with the mechanical action of toy dolls. . . . There they stood, automata, representatives of the society which streamed past them." On New Year's Day, the Fourth of July, and at the fortnightly levees, when the whole world might come, the crush was ruinous to gowns and tempers.[11]

Mrs. Grant, a comfortable, matronly woman with an unhappy squint and very plain manners and tastes, had her reception day first on Tuesdays, and after 1875 on Fridays. These afternoon receptions were also open to the entire public, though most of the guests were Washington women. Until this time Presidents' wives had almost always received alone. But Mrs. Grant usually invited several women of prominence, the wives of Cabinet members or Senators, to receive with her, thus pleasing them and her guests while lightening her own burden. As the Cabinet also met on Tuesday afternoons, not infrequently the President and some of the Secretaries, as it broke up, would come in to help her greet the visitors. Fish liked to do so. These afternoon receptions were highly popular, and contributed to the warm liking of Washington for the Grants. When not entertaining, the Grants dined regularly at five, and went to bed at ten o'clock.[12]

White House dinners were more elaborate than they have been under most subsequent Administrations. The Italian steward, Melah, whose salary was paid by the government, delighted to serve a repast of twenty-five or even thirty-five dishes, beginning with soup, fish, filet of beef, leg of partridge, and other meats, and ending with frozen punch, Melah's own famous rice pudding, peaches, confectionary, nuts, ices, and coffee. Six wine-glasses were placed at every plate, and a new wine was poured for every third course.[13] The state dining-room, one of the handsomest apartments of the White House, truly baronial in proportions, was then furnished with sombre heaviness.[14] But the horseshoe-shaped table, with its large flower-decked mirror in the centre—an ornament which could be so placed as to shield the President from any guest with whom he did not care to talk—was laid with beautiful crystal, china, and silver. The President and Mrs. Grant always occupied seats on either side the centre of the table, for they could bet-

[11] Marion Gouverneur, *As I Remember,* gives impressions of social Washington in this period; see also Emily E. Briggs, *The Olivia Letters.*
[12] Bryan, *National Capital,* II, 571; cf. Jesse Grant, *In the Days of My Father.*
[13] Briggs, *Olivia Letters,* 204 ff.   [14] Martin, *Behind the Scenes in Washington,* 376.

ter direct the conversation from these points. Dinner was at seven; it seldom occupied less than two hours; and after it was over the guests repaired to the Blue or Red Room, where they conversed for perhaps fifteen minutes before the President gave the signal for breaking up. These entertainments were costly and the doubling of the President's salary in 1873 came none too soon.

President Grant had no hesitation in violating long-standing customs of the White House, for he disliked to be bound by tradition. Previous executives had felt constrained to entertain all Senators and Representatives at dinner, but as Congress grew, the difficulties had increased. Andrew Jackson had invited the members in alphabetical order, and by giving two dinners a week had fulfilled his assumed obligation to all. But Grant adopted an entirely new course. He invited only what Senators and Representatives he pleased, and asked their wives with them. Considerable tact was shown in making up the lists of guests, those who were asked felt that they were really wanted, and the innovation pleased Congress instead of offending it. Another precedent, dating from Washington's day, bound the Chief Executive to accept no invitations to dinner outside his official family, and to pay no visits of ceremony unless another chief of state came to the capital. But Grant and Mrs. Grant—particularly the former—dined out at their pleasure, and without hesitation accepted invitations to evening parties.

While the President's household life necessarily had its glittering side, while on the evening of a reception or dinner there was something impressive in the driveways crowded with carriages and finely matched bays or blacks, the brilliantly illuminated rooms brave with flowers, gowns, and gold braid, the scented conservatory, the Marine Band in its scarlet uniforms, nevertheless the Grants were essentially very simple folk. The family was interesting. When they entered the White House Nellie, whose bright eyes, sweet face, and quick ways made her remarkably attractive, was seventeen; Fred was nineteen; Ulysses S., Jr., familiarly called Buck, was sixteen; and Jesse, the youngest, was eleven. Even Jesse could remember the pinched days in Galena when his father came home tired and discouraged from the leather store,[15] while Fred could recall the still harsher years in the log cabin a few miles outside St. Louis, where Grant was unsuccessfully tilling the

[15] Jesse Grant, *In the Days of My Father*, 9 ff.

farm he named "Hardscrabble." Besides the children, there was the grandfather, "Colonel" Frederick Dent, onetime slave-holder, owner of the large plantation "White Haven" near Jefferson Barracks in Missouri, and in his own estimation a Southern gentleman. He had been a Jacksonian Democrat and a Confederate sympathizer, and had called his son-in-law a renegade when he went into the Union Army; now he liked to loaf in the big reception hall with the politicians, smoke cigars, drink juleps, read newspapers, and abuse the Yankees. "The General's really a Democrat, only he don't know it," he would tell callers confidentially.[16] There were other Dents, some transitory, but one a permanent inmate of the Executive Mansion—Frederick Dent, Jr., Grant's brother-in-law, who made appointments and received callers. Occasionally the President's father, Jesse, postmaster at Covington, Kentucky, came to Washington. But he seldom slept in the White House, observing spitefully that it was too full of the Dent tribe.

Of the children, "Buck" in time entered Harvard; Fred was soon in West Point; Nellie was all too early considered marriageable; but Jesse remained, making friends with Albert the coachman, amusing the household with his pranks, and looking after his pets—several dogs, two gorgeous gamecocks, and an ill-tempered parrot given him by the Mexican Minister, Senor Romero. Once he ordered some stamps from a Boston dealer, and when the advertiser kept his five dollars but sent no stamps the President playfully suggested that he bring the matter before the next Cabinet meeting:[17]

Promptly on the hour I presented myself at the Cabinet meeting. Hamilton Fish . . . and William W. Belknap . . . were great friends of mine. "Jesse has a matter which he wished to bring before you, gentlemen," said my father. Breathlessly I told my story, ending with the suggestion that either the Secretary of State, the Secretary of War, or Kelly (the policeman on special duty at the White House) write a letter.

"This is plainly a matter for the State Department to attend to," said Mr. Fish. To this Mr. Belknap promptly took exception, declaring it his intention, as head of the War Department, to act at once.

Followed a general debate, in which the other Cabinet members stood solidly for Kelly. I shall never forget with what interest I listened to impassioned speeches in which Mr. Kelly's virtues, his power and influence, were extolled. He was declared to have wider powers than the Constitution be-

[16] W. E. Woodward, *Meet General Grant*, 403. Newspapers of the day contain much appreciative matter on the Dent family.
[17] Jesse Grant, *op. cit.*, 69, 70.

stowed upon either the Department of State or the War Department, and his personal ability and influence were proclaimed to be greater than that of the Secretaries who sought to usurp his prerogatives. When the question was put to vote, Mr. Fish and Mr. Belknap voted for their respective departments, but the rest of the Cabinet voted for Kelly.

Second only to the President and Mrs. Grant in Washington society stood Secretary and Mrs. Fish.[18] Both had been born to the polite world; social graces as well as moderate luxury were a matter of course to them; and Mrs. Fish helped Mrs. Grant over many a rugged spot of social management. Their house, formerly Senator Morgan's, was one of the finest in the capital, and contained perhaps the best single room for receptions outside the White House. Mrs. Fish, of but medium height but commanding presence, with features that were classical and intellectual rather than beautiful, was always stately, serene, and perfectly poised. She was polite and gracious to all, and in her house the polished European diplomatist and self-made Western leader felt equally at home. Beside the somewhat dumpy Mrs. Grant she made a striking appearance, her wonderfully pure and pale complexion slightly flushed, her gray hair surmounted by a coronal which only she could have worn. But she was not at all austere, and her goodness of heart soon became famous; for despite her incessant social duties she found time for church work, for visiting sick rooms, and for much attention to charities.

At the house on Scott Square Mrs. Fish received every Wednesday afternoon, assisted usually by her only unmarried daughter, Edith.[19] She and Secretary Fish gave two formal dinners weekly through the season, managing them with great method; and at receptions by card there were sometimes fifteen hundred guests. Their engagement book for 1869–70 shows how heavy was the burden of entertaining, and how varied their list of guests. On September 9 they gave a dinner for the President, three of the Cabinet, Judge Richardson, and Generals Porter and Sherman. In October the diplomatic dinners began, the whole corps being entertained in order; while that same month they dined the Justices of the Supreme Court. Among others at their table during the autumn were Judge Edwards Pierrepont, Colonel Babcock, the banker W. W. Corcoran, James Watson Webb, Senators Sumner, Schurz, and

18 Helen Nicolay, *Our Capital on the Potomac,* 406 ff.
19 Ben Perley Poore, *Reminiscences,* II, 298. Edith later married the son of Sir Stafford Northcote.

MRS. HAMILTON FISH

Conkling more than once, many other Senators once only, Bancroft Davis, and Colonel J. W. Forney. But with January 1 the dinners really began! At one of the most notable, on January 27, were Prince Arthur of Connaught, Speaker Blaine, Chief Justice Chase, Senator Sumner, General Sherman, Admiral Porter, most of the Cabinet, Minister Thornton, and General Banks. It is evident that Sherman, Schurz, and Bancroft Davis were favorite guests, their names turning up again and again. But there are other names which could have given Secretary Fish little pleasure, such as Ben Butler's. At the dinner on February 8 to a long list of members of Congress, Senator Sprague of Rhode Island and Senator Roscoe Conkling sat down together; but this was before Conkling's attentions to his beautiful wife had begun to annoy Sprague.

Twenty guests were usually asked to large dinners, and the ordinary hour was seven; smaller dinners sometimes began at six. Diplomatists, Cabinet members, and Supreme Court Justices in general brought their wives, but Senators and Representatives came alone. Although the President dined repeatedly at Fish's during the winter, he did not bring Mrs. Grant with him. Grant, indeed, often came to the house informally. He loved in the evening to walk across Lafayette Square and down Fifteenth Street, two blocks in all, to Fish's house. He would greet the Secretary, chat a few minutes in his study, and then cross the hall for a much longer talk with Mrs. Fish, whom he found highly congenial.[20] Despite his reputation for taciturnity, when with friends on whose sympathy he could count he became talkative, while in commenting on questions of the day he showed a surprising amount of humor. But Mrs. Grant loved her home, and stirred out of it as little as possible.

Other members of the Cabinet, as at first constituted, cared little for social life.[21] Attorney-General Hoar was wealthy, and married to a charming woman; but with seven children and a passion for quiet labor he detested entertainments. He liked to stick to his desk, and became

[20] Hamilton Fish 2d to author, June 4, 1933; as secretary to his father, Mr. Fish formed many impressions of value to the author.

[21] Among the names most frequently seen in the society columns were the Spragues, Dahlgrens, Chandlers, Anthonys, Corcorans, and Riggses. Kate Chase Sprague was the most striking woman of the period in Washington, uniting the animation of Dolly Madison with the audacity and charm of Jessie Benton Frémont. By 1870 it was well known that her marriage was unhappy, for her erratic husband was addicted to drink, but she plunged with all the more vigor into social life. Of the diplomatists the British Minister, Edward Thornton, took the leading place—tall, erect, and military-looking. His wife, the daughter of an English clergyman, was tall, thin, and of quiet tastes. Thornton was universally liked, and Fish was much pleased when in 1871 he was knighted.

irritable over interruptions. Secretary Boutwell, an angular, nervous man, had few friends and did not care to make more. Postmaster-General Creswell was deservedly popular, possessed wealth, and entertained well. Of General Belknap we shall say more later. When he first entered the Cabinet in the fall of 1869, succeeding Rawlins, his wife, who had been a Kentucky belle, had leased the Rogers house on Lafayette Square. Here she charmed everyone with her grace and cordiality; but her health was failing, and before the year 1870 ended she was dead. Secretary Fish and General Sherman were among the pallbearers who carried her coffin into St. John's Church. Her household remained in the care of her sister, an equally charming and dashing young woman; and soon she and the heavily-whiskered, barrel-shaped, jovial Belknap were married.

III

North and West of the capital spread a land that throughout Grant's first Administration was vitalized by one of the great booms of our history. The electric current of business enterprise flowed into Washington as from a million generators. Men's hair crackled with it. Far more important than the slow reconstruction of the South was the rapid reconstruction of the North and Northwest by capital, technology, organization, and immigration. The first transcontinental railroads; the great Western ranges; bonanza mining; the petroleum industry; Besemer-Kelly steel—all these were newborn. The packing industry, the milling industry—these were reborn and grew into giants. Before Grant left the White House men had used the first telephones and typewriters, sat in the first parlor cars, read the first truly national magazines, debated the first legislation against monopoly, welcomed the Middle West and Far West into literature, heard the first dynamo hum. Crude and undisciplined are adjectives which must be interpreted as variables. Had a nation so full of new wealth, new technology, new social forces as was the United States of 1870 lacked crudity, exuberance, and recklessness, something would have been wrong with it.

But just how would all these forces play upon Grant? In general, the political vitality of the Federal Government has been lowest at precisely those times in which our economic energy has been greatest. The powerful business forces which were steadily taking control of the

United States did not wish a strong President, an alert and aggressive central government. They wanted passivity. Given that, they would know how to enforce coöperation when and where it was needed. The richest interests of the country had little to ask of Grant save that he sign instantly whenever requested; and he knew so little of government or economics that he would have done that anyway. It was upon Congress that the special interests focussed their chief efforts. Congress made the tariff schedules, the tax laws, the land grants, the appropriations. It was only the lesser fry—the claim agents, the office-mongers, the departmental contractors, the Carpetbaggers—who haunted the White House anterooms. A few of those who had hoped to angle in muddied international waters, profiting by tropical annexations or a Cuban war, still hung about there, cursing Fish; but by 1872 they had ceased to wear a hopeful look.

Not once does Fish's diary offer us an explicit opinion of Grant as a President. Reticence inhered in his definition of a gentleman; prudence inhered in his conception of a Secretary of State—for diaries are sometimes stolen. He later told his daughter that he did not put down the worst facts about Grant.[22] But in a thousand entries he presents his implicit opinion. Be it remembered that the diary was kept as an office day-book, as a record of business transacted, a transcript of conversations to guard against misquotation or misrepresentation. It was unnecessary to write much about Grant; only on exceptional occasions, as when irritation demanded some outlet, did Fish do so.

From Grant an admiring nation had expected, above all else, grasp and decision. His might not be a subtle intellect, but it would prove diamond-clear, firm in its hold upon essentials. Where book-taught generals failed, he had grasped the situation before Donelson, before Vicksburg, before Richmond; surely he would grasp the essentials of civil problems in the same way. What are the facts? Fish's diary is replete with illumination upon Grant's grasp of problems.

On January 10, 1871, the Cabinet took up foreign affairs.[23] "I hear that Spain is sending troops out to Cuba," ejaculated Grant. "Is that a fact?" Few facts in contemporaneous history were better known, and Fish said as much. "Spain is pardoning convicts on condition that they join the army and go to Cuba," he remarked. Grant flared up in-

[22] Memorandum by Mrs. Sidney Webster in Fish Papers.
[23] Diary.

stantly. "Well, I want a strong protest made," he exclaimed. "And I want a demand sent for early settlement of the claims of our people." The diary brings before us Fish in agitated expostulation. General Sickles, he pointed out, was working night and day in Madrid to negotiate a convention on the claims; his latest dispatches were encouraging. A protest just now, with King Amadeus barely seated on the throne, would seem discourteous and be interpreted as an effort to pick a quarrel. "Well," growled Grant, "I don't wish anything done at present."

Or again, take an earlier episode; on June 7, 1870, Grant was trying to rewrite Fish's message on Cuba, which did not need rewriting. He uneasily shuffled his sheets, a mass of "obliterations and interlineations." Reading a fragment to the Secretary, he promptly fell into difficulties. He referred to "captures" of American vessels; when Fish protested, to "seizures"; finally Fish told him the correct word was "arrests." His facts were also garbled. A few days later he interfered again. We find Fish on June 17 describing the results:

On Monday the President wished to insert in the message sent to Congress on the Cuban question a statement which he had prepared, to the effect that Spain had captured three of our vessels on the high seas (*Mary Lowell, Lloyd Aspinwall,* and *Mary Connery*), and refused the papers in the first and reparation in the second. I obtained with some difficulty the exclusion of any *specific* allusion to these cases, and the substitution of the general statement, toward the close of the message, of the reference to arrests on the high seas. The *Mary Lowell* papers were received on Tuesday, and on Thursday we have the submission by Spain to arbitration of the question of her liability for the *Aspinwall.*

In short, Fish had saved Grant from looking like a fool.

At best the President was never the soul of discretion. Such diary-entries as that under March 15, 1870, are not infrequent. The President read Fish the draft of a proposed message on the decline of American shipping. "It contains," records Fish, "a severe passage with regard to Great Britain, to which I take exception, as unnecessary to the argument, and calculated to excite unpleasant feelings between the two countries." Or we may cite a droller instance. Grant was much hurt when Charles A. Dana, who as Assistant Secretary of War had done so much for his promotion and fame, began to assail him in the *Sun.* One wintry day late in 1870 he talked with Fish about Dana.

The editor was a blackmailer, he declared. He knew a former employee of the *Sun,* a Venezuelan by birth, now a naturalized citizen, who possessed memoranda showing the precise sums of hush-money paid to Dana on various occasions, with details of the circumstances. According to this ex-Venezuelan, an attack upon Jim Fisk, Jr., had once been prepared for the *Sun,* and proof-sheets had been sent him with word that unless he made some "arrangement," it would appear next morning. Fisk had told the *Sun* to go to hell. A large edition was printed. But just before it went on the streets, in the small hours of the morning, Fisk drove down to Park Row and paid $5,000 for suppression of the article. Though the first edition was destroyed, the ex-Venezuelan had kept a copy. This was a curious tale, but Fish attached little significance to it. A few days later, however, came the sequel:

December 20, 1870.—. . . . Received a note from the President requesting me to call and bring the nominations of James R. Partridge as envoy extraordinary, etc., to Peru and Antonio M. Soteldo for Venezuela. The latter name I had never heard, and did not know who or what or whence he is; carried the nominations to the President; find that Soteldo is the person who has been engaged as an assistant editor of the New York *Sun,* and is now making public certain disclosures relating to that paper and its editor; that he was one of its reporters in Washington last winter. The President in his note has expressed a desire to *consult* [me] with regard to the nomination. [On my] seeing him, he stated as a reason that Soteldo imagined himself in danger of violence from some of the "roughs" who may be instigated by the parties who may be exposed by his statements; hands me the recommendations in his favor, utterly insignificant. . . .

I remonstrate against the appointment; [I say] that it will bring the whole diplomatic appointments of the government into disrepute and contempt; will be severely and justly criticized in the Senate; will be taxing his friends in the Senate too heavily to sustain it, under the opposition it must meet; that to appoint a man thus unknown will be considered as the price paid for the disclosures which the man proposes to make (the *Tribune* of a day or two since contained a chapter of his forthcoming pamphlet), and will be regarded as making the President responsible for, or at least as having paid for, the disclosures, by this appointment. He admits the force of these objections, especially the last. I further urge the fact of his being a Venezuelan as an objection to his being sent to Venezuela.

Grant's knowledge of the Constitution was as defective as his sense of the courtesy due to other nations. In his first draft of his annual message of 1870, discussing Santo Domingo, he proposed a new treaty, "to be submitted to Congress." Fish gently pointed out that treaties can be submitted only to the Senate. The President also asked Congress to authorize a commission to negotiate this treaty; Fish reminded him that he had full Constitutional power to negotiate a treaty by commissioners or otherwise, and that Congress needed only to appropriate money for expenses. In the same draft, Grant attempted to frighten Congress with the bogey of European seizure of Samaná Bay, and bluntly named Prussia as the government which was intent upon obtaining it—a serious charge against a friendly nation. Fish insisted that he take the name out. When Congress later asked him for confidential information about the threatening Power, Grant sent it a letter written in New York by the rascally broker Hartmont to the rascally Fabens, suggesting that Prussia desired the port. This was all the evidence he had! And even this had a cooked-up look; for why should Hartmont write Fabens when he was seeing him every day, and what did Hartmont know about Prussian policy? [24]

The President at times showed a curious forgetfulness, even of his own decisions. At the Cabinet meeting of April 14, 1871, for example, he and Fish discussed the choice of an attorney to represent the United States in the adjudication of claims against Spain. Fish writes drily: [25] "I ask the President if he has anyone he wishes for counsel, remarking that he should be a first-class lawyer and familiar with Spanish. He asks if Cushing would serve, and authorizes his appointment if he will. The last time I spoke with him on the subject I suggested Cushing, and he objected." Sometimes Grant seemed even to forget that he was President of the United States. In the fall of 1870 a newspaper dispatch, quoting him on foreign affairs, greatly annoyed Fish. He asked the President about it. Grant explained that the previous Sunday, while he was taking a walk, "some person, a stranger to him, joined him." The man tried to draw him out; Grant was reticent, avoiding most of his questions. The stranger remarked that it had been rumored that the United States would not press the *Alabama* Claims. Grant replied, "That is pure fiction." And the newspaper story indicated that he had told this total stranger a good deal more!

His management of Cabinet meetings left much to be desired. Again and again they were occupied chiefly with gossip; it was entertaining

---

[24] Senator Anthony of Rhode Island wrote Fish a letter of grieved astonishment on this occurrence.

[25] The material in these pages is drawn throughout from the Diary.

gossip, but Fish chafed under it. One typical groan from his conscientious spirit will suffice. On December 20, 1870, he asked for discussion of a dispatch from the Minister to Hawaii upon reciprocity and eventual annexation. The United States, he remarked, was losing its trade and influence in Hawaii; the ruler there was the last of his dynasty; and while the islands on his death would be likely to drop into American hands, it would be easy to lose them through indifference. He looked about hopefully. Silence. "No one responds, and the subject is dropped. The indisposition to consider important questions of the future in the Cabinet is wonderful. A matter must be imminent to engage attention; indifference and reticence. Alas!"

IV

But what most worried Fish and other astute observers in Washington was Grant's natural friendliness to many people intellectually and morally below him, to all hail-fellows-well-met, and to everyone who pretended an enormous loyalty. This tendency was the scar left by long years of failure and humiliation. He took naturally to the adroit, flattering, calculating Ben Butler. Butler was interested in various private claims; he was interested in Lower California lands; and he was interested in Santo Domingo real estate. By his influence with Grant he had his brother-in-law, Webster, made consul-general in Frankfort; he had a nephew, Butler, made consul-general in Egypt; and he had another brother-in-law appointed to office under Grant's own brother-in-law, Casey, who was collector of the port in New Orleans. Though he was notoriously a schemer, Grant liked him and gave him free run of the White House offices. Grant also liked the breezy and scheming Alexander R. Shepherd; he liked the scheming Henry D. Cooke, brother of Jay Cooke. Early in 1871 Fish was worried lest Henry Cooke be given an important diplomatic appointment; and he drew a sigh of relief when Grant told him on February 26 that the man would accept a berth in the District of Columbia government instead. "A good escape from a number of embarrassments and some perils," Fish wrote in his diary. Grant immensely liked his devoted but scheming secretary, Orville E. Babcock, and Babcock's scheming friend Rufus J. Ingalls. All these men by 1871 made up a happy, busy, ambitious White House coterie.

It need not be said that the President liked and patronized his kins-folk, who were numerous. One brother-in-law, A. R. Corbin, had come near bringing disaster on the President in the Black Friday affair. His brother Orvil Grant was hungry for the crumbs of power. So were three other brothers-in-law, Michael J. Cramer, the before mentioned James F. Casey, and Louis Dent; all selfish, greedy, and irresponsible. Early in 1871 Roscoe Conkling and Fish had a frank talk about the matter. The Secretary writes: [26]

He refers to a recent publication of a letter of Orvil Grant to the President in terms of regret; [says] that the President is being injured by such things, and expresses the hope that something may be done to arrest such interferences; [says] that the popular mind is arrested by and holds such trifling incidents to the disadvantage of the President; that he is being injured by the Dents, etc., etc. [He asks] whether I cannot say something to him, etc.

It is a very delicate matter. I appreciate what he says and wish it could be prevented. I am aware of the feeling on the subject and on the retention of so much of the military about the personnel at the White House, but do not see how it can be remedied.

Cramer, appointed Minister to Denmark, once disobeyed instructions. Fish had sent him a confidential dispatch relating to the recall of Catacazy, which he promptly read to officials in Denmark—that is, ran cackling to them with it, as John Hay would have said. The contents thereupon became known in St. Petersburg, and gave our Minister grave embarrassment. When Fish laid the case before Grant, the President, to his credit, instantly assented to a reprimand.[27]

But by far the most obnoxious relative was the peripatetic Judge Louis Dent of California, Mississippi, and Washington. After his exploit in wrecking the moderate Republican cause in Mississippi, he settled in the capital and entered the claim-agent business with a former newspaper man named Paige. We have mentioned his connection with the Perkins Claim against Russia. Fish's diary for May 4, 1870, describes how frostily he received Dent and his associate Stewart when they called at the State Department to press it. The Secretary omitted no precaution. "I have Mr. Barrows present," he writes, "to take down in shorthand the conversation."

Dent and Paige also pushed various claims against Spain. The most

26 Diary, January 8, 1871.   27 Diary, January 16, 1872.

noted of these was in behalf of José Garcia Angarica, a naturalized citizen in the commission business at Cardenas, Cuba, whose property there had been seized. The Spanish Minister complained bitterly throughout the first half of 1871 of their activities.[28] Because he resisted the Angarica claim as fraudulent, he told Fish in May, they had inspired an article in the New York *Tribune* roundly abusing him. Worst of all, they had hinted to clients that if they wished their claim allowed promptly by the Joint Commission, they must furnish money for bribing Caleb Cushing and Sidney Webster! Fish was still wrathful over this disclosure when a few hours later he went to a Cabinet meeting. There Grant handed him a letter from Dent and Paige upon the Angarica claim, insolently attacking Caleb Cushing and the Spanish Minister for obstructing justice! The Secretary restrained himself with difficulty. He told Grant that a State Department investigation had shown that Angarica's claim possessed highly dubious features, and demanded cautious treatment. Thereupon the President explained that he had not read the letter. Louis Dent had been at the White House two evenings before; "he spoke about the claims, and I asked him to make a statement in writing." This heightened Fish's resentment.

"Dent & Paige," he said bluntly, "are speculating upon claims on the ground that Dent is related to you and that they have special influence. They are also making appeals to public passion by anonymous articles in the press. In these they print utterly false statements."

"It's Paige does that," protested Grant. "He was a newspaper man."

"I will tell you just what these gentlemen are doing," proceeded Fish. "They are accusing irreproachable men, including my son-in-law Mr. Webster, of corruption. They are trying to connect me, the Secretary of State, with similar charges. "Here"—drawing the *Tribune* article from his pocket—"let me show you the article they wrote. The Spanish Minister inquired at the *Tribune* office, and the editors told him this article had been sent them from the White House."

Grant declared that he had not seen it, or heard of it.

"I was sure you had not, and I told the Spanish Minister so," concluded Fish. "But I wish you to know how much presumption these men are showing, and what unjustifiable liberties they take on the basis of Dent's connection with you."

Grant made no recorded reply, but when the Cabinet meeting broke

28 Diary, January 19, 1871, and dates following.

up he kept the Dent & Paige letter.[29]

Every palace cabal, every Kitchen Cabinet, requires a dominating mind, a leader like Amos Kendall in the Jackson Administration or Harry Daugherty in Harding's. In 1872 no one was yet certain that a Kitchen Cabinet existed. But everyone knew that if it sprang into existence Orville E. Babcock would be its head. Louis Dent cultivated a suspicious intimacy with Babcock. So did Fabens, who, calling at the State Department on April 29, 1870, explained certain irregularities in his handling of Dominican affairs as due to Babcock's advice. So did Ben Butler, Henry D. Cooke, and Colonel Forney, editor and lobbyist. It was Forney who told Caleb Cushing in February, 1870, that Dent and Paige had assured him that Grant was about to revolutionize the Cuban policy of the government, adding: "You had better be in time. There's money in it." Cushing repeated this to Fish with a covert sneer, saying, "In France the Empress makes some politics." [30] Babcock had every advantage of position, he was a friend of the ablest Congressional politicians, and Grant implicitly trusted him. He could easily form a cabal. But would he?

Fish's attitude toward Babcock was soon determined. After Santo Domingo, the Secretary knew that he was a blunderer, and suspected that he was corrupt. After June 3, 1870, when he caught Babcock lying to Grant about Fish's proposed message on Cuba—that is, trying to prejudice Grant against it by saying that Bancroft Davis was the real author—Fish knew he was a double-dealer and mischief-maker. He never forgave Babcock for misrepresenting Rockwell Hoar's resignation. Repeatedly during 1870–72 he blamed him for the leakage of state secrets from the White House, the circulation of rumors embarrassing to our foreign relations, and pressure upon Grant in improper directions. The diary gives us a vivid little vignette of Washington's birthday, 1871, in the White House: snow falling outside; the bustle of Mrs. Grant's reception in the East Room; behind the palms in a corner Jacob D. Cox and Fish having a long, anxious talk about Dent, Paige, Babcock, and Banks—about their furtive machinations to begin a war with Spain. Early in 1871 Fish discovered evidence that the Haitian Minister had used $20,000 to help defeat Dominican annexation. Resenting this, he equally resented the vehemence with which Babcock urged criminal proceedings against the Minister (who' was

[29] Diary, May 25, 1871.   [30] Diary, February 19, 1870.

of course protected by diplomatic immunity) for interfering with our foreign affairs.

v

Fish knew by 1871 that a group of Senatorial politicians were eager to get him out of the Administration, and were finding allies in all sorts of dubious quarters. The press that spring printed constant rumors of his resignation. We have quoted his statement that these reports were inspired by men who had all too much of Grant's confidence, "who exercise more influence than will prove for his good or that of the Republican Party." He meant the three musketeers of Stalwart politics, Oliver P. Morton, Zach Chandler, and Matt Carpenter, Westerners all. When the first two quarreled, he felt that it was for the public good. He did not hesitate to tell Grant this spring his frank opinion of Morton. The Secretary likewise thought Cornelius Cole of California anything but a judicious adviser for Grant. Quietly but assiduously, he urged the President toward safer advisers. The Senators he trusted best were George F. Edmunds, H. B. Anthony, Lot M. Morrill, Timothy O. Howe, and W. B. Allison.[31] He also liked Conkling. Behind his surface faults—his imperious pride, fierce temper, and love of political domination—he saw another man whose advice to Grant would be unselfish and shrewd, though decidedly partisan.

As for the Cabinet, by 1872 it had sadly deteriorated. Since the loss of Cox and Hoar, Fish felt little admiration for any of his associates. Creswell was able and cultivated, but dangerous—an expansionist in foreign affairs, a harsh Radical upon Southern Reconstruction. Boutwell showed industry and incorruptibility, but was secretive,[32] narrow, and two-faced. He rarely said a word in the Cabinet upon his financial policy, and when he did it was likely to be misleading. Fish's diary for March 11, 1870, contains an illuminating bit:

Nothing done in Cabinet, except discussion on the resumption of specie payments. Robeson favors immediate return, and that the government lend its assistance thereto. Boutwell does not favor early resumption; Cox doubts if it can be retained if resumed very soon. The President intimates to Boutwell a wish to throw two or three millions of gold on the market (the price having advanced today some two per cent, or thereabouts) in order to break the efforts of the "bulls" to put up the price. Boutwell says "he does not

[31] Hamilton Fish 2d to author, June 20, 1934.
[32] Cf. *The Education of Henry Adams* on Boutwell's secretiveness.

think that would be wise," and there it rests. Boutwell gives no reasons, and rarely indicates or explains anything of his policy.

Night before last Judge Hoar was at my house, and referring to this habit of Boutwell's, said that he had much respect for Boutwell, and considered him in many respects able. But he reminded him of a certain lawyer in his town, who had acquired an amount of local reputation, but who, when consulted, always looked wise, shook his head, and said, "Well, I don't know; I don't know about that." A clever young man, a student in this lawyer's office, being asked about him and as to this habit of mystified silence and wise looks, with the habitual answer of "I don't know," he said: "Well, it is literally true in every case, for damn him, he don't know."

A year later (April 11, 1871) we find a similar entry:

At the Cabinet yesterday I asked Boutwell what his monthly statement would exhibit; how much of diminution of debt. He evaded a direct answer, saying: "It will probably show enough to lead to a repeal of the income tax, if there were time for Congress to act, but there is not." He then added, "I think the reduction will amount to six millions." Today the statement is published, and the reduction exceeds eleven millions. Boutwell's reticence and concealment from his colleagues of information to which they are entitled are remarkable, to say the least; there is something about this which time will develop. I do not care to record my own apprehensions.

His remark about the income tax is characteristic. Last Tuesday evening the President told me that he had authorized Pleasanton [Commissioner of Internal Revenue] to urge upon Congress the repeal of the income tax, and that he himself had urged it upon several members of both houses. His Secretary of the Treasury opposed and defeated the repeal, and now admits a state of the Treasury which he thinks would lead to the repeal, but conceals the extent from his associates in the Cabinet, although it must be made public the following day.

In other ways Boutwell showed a duplicity that disgusted the straightforward Fish. For example, at a Cabinet meeting late in 1871 he warmly praised Edwards Pierrepont to Grant; yet a few weeks earlier he had told Fish that he felt a deep distrust for Pierrepont! "That is just what I should expect from Boutwell," comments the Secretary.[33]

As time showed, two Cabinet members were a real liability to the government. Fish always regarded that breezy Iowan with a Princeton background, Belknap, with coldness; he was essentially a military man, and Grant was surrounded by too many army officers. Attorney-

[33] Diary, November 21, 1871.

General Akerman was apparently incompetent. He was a fatuous gossip. He once entertained the Cabinet with a long tale, allegedly told him by Robert Toombs, of how Jefferson Davis and Judah P. Benjamin during the Civil War had transferred funds and other property of the Confederacy to Europe for their private use if defeated; these funds, he said, made Benjamin rich when he went to England after the war. Fish did not believe the story. A lily-white Republican, the Georgian kept harping upon Democratic outrages in his section. "Akerman introduces Ku Klux," runs one entry.[34] "He has it on the brain. He tells a number of stories, one of a fellow being castrated, with terribly minute and tedious details of each case. It has got to be a bore to listen twice a week to this thing." He made almost incredible blunders. Soon after taking office he prepared for Grant a proclamation suspending the writ of habeas corpus in nine South Carolina counties. He put in a wrong county name! As a result, a new proclamation had to be issued releasing Marion County and including Union County.[35] He was always bringing up absurd questions:

December 1, 1871.— . . . Akerman reads letters from the acting Governor of Georgia asking whether he can rely upon the support of the Federal Government in his contest for the possession of his office, he having been President of the Senate when Governor Bullock resigned, and the legislature on the following day having elected another person president of the Senate. The President thinks (as anyone would suppose) that he has nothing to do with a speculative case of the kind. It is for the State to settle. . . .

Yet the reason for Akerman's ultimate dismissal did him credit. Under grants made by Congress in 1862–64, certain Western railroads attempted to obtain large areas of land to which their title was dubious. The Secretary of the Interior, Delano, referred the matter to Akerman, who made an adverse report. When asked by Delano to consider the matter again, Akerman became more convinced than ever that the claim was illegal. Gould, Huntington, and other railway magnates began a campaign against him, and placed heavy pressure on Grant to remove him. Delano joined the attack; a newspaper he owned, the Baltimore *American,* opened fire on Akerman. The assault became irresistible.

On the evening of December 10, 1871, the President walked over to Fish's rooms—for the Secretary had given up his house and was in

---

[34] Diary, November 24, 1871.   [35] Diary, October 31, 1871.

temporary lodgings. "I shall be obliged to make a change in the Attorney-Generalship," he announced. Fish made no comment. "I have decided to appoint Judge Williams of Oregon." Fish betrayed a spasm of pain. Just six weeks earlier they had talked of Williams, a lame-duck Senator. Grant, mentioning him in connection with the English legation, said, "He is hardly big enough for the place." Fish had emphatically agreed that he was not. But now he was big enough for the Attorney-Generalship! On December 13 all details were settled. The President strolled through the wintry gloom to Fish's quarters again, and asked him to come to the White House, remarking that Akerman had resigned—by request—and would leave soon after New Year's. Williams, Colfax, and Boutwell all came in. After Williams had been closeted with the President for a time, he emerged looking as pleased as a cat with cream. "I have accepted the Attorney-Generalship, gentlemen," he said. Some men traced the curious appointment of Williams to the fact that he was counsel to the Alaska Improvement Company, in which Grant was a stockholder.[36]

VI

But most dismaying of all was the growing aroma of corruption which tainted the air in Washington. Sensitive men by the summer of 1872 had a premonition that scandals lay everywhere just below the surface. Whitelaw Reid had written a friend that "the depth of corruption" in the Administration was "scarcely suspected as yet even by its enemies." [37] Gossip about the Whiskey Ring and Credit Mobilier broke forth and then was hushed up. Occasionally some significant incident profoundly alarmed Fish. For example, on November 17, 1871, Belknap and Akerman read the Cabinet letters from Edwards Pierrepont, Federal Attorney in New York, advising that the Government dismiss its criminal proceedings against Polhemus & Jackson, a brokerage firm through which an army paymaster had made extensive speculations with government funds. The firm had known that it was using government money. But Pierrepont intimated that the prosecution would involve prominent Republicans, including Jay Cooke & Company. Fish and others protested so indignantly that Grant ordered the

[36] Bowers, *The Tragic Era*, 371; Oberholtzer, *United States*, II, 311; information given me by Mr. Warren Grice of Georgia, a student of Akerman's career.
[37] To John Bigelow late in 1871; Royal Cortissoz, *Life of Reid*, I, 204.

prosecution to be pushed. "Pierrepont has done himself no credit by his action in this matter," writes Fish.[38] But the most disturbing fact of all was that he had obviously expected Grant to approve of his dishonest suggestion.

That he had a certain ground for this expectation was indicated by the affair of Governor E. S. Solomen of Washington Territory. Solomen, for whose appointment Grant was responsible, was shown to be guilty of attempting to bribe a Treasury agent. In the first days of 1872 Grant handed Fish the man's resignation to take effect three months later, on April 1. Since he deserved summary dismissal, the Secretary was amazed. "Do you intend to allow him to remain in office until that time?" he inquired. Grant did. "I regret that," expostulated Fish. "He has misbehaved and ought to be removed at once; not allowed to defer his departure as if it were his own choice." Grant set his jaw and made no reply. He merely directed the nomination of another man in his place.[39] The episode disclosed a curious attitude toward corruption in office—if it was a friend of Grant's who was corrupt.

The New York Custom House investigation early in 1872 indicated some of the grim possibilities of the situation. It was an interesting story. We have seen that in 1870 Grant removed the respected Moses H. Grinnell as Collector of the Port of New York, and appointed Tom Murphy in his stead. He did so primarily because of personal regard for Murphy, and secondarily because the politicians, including Conkling, were dissatisfied with Grinnell. Senator Fenton took the appointment as a heavy personal blow. He and Murphy had been enemies for years. But Conkling, thirsty for absolute power, forced Murphy's confirmation by a vote of 48 to 3. He thus won Grant's gratitude, cemented the loyalty of Murphy, and became master of the custom-house, with its thousand employees, for the solidification of his own political authority. Thenceforth the Conkling faction was supreme in New York. Murphy dismissed Fenton men in droves. With a brave show of virtue General Porter wrote him [40] on July 13, 1870, that many persons seeking office would use "the President's name or mine," but without authority; "you will never hear from me on the subject of office." But he significantly added: "My only desire is to see you so distribute the patronage of your office as to render the most efficient service to the country and *the cause of the Administration.*" Murphy duly filled the

[38] Diary, November 17, 1871.   [39] Diary, January 9, 1872.   [40] Grant's Letterbooks.

offices with men who would labor for Grant's reëlection.

A conspicuous colleague of Murphy's was Colonel George K. Leet, who soon became famous. He had been a minor member of Grant's staff during and following the war. Just after Grinnell's appointment he had come to the Custom House with a letter from Grant. As a result, Grinnell gave him part of that juiciest of plums, the general-order business. This was the business of storing imported goods which were not called for at the New York docks within twenty-four hours after arrival, and which under the law were sent to warehouses specified by the Collector. Few large importers being able to remove their consignments at once, most of their goods were stored for some time, at rates profitable to the warehousemen. But Leet soon became dissatisfied with his share, and began badgering Grinnell for a monopoly of the business. He even declared that if Grinnell did not make his warehouse the sole depository, there would soon be a new Collector. Probably this was empty vaporing. But Grinnell went out; Murphy came in; and Leet promptly obtained his monopoly! Estimates of the profits made by his firm, Leet, Stocking & Co., ranged from $60,000 to $200,000 yearly. Deputy Collector Clark, indeed, called this monopoly the most profitable of all perquisites in the gift of the government. Vigorous complaints were soon made by merchants of extortionate charges, and their protests were taken up by the *Tribune* and other journals. At least twice A. T. Stewart personally spoke to Grant. Finally the President told Murphy: "There is so much talk and scandal about this young man Leet in New York having the general-order business there, on account of his being with me during the war, that I have come to the conclusion that this young man had better leave." But Murphy assured Grant that the discontent had been artificially worked up by steamship companies desirous of seizing the general-order profits; and Leet, Stocking & Co., remained undisturbed until the Custom House Investigation early in 1872.[41]

This Congressional inquiry, in which Senator Bayard was prominent, brought out shocking facts. It showed that the Custom House had two heads, the nominal Collector being Tom Murphy, the real executive an industrious Democrat named Clinch.[42] Murphy looked after primaries, conventions, and campaign collections; Clinch, whom Murphy

[41] For this Custom House investigation, see Senate Report No. 227, 42d Cong., 2d sess.; N. Y. press, January–February, 1872.
[42] *Ibid.;* see also George F. Howe, *Chester A. Arthur,* 45 ff.

admitted to be "the practical working Collector," looked after the Custom House. In practically all of Murphy's appointments merit was disregarded. As the merchant William E. Dodge declared: "The slightest fitness for the post or adaptness to the work is not thought of for a moment. They do as little work and get the most they can." Petty bribery was general; nearly everyone took douceurs. Though the 250-odd inspectors received an average salary of but $1400 yearly, Charlton Lewis of the *Evening Post* stated that their places were more sought after than the office of United States Senator. The three highest functionaries, the Collector, Surveyor, and Naval Officer, together with special agents, profited richly from the moiety system—their share of the fines imposed. Naval Officer Laflin, for example, admitted collecting about $18,000 in ten months as his share of the fines, which was less than the usual figure. While the moieties were legal, they encouraged minor Custom House employees and informers to set up a terrifying system of blackmail. In short, the chief revenue-collecting agency in the nation was full of scandal, full of inefficiency, full of machine politics. It was also shown that Murphy had been hand-in-glove with the infamous Tweed Ring conspirators, Tweed, Sweeny, and Connolly.[43] However valuable his appointment was to Conkling, to the Republican Party as a whole it proved a disaster. William E. Dodge testified that he could hardly name one intelligent acquaintance who had voted for the party in the fall of 1870, and this because "the Administration was represented here by such a venal, corrupt machine as the Custom House."

The inquiry justified Fish, who had opposed Murphy's selection. When Conkling had come to him resentfully, he had said that it was a passive opposition; but it had been active enough, for he told Grant his frank opinion of Murphy. When he declared that the man had made his money as a profiteering wartime contractor, Grant had assured him that Murphy said he had made it in real estate!

A vulnerable Southern policy, a discredited Dominican policy, a weak Cabinet, a deplorable set of political associates—with these handicaps Grant entered the campaign of 1872. The legend was still untouched; he was the only regular Republican who could possibly be elected, and the machine leaders rallied about him. But a formidable revolt had

[43] He had gone into real estate purchases with members of the Tweed Ring, and accepted a place on two commissions used by the Ring to rob the city; see N. Y. *Tribune* and *Herald,* January–March, 1872.

broken out among Republicans who prized liberalism more than regularity. If the followers of Schurz and Sumner, of Greeley, Bryant, and other reform editors, could agree with the Democrats upon a leader of high ability, the outlook for Grant would be dark. Meanwhile, Fish occupied an uncomfortable position. Among the raffish crew in Washington this son of a patriot who had fought at Monmouth and Yorktown, this survivor from a more austere age, moved with dignity and poise, but with growing inner anxiety. It was still his intention to retire on March 4, 1873, whether Grant were reëlected or not.

WHILE Fish was most worried by the indirect claims, the Liberal Republican Convention gathered in Cincinnati on May 1, 1872. An impressive list of men had aligned themselves with the revolt against Grant.[1] The names of such sympathizers as Salmon P. Chase, Gideon Welles, Montgomery Blair, William Cullen Bryant, Jacob D. Cox, and Charles Sumner bore out the view that it represented à revival of the initial idealism of the Republican Party. The opening scenes, as Carl Schurz, who was permanent chairman, pleaded for a candidate of "superior intelligence coupled with superior virtue," were full of enthusiasm. Had the convention nominated Charles Francis Adams or Lyman Trumbull, the movement would at once have gained a brilliant prospect of success.[2] But as a result partly of the machinations of professional politicians, partly of the adroit moves of Whitelaw Reid, and partly of one of the spontaneous impulses which often sweep over ill-organized gatherings, the convention on May 3 selected Horace Greeley. A majority of the delegates instantly repented—but it was too late.

Fish breathed a sigh of relief and amazement when he learned of the nomination. He realized immediately that Grant was saved. Greeley possessed qualities of greatness as an editor, and qualities also of popular strength. But his impulsive judgment, lack of political experience, fluctuating Civil War record, and personal eccentricities, made him a weak rival of the nation's military hero. "Is the Cincinnati Convention to be a stupendous farce, or the prelude to a fearful casualty?" Fish demanded of Thurlow Weed.[3] If Greeley gained wide support, he added, it would prove that the popular conception of qualifications for the presidency was falling toward "those which elevated a horse to the Roman Consulate." He wrote John Jay that it would be difficult to find any American of high intelligence and honesty who was worse equipped for the Presidency than Greeley.[4] "Erratic, uncertain, violent

[1] E. D. Ross, *The Liberal Republican Movement, passim.*
[2] C. F. Adams, Jr., *Charles Francis Adams,* 372; Schouler, *United States,* VII, 212, 213.
[3] Fish to Weed, May 27, 1872; Letterbooks. This parallels John Sherman's statement in a letter to General Sherman that Greeley was "probably the most unfit man for President, except Train, that has ever been mentioned." *Sherman Letters,* 399.
[4] Fish to Jay, June 2, 1872; Letterbooks.

in his temper and unwise in his judgment, a bad judge of men and open to the influence of the grossest flattery and personal adulation, with an ambition and craving for office—not dangerous for want of personal courage—he has now turned upon all the principles for which he has ever contended. . . . I do not think he can be elected—but it will be a hard and bitter contest."

Thurlow Weed expressed the same view.[5] He did not think that any considerable body of men "outside a lunatic asylum" would nominate Greeley, and yet it had been done. "This alarms me. The spirit of unrest is abroad. Everybody had persistently conceded honesty to Mr. Greeley. The unreasoning masses show signs which disturb me. Most of my friends I see say there is no danger. Surveyor Cornell told me yesterday that the President desired Greeley's nomination by the Democratic Convention. I think that such a nomination even by one convention is a dangerous experiment." Still harsher terms were used by the historian Bancroft.[6] "Greeley will rally to his support all the worst elements in our society," he wrote; "the rogues in New York and in Brooklyn, and all the Catholic priests that meddle with politics, and all the friends of disorder in the South. I look upon him as the stalking-horse of the secessionists."

I

Before the campaign began Grant and his associates had taken adroit measures to strengthen their position. In New York Senator Fenton had shown frank resentment of the President's favoritism to Conkling; in Louisiana, the Republican faction under Henry Clay Warmoth still more bitterly resented the Administration's support of the faction headed by William P. H. Kellogg and Grant's brother-in-law Casey. Such sore spots required careful attention, and they received it. Fish's diary states:

Wednesday, March 20, 1872.—On Monday in conversation with the President, I mentioned the danger of losing the vote of New York by reason of Fenton's attitude, and that Boutwell had told me on Sunday that Fenton had called upon him within a day or two previously, and said he did not desire to oppose the President, but complained that he was ignored, etc., by the Administration; that Boutwell was convinced that Fenton desired to be recon-

---

[5] May 22, 1872; Fish Papers.
[6] Bancroft to Fish, June (no day), 1872; Fish Papers.

ciled, and that some very slight recognition would be sufficient. I urged that some effort be made to that end. After some conversation he requested me to see Boutwell again and that he and I, either jointly or separately, see Conkling and ascertain how he would regard such recognition, and also see Fenton and ascertain what he wants.

Last evening I went to Boutwell's; being absent, he called on me this morning. I mentioned the conversation with the President, and suggested that he had better see Conkling first.

Boutwell says that he has had an interview with Warmouth of Louisiana; that Warmouth professes an entire willingness to reconcile and unite the party; that he has (as Boutwell thinks) just grounds of complaint; that Casey and Packard have behaved badly to him. Says that a fund of $50,000 was raised, of which $18,000 was appropriated for the Senate ($1,000 for each member) and the remainder for the lower house of Louisiana, to secure the passage of what was called the Levee Bill; that this money (which he calls a "corruption fund") was held by Casey and actually locked up in the Government safe in the Custom House. He thinks Casey ought to resign, and Packard to be removed, in which case Louisiana will be ensured for the Republican ticket.

In dealing with the tariff and taxation Grant had also taken steps to strengthen his political position. As early as October 23, 1870, he had shown an uneasy responsiveness to the attacks of the tariff reformers —who included leading Republican editors of the Northwest. Calling at Fish's house in the evening, he remarked: [7] "I am not half as much a protectionist as I was a year ago. But I do think that free trade is impracticable, and would ruin the country." Fish asked him what he meant by free trade. "Why," replied Grant, "I mean entire free trade, and Nordhoff's idea that we should burn the custom houses." Perhaps he had at last profited by David A. Wells' expert reports as Special Commissioner of the Revenue, though the previous June he had unwisely acquiesced in Boutwell's refusal to continue Wells in office. A month later he showed that his enlightenment had been real if slight:

November 24, 1870.—Cabinet . . . President says he had intended to read his message as far as completed, but will wait until the Cabinet be more full. . . . Says that he recommends the abolishing of all internal revenue taxes except those on spirits, wine, malt liquor, tobacco, and stamps; that he recommends a reduction of revenue from imports by abolishing duties on those articles not produced in the United States which enter into the arts and manufactures, and reducing or abolishing duties which are not productive on other articles entering into manufactures; that he thinks a more grad-

[7] Diary.

ual reduction of the debt than hitherto is now sufficient; that he recommends reduction of duty on salt, one half the present duty, and on coal to fifty cents a ton. Creswell thinks the reduction on coal will be unpopular as interfering with our own production. The President says the coal producers do not care a particle for the duty, but Creswell says the reduction will affect the Maryland coal.

The result, after much delay in Congress, was the ten per cent horizontal reduction in the tariff on many classes of manufactures, passed in May, 1872. It was better than nothing.

In the same spring session of 1872 the assailants of the income tax were placated by its discontinuance. It is to Boutwell's credit that he had long opposed dropping it, though his reasons were founded on expediency alone. "He warmly denounces the repeal of the income tax," runs Fish's diary for June, 1870, "but wholly on political grounds; that the substitution or continuance of the other taxes which affect a larger number of persons will be unpopular. (The question of equity or right did not constitute any part of his reasoning; whether it did of his judgment was not apparent from what he said.) He thought it would be used against the Republican Party on the stump. Belknap concurred in this opinion." By 1872, however, when Grant needed the support of the great moneyed interests, the income tax was plainly a political liability. It was the fairest single element in the revenue system, as the fervent opposition of these interests proved, and it was a misfortune that it was not revised and strengthened. But it was unpopular, evasion had become widespread, and the Administration and Congress simply jettisoned it.

Another bit of political fence-mending was Grant's sudden espousal of civil service reform. In his message of December, 1870, he recommended action; Congress responded; and in 1871 he appointed a Commission under George William Curtis to devise rules for civil service examinations. On January 1, 1872, after Curtis had attended two Cabinet meetings to make explanations, Grant put these rules into effect. Yet Fish's diary shows that neither the President nor his Cabinet felt any real faith in the projected reform. We read:

December 22, 1871.—Friday. Cabinet. All present except Robeson. Nothing done except that Delano raised question as to the effect of civil service rules upon the Indian Agents, etc., appointed on the nomination of the various religious societies. The President directs that an executive order be issued reappointing the same persons as the advisory board under the system to be inaugurated on January 1, and that Indian agents and superintendents for the present be exempted from the requirements of competitive examination.

January 23, 1871.—Cabinet . . . I mention that several vacancies exist in consular agencies which ought to be filled, and nominations have been received, but that the civil service regulations prohibit the appointment without examination; that the parties reside at great distances from here; the offices are of little value, the candidates probably would not come here for examination, and no board of examiners exists. The President advises that they be appointed at once, subject to such rules as may be adopted hereafter for examination. I object, and propose to refer the facts to the Advisory Board, wishing to oblige them to realize the impracticability of their rule as applied to the consular service.

Much conversation ensues as to the general nature and the impracticable character of the scheme proposed by the late Commission. Among other things it is suggested that they be asked for an estimate of the expense necessary to establish their examining boards, etc., with a view to laying it before Congress for an appropriation, and thus throwing upon Congress the decision whether they will carry out the proposed scheme.

To unprejudiced observers, the weakest portion of Grant's record was its Southern chapter. No one could gaze at the poverty, misgovernment, and violence which reigned in 1872 throughout the lower South without realizing that he had fallen far short of the goal he had announced in 1868. Military reconstruction and Negro suffrage were bearing their full fruit; in State after State the whites, in desperation, were using force to throw off the intolerable yoke of Negroes, Scalawags, and Carpetbaggers. The Congressional Radicals and Grant had replied to their efforts by the harsh Ku Klux legislation of the spring of 1871.

All this was quite outside Fish's province. But a single significant entry in his diary, February 24, 1871, indicates the temper in which Grant had written his message of the following month asking for the Ku Klux law, and shows that already he was trying to moderate the President's policy. "The President refers to the condition of affairs in the South, especially in South Carolina," it runs. "Reads the report of the State Constable of the condition in several counties; murders, whippings, and violence. He expressed a determination to bring a regiment of cavalry and perhaps one of infantry from Texas, where (he says) they are protecting from the Indians a population who annually murder more Union men, merely because they are Union men, than the

Indians could kill of them. The question of bringing colored troops is considered. On the one side it is urged that the presence of colored regular soldiers will encourage the Negro population, and give them more courage and self-reliance; on the other it may irritate the white population, and provoke collisions, in which case many at the North will say it was unwise to provoke a prejudice. I present the latter view, Robeson and Delano incline to the former." Sixteen companies of white troops were sent into South Carolina.

While in his last annual message before the campaign Grant proposed the removal of disabilities from all Southerners except "the great criminals," otherwise he stood adamant on his rigorous policy. Rutherford B. Hayes was probably correct in believing this policy popular in the North. Prejudice against the "rebels" was still intense. Even Fish rather frigidly defended Grant's course. Writing October 26, 1872, to Edward S. Baker of Mississippi, who had denounced the Carpetbag tyranny, he offered some unconvincing arguments: [8]

You have had four years' experience of General Grant's Administration. Going into office at a period when much of the animosity excited by the War still remained, when the States which had seceded were still out of the Union, when vast numbers at the South were disfranchised and incapacitated from holding office, we now see a general feeling of kindness and a return to the fraternal recognition between North and South which marked the era of the past. Every State is now represented in the Senate of the U. S. Every Congressional District has its representative in the House of Representatives. No man at the South is disfranchised by any laws of the United States, and with the exception of a very few (probably not to exceed a hundred) no man is disqualified from holding office. . . .

You say that Mr. Greeley promises you relief from these "Carpetbag Vultures," but General Grant says nothing. Mr. Greeley is in a position where he or friends for him may and do promise all sorts of things. General Grant is a very different man from Mr. Greeley; he will make no promise that he does not think he can execute. . . . I am sure that General Grant does not desire to subject you to the government of persons among you whom a majority of your own people do not desire as rulers. If, as you say, he is silent while Mr. Greeley is profuse in his promises, it is because he does not mean that a promise of his shall be thrown in his face, because it was impossible to execute it. Neither the President nor Congress can prevent the moving into your State of such persons as desire to settle among you, nor can the President or Congress prevent the people of your State selecting whom they choose for local rulers. . . .

[8] Letterbooks.

II

Foreign affairs fortunately played little part in the campaign. Just before the Liberal Republican Convention met, Blaine believed that the British demands on the indirect claims would become an issue. "Your father," wrote Mrs. Blaine to her son on May 1, 1872,[9] "was so impressed with the fatal influence which any concession on the part of Mr. Fish would have on our political situation, that he went in to talk over matters with him Sunday evening. Was there till a very late hour." But this question was quickly disposed of to general satisfaction.

The Congressional inquiry into the sale of War Department arms to France, pushed to the utmost by Sumner and Schurz, proved a disappointment before the campaign really began. Doubtless Sumner's principal object in originating it was unimpeachable. But some of its supporters hoped it would arouse German-American hostility against Grant; and the Senate discussions of February and March, 1872, turned quite as much upon its political aspects as upon law and fact. The War Department, not the State Department, was the object of attack, and politicians who knew the inner facts feared that Rufus Ingalls, Grant's and Babcock's friend, might be brought to bay. Fish's chief concern was lest it might embarrass our relations with Germany.

At the outset, as Fish's diary shows, Grant came near making a characteristic blunder. On February 13th the Cabinet discussed the investigation at length. Secretary Belknap stated that most of Sumner's information had been furnished by the Marquis de Chambrun, counsel to the French legation. According to de Chambrun, employees in the War Department had taken bribes and otherwise profited by the sale of arms. "Well," said Grant, testily, "I want you, Boutwell, and you, Williams, to order the immediate prosecution of all persons in New York who testify that they gave bribes to government officials. I want all persons accused on good evidence of either giving or taking such bribes prosecuted." Boutwell and Williams acquiesced, and the latter asked: "Shall we make a public statement that such orders have been given?" Grant was about to say yes when Fish interposed. "No, no," he exclaimed. "Such a public order would be a dreadful mistake. If the rumor got abroad that there was such an order at all it would give our

[9] *Letters of Mrs. James G. Blaine*, I, 123–24.

enemies an opening. They would say that the Administration is intimidating witnesses, and trying to prevent them from giving testimony." He was so obviously right that no more was heard of the order.[10]

In the end the investigation was carried out by a thoroughly "safe" committee. Sumner, now ill and broken, declined to sit on it, and Schurz was denied a seat, but both were asked to testify. Secretary Delano told Fish [11] that he had seen Schurz and Lyman Trumbull in frequent consultation with men he knew to be "infamous characters." After thirty-one sessions, the committee made a whitewashing report which Sumner and Schurz denounced in fierce terms.[12] Their indignation was justified, for the report not merely covered up suspicious facts, but contained much bad international law. The best authorities hold that a government vending large quantities of arms during a war must know that the purchasers intend them for one of the belligerents, and is guilty of a dereliction. But the controversy attracted little attention, and the German-Americans continued to prefer Grant to Greeley.[13]

The reasons for this were simple. Administration leaders had handled the inquiry in a way to minimize the evidence of dishonesty; the war was over; the arms sold to France had done her little good; and above all, the German Government itself made no written complaint. For this last fact George Bancroft tried to take all the credit. He wrote Fish that while the investigation had impaired the good feeling of the Germans for the American people, it had not injured "me personally" at all.[14] "The Emperor treats me with the kindness which has never varied; Bismarck invited me (and I believe no one else) to visit him at his new acquisition; and the Emperor's son-in-law, the reigning Grand Duke of Baden, passed an hour with me a few mornings ago on a voluntary visit that was as friendly as possible. So you need have no anxiety about the Emperor's fidelity in our San Juan reference. As to the sale of arms, I had to use all resources to prevent official complaint during the winter of 1870–71, but I succeeded; and you can say with the utmost truth that no complaint or remonstrance was made to me. On the contrary, our friendly relations were unbroken." The inquiry

---

10 Diary, February 13, 1872.   11 Diary, March 26, 1872.

12 *Congressional Globe*, May 30, 1872. Senate Report 183, 42d Cong., 2d Sess. See Thornton's report in *Br. and Foreign State Papers*, Vol. 61, 925; Hall's *International Law*, 5th ed., 598.

13 Cf. Pierce, *Sumner*, IV, 513.

14 Bancroft to Fish, about April 15, 1872; Fish Papers. Bancroft had a habit, especially reprehensible in a historian, of leaving letters undated.

had after all done something—it had given Bancroft an opportunity to plume his vanity. But in America it probably did not change a thousand votes.

Inevitably the Liberal Republican and Democratic assaults on the Administration included some thrusts at the State Department. Throughout the summer the Geneva Tribunal was hard at work; Bancroft Davis, Evarts, Cushing, and Waite were presenting the American case with the utmost ability. Why should anyone wish us to fail there? Yet while the game was being played out, the New York *World* published offensive articles, printed garbled extracts from State Department despatches, offered a pro-British interpretation of the evidence, and arrived at unfair conclusions.[15] Fish asked a trusted journalist to expose the unfair statements of the *World, Tribune,* and *Herald*.[16] He believed that Administration organs would be glad to print a short, strong article, which the National Committee might broadcast in pamphlet form. Washington newspapers used this article, but the press in general was reluctant to copy an article inspired by the government. To Bancroft Davis, just after his triumph at Geneva, the Secretary wrote in sympathetic terms.[17] "You have had an over-full measure of personal abuse, but your work and its results will vindicate you as soon as the bitterness and the blackguardism attendant upon the Presidential contest shall have passed. I have had my share and know how unpleasant it is, but I know that the thinking and substantial part of the public form their own opinions and approve what has been done. . . ."

The decision of the Geneva Tribunal on September 14 of course redounded enormously to the credit of the Administration. And another diplomatic victory came soon enough afterwards to assist the Republican fortunes. The German Emperor on October 21, 1872, decided the question of the San Juan channel in favor of the United States. The line was to pass through the Haro Canal, and San Juan Island, after a dispute of twenty-six years, was safely American.

III

As soon as Greeley was nominated, most Eastern business men had rallied impressively to Grant. Some of them feared the South; all of

---

[15] See, e. g., the N. Y. *World*, August 18, 1872.
[16] To Henry O'Connor of Washington, Garrison, September 21, 1872; Letterbooks.
[17] September 21, 1872; Letterbooks.

them feared that the reformers would pursue tariff and taxation policies inimical to vested interests. John C. Hamilton, who typified the wealthier men of New York City, wrote Fish on May 31 [18] that while he felt a kind regard for Greeley personally, he shuddered at the thought of his election, for as Grant was pledged to the Union, Greeley was pledged to disunion. A more important reason came out in the next sentences. "I wish the income tax could yet be repealed. Our Union League has denounced it unanimously. They contribute very largely at elections, and when we are to pay a city tax of 2.75 per cent, it is unfortunate this income tax is now to be called for. But I suppose, though we probably will lose this State, it is too late." It was not too late. Union League members were soon blessing the Republican policy that placed the principal burden of taxes on the farmers and workingmen; they perceived more than ever that Grant meant safety.

The rally of other groups was equally striking. Most colored voters preferred their military liberator to the editor who had demanded a truce in 1864. Most Northern veterans were with Grant. The Middle West remembered that he was its son. William Cullen Bryant, after a sharp editorial upon Greeley's uncouth manners, presided over a meeting of disgruntled liberals who repudiated his candidacy. On June 1 Thurlow Weed assured Fish [19] that the nation as a whole was behind the Administration, and that his only uneasiness was over the polyglot metropolis. "The Tammany thieves hope by this movement to bridge over the great gulf that separates them from all creditable personal or political associations. They have evidently made their bargain with Greeley. If the Baltimore Convention should endorse him, the Irish will break loose and go for him wildly." Yet many Irishmen gratefully recalled Grant's moderation in 1870 toward the Fenian prisoners.

As the skies brightened, the chief anxiety of the President's friends was lest he might make some costly blunder. All summer he was under a galling fire from the reform press for his nepotism, his easy acceptance of gifts, the military atmosphere of the White House, the lack of vigilance, efficiency, and high purpose in his Administration. Critics dealt sharply with his love of "fast trotters" and of the Capuan ease of Long Branch. He might have replied. But with marked unanimity, his friends refrained from asking him to make campaign trips, deliver speeches, or indeed do any public act. Their attitude may be judged

[18] Hamilton to Fish from New York; Fish Papers.   [19] Fish Papers.

from a single episode recorded in the diary. On July 15 Fish, half ill from overwork, returned from a brief visit to Garrison to attend a Cabinet meeting scheduled for the 16th. At the appointed hour he trudged up the White House steps. Creswell and Delano were waiting in the hall—but no President! Grant had decided that business was not sufficiently urgent to call him from Long Branch, and had telegraphed Horace Porter that he would not come until the next week. The Cabinet members (Williams was in the city ready to attend) discussed the matter. Fish might well have been irritated. The President had notified him that the Cabinet meeting would be held, and had made no reply to his letter announcing that he would travel 300 miles to attend it. But he had only one thought: "If the Democratic papers get hold of this," he wrote,[20] "they will make capital out of it."

As the summer passed all the news which reached Fish was favorable. Senator Howe wrote in August [21] that while some Republicans had left the party, the great mass were more earnest than ever, and "my belief is the demoralized Democracy will supply all losses from defection." Some New York leaders still felt uneasy. But Fish informed Bancroft Davis in midsummer that from what he could observe, "we shall gain at least three from the Democrats for every Republican who votes for Greeley. . . . It was by audacious bragging and political trickery that the Greeleyites captured the Cincinnati Convention. The hungry appetite for office and patronage brought the Baltimore Convention into condition to surrender without demur to the Greeley men. The movement, however, is formidable." Seward pronounced for the Administration, and a prominent Democrat shortly assured Fish that Grant would carry the State by a hundred thousand.[22]

IV

Thus the October elections in Ohio, Indiana, and Pennsylvania drew on. Greeley's tour of these States had attracted huge audiences, and his speeches had made a strong impression. The Administration was still distinctly nervous. Particularly did Pennsylvania and Indiana seem doubtful; Ohio, where Secretary Delano had great prestige and Gree-

---

[20] Diary, July 15, 1872.
[21] From Green Bay, Wisconsin, August 2, 1872; Fish Papers.
[22] Fish wrote Bancroft Davis, August 6, 1872, that he had made inquiries in the neighborhood of Garrison, and that if it offered any index, Greeley could not carry New York —which was vital to his success.

ley was in ill-favor, was fairly safe. In Pennsylvania, Andrew G. Curtin, the war governor and "soldiers' friend," had returned from Russia eager to continue his political career and nervous lest Grant give all the patronage to the Cameron machine. Fish urged the President to see him and make sure of his support, for conquest of the State in October "will make easy work throughout the country in November." Other precautions were taken. Speakers were poured in, manufacturers were forced to make large contributions, and Negro workers were brought from Virginia and Maryland. The *Tribune* declared that "there was nothing in Pennsylvania which was not bought."

The night before these elections, October 8, Fish wrote Elihu Washburne: [23] "I am very hopeful, but not without anxieties. The consequence in one direction or another will be significant."

It was more than significant. It decisively shattered the hopes of the coalition behind Greeley. The Republicans carried Pennsylvania and Ohio by heavy majorities, while the slenderness of Hendrick's majority for governor in Indiana presaged a Republican victory there in November.[24]

Fish expressed a glowing elation.[25] "The Presidential election may be considered as decided. Yesterday's work in Pennsylvania, Ohio, and Indiana can leave no question; the campaign henceforth is easy. White coats and hats are now at a discount. Was there ever a more barefaced, profligate, unprincipled coalition?—or a more shameless sacrifice of principles and of profession in a wicked effort to obtain spoils? The Republican Party is stronger as well as purer by reason of the men who have gone out from it." But he wrote his friends that there must be no relaxation of effort—that the "amalgamation party" and the "Dolly Varden ticket" must not merely be defeated, but crushingly defeated. "The snake is scotched but not killed," he warned Senator Anthony.[26] "In 1868 the rebels tried to regain power under Horatio, and now they are trying under Horace; a very slight change of name, none of principle."

To the very end the Liberal Republicans continued to assail Grant for tyranny at the South, Caesarism at the North, and general laxity and favoritism. The Republicans continued to ridicule Greeley's Fourierism, vegetarianism, and other isms, his linen duster and white hat,

[23] Letterbooks.   [24] Schouler, *United States*, VII, 216.
[25] Fish to Elihu Washburne, October 12, 1872; Letterbooks.
[26] Fish to Anthony, October 13, 1872; Letterbooks.

his political vagaries, and his softness toward "rebels." But the outcome became more and more certain. In choosing a President most Americans are conservative; and even malcontents thought it more conservative to stay in the frying pan than jump into the fire. W. T. Sherman remarked: "I prefer the ills we have rather than those threatening us." [27] As the campaign closed, its bitterness increased. Nast's caricatures of Greeley as a combination of simpleton and knave stung the editor deeply. Grant's opponents, especially the Democrats, revived the report that he was a drunkard. On this point Fish wrote an emphatic letter to a Southern inquirer: [28]

I have known General Grant very intimately since the close of the war. I have been much with him at all hours of the day and night—have travelled with him days and nights together—have been with him on social and festive occasions as well as in hourly intercourse of close official relations. I have never seen him in the most remote degree under any excitement from wine or drink of any kind.

I have never known either exhaustion and fatigue of travel, or of continual anxious labor, to lead him to any undue indulgence in any stimulant of drink. The very close personal association which I have had with him for many years justifies me in saying that the imputation of drunkenness is utterly and wantonly false, and that his use of wine is as moderate and proper as that of a gentleman need be.

The Republican candidate for Vice President was Henry Wilson of Massachusetts, "the Natick cobbler," supposedly an austere embodiment of all the virtues. Beyond doubt he was a highly estimable man; but Democratic campaigners would have given much for an entry in Fish's diary for May 12, 1870, upon him. James Watson Webb that day had told the Secretary of a recent conversation with General Thomas Jordan, who in 1861 had been adjutant-general of the Confederate forces at Manassas, and chief of staff under Beauregard. According to Jordan, at the outbreak of war he had found that an intimacy existed between Senator Wilson and one Mrs. Greenhow. He established "the same kind of intimacy" with her. He then induced her to extract from Wilson all the official news that she could get; and, provided with a cipher, she sent this to the Confederate authorities. Thus she obtained from Wilson in-

[27] *Sherman Letters,* pp. 337, 338. A writer in the *Atlantic* for September similarly wrote: "Thousands, perhaps hundreds of thousands of citizens will abstain from voting at all because they believe both candidates personally unqualified, or disqualified, for the Presidency."
[28] Fish to C. C. Amsden, October 25, 1872; Letterbooks.

formation that McDowell had been ordered to advance upon Manassas, which she immediately communicated. The Confederates knew all about McDowell's plans within a few hours after the orders were given, and in this way were able to concentrate their troops and win the battle of Bull Run. Fish of course put this dubious story in his diary for what it was worth. But if it had leaked out, it might have enlivened the campaign immensely.

When Fish seized his newspaper on November 6, he found that Grant had been reëlected by a sweeping popular vote, while his majority in the electoral college was still more overwhelming. Greeley carried only six States, all in the former slave area. His defeat plunged him into depths of humiliation. Almost simultaneously the death of his wife plunged him into depths of sorrow, and the prospective loss of his editorship of the *Tribune* into depths of despair. His mind gave way, and the country had hardly learned this before still more tragic news arrived. In Fish's papers is a brief note from Grant dated November 29. "My dear Governor," it read, "under the circumstances, Mr. Greeley having died this afternoon, Mrs. Grant, Nellie, and myself send our regrets for not attending Mrs. Fish's party this evening."

Grant accepted the victory as merely his due. He had returned from Long Branch shortly before election day as imperturbable as ever. But it was obvious that he had never regarded the Liberal Republican movement as a rebuke; he thought of it as simply an impertinence. He had told Garfield that it reminded him of a Western experience with coyotes. Once when he had believed that he heard a hundred of them howling, he found that there were only two! His gratitude to the politicians who had carried him through the crisis was frankly expressed, and both he and they took the verdict as a complete vindication. Fish wrote the rector of St. Mark's:[29] "The overwhelming numbers by which the people have expressed their approval of his course do not seem to move him so much as the quiet, thoughtful congratulations of those who from the retirement of their studies tender him a tribute of approval which come from unselfish patriotic emotions."

The President's complacency was increased by the heavy blow which fell upon Congress immediately after the election. He had deeply resented the readiness of Congress to investigate the executive branch of

[29] Fish to Dr. T. E. Vermilye, November 9, 1872; Letterbooks.

the government. The inquiries of the previous spring into the New York Custom House and the sale of arms had irritated him. He therefore felt no sympathy when the Credit Mobilier scandal exposed Congress itself as wearing sadly besmirched garments. Rumor had been busy ever since 1868 with the name of the Credit Mobilier, a corporation used by Representative Oakes Ames and other promoters of the Union Pacific Railroad to construct its line in a fashion highly profitable to a few inside men. During the campaign these rumors had grown into categorical charges in the New York *Sun*.[30] On the day Congress met in December, 1872, the House at Speaker Blaine's instance, and without a dissenting vote, ordered an investigation. This was conducted by a committee of five under Luke P. Poland of Vermont, assisted later by a similar Senate committee under Jeremiah M. Wilson of Indiana. It showed that Oakes Ames, wishing to protect the Credit Mobilier from Congressional scrutiny or unfriendly legislation, had offered fellow-members of Congress blocks of stock on terms so generous as to constitute bribery. A considerable number had taken shares. Some now brazened their course out; others attempted a denial—until Ames produced a memorandum book and other evidence which implicated them.[31]

Within six weeks the investigation had proved shockingly destructive. The *Nation* of January 30, 1873, summed up its first effects as "total loss, one Senator; badly damaged and not serviceable to future political use, two Vice Presidents and eight Congressmen. The condition of Ames's reputation language is inadequate to describe." The Senator was Patterson of New Hampshire; the Vice Presidents were Schuyler Colfax and Henry Wilson; and the damaged Representatives included James A. Garfield and Grant's critic Henry L. Dawes. Fish, shocked though not astonished, reflected the Administration view when on February 20, 1873, he sent Schenck some caustic observations upon Congress.[32] "Last winter it was 'investigating' the Executive Departments; now, on the Christian maxim of rigid self-examination, it is investigating itself. And what developments! Since the early days of the church, has there been such a

---

[30] Beginning September 4, 1872.

[31] For the House (Poland) findings see House Reports Nos. 77, 78, 42d. Congress, 3d. Session; for the Senate (Wilson) findings, Senate Report, No. 519, 42d Congress, 3d. Session.

[32] Letterbooks.

slaughter of 'Christians'? Cold water does not seem to wash away all suspicion (?) of wrong. 'Tis sad and sickening to see reputations which one had loved to believe well-earned and pure knocked to pieces, and leave no chance for friends to say a word. For most purposes the present Congress is practically demoralized. So many are struck at, and they too leaders, that little beyond the appropriation bills seem *really* to engage attention."

Congress was further discredited as its session ended by the disgraceful "Salary Grab." To the country it seemed bad enough that Grant should allow his salary to be raised from $25,000 to $50,000 a year, when the spirit though not the letter of the Constitution forbade a President to sign a bill increasing his own emoluments.[33] But it was far worse for Representatives and Senators to vote themselves a virtual bonus. They not merely lifted their future salaries from $5,000 to $7,500, but made the increase retroactive for two years—each member thus receiving $5,000 in a lump sum. The bill passed March 3, 1873. A storm of anger swept the nation, and the reputation of Congress sank to the lowest point since slavery days. Grant's shortcomings for the moment seemed slight by contrast with this shameless theft.

The next day, March 4, Grant rose in front of the Capitol to read the most complacent and fatuous of all his public papers, his second inaugural. Though Fish nowhere commented upon it, we cannot doubt that it filled him with pain and disquiet. Half of the press treated it with contemptuous sarcasm. Of all the documents in that variegated compilation, Richardson's *Messages and Papers of the Presidents,* it is the most remarkable. With the one merit of brevity, in two and a half pages it presented an appalling array of empty clichés, shallow thinking, and bad grammar. Grant could write like a great commander when his mind was filled with his subject—the principal part of his *Memoirs* proves that; but when he tried to generalize upon politics and economics he wrote like a tanner of Galena. And worse than the intellectual defects of this paper was its evidence that he was in a cocksure and self-satisfied mood. He had written it without advice from anyone. Speaking of the recent election as "my vindication," he made

---

[33] The President is not permitted to approve a bill raising his salary during the term for which he has been elected; Grant on March 3, 1873, approved a bill doubling his salary for the term beginning March 4. Salaries of Cabinet officers and Supreme Court justices were simultaneously raised to $10,000 a year. *Congressional Globe,* 42d. Congress, 3rd Session, pp. 1671 ff.; 2045 ff.; 2101 ff.; 2179.

it plain that he intended to take the reins of government into his own hands.

He began in patriotic vein. "The past four years, so far as I could control events, have been consumed in the effort to restore harmony, public credit, commerce, and all the arts of peace and progress. It is my firm conviction that the civilized world is tending toward republicanism, or government by the people through their chosen representatives, and that our own great republic is destined to be the guiding star to all others." This echo of Jefferson Brick, "We air a great people and we must be cracked up," would have been strange at any time. But it was particularly queer just after the Credit Mobilier and Salary Grab. Grant threw out a few philosophical truths. Thanks to the telegraph and "rapid transit by steam," all parts of the continent had been "made contiguous for all purposes of government." He offered one sentence upon the Negro. He would not ask any action for improving "the social status of the colored man, except to give him a fair chance to develop what good there is in him, give him access to the schools, and when he travels let him feel assured that his conduct will regulate the treatment and fare he will receive." He then returned to ungrammatical generalizations—"I believe that our Great Maker is preparing the world, in His own good time, to become one nation speaking one language, and when armies and navies will no longer be required." And he concluded with a plaintive reference to his faithful performance of many heavy duties:

Notwithstanding this, throughout the war, and from my candidacy for my present office in 1868 to the close of the last Presidential campaign, I have been the subject of abuse and slander scarcely ever equalled in political history, which today I feel that I can afford to disregard in view of your verdict, which I gratefully accept. . . .

Another act of Grant's made the judicious grieve. No man had fared worse in the Credit Mobilier scandal than Schuyler Colfax. He had accepted Oakes Ames's bribe of stock. He had lied about it afterwards. When his story was investigated, it was shown that he had also sold his influence as Speaker to a manufacturer of envelopes who held a large contract with the postoffice. Yet Grant now gave him a letter expressing the strongest faith in his integrity; the more unfortunate because it recalled that, just after the Custom House investigation, Grant had written Tom Murphy a missive expressing affectionate admiration and respect, and just after the Black Friday affair, a similar letter to Daniel Butterfield.

Altogether, the prospect for the coming four years was not without its shadows.

WITH the Geneva Arbitration triumphantly ended, and Grant safely reëlected, Fish turned back, doubtless with a sigh, to the one great problem which confronted him every year, without respite, from 1868 to 1877. Diplomatically, but a single cloud hung in the sky; it lay in the familiar quarter above Cuba—a thick and sable cloud, lit up momentarily by jagged thrusts of lightning.

Cuba!—every American, thanks to a torrent of books, magazine articles, and newspaper correspondence, fitted a lurid picture to that word. In 1872–73 it was probably the most tragic spot on the globe. The four-year-old insurrection was maintained as ferociously as ever by guerrilla bands. Armed with machetes, variegated firearms, and scanty doles of ammunition; commanded by the indomitable Gomez, Garcia, and Agramonte; holding the mountains of the east in force, roving the woods, and pouring out of ambuscades; still hopeful of American intervention, the Cubans struggled on.[1] For every man their hornet bands lost in battle the Spaniards lost two; for every man they lost by disease the Spaniards lost five. Adventurers, Creole patriots, and escaped slaves steadily filtered into their ranks. Deep in the rugged highlands between Cabo Cruz and Santiago de Cuba stern little President Cespedes, in a hut with a hammock, a stick-table, a lath stool, a few valises for clothing, and a repeating Winchester, gave their cause a touch of civil dignity. In New York their Junta boasted of "three army corps" of well-drilled men, controlling two-thirds of Cuba.[2] This was absurd, for they had lost ground; but their battalions of fluctuating strength—now not more than 10,000 men in all—did half-control, half-terrorize one-fourth of the island.

And what of the Spaniards? In four years 76,000 lads and men had been mustered in Spain and sent clattering down the gangplanks in Cadiz and Vigo; in the same years 46,000 had been shovelled into sandy graves, or sent home emaciated wrecks.[3] To the 30,000 ill-fed men who remained, almost all infantrymen, with little artillery, fell

[1] Cf. F. V. Aguilera and Ramon Cespedes, *Notes About Cuba* (1872); Cuban Junta, *Facts About Cuba* (1870); J. J. O'Kelly, *The Mambi-Land, or Adventures of a Herald Correspondent in Cuba* (1874).
[2] Aguilera and Cespedes, *op. cit.*   [3] Gallenga, *Pearl of the Antilles.*

the bloody field-fighting. The Volunteers maintained the "home front" in cities and towns, with more of marauding expeditions, lynchings, and other outrages than of real encounters. Though they seldom lost any men, they insisted on killing captives, hunting rebels with blood-hounds, and cowing the Creole population with sudden bloody strokes. Most of them had left Spain as adventurers, eager only to make money, and were as fierce of temper as Pizarro's men; chiefly bachelors, they had lived as turbulently as California gold-diggers. War now brought out the worst in them. They were largely controlled, moreover, by the harsh ruling oligarchy, representing the great land-holding, slave-owning, and commercial families. Neither civil nor military leaders from Spain dared interfere with the Volunteers or oligarchy, for their support was essential to the mother country. Year after year, the oligarchy could hold the rich sugar-districts and the great importing and exporting businesses by spending say 15,000 lives and $20,000,000. The lives came from Spain; the money was wrung out of the Cuban people; those who crowded the Casino Espagnol in Havana and Santiago risked little and gained everything.[4]

One incompetent captain-general succeeded another. De Rodas, forced by Volunteer pressure in 1871 to resign, was replaced by Count Valmaseda, whose bloody proclamation had so horrified America. The new leader was pungently described by Sickles in a letter to Bancroft Davis.[5] "Valmaseda out-telegraphs De Rodas. The latter put down the insurrection every month *morally,* the former demolishes it every night *materially.* Yet it still lives and will not die. The poor fat count is only appointed *ad interim,* and of course he has to put down the rebellion *ad interim* or lose his place with its $100,000 a year, a palace, and a vice-royal establishment—besides innumerable perquisites out of which a fortune is always gained. Valmaseda is even less a soldier than de Rodas; . . . they say he is not only without capacity, but that he lacks pluck." Happily, Valmaseda did not last long. Late in 1872 he was replaced by Concha, who had served twice in the same office before; a man less a pet and tool of the Volunteers, but far from a great statesman.

    [4] The Cuban Consular Reports, Vols. 61–64, State Department Archives, contain a mass of valuable material. H. C. Hall and Thomas Biddle sent especially valuable papers from Havana. They were impressed by the guerrilla character of the war and the apparent hopelessness of ever ending it.
    [5] March 7, 1871; Davis Papers. Cf. London *Times,* January 25, 1873, on Valmaseda.

Estimates of the aggregate losses in Cuba vary. The best authority states that the war cost 150,000 lives in the first four years, including Spaniards, Cuban rebels, and the non-combatants crowded by Spanish orders into the towns. Wealth was poured out in floods; devastation wrecked villages and countrysides. But the contractors, bureaucrats, and generals prospered; and so, with sugar prices rising, did the planters. Slaves, after a temporary depression, were worth as much as at any time in the previous dozen years. The Moret law of June, 1870, emancipating all aged slaves and all slave children born after its enactment, was kept a dead letter. Indeed, the Volunteers did not even permit its publication for nearly two years.[6] A ten years' war sounds horrible, but some men always find any war too short, and in Cuba this group were all-powerful. In distant Spain the people, haughty and ignorant, quarreled over every issue save one—they would hold to the pearl of the Antilles. Neither merchants nor politicians, church nor military, King Amadeus nor the republicans, could afford to lose it. The peasants and workmen whose sons died under its palms could not afford to keep it, but this they had not yet learned.

To the end of his career General Prim had believed in selling Cuba to its own people. After he had brought about the election of Amadeus as king in 1870, he had again occupied himself with the Cuban question from the same point of view from which he and Sickles had previously studied it. Frankly and openly, he sent an agent, a Cuban liberal named Nicolas Azcarate, to the New York Junta with an offer of autonomy. Secretly, he sent other agents to the Junta who were authorized to offer full independence if the Cubans would indemnify Spain by a payment of $200,000,000 (the price had gone up!) guaranteed by the United States. In November, 1870, the poet Juan Clemente Zenea went to Cuba to negotiate with the insurgents in the field. He carried a safe-conduct from Don Lopez Roberts, and both Roberts and Azcarate guaranteed his life in the name of General Prim. The ruling oligarchy in Cuba were desperately frightened by the possibility that his mission would succeed. But on December 27, 1870, Prim was mortally wounded in Madrid, and died three days later. The day of his death the Spaniards threw Zenea into a Cuban prison; and there the irreconcilable Valmaseda held him

---

[6] Foreign Relations, 1872; see London *Times,* October 11, 1872, on Cuban slavery. Consul-General Thomas Biddle sent May 7, 1870, a British estimate that the war had cost not less than 54,850 lives in its first twenty months. He thought this too low, for Spanish officers notoriously reported many dead men alive that they might draw their pay.

for eight months, until in August, 1871, he was shot. With Prim died all hope of the purchase of Cuba.[7]

In the United States the Junta, with the aid of Colonel Ryan and other leaders, was as busy as ever, and Congress and the press remained sympathetic. At times general indignation was aroused by some outrage. Thus in November, 1871, a party of medical students of the University of Havana entered a cemetery. In a frolic they scratched some satirical verses (so it was alleged, and also denied) upon the tombs of two Spanish patriots. The Volunteers rose in "a ferocious and riotous mob," "a savage rabble," to use phrases applied to them in the Spanish Cortes itself. Defying the Spanish commander, they had eight of the students, including one boy who had been in Matanzas on the day of the episode, summarily shot; while some thirty others were sentenced to hard labor in the chain gangs. Other occurrences indicated that Havana was ruled not by Spain but by irresponsible Volunteer leaders. So long as Madrid controlled Cuba, it was the duty of the United States to refrain from intervention. But if the mob took control, intervention to protect American lives and property would be imperative; the more imperative because the Volunteers were savagely hostile to Americans.[8]

The danger of some "incident" was increasing. Formidable naval forces now lowered at each other in Cuban waters. During 1872 four Spanish ironclads, British-built and well armed, had been based on Havana.[9] In fact, most of the fleet of the monarchy was there. The American Government early that year sent seven ironclads, with nine unarmored vessels, to southern waters—"a formidable force," Thornton wrote Lord Granville.[10] Admiral Porter told a British naval officer that fourteen monitors could steam for Havana on a few hours' notice. Though Fish and Robeson heard that many Spanish commanders were spoiling for a fight, experts in Washington and London agreed that the American navy was superior in armament and personnel.[11] Spain notoriously had to employ Britons and Americans for engineers; little coal was available in Cuba; and the ships would soon be sunk or

---

[7] I have received valuable information on Prim's last offers from Dr. Luis Fernandez Marcané of Havana, Cuba.

[8] Nation, December 7, 1871.

[9] Two ironclads had been there; early in 1872 Spain sent two more. Layard to Granville, December 8, 1871; PRO, FO 115, 550.

[10] Thornton to Granville, January 9, 1872; PRO, FO 5, 1361.

[11] Cf. Annual Reports Secretary of the Navy, 1870, 1871, 1872.

helpless. Probably no leader in Madrid doubted that a war would end in quick defeat.[12]

Even so, Spanish leaders could think of worse calamities. All would be lost save honor—and the significance they attached to honor was enormous. Fish heard in the summer of 1872 of an interview which had just taken place in Madrid between Foreign Minister Martos and the British Minister, Layard. The latter stated that Great Britain fully supported the American position upon slavery in Cuba, and did not believe that further delay could be excused. "I can see but one way out of the predicament in which the Spanish Government is placed. That is to make so public and explicit a declaration upon your future policy in Cuba, especially with reference to slavery, as will satisfy Great Britain and anticipate the demands of the United States." But Martos confessed that his government did not *dare* make such a declaration.[13] Not only would it alienate the Volunteers and the Spanish Party in Cuba, and lead at once to the loss of the colony, but it would probably cause a tremendous insurrection in northwestern Spain, whose interests were closely connected with Cuba. The complete suppression of the insurrection was the only question upon which Spaniards of all political parties agreed, and even a popular government could not hold power a day if it laid itself open to the suspicion of leaning toward the Cuban insurgents. Layard spoke of the danger of war. But Martos replied: "If we lose Cuba by mismanagement and by alienating the affections of the loyal inhabitants, we should be looked upon as traitors; if the United States choose to deprive us of our colony, we may have to yield in the end to superior force, but we shall have preserved our national dignity."

In short, it would be more honorable to lose Cuba by fighting the United States in behalf of slavery than to lose it by forcing emancipation upon the Volunteers! [14]

I

A happy feature of the situation was that Spain was now represented by perhaps the ablest Minister she has ever sent to Washington, Ad-

---

[12] H. C. Hall, Confidential Report, April 18, 1872; Fish Papers.
[13] Layard to Granville, Madrid, June 24, 1872; PRO, FO 115, 536. Austen Henry Layard was a man of high distinction—one of the first great archaeologists, the excavator of Nineveh, a former M.P., and twice Under Secretary for Foreign Affairs.
[14] See *Ibid* for Layard's contempt for Spanish promises.

miral Don José Polo de Bernabe. Fish had been apprehensive when he heard that Lopez Roberts was to go, for they had gotten on well, while the press reported that Polo was hostile to the United States. But a sinister reason for Roberts' recall was soon reported to Fish by the Turkish Minister, Blaque Bey.[15] Roberts' brother was civil governor of the city of Havana, lining his pockets like the rest. It was said that this brother had instigated the arrest of the eight medical students as a blackmailing operation, had demanded $50,000 each from the parents, and on failing to get it, had caused the executions. With this tale circulating behind his back, Lopez Roberts departed in April, 1872. And Fish no sooner welcomed Admiral Polo than he perceived that the change was for the better.[16] Tall, handsome, speaking fluent English, Polo exhibited dignity, cordiality, and understanding. He "seems a frank, true-hearted, and just man," wrote Fish. In the trying months that followed, his honesty, tact, and intelligence smoothed the path of Spanish-American relations.

Early in 1872 it seemed that America also would have to change her Minister. Sickles had offended Don Mateo Sagasta, chief power behind the throne of Amadeus,[17] and Sagasta sent word that he wished him recalled. Polo made the request on April 26, explaining that Sickles had written rash letters, uttered injudicious remarks, and shown too much sympathy with the Spanish republicans; in fact, was an open partisan of Castelar's.[18] A little more, and he would be running for office in Spain! Fish did not need to say that he could believe anything of Sickles. The Minister had just been home on leave to look after Erie Railroad affairs. As head of a powerful group trying to gain control of the line, he had bribed directors behind Jay Gould's back, and forced even that astute manipulator to come to terms with him![19] But while Fish did not defend Sickles, he made it clear that American patience with Spain was exhausted. After recapitulating a long list of grievances, he told Polo that when Sickles left, the United States would probably not trouble to replace him. "Really, it scarcely seems worth while to have a representative at Madrid. If we send another Minister, he will meet the same excuses, delays, and denials, and I see no reason to think that he will accomplish more than Sickles has done."

[15] Diary, May 2, 1872.   [16] Diary, April 4, 1872.
[17] See London Spectator, June 22, 1872, for review of the Serrano-Sagasta régime.
[18] Diary, April 26, 1872.
[19] The Nation, December 12, 1872, describes Sickles' activities in Erie.

And Fish was as good as his word. When Sickles sailed for Spain on April 27, 1872, he was instructed to deliver his letter of recall, and along with it a note informing the Spanish Government that until it was ready to pay greater heed to American pleas and protests, President Grant would not send another Minister to Madrid.[20] This was not intended to rupture our relations with Spain. The capable Alvey A. Adee would remain at the Legation as chargé.[21] But it was a distinct threat that a diplomatic rupture might presently follow.

Fortunately, the stiff Sagasta fell from power before Sickles could follow his instructions. Ruiz Zorrilla became Radical Premier in June, 1872; the Cabinet was reconstructed with a large republican element; and the before-mentioned Sr. Martos, one of these republicans, took charge of foreign affairs. Martos wished Sickles to remain in Madrid; as he ingenuously remarked to Layard, "He and I speak the same language of democracy. We can understand each other." [22] The doughty general plunged deeper than ever into Spanish politics. Representatives of other nations were soon describing his activities in scandalized dispatches. He was hand in glove with republican leaders and agents of the Cuban insurgents; both groups met frequently at his house, consulted him upon their plans, and wrote many of their documents under his supervision. All over Europe, since France had deposed Napoleon III, radical movements showed tremendous vigor. If a republic could be set up in Spain, Sickles intended to be one of its founders.[23]

Fish, who knew nothing of these intrigues, was relieved that Sickles had been permitted to remain. Throughout the spring and summer of 1872 his eyes were fixed chiefly upon Geneva. But whenever he turned them to Madrid, he felt a rising impatience. Talking with Thornton in May, he grumbled that the accumulation of American grievances was becoming "intolerable." [24] Some American estates had now been embargoed for two or three years, the proceeds impounded, and the property itself heavily damaged. Slavery continued to flourish and the treatment of the Chinese coolies amounted to servitude. Spanish prisons were being emptied into Cuba, and many of the worst con-

20 N. Y. *Tribune*, April 27, 1872, stated he would not remain long.
21 Thornton to Granville, May 6, 1872; PRO, FO 5, 1363.
22 Layard to Granville, Madrid, February 16, 1873; PRO, FO 115, 550.
23 See Sickles Papers, Letterbook 2, *passim*.
24 Thornton to Granville, May 6, 1872; PRO, FO 5, 1363.

victs escaping to the United States.[25] "The drift of Mr. Fish's observations," Thornton reported to Lord Granville, "seemed to be that the Spanish Government was utterly powerless to protect American citizens in Cuba, and that the United States would finally have to demand satisfaction of the Volunteers, who appear to be the real masters of the island." Repeatedly the Secretary expostulated with Polo in severe terms.

Even petty cases springing out of the tyranny and disorder in Cuba often gave him enormous trouble. That of Dr. J. E. Houard was typical. A native Philadelphian practising medicine in Havana, he had been jailed in December, 1870, on the unfounded charge of supplying medicines to the insurgents. Two and a half years later the case still dragged its slow length along. Congress had demanded information; Fish had compiled a report embodying fifty-odd notes and other documents; Houard was now imprisoned in Ceuta, Morocco—and yet he was innocent! Because an old box of pills bearing his name had gotten into a rebel camp, Fish had wasted days of toil, our consul in Havana and our Minister in Madrid had spent sleepless nights, and Congress itself had staged a resentful debate.[26] Such Jenkins-ear cases were all too numerous. Moreover, the policing of the Atlantic and Caribbean against filibusters and arrogant Spanish captains was costly. Admiral Polo admitted to Thornton that the United States enforced its neutrality as effectively as could be expected.[27] Fish could boast that since the *Perrit*, no filibustering expedition of a really stoppable kind had gotten to Cuba. But this record was achieved only through constant expense and anxiety, all chargeable to Spain.

Americans in the spring of 1872 read curious items in their newspapers. One described the excitement in Aspinwall as the ship *Virginius* put to sea escorted by the warship *Kansas*, every gun shotted, and followed (at a safe distance) by the Spanish cruiser *Pizarro*. The *Virginius* was accused of filibustering operations, but the navy was not going to see her fired upon so long as she flew the American flag and kept outside Spanish waters. Another item told how the warship *Wyoming* convoyed the *Edgar Stewart* into *Key West*, the Spanish cruiser *Borgia* hovering in the rear.[28] But what if a Spanish cruiser should ar-

---

[25] See pamphlet, *The Cuban Question in the Spanish Parliament* (1872).
[26] House Exec. Doc. 223, 42d Cong., 2d Sess., is devoted to Houard.
[27] Thornton to Granville, August 26, 1872; PRO, FO 5, 1365.
[28] N. Y. *Times, Tribune,* June, 1872; Thornton to Granville, June 17, 1872, PRO, FO 5, 1365.

rest some American vessel on the high seas (as had happened before), and an American warship suddenly arrived upon the scene?

For its part, the Spanish Government continued to lodge protests against filibustering expeditions. On June 9, 1872, for example, the U.S.S. *Moccasin* overhauled the 130-ton vessel *Pioneer* in Narragansett Bay flying the Cuban flag.[29] Bought shortly before by Cuban agents, she carried three cannon, some small arms, and a ton and a half of gunpowder. Polo hurried to Glenclyffe to urge that the government take rigorous steps. The ship was simply a pirate, he declared. Fish assured him that the neutrality laws would be enforced; but he pointed out that there had been no act of piracy, and that it would be unwise to prosecute men who were merely sailing under an unrecognized flag for that crime. Polo reluctantly agreed.[30]

A little later, Fish had an interview with an officer who sent in a card engraved "Captain Norton: The Cuban Navy." The Secretary declined to receive him except as a private gentleman. Norton entered an eloquent plea for his little ship *Pioneer*. "Several of the South American republics have recognized Cuba as an independent Power," he argued. "This recognition must be admitted by other Powers, and gives Cuba the right to carry her flag on the high seas. The *Pioneer* goes out in the same way that the United States sent out Paul Jones in the Revolution, when the United States was recognized by France but not by the Powers in general." Fish replied that the issue might have to go to the courts; meanwhile, the government intended to fulfill its obligations to other nations. The *Pioneer* never put to sea again under the Cuban flag. Thornton wrote Granville this summer that the circumspection of the Grant Administration in enforcing neutrality was not unconnected with the great adjudication at Geneva. But there is no evidence whatever for this view; it was part of Fish's consistent policy

II

Fish was soon deeply disappointed in the Radical Ministry headed by Sr. Zorrilla. It had come into power with a great blare of reform trumpets; but before the end of the first month the Prime Minister affirmed, like his predecessors, that he would grant Cuba no concessions whatever until the rebels had laid down their arms. This announcement

[29] *Ibid.*   [30] Diary.

was echoed by Sr. Martos. On a hot midsummer day, August 22, Thornton drove up the hill at Garrison with the latest news from London. The Spanish Minister there had told Granville that Spain was anxious to liberate the Cuban and Puerto Rican slaves, but could not do so while the insurrection raged, and that it raged because fanned by American sympathy. Such impudence was too much for Fish. He treated Thornton to an outburst: [31]

I say that I think this government has done all that a government can be called upon to do in such circumstances; that for nearly four years we have abstained from recognizing belligerency; we have exerted the inherent power of a government to arrest expeditions and seize vessels, have broken up the Junta, and done all that a government can be called upon to do; that the continuance of the insurrection is a great cause of disturbance to the country; that Spain has not exercised proper energy to repress it; that it could have been repressed long since, but that her officers in Cuba have found its continuance pecuniarily profitable. He assents to what I say. . . . I state that . . . unless Spain is more successful in subduing this insurrection than she has been, or shows more capability to do so, I cannot say that we may not be obliged to adopt a different line of policy. '

Fish had instructed Sickles to continue to demand the abolition of slavery and other reforms.[32] The general was ably seconded by Republican Deputies and Senators who maintained a continuous fire upon the conservatives. They showed that army officers had embezzled large sums in Cuba. They denounced the murders by the "slaver Volunteers." They asked how long the Cabinet would protect a system of servitude which disgraced the nation. "Let me remind you," cried Eduardo Benot in the Senate on October 18, "that when Spain was the most powerful nation of the earth and the sun never set on its dominions, we lost Flanders through the Duke of Alva's cruelty. How then shall we hope to hold Cuba by fire and sword, and not by right and justice?" [33] When the Cabinet again stated that reform was impossible until the revolt ended, Sickles denounced this "declaration of a war of extermination." He told Spaniards that they must not be surprised to see the American Government revise its Cuban policy sharply.

It is little wonder that on October 24, 1872, Fish warned Polo that the situation was becoming unendurable.[34] "I tell him that, not speak-

[31] Diary, August 22, 1872.
[32] State Department MSS, Diplomatic Drafts, Spain, 1872.
[33] Cortes Proceedings.   [34] Diary, October 24, 1872.

ing officially, I think the continuance of the contest in Cuba without apparent possibility of success on either side is producing a state of things which will justify, if not require, a recognition of belligerency. That four years of contest without any advantage of arms by Spain over the insurgents exhibits a condition under which no complaint can be made if other Powers recognize it as war." Polo anxiously protested. He declared that Cuban independence would result in a bloody war between blacks and whites. He added that the new Zorrilla Government was the most liberal Spain had ever had; that it was sincere in endeavoring to ameliorate the condition of Cuba; and that rigorous American steps would probably cause its overthrow, and bring in a reactionary régime. All this had force, but Fish again expressed his irritation:

I remind him of our patience and endurance; of the disappointment we have met with; the promises Spain has made of granting more liberal government, of emancipation; of relieving embargoed estates, etc.; that nothing is done; the emancipation decree is made null by the regulations for its enforcement; estates are still held and in some instances where we have been promised that they should be released, it is now alleged that these cases are to be recommitted for consideration by the Junta to be convened in Havana; that we cannot submit to this; it would be a violation of faith, and an indignity to this government; that all these things look like procrastination, and we meet with no results. He urges me to write to Sickles, who he says is on the best of terms with Martos, and that Sickles will support what he will urge in favor of action and the settlement of questions.

On October 29, with Congress five weeks away, Fish sent Sickles the instruction soon to become famous as "No. 270." [35] This was decidedly the most menacing document which had come from the State Department during the Grant Administration. Listing at length all the American grievances, he spoke in sharp terms of the "grasping cupidity" of Cuban planters and expatiated upon the non-enforcement of the feeble emancipation law:

The United States have emancipated all the slaves in their own territory, as the result of a civil war of four years attended by a vast effusion of blood and expenditure of treasure. The slaves in the Spanish possessions near us are of the same race as those who were bondsmen here. It is natural and inevitable for the latter to sympathize in the oppression of their brethren, and espe-

[35] State Department MSS, Diplomatic Drafts, Spain, 1872.

cially in the waste of life occasioned by inhuman punishment and excessive toil. Nor is this sympathy confined to those who were recently in bondage among us—it is universal as it is natural and just—it rests upon the instincts of humanity and is the recognition of those rights of man which are now universally admitted. Governments cannot resist a conviction so general and so righteous as that which condemns as a crime the tolerance of human slavery. . . .

He also argued that another view might be taken of the subject. Great vested interests had for nearly two and a half years defeated one of the most important laws ever enacted by Spain. These interests were the most defiant of all in insisting upon continued Spanish domin- ion over Cuba.[36] "The example of disregard to laws thus set cannot be without its influence. If Spain permits her authority to be virtually and practically defied in that island . . . is not this tantamount to an acknowledgment of her inability to control?" He protested against Zorrilla's recent statement that pacification must precede reform as illogical, inexpedient, and indefensible; and he closed upon a threaten- ing note:

It is hoped that you will present the views above set forth . . . in a way which, without giving offence, will leave a conviction that we are in earnest . . . and that we expect redress, and that if it should not soon be afforded, Spain must not be surprised to find, as the inevitable result of the delay, a marked change in the feeling and in the temper of the people and of the gov- ernment of the United States.

Even before Sickles received No. 270, Zorrilla and Martos had of- fered a few concessions.[37] On October 20 they asked him to ascertain whether President Grant would be willing to mediate for peace in Cuba on the basis of a municipal franchise for all freemen, provincial auton- omy, and a gradual abolition of slavery. Two days later Martos added a written memorandum of a programme which the Cabinet had decided upon for Puerto Rico. It embraced four points: (1) Civil authority to supersede the military; (2) The towns to elect their own municipal governments; (3) A provincial assembly for the island; (4) Abolition of slavery. The first three reforms were to be decreed as soon as the Cortes acted, but the Cabinet was undecided whether abolition should be immediate or progressive. Sickles hastened to send this encouraging

[36] Cf. London *Spectator*, June 29, 1872, for Zorrilla's difficulties.
[37] On the Spanish background, see Hannay, *Castelar*, Ch. VI.

news to Fish, Sumner, and sundry lesser friends [38]—for he was never cursed with secretiveness. When the proposal was discussed in the Cabinet on November 12, 1872, Grant expressed impulsive willingness to extend his good offices. But Fish stopped him. He reminded the President of Paul Forbes' fiasco three years earlier. "Do we have better ground now for asking the Cubans to ground arms?" he asked. He pointed out that if Madrid were in earnest, it should be definite about the intended reforms and proffer a formal request for Grant's services. "I suggest," he said, "that we send Sickles instructions giving Spain a clear choice. Either she can apply formally for your good offices, and indicate specific reforms which meet your approval; or she can reconcile herself to our announcement that we see no reason for continuing an envoy who is unable to persuade her to redeem her promises, and that Sickles' recall will probably be deemed advisable." [39] The upshot was that Grant decided to have nothing to do with the proposal.

Nor did Martos follow up his trial-balloon. Other Cabinet members opposed any move, and American mediation would have wrecked the Ministry. His inquiry had just one result. Combined with Sickles' friendship for him, with Layard's warning to Sickles that tact would gain more than threats, and with Sickles' participation in the advancing republican movement, it brought about a partial suppression of No. 270. Sickles did not read that stern document to Martos. "I communicated the purport of it to him verbally only and in conversation," he later wrote Fish, "confining myself mainly to the grievances and touching very lightly on the admonitions." This was wise. All Spain was soon engaged in a fiery discussion of the proposed reforms in Puerto Rico. The conservatives hurriedly organized a league to maintain the status quo. The Spanish Colonial Clubs in Madrid, Cadiz, Seville, Barcelona, Valencia, and other cities—really branches, Sickles wrote, of the Casino Espagnol in Havana—rallied behind it.[40] They drew Serrano, Sagasta, and other leaders to their aid. They bought up every purchasable editor. They fomented a riot in Madrid in which ragged hirelings were bloodily dispersed by the military.[41] No. 270 would have played into the hands of these reactionaries.

[38] Sickles to Sumner, October 21, 1872; Sickles Papers, Letterbook 2.
[39] Diary, November 12, 1872.
[40] See *Cuban Question in the Spanish Parliament*, 31, 32, for the progress of manumission in Puerto Rico.
[41] Sickles to Cooper, December 17, 1872; Sickles Papers.

III

When Fish found that No. 270 had accomplished nothing, he was brought to the question of his next step. He must do something; but what? The more he considered his initial suggestion of recalling Sickles, the less he liked it. If he did this just before Congress met, the interventionists would make excited use of it. Colonel Ryan had been in Washington talking noisily of Cuban wrongs. The New York *Herald* had succeeded in getting a correspondent named Henderson arrested in Havana. Banks, Butler, and the rest were ready to make the welkin ring on ten minutes' notice.[42] The Secretary's object was to bring Spain to terms, not to bring the United States to a declaration of war. But how?

By prolonged study, and with the aid of some suggestions from Consul Hall in Matanzas, Fish hit upon what seemed a solution of the problem. His plan was to ask Congress for high discriminatory duties upon goods from all slaveholding countries—Cuba, Puerto Rico, and Brazil being the chief. This would satisfy the Congressional friends of Cuba without encouraging jingoism. It would healthfully jar the Zorrilla Ministry. Above all, it would strike the pocket nerve of the Casino Espagnol patriots in Cuba an excruciating blow. For years the United States had bought fully three-fourths of the Cuban sugar-production. It consistently paid high rates. Indeed, sugar-cultivation had never been more profitable than in 1872; prices in Havana throughout the autumn were fully thirty per cent above those of 1869–70. On these profits slavery and the clandestine slave-trade flourished.[43] It was the sugar-planters, sugar-factors, and dealers in sugar-hands who were obstructing reform and peace in Cuba. A few Americans, even, owned plantations and slaves in Cuba.[44] As Boutwell informed the Secretary, discriminatory duties would cost something; they would be paid in part by American consumers and in part by Cuban growers. But it would be worth the sacrifice to throw the greedy slave-drivers into bankruptcy. On November 19 Fish brought the proposal before the Cabinet. Presi-

[42] Fish was told of plots to create excitement in Congress; some Americans had agreed to go to Cuba and get themselves arrested. Fish to H. C. Hall, October 25, 1872; Letter-books.

[43] H. C. Hall, Confidential Report, April 18, 1872; Fish Papers. Epidemics in western Cuba drove up the price of slaves. Thomas Biddle had reported December 21, 1870, that adults fetched $400–$600 in Havana, and they soon advanced.

[44] Action against them had been proposed in Grant's annual message, 1871.

dent Grant at first demurred. But as the Secretary persisted he gave way, and prepared to incorporate the recommendation in his annual message to Congress.[45]

Senators and Representatives were again crowding into Washington, and leading men were confidentially informed of the tariff plan. They expressed approval. On November 21 the Secretary talked to Admiral Polo with significant asperity. The latter had brought a letter from Captain-General Concha, asserting that the Moret Law was at last in operation and that all slaves who had reached sixty years were free. Fish scornfully replied that the law was dismally ineffectual; that all regulations for its enforcement had been drafted in the interest of the slaveholders; and that the rules for recontracting Chinese coolies meant their complete enslavement.[46] Obviously the sands were running out. Grant's message was to go to Congress at noon on December 2 with a forcible recommendation for discriminatory duties. Both houses would act without delay.

Admiral Polo unquestionably heard the current intimations that a blow at the great Cuban sugar interests was coming. In frantic communication with Madrid, he obtained an answer in the nick of time. The chill dawn of December 2 had hardly lighted I Street when his carriage whirled to a stop before Fish's door.[47] The Secretary rose hastily from the breakfast table to greet him. Polo held a dispatch which had come during the night. The Spanish Ministry had at last made up its mind.[48] Without waiting for legislation by the Cortes, but acting by executive decree, it would forthwith separate the civil and military power in Puerto Rico, extend the provincial laws of Spain to the island, and erect municipal governments there. It would also introduce a bill into the Cortes for abolishing slavery in Puerto Rico; a majority of the Cabinet being for immediate emancipation, a minority for gradual steps. This bill would be sent in as soon as a pending loan had been floated, and a new conscription of troops completed—that is, Polo hoped, soon after December 15. "My dispatch adds," the Admiral said, "that these concessions to Puerto Rico are evidence of what Spain is willing to concede to Cuba." He begged that the President's message

[45] Diary, November 18, 1872.   [46] Diary, November 21, 1872.
[47] Diary, December 2, 1872.
[48] On November 21 Fish lectured Polo severely; on November 22, Martos handed Sickles the plan of Puerto Rican reforms. Sickles to Cooper, November 23, 1872; Sickles Papers.

might contain nothing to create an impression that these steps had been produced by American threats.

Fish was pleased. He had received similar information from Sickles the previous day. Moreover, he had been softened by some recent cordial words of Martos for the United States, and by Sickles' faith in the Spanish promises of reform. "Nothing will appear in the message that can be construed as a threat," he told Polo. Speaking confidentially, he added that in view of this new information, some passages prepared for the message "will have been modified." He spoke of the plan for a discriminating tariff. "This will now be suspended," he announced. "It will be held for further consideration awaiting the action of the Spanish Government." Grant's message, spread in the afternoon press, contained nothing of note on Cuba save some approving words upon the new regulations to enforce the Moret Law, and a hope that Spain would "voluntarily grant additional measures of reform." [49]

The Radical Ministry in Madrid lost no time in translating its words into deeds. Executive decrees upon Puerto Rico were issued at once. On December 21 a bill for the *immediate* emancipation of the 50,000 slaves was introduced in the Chamber. It provided for indemnifying the holders; the amount, estimated at $8,000,000, to be raised by a loan secured on the revenues of the island, and guaranteed by the Spanish Government. As Puerto Rico had about 600,000 people, predominantly white, and was peaceful, rich, and almost debt-free, the loan offered little difficulty. Sickles, with a keen eye to business, hurriedly wrote a financial friend: "The security is perfect. . . . Britain offers to take the issue at 80 (Anglo-Spanish Bank). What will you offer?" [50] Before Christmas both houses in Madrid voted for emancipation "in principle" by large majorities; 60 to 6 in the Senate, 214 to 12 in the Chamber. In March the emancipation law passed, and the fetters fell forever from the limbs of the Puerto Rican blacks. [51]

But the lash and the slave-pen still existed for half a million Cuban Negroes. [52] We have seen that Fish had already urged that emancipation be applied to the "loyal" part of Cuba. Polo talked with the Secretary on December 6. "He suggests," states the diary, "that the re-

[49] Richardson, *Messages and Papers*, VII, 189 ff.
[50] Sickles to De Laski, December 21, 1872; Sickles Papers.
[51] The slaves were free four months after the bill became law.
[52] According to the Spanish Abolition Society, "the insurrection in Cuba has produced the dispersion or death of two thirds of the slaves of the Central and Eastern Departments of the island, who in 1862 amounted to nearly 180,000 persons."

forms promised might be introduced into that part of the island where there are no insurgents. I had once before thrown out this idea, but he had not apparently noticed it, and I desired to let it not appear as my proposal." At once Fish urged a logical further step. Spain had built a *trocha* of forts and entrenchments to cut off the eastern end of the island; let her now extend the Puerto Rican reforms to the broad regions lying west of this line. This would remove the temptation to slaves to engage in the revolt, and make it unprofitable for slaveholders to prolong it. On January 2, 1873, Fish asked Thornton to have Great Britain exert her influence in Madrid for this measure; and he tried to enlist Italian influence with King Amadeus.[53] But all this effort came to precisely nothing. The Spanish Ministry might carry reforms in little Puerto Rico; it could not carry them in Cuba.

IV

Thus the familiar *impasse* reasserted itself, with more irritating accompaniments than ever. Not only were American-owned estates still embargoed; the authorities were actually about to lease some of them and impound the proceeds. American shipping interests were in arms against outrageous exactions by Cuban port authorities. All fall the *Herald, Tribune,* and *Sun* had grumbled over the inaction of the State Department; Thornton wrote home that a concerted campaign was under way to prevent Grant from retaining Fish in the Second Administration. On December 23 Fish told Polo [54] that unless American rights in Cuba were better respected, "it will be impossible to keep the matter out of Congress, and probably impossible to abstain from executive action." The Colombian Government was addressing circulars to all the republics of Latin-America, proposing union under the leadership of the United States to urge measures leading to Cuban emancipation and independence. This got into the newspapers. Senator Frank P. Blair had already introduced a troublesome resolution in the Senate, and Chairman Banks was soon to bring one forward in the House.

To protect himself, on January 9, 1873, Fish made public his recent correspondence with Sickles, including No. 270.[55] This threatening note produced a deep impression. "One of the most unrelentingly truthful and candid documents recorded in diplomatic annals," said the

[53] Diary, January 2, 1873.　　　　[54] Diary, December 18, 23, 1872.
[55] See N. Y. *Tribune* for hostile, *World* for friendly treatment, January 10–14, 1873.

Tribune, praising "the blade of fact very scantily wreathed in garments of courtesy." Editors agreed that Fish had delivered a terrible arraignment and challenge. If severe notes could produce any effect, his pen had served the nation well. Polo, grieved and apprehensive, received a frank explanation from Fish. I say, writes the Secretary,[56] "that the publication of the letters which were sent in with the message was necessary to satisfy Congress that the Administration had the matter in hand; that the danger had been and is of the question becoming one of Congressional debate, which would give occasion for the utterance of many harsh things and would agitate the public mind; that the publication had thus far had the effect of preventing any debate in Congress; that the effort of the opposition press (the *Tribune, Herald,* etc.) was to agitate the question; that any contradiction of what they have uttered would lead to further assertions. . . ." Again he had acted shrewdly.

But upon liberal circles in Spain the publication of No. 270 fell like a bombshell. It exposed the Zorrilla Ministry, the best since the revolution, to a terrific new storm. For months it had been assailed by a furious coalition of reactionaries. Now Fish, however unwillingly, had supplied them with fresh weapons. They could assert that the reforms they fought had been dictated in Washington, in such language as no Spanish Government had ever before tolerated. Zorrilla had protested on December 30 that foreign intervention could never be suffered in the affairs of the colonies. Striving to save himself, he now denied that he had ever received any such humiliating representations as those contained in the note of October 29.[57] Martos echoed his denials. As Sickles hastily explained to Fish, these statements were half-true; not until recently had he shown the full text of No. 270 to Martos.[58] But such disclaimers did the Zorrilla Ministry little good in Spain, and increased the hostility in America. At Fish's earnest request, Admiral Polo telegraphed Madrid asking it to avoid any more denials or controversial statements whatever.[59]

By February 1, 1873, the situation presented the unhappiest mess imaginable. Neither Spain nor Cuba had a government which could be held fully responsible, or counted upon to maintain any policy a month in advance. In both lands revolution was seething. In both, resent-

[56] Diary.
[58] Sickles to Fish, January 22, 1873; Sickles Papers.
[57] *Nation,* January 16, 1873.
[59] Diary, January 23, 1873.

ment against the United States had reached a fiery pitch. American feeling, indignant and disillusioned, was fast hardening into a determination to intervene, liberate Cuba, and restore peace. Grant was expected to take a firm stand in his inaugural address of March 4. Sickles, indeed, served notice upon Madrid that he would do so. As February opened Polo was alarmed to hear that the Cuban agent Macias was in Washington buttonholing members. On the 3rd he hurried to Fish's house before breakfast. He reported that a surprise move was under way—Macias was boasting that before night one of the houses of Congress would pass a resolution recognizing either the belligerency or independence of Cuba. Fish dismissed him impatiently. Nevertheless, he called his carriage, picked up Bancroft Davis, and hurried to the White House. Grant, who intended going to the Capitol that day, assured him that he would ask influential members to block any sudden move.[60] That afternoon Banks reported a resolution asking the President to sound European governments upon joint measures to protect non-combatants in Cuba, enforce the rules of civilized warfare, hasten emancipation, and bring about peace. The House quietly referred it to the Foreign Affairs Committee. But the episode had been ominous.

v

Yet Providence was always with Fish in preventing a Spanish war. At this critical moment occurred an event which instantly revolutionized American feeling toward Spain—the erection of a republic. For months Amadeus' reign had been visibly closing. This able, conscientious son of Victor Emmanuel II held an impossible position. What Spain temporarily needed was an iron dictatorship, not the constitutional rule of a well-meaning foreigner. A quarrel of the Zorrilla Ministry with the officers of artillery, the most powerful caste in the army, gave the signal for the overturn. Early in February Polo was manifestly plunged in gloom. He shook his head sadly, and spoke to Fish of a coming "catastrophe" at home. February 13 brought definite news. That night a reception was held at the White House. Amid music, flowers, and brilliant lights, Polo pushed his way between uniformed men and beautifully-gowned women, bowed to Fish, and handed him a telegram. In Madrid all was over. Amadeus had resigned the crown and fled to Portugal; the two chambers had constituted themselves a

[60] Diary, February 3, 1873.

National Assembly; and by an overwhelming vote it had proclaimed a republic.[61]

Though Fish did not know it, Sickles had played a leading rôle in the revolution. He had incessantly advised the republican leaders. Taking a hand in the artillery question, he had urged his friends in the Cabinet to maintain their defiance of this aristocratic corps. He was also privy to the premature attempt to resolve the Cortes into a National Convention on January 31, and to the vote in the Cortes on February 9 which led to Amadeus' abdication. On learning of this vote he ostentatiously drove to congratulate the President of the Council. Layard wrote in shocked terms to Lord Granville: [62] "He was, no doubt, already acquainted with the plot that had been prepared, and was so sure of its successful result that he could not abstain from showing his hostility to the King and the monarchy by abstaining on a frivolous excuse from taking part with his colleagues in the ceremony of the baptism of the infant prince and at the royal banquet. It is unnecessary for me to mention other instances of his studied disrespect for the King."

Warned by Sickles that the overturn was imminent, Fish had cabled him to recognize the republican Government whenever it was "fully established and in possession of the power of the nation." [63] The wires soon hummed with the unprecedented honors paid Sickles. On February 15 he let it be known that he would visit the "President of the Executive Power," Sr. Figueras, to announce American recognition. Madrid was all pomp and jubilee. Officials of the republic hurried off with carriages to bring Sickles. A regiment drawn up before the Presidency presented arms. Bands played the Star-Spangled Banner and the Marseillaise. Officers resplendent in gold lace awaited Sickles at the foot of the staircase. The President, surrounded by Cabinet members, greeted him at the top. Sickles and Figueras exchanged declamations upon liberty, democracy, fraternity, the new era, and the bonds of union between their sister republics. According to the Spanish press (though no such statement appears in his published address), Sickles declared: "From this day the filibustering policy has ended in America, and the United States have determined to coöperate as far as it depends upon them in bringing the insurrection in Cuba to an end." He then

[61] Diary, February 13, 1873.
[62] Layard to Granville, February 16, 1873; PRO, FO 115, 550.
[63] State Department MSS, Diplomatic Drafts, Spain, 1873.

paid an equally ceremonious call upon Martos, now president of the National Assembly.[64]

Later that day the National Assembly heard with excitement the news of American recognition. The speeches by Sickles and Figueras were read amid salvos of applause. Martos and Castelar delivered congratulatory orations. The former declared that he and Sickles had talked confidentially upon Cuba. "And without any indiscretion I can say that, now more than ever, we may consider as dissipated those shadows, those apprehensions that patriots may have felt as to the integrity of our territory; which if always protected by the valor and resolution of Spain, is now safer than ever by reason of the new-born affection of a nation which until today might have formed views hostile to our sovereignty." If Sickles authorized any such statement, he had taken a good deal upon himself. Fish had instructed him on the 13th: "You will not fail to urge upon a government already committed to the principles and the expediency of emancipation and of political reforms the immediate enforcement of practical and efficient reforms and the abolition of slavery in the colonies. The present seems to be the moment when the government can accomplish great results. Endeavor to have the decrees self-acting and not dependent upon further regulations. . . ." [65] But Sickles was always ready to take a great deal upon himself!

To most Americans "republic" was a word more blest than Mesopotamia. Well-informed European observers felt certain that the new government would prove feeble. Castelar was a rhetorical idealist; he and half of the Cortes believed that the mere Hugoesque declamation of such words as "republicanism," "brotherhood," and "justice" would usher in a golden age. Actually Spain faced some of her most tragic years. Until the first days of 1874, when Castelar went back to his modest bachelor flat and his lectures as professor of history in the University of Madrid, the republic waged a desperate war against disintegrating elements—Bourbons, Carlists, adherents of a military dictatorship under Serrano, and others.[66] Anarchy overspread much of the peninsula; the credit of Spain sank lower than that of any other great nation. In Cuba, left largely to itself, the reactionary forces became stronger than ever. But a host of Americans were loath to think

[64] Layard to Granville, *ut supra*, with enclosures.
[65] State Department MSS, Diplomatic Drafts, Spain, 1873.
[66] See the excellent pages in Hannay, *Castelar*, Ch. VI.

that a republic would not solve all of Spain's problems.

Congress hastened on March 1–2 to pass resolutions congratulating the Spanish people. The press teemed with cordial articles. President Grant, to Polo's gratification, made no reference to Cuba in his inaugural address of March 4, 1873. Sickles in a moment of exuberance had suggested to Fish that the United States might now guarantee to Spain the cost of emancipating the Cuban slaves,[67] and the Cabinet of course scoffed at the idea.[68] Nevertheless, the Cabinet discussions were exceedingly friendly to Madrid. The measure of this friendliness is afforded by one striking incident. Certain European Powers were distinctly hostile to the new Spanish republic. In March, Sickles reported that Castelar had spoken to him of a possible revolution in Lisbon, and had expressed fear that if it broke out Great Britain, long Portugal's protector, would intervene in Peninsular affairs. What course would the United States take if Europe tried to crush the Spanish and Portuguese republics? Grant seemed to think that the United States might well object. He told the Cabinet that considering the importance of Spain's possessions in the New World, and the interest of the United States in seeing Cuba and Puerto Rico under republican government, he might deem it his duty to protest against any attempt to deprive these islands of political institutions which harmonized with those of American nations.[69]

Even the ever-cautious Fish was pleased by the first fruits of the new régime. Castelar gave Sickles assurances of prompt action upon all issues between the two nations. An early decree liberated about ten thousand Cuban Negroes illegally held in slavery—"emancipadoes" brought from Africa in violation of the law. All this bore a hopeful look.[70] When the Colombian Minister called to present again his scheme for a grand Pan-American combination to bring pressure upon Spain, Fish rebuked him. "I replied," he writes in his diary, "that some of the most earnest and intelligent republicans of the present age had inaugurated the revolution in Spain, and were now endeavoring to establish permanently a republican government; that . . . the future of a republican government in Spain and its dependencies was hang-

[67] Sickles to Fish, January 22, 1873; Fish Papers.   [68] Diary, February 14, 1873.
[69] Sickles to Fish, March 17, 1873; Fish Papers.
[70] Sickles' dispatch No. 387, February 12, 1873, describes the Spanish anxiety for American support; No. 390, February 15, describes his official reception. *Foreign Affairs*, 1873, II, 889–891.

ing upon this issue, involving not only the question of a republic for 1,500,000 in Cuba, but for 14,000,000 in Spain. It behooves those who were considering this question to think of the effect of pressing Spain in her present emergency with questions such as he contemplated."

But from the forgotten Cuban insurgents came a cry of anguish. Deep in the mountainous jungles of Oriente, poor Cespedes learned that the American Government was striking hands with the new leaders in Madrid. Pacing the hut that represented Cuba's capital, he dictated an eloquent letter to Grant which—dated March 22, 1873, in the District of Bayamo—is still in Fish's papers. Once more he pleaded for intervention. He declared that the new régime in Madrid was as intent as the old upon exterminating the Cuban patriots and riveting its fetters upon the slaves of the Antilles. "In the name of humanity, of respect for republican principles, of civilization," he adjured the United States to halt the war still raging in Cuba.

VI

The short special session which followed Grant's second inauguration ended. A quiet spring descended upon Washington. The opposition press, forgetting foreign affairs, centred its attention upon corruption and the Southern question. Looking back upon his four and a half years of struggle with the Cuban problem, Fish could but marvel at the way in which fortune—aided by his own resourcefulness—had repeatedly averted imminent war. In the autumn of 1869 the sudden preoccupation of Grant with the Dominican situation and the death of Rawlins had saved the situation. In the early summer of 1870 it had been saved by the special message to Congress which he had forced upon Grant. Now in the spring of 1873 an equally dangerous crisis had been dispelled by the sudden creation of a republic in Spain. The lessening of tension came none too soon; for within six months the *Virginius* affair was to bring Americans to such a pitch of righteous anger as they had not felt since the bombardment of Fort Sumter.

THE representative of a sterner, simpler American age, Hamilton Fish at times took a just pride in his old-fashioned conceptions of integrity and morality. "No, I did not receive any Credit Mobilier," he wrote John C. Hamilton on January 28, 1873. "So much for what some people regard as . . . being an old fogey, which, with many, in these days of bargaining and of the domination of the Almighty Dollar, signifies the retention of some old-fashioned notions of common honesty. But what a development is being made! Sad! sad! sad!"

During his first four years in office, Fish had been incessantly harried by foreign problems. During his last four years, he had wider opportunity to observe events in Washington, and to concern himself with other departments of the Administration. In foreign relations he was destined to perform one more great service: to save the United States from war with Spain when at last American blood was shed with unforgivable barbarity. But his principal interests and activities now swung slowly from external to domestic affairs. His diary and letters show him a more and more anxious observer; they reveal him as trying more and more earnestly to save Grant from his worst impulses and advisers. His official career may roughly be divided into three parts: One year in which he wrested full control of the State Department from Grant; four years in which he used that control to preserve peace with Great Britain and Spain, and to accomplish other important tasks; and three years in which he reached out for a larger measure of authority in an Administration that was increasingly disgraced and demoralized. As he comprehended the forces that surrounded Grant, all thought of resignation vanished from his mind.

The festering corruptions of the post-war period sprang up in every part of America and in almost every department of national life. Other loose and scandalous times—in Buchanan's day, in Hanna's, in Harding's—have been repellent enough; but the Grant era stands unique in the comprehensiveness of its rascality. The cities, half of which had their counterparts of Tweed; the legislatures, with their rings, lobbyists, and bribe-takers; the South, prey of unscrupulous Carpetbaggers and Scalawags; the West, sacked by railway and mining corporations;

Congress, with its Credit Mobilier, its salary-grab, its tools of predatory business; the executive departments, honeycombed with thievery; private finance and trade, with greedy figures like Jay Cooke and Collis P. Huntington honored and typical—everywhere the scene was the same. Why? Beyond doubt the reasons for this pervasive malady were numerous, deep-rooted, and complex, and we can list but a few. The war explained much: its terrible strain upon all ten commandments; the moral exhaustion which it produced; the waste and jobbery which it bred; its creation of vast new Federal responsibilities. Washington became an irresistible lodestone for crooked men. The fecund war contracts, the tariffs, subsidies, and bounties, the huge appropriations for speculators and claim-agents, the opportunities for theft in both collecting and spending the swollen Federal revenues, drew them as honey draws flies.[1] Moreover, the sixties were the decade of the most violent turmoil in American history. The South was ruined, and the fine principles and traditions of its aristocracy were engulfed. The industrial revolution in the North brought the roughest, most aggressive business elements to the front. As the West was settled with amazing rapidity, a more extensive and influential frontier than ever before gave manners a cruder cast. Cities were filling up with immigrant communities, subservient to machine politicians. Everywhere tested standards, restraints of public opinion, the cake of custom, were broken down.[2] Conditions of the day produced a new and flashier political leadership. They brought demagogues and pushing brigadiers into office; generals like Ben Butler and "Black Jack" Logan, vote-getters like Oliver P. Morton and Zach Chandler, speculators like Oakes Ames.[3] The contrast between such men and the austere, scholarly, conscientious Hamilton Fish was the contrast between two eras of national life.

But one fact must be emphasized. Contemporaneous with this corruption, geared to it as a motor is geared to the conglomerate machinery of a factory, was the tremendous industrial boom which followed the war. For eight years Northern business rollicked amid a flush prosperity. With money easy, with fortunes rising on every hand, with the temptation to speculate irresistible, the whole tendency of American life conduced to greed. We may say of the United States after the upheaval of civil war what John Addington Symonds says of Renaissance

[1] Allan Nevins, *The Emergence of Modern America*, Chs. 1–6.
[2] Schouler, VII, 209 ff.
[3] "The moral law had expired—like the Constitution;" *Education of Henry Adams*, 280.

Italy: "Vehement contention in the sphere of politics, restless speculation, together with the loosening of every tie that bound society together, emancipated personality and substituted the freedom of self-
centred vigor and virility for the prescriptions of civil or religious
order." But the boom gave this age of license its special money-getting
tendency. The panic of 1873 fell as a chilling blight on corruption as
on business. The worst scandals were not exposed until after this date.
But almost all of them took root in the flush years of business expansion.[4]

This connection between the riotous boom, 1868–73, and the mani-
fold corruption is easily demonstrated. The "Erie War" of Gould and
Fisk against Vanderbilt was fought out in 1867–68. Oakes Ames began
his Credit Mobilier bribery in the first weeks of 1868. In 1869 the
Tweed Ring thefts became most brazen and unrestrained. In the spring
of 1868 Speaker Blaine made his famous ruling in favor of the Little
Rock & Fort Smith Railroad, and that summer asked his first favors of
two Little Rock officers. During 1870 the Whiskey Ring took definite
form in St. Louis. In the fall of 1870 Secretary Belknap's wife accepted
the first corrupt payments in connection with an Indian post-tradership.
In 1870 also the Freedman's Bank charter in Washington was amended
by Congress, and the theft of its assets began. The year 1871–72 witnessed the Leet & Stocking exactions in New York, and toward the
close of 1872 Minister Schenck was drawn into the toils of the Emma
Mine promoters. The summer of 1872 produced that ludicrous knav-
ery, the Southwestern diamond-field swindle which Clarence King so
neatly exposed.[5] The looting of Eastern savings banks and insurance
companies was then almost completed. In brief, the years 1868–73
were the years in which corruption kept pace with the upward curve
of the business cycle; in which the lax morals of the financial world
were transferred to the political world. After the panic of 1873, virtue
reasserted itself in the chilly air of the depression. It is an illusion to
think of 1875–76 as the scandalous years. They were merely the years
in which the great scandals of the earlier period were dragged to
light.

The word epidemic, applied to this frolic of corruption, is singularly

[4] Oberholtzer, *United States*, Vol. I, gives the fullest account of this boom.
[5] For this swindle, see John Hays Hammond, *Autobiography*, I, 170.

accurate. As Fish's just-quoted words imply, a contagion filled the air. "The continent spills riches for everybody; everybody is grabbing his share; I must get mine"—so men argued. Why be over-scrupulous in making money when it was so plentiful? Why should politics be more honest than business, or business than politics, or Tom than Dick and Harry? Everybody was prosperous (poor farmers and laborers did not count); everybody was easy-going; everybody agreed that it was a duty to "develop the country." The nation as a whole was to blame, not merely the Grant Administration; and the nation was behaving just as in other boom periods—before 1837, 1907, 1929—and as it will behave again.[6] Through it all, it had a few such Roman figures as Hamilton Fish to remind it of a more disciplined past; but they were ignored.

President Grant is chargeable with a heavy responsibility for some scandals of the day; just how heavy Fish soon saw, and subsequent pages based upon his diary and letters will show. Honest as to money himself, he was the source of more dishonesty than any other American President. His responsiveness to such great moneyed interests as Jay Cooke represented was a national calamity.[7] But when we look at the scandals, his responsibility was for the most part general, not specific; indirect, not direct. At some points he cannot be defended. The rôle he played in crippling both the Whiskey Ring prosecutions and the impeachment of Belknap offers the darkest single page in the history of the Presidency. For this and for his arbitrary acts in the South, he was far more worthy of impeachment than Andrew Johnson. But with most scandals of the time he obviously had nothing to do. The Credit Mobilier affair can as little be laid at his door as the Tweed Ring thefts. Unfortunate as his selection of Belknap as Secretary of War proved, it had been recommended by General Sherman and praised by Middle Western Senators. His chief errors were of omission, not commission; he was more blameworthy for the general laxity, the want of vigilance and high purpose, which characterized his Administration, than for wrongful acts. The American people always derives much of its tone from its President. It is strenuous under a Theodore Roosevelt, idealistic under a Wilson, slothful under a Coolidge. Lowell was correct in these

[6] A neglected novel published soon afterward, *The Money-Makers*, (an answer to John Hay's *The Bread-Winners*), offers a vivid picture of this competition in laxity.

[7] V. L. Parrington, *Main Currents in American Thought*, III, 27 ff.

years in writing, "A strong nation begets strong citizens, and a weak one weak." [8] Fish perceived clearly enough that Grant's casual way of performing his duties; his easy acceptance of vicious personal influences; his negligence and favoritism in appointments; his careless inconsequentiality in handling Cabinet affairs; his detestation of reform because reformers were critics—all this, taken together, constituted the heaviest count against him. He was upright according to his lights. But the lights were murky, and the tone of his Administration delighted knaves and discouraged honest men. [9]

I

Fish's eyes were opened to the evils of the day even before the Credit Mobilier inquiry, and before grave charges were levelled in 1872 against Robeson's and Creswell's handling of naval and post-office funds. [10] He was deeply pained by three scandals connected with the foreign service—the Webb scandal, the Van Buren scandal, and the Schenck scandal. For none did he have any responsibility, but all injured the United States abroad. The first had a particularly nasty look. James Watson Webb, the mercurial, quarrelsome Captain Bobadil who had edited the *Courier and Enquirer* between duels and street-affrays, had been made Minister to Brazil—1861–69—by Seward. Everybody knew that he lacked discretion; in 1872 charges of corruption were levelled against him as well. [11]

When Webb reached Rio de Janeiro, he had found among the unsettled business of his legation the so-called *Caroline* claim. The *Caroline* was a Peruvian ship condemned in 1842 in a Brazilian seaport as unseaworthy, and sold, the heaviest loss falling upon American insurers.

[8] James Russell Lowell, *Writings* (Riverside Edition), V, 281.

[9] So stern a member of Congress as Justin Smith Morrill, says his biographer, wished to hurry over the Credit Mobilier, Whiskey Ring, and other scandals; "he had no taste for muck-raking, and his love of the Republican Party would have led him to ignore them if he could." W. B. Parker, *Life and Public Services of Justin Smith Morrill*, 244.

[10] For these charges see Oberholtzer, *United States*, II, 70, 71. Those against Robeson were the more serious; House Misc. Docs., 42d Cong., 2d Sess., No. 201. The Secors, a firm of naval contractors, had built three monitors during the Civil War for an agreed price of $1,380,000, but complained that owing to the rise in costs they had lost money. Congress directed an inquiry by a board of officers, and on its recommendation appropriated $115,000 additional to the Secors "in full discharge of all claims." Robeson was hardly settled in office before he ordered a reinvestigation. On the report of officers in his department he paid the Secors in 1870 $93,000 more. This may not have been corrupt, but it was certainly a flat violation of law.

[11] Webb published a pamphlet, *The Case of General J. Watson Webb vs. Hamilton Fish and E. R. Hoar*, which I have found far from convincing.

They had brought suit against the captain for fraudulent and barratrous conduct, and finally obtained a judicial order in Brazil nullifying the former judgment. But it turned out that neither the vessel nor pecuniary damages could be recovered. The underwriters about 1854 assigned their claim to Lemuel Wells, former American consul at St. Catherine's, Brazil, who had been dismissed for cause. He presented it as one against the Brazilian Government, urging the State Department to support it on the bizarre ground that the Brazilian court which had condemned the *Caroline* was corrupt, and the Government therefore answerable for the loss. Though the Department gave some attention to the claim, Washington was never really convinced of its validity.[12] Secretary Seward, in fact, was suspicious both of it and Lemuel Wells.

But ultimately Webb plunged ahead in his own bellicose fashion, for he had come to a private agreement with Wells. In 1867, while Brazil was at war with Paraguay, he revived the claim, threatened to break off diplomatic relations, and finally demanded his passports. Brazil being in no position to resist, her government protestingly complied. Webb, reporting this settlement on October 1, 1867, wrote the State Department that he was sending it "a bill on London for £5,000," to be paid over to Wells. The "sum agreed upon" by Webb and the Brazilians was not otherwise stated, and the State Department assumed that the total was only £5,000. But Seward, still suspicious, wrote Webb that the Department would hold the £5,000 in trust until he learned more about the whole affair; and it was invested in United States bonds.[13]

When the Brazilian Government, outraged by this piece of extortion, renewed its protests, Seward had the subject submitted to the counsel for the State Department. He reported the claim invalid. The State Department then submitted the question to the Attorney-General. Not until January 2, 1872, did the latter announce his decision. It was wholly in favor of Brazil. Fish agreed with this decision, and Grant ordered the money repaid to Brazil with interest. But when the Brazilian Minister, Sr. D. J. G. Magalhaens, heard that the sum returnable was £5,000, he threw up his hands. As he immediately proved, Brazil had paid Webb no less than £14,252!

The result was a curious drama. Fish penned a peremptory demand

[12] A large envelope of documents in the Fish Papers treats this subject; see also the speech reviewing it by Rockwood Hoar, *Congressional Globe*, May 16, 1874.
[13] Seward to Webb, Dec. 7, 1867; State Department MSS, Diplomatic Drafts.

that Webb account for the missing moneys. After much delay, Webb sent back a blustering and defiant reply.[14] In a series of letters, full of threats and swagger, he admitted that he had received £14,252 from Brazil and concealed the fact from Seward; but he refused either to account for the money or to pay it over. His defence was that large payments had been made to Brazilian officials to procure allowance of the claim, but he refused to give names or amounts. In short, he pleaded guilty to bribery while declining to supply evidence to exonerate himself from the charge of theft! What Fish thought of the Minister may be imagined. Webb quoted an expression from one of Seward's dispatches (December 7, 1867) as evidence that Seward approved of the bribery: "You have shown much energy and sagacity in the adjustment of the claim." But Fish pointed out that Seward had expressly instructed Webb to do nothing to weaken the moral or legal right of the government to intervene in behalf of the claim.[15] No Secretary of State in our history but would have scorned bribery to obtain money from an impoverished sister-republic, and Webb knew it. Fish then and later was convinced that Webb had pocketed most of the missing money. So were leading newspapers, whose comments were stinging.[16]

The Administration was determined to have justice done, and Congress, after investigation by a sub-committee of the House Foreign Affairs Committee, voted $96,406.73 to reimburse Brazil.[17] Rockwood Hoar in a blistering speech to the House on May 16, 1872, reviewed the subject. When the Cabinet discussed the "misappropriation," Grant directed that the case be given to the Department of Justice for prosecution.[18] Webb was in Europe, and Federal officers found that he had left no attachable property. The Cabinet discussed the possibility of having him extradited, but decided against so rigorous a course—particularly as his son announced that he was coming home to confute his enemies.[19] Meanwhile, the Brazilian Government pronounced Webb's story false and dishonorable, and declared that it held direct evidence of his dishonesty. He had received three drafts in payment of the claims —one for £5,000, one for £3,252, and one for £5,900. He alleged that he had sent the first to Seward, and paid the other two to certain Bra-

---

[14] Fish to Webb, June 20, 1872; Webb to Fish, July 20, 1872; Fish Papers.
[15] Fish to Webb, September 3, 1872; Fish Papers.
[16] "The defence, so far as it can be judged from this instalment of it, is certainly no defence at all"; *Nation*, July 2, 1874.
[17] *Congressional Globe.*   [18] Diary, August 6, 1873.   [19] Diary, October 31, 1873.

zilians by order of Lemuel Wells. But the government furnished evidence that he had remitted the £5,900 to Baring Brothers, his London bankers, for deposit in his private account.[20] Webb then explained that Barings had used the £5,900 to buy United States bonds which he handed to the Brazilians! Both Fish and the Federal Attorneys, after inquiry, were satisfied that Webb had kept the bonds—which could not be traced —for himself.

Fish regarded the case as perfectly clear. When Webb accused Rockwood Hoar of falsehood and slander, the Secretary wrote that he evidently did not realize that every paper connected with the *Caroline* claim had been in the possession of the Foreign Affairs Committee for weeks before its action, and that House members had seen a copy of the draft for £5,900 which he remitted to London with his own endorsement on it. "This reticence of Mr. Webb's as to what became of the money may be evidence of the 'sagacity' of which he speaks so frequently; *if it be,* it is of that kind of 'sagacity' familiar to the police and to prosecutors of felons." Webb had said that the Secretary charged him with embezzlement. This was untrue, replied Fish; he was in doubt whether the proper term was theft, embezzlement, or breach of trust. Whatever the term, "the affair of the *Caroline* is not the only instance of abuse of his position as the Representative of his government by being pecuniarily interested in claims which he endeavored to enforce against Brazil. It is known that he had a pecuniary interest in the claim for the ship *Canada*." [21]

Unhappily, Webb proved out of reach of American law. He retained William M. Evarts.[22] Suit was brought in the Federal District Court to recover the money. After long delay, an order was obtained for his examination before a referee. He confessed to the sums he had received, but still maintained that, in accordance with Wells's instructions, he had used all but £5,000 in bribery. To be sure, £5,900 had gone into his

---

[20] Sr. Borges to Fish, Diary, December 2, 1874. The feeling of Brazilians may be gathered from Fish's conversation with Sr. Borges on this date: "He says his Government is very indignant at suggestions and imputations made by Webb of payment of money to procure the allowance of the claim, and that they inform him that the draft which Webb negotiated in Rio and which bore the endorsement of the money having been received there, was in point of fact exchanged by Webb for a draft at short sight on London which he remitted to, and deposited directly with his private bankers, Messrs. Baring Brothers & Co. . . . He mentions several things as stated by Webb, which he denounces as untrue and impossible, and promises to procure confidentially a memorandum of facts and dates which will expose the falsehood of those statements in Webb's letters."
[21] Fish to Hoar, Washington, June 22, 1874; Letterbooks.
[22] Evarts to Fish, November 8, 1874; Diary, November 10, 1874.

private account—but he waved that detail aside. To be sure, the bribery itself was dishonorable and unauthorized—but he replied that it violated no American law. It was useless to ask him to name a single Brazilian to corroborate his story—he simply stuck to it, with many explosions, objurgations, and denunciations of his enemies.[23]

District Attorney Bliss finally asked Judge Blatchford to *compel* Webb to name the Brazilians involved; but Blatchford ruled that he need not disclose the identity of the Brazilians, for it was irrelevant to the issue whether he owed money to the United States.[24] In one sense it might have been irrelevant. In another it was not, for unless his tale were thus brought to the touchstone there existed no means of proving it false. He left the courtroom legally innocent. But unkind men still believed that he had split the money in three parts: £5,000 going to the United States for Wells, £3,252 to various Brazilians, and £5,900 to himself. Brazil had her money back; the United States had a bill for reimbursing her; and Webb had his Baring bank-account—and what was left of his reputation.[25]

Meanwhile, the sorry story of General T. B. Van Buren was being disclosed. The Austro-Hungarian Government had invited the United States to participate in an international fair in Vienna in 1873, and Congress in June, 1872, authorized the President to send one or more representatives.[26] Grant characteristically selected Van Buren, a strutting, windy New York politician who had no acquaintance whatever with American art, science, industry, or letters. Van Buren hastened in turn to nominate unfit associates, the chief being another politician named William Mayer. Very belatedly, on February 14, 1873, Congress appropriated $200,000, stipulating that no one should receive more than $5,000 for salary and expenses. At first all went well. The Viennese authorities set aside a commodious "American Transept" in the Palace of Industry. Minister Jay took great interest in filling it; [27] and encouraged by our government, some 700 American manufacturers, mining companies, and civic bodies prepared exhibits, which in March, 1873, were sent by U. S. S. *Guard* to Trieste. Van Buren shortly fol-

23 For matter on the Webb suit, see N. Y. *Tribune*, December 20, 1875.
24 N. Y. *Tribune*, February 7, 1876.
25 The government was unable to find Wells, whom the Brazilian Minister thought dead. Webb might easily have given the names of bribed Brazilians, with sums and corroboratory letters, to the court or State Department *in confidence*. He never offered to do so.
26 Act of June 10, 1872; *Congressional Globe*.
27 Jay to Fish, November 11, 1872; No. 489.

lowed on a steamer to England.[28]

Nobody had supposed that our participation in a European exposition could give rise to scandal. But it shortly appeared that Van Buren was preposterously incompetent, that Mayer was a knave, and that Minister Jay was a jealous, loose-tongued busybody. When Van Buren left Washington he had given Fish a bond for the proper disbursement of the appropriation. It was so defective that Fish sent it after him to be executed in due form, meanwhile granting Jay control over the money. Jay and Van Buren promptly quarrelled,[29] and Jay soon cabled that he had discovered corrupt practices—that William Mayer had sold a restaurant concession to an American for a large sum. Other excited cablegrams followed. Jay, who was disposed to wash all the dirty linen in public, recommended a special investigating commission. Fish in great distress suspended Mayer by cable, and at once empowered Jay and another New Yorker in Vienna, Thomas McElrath, to make an inquiry. "You will inform General Van Buren," he wrote Jay, "that your approval will be necessary to all liabilities hereafter incurred." [30]

The episode thereupon became a sensation. On April 21 the New York *Herald* published a Vienna dispatch alleging that places on the American Commission had been sold; one man had paid $6,000 for his appointment, and others lesser sums. Fish cabled Jay the same day: "You and McElrath must investigate this thoroughly. Ascertain who are the persons alluded to. See the reporter and get all the information you can. . . . The Commission must be free from taint. Your action in suspending any suspected party will be sustained no matter what may be his position. The honor of the country requires thorough examination, and decided action. Report fully." Three days later he suspended Van Buren's entire Commission, fifteen in all, and named a new Commission in their stead. This body included Theodore Roosevelt, Sr., Jackson S. Schultz, and James Renwick, names far different from any in the original list. Meanwhile, Jay and McElrath were taking testimony, and the European press was rolling the sweet morsel under its tongue.

Fish's ruling emotion was anger against Van Buren and Mayer in causing the scandal; Grant's ruling emotion was anger against Jay in noisily exposing it. Van Buren's political friends immediately descended

[28] London *Times*, March 18, 1872.   [29] April 8 *et seq.;* Fish Papers.
[30] Cablegram, March 26, 1873; dispatches March 26, April 9, 11, 1873; State Department MSS, Diplomatic Drafts, Austria-Hungary.

upon the President at Long Branch. They assured him that the charges were false, and had arisen from jealousy; that Jay and McElrath were holding their hearings in secret, and stacking the cards against Van Buren. Grant listened readily, for he liked Van Buren and disliked Jay, and knew that he was blameworthy for appointing the former. He wrote Fish [31] that "it seems to me they have much justly to complain of. . . . I confess to a prejudice against McElrath and an entire want of confidence in the judgment and discretion of Mr. Jay. I do not believe that our country would have been so scandalized before the world nor would have got into such a complication, if Mr. Jay's place had been filled by a man of tact and discretion."

But the investigation remained under Fish's control, and was carried forward vigorously. He was supported by the best newspapers. "I see," John Murray Forbes wrote him,[32] "that the friends of the killed and wounded at Vienna are making all the clamor they can through the press against your action. Let me say, however, that all the sound men I see are entirely with you, and highly applaud the telegraphic promptness with which you repudiated the doings of the speculators who had crept into the Commission." Jay celebrated the Fourth of July, 1873, by bringing the long-drawn inquiry to a close. The State Department had meanwhile published letters from Van Buren which, with sweeping denials, ascribed all the troubles to Jay's "accursed malignity, unhallowed vanity, and ambition." [33] He had acted with more haste and clamor than were necessary, but the full testimony spoke for itself in conclusive fashion.[34]

As Jay and McElrath reported, both Van Buren and Mayer had accepted money for certain restaurant concessions—an "American Indian Wigwam," an "American Pavillion," and an "American Bar," all specializing in mixed drinks. Europe was eager to taste American cocktails, flips, juleps, and cobblers. Mayer had taken most of the money, part of it paid as a "loan" or "tax" without receipts, and part as "schoolhouse donations." The Special Commissioners characterized him as a thief in the plainest language. They were gentler with Van Buren, but left no doubt of his incompetence. He had left too much of the management to his subordinates, and permitted "a looseness in contracts, in instructions, and in accounts, calculated to ensure the ruin of any private

[31] Grant to Fish, Long Branch, June 28, 1873; Fish Papers.
[32] Forbes to Fish, Boston, April 30, 1873; Fish Papers.   [33] *Nation*, May 22, 1873.
[34] MS Report, Special Commissioners of the Vienna Exposition; Fish Papers.

business, and which in a great national trust . . . was to the last degree discreditable." [35] Fish summed up the whole episode with his usual shrewd judgment: [36]

The Vienna business is nasty; there has been dirty work and much lying. Van Buren has no capacity for the organization of such an affair and fell into the hands of others who were rogues; and, while perhaps not intending wrong, admits having received money, which he attempts to justify, and then denies plumply and positively that he took anything. He is an impulsive, dash-ahead creature, full of self-esteem and gas, but not naturally vicious or corrupt— bad-tempered, possibly. He foolishly undertook to justify and defend his subordinates, who had had the cunning to entrap him, and held him in their power, and who have since denounced him. Jay might, I think, have used a little more forbearance, and have prevented the publicity which he forces upon us, and which damages us before the world.

The episode was soon forgotten, but it showed how easily the appointment of a weak man to even a minor post might besmirch the name of the republic.[37]

II

Meanwhile, a third scandal was threatening, and this time one which Fish unfortunately did not treat so vigorously. It involved Robert C. Schenck, Minister to Great Britain. For no member of the diplomatic service did Grant feel a warmer personal liking. A fellow-Ohioan, an old companion in arms, he was a bluff, hearty, practical man, full of good sense, and devoted to the Administration. This liking Fish shared. Schenck had been sent to England at a time when no difficult tasks were likely to fall upon him; but he discharged his duties loyally, tactfully, and ably. He obeyed instructions, kept on good terms with Granville, and sent back letters full of shrewd insight. There is ample evidence in the Foreign Office papers that the British Government respected his abilities; he was a firm and dexterous defender of American rights and policies. It was a calamity when he laid himself open to attack.

Schenck had reached his legation in June, 1871. In November, Fish's

[35] The London *Times*, August 29, 1873, gives an English view of the matter.
[36] Fish to Schenck, June 15, 1873; Letterbooks.
[37] It was generally understood thereafter that Jay would not remain long in Vienna. His course in other diplomatic matters was displeasing. For example, he kept pushing a plan for an international patent convention in Vienna although the United States, Britain, and Austria-Hungary herself resisted it. "Cannot something be invented to drive the notion out of his head?" Fish finally demanded; "It seems to me that he has committed as great a diplomatic blunder in this affair as his ill-judged precipitancy in the Van Buren matter was a blunder of judgment and want of discretion."

eye fell upon an article in the London *Economist* criticising the Minister because his name had been advertised among the directors of the Emma Silver-Mining Company, a corporation selling shares in the Emma Silver Mine of Utah to British investors. The Secretary was disturbed. He read the article to the Cabinet on November 4, 1871, expressing uneasiness.[38] As he told his colleagues, no law or departmental regulation prohibited a Minister from being concerned with a business corporation. "But," he added, "it is unfortunate that this advertisement, which shows the Emma Company to be an inchoate and possibly speculative concern, should be published in London. It will be supposed that his name is on it to bolster up a weak concern with the prestige of his official position." Before he could do anything more, Schenck himself acted. The American press had taken up the subject, publishing some sharp criticisms. In a telegram apparently full of bluff honesty,[39] Schenck stated that he was "surprised and pained," and added: "Have no pecuniary interest except some shares, for which, after investigating fully, I paid dollar for dollar. Having thus decided and raised means to invest, was solicited by respectable Americans to act with gentlemen of known high character as director, to protect their interests and my own in what I believe very valuable property. Perhaps made mistake. . . . Will withdraw from board or do whatever you advise."

Fish read this telegram to the Cabinet on November 28,[40] and a reply which, with Grant's approval, he sent next day. After stating that a diplomatic officer might buy shares in any honest enterprise, he delivered a sharp warning and a clearcut if tactful command: [41]

The advertisement of the name of a diplomatic representative of the Government, as a director of a company seeking to dispose of its shares in the country to which he is accredited, is ill-advised and unfortunate, and is calculated to subject him to criticism; but it is assumed that the advertisement of the mining company in the London journal was not your act, but that of the agents of the company without consultation with you.

You are earnestly advised to withdraw your name from the management of the company.

This left Schenck with but two courses; he could resign as director, or he could resign as Minister. Naturally he took the former. But

---

[38] Diary.   [39] Schenck to Fish, November 27, 1871; Fish Papers.   [40] Diary.
[41] November 29, 1871; State Department MSS, Diplomatic Drafts, Great Britain.

though he sent his resignation to the company on December 6, 1871, he gave it no publicity until January 12, 1872, when it appeared in the London *Times*. The delay could be construed as giving insiders time to sell their stock before his withdrawal brought the price down; and the form of his letter was also censurable. "My resignation," wrote Schenck, "is upon grounds purely personal to myself. In consenting to become a director, I know that I but exercised a private and individual right, in no way incompatible with public or official duty; but I prefer to take away from some who have criticized me even a pretext for their comments and attacks. I beg, therefore, to record my assurance to . . . members of the board that I continue to have the fullest confidence in the value and profitableness of the property they have in charge, in which I hold all the shares I have been able to take." [42] Though Fish had told him that it did not befit a Minister to promote stocks, in resigning he had seized the opportunity for more promoting! Moreover, his statement that the resignation was "upon grounds purely personal to myself" was false. It had been dictated by the Secretary upon public grounds.

But the great point was that he had resigned. Fish was satisfied with this, and did not greatly mind Schenck's use of the face-saving phrase about personal grounds. Doubtless he never knew of the tardiness with which the resignation was published in the London *Times*. He was the more inclined to drop the matter because the storm over the indirect claims began at this moment, and he valued Schenck's ability to help him to deal with it. Moreover, Fish realized how hard Schenck's position was. His salary was but $17,500 a year; the cost of maintaining a dignified position in London, as various successors testified, was at least $45,000 a year.

But a revival of the subject proved unescapable. The Emma Mine paid dividends at the rate of 1.5 per cent a month until December, 1872. Investors then learned not only that the treasury was empty, but that the ore had given place to limestone and the mine appeared "played out." Within a short time the stock had dropped from £33 a share to £4. A new storm of criticism arose. An English stockholder addressed a scathing open letter to Schenck, which the American press reprinted.[43] Other Britons in the spring of 1873 published figures to show that of the

[42] This and many other documents in the matter are printed in House Report No. 579, 44th Cong., 1st Sess., report of Abram S. Hewitt's sub-committee on the Emma Mine.
[43] *Nation*. June 12, 1873.

£1,000,000 their countrymen had paid for the mine, £840,000 had been lost.[44] It was evident that the American Minister had signed statements in the original prospectus which were totally untrue. Louis Jennings of the New York *Times* returned from London in the summer of 1873 with disturbing reports which he imparted to Grant at Long Branch. The latter sent an alarmed letter to Fish: [45]

> I think I should see you either the last of this week, or early next, in regard to some unpleasant rumors that have come to me in regard to the position occupied by General Schenck in England. It will be necessary at least to let the General know of them, and get his statement, so that if the attack should come upon him, as I understand it will, we should be in a position to justify his retention. The story in a few words is, that many English capitalists were induced to invest in stock in the Emma Mine because the American Minister headed the list of Directors; that the concern was bogus, and no returns came to the investors except a few dividends from funds they had payed in; that Schenck from being a poor man has become rich, and I am told, asserts that his receipts from these subscriptions was £100,000 sterling.

The next Cabinet meeting, August 5, witnessed a warm discussion of Schenck's unhappy position.[46] Jennings had told the President that the *Times* would not exploit the charges unless other newspapers did so, but they were now common property. While Secretary Delano defended Schenck, the others were suspicious of him. Grant wished to obtain statements which could be used in defending him when the storm burst. He directed Fish to write a suitable letter, and the Secretary brought a draft to the Cabinet next day. In this Fish detailed the principal allegations, which included the charge that Schenck had profited largely from the sale of Emma Mine stock, and was now living in a style which his mere salary as Minister could not justify. "In directing this communication to be made to you," he concluded, "the President directs me to say that his confidence in your personal rectitude and integrity is not diminished, but that as the information comes from an intelligent person who professes to be actuated by a friendly disposition . . . he deems it an act of justice as well as of friendship and of confidence to communicate to you what is thus reported." [47]

By this time Fish could no longer doubt that Schenck had been guilty of serious offences. He had read the evidence against the Minister in the New York *Herald, Tribune,* and *Nation.* He knew that Schenck's in-

[44] *Ibid,* July 17, 1873.　[45] Grant to Fish, Long Branch, July 23, 1873; Fish Papers.
[46] Diary.　[47] The draft is copied in the Diary for August 6, 1873.

come had been unexpectedly augmented. For example, the Minister had written Fish in the fall of 1872: [48] "At the time of my acceptance . . . of the President's appointment, I was well aware that I could not support myself and family on the salary allowed, and live as decently and becomingly, with the strictest economy, as was proper in the position, and would be expected of the American representative in London. My expectation in that regard has been fully verified. But I fortunately last year made an investment which added something, and may yet for a while continue to add so much to my personal income, as to enable me to eke out the deficient government allowance. . . ." Fish knew also that Schenck was avid of money. The Minister had asked an extra appropriation of $2,500 for an amanuensis; as soon as it became available on June 30, 1873, he hastened to draw upon it. "This has been a hard quarter for me financially," he wrote,[49] "and so I am reminded of this resource." He lived expensively. He had a handsome house in London; his three daughters were being educated on the Continent; he made extensive pleasure-trips. At the very time the Cabinet was discussing his conduct, he and two daughters were setting out with their carriage, horses, coachman, footmen, and ladies' maid for a tour of southern England and Wales.[50]

Yet if the letter went, Fish knew what the result would be. Schenck would vigorously assert his innocence. He would say again that he had acted in good faith and in exercise of an indubitable private right; he would demolish the exaggerated portion of the charges. His self-righteous reply would be just what Grant desired. Schenck's defence would be converted into an Administration defence of its Minister, and the State Department would be thrust into an untenable position.

On August 6, Fish read the Cabinet the draft letter; but in doing so, he remarked that when he concluded he would like to raise a question. "That draft is just right," said Grant, when he had finished. "But the question you wish to raise is whether to send any letter at all on the subject." Fish replied: "Precisely that. And I am clearly of the opinion that it is better not to write any letter, or to take any notice of the communication by Jennings. If General Schenck makes a denial, the Administration will be bound to accept his denial and stand by it; if he explains his course, the Administration will be bound to examine the

[48] Schenck to Fish, November 30, 1872; Fish Papers.
[49] Schenck to Fish, London, June 26, 1873; Fish Papers.
[50] Schenck to Fish, London, August 8, 1873; Fish Papers.

matter and become a prosecutor."

"Do not send the letter," said Grant. "I will not become the accuser of General Schenck. If he is accused, we will call upon him and will investigate." [51] And Fish, after copying the draft into his diary, destroyed the original.

It was certain that Schenck would be accused by others, for the outcries of defrauded investors became louder. In the fall of 1873 an Englishman, S. T. Paffard, published a pamphlet history of the Emma Mine in which Schenck was handled without gloves, and the *Nation* thereupon gave four columns of fine print to a searching analysis of its record.[52] No evidence as yet appeared that Schenck had received an improper reward for the use of his name; it seemed that he had merely been deluded into joining the enterprise. Fish would have shown more wisdom and courage had he taken steps to bring about a severe investigation. But at any rate he had prevented the Administration from being manoeuvred into defending the Minister. The matter was left in abeyance; he still thought Schenck fundamentally honest, and believed that he had learned his lesson.

III

All these scandals in our foreign representation were deplorable. But after all, Schenck was Grant's appointee, not Fish's, and had been chosen after the Secretary had fruitlessly proposed Rockwood Hoar and Andrew D. White. Van Buren was Grant's appointee. James Watson Webb was Seward's. Indeed, not more than half a dozen appointments had been made in the foreign service at Fish's instance—and they were all sound. As a witty observer remarked, Grant applied the "nebulous test" in making nominations to office. The long-suffering Secretary sometimes grew impatient as he tried to work with the tools that were given him in foreign capitals; but he realized that his was only the common lot of all Secretaries since John Quincy Adams.

The worst of Grant's appointments were those to consulships. Though the character of our consuls had been a standing jest for decades, the derision of Congressmen, State Department, and foreigners alike, Grant actually lowered it. In 1873 Fish asked the President, "Do you really wish George S. Fisher of Georgia given a place?" "Yes," ex-

[51] Diary, August 6, 1873.
[52] "True History of the Emma Mine," *Nation,* December 18, 1873.

claimed Grant, *"I want to get him out of the country."* "Well," said
Fish, "La Guayra will do." [53] Too many appointments were made in
the spirit of Grant's remark. Moran was horrified by the first consular
representatives to pass through London in 1869. The intelligence of
many Latin-American consuls was typified by the gentleman who sent
the State Department eggs of a particularly destructive termite—and
was dismissed for his pains.[54] When the consul at Demerara presented
Bancroft Davis with a monkey, Davis wrote Fish that he did not know
what to do with the animal unless he could pass the civil service examination for a consulate. "No doubt," he added, "he will be as good
as some who have held the commission in the past." [55]

The learned George Henry Boker, Minister to Turkey, wrote Fish
in criticism of our consul-general there.[56] "How Goodenow has managed to live in Constantinople for nine years without having any foreign language forced into his head is a mystery to me. It shows an
amount of ingenuity at escaping undesired knowledge that is really
commendable." Remonstrances from foreign sources were frequent. In
June, 1873, for example, Thornton reported that the officials of Ceylon
could not receive Grant's new Commercial Agent in Colombo socially.
"He is a gambler, a heavy better and sporting man, a farrier with
rather low associations." And some remarks by Ben Butler that autumn
show how American politicians viewed the consuls. Butler had impu-
dently tried to collect $700 from the State Department upon the claim
of his nephew, recently consul at Alexandria, for travelling expenses
up the Nile. Fish refused payment. The result was a peevish outburst:

General Butler remarked that it was desirable that some of our Ministers
should be able to speak at least some other language than bad English, adding that he believed Boker may be said to speak two, bad English and the
profane. He alluded to the recent appointment of a consul at Havre, remarking with bitterness that Indiana was getting everything; denounced Bridgland
. (lately appointed consul at Havre) as a swindler and a thief; says he was
under indictment and saved from conviction only by the fact that the District
Attorney was not continued in office to prosecute him; that he had held some
office in the Internal Revenue Department in Texas, where he had been a
defaulter and a swindler; he enumerated other offices held by persons from
Indiana, and among them Beardslee, who superseded his nephew at Alexandria. I remarked that Beardslee was a very excellent officer, and was the only

[53] Diary, October 2, 1873.   [54] Fish to Davis, Garrison, July 28, 1873; Letterbooks.
[55] July 23, 1873; Fish Papers.
[56] Boker to Fish, Constantinople, August 14, 1873; Letterbooks.

person whose appointment had been asked of the State Department by Mr. Colfax during the whole time of his Vice Presidency. He replied that Colfax had stolen money through the Credit Mobilier and got pay besides from the government in offices. . . .

Yet Fish succeeded in stopping some improper appointments. For example, in the fall of 1873 he tactfully prevented Grant from appointing Dr. Samuel Gridley Howe as Minister to Greece. A long feud had raged between Dr. Howe and the head of a large American mission school in Athens; the Greeks took exception to Dr. Howe's administration of a fund raised at the time of the Cretan revolt; and Fish distrusted the man's perfervid temperament. A few months earlier Howe had become head of a company to "develop" Santo Domingo. In 1873 the President wrote from Long Branch that he wished the consulate in Jerusalem given to the Rev. Dr. Frank S. De Hass of the Methodist Church.[57] Grant had known De Hass since the war, for he had been pastor of a church in Washington. Fish at once protested. It was unwise, he pointed out, to send any clergyman to a non-Christian country as Minister or consul. "Turkey is very sensitive, and unless a clerical consul is a *very* wise and discreet man, he can very easily get himself and his country into trouble at Jerusalem." Grant dropped De Hass. A little later the creation of a Court of Commissioners of *Alabama* Claims became necessary. Fish suggested several able men to the Cabinet. "Stop," suddenly cried Grant, "I want to put Cornelius Cole on." The California legislature had refused at the beginning of 1872 to reëlect Cole to the Senate. His integrity had long been under attack. He was one of the few Republicans who had voted against the Treaty of Washington. Fish indignantly objected. "Well," said Grant, anxious to do a favor for a friend, "how about making him counsel to the Commission?" This brought a protest from the Attorney-General. "I begged the President," writes Fish, "to look in some other direction for a place for Cole."

During 1872–73 Fish became convinced that many of the bad appointments which Grant tried to force upon him were suggested by Ben Butler, Orville E. Babcock, the Dents, and others who maintained a shrewd influence in the White House. The Kitchen Cabinet was developing. Bancroft Davis shared this suspicion. They believed that Babcock, Louis Dent, and others hoodwinked the President; that they

[57] Grant to Fish, July 11, 1873; Letterbooks.

wrote letters for him to sign; and that they induced him to authorize letters, and then included new matter in them. In July, 1873, Davis informed Fish at Garrison that the White House had just sent over a demand for two minor appointments. One man was wholly unknown, the other wholly unfit. "Shall I make out the appointment? It is a very peremptory order, and I do not believe the President ever ordered it. . . . Brimm is a rascal and ought not to be appointed. I do not believe the President sanctioned such an imperative order in his case." [58]

Entering his second term with increased disinclination to defer to public opinion,[59] Grant seemed willing to brave any censure except that of the professional politicians and the backstairs White House cabal. Two striking illustrations of his tenacity in error were supplied in 1873 by his treatment of the Casey scandal in Louisiana, and the "Boss" Shepherd scandal in Washington. James F. Casey, Grant's brother-in-law, presided over the granite custom-house in New Orleans as Collector of Customs. Like Murphy in New York, he controlled local politics in the interests of the Administration. His gross misconduct in office, involving clear corruption, was frequently dwelt upon by the press.[60] In 1872 his activities were investigated by a Congressional committee, which made a very damaging report. This was withheld in the hope that he would resign, and when he did not, was published. Yet in March, 1873, the President shocked Washington by reappointing him for another four-year term. The independent press expatiated upon the "indecency" of the nomination. Many Washington observers expected the Senate to reject it, especially as West, the only member from Louisiana, opposed it; and so many of Grant's disgusted followers shirked the vote that a quorum could hardly be obtained. Yet Casey was confirmed by a slender margin. The *Nation's* correspondent voiced the general sentiment: "We may set it down as a certainty now that the moral tone of General Grant's second Administration will not be a particle above the first." [61]

At least the Boss Shepherd affair did not involve a relative of the President. In 1871 Congress had created a new and more efficient government for the District of Columbia. The law vested the greater part of the practical administration in a Board of Works, whose nominal head was President Henry D. Cooke, but whose actual director was

---

[58] Davis to Fish, July 11, 1873; Letterbooks.
[59] E. L. Godkin, *Nation*, January 15, 1874.
[60] *Nation*, 20, 1873. [61] *Nation*, January 27, 1873.

the masterful contractor, Vice President Alexander R. Shepherd. Without delay it undertook a much-needed system of public improvements,
grandiose but practical, which began the transformation of ramshackle,
straggling Washington into a beautiful and impressive capital. Unfortunately, this renovation soon piled up a debt of some $17,000,000 and
threw the Federal District into virtual bankruptcy. A brisk bombardment of charges fell upon Boss Shepherd—extravagance, jobbery, illegality, the making of a fortune by real estate "speculations," and
other dishonest acts. As the uproar rose to its height in the late summer of 1873, with thousands of citizens signing petitions for relief,
Cooke resigned. He also received the testimonial letter of praise which
Grant delighted to give to every man who left Federal office hurriedly
and under fire.

Whom should Grant name in his place? The country assumed that
it would be someone who would strike a ringing blow at the alleged District "Ring" of corrupt politicians and contractors, and pry into Shepherd's dubious operations. Precise and detailed charges had been made
against Shepherd. They connected him with flagrant violations of the
law to his own benefit. Hence the consternation of confiding citizens
when in September, 1873, the President named as Cooke's successor—
Boss Shepherd himself! The public did not know, as Fish did, that this
appointment had been brought about by Babcock's adroit manoeuvring
and cajolery.

Few aspects of Grant's career as President are more remarkable than
his rapid induration against criticism. During his first year in the White
House he showed repeated spasms of pain; he positively writhed under
the talons of Dana's *Sun,* and once warned his Cabinet that he wished
no office given to any friend of any stockholder of that journal. Fish
records on February 8, 1870, for example, that Grant spoke with the
deepest feeling of the abuse to which he was subjected. Calumnies were
being heaped upon him, he said; his enemies were inquiring into his
private investments; somebody had even charged that his nomination of
J. Russell Jones had been bought by a gift of land near Chicago—the
fact being that he and Jones had purchased the tract in partnership. "He
says," Fish writes, "that he has very seriously been contemplating a
resignation of his office." Nearly all our Presidents have suffered from
foul attacks, and nearly all have developed some defensive armor.
Grant's became so heavy that after 1872 few records of his sensitiveness

to the slings and arrows of his enemies can be found; and to an unfortunate degree he disregarded just criticism from responsible sources.

Very early in the second Administration the rickety structure of civil service reform crashed in complete ruin. The President had never paid the ideal more than lip-service; he had always regarded George William Curtis, head of the Civil Service Commission, as a nuisance. In March, 1873, he cruelly humiliated Curtis. The Surveyorship of the Port of New York had fallen vacant. Grant had at first nominated the Deputy-Surveyor, a faithful public servant for many years, and the press warmly praised this adherence to "the rules." Then the politicians became active. They began to predict that the President would withdraw the nomination. He did so—but critics were silenced by the announcement that the place would still be filled "under the rules," for the next-best man would be selected by a committee consisting of Mr. Curtis, Jackson S. Schultz, and Collector Chester A. Arthur. The public waited. Finally Grant nominated George H. Sharpe, a professional politician of no special fitness whatever. Curtis immediately authorized a statement in the *Tribune* that this nomination had been made without his knowledge or consent, and that "men do not willingly consent to be thus publicly snubbed." A few days later he resigned from the Commission. The little farce was ended; the officer-mongers' business flourished as much as ever, and when reform was mentioned, those in influence at the White House wore a derisive smile.

IV

But as we have said, what chiefly worried Fish was not Grant's specific acts, but his general negligence and laxity. The nation could endure the appointment of incompetent diplomats, of a Casey or a Shepherd, without material injury. But could it long endure the gross carelessness with which Grant administered his high office? Might it not sustain grave damage from such treatment as in 1873 he gave the choice of a new Chief Justice of the United States?

For within a few months after his second inauguration, Grant had to make by far the most important single appointment of the Administration. Salmon P. Chase, Chief Justice since 1864, died of paralysis on May 7, 1873. A man of brilliant if uneven powers, and of commanding if by no means winning personality, he had been even greater as Chief

Justice than as Senator from Ohio or Secretary of the Treasury. In the trial of President Johnson he had evinced a signally high sense of constitutional propriety and judicial responsibility, withstanding the clamor of the Radical politicians and editors with courage and dignity. In several far-reaching cases he had supported humble citizens against the use of arbitrary war powers by the Executive. With equal firmness, he had supported the President and Supreme Court against the attempted usurpations of Congress under Wade and Stevens. For nine years in his great office he had been wise, liberal, and just. Men realized that a mighty leader had fallen; the last of the three giants, Seward, Stanton, and Chase, who had borne the heaviest departmental labors during the Civil War, and whose exertions had shortened their lives. Men also realized that during the past seventy-five years the Supreme Court had been presided over by three jurists of consummate ability. Could Grant find a leader worthy to stand beside John Marshall, Roger B. Taney, and Salmon P. Chase? The nation expected him to try. Distinguished men—Swayne and Miller of the Supreme Court, Emmons of the Circuit Court, Curtis, Rockwood Hoar, and Evarts at the bar—furnished a field of selection.

Characteristically, Grant passed over such names in favor of Roscoe Conkling. He had formed a strong personal friendship for Conkling and was grateful to him as an Administration pillar in the Senate. The press was soon filled with reports of Conkling's hesitation, and filled also with surprised protests. Conkling had brilliant abilities. But his interest in the law had always stood subordinate to his interest in politics; while he displayed the very antithesis of the judicial temperament.[62] A passionate partisan, proud and autocratic, a veritable Hotspur in temper, he was about as well fitted for the bench as for a monastery. Reckless, headstrong, full of dash and prone to splenetic quarrels, he could never be trusted to furnish a balanced judgment. For years he had practised but casually, his name appeared in few reported cases, and he had made only one argument before the Supreme Court. A hard student might atone for these deficiencies, but Conkling was not a student. And his whole bent ran counter to the tendencies which liberal men hoped would stamp the coming age. He had fought reform at every step, was wedded to machine politics, knew nothing of economic or social forces, and had never originated a single constructive meas-

[62] *Nation*, October 2, 1873.

ure. Amid general relief, the Caesar of New York politics declined the post. His motives were mixed, but one which did him credit was his candid recognition that he was not equipped for the Chief Justiceship.

Grant thereupon made a creditable move. On November 30, 1873, after a Cabinet discussion, he impulsively turned to Fish. "He spoke of the Chief Justiceship," runs the diary, "and said he thought of offering it to me if I would accept it. Thanking him very cordially, I told him that I could not, that I did not feel myself competent for the place; he replied that he would be the judge of that, and he thought I was. I insisted that I could not accept it; that it was upwards of twenty years since I had had any connection with the bar or practise, and I had no familiarity now with the proceedings of the courts, and I felt that it would be important to put a younger man in the place." It was perhaps unfortunate that Fish declined. Unlike Conkling, he was a student. He could have mastered his judicial duties as quickly as he had mastered the State Department. His great work in foreign affairs having ended with the Geneva Arbitration, he could have embarked on a new career long outlasting.the Grant Administration. But although several Cabinet members urged him to consent, he was adamant.[63]

The President's next step was equally impulsive and less discreet. Ben Butler's influence over him at this time greatly puzzled observers. The two men should have been enemies; Grant during the war had sent Butler home from City Point discredited, and long years afterward *Butler's Book* contained a savage attack upon Grant's war record. "Butler says he has a hold on you," Rockwood Hoar once remarked as he sat beside the President. Grant set his teeth, drew down his jaw, and without changing countenance looked Hoar steadily in the eye during a long and painful silence—his way of expressing anger. At least partially, Grant's liking for the man is easily explained. The President and Butler agreed in detesting Sumner. Butler's very crassness of speech and act had its appeal to Grant. Above all, Butler supported most of the Administration measures, he flattered the President's prejudices, and he carefully allied himself with Babcock and the Dents. Now he proposed Caleb Cushing for the Chief Justiceship. For years he and Cushing had been close friends; Cushing had supported him for the governorship of Massachusetts in 1860, and defended him in a court action in 1868. Butler suggested that Grant might give Cushing

[63] Diary, November 30, 1873.

a "temporary" appointment. It would be understood that he must resign before Grant left office, and the President could meanwhile find somebody else. Grant accepted the idea!

But when Grant made the suggestion his Cabinet rose in opposition. Without exception they were opposed or dubious. Fish writes of his own stand: "I expressed a very high estimate of Cushing's ability and fitness and the appropriateness of some recognition of those who represented us at Geneva, but felt the force of the objection to Cushing's age, and the question of the propriety of dispensing an office of that character on a conditional tenure." Grant dropped the name.[64]

His fourth step was very nearly the worst possible, for he nominated Attorney-General Williams. A storm instantly arose in the Senate, now just convened, and the press. Williams's reputation as a lawyer did not extend beyond rural Oregon. Whenever tested as Attorney-General he had signally failed. For example, after the Credit Mobilier inquiry Congress had ordered suits against the company, which had manifestly defrauded the government of millions. Yet Williams had so shamefully mismanaged the case that the government lost it.[65] Moreover, charges were soon made against his integrity. His wife was socially ambitious, and they had been living far beyond his meagre salary. On December 26, 1873, Fish went to the White House early for a Cabinet meeting, and found the President alone and much agitated. The reasons for his excitement are succinctly stated in the diary: [66]

He . . . asked if Senators Conkling and Frelinghuysen had called upon me. [On my] answering in the negative, he said they would do so to speak with reference to the appointment of a Chief Justice; that Judge Williams would probably not be confirmed. He did not think he (Williams) had done anything corrupt or illegal, but that there had been indiscreet things done. That Mrs. Williams had given orders for the purchase of an expensive carriage and liveries for two servants and that the expenses for those had been paid out of the contingent fund of the Department of Justice; as were also the wages of the two men who were employed as private servants. He manifested much regret at having learned this. . . . It was also alleged that Judge Williams had mingled his accounts with those of the Department, and that during the panic, when the banks were not paying private checks, it was said that the money for meeting the expenses of his house had been paid from the funds of the government; that he understood it had all been made good, but that this appropriation of government funds was unjusti-

[64] Diary, December 1, 1873.   [65] *Nation,* December 11, 1873.
[66] Diary, December 28, 1873.

fiable; that these Senators had mentioned the fact to him, and he thought it necessary to bring them to Judge Williams' notice; that they (Conkling and Frelinghuysen, as I understood) thought it had better be done by myself as the senior member of the Cabinet, and they would call upon me to give me the facts.

Williams, frightened and angry, lost his head and announced at the next Cabinet meeting that he intended to submit to the Senate Judiciary Committee a detailed statement of his personal and family expenditures since taking office. This would simply have offered fresh ammunition for the attack. Fish and Belknap persuaded him to refrain.[67] Mrs. Williams, a woman of temper, was meanwhile spreading spiteful gossip about Conkling. She told Mrs. Fish that he ought not to talk about misuse of money—he had used the secret service funds of her husband's department to gain his recent reëlection. When Grant heard this malicious tale he was angry. "It is a falsehood," he told Fish. "The only use made of that fund was to pay Davenport for the registration of voters in New York City. That was perfectly legitimate, and I stand ready to defend it." [68]

Williams's position was hopeless, and the only question was how to extricate him with the least possible damage to the Administration. The Senate Judiciary Committee held a conference with Fish, Edmunds acting as the principal spokesman; [69] and they exhibited two letters from Williams, floundering and unsatisfactory attempts at excusing his conduct. They told the Secretary that if they had to make a report, they would unanimously advise rejection. They preferred not to report, and asked that the name be withdrawn. Even if Williams withdrew, however, they would say nothing to whitewash him. The Committee was convinced that he had shown the most culpable negligence and indiscretion, and that while his intention might not have been criminal, his use of the contingent funds of the Department of Justice for personal expenses was at least a technical violation of the Act of 1846.[70]

When Grant learned of the implacable attitude of the Senators, he placed the unpleasant task of closing the incident squarely on Fish's shoulders. The Secretary was to see Williams, and ask him to request the withdrawal of his name. "He might put it on such ground as he saw fit, but he thought Williams might say that the nomination had been

[67] Diary, January 2, 1874.   [68] Diary, January 5, 1874.
[69] Diary, January 6, 1874.   [70] Diary, January 7, 1874.

conferred upon him without solicitation, and that finding opposition
in the Senate, and an amount of criticism in the press and from a portion of the Bar, that it might be a relief to the President to send in
some other name." None too gracefully, Williams consented. His usefulness either within or without the Cabinet had of course been destroyed. The charges against him at once became public property, and
the press thenceforth dubbed him "Landaulet" Williams—for it was a
landaulet he had bought with government money. Yet Grant inexpli-
cably and inexcusably permitted this delinquent servant to remain as the
chief law officer of the government.

The President was now angry—Tom Murphy remarked that "the
old man got mad" [71]—and more ready than ever to listen to Butler,
Babcock, and the Dents. While Fish vainly urged him to nominate
Rockwood Hoar, he returned instead to Caleb Cushing. Giving the
excuse that the Senate would reject Hoar, he finally sent in Cushing's
name; the reluctant but loyal Cabinet, Fish writes, "all assenting." The
nomination was highly unpopular. Cushing stood high among the small
group of really eminent American lawyers, but for this position he was
the worst man in the group. Acute of intellect, saltily individual, as
learned as Evarts or Jeremiah Black, still strenuously active in mind
and body, he was an impressive figure; but he was more renowned for
erudition than for wisdom, for shrewdness than for principle. His name
was a synonym for crafty and shifting partisanship. He had left the
Whigs to follow Tyler; in 1860 he had presided over the Democratic
Convention; in 1868 he had been for Grant. His grave defects of temper had recently been exemplifid in his book on the Geneva Arbitration. For thirty years he had made enemies on every side, and they now
joined hands to defeat him.

In the midst of a Cabinet session two days after the nomination went
to the Senate, a message was handed to Secretary Belknap. It was
from Senator A. A. Sargent of California, who had been reared in
Cushing's town of Newburyport, Mass., and had there learned to hate
him. He asked for a copy of a letter in certain Confederate archives
which the government had purchased in 1872 in the hope that they
would contain material damaging to Horace Greeley; a letter which
Cushing had written to Jefferson Davis on March 20, 1861. Belknap
had a copy in his pocket.[72] It was merely a polite note of introduction.

[71] *Nation,* January 22, 1874.   [72] Diary, January 13, 1874.

Cushing, who had then recently been the Democratic Attorney-General, presented a Washington clerk named Archibald Rowan to Davis as a gentleman deserving of confidence. That was all. The letter did not begin "My dear friend," as a lying version published immediately in the Washington *Chronicle* stated; it did not commend Rowan as a man of seven years' experience in the Ordinance Department and hence likely to be "of special service." [73] It was a mere act of kindness to a jobless clerk. But it was enough that Cushing had written a friendly note to Jefferson Davis a few days before the Civil War began. "It looks pretty black for Cushing's chances," Fish commented.[74]

Next day the Cabinet held a special session. Grant had written a resentful letter withdrawing the nomination. Various members exerted themselves to soften its language. But in the midst of their expostulations Ben Butler was announced with a letter of withdrawal from Cushing himself; and Grant sent this with a brief note to the Senate. Once more Fish urged the name of Rockwood Hoar, but this time the President had a fresh excuse. He said that Hoar had told him only the day before that he was preparing a speech in which he would shortly deny the power of Congress to emit legal tenders. The Supreme Court had by this time, reversing itself, declared the legal tenders constitutional; and as Grant strongly held to this view, Hoar's opinion was repugnant to him.[75]

It was now the middle of January, 1874. Nearly nine months had passed since Chase's death; two men had refused the Chief Justiceship, two more had been defeated as unfit; Grant must obtain somebody at once, or become a laughing-stock. After the wise precaution of consulting Senate leaders, he finally nominated Morrison R. Waite of Ohio, who was immediately confirmed. "It has been a hard parturition," wrote Fish, "I hope that what has been produced may prove successful." [76] Waite inspired mixed feelings; thankfulness when men thought of Conkling and Williams, discontent when they thought of Curtis or Hoar. It could fairly be said of the new Chief Justice that he stood in the front rank of the numerous second-class lawyers of the country. He would have been little known if Delano had not insisted upon him as one of the counsel at Geneva; but his character was unassailable, his standing at the Ohio bar was high, and he had just been chosen chair-

---

[73] Fuess, *Caleb Cushing,* II, 370–374.   [74] Diary, January 13, 1874.
[75] Diary, January 14, 1874.   [76] Fish to Schenck, January 19, 1874; Letterbooks.

man of the Ohio Constitutional Convention.[77] If in some respects commonplace, he quickly proved that he possessed industry, sense, and above all liberalism.

V

Plainly, Grant's administration was one in which almost anything might happen. More and more, it carried about it an atmosphere of stratagems and spoils. What, for example, was to be said of the scheme which Ben Butler confidentially broached to Fish one spring morning in 1873? He asked whether the State Department would object to the formation of an Anglo-American company to purchase the three northern States of Mexico and organize an independent government there! "This," he remarked, "would eventually result in the annexation of these States to the Union." Fish drily pointed out that there were five Mexican States bordering on our territory. Butler hastily corrected himself and said that he meant five! He promised that there would be no fighting, no filibustering, and no complications—that the company would use nothing but money and reason. It was part of his plan to induce Brigham Young and his Mormon associates, who had become discontented with Utah, to remove to this Mexican area. Fish could hardly take Ben Butler seriously in the rôle of Aaron Burr. And yet when he recalled Butler's connection with the backstairs group at the White House, he could not avoid a certain uneasiness.

Uneasiness, in fact, henceforth haunted him. What if the backstairs clique really took control of the government? But Fish was of a religious temperament; and he may have heard of Bismarck's statement that a special Providence existed for fools, drunkards, and the United States.

[77] *Nation*, January 22, 1874.

SECRETARY FISH was to have one more opportunity to serve the cause of peace in a great international crisis. A new Cuban imbroglio, arising with dramatic suddenness, for an anxious month threatened war, and tested his sagacity, calmness, and patience to the utmost.

Late in the evening of November 5, 1873, Fish received a telegram from Consul-General Henry C. Hall in Havana announcing that the Spanish gunboat *Tornado* had captured the ship *Virginius* and brought her into Santiago.[1] Hall had no later news. As Fish was aware, the *Virginius* was notoriously engaged in the business of carrying arms to the Cuban rebels; his files were full of Spanish complaints about her.[2] On the 6th, the Secretary accompanied Grant to a fair at Leesburg, Va.[3] He returned that night to find a dispatch from Sickles announcing that the Madrid Government had instructed Captain-General Concha to inflict no penalties without its sanction.[4] This looked hopeful, and while somewhat disturbed, he anticipated no serious trouble.

But next day, Friday the 7th, while the Cabinet were discussing the dispatches from Havana and Madrid, the correspondent of the Associated Press sent an envelope marked "urgent" in to Fish. It contained a dispatch filed in Havana a few hours earlier, stating that the Santiago authorities had condemned four of the prisoners, including the noted "General" Ryan, to death, and they had been shot on the morning of the 4th. This was alarming news. An excited discussion ensued upon the legal responsibility which Spain had incurred in the capture of the vessel and the summary execution of the four men, one an American.[5] Grant wrote on a card: "Would it not be well to telegraph Sickles that the summary infliction of the death penalty upon the prisoners taken from the *Virginius* will necessarily attract much attention in this country, and will be regarded as an inhuman act, not in accordance with the spirit of the civilization of the 19th century?"[6]

Sir Edward Thornton and Admiral Polo that afternoon, hearing the

[1] Fish Papers; *Foreign Relations*, 1874, 930 ff.
[2] See *Foreign Relations*, 1874, 1003–1030, for her activities.
[3] Diary, November 5, 6, 1873.
[4] Sickles to Fish, November 6, 1873; *Foreign Relations*, 1874, 920.
[5] Diary, November 7, 1873.   [6] Fish Papers.

news, hurried to the State Department. Thornton told Fish that he had strongly condemned the precipitate shooting of the four captives. When Polo arrived, Fish closed the door and spoke in the most serious tone. "I told him the case promised to be a grave one, but I hoped it would be discussed calmly and on its merits; it was not to be denied that the precipitate action of executing four of these men would excite a great deal of feeling in this country and elsewhere. He inquired whether I knew whether she had been arrested in British waters or not. Informing him that I had no positive information on the subject, I referred to the official publication in Madrid which states that she had been captured six miles out from Jamaica. . . . I was not prepared to admit the right of capture on the high seas even though the chase had begun in Spanish waters. He thought the *Virginius* was not properly carrying the American flag. I asked him confidentially if he would furnish me any evidence on that point, which he agreed to do." [7]

But while it was a serious affair, it did not even yet seem to hold a grave threat of war. Suspected ships had been captured before; Americans more innocent than Ryan had been shot. Communication with Santiago remained interrupted throughout the 9th, 10th, and 11th. Fish meanwhile heard from Sickles that President Castelar had been deeply agitated by the news of the shootings, and had sent strict orders to stay further proceedings. He had at once called upon the American Minister.[8] "How deeply I deplore the execution of the four prisoners!" he exclaimed. "What a misfortune that my order was not received in time to prevent such an act! It was against the law. . . . Such scandals must cease." This was a gratifying attitude. The Cabinet on the 11th showed calmness. Fish writes in his diary: [9]

The affair of the *Virginius* and our relations with Cuba and Spain were discussed. I read a private letter addressed to me by Hall . . . in answer to one of mine inquiring as to the present and possible future of our relations with Cuba and Spain. Long and serious discussion was had, in which all the members present more or less took part. A concurrence of opinion that war was not desirable, but might be within the contingencies, was expressed, and the question of the recognition of belligerency was discussed, and so far as any opinion was expressed, it was to the effect that there was not sufficient evidence of Government and Authority in the insurgents to

[7] Diary, November 7, 1873.
[8] Sickles to Fish, November 7, 12, 1873; *Foreign Relations*, 1874, 922.
[9] Diary, November 11, 1873.

justify a recognition; in a word, that the *fact* of belligerency does not exist; although this conclusion was reached with much difficulty and after a presentation of opposite views.

In answer to a request for my views as to what should be done, I suggested a recommendation for the discontinuance of all commercial intercourse with the island of Cuba, to be accompanied with expressions of kindness and sympathy with the present Republican Government of Spain, and the pointing out that the outrage and wrongs in Cuba are the result of a secondary insurrection against the power of Spain; viz., that of the Casino Espagnol and the Spanish Volunteers. The proposition was considered in various lights, and arguments for and against were advanced. I advised that no decision should yet be reached, for unless Spain should be able to release the embargoed estates of American citizens before the meeting of Congress, it might become necessary to recommend some still more positive measure.

I

Then on November 12th fell a thunderstroke. The State Department received news from the consul-general in Havana that five days earlier Captain Fry of the *Virginius* and thirty-six men had been executed in Santiago as "pirates," and four days earlier twelve more—making fifty-three in all shot. The press that day blazoned the news to a startled nation. The anger of the country mounted as additional details came in. Behind the veil drawn by severed telegraphs one of the most brutal crimes of the period had been enacted, and now was suddenly disclosed to the world.

It appeared that the *Virginius* had carried 52 officers and men and 103 passengers, many of the crew being American and British subjects and most of the passengers Cubans.[10] The captain was Joseph Fry, an attractive Louisianian, who after serving twenty years in the American navy and four with the Confederacy had just joined the ship.[11] The vessel carried regular American papers and the American flag, though her right to both had long been questioned. Her errand had been obvious: arms and ammunition had been thrown overboard during the chase, while many of the Cubans looked like rebel recruits. The governor of Santiago, General Juan Burriel, convoked a court-martial to decide the fate of the prisoners. The first four men, Gen. W. Ryan and three Cubans, had been tried and sentenced some two

[10] For documents on the *Virginius* see House Ex. Doc., 43rd. Cong., 1st session, No. 30, *passim.*
[11] J. M. Walker, *Life of Captain Joseph Fry* (1875).

years earlier, and were now shot as soon as identified. The others were given a secret trial, without counsel or opportunity to be heard in their own behalf; a flat violation of the treaty provisions of 1795 with the United States guaranteeing civil trials to Americans. Vigorous protests by the British consul and American vice-consul had availed nothing.[12] The men were lined up against a wall, and a volley poured into them. "Then ensued a horrible scene," later wrote an onlooker.[13] "The Spanish butchers advanced to where the wounded lay writhing in agony, and placing the muzzles of their guns in some instances in the mouths of their victims, pulled the triggers, shattering their heads into fragments."

Burriel, a martinet who mingled sadism with Catholic fanaticism, refused to let the American vice-consul telegraph Jamaica for evidence. He at first ignored the vice-consul's written protest, and finally, after the killings, replied with insulting arrogance. He had been too busy to answer letters, he wrote.[14] Moreover, "the past two days were holidays, upon which the officials do not come to their offices, being engaged, as everyone else, in the meditation of the divine mysteries of All Souls' day, as prescribed by our holy religion. . . ." Other executions would have occurred had not the British warship *Niobe* under Captain (later Sir) Lambton Lorraine arrived in port on the 7th. He had sailed from Jamaica in such hot haste that he left several of his crew behind. He at once delivered both oral and written protests against Burriel's acts. Spain had no right, he declared, to capture the *Virginius* on the high seas; and even though she carried arms and recruits, her crew were not to be treated as prisoners of war—much less as pirates. Burriel sent him an insolent answer: "I am not in the habit of allowing myself to be overawed." Thereupon Lorraine swung his ship about, trained his guns upon Santiago, and though he made no explicit threat, let it be understood that further executions would mean the bombardment of the city. One of its principal avenues is honored today by the name of this resolute British officer.[15]

To understand these savage murders we must grasp a number of

[12] Chadwick, *Relations of the United States and Spain* (Diplomatic), 318 ff.
[13] Walker, *Fry*, 281.
[14] The full correspondence, which presents Burriel in a sickening light, is in House Ex. Doc., 43d. Congress, 1st Sess., No. 30. Eight American citizens had been slain.
[15] Lorraine was later banqueted and presented with a service of plate by the people of New York City; H. T. Peck, *Twenty Years of the Republic*, 535. For his course see House Report 781, 43d Cong., 1st sess.

facts. One of the most important is the reckless and fanatical character of the government in Santiago. Cuba was no longer ruled from Madrid. In Havana and Santiago the Volunteers carried affairs with a high hand; they felt as insensate a hatred of Americans as of the Cubans; and they had long defied the laws of humanity. Burriel was merely an extreme representative of their cruelty. We must remember, again, that many residents of both Spain and Cuba yet belonged rather to the Middle Ages than to modern life. Both lands had long been a seat of desolating civil strife. In both illiteracy, religious superstition, official corruption, and poverty had combined to retard progress toward humane principles. In Cuba atrocities of the most fearful kind had long ceased to excite comment; in Spain itself the Carlists were responsible for executions as brutal as those in Santiago.[16] When the news of the capture of the *Virginius* reached Madrid, much of the press set up a clamor for blood. Indeed, even the best Spaniards probably thought that the execution of a few dozen men for transporting arms to the insurgents was a trifling matter.

Moreover, the *Virginius* had long been the very symbol of the much-hated work of American filibustering. A former blockade-runner, built (like its captor the *Tornado*) on the Clyde, and captured at Mobile in 1865, she had been sold by our government in 1870 to one Patterson for $9,800, and "chartered" by the Junta. She had immediately become famous for her activities in Cuban waters. In one trip she had landed ordnance stores near Santiago for the rebels; in another needle-guns, Remingtons, and ammunition. She had even helped the Venezuelan dictator, Guzman Blanco, quell a revolt on the understanding that he would later assist the Cuban cause. For three years she had been a thorn in the Spanish side.[17] Efforts by Madrid to have her held by the Venezuelan and Colombian authorities had been resisted by the American Ministers to these nations. We have noted how the *Kansas* escorted her out of Colon when she was threatened by a Spanish cruiser. This was done because her papers had been declared correct by the American consul. Yet her character was such that in 1872 the British Minister to Venezuela had prevented her nominal sale to an Englishman by declaring that she would be seized as an outlaw if she hoisted British colors! Naturally the Volunteers had

[16] This aspect of the matter impressed England, which had lost subjects in Spain itself; London *Times*, November 14–20, 1873.

[17] Fish's Diary, 1871–73, contains repeated entries on Spanish complaints of the *Virginius*.

long boasted of what they would do if they laid hands on her. It was Captain Fry's fate to be haled before the most vengeful of the island's local despots at the very time that communication with Havana and Madrid was broken by the insurgents. Burriel had a clear field, and ran amuck without hindrance until the *Niobe* interposed.

When Fish received the Havana dispatch upon the "butchery and murder" (as he later termed it) at Santiago, he showed it to Grant, and thence hurried to the Navy Department to see Secretary Robeson. Two days earlier he had asked Robeson to send a warship to Santiago immediately. The *Kansas* was to sail on the morrow, and a messenger was now rushed to New York with fresh instructions to the captain.[18] Robeson had assured Fish that the navy was prepared for any emergency, and that several ironclad monitors could sail for Cuba on brief notice. The Cabinet the day before, indeed, had discussed the mobilization of troops, and Belknap had postponed the transfer of certain army units until the situation cleared.[19] A fleet-encounter would have provided an interesting test of the comparative merits of the old-style American monitors and the new-style armored ships of Spain. But America had all the advantages of position, greater tonnage, and—no doubt—better gunnery.

Returning to the State Department, Fish sent an ominous message to Sickles. "If the report be confirmed," he directed, "you will protest, in the name of this government, and of civilization and humanity, against the act as brutal, barbarous, and an outrage upon the age, and will declare that this government will demand the most ample reparation of any wrong which may have been committed upon its citizens, or upon its flag." [20] But he added that grave suspicion existed as to the right of the *Virginius* to her flag and papers, and that Sickles must bear this in mind in whatever he said to the Ministry. American indignation was fierce and deep. The flag had been insulted, and even men who cared nothing for freeing Cuba were aroused.[21] Bancroft Davis informed Fish from New York that he heard the expression of a powerful emotion "on every side and from all classes of people." The correspondent of the London *Times* wrote that the executions had caused

[18] Diary, November 12, 13, 14, 1873.
[19] British authorities agreed that the American Navy, antiquated as it was, could easily dispose of the inefficient Spanish Navy; see London *Times*, November–December, 1873.
[20] House Ex. Doc., 43d Congress, 1st Session, No. 30, 15 ff.
[21] Oberholtzer, *United States*, III, 123, 124.

"an outburst of indignation from the press and the people that is ominous for Spanish rule in Cuba." Indignation meetings were held in Pittsburgh, Boston, Baltimore, New Orleans, and other cities. The press immediately gave great space to naval preparations and the strengthening of coastal fortifications. For some days the New York *Times* reported "intense excitement" in Wall Street.

Under other circumstances this excitement—matched in Spain by popular feeling which at one moment threatened a mob attack on the American Legation—would have touched the match to war. But the danger of a conflagration was far smaller than would have seemed possible a year earlier. The United States had just suffered a severe financial panic, and was preoccupied with the grim depression now rushing upon it. Since the establishment of the Spanish republic the previous spring, the movement for intervention had almost collapsed, and sympathy with Madrid had become widespread. Faith in the Cuban rebellion had diminished. The uncertain status of the *Virginius* was soon borne home to the American people, who also shortly realized that Castelar was honestly willing to make whatever reparation was politically feasible. Nor did any such latent jingoism exist as was to respond to the sinking of the *Maine* in 1898; Americans were too close to their last war. Trustworthy observers were agreed that the general wrath stopped short of a demand for hostilities. *Harper's Weekly,* the New York *Tribune,* the *Nation,* and other organs declared that no real demand for a conflict existed outside Junta circles.[22] Dana's *Sun* was almost the only journal of influence which called for unsheathing the sword.

II

Fish's position in the crisis passed rapidly through three phases. Comprehending the weakness of Spain, he reserved his anger for the irresponsible officials of the island. At the outset he expressed the view that the outrage proved Spain's inability to govern there, and that if she could not call her subordinates in Havana and Santiago to strict account, she would do well to take her hands off and let the United States deal with them. When Madrid asserted full responsibility, he determined to require a full atonement. Arbitration, he held, was inadmissible, for the question was one of national honor. Madrid

[22] N. Y. *Times, Tribune, Herald,* November 14–30, 1873.

must apologize for the insult to the flag, must restore the ship and pay for the blood spilt, and must furnish "some speedy and signal visitation of punishment" on the guilty officials. This second policy resulted in peremptory demands upon Castelar's government, with a time-limit attached. Then, discovering how dubious was the *Virginius's* title to the American flag, and realizing that too harsh an attitude would cause the fall of the Spanish republic, he greatly modified his demands. But throughout the three phases of his policy he was intent upon preserving peace. His greatest difficulty lay not with American sentiment, which was moderate, nor with Grant, who supported him, but with the pride and stubbornness of Spain.

The first phase was brief. On November 13th Polo was at the State Department, full of anxiety.[23] Eager to present some excuse, he declared that the United States had not used due diligence to prevent the filibustering expedition. Recruits had left New York for it on the *Atlas,* despite Spanish warnings to the Federal Attorney. It turned out that no sworn evidence whatever had been presented to the Federal Attorney. Fish spoke in severe condemnation of Burriel's course—his brutality, his refusal to let the American consul telegraph to Jamaica, and so on. He pointed also to the failure of the Captain-General to move energetically. "All this looks like premeditation," he said. He then descanted upon Spanish impotence in the island. "The Volunteers and Casino Espagnol have usurped the powers of your government," he told Polo. "They have accomplished a successful revolution." Why not admit it? Why should Spain not confess to the indignant world that the Volunteers were in rebellion against her no less than the insurgents, and that the home government was temporarily powerless? Madrid might then inform the United States that it was at liberty to avenge any wrongs perpetrated by the Volunteers. Fish added that while he could not make this suggestion officially, it seemed to offer a means of maintaining peace between Spain and the United States, and at the same time of reducing Cuba to such a position that the Spaniards could carry out their reforms. And he could assure Polo of one fact; the United States was determined to have "most ample reparation" for all the wrongs she had suffered.

As Polo was ushered out the Peruvian chargé entered. Latin America, when the news of the crisis reached it, had felt a thrill of hope

[23] Diary, November 13, 1873.

that the United States would now liberate Cuba; and the chargé brought word that his country would furnish the fullest support. "Do you mean that Peru will go to war with Spain?" asked Fish.[24] The chargé unhesitatingly replied yes. "I encouraged him to suppose," Fish writes, "that in case any action is determined on I might communicate with him." A few days later similar assurances of aid came from our Minister to Mexico.

The 14th brought the first Cabinet meeting since news of the massacre. Fish exhibited a draft-message to Sickles, written with sufficient asperity to impress Madrid with the gravity of the crisis.[25] The Minister was to demand the restoration of the *Virginius,* the release and delivery to the United States of the survivors; and a salute to the American flag in the port of Santiago. If satisfactory reparation were refused, he was to close the legation and leave Madrid.

President Grant at once approved this. Creswell wanted something more prompt and decided, but could not explain what; he said that he was afraid Spain would comply with the demands! What he actually wanted was war. Robeson and Williams at first thought that it would be better to make a mere general demand for ample reparation. Time soon proved that they were right; but after Fish had offered some arguments, and Grant had declared an emphatic preference for specific demands, they yielded. Only one amendment was made. Fish had inadvertently omitted any reference to penalties, and to the first sentence was added a demand for "the signal punishment of the officials who were connected with the capture of the vessel and the execution of the passengers." Spain was given a time-limit of twelve days. Thereupon the Cabinet again fell to discussing preparations for war.[26] Robeson was directed to collect the entire available navy in Florida waters at once, Grant and Fish assuring him that Congress would legalize any overdraft upon his appropriations. The West Indian fleet under Rear-Admiral Scott comprised five ironclad monitors, and twelve wooden ships; it was at once heavily reinforced, while nine colliers were hurried to Key West with fuel.[27] Troops were concentrated at Fortress Monroe; Fort Jefferson and other Gulf posts were strengthened and re-garrisoned. Official circles in Washington not only believed the navy able to crush the Spanish fleet without difficulty, but anticipated no difficulty in landing an initial army of ten

[24] Diary, November 13, 1873.   [25] Diary, November 14, 1873.   [26] *Ibid.*
[27] Report Secretary of Navy, 1874.

thousand men in Cuba within a few weeks.

At the State Department Fish immediately placed his dispatch upon the wire. It was virtually an ultimatum; if Spain did not meet his requirements within twelve days diplomatic relations would be severed— and that meant war. Edwards Pierrepont had written offering to help arouse public sentiment.[28] Fish replied: [29] "The Administration does not need the stimulus of public meetings. It is 'fired up!' and you will see monitors and vessels of war moving toward the Antilles as fast as they can be put to sea. We appreciate that a certain class of negotiations are best conducted by a nation, its full armor on its back, and *we are in thorough earnest*. If the armor does not secure peacefully what will be satisfactory it will at least be ready for consequences." He was deeply aroused. Three days later he wrote William Cullen Bryant that the Administration was occupied with "the horrible butchery" at Santiago.[30] "I think that it marks the end of Spanish rule in Cuba. It throws grave responsibilities on this government, and opens a difficult question as to the future of the island. . . . But it is evident that Spain cannot govern it, in fact that Spain has not for some time past been able to control it. Should not then the *nominal* supremacy of Spain over the colony be denounced by other Powers—even if not renounced by her?"

No one who knew the Spanish temper expected prompt action from even Castelar's liberal régime. Sickles received Fish's dispatch of the 12th, instructing him to protest against the executions as brutal and barbarous and to demand "the most ample reparation," on the 14th. Already he had talked with Foreign Minister Carvajal, voicing the indignation of the United States, and questioning him as to the real extent of Spanish authority in Cuba.[31] He had made no demand, however, expecting that Spain would spontaneously offer reparation; for both Castelar and Carvajal had expressed deep regret over the shootings. But on receipt of Fish's dispatch of the 12th, with its stinging epithets, "butchery and murder," "barbarous," and so on, he sent Carvajal a note which reproduced its language almost verbatim. When the Foreign Minister read this note he bristled defiantly. Regarding its phrases as insulting, and believing that the hot-tempered Sickles had written it without due authority from Washington, he took a resentful attitude which gave the whole situation a new tension. That same day, Novem-

28 Pierrepont to Fish, November 13, 1873; Fish Papers.
29 Fish to Pierrepont, November 14, 1873; Letterbooks.
30 Fish to Bryant, November 17, 1873; Letterbooks.   31 Chadwick, op. cit., 327–329.

ber 14th, he penned a heated reply. In this he indignantly rejected the protest. He commented upon its harsh and insulting style. He denied the right of the United States to characterize Spanish acts in any other terms than those which Spain herself thought just; particularly when neither the State Department nor Sickles possessed sufficient information about the *Virginius* affair to support a complaint. He regretted that the American Minister had not waited, as he had at first intended, for spontaneous action by the Spanish Government; and he stated that he would tolerate "no disparagement of any right."

This violent reply in turn angered Sickles. He hastened, in a new note of November 15, to correct Carvajal's view that he had gone beyond his instructions, pointing out that his language was almost a precise transcript of Secretary Fish's instructions. He rebuked Carvajal sharply. "When His Excellency proceeds to affirm that neither the government of the United States nor the undersigned are sufficiently informed of the nationality of the *Virginius* or of the circumstances attending her capture . . . to warrant a reclamation or protest against these acts, the undersigned can do no less than point out to the Minister of State that he thus assumes to speak of matters not within his cognizance." By this time Fish's dispatch of the 14th, the virtual ultimatum, had arrived, and he notified the Foreign Minister of its demands in blunt terms. He also sent a note calling attention to the refusal of General Burriel at Santiago and the Captain-General at Havana to listen to the requests of the American consul and consul-general. Altogether, Carvajal must have felt overwhelmed that November day. The notice that his government had less than a fortnight within which to restore the *Virginius* and her surviving men, to salute the American flag, and to punish the responsible officials, showed Spain on the beetling verge of war.

And Fish was as indignant as Sickles. At the same time that he learned from Madrid that Spain had rejected his first protest, he received a report (which happily proved erroneous) that fifty-seven more prisoners had been executed in Santiago. He telegraphed this news to Sickles as evidence of the necessity of speedy reparation, adding: "There is but one alternative if denied or long deferred. If Spain cannot redress the outrages perpetrated in her name in Cuba, the United States will. If Spain should regard this act of self-defense . . . as necessitating her interference, the United States, while regretting it, cannot avoid the result. You will use this instruction cautiously and discreetly, avoiding unnecessarily exciting any proper susceptibilities, and avoiding all appearance of menace; but the gravity of the case admits no doubt, and must be fairly and frankly met." [32] The United States might have to land troops at Santiago and discipline Burriel, whatever the consequences for peace or war.

The result of Fish's stand was that within three days the Spanish Government climbed down from its first defiant position. It is true that Carvajal on the 17th loosed another rhetorical note at Sickles, characterizing the American demands as humiliating and unjustified, and asking for a suspension of judgment pending an investigation. Spain, he wrote,[33] "will decide upon nothing to relieve the flag of the United States from an offence until she is certain the offence exists"; but if her officers had violated any obligation whatever, "she will be glad to repair the wrong according to its just importance." The hotheaded Sickles cabled to Fish: "Regarding this as a refusal within the sense of your instruction, I propose, unless otherwise ordered, to close this legation forthwith, and leave Madrid, embarking at Valencia for France. . . ." Next day he added: "Popular feeling runs high here against the United States and this legation. Press violent and abusive, advising government to order me out of Spain. Last night a mob was collected to attack and sack the legation. The authorities interfered and preserved the peace." But the Spanish Government at last realized that the United States was in earnest. On the 18th it therefore offered to transfer the negotiations to Washington. Admiral Polo was directed to ask for a proper period in which to ascertain the facts. But he was also instructed to assure the American Government, in positive terms, that Spain would comply strictly with her treaties and the principles of international law; that she would punish all officers who deserved it, regardless of station, and that she would make full reparation for all proved offences.[34]

Fish felt that this plea for an interval to permit of investigation was reasonable, and directed Sickles to tarry in Madrid for further instructions. He was also glad to have the negotiations brought to Washington. For one reason, personal feeling evidently existed between Sickles and Carvajal. For another, some telegrams from Sickles were

[32] Fish to Sickles, November 15, 1873; *Foreign Relations*, 1874, 941.
[33] *Foreign Relations*, 1874, 947–949.   [34] *Foreign Relations*, 1874, 951, 954, 979.

arriving in very distorted shape, and were excited in tone; Fish distrusted him, and was glad to have Spanish statements reach him direct from official Spanish sources, not through a medium. With Congress about to meet and much of the press violently aroused, he wished to hold the reins firmly in his own hands.[35]

In fact, Fish and Polo were as likely to find a peaceable solution as the nervous Carvajal and testy Sickles were likely to come to a rupture. Both men were calm and reasonable; Fish had been striving for years, Polo for months, to avoid hostilities over Cuba, and each was aware of the weakness of his government's case. At best, the outlook remained sinister; but there were certain factors making for mutual forbearance.

Admiral Polo knew well that the *Virginius* could be convicted of nothing worse than an intent to violate the municipal laws of Spain. Her chase, as was later proved, had begun outside Cuban waters. She had offered no resistance, and was in fact unequipped for offense or defense. No recognized state of war existed in Cuba, and the ship's cargo could not be regarded as contraband of war when there was no war and no blockade. No proof could be offered that any of the Americans on board had accepted commissions in the Cuban army—which was not a recognized army anyway—or meant to levy war against the Spanish Government. The Spanish navy would have been justified in watching the vessel, in seizing her had she entered Cuban waters, or possibly even in a precautionary seizure on the high seas; but the authorities had no excuse for visiting such a fearful punishment on her men. As one of the best authorities states: [36] "Had they even been seized while in the act of landing the passengers the business in which they would have been engaged would not have amounted to piracy. The element of violence would have been wanting." Fish had repeatedly warned Spain not to treat Americans running the patrol as "pirates."

For his part, Fish knew that the status of the *Virginius* was highly dubious. What real title had she to her American papers and her American flag? If none, what right had the American Government to interfere in her behalf? The papers seemed in proper order, and American consuls and American naval officers had recognized her as entitled to them and to the flag; but what if the title rested in fraud? Fish knew that one or two of our consuls in Caribbean waters had for many months felt that the *Virginius* possessed a dubious legal claim to American protection, and no moral claim at all. He knew that journals like the *Nation* were questioning whether the legal title were valid. And on November 15 he received a rude shock in the matter. He writes in his diary:

Pearne, last consul at Kingston, called at the Department and in the course of conversation respecting the *Virginius* mentioned that the papers were all regular, and he had placed Frye in command of her when Williams gave up. On my inquiring how he came to do so, he stated that he had acted in strict accordance with the consular regulations, and at the request of the owners of the *Virginius*—adding that he had refused to do so until requested both verbally and in writing by Mr. Quesada. I asked if Mr. Quesada was the owner; he said that he appeared to be, and on my reminding him that the vessel was registered in the name of Patterson he remarked: "So it was. That never occurred to me. Had I thought of that I could not have made the transfer."

General Quesada was a member of the Cuban Junta in the United States! As it appeared later, he, José Mora, and other Cubans were the real owners, and Patterson's sworn statement that he was the sole proprietor and that no foreigner was interested in the vessel was false.[37] A ship owned by the Junta, and employed in landing not only arms but armed men to fight against Spain—Pedro Cespedes, Ryan, and others were notoriously Cuban soldiers—was making fraudulent use of our flag.

Various influential Americans argued with the State Department that the disreputable character of the *Virginius* gave it a weak case. The distinguished attorney John Norton Pomeroy contributed a well-balanced article to the *Nation*.[38] In a letter to Fish he pointed out that during the long *Alabama* controversy the United States had strongly condemned the fraudulent use of neutral flags and papers in aid of combatants; and that for our government to abandon these principles in response to a sudden feverish clamor would largely obliterate our triumph in the Treaty of Washington.[39] Edwards Pierrepont sent Fish

[37] *Foreign Relations*, 1874, 1001–1009.   [38] *Nation*, XVII, 332–34, Nov. 20, 1873.
[39] Pomeroy to Fish, Rochester, N. Y., November 21, 1873; Fish Papers.

similar advice. It was true, he stated, that every ship with papers of *prima facie* regularity was part of the soil of her apparent nationality, and that an attack upon her was good cause of war. "But because there is no precedent to support the contrary proposition, it does not follow that none ought to be made. The great volume of the Common Law was swelled to its present proportions by *new precedents* arising out of new circumstances. Suppose the Spanish Volunteers in Cuba, inflamed against the citizens of the United States, should send an armed expedition intended to aid a bad riot in New York and to burn the city, and a United States ship of war should sink the ships of this expedition off Sandy Hook in an attempt to capture them, would Spain have just cause for war when it appeared that the ships with Spanish register and Spanish flag were in fact owned by lawless men in New York who planned the riot? . . ." [40]

Knowing how treacherous was the ground they trod upon, both Polo and Fish were inclined to move cautiously. When Polo received news of the transfer of negotiations, Fish in a long conversation impressed upon him the importance of definite Spanish action in place of mere promises. The United States was tired of the postponements of recent years, he said. At the Cabinet meeting that afternoon, the 18th, as he was reading the latest message from Spain, a note was handed him from the Associated Press. It contained a Madrid dispatch saying that the Spanish Cabinet were unanimously in favor of a satisfactory and honorable settlement, but were resolved to protect the integrity of Spanish territory. Fish then turned to the task of convincing Grant that patience was necessary: [41]

I express the opinion that these representations may probably lead to the necessity of extending the time at which Sickles has been directed to close his legation. The President replies that this is only the same sort of procrastination to which we have been accustomed. Admitting the fact, I observe that this government cannot afford to go to the extreme of war in view of an official representation that Spain is prepared to make honorable satisfaction by means of which damaged interests will be reëstablished and national susceptibilities appeased; that we owe it to ourselves and the world to be right, before resorting to the extreme measures of war; and that if Spain declare her readiness to make atonement we should not be justified in withdrawing our Minister until she had ample time to obtain from Cuba full official re-

[40] Pierrepont to Fish, November 24, 1873; Fish Papers.
[41] Diary, November 18, 1873.

ports of the occurrence. I then read the "private and confidential" of November 15, addressed to me by Captain Edwin L. Brady, and mention what was stated to me by Mr. Pearne on Saturday last respecting his placing Captain Frye in command of the *Virginius* on the request of Mr. Quesada, who assumed to be the responsible owner of the vessel, and that if Quesada was the owner Pearne was wrong in granting the papers, inasmuch as the fact showed a change of ownership which deprived the *Virginius* of her right to the register which she bore.

The President said there would be time enough before the 26th to decide whether to extend the time.

The next day Fish and Polo, anxious to reach a peaceful settlement, had another long discussion. The Minister asserted that the vessel belonged to Quesada, and that her papers had been obtained by fraud. "Well," said Fish, in effect, "it seems to me there may be an easy way out. Your government can say that it believed the *Virginius* had no regular American papers and was sailing under false colors. You can apologize for the mistake—for it really did have regular American papers. You can thereupon restore the ship, and salute the flag as having been unintentionally assailed. But General Burriel should at all events be punished for his brutality, and the surviving passengers should be surrendered." [42] The Secretary of State was trying to build an easy bridge for the Spanish retreat.

Thereafter he and Polo acted in close coöperation. They saw each other every day, and sometimes several times a day; they concerted steps which they believed would circumvent refractory members of their two governments. For example, on November 20 Polo called with a proposal by Madrid for arbitrating the dispute. Fish could not accept it, but he was unwilling to rebuff the Castelar Government sharply. He and Polo therefore agreed upon the following mild telegram, which Polo sent back to Madrid: "Read the telegram to Mr. Fish, who will take it into consideration, with a sincere and earnest desire to reach an honorable and amicable adjustment, but he cannot conceal the fact that there is great difficulty attending it. He says that he has no knowledge as yet of the release of the embargoed estates, or any manifestations of the power of Spain to enforce in Cuba her orders or the reforms of which assurances have often been given, or to give hope of the early pacification of the island, or to assure the protection of the lives and rights of American citizens therein." A few days later Fish, in

[42] Diary. November 19, 1873.

accordance with the decision of the Cabinet on November 21, formally replied that a question of national honor was not arbitrable; but the sting of this refusal had been drawn in advance.[43]

III

Meanwhile he was taking measures to reduce the demands originally made upon Spain. As a result of his arguments, the same Cabinet meeting that pronounced against arbitration decided that he was "to hold the door open for further propositions, conditioned upon an apology for the indignity to the flag, and the delivery of the vessel to the United States." [44] When he handed Polo the note upon arbitration, he carefully abstained from restating therein the various demands for reparation made in the quasi-ultimatum. Polo remarked upon this omission. The Secretary then jotted down informally the three demands "which the United States feels itself justified in expecting from Spain"—the restoration of the *Virginius* and its survivors, a salute to the American flag, and the signal punishment of the delinquent Spanish officials. He read this to Polo, who hastily agreed that it was inadvisable to repeat them; and Fish therefore gave him no copy of the paper.[45] He was trying to keep the situation as fluid as possible. He had requested the British Government to bring pressure upon Spain for a prompt compliance with the wishes of the United States, and Lord Granville had immediately sent word that it would do so.[46] The influence of the British, whose citizens had also been slain but whose flag was not involved, might be potent. A dozen guarded entries in the diary show that Fish was exerting every effort for peace.

But he was fearful of the malign influences surrounding Grant. Some men near the President were eager for war. On November 9 Bancroft Davis wrote from New York: [47]

My dear Governor:
A little incident took place on the train yesterday which it is just as well you should know. Among the passengers was General Dent, who started from Washington so drunk that he couldn't speak plainly, and left the train in Jersey City so tipsy that he staggered through the station to the boat. He took his drinks in the forward compartment of our car, and spent most of

[43] Diary, November 20, 1873; *Foreign Relations*, 1874, 958.
[44] Diary, November 21, 1873.   [45] Diary and Memorandum, November 22, 1873.
[46] Diary, November 21, 1873.   [47] Fish Papers.

the day there—but when we were near Baltimore he emerged and spied us. He came up to me and in quite a loud tone said, "What are you going to do with the *Virginius?*" I don't attempt to give his pronunciation. Imagine Dick Taylor on the night he dined with you trying to say "National Intelligence" and you may fancy it. . . . I said in reply to him, "I don't know, General; that is a matter for my superiors to decide," and tried to turn the conversation. He came back to it, however, and said: "I understand you. You may pretend not to know—that's all right for you—but I know all about it. I was in the next room at the last Cabinet meeting, and I heard all that was done. I hope we shall not stand this. I want to be sent down there with my battery. I should like nothing better than to pitch into Morro Castle." This he said in a tone of voice loud enough to be heard by people about me. Fortunately nobody, probably, was able to comprehend his thick speech.

To which Fish replied: [48]

The little incident of eavesdropping explains some things. What a nasty crew to have about one! Drunken, stupid, lying, venal, brainless. Oh! that "Somebody" were rid of such surroundings!

But within a few days, despite the devoted efforts of himself and Admiral Polo, and despite the British pressure in Madrid, a rupture of relations seemed imminent. It had been understood on November 21 that Fish would give the Spanish Government until the 26th to take satisfactory action. But Madrid insisted upon delay; it asked the United States to wait "for our solution, which would be immediate on receipt of the facts in the case." Fish replied that past experience with the Spanish Government did not warrant the United States "in entering into an agreement which practically amounts to an indefinite postponement." Castelar's Ministry again protested against haste, declaring that it would promise to make full reparation if Washington would only wait for proof that the vessel really had the right to carry the American flag. To this Fish quite properly replied that search for such proof was irrelevant. The documents of the vessel were in due form, our consul had given her the right to carry the American flag, and her capture was an insult to the United States whether the papers had been fraudently or correctly obtained.[49] And Grant now sternly intervened. At the Cabinet meeting on the 25th he gave orders that Sickles be instructed to leave Madrid unless a satisfactory answer came by the end

[48] Fish to Davis, Washington, November 14, 1873; Letterbooks.
[49] *Foreign Relations*, 1874, 983–985.

of the following day.[50] Fish sent this order. But he added in his message to Sickles: "Should a proposition be submitted to you tomorrow, you will refer it here and defer action until it be decided upon." [51]

The essential dispute between Spain and the United States had by this time been narrowed to a very small point indeed. Fish was insisting that reparation for the indignity to the American colors must procede the investigation into the ship's right to carry them; the Spanish Government was insisting that the investigation should come first. On November 26 a new proposal arrived from Madrid, and Sickles delayed his departure. In this note the Spanish Government tried to remove Fish's objection to an "indefinite postponement." It promised that if within a month—by December 25—the illegality of the *Virginius's* registry had not been proved, it would deliver the vessel and crew, furnish the required salute, and punish all officials concerned in the affair. This showed progress, but it still fell short of the mark. Receiving it on Thanksgiving Day, the 27th, Fish at once showed it to the President, who agreed that it could not be accepted. The Secretary declared that no Power had the right to molest on the high seas in time of peace a ship bearing American papers; and that Spain was virtually asking the United States to consent to her retention of the *Virginius* while she sought evidence to justify her act.

Fortunately, Polo was prepared with an alternative proposal, which had been sent him in a strictly confidential communication. Spain should give up the vessel and men at once; the United States should institute an inquiry into the *Virginius's* ownership, and if it found any violation of Amercan laws, inflict proper punishment; and the salute to the American flag should be postponed until the end of the inquiry.[52] Fish and Grant agreed that this plan was acceptable. Light had dawned at last.

Next day, November 28th, this last-minute action of Madrid and the cool firmness of Fish brought the whole negotiation to a satisfactory close. Some confusion was produced in the morning when Polo called with a telegram from his Government stating that the discussions had been re-transferred to Madrid. Fish exclaimed that this was preposterous; he believed that Sickles had already left his post, and even if he had not the telegram showed both vacillation and misunderstanding.

---

[50] Diary, November 25, 1873.   [51] *Foreign Relations*, 1874, 958.
[52] Cabinet Memorandum in *Foreign Relations*, 1874, 986.

Polo himself did not know what it meant, and they agreed to ignore it. Fish therefore went to the Cabinet in an unperturbed mood, and stood staunchly by his promise to Polo that the United States would defer the salute if ship and men were surrendered at once. He wrote in his diary: [53]

Cabinet. All present. I hand to the President a memorandum for his message on matters connected with this Department, except on relations with Spain and the affair of the *Virginius,* which I tell him cannot be completed as the subject is assuming different phases from day to day, and as our information comes by telegraph where frequently words and sentences are unintelligible and have to be guessed at, and which it would not do to communicate to Congress in this imperfect form. I read all the telegrams and memoranda respecting the *Virginius* received and sent since the last meeting. Mr. Creswell exhibits some impatience, but after discussion confesses that nothing more could be asked than has been, and that if the arrangement be made, as indicated in a conversation with Admiral Polo of yesterday, the country will not be justified in standing up on a question of punctilio as to the salute to the flag. He still indicated a desire for some further assurance of the punishment of those connected with the executions at Santiago de Cuba, but finally yielded, admitting that we claimed all that we justly could claim.

And immediately afterward the Secretary reaped the reward for his patience. His diary continues: [54]

Early in the evening (between six and seven) Admiral Polo called at my house and with much earnestness of manner expressed his satisfaction at being enabled to say that the question between the two governments respecting the *Virginius* would be settled according to our request, and that he had received a telegram of which he gives me a copy, as follows:
Telegram from Secretary of State, Madrid, to Spanish Minister, Washington. Received 28th November, 1873, 6:30 P. M.
"We can accept the restitution according to the terms of your telegram. Inform Mr. Fish at once and express the satisfaction with which I see happily terminated the negotiations between two nations who have been at peace during a century under different forms of government and could not forget that they now happily live under the same institutions."

Actually Sickles had never left Madrid. He had requested his passports on the 26th, but had agreed to a postponement of their delivery. Early on the 28th he had presented a little ultimatum of his own, telling the

[53] November 28, 1873.   [54] *Ibid.*

Foreign Minister that he would renew his request for passports in the afternoon unless the original American demands were accepted in full. But before he could do so he was informed of the new agreement in Washington. When he suggested to Fish that an unconditional acceptance might yet be obtained, he was summarily ordered to remain at his post and await instructions. Nor had the Spanish Government ever attempted to re-transfer the negotiations to Madrid. What it had done, as the situation became threatening, was to try to use the agencies of both capitals simultaneously to arrive at an immediate understanding. When the Foreign Minister had telegraphed Polo,[55] "Negotiations renewed in Madrid. Confer again with Mr. Fish on the basis of last official note. . . . " he had meant simply that he wished negotiations to be carried on in both Madrid and Washington at once. Polo had misunderstood him. But it was an instance of all's well that ends well.

IV

For after the fateful 28th, despite a few new delays and vexations, the *Virginius* affair was quickly brought to an end. Polo and Fish at once prepared a protocol, which Grant approved.[56] It provided that the Cuban officials should forthwith restore the *Virginius* and her surviving company; and that on December 25, 1873, Spain must salute the American flag unless it were proved that the ship had no right to fly it. In that event a salute would be waived, and the United States would accept a mere disclaimer of intended insult to its ensign. It was further agreed that Spain would investigate the conduct of the officials accused of infringing laws or treaty obligations, and inflict due punishment on all guilty persons. The United States, if the *Virginius* were not entitled to the American flag, would for its part take proceedings against the vessel and the owners. Other reciprocal "reclamations" were to be the subject of negotiation.

The news of this partial Spanish surrender filled the Volunteers in Cuba with fury. The loyalist press raged at both governments; the authorities in Santiago ordered all men over twenty-two enrolled as soldiers.[57] On December 4 Polo called at the State Department looking very sad and ill. Alarming news from Havana had kept him up all night. The Captain-General had cabled that the excitement was intense

[55] *Foreign Relations,* 1874, 987.   [56] Diary, November 29, 1873.
[57] *Foreign Relations,* 1874, 1082–1090.

and universal, that he feared he could not deliver the *Virginius* in Havana harbor without violence to the American ship sent to receive it, and that Polo should gain more time. Fish was adamant in resisting delay. When Polo asked if .the vessel could not be sent to Spain or at least Puerto Rico for delivery, he objected; but he said that the United States would receive her at any small port in Cuba.[58] Next day the Spanish Government inquired, through Polo, whether the United States would not let the *Virginius* be delivered to a consul of another nation. Of course Fish again refused. The situation still held elements of danger, as President Grant's peremptory attitude at the Cabinet meeting that day showed. Fish writes:

> I read all telegrams, dispatches, and memoranda respecting the *Virginius*. . . . The question is raised whether we might accept surrender in New York or some other American port. Robeson and Creswell think she should be delivered in Cuban waters. The President, however, is of opinion that the surrender in an American port would be sufficient, and repeats with some energy, that he would not allow a question of that nature to stand in the way of a friendly settlement. I read also a draft of a memorandum of terms as to time, place, and manner of carrying out the Protocol, including the ceremony of a salute to the flag. . . .
>
> The President suggested that Admiral Polo should be told that, unless the matter was adjusted on Monday, the question would be referred to Congress for its decision. On my suggestion that in that case it would be necessary to make a recommendation to Congress, and inquiring what action he would recommend, he said reprisals, recognition of independence of Cuba, and a temporary suspension of the Neutrality Acts, so far as regarded Spain. I objected to reprisals . . . as a half-way measure of war, and advanced the opinion that if it became evident that war was to result, it would be desirable to bring about the first act of hostility from Spain.
>
> On discussion it was decided not advisable to intimate any limited time to the Spanish Minister for positive decision, but to hold out the importance of an early decision, and make it as urgent as possible without committing the government.

Finally, on December 16, the *Virginius* was surrendered to the American navy at Bahia Honda, sixty miles west of Havana. Convoyed thither by the Spanish warship *Isabel la Catolica,* she was delivered, as Fish had insisted against Spanish objections, with her flag flying. On December 18 the survivors, most of whom had been confined in Morro Castle at Santiago, were given up to the American warship

[58] Diary, December 4, 1873.

Juniata at that port. The *Virginius,* long misused and in bad disrepair, foundered on her way to New York.[59]

Meanwhile, government officers had begun a thorough inquiry into the ownership of the vessel. Testimony taken in New York was laid before Secretary Fish and Attorney-General Williams. When the latter reported that her papers had been fraudulently obtained and that she had no right to the American flag, the demand for a salute was dropped. Nevertheless, the Attorney-General held—of course correctly—that her capture by Spain on the high seas had been as illegal as if her registry were unsullied. Spain had to admit this illegality; and this involved admission also of the wrongfulness of the executions. The United States pressed for an indemnity, and in 1875 obtained $80,000, which was distributed to the proper persons. Great Britain also, nineteen of her subjects having been slaughtered, demanded and received payment.

There remained the question of the punishment of General Burriel, and here Spanish procrastination appeared at its worst. The London *Times* justly said in 1876 that if the author of this crime had been an Englishman, "he would assuredly have been hanged; yet he is still at liberty, and we believe has some sort of command." The United States insistently urged that he be brought to trial. He was recalled from Cuba at the end of 1873; in the spring of 1874 he replied to a severe arraignment of his conduct published in the *Revue des Deux Mondes*; and he then retired to an obscure corner of Galicia, mortified, the American Minister reported, "by seeing that his government is humiliated on account of his acts." [60] But in spite of solemn promises in Madrid he was never tried, and in 1875 was actually promoted to the rank of major-general. When he died in 1877 his atrocious deed still had warm defenders in the Spanish press.

American sentiment instantly accepted the settlement of the *Virginius* affair as just. Had the event occurred twenty years earlier, when the Southern slave-barons were in power, Cuba would immediately have been conquered. But public sentiment was now—thanks largely to Fish—in such a state that efforts to whip up a belligerent emotion met no success. The principal mass-meeting during the crisis was that in New York on November 17, which filled Steinway Hall and Tammany Hall. The crowd cheered S. S. Cox's attack on the Adminis-

[59] Diary, December 17, 19, 1873. [60] Chadwick, *op. cit.*, 351, 352.

tration for its hesitancy, and Governor Hendrick's telegram demanding armed intervention. But William M. Evarts made a conciliatory speech, while a letter from Sumner deprecated the "belligerent preparations of the last few days" and pointed out that the Spanish republic was struggling for existence.[61] John Murray Forbes mailed Fish an editorial of the Chicago *Tribune* in favor of moderation, writing that he did not doubt that this was "the sober second thought of the country, nor that all sound men are looking to your steadiness to resist the senseless outcry for war." [62] Gouverneur Kemble sent his assurances that in spite of the excitement, "we are not all mad, and therefore hope you will not be affected by it, or swerve from the neutral policy hitherto maintained . . . ;" [63] and Reverdy Johnson made a similar statement.

Fish had been certain that he could appeal to this sober conservatism among thoughtful Americans. When he wrote William Cullen Bryant of the *Evening Post* on November 17 that he thought the "horrible butchery" at Santiago marked the end of Spanish rule in the island, he added that he was still against violent steps. He had been much abused by Cuban partisans, but while determined to vindicate the honor of the republic, he would not be "carried away by temper or excitement," or swerve from the legal path. "The recognition of belligerency would have been the assertion of what does not exist; there is not at this day the evidence of any organized government of what is called the republic of Cuba; no seat of government, no legislature, no courts, no cities, no seaports, no means of communicating with other Powers; simply a brave, persistent defiance of Spanish rule, and a long-continued guerrilla fighting. I have endeavored to persuade these Cuban gentlemen . . . that recognition of belligerency would not benefit them—at least Mr. Lemus admitted to me that he agreed with me in this view. Recognition would have contradicted the arguments, in fact the whole history of the diplomacy and of the position of this government. . . ." [64] Bryant had replied sympathetically.[65]

"In relation to the main subject of your letter," he wrote, "let me say that I fully comprehend the embarassing position in which the butchery of the men found on board of the *Virginius* placed the Administration. A war with Spain would be a real disaster to the country,

---

[61] N. Y. *Tribune,* November 18, 19; *Nation,* November 27, 1873.
[62] Forbes to Fish, Chicago, November 17, 1873; Fish Papers.
[63] Kemble to Fish, Cold Spring, N. Y., November 17, 1873; Fish Papers.
[64] Letterbooks.   [65] Bryant to Fish, Roslyn, L. I., November 19, 1873; Fish Papers.

FISH VS. SICKLES

John Bull to Spain: "It's difficult Fishing here!"

(Nast in *Harper's Weekly*)

and we do not want Cuba, with her ignorant population of Negroes, mulattos, and *monteros* or white peasantry, alien to our own population in language, manners, habits, and modes of thinking. . . . I for my own part, and I am sure that I speak for great numbers of our people, have admired the wise deliberation with which the Administration has proceeded in this matter, and I am confident that the great mass of the people will ultimately approve its course. It will look well in history."

Congress fortunately did not meet until after the settlement of November 28th, and when it did the members showed a signally pacific temper. The only dispute then remaining was over the place of delivery for the *Virginius*. Chairman Cameron of the Foreign Relations Committee and Oliver P. Morton called at the State Department to express their desire for a friendly agreement upon this matter; and Morton even proposed introducing a Senate resolution to advise some mode of accommodation.[66] Garfield suggested to Bancroft Davis the same day that the subject be carried along until Congress broke up for the Christmas holidays, when it could better be adjusted. In fact, Congress proved so lamblike that Grant expressed amazement. With one of his rare glints of humor, he said he believed that if Spain sent a fleet to New York and bombarded the city, the Senate would pass a resolution of regret that she had been put to the trouble, and offer to pay her for the expense of the operation.[67] As we have said, the panic and industrial depression accounted for part of this meakness of temper; the friendliness toward Spain's republican government for still more.

v

And when peace was assured, a shower of congratulatory letters fell upon Fish. Edwards Pierrepont wrote that "this will more than compensate you for all your anxieties and give you an enduring eminence among great statesmen." [68] William M. Evarts sent warm felicitations. The veteran journalist Nathan Sargent declared: "It falls to the lot of but few men in office to accomplish two such gratifying victories as you have achieved—first in the settlement of our difficulties with England, and second, this Spanish imbroglio." [69] Oliver P. Morton pointed out

[66] Diary, December 5, 1873.   [67] Diary, December 7, 1873.
[68] Pierrepont to Fish, New York, November 29, 1873; Fish Papers.
[69] Evarts to Fish, New York, November 30, 1873; Sargent to Fish, Washington, November 30, 1873; Fish Papers.

that the situation had been peculiarly difficult. War would have been a calamity "and most likely unpopular;" demands too rigorous would have overthrown Castelar's republic; and yet vindication of the national honor was imperative. "Your success in this matter, and in the settlement of the *Alabama* Claims, are among the greatest achievements of American diplomacy." Wayne MacVeagh wrote that he recalled no other instance in diplomatic history of such large concessions being obtained upon so small a foundation without resort to arms. "I am sure the country will not soon forget the inestimable service you have rendered her. . . . Such victories of peace are 'no less renowned' and far more blessed than those of war." [70]

The one American figure who emerged from the affair with discredit was General Sickles. His attitude toward Spain had undergone a sudden change. As late as September 10, 1873, he had written that Castelar "is one of the greatest men of the epoch," and been full of hope for the republic under his leadership. But by mid-November he thought Castelar a failure and his government done for. He blamed Fish and Grant for being "sentimental" over the republic, which had "utterly failed," so that it was "a mere question of days and hours, of opportunity and pretext, for the Dictatorial Reaction to assume power." Thus disillusioned, he had favored a peremptory course toward Spain from the outset. He was offended by the transfer of negotiations to Washington, and bitterly disappointed when Fish receded from the drastic demands of his quasi-ultimatum. Thirty-five years later, addressing a historian of the affair, he still condemned the Secretary's moderation.[71] Feeling convinced that the moment had come to humiliate Spain or go to war with her, he had gravely misused his official powers. He had sent dispatches of a character to arouse the State Department, to misrepresent the Spanish position, and—if any leakage occurred—to excite American sentiment. For example, he had described Carvajal's reply to Fish's semi-ultimatum as a statement that the American demands were "without foundation, imperious, arbitrary, compulsory, and humiliating." This did great injustice to the dignified if controversial character of Carvajal's reply, which

[70] Morton to Fish, Washington, November 30; MacVeagh to Fish, Harrisburg, December 12, 1873; Fish Papers.
[71] See Sickles to Chandler, September 10, 1873, December 10, 1873, for his views of the republic; Sickles Papers. For his statement thirty-five years later, see J. M. Callahan, *Cuba and International Relations*, 410.

had ended with a courteous request for delay and not a flat rejection. The most disagreeable and stubborn portion of the Spanish communications Sickles cabled; the explanations and conciliatory expressions he sent by mail. Castelar's two earnest expressions of regret over the executions, for example, did not reach Fish until November 28 and December 8. In proposing on November 19 to "close the legation forthwith" Sickles was trying to force the Secretary's hand.[72]

Moreover, as Fish wrote later: "Several of Sickles' communications to me appeared somehow or other in the press in this country simultaneously with their reception at the Department. It really appeared as though he took the violence of the *Herald*, the *Sun*, and other kindred sheets as evidence of the popular sentiment." [73] When the final settlement was made, Sickles's position had become untenable. He resigned on December 6. Fish, with the final negotiations to carry through, then asked him to remain. But when a fortnight later he repeated his resignation, it was gladly accepted.[74]

Fish welcomed the opportunity to send an abler man to Madrid. Knowing how soon the office-hunters and patronage-brokers would descend upon Grant, he hastened to propose a successor. "I venture to suggest to you the name of General Cushing," he wrote the President on December 22, 1873. "Among his many and varied accomplishments he is a thorough Spanish scholar, and I think that his appointment will give more confidence to the country, and will be more likely to result in satisfactory decisions, than that of any other man of whom I can think—probably than any other man in the country. He is in entire harmony with your own views and policy with regard to Cuba as well as with regard to other questions." On January 6, 1874, the nomination went to the Senate.

The new appointment was nearly ideal. Cushing, with all his faults, was intellectually one of the most distinguished men in the country. He had spent much time in Spain in early life and had published interesting reminiscences of his travels there.[75] He was widely read in Spanish literature, and on terms of intimacy with many Spanish leaders. For many years he had been an aggressive opponent of filibustering or intervention, and while Attorney-General under

[72] Cf. Rhodes's condemnation of Sickles, *United States*, VII, 33–35.
[73] Fish to Washburne, February 12, 1874; Letterbooks.
[74] Grant to Fish, December 20, 1873, for Grant's assent; Fish Papers.
[75] *Reminiscences of Spain* (1833).

Pierce had acted energetically to repress such unlawful enterprises.

Three years earlier two great nations, boasting themselves in the forefront of civilization, had plunged into war because of a mere punctilio—the shadowy point of honor involved in the Ems telegram. It would have been easy to plunge the United States and Spain into war because of another punctilio—the shadowy point of honor involved in the affront offered to the flag of a vessel which had no right to fly it. Brave young Americans, brave young Castilians, would have bit at the gore-soaked earth in their last agonies because their national leaders lacked a sense of proportion. In a quarrel over a few words, a gesture, the drifting cannon-smoke of a salute, two nations which had each learned by recent experience how much war costs in blood, in money, in sorrow, above all in moral retrogression, would have leaped back into war. Whatever Spirits shake their heads over the woes and follies of this spinning bit of planetary dust would have lamented a new irony. But this unhappy result was averted. It was seldom that Hamilton Fish revealed his deeper feelings. Yet just before Christmas, the Day of Peace, he wrote his son in terms that were less restrained than usual. "I do not expect that the fugitive-from-justice editor of the New York *Sun,* or the wild Irishmen who run the New York *Herald,* or the Spaniard who edits *El Cronista,* will be satisfied," he declared, "but I have thought of the tens of thousands of wives who might have been made widows, and of the hundreds of thousands of children who might have been made orphans, in an *unnecessary* war undertaken for a dishonest vessel. . . . There *is* a national evil worse than war, but unless the national honor, or the national existence, require war (and when either is endangered or attacked, war becomes a necessity), then the nation should do all that it can to avoid the terrible evil. That is what I have endeavored to do."

LIKE most Americans, Fish had hoped that Grant's last four years would be comparatively uneventful. It has often been observed that no President has been happier in his second term than in his first, and for obvious reasons; the lustre of his initial popularity has been dimmed, his enemies have had time to join hands, and his special policies have lost their first impetus. Fish would have been content had Grant faced no problems graver than those of Monroe in his second Administration. But all such hopes were scattered by the financial tornado which descended upon the nation in September, 1873. For eight years the country had been more expansively prosperous than ever before. Railroads had shot out from the Mississippi, great new industries like steel and petroleum had arisen, mass-production had been organized in the shoe, clothing, meat-packing, and flour-milling industries, agriculture had covered the prairies, and cattle-ranching was driving the buffaloes from the plains. Mills were running at capacity, labor was fully employed, immigration was brisk, and wages were making much-needed gains. A multitude of industries were distributing their securities at high interest rates among a host of small investors never before able to buy. Until midsummer of 1873 few clouds had dimmed the horizon. Then in a twinkling the scene changed to gloom and anxiety, and Grant faced a vista of trouble.

Fish was at Garrison when on September 13 Kenyon Cox & Co. failed, and from that coign of vantage during the next few days watched an ominous decline in stocks.[1] On the 18th the banks began to call their temporary loans in large numbers, and at noon that day the country heard the stunning news that Jay Cooke & Co. had closed their doors. The night before this failure, Grant had been a guest at "Ogontz," Cooke's palatial house near Philadelphia. Though Cooke had received warning telegrams early on the 18th, his courtesy forbade him to breathe a word to the President, and Grant proceeded to Washington unaware that he had slept in a doomed house. Next day the New York bankers Fisk & Hatch failed. These announcements were precursors of a general crash, and at noon on September 20th the boiling Stock

[1] *Commercial & Financial Chronicle,* August, September, 1873.

Exchange in New York was closed until further notice. The worst panic since 1837 was on, and in its wake came a grim depression that was not to lift until 1878, long after Grant had left Washington.

What could the government do about the calamity?—that question instantly occurred to Fish as to others. But the Secretary of State knew better than others how unprepared the Administration was. At best no government can do much to shorten an industrial depression; the storm has to blow itself out, the cycle to complete itself. In the seventies, with *laissez faire* still unchallenged, the Administration was not expected to furnish even palliatives. Men asked merely that it hold the tiller of public finance steady; that it keep confidence in the value of the dollar and the stability of the Treasury unimpaired. Grant obviously knew nothing whatever about finance. Did the Secretary of the Treasury possess more knowledge, and was he a leader upon whom the nation could rely for sound judgment and courage? It was the country's misfortune that at this critical moment it had no Chase, no Hugh McCulloch, not even a Boutwell, in the Treasury, but a new and untried man: William A. Richardson, who had succeeded to the office only six months earlier. All the greater was the responsibility resting upon Grant.

I

That Richardson was the merest stopgap, named temporarily as a *pis aller*, is made clear by Fish's diary. A Harvard graduate, long a plodding, methodical lawyer in Lowell, Massachusetts, a probate judge there, a friend of Boutwell's, who appointed him Assistant Secretary of the Treasury in 1869, he was little known. He had first come into general notice when he performed Boutwell's duties for several months in 1872. He then reissued about $5,000,000 of the $44,000,000 in greenbacks wisely retired by Secretary McCulloch, ostensibly because the fall crop movements required more money, but really to affect the fall elections in the inflationist West. He had been rebuked by the Senate Finance Committee and the conservative press,[2] and was thereafter distrusted in financial circles. Early in 1873 it became evident that Boutwell was about to succeed Vice-President-elect Henry Wilson in the Senate. Various men were suggested for the Secretaryship. One was Henry Clews of New York, another A. J. Drexel of Philadelphia

[2] N. Y. *Tribune, Nation,* December, 1872.

Jay Cooke, alarmed by the latter suggestion, for Drexel & Childs were rival Philadelphia bankers, instructed his brother Henry to make every effort to defeat it. "It would be cruel to permit such a party to get into the Treasury," he wrote.[3] In consequence, with Ben Butler and Henry Cooke joining hands in Richardson's support, rumors of his appointment—very alarming to most Eastern bankers and editors—had gained currency. Richardson meanwhile actively canvassed for the position.

Ordinarily the wiles by which a politician gains Cabinet office are no more interesting than edifying; but with the black cloud of panic lowering over the unconscious nation, Richardson's efforts and Grant's surrender to them have striking significance.[4] Fish's diary relates how on Sunday evening, March 16, 1873, Richardson had rung his doorbell.

He said that Grant would decide upon the Secretaryship within a few days; that Fish would be consulted, and would be able to determine his fate; and that he wished to make a personal plea. His position was very trying. He declared that Grant had spoken of appointing him, "that the public generally expected it, that the whole press of the country with the exception of the New York press favored it, that a great portion of the Senate favored it and had spoken to him in relation to it, that within a few days the President had told Senator Morrill of Maine that he would appoint him, had given Mr. Boutwell to understand the same thing, and that if now disappointed it would be utter disgrace and ruin to him, and to his family who had been led to count upon it." He showed deep emotion. "I have taken the odium of the overissue of greenbacks, a party measure of which you know the real history," he told Fish. As a matter of fact, Fish had known nothing about it until a few days earlier, and said so. "Well, it was insisted upon as a party measure, and I took all the censure and odium of it," continued Richardson; "now I think I am entitled to recognition and consideration for my services." He added that after holding the office a short time he could resign and go at once to Paris as head of the house of Monroe & Co., and would therefore be content with an *ad interim* appointment. All this irritated Fish, who records:

I told him that I knew of no such thing as an *ad interim* appointment; that some months since, early in the session, the President in speaking with

---

[3] Oberholtzer, *Jay Cooke*, II, 364–365.

[4] See Storey and Emerson, *E. Rockwood Hoar*, 243, for Richardson's lack of reputation. Someone asked Hoar if he were known in Massachusetts. "No," said Hoar, "his reputation is strictly national."

me [said] . . . that he thought of appointing him (Richardson) *ad interim,* and, in reply to a remark of mine that there was no such thing as an *ad interim* appointment, the President had said he meant a temporary appointment, from which I inferred (not telling him what in fact the President had said, that he would not think of him for a permanent appointment) that the President meant until the end of the then existing session of Congress from the time of Boutwell's election. He (Richardson) then said . . . that if appointed he would resign at the end of one day or at any time the President might name.

I told him that one day last week . . . the President had expressed his wish to recognize his services by giving him an *ad interim* or temporary appointment, [and] that I had felt it my duty to say to the President that whoever was to be the permanent Secretary ought to have the confirmation of the Senate and not [be] left during this long recess without the moral support of such confirmation, and subject to all the intrigues of politicians and of financial cliques which would weaken his power and make his position uncomfortable and feeble. . . . That we could not disguise to ourselves that the Republican Party had suffered during the past winter from the allegations of fraud in the Kansas election, the extravagance of appropriations, and especially the Congressional back-pay, all of which placed the party on the defensive, and care should be taken to avoid any further subjects of attack. He (Richardson) replied that he feared my views would defeat him, but that he would be quite content to resign before the adjournment of the Senate to allow a permanent appointment to be made. . . .

Later that evening Boutwell had called. He remarked that Richardson was competent because of his familiarity with the business of the office and the personnel of the department, and in especial because of his close connection with the work of loan-conversion. He did not believe him the best man for the place, "but at the present time his would be the best appointment that could be made as a temporary one." Fish still raised objections. He said that he knew from conversations with Senators and Representatives who had asked him to prevent the nomination that it would be unpopular. Moreover, he feared that Richardson was unable to keep his own counsel. "Yes," admitted Boutwell, "it is true that precisely there Richardson fails, but I am at a loss to know who else can be named." Obviously Fish was hostile. But Grant showed the very next day that he had no hesitations. Fish again records:

March 17, 1873 (Monday).—Cabinet . . . The President stated that he had requested our attendance in order to send to the Senate all nominations, and that he had concluded to name Judge Richardson as Secretary of the

Treasury to hold the office temporarily, thinking that he was quite competent to the discharge of the duties, especially with reference to the issuing of the new loan and its negotiation, with the details of which he supposed him to be more familiar than with any person excepting Governor Boutwell and possibly even more familiar than he. That his nomination would indicate to the country an adherence to the financial policy which had been established and would thereby quiet many expectations and efforts toward a change in that policy; that he desired him to hold the office until the negotiations for the loan should be completed, which he thought might occupy some months and possibly until the next session of Congress.

Richardson had been promptly confirmed. The country thus faced its grave new financial problems under a Secretary who was widely distrusted, who seemed unable to keep secrets, and who had claimed his position as the reward for executing a discreditable party manipulation of the currency.

As Fish at once realized, the panic was not merely a trumpet announcing the onset of depression, but was also a drum-beat summoning the inflationist and contractionist forces of the land to a desperate battle. Their chronic post-war skirmishing had ended some years earlier in a precarious truce. After the war, when Secretary McCulloch had begun retiring greenbacks, the statutory limit of the greenback circulation was $400,000,000. He withdrew $44,000,000 before he was halted in 1868 by an act of Congress. That left $356,000,000, which Boutwell and Richardson had temporarily increased by small amounts. Eastern contractionists had talked of the dangers of inflation and a speculative currency; Western inflationists had denounced the retirement of the greenbacks as the Sangrado practise of bleeding a patient to death.[5] Moderates like John Sherman had taken a median path. What course would Grant now choose? Hitherto he had approved of Boutwell's conservative policies and emphasis on debt-reduction; but he was a Westerner himself, and readily accessible to inflationists like Oliver P. Morton and John A. Logan. The country waited anxiously. During the panic of 1857 the government had taken a passive rôle. But now it was in direct control of the volume of currency, able to contract or expand it instantly. A wild clamor arose from men eager to influence the Administration.

[5] Foulke, *Morton*, II, 319 ff.

II

The President and Secretary Richardson, accompanied by Reverdy Johnson, reached New York on September 21 to consult with business men and bankers at the Fifth Avenue Hotel. Many industrialists and politicians implored them to relieve the money-market by releasing a large part of the $44,000,000 in retired greenbacks, still held in the Treasury under the name of a "reserve." Others objected vehemently to the emission of a dollar. Secretary Richardson, to the relief of conservatives, shortly announced that he would reissue no greenbacks; instead, he merely began buying government five-twenty bonds with the surplus currency in order to relieve the general tightness.[6] The banks had quickly done their part by issuing large quantities of clearing-house certificates usable as money—an expedient which carried banking-houses through the first "runs" by panicky depositors, and provided ample funds for business transactions. By October 1 the net addition to the currency by clearing-house certificates, use of government money, and other expedients was estimated at $50,000,000.[7] Experienced financiers also pointed to the indications of a coming plethora of money. As in all depressions, excess funds soon began flowing into savings banks and other depositories, where a deficiency of confidence kept them immobilized.

Grant meanwhile conferred with various men, including that great financial authority Mr. Tom Murphy. His position was unhappily less clear than Richardson's. He soon wrote a letter to the New York banker H. B. Claflin which implied his approval of a common violation of the banking laws. National banks were required to keep a reserve equal to a fourth of their note-circulation and deposits, and were forbidden to make new loans if the reserve fell short. But nearly all had been granting loans in excess of the legal allowance, and Grant indicated his acquiescence in the practice. In still other ways he showed his sympathy with the demand for an expansion of currency and credit.

Fish, half-ill at Garrison, knew of the clamorous demands upon Richardson and wrote encouragingly on September 24th: "By all means I trust you will not issue more greenbacks. Such is the desire of the soundest thinking people." By return mail he had a pathetic letter.[8]

[6] Rhodes, United States, VII, 43–47.   [7] Nation, October 2, 1873.
[8] Richardson to Fish, Washington, September 25, 1874; Fish Papers.

"I can hardly express to you the regret which I feel at your not having been here through this severe panic, during which I have been overwhelmed with telegrams day and night, making all kind of wild and absurd propositions. I have resisted the pressure to the fullest extent in my power." Richardson added that "I know you would have been a great support to me in stemming the torrent"; that "I have stood here alone most of the time and have borne the brunt of the battle"; and that he hoped that Fish would soon return to Washington, for "We shall be asked to do the wrong thing again and again." Fish wrote once more on September 26 applauding the press statement that he would issue no more greenbacks and urging him to stand firm: [9]

I am in the receipt of your letter of yesterday. I sympathize warmly with you in the cares pressing upon you and trust that you will firmly resist any expansion of the currency. We are going through what was as inevitable as the succession of night and day. The losses thus far sustained cannot now be repaired. Any expansion would only bolster up some now tottering concerns, and would encourage new speculations, and the trouble would be deferred for a very short time to return with increased severity. It appears to me that we are now passing through a tremendously severe ordeal, at the end of which are to be seen brighter skies and a more wholesome condition than we have experienced for some years.

The country has large crops of grain and of cotton; bread must continue to be cheap, while wages must fall and the excess of our crops will be bought abroad at fair prices.

The pressure of the speculating classes and the anxieties and honest fears of many in legitimate business will continue to urge expansion and to suggest expedients which may not be authorized by law. But I assure you that nothing the President has ever done seems, so far as I hear from persons of all classes, to give more satisfaction than the decision which he and you reached on Sunday last. I hear from everyone, except those interested in speculation in stocks and bonds, one universal approval of the "heroic action" of the President and Secretary of the Treasury and but one expression of hope that you will adhere to the policy of non-expansion. It may be a severe remedy, but severe cases require severe remedies.

I expect to be in Washington on Tuesday morning. . . . I agree with Henry Wilson in urging you to stand like a rock. Hoping to see you Tuesday, and in the meantime ready to do what I can to aid and sustain your hand, I am . . .

Fish was back in Washington for the first Cabinet meeting after the panic on September 30, and lent energetic support to a conservative

[9] Letterbooks.

policy. The discussion showed that two members, Belknap of Iowa and Delano of Ohio, were for inflationist measures, and that Grant was still hesitant. All agreed that reforms in banking practice were much needed, and Fish tried to divert attention to them. He urged that New York banks be estopped from one general and quite illegal course. They had been accustomed to assist stock-brokers by certifying large checks early in the day, with the understanding that the necessary money or securities would be brought in by three o'clock; in other words, they had been making heavy unsecured loans for hazardous speculations.[10] On Fish's mention of this fact Grant remarked with an air of sudden illumination: "Ah, I suppose that is what Murphy called my attention to, and tried to explain to me, but I didn't understand it at the time. My opinion is that it ought to be stopped." Both the President and Richardson believed that the country was now close to the resumption of specie payments. Actually resumption was more than five years distant; gold had fallen at the first onset of the panic, but immediately rose again.[11] No decision was made on the greenback policy, and Richardson's negative decision temporarily stood.

After the meeting Richardson drew Fish aside to tell him of the President's uncertain position. He confided that "there had been great difficulty in reaching a solution . . . ; that there had been some adverse and powerful influences very near to the President, urging a very wide expansion and general inflation." The previous Sunday, September 28, Grant had almost surrendered. "They were in conference for many hours, and at one time he feared that all was gone, but [Attorney-General] Williams had stood up manfully, and with great difficulty had restrained the President to that which appeared in his letter to Claflin." Secretary Delano had besieged the White House, and his influence had been especially pernicious. Full of Western doctrines, he had been excited and violent in urging inflationist schemes. Orville E. Babcock had given him all too effective support. "Who is behind Babcock?" asked Fish, suspiciously. "I suppose it to be Porter," replied Richardson.[12] But this was probably an unjust aspersion upon Horace Porter, who had left his White House position the previous year to join the Pullman Company.[13]

On October 2 Fish learned that $2,000,000 in greenbacks had been

---

[10] *Nation*, October 2, 1873.   [11] Diary, September 30, 1874.   [12] *Ibid.*
[13] Elsie Porter Mende, *Horace Porter*, 126 ff.

reissued after all. He also learned that Secretaries Delano and Richardson were on the very verge of a breach. They had glared at each other across the Cabinet table. That day they exchanged hot words on the White House stairs. "Sir," said Delano in an offensive manner, "you must remember there is a West." To which Richardson retorted: "I know it, sir, but I remember there is also a country!" [14]

Grant for some weeks seemed if anything to favor the moderate inflationists. Early in October he gave an interview to the Associated Press. He startled the conservatives by declaring that if Congress were in session he would ask it to legislate for the reissue of the whole $44,-000,000 "reserve," bringing the greenback currency back to $400,-000,000. He believed that the country was still fundamentally prosperous, and spoke of the panic as a "passing event" which might yet prove salutary; for a return to specie payments was impossible without a shrinkage of values, and this shrinkage had now taken place. He wondered why silver, now worth as much in currency as in bullion, was not "pouring out." When it did begin to flow, he believed that the nation could absorb $200,000,000 to $300,000,000 of it, thus expanding our currency and simultaneously benefiting the Western mine-owners. He spoke also of asking Congress to pass a free banking law, with a repeal of the old requirement of a reserve for the protection of depositors; and said that he would probably recommend a postal savings bank to pay four per cent on all money sent to it. The interview was not merely inflationary in tone, but painfully crude in some of its ideas; yet it breathed an extraordinary self-confidence in dealing with these difficult subjects. [15]

During November, Fish, Richardson, and other conservatives of the Cabinet labored to keep ill-considered demands for currency-expansion out of the President's annual message. Early that month Grant had a long talk with President John E. Williams of the Metropolitan Bank of New York. Williams understood him to urge the banks to help relieve the stringency, and to say that the government would aid them "by issuing three or four millions a week of the reserve." When the banker published this statement Richardson denied that any such issue was contemplated, and Grant had to say that Williams had misunderstood him. But the President had doubtless used these very words, for he was presenting even more reckless ideas to the Cabinet.

[14] Diary, October 3, 1873.   [15] *Nation*, October 16, 1873.

The meeting on November 7 left Fish dejected. Richardson, he records, read a proposed report to Congress upon the recent panic and the course of the government. It embodied "some suggestions toward the prohibition of national banks from paying interest on deposits, and as to the right of issuing the reserve of $44,000,000 currency and the expediency of government's having the power to use such reserve in case of necessity." This was bad enough, for it showed that Richardson was vacillating. But worse followed: [16]

"Discussion arose as to obtaining what is called an elasticity in the currency, and the President stated that in his opinion it would be advisable to authorize the issue of convertible bonds bearing 3.65 per cent interest. Mr. Creswell inquired whether that would not amount to an expansion of the currency. On explanation of the *modus operandi* it was thought that it would, and that it would simply be throwing upon government, in times of redundancy of currency, the payment of interest on a surplus currency which the banks now paid. On consideration this project was abandoned."

In espousing this 3.65 convertible-bond scheme Grant was adopting a favorite plan of the greenbackers! It assumed a protean variety of forms, the scheme shortly offered in Congress by William E. Kelley of Pennsylvania being typical of many. He proposed that the government sell at least $50,000,000 worth of bonds bearing 3.65 per cent interest, and issue $50,000,000 in greenbacks as a reserve for their redemption; using the $50,000,000 received for the bonds in buying up older bond issues—that is, returning it at once to circulation. The result would be to add $50,000,000 to the greenback currency.[17] Peter Cooper wished to emit indefinite quantities of greenbacks and maintain their credit by making them convertible into 3.65 per cent bonds at the will of the holder. Clearly, Grant's financial ignorance was profound and his inability to conceal the fact explained his hasty retreat from his 3.65 per cent proposal.

While the President's message in December, 1873, happily contained no concrete proposal for new greenback issues, it distinctly leaned toward currency expansion.[18] To be sure, Grant warned the nation that "undue inflation" would be folly, for even if it gave temporary relief it would lead to price inflation and eventual hardship. What was

---

[16] Diary, November 7, 1873.   [17] *Nation*, January 15, 1874.
[18] Richardson, *Messages and Papers*, VII, 243–248.

needed was "elasticity," and he suggested several modes of gaining it. During the four preceding years, he argued, the currency had been diminished in measurable ways by about $63,000,000; and comparatively speaking, there had been a much larger contraction, for population, commerce, and manufacturing had greatly expanded. His statement that he hoped "the best method may be arrived at to secure such an elasticity of the currency as will keep employed all the industries of the country and prevent such an inflation as will put off indefinitely the resumption of specie payments," showed that he really wanted a moderate inflation, or reflation. Most commentators instantly placed that interpretation upon the message. By this time, indeed, Richardson had reissued $8,000,000 of the $44,000,000 greenback "reserve."

III

In Congressional debate the inflationists and conservatives grappled like rival condottiere.[19] Senator Ferry of Michigan wished to bring the irredeemable greenback currency up to $800,000,000 by substituting governmental legal-tender notes for the national banknotes then in circulation; to release the banks from all restrictions; and to float an issue of 3.65 bonds. Wilson of Indiana proposed a government fund of $100,000,000 to be lent in times of stringency to all applicants who could offer Federal bonds for security. Senators Wright of Iowa, Carpenter of Wisconsin, Logan of Illinois, and Morton of Indiana gave enthusiastic support to general demands for inflation. The opposition was led by Carl Schurz, John Sherman, and Morrill of Vermont, who pointed out the dangers of a huge irredeemable currency.[20] Meanwhile, a quarrel had developed between Secretary Richardson and the House Ways and Means Committee over the best method of replenishing the Treasury. It was nearly empty, and the national debt had increased rapidly during the past two months. Richardson declared for an immediate levy of new internal revenue taxes, but the House, fearing the political consequences, clamored for economy as the true road out. While the quarrel persisted, Richardson, to meet expenses, kept on reissuing greenbacks until early in 1874 the new emissions totalled $26,000,000!

The more conservative of the two houses was the Senate, where John

[19] Foulke, *Morton*, II, 323 ff.; John Sherman, *Recollections*, I.
[20] W. B. Parker, *Justin Smith Morrill*, 227–229.

Sherman held a strategic position as chairman of the Finance Committee. None of the ill-considered schemes which Congressmen like Kelley were pushing could pass the upper chamber. Led by Sherman, the Finance Committee shortly reported a creditable bill.[21] It provided that the existing greenback circulation, now $382,000,000, should not be exceeded; that national banks might be organized in all States and Territories until each had as much banknote circulation in proportion to its population and wealth as New York State; that for every $1,000,000 issued by such banks $750,000 in greenbacks should be withdrawn from circulation until the total was reduced to $300,000,000; and that the national banks must keep a fourth of the coin which they received in interest on government bonds as part of their reserve. This measure offered a considerable expansion of the banknote currency, and yet by its gradual contraction of the greenbacks would protect the Treasury. But the inflationists sternly rejected it. The House immediately organized a counter-offensive, and on March 23 voted by 171 to 70 a bill for increasing the greenback circulation to $400,000,000.[22]

This, said the inflationists, represented their minimum terms.

In both chambers a majority quickly rallied to the $400,000,000 clause. After many amendments, the pending legislation was reduced to simple form. It provided in twenty lines that the maximum amount of greenback currency should be $400,000,000, and that $46,000,000 should be added to the circulation of the national bank notes, raising their total also to $400,000,000. The country would then have a circulation of $800,000,000 in legal tender notes and national bank notes combined. Theoretically this would be an increase of about $100,000,000. Passing House and Senate by wide margins, the bill went to the President on April 14, 1874.

Grant was generally expected to approve the bill. What did all his recent inflationist statements, what did his encouragement of Richardson's reissue of $26,000,000 in greenbacks mean, if he would not sign it? His annual message had fairly committed the Administration to the view that $400,000,000 was the proper legal-tender level. As for the proposed increase in the national banknote circulation, that would after all depend upon the ability of people who wanted the notes to buy United States bonds for deposit; and a good market for the bonds was so desirable that Grant might well hesitate to interfere with the

[21] *Nation,* March 19, March 26, 1874.   [22] *Nation,* March 26, 1874.

process. It soon appeared, moreover, that the measure was less inflationist than had been supposed. Comptroller Knox pointed out that
a clause which required national banks to keep three fourths of their
reserves on hand would cause an immediate contraction equal or almost
equal to all the new circulation authorized.[23] This made it possible to
defend the bill as a rather mild measure. Actually it remained a bad
bill. Legalizing a circulation-increase of about $100,000,000, it would
unsettle values and raise a speculative spirit. If it failed of an inflationary effect the cry for "more money" would soon be raised again. And
it violated all the promises of the party. The Republican platform of
1868, Grant's utterances in 1869–70, had looked toward an early resumption of specie payments, for which all wise citizens hoped. This
bill looked away from it and toward a cheaper paper currency than
before, toward cheaper money instead of the world standard. There are
times, as in 1933, when a grave deflationary crisis demands a reduction in the unit of value. But the United States in 1874 was not pinned
to gold; deflation had not yet moved far; and what the Carpenter-
Morton-Ferry group proposed was an opening wedge for drastic inflation. Closely examined, the bill was indefensible.

If Grant believed in principles, here was one worth fighting for if
it took all summer; but did he? At first the answer seemed no. Both
he and Richardson spoke approvingly of the bill. At a Cabinet meeting just before it passed, April 10, 1874, Richardson indeed valiantly
defended it.[24] "It will not have an inflationary effect," he argued. "It
merely legalizes the issue of the full $44,000,000 reserve which the
Administration claims to be legally issuable anyway. It is true that the
provision for more national bank currency seems to contemplate expansion, but this is illusory. The requirement that the banks must not
deposit more than a quarter of their reserves in New York or other
redeeming depositories, with other features, will operate practically
in the direction of contraction." Grant accepted this view. The day
after the bill passed he chatted with Fish, who sternly opposed it: [25]

He says that he had examined the bill as printed in the papers with some
care; that the main objection is the animus or intent of the bill, which in
itself is comparatively harmless, and is rather one of contraction than of
expansion. Unfortunately, it has been passed by almost a geographical division, and that a veto would tend to array one section of the country against

[23] *Nation*, April 16, 1874.   [24] Diary, April 10, 1874.   [25] Diary, April 15, 1874.

the other. His present idea is not to be in a hurry to sign the bill, and not to sign it without assigning his reasons. His present intention is to prepare a message reviewing the bill, and pointing out such conservative features as it may possess, and forestalling any measure of expansion which may be in contemplation.

IV

At this moment, with inflation apparently imminent, another great scandal broke—the Sanborn Contract scandal. It left Richardson heavily besmirched, and with his resignation unescapable, the dreadful danger loomed up that he would be replaced by the inflationist Delano of Ohio. Truly, troubles never came singly while Grant was President!

A few words will suffice for the scandal itself. John D. Sanborn was a Massachusetts politician, an old agent of Ben Butler's in Southern speculations during the war, and now connected with his machine.[26] At Butler's suggestion, Richardson had made contracts with him to collect internal revenue taxes evaded by railroads, distillers, legatees, and others. Sanborn and the Treasury, under the moiety-system, were to divide all collections equally. This system, a fertile source of corruption, had already been condemned by public opinion and discarded by the Administration, but a special exception was inserted by Butler in an appropriation bill. Early in 1874 the House Ways and Means Committee investigated Sanborn's work. They learned that Treasury officials had virtually warned collectors to neglect their duty so that Sanborn might have more money to collect, and that most of the $427,-000 which he had recovered would have come to the government in due course anyway. He had gotten much of it by simply sending demands to 592 railroads listed in *Appleton's Railway Guide,* together with a false oath that he had received information of tax-evasion, and thus extorting money from many of them! Sanborn testified that of his share, $213,500, he had paid $156,000 for "expenses" to men whom he would not name. A faint suspicion arose that Butler had received part of it!

The whole affair looked like a conspiracy, connived at by Boutwell and Richardson, for defrauding the Treasury and the taxpayers simultaneously for the benefit of a few men.[27] It was more than suspected that the contract had been a *quid pro quo* for Butler's aid in the Senate in raising Richardson to the coveted Secretaryship. The way in which

[26] Bowers, *The Tragic Era,* 422, 423.
[27] Schouler, *United States,* VII, 239; Hesseltine, *Grant; Nation,* April 2, 1874.

shrewd men regarded it is illustrated by a letter which Fish received late in March from Thurlow Weed: [28]

The Administration is falling into disrepute. You have done well and wisely in resisting all and averting many mischiefs, but without more elevation and a higher tone in the head of the Administration, one of its arms, however strong, cannot save it.

Sanborn was with Butler at Fortress Monroe and New Orleans with "tobacco and cotton permits." Tweed, Connolly, and Sweeny rolled into one would not make a more rapacious man than Butler, who is now working destruction to the Republican Party as surely as he ruined the Democracy at Charleston in 1860.

Early in April Butler, squint-eyed, alert, and impudent, swaggered into Fish's office with Representative John M. S. Williams of Massachusetts.[29] The latter had a detective-friend, one Donahue, whom he wished sent to Canada to spy upon smugglers. "A sharp fellow, this Donahue," said Butler, approvingly. "One might need a saint to find out what saints are doing, but that information is not worth seeking for. We want to find out what the other class is after, and a saint can't do that but Donahue can." Fish declined the man's services.

When Williams had departed, Butler leaned forward confidentially. He first said that Williams had special reasons for wishing Donahue sent to Canada. Donahue knew a few facts about him, and Butler, winking in his cross-eyed fashion, added: "You know, Credit Mobilier matters; and money on which no income returns were made." Butler then turned to the Sanborn Contract scandal. He scoffed at the investigation. "It's all a put-up job for the purpose of getting Delano into the Treasury," he said. "Fellows like Foster of Ohio and Beck of Tennessee have been engineering it. The committee at first intended to make a severe report. But they have found that they had better not. Old Fernando Wood was especially eager to attack my friend Sanborn, but he has thought better of it." And with another wink he went on: "One of Sanborn's friends called on Fernando. He suggested that perhaps it would be just as well if he kept his hands off; that there are parties who hold evidence that Wood made upwards of $60,000 on various deals and has failed to pay a cent of income tax. You can bet that Wood dropped the Sanborn affair immediately." Butler's face lost its amused leer and became set and determined. "I can tell you this,

[28] Weed to Fish, New York, March 25, 1874; Fish Papers.   [29] Diary, April 10, 1874.

Mr. Fish," he concluded. "Grant ought not to remove Richardson while this persecution is going on, and Richardson ought not to resign."

"Mr. Butler," said Fish severely, "I think that the clamor which has been raised against Richardson, just or unjust, has ended his usefulness as Secretary."

Butler grunted. "A satisfactory report will be made in a few days," he rejoined. "Its general purport will be that contracts may have been improvidently made, and that the law authorizing them may have been improvident, but that it was Boutwell who made them, and nobody supposed at the time that much if any of the unpaid taxes could be collected. Richardson will be relieved from censure, and he can then do as he pleases about resigning." And he swaggered out of the office.

Knowing Grant thoroughly, Butler was aware of his stubborn aversion to dismissing any officer "under fire." Whatever the reasons for this—his instinct for military solidarity, the loyalty of a long-friendless man for his supporters, his disinclination to admit a mistaken appointment—it was a salient trait. Circumstances seldom altered it, and it led him to defend men like Babcock, Belknap, and Richardson long after he should have repudiated them. Of course, it was grossly inaccurate to say that Richardson was merely under fire. He had been tried and found wanting. He was a negligent and faithless official, who had lent himself to the operations of a gang of designing men engaged in mulcting private business and the Treasury. But his friends set up the usual cry that he had been misunderstood and imposed upon, and must not be abandoned to a pack of Administration enemies; and this was enough for Grant. On April 15, Fish wrote that he had just talked with the President:

The question of a possible change in the Cabinet arising, he says that Richardson is shortly to leave the Cabinet, and would probably have presented his resignation before this time but for the pending investigation in Congress; that he had spent last evening with Messrs. Dawes and Boutwell, in which Dawes [chairman of the Ways and Means Committee prosecuting the Sanborn investigation] said that there was no evidence affecting the character or honesty or charging corruption upon the officers of the Treasury in connection with these claims, although there had been much looseness and improvidence; and that they had come to the conclusion that Mr. Richardson had better withhold his resignation until the close of the investigation.

In other words, Grant had reached precisely the conclusion Ben Butler wished him to reach. Worst of all, the President told Fish that he thought of making Delano the new head of the Treasury. Fish remonstrated vigorously; he cited various objections and expressed doubt even of Delano's honesty. "At the close of the interview," the diary succinctly records, Grant "decided that it would not be advisable to make such an appointment." But he gave Fish new dismay when, saying that he would select no New Englander, he suggested two Pennsylvanians.[30] They were Joseph Patterson of Philadelphia, a nonentity, and Don Cameron, son of the ruling boss of the State—a man later distinguished for his ardor in the free silver cause.

v

On April 17 the Cabinet again discussed the currency bill. Grant was still inclined to approve it, and was encouraged by Secretaries Richardson, Delano, and Belknap, while Fish and Creswell favored disapproval. The President that very day had received a New York delegation with a petition signed by 2,500 leading commercial firms asking him to veto the bill. When he met them, Butler, Ferry, Logan, and Carpenter somehow managed to be present also. Grant had received the delegation coldly; he had intimated to them that what was good for New York was not good for the rest of the country, and had spoken sharply of the impertinence of a previous Boston delegation which had dared to condemn the reissue of greenbacks as of doubtful legality. The New Yorkers had retired in a chastened mood. Yet the imposing New York petition had made an impression on Grant. In the course of the Cabinet discussion Richardson and Delano assured the President that the bill would tend to contraction; they predicted that if it became law the quarrel between East and West on the currency question would disappear; and they declared that he could settle the question once and for all by this "compromise." Fish and Creswell argued at length that the measure was clearly inflationary, that it broke the party's word, and that it would merely whet an appetite for more paper money.

Fish was deeply aroused, and when the meeting ended felt that he

[30] Diary, April 15, 1874.

had shaken the President. Grant kept the subject under advisement. But Fish was greatly encouraged by the evidence that he was now genuinely hesitant. The Secretary's feelings were so strongly enlisted that he thought of resigning if Grant signed the bill. He wrote John M. Francis of Troy [31] that while it might do no practical harm, it was "vicious in intent," was "a departure from the pledges which Congress, the President, and the Republican Party have given," and furnished "an entering wedge for any amount of 'wildcat' and 'red-dog' irredeemable rag-and-lamp-black legislation." In great suspense he went to the Cabinet meeting of April 21.

Grant at once took up the currency bill,[32] announcing curtly that he wished to dispose of it that same day. He said that he had given it the most exhaustive consideration; that desiring to approve it, he had first written a message embodying the best arguments he could devise for signing it; that the more he wrote, the more convinced he had become that the bill was bad; that having completed the message, he had decided that it was quite fallacious; and that he had therefore discarded it and written another vetoing the bill. He picked up the paper and began reading it. Fish felt a special exultation when the President, after mentioning that some authorities thought the bill deflationary, reproduced the very argument he and Creswell had used at the previous meeting. Grant wrote that the measure had been passed to furnish a generous increase of circulation; and that if it failed to do so, its friends, particularly outside Congress, "would clamor for such inflation as would give the expected relief."

The Cabinet inflationists sat stunned as Grant announced this *volte-face*, and as Fish hastened to express his gratification. Then they roused themselves to battle. "Delano," he writes in his diary,[33] "fought it from the jump. Williams decidedly objected. Robeson expressed the wish that the President had reached a different conclusion; Belknap thought it would array the entire West in opposition." Richardson, who had no convictions, "acquiescently approved." Creswell alone aligned himself firmly with Grant and Fish. The inflationist members, perceiving that they could make no stand on principle, retreated to considerations of expediency, and the following dialogue ensued:

Delano (after various suggestions in opposition).—"Mr. President, you ought to remember that the use of the veto power is not popular except

---

[31] Washington, April 18, 1874; Letterbooks.   [32] Diary, April 21, 1874.   [33] *Ibid.*

when exercised on the ground of the unconstitutionality of a bill."

Fish.—"Whether that is so or not, the good faith of the nation is above the Constitution."

Grant.—"That is true, and I shall stand by my veto. I wish to send it in today and have done with it."

Robeson.—"It seems to me, Mr. President, that it is always wise to lay a paper aside after writing it to think it over. And like Secretary Delano, I wish to raise the question of the political effect of a veto. The Congressional elections are just ahead."

Delano, Williams, and Belknap (more or less in chorus).—"A veto will certainly injure the party and the Administration politically."

Fish.—"I dissent utterly from that view. The honest sentiment of the country, irrespective of section, will sustain it. On the other hand, if you sign the bill the Democratic Party throughout the land will rally to their old Jacksonian doctrine of hard money, and your action will give the Democrats the whole capital now in the Republican Party."

Grant.—"I dare say the first result will be a storm of denunciation. But I am confident that the final judgment of the country will approve my veto."

To three agencies we may attribute the President's action: to the impressive New York protest, to Fish's eloquent arguments, and to Grant's own common sense. The decision, while falling like a thunderbolt upon inflationist leaders, was received with enthusiasm by most Eastern and many Western newspapers. It was all the more refreshing because ten days earlier not one citizen in a hundred had doubted that Grant would sign. "You can hardly believe," Edwards Pierrepont wrote Fish,[34] "what a perilous load is lifted from the hearts of sober men in this city. No braver battle did the President ever fight and no victory did he ever gain which history will record as more illustrious. I know you helped it—God bless you." John M. Francis wrote that he had been in Chicago when the veto was received there.[35] "It caused almost general rejoicing among the business men of that city. Chicago is sound upon the currency question, Logan to the contrary notwithstanding." The opposition announced that they would issue a reply, but they thought better of this. As they read the message, they saw that it closed the door not temporarily but permanently. For Grant did not rest his veto upon special defects which might be remedied by amendments; he rested it on the ground that he had always opposed an irredeemable paper currency and that the party had repeatedly de-

[34] Pierrepont to Fish, New York, April 23, 1874; Fish Papers.
[35] Francis to Fish, Troy, N. Y., May 4, 1874; Fish Papers.

clared for a speedy return to specie payments. Fish wrote General Schuyler: [36]

You are quite right in placing me in the most ultra position in favour of the views and the policy on which the President rests the withholding of his approval from the late currency bill. I had no hesitation in the expression of my views, but you must give the President the undivided credit for what he did. Never did a man more conscientiously reach his conclusions than he did in the matter of that bill, and this in the face of the very strongest and most persistent influences brought to bear upon him; and you can scarce imagine the extent and the variety of the sources which were drained to influence him; and now that he has decided, *many* who were *very urgent* to persuade him to an opposite course from that which he took, are either silent or professedly in approbation. He has a wonderful amount of good sense, and when left alone is very apt to follow it, and to "fight it out on that line." He did so in this recent matter, and astounded some who thought they had captured him.

VI

This victory for a cautious financial policy rendered the appointment of an able and conservative Secretary of the Treasury more important than ever. Ben Butler fortunately proved a false prophet as to the action of the Ways and Means Committee upon Richardson. In June it made a scathing report. The Secretary of the Treasury was accused of violating the law, and of assisting Sanborn and his partners in "marauding upon the public treasury." Through Representative Charles Foster of Ohio, the committee presented a resolution censuring Richardson and two departmental subordinates. It also offered a resolution declaring that since the Sanborn Contracts had resulted in a fraudulent abstraction of government money, the government should institute legal proceedings to recover it.[37] This made Richardson's position impossible. He resigned forthwith—and Grant characteristically appointed him to the Court of Claims! The judicial bench was obviously the place for an officer found guilty of gross misconduct. But who should succeed him?

Robeson urged Elihu Washburne for the office, and Fish, with some misgivings lest Washburne neglect the laborious details of the Treasury, approved the suggestion. The President requested him to sound Washburne out, and the Secretary cabled: [38] "In my judgment you are the

[36] Fish to General L. Schuyler, April 25, 1874; Letterbooks.
[37] *Nation,* May 28, 1874.
[38] Fish to Washburne, May 5, 1874; State Department MSS, Diplomatic Drafts, France.

man who combines personal, political, and geographical qualities beyond any other and who will meet the exigency." William E. Chandler also wrote Washburne urging him to accept.[39] "Up to the time of the President's veto," he pleaded, "we were drifting helplessly on a lee shore; and were tolerably sure to lose the next House, and after that possibly, probably, the Presidential election. Now the President's veto has changed all that. With a vigorous administration of the Treasury by a Western hard money man we can save the House. . . . Another thing, if you don't accept no man can tell whom the President will select." But Washburne declined.

Meanwhile Delano continued his eager wirepulling, and showed increasing petulance as the place was not offered him. Calling at Fish's house early on May 1, 1874, for advice, he frankly unbosomed himself: [40]

He says that last year, when Richardson was appointed Secretary of the Treasury or about that time, Carpenter and other Senators had told him the President had said that Richardson was to remain until July only, then he should appoint Delano; the same thing had since been repeatedly told him, and it had also got into the newspapers; that now there seemed a doubt, and should any other appointment be made he should have to regard it as a want of confidence and an intimation on the part of the President that he wished him to resign his present position. He wished my advice as to whether he should go to the President and speak with him on the subject.

Fish of course declined to offer any advice, but inquired whether the President himself had ever given Delano any assurances, or authorized any of the intimations made to him. Delano confessed that Grant had not. Fish then told him that he had no right to regard the expressions of others as indicating any fixed intention on the part of the President. Grant might or might not have said what was reported; he might have changed his mind since on grounds of public policy. "At any rate," concluded Fish, "your decided opposition to the policy of the President's veto would unquestionably now embarrass him in carrying out any such intention." Delano thereupon gave the measure of his honesty. "He protested that he was not an inflationist but a contractionist, and opposed the veto because he thought the bill was in

[39] Chandler to Washburne, Washington, May 4, 1874; Washburne Papers, Vol. 90.
[40] Diary, May 1, 1874.

the direction of contraction." [41]

On June 1 the President ended all suspense by nominating Benjamin H. Bristow of Kentucky to the Treasury Department. No better choice could have been made. Bristow was a man of forty-two; a graduate of Jefferson College in Pennsylvania, a veteran of Fort Donelson and Shiloh, and a distinguished lawyer, who had made his mark as Federal Attorney during the Ku Klux troubles, and had been the first Solicitor-General of the United States, 1870–72. Though in no sense an expert upon finance, he was shrewd, experienced, and conscientious; he possessed a good practical knowledge of business and commerce, and he had proved himself an excellent administrator. Fish was greatly pleased, and had occasion at the first Cabinet meeting which Bristow attended to note how well he was grappling with the problems of his office, and how quickly he was instituting healthful changes.[42] He was masterful, energetic, and ambitious. By this time the depression was felt in every department of national life; but men breathed more freely when they reflected that the President would stand like a rock against runaway inflation, and that the Treasury was in thoroughly safe hands. Grant had done something to redeem his record. In after years men were to remember the veto of the inflation measure (followed as it was in 1875 by a Specie Resumption Act) as standing next to the Treaty of Washington among the Administration's achievements.

[41] *Ibid.*   [42] Diary, June 5, 1874.

PRESIDENT GRANT'S decision to veto the inflation bill came in the nick
of time to prevent the resignation of Fish. Increasingly uneasy, the
Secretary had intended in any event to retire before the winter of
1874–75, and probably soon after the summer adjournment of Congress.[1] Convinced that the bill was vicious and would lead the Administration into a Serbonian bog of financial malpractise, he was determined to leave as soon as Grant signed it. His own public reputation
would thus remain uncompromised. But when on April 21, 1874, Grant
took his gratifying stand against the bill, Fish instantly decided to postpone his departure. Circumstances demanded it. A majority of the
Cabinet were arrayed against the President; Richardson, naturally
irresolute, and his reputation now shattered, could give him no support; it was important for Fish to remain temporarily at his side. "But,"
Fish wrote, "my expectation of withdrawing . . . during the coming
summer or autumn remains unchanged." [2]

Yet the next few months were to place before him a perplexing question of duty, and finally to lead him to a different conclusion. Duty—
that word his family, his church, the aristocratic code of old New York,
had always emphasized. He felt for it all the devotion enshined in the
poetry of the race: "stern daughter of the voice of God"; "not once
or twice, in our great island story, the path of duty was the way to
glory." Well, where did duty lie? In quitting a leaderless Administration, irresponsible in spirit, permeated by corruption, apparently certain of disaster? Inclination certainly pointed that way; he had done
his great work in the State Department, he loved peace, and he could
retire with unspotted honor. Or did duty lie in staying with the ill-
managed vessel, lending a hand with the tiller, pointing out false lights,
doing what he could to prevent disaster from becoming utter wreck?
That course meant heavy labor, heartbreaking anxiety, and no thanks.
It meant risk of his own good name, for when an Administration falls
into disgrace men do not easily distinguish between its members. Yet
Fish remembered Rockwood Hoar's words in the gloomy summer of
1870—"Hold fast; you are the bulwark now standing between the

[1] Postscript to Diary, April 21, 1874.   [2] Diary, April 21, 1874.

country and its destruction." As his sense of the perils environing Grant increased, his decision became more and more certain.

The Secretary was increasingly disturbed in 1873–74 by Grant's carelessness and laxity. He was disturbed by the President's imperiousness and self-sufficiency, unquestionably enhanced by his reëlection. But what alarmed him most of all was the growing evidence of a government within a government, or rather of a backstairs group at the White House which more and more undertook to control the Executive Office itself.

I

Grant's negligent, casual ways, and his lack of vigilance, were often amazing. Fish's diary for the autumn of 1873 supplies a striking instance. On September 5, the Secretary had written the President at Long Branch that the British expected to pay the Geneva Award on the 9th, and asked if he had any instructions. On the 9th Fish received a reply (dated the 8th) saying that although the letter had been on Grant's table since the 6th he had not opened it. Grant offered no instructions. But to Fish's amazement, he reopened the question of Cuba. He wrote in characteristic style:

There is only one matter that I think about which I would like to consult about at this time, that is the recognition of belligerency to the Cuban Patriots. It looks to me that the republic of Spain is by no means assured. Should a monarchy prevail money in the shape of a new loan would be a necessity to the new government. All the European Powers and the European moneylenders would be interested in sustaining a monarchy but would not lend without security. What else has Spain left as collateral but Cuba? That once pledged, nations furnishing money would become interested in supporting their debtor. I am very well aware however that these are not proper reasons to assert for recognizing belligerency but they are proper ones to consider as bearing on the subject.

In great alarm, Fish wrote that he would disengage himself from imperative business at the State Department and arrive in Long Branch for a conference, if convenient, early the following week. This letter was mailed the 9th. On the evening of the 14th, no word having come, he left Washington, still worried. On reaching Long Branch next day he found Grant insouciantly entering a train with General Sheridan for Pittsburgh. A few minutes more and the Secretary of State would have had his journey for nothing. The President said that he supposed Fish's letter had been on his table for several days (it had certainly been there four!) but that he had not opened it until that morning. "I make this note," Fish writes in his diary, "thinking how little the affairs of the government trouble the President. Had my letter gone to his secretaries they would doubtless have laid it before him, but . . . the secretaries as I understand do not open letters addressed in my handwriting; they go to the President's table with other private and confidential correspondence, and lie there until sometime when there is nothing else to do, and then the matter on the table is taken up and all disposed of at once. Fortunately no great harm has resulted . . . but it is strange that letters from one of his constitutional advisers should be allowed to lie upon the President's table unopened day after day. Would it have been the same whatever might have been the subject of the letter?"

As for Grant's self-sufficiency, his imperious method of handling public business, that kept cropping out in a variety of ways. One unhappy event of June, 1874, was the sudden resignation of Postmaster-General Creswell. Grant called the Cabinet together to announce the fact, giving no explanation, and Creswell sat silent.[3] Fish believed the other Cabinet members as genuinely grieved as himself. Not only had Creswell proved one of the most enterprising Postmasters-General in the long history of his office; he was a reformer, who had attacked the franking system as the "mother of frauds," and urged a postal telegraph against the opposition of the Western Union monopoly. His breadth and cultivation would be sorely missed. When soon afterward Ben Butler called, Fish remarked that the resignation had been a general surprise. "Yes," said Butler drily, "and to none more so than to Creswell himself."[4] He had been dismissed by Grant! And Butler had of course been given inside information by Babcock.

Eager to forestall an unfit selection, Fish proposed Eugene Hale of Maine, a brilliant young Congressman, son-in-law of Zachariah Chandler and close friend of Blaine. Grant accepted the suggestion, but Hale declined on the ground of ill-health. Fish also proposed Wayne Mac-Veagh of Pennsylvania, who had made an able Minister to Turkey, and who was Simon Cameron's son-in-law—but this suggestion met less favor. After some hesitation over two Southern Republicans, Grant

[3] Diary, June 24, 1874.   [4] Diary, July 22, 1874.

finally pitched upon a third man proposed by Fish—Marshall Jewell. He was an admirable choice. A leather manufacturer who had gone into politics, he had made a businesslike governor of Connecticut, and for a year a highly efficient Minister to Russia. He had done much in that country, for example, to assure complete patent-protection to American inventions. He possessed high executive talent, was politically liberal, and showed a business man's impatience with mere politicians. Spoilsmen were soon grumbling that he ran the postal department "like a factory." [5] He was an even better man than Creswell—the Cabinet had after all lost nothing.

But Jewell, like Bristow, soon began meeting criticism and opposition in quarters close to the President. Bristow was already showing remarkable zeal in the Treasury, where the dirt and débris of years rose in clouds before his unresting broom. He made some queer discoveries. For example, he imparted to the Cabinet on July 1 the shocking fact that Boutwell's and Richardson's private secretary, one Bartlett, had been a detective employed by Pinkerton's Agency! "This," he commented, "will explain many of the leaks and failures of justice." [6] No clearance of supernumeraries had occurred in his department since the war. Taking advantage of reduced appropriations, Bristow set about a general house-cleaning and dismissed between 700 and 800 persons. The step required courage, for a chorus of protests arose; but it made the Treasury a businesslike branch of the government instead of an almshouse for women, old soldiers, and political favorites. [7] In letting out the bonded warehouse business, Bristow required a guarantee that successful applicants should personally superintend it, thus making impossible the sub-letting which had been one of the scandals in Leet & Stocking days.

When Bristow took office the six per cent bonds were being converted into fives. By a bold innovation, he offered the residue of the conversion loan—$179,000,000, or any part of it—to bankers in general without the intervention of a syndicate. This had a healthy look, and spoke well for the purity of his policy. The new method proved a general success. Before the close of July scattered bids for about $10,000,000 had been accepted, while Rothschilds in London and J. W. Seligman in New York had jointly taken $45,000,000, with an option

[5] *Dictionary of American Biography.*   [6] Diary, July 1, 1874.   [7] *Nation*, July 9, 1874.

on the remainder at any time during the next six months.[8] But the Secretary's policy was insidiously attacked. "Great efforts," he told Fish, "have been made to induce me not to adopt this course, but to accept certain proposals made by individuals instead." He added, significantly: "I can't afford to do such things, and I was sorry that the pressure was brought to bear in the quarter whence it came."[9] Fish had little difficulty in surmising the quarter he meant. Boutwell had set up a machinery of private contracts with syndicates, and the men who had profited from it had gone running to him, to Ben Butler, and above all to the secretaries' room in the White House.

Having finally taken the right course in financial matters, Grant maintained it with courage—sometimes more courage than discretion. All spring he stood by the principle of his veto, refusing to let Congressional pressure budge him an inch. A new bill had been hurriedly written to replace the one he had killed. Leaving the greenback currency at $382,000,000, it contained provisions upon national banks which were considered inflationary by some and contractionist by others.[10] On the whole, however, it was sound; its tendency—what Grant called its *animus*—was as good as that of the previous bill had been bad. Grant, with Fish and Bristow standing beside him, insisted on a number of amendments to improve it. For since the "sound money" men had rallied about him, the President now took bold ground against inflation and in favor of an early resumption of specie payments.

At some points he went further than his party dared. At the beginning of June, saying that he wished to avoid misrepresentation, he embodied his opinions on the bill in a letter to Senator Sherman and Representative Maynard of the conference committee.[11] He called for strict economy, judicious taxation, repeal of the legal tender acts, abolition of small notes, and early specie resumption. Though Fish approved these views, he and other Cabinet members counselled Grant not to send it, but to convert it into a private memorandum to be shown to Sherman and others. This was done. The result of even this mild step was a revolt among Congressmen. Fish writes:

Sunday, June 7, 1874.—I received a note from Speaker Blaine asking to see me; not being well, I requested him to come to my house, which he did.

---

[8] *Nation*, July 30, 1874.
[10] *Nation*, July 30, 1874.

[9] Diary, July 3, 1874.
[11] Diary, June 1, 1874.

He speaks of the President's memorandum on finance, exhibiting considerable feeling, saying that if carried out it would be ruinous to the Republican party and the country; he said he should be inclined to adopt the words of Mr. Webster and say that when his leader turned a sharp corner into a dark lane and changed the light which he had been accustomed to follow, that it could not be expected that they should keep company longer.

I told him that without adopting all the details of the President's plan, I believed the principles underlying it were the only safeguards of the country. We then considered the bill, he defending most of the provisions to which I took exception, admitting that personally he would not object to some of them. Our interview was interrupted by Mrs. Fish's illness, and I subsequently received from him a copy of the bill, and later in the evening he called again, and I submitted to him certain proposed amendments all of which he thought were improvements to the bill, and expressed the opinion that they might be assented to by the Committee, and he would endeavor to urge their acceptance.

Still difficult to restrain, the President at the Cabinet meeting of June 9, reiterating "the firmest adherence to the principles of his veto," induced most of the members to approve of drastic proposals—one being for the gradual reduction of the outstanding greenbacks to $300,-000,000. Next day Senators Jones and Stewart of Nevada came to Fish in great alarm. They reported that the President had demanded that an entirely new currency bill be drawn up embodying the views of his memorandum. Fish agreed that this was quite unadvisable. On the 11th he went to the White House, at their request, and labored to convince Grant of the impolicy of throwing a wholly new measure into the arena; "in which view," he writes, "he finally concurs." [12]

II

But while giving Grant credit for firmness on the currency, Fish was irritated by his pliability in other matters, some of them closely affecting the State Department. Throughout the spring of 1874 the Secretary felt a growing concern over the Cuban question. He had gone to New York on business early in April.[13] While there he learned that ex-Senator S. C. Pomeroy of Kansas, nicknamed "Old Subsidy" and at this moment accused of offering an $8,000 bribe in the Kansas legislature to gain reëlection, had been negotiating with the Cuban Junta. Though Pomeroy's reputation was decidely fly-blown, he held a certain influence with the raffish element of Congress. He had as-

[12] Diary, June 9, 10, 1874.   [13] Diary, April 7, 1874.

sured Sr. Aldama, leader of the Junta, that he could obtain the recognition of either Cuban independence or belligerency for $30,000 in cash, with a guarantee of $150,000 more in cash and $150,000 in bonds on the issuance of the proclamation.[14] He gave Aldama a list of men close to the President whose opinions he pretended to know; he claimed to speak with Grant's approval; and in support of this claim, pointed to the fact that Grant's brother Orvil was staying with him in New York.

All this, reported to Fish, had deeply disturbed him. So had a series of articles which immediately began appearing in the Washington *National Republican,* edited by William J. Murtagh, who was so close to Babcock and the Dents that the paper was spoken of as the Administration organ—close also to Boss Shepherd's District of Columbia Ring. These articles attacked the State Department policy and argued for a bolder line. One on April 13 abused Fish personally, and demanded recognition of Cuban independence by Congress. "The present moment is opportune," it declared, "and it would be a grave blunder to suffer it to escape." That evening Murtagh, a slippery-looking old Irishman, called at the Secretary's house to apologize. He professed to be extremely mortified and angry. The previous night, he explained, he and the chief editor had both been absent. James F. Casey of New Orleans, the President's brother-in-law, had come into the office and caused the publication of the article.

So while Frederick T. Dent eavesdropped next the Cabinet room, Casey wrote attacks on the State Department! Fish made his indignation so plain that the abashed Murtagh finally promised to insert a notice next day stating that the article had appeared unintentionally, and was not to be regarded as expressing the opinion of the Administration or the *National Republican!* [15] But no such notice ever appeared.

At the first opportunity Fish asked Grant if he had seen the offensive article. He said he had not—a surprising statement for so inveterate a newspaper reader. Fish concluded that his secretaries had hidden the issue. Grant added that a recognition of belligerency would be absurd, but that he "was not sure that recognition of independence might not soon be necessary." [16] The Secretary could have explained for the

---

[14] Fish to Bancroft Davis, New York, April 3, 1874; Letterbooks.

[15] Diary, April 13, 14, 1874. Grant had appointed Murtagh a Police Commissioner of the district of Columbia; Grant Letterbooks, March 13, 1869. He was thus a link between Shepherd and Babcock.

[16] Diary, April 14, 1874.

hundredth time why it would be highly improper, but he contented himself with repeating what he had heard about Pomeroy. Grant's response was that if Sr. Aldama or anybody else trusted Pomeroy, or supposed he had any power, they were likely to find themselves out of pocket and grievously mistaken. He evinced no moral indignation. Within the next few days other suspicious events occurred. Senator Carpenter introduced a resolution for the recognition of Cuban independence.[17] Rumors of the use of Cuban bonds in Washington again became rife; and men were named in the affair whom Fish considered open, as he wrote in his diary, to the "improper influence of pecuniary advantage." [18] The tracks of Pomeroy, of his housemate Orvil Grant, of Murtagh, of Casey, and of Carpenter all led back toward one common starting-point.

The subject died away in May. But early in June Representative Orth, driving with Fish one evening, remarked that "a considerable movement" was again manifest in the House upon Cuba.[19] Casey, the President's brother-in-law, had spoken to him repeatedly. He had intimated that the President would like to see him about Cuba. It should be said that Godlove S. Orth was a man of influence. An oldtime Whig, he had entered Congress from Indiana in 1863. He took a keen interest in foreign affairs, labored for years to induce European governments to recognize the right of expatriation, and in 1868 had framed legislation for reorganizing the diplomatic and consular service. He had supported Dominican annexation, but thus far had opposed the recognition of the Cuban rebels. Anything he said was to be taken seriously. And by this time Fish knew that the sooner the bull were taken by the horns the better. Next day he went to the White House for one of those interviews which would seem incredible if we did not have the record in black and white—an interview in which Grant appeared like a contrite schoolboy: [20]

I mention what was told me by Orth relative to Casey and Cuba, and ask whether Casey was authorized to speak on the subject. He emphatically denied any authority to Mr. Casey to speak on the subject. I inquired whether he had authorized any expression of opinion or had said or done anything, and referred to the articles in the *Republican;* indicating one as having been very offensive inasmuch as it assailed measures which he himself had authorized and directed, particularly with relation to the gunboats. He had not seen

[17] *Congressional Globe.*   [18] Diary, April 21, 1874.
[19] Diary, June 9, 1874.   [20] Diary, June 10, 1874.

that article—said that the only person with whom he had conversed was Carpenter, who had spoken to him very warmly in favour of some expression of sympathy in favour of the Cubans, and that he (the President) said to him (Carpenter) that "he might go ahead," though not for recognition of belligerency, but for some expression of sympathy, or even a recognition of independence.

Even a recognition of independence! Carpenter, flighty, impetuous, was notoriously lacking in judgment. He had become famous the previous year by actually making a defence of the Salary Grab and Credit Mobilier. He knew nothing of foreign affairs. Yet Grant had notified this irresponsible Wisconsin Senator of the most important change possible in our foreign policy without consulting the Secretary of State! Fish continues: [21]

I told him that a recognition of independence would really be a stultification of ourselves and a falsification of facts. I went at length into the question and into our present relations with Spain, telling him that I thought it doubtful whether under his instructions General Cushing would not find himself obliged to quit Madrid before Congress convenes in the autumn; that we will put ourselves wrong before the world and in history by recognizing either belligerency or independence; that if Spain could not act up to her promises the moral effect of the breaking off of relations by the United States would be far more serviceable to the Cubans than the indirect and cowardly mode of declaring that to be a fact which is not.

He concurs and says he will send word to Carpenter to let the thing drop.

The Secretary was further irritated by Grant's attitude toward the moiety system—the system by which informers were paid a percentage of taxes they helped collect. Congress, after the Sanborn Contract scandal, passed a bill abolishing this wretched device. Fish had long detested the system. He had publicly denounced it as one "under which great oppression has been visited upon individuals and great fortunes have been made by some favored few." It bred nests of spies and blackmailers; it tempted every clerk, bookkeeper, and confidential agent to betray his employer if guilty, and to falsify transactions if innocent; it was corrupting in the extreme.[22] Yet when the bill reached Grant in June, 1874, he astounded the Cabinet by saying that he would not sign it; that it had been drawn in the interests of smugglers and would cost the country twenty millions a year in revenue. He was obviously re-

[21] *Ibid.*   [22] Fish to Weed, Washington, March 14, 1874; Letterbooks.

peating what Ben Butler, or somebody like Ben Butler, had told him.

Fish whispered across the Cabinet table to Bristow, in whose department the matter fell. And Bristow bravely took issue with Grant. He said that in his opinion it would not do to refuse assent to a bill which had passed the House unanimously and the Senate with only three dissenting votes, and which the commercial community and the press had enthusiastically endorsed. He recalled that Grant himself had once recommended the abolition of moieties! Fish vigorously seconded these statements. Grant said nothing, but was obviously shaken. "In connection with this," wrote Fish in his diary, "it is to be noted that Tom Murphy, Rufus Ingalls, Frank Howe, and others have been for days hanging about endeavoring to prevent the signing and passage of the bill."

III

But worse was to come. At the beginning of July Fish heard of a new backstairs intrigue which placed a special humiliation upon the much-suffering State Department. "General Babcock," he wrote in his diary,[23] "is anxious to have General Meigs appointed to some diplomatic position in order to make a vacancy in the quartermaster-generalship for Rufus Ingalls." Ingalls was the West Point classmate of Grant's who accompanied Babcock on the famous trip to Santo Domingo. As chief quartermaster in New York, he wished a better post. The Russian legation was now vacant, and on July 7 Fish had a characteristically casual letter from the President:[24]

I understand that Gen. M. C. Meigs, Qr. Mr. General, is a candidate for diplomatic honors now that he is eligible for retirement. He is a highly educated man and I think would be well qualified for such service. You may therefore if you please tender him the mission to Russia. I know that the Sec. of War is anxious that he should be relieved from his present duties, for which his early education never fitted him. Graduating in the Engineer Corps he has never served with troops and knows therefore nothing of their wants.

Grant's statements about Montgomery C. Meigs's unfitness were astounding. A West Point graduate who had made a brilliant early reputation, including the supervision of the building of the Capitol wings and dome in 1853–59, he had served as quartermaster-general

---

[23] Diary, July 3, 1874.   [24] Grant to Fish, Long Branch, July 7, 1874; Fish Papers.

of all the Northern forces from beginning to end of the Civil War. He had spent more than $1,500,000,000 without a breath of scandal. He had performed a stupendous task with the completest success. Stanton wrote later that he had been absolutely indispensable, and Seward testified that without his services the national cause must have been "lost or deeply imperilled." [25] And now Grant wished to displace the man who had clothed and supplied all the Union armies on the ground that he "knew nothing of the needs" of soldiers! It was certain he knew nothing of diplomacy. Filled with indignation by this transparent intrigue of Babcock and Belknap to find a fat office for their friend Ingalls, Fish wrote two letters. One, to Belknap, was curt and icily polite. He pointed out that Federal statutes made it impossible for a military officer, whether active or retired, to accept a civil post without resigning his commission. He also protested against the transfer to the State Department—"that refuge for all for whom no place can be found elsewhere"—of a purely military figure. "Between ourselves I am pretty well tired of taking charge of the incurables and confirmed invalids." The other letter was to the President, and was phrased with unusual candor: [26]

With the highest estimate of General Meigs's character, ability, and attainments, I think that if the special education he has received, and the experience of so many years in the quartermaster-general's department have not fitted him for the duties of his present office, it is not to be expected, at his time of life, that he will be able to fit himself for the very delicate and important duties of a diplomatic position near one of the first Powers of the world— duties requiring great practical adaptability, as well as previous study and experience in public laws, and a familiarity with international politics and policy. Mr. Disraeli has lately stated in Parliament that an international crisis was nearer at hand than is generally supposed. Russia and the Eastern question will figure in such a crisis.

Pardon me, my dear General, should I seem a little sensitive in respect to having one who is held to be unfit to discharge the duties of a Bureau in the War Department as competent to the most important diplomatic duties under the Department of State. This, however, is only half serious.

But there is an objection, to which I allude with some hesitancy, but under a firm impression of its real seriousness.

The interests of the country and the continued ascendancy of the Republican Party, in my judgment, are identical, and we cannot shut our eyes to the fact that the hold of the latter upon public sentiment and sympathy is not as

[25] *Dictionary of American Biography.*   [26] Fish to Grant, Garrison, July 13, 1874.

strong as it was. There is a deep and growing restlessness and jealousy of military influence and ascendancy, and this jealousy is being fostered and worked upon by the Democratic press, and will be turned to the disadvantage of the Republican Party in every possible way.

General Meigs's appointment to a diplomatic mission will not be recognized as a concession to any peculiar eminence, or to any prominence as a statesman, or politician, or a diplomatist, in neither of which capacities is he known. It will be very far from satisfying the politicians of the Republican Party, and will be attributed, erroneously no doubt but none the less certainly, to another consideration.

These objections are so strong to my mind that I feel it a duty to suggest them. If, however, in view of what appear to me very strong reasons for not making the appointment, you still desire the tender of the position to be made, I will make it on my return to Washington whither I expect to go within a few days—so soon as I can arrange some matters of business here.

This outspoken letter had no effect whatever upon Grant. But fortunately the Federal law requiring an army officer to resign his commission upon taking civil office did have its effect upon General Meigs. He was not willing to exchange a permanent military position for a temporary diplomatic berth. Belknap and Babcock wrote letters to explain that the statute did not mean what it said, but Fish quickly demolished their flimsy readings of the law.[27] Grant invited poor Meigs by telegraph to Long Branch. After he had resisted all blandishments for two days, he was requested to take further time to consider. It would have been disrespectful to refuse. But after deliberation, he still said no. On September 7 Fish was able to write Bancroft Davis: "The little scheme for putting somebody into the quartermaster-general's place . . . has failed." But he confessed that he did not know what would happen next, and hinted that another man now exercised more power over diplomatic appointments than himself. The post at St. Petersburg was still open. "I have suggested James Russell Lowell, but know not whether 'Bab' will allow it."

In the coterie which exerted so potent a backstairs influence over Grant, Babcock was now dominant, Louis Dent having died suddenly in the spring of 1874; and having assisted to eject Creswell from the Cabinet, he was actually ready to try conclusions with Fish. It is difficult to place any other construction upon his behavior. In August Bancroft Davis, who had been rewarded for his work at Geneva by appointment as Minister to Germany, wrote Fish from London. He had

27 Fish to Babcock, July 13, 1874; Letterbooks.

talked there with J. Russell Jones, Minister to Belgium.[28] He opened the conversation, wrote Davis, "by asking when Jay was to resign. I replied that Jay had told me he might possibly remain till spring. He asked me if I had heard that he, Jones, was to have the place. I said that I had not. He expressed great surprise at that, and added that he had received a letter from Babcock telling him that Jay was to resign, and asking if it would be agreeable to him to have the place. He said that the letter was written in such a way as to lead him to suppose that it was done by direction of the President, and he added that he understood that you had been consulted about it and favored his appointment. He is in the field for it now, and will be pressed whenever the vacancy occurs, unless it is created for the purpose of filling it with Orth or someone else." Davis concluded: "Babcock seems to be running things into the ground."

That was Fish's conviction. When he read this letter the thread of his patience snapped. He had become thoroughly tired of Babcock's interference with all the affairs of government; when the man presumed to decide upon ministerial transfers without a word to the State Department, it was too much. Fish resolved to bring the issue to a decision as soon as the President returned to Washington.

His determination was fortified by another talk with Murtagh, owner of the *National Republican,* whom he called to the State Department on September 9. The Secretary began by saying that the Department would no longer send the *National Republican* to legations abroad. He did not wish to influence Murtagh's course, but of late the *National Republican* had frequently opposed his policy upon Cuba, and had criticized and misrepresented him, and he could not mail to our Ministers a journal which differed from the State Department on an important policy.[29]

Murtagh was at once all explanations. He said that "in every article which had appeared in reference to Cuba, he had been countenanced by the Administration and had its previous approval." He repeated with emphasis "that he had published nothing about Cuba that had not the previous sanction of 'the Administration.' " The Secretary asked how that could be, when the Administration indicated its foreign policy only through the President's messages and the State Department. But

28 Davis to Fish, London, August 14, 1874; Fish Papers.
29 Diary, September 9, 1874.

Murtagh persisted in saying that the "Administration" had inspired or approved all that he printed. Evidently he meant the White House. His asseverations finally provoked Fish to some plain speaking.

"I deny," writes the Secretary, "that he had the authority of the 'Administration'; that I probably know who communicated with him; in the course of the conversation I named Babcock and Carpenter (with other names intentionally mentioned, but not because of any suspicion of connection on their part with the publication). He makes no allusion to Babcock, but very positively says that Carpenter 'had not been in his office since he had defended him against the Long Branch story.' (The President had told me that Carpenter was the only person with whom he had spoken with reference to Cuba.) I told Murtagh that someone had been playing double; that I believed I understood the matter." [30]

IV

We can understand the bitterness with which the Secretary set down this entry, and we can also comprehend his sense of the dangers encompassing the Administration. If Babcock were to determine our Cuban policy and fill our legations abroad, ruin lay ahead. Fish had just learned from Gibson, the astute Washington correspondent of the New York *Sun*, that as soon as Congress met there would be another concerted movement to force the recognition of Cuban belligerency or independence; that large amounts of Cuban bonds had been placed, and more would be used; and that the *National Republican* had received a share of them.[31]

Fish's intention was to protest, and if that availed nothing, resign. Calling at the White House the very day Grant returned, September 14, he used the most vigorous language at his command. The President, began, as he expected, by asking what he thought of transferring Jones from Belgium to Russia, and J. Meredith Read from Greece to Belgium. Fish said flatly that it would be a great error. Jones did not deserve promotion; placed since 1869 in the most important post in Europe for news, he had never sent the State Department anything but press clippings. Moreover, Illinois ought not to have two of the five major missions, Paris and St. Petersburg. As for Read, he was a selfish climber, continually keeping his name in the press, and his advance-

[30] *Ibid.*   [31] *Ibid.*

ment would not be popular. "It would be wise," he told Grant, "to appoint to Russia a man whose name would at once impress cultivated people, perhaps a distinguished literary man. James Russell Lowell would be excellent. His nomination would conciliate a large body who at present are not exactly hostile to the Administration, but chilly and disappointed." [32] Grant maintained the silence which was his habitual mark of disapproval. Lowell had been Sumner's and Motley's friend. Sumner had died in March, 1874, while Motley had resumed his pen and just published *John of Barneveld,* but Grant remained unforgiving. Dropping the subject, Fish asked if the President had authorized the tender of the Austrian mission to Jones. On being told no, he mentioned that Jones had boasted in London of receiving a letter, which he understood had the President's sanction, offering him the place. Again Grant was silent, but this time for a different reason.

The Secretary then referred to that precious ornament of the diplomatic service, Rumsey Wing of Kentucky, Minister to Ecuador. Authorities in Quito had reported that he was suffering from delirium tremens; that as he constantly went armed he was a menace to the city; and that he had committed a murderous assault on the British Minister.[33] Grant had been responsible for his selection. "O, yes," said the President. "General Babcock told me about him. I must make a change there, and I will give the place to Kentucky again." Fish started. Only two or three men in Washington knew of the impending vacancy, yet Babcock had already seized upon it. The Secretary protested that Kentucky held the Danish mission, and was a hopelessly Democratic state. "Yes," replied Grant, "but the politicians do not count Cramer in Denmark to Kentucky's credit. He is my brother-in-law and a personal appointee. Besides, I have a man in mind for Ecuador. He is a brother-in-law of Belknap's, a lawyer, a good man; I think the name is Bowen."

That night Fish attended a White House dinner.[34] Columbus Alexander, from Kentucky, sat next him. The Secretary inquired if he knew a brother-in-law of Belknap's, a lawyer named Bowen. "Oh," said Alexander, "I know him, but your details are wrong. His name is Bowman, not Bowen; he is not a brother-in-law, but a brother of a brother-in-law; and he is not a lawyer but a farmer living at or near

[32] Diary, September 14, 1874.
[33] Sr. Francisco Xavier Leon to Fish, Quito, August 19, 1874; Fish Papers.
[34] Diary, September 14, 1874.

Harrodsburg." So much for the accuracy of Grant's information.

And at this moment Fish learned of another slight upon the State Department. John A. Bingham, Minister to Japan, wrote announcing the arrival of General Meyer and Colonel Lyford with commissions from the War Department authorizing them to present to the Emperor certain military equipment. Fish knew both men. "Meyer, you know," he wrote Bancroft Davis, "is an intimate friend and pet of Babcock, as Lyford is of Belknap; the former was a frequenter of the room adjoining the President's."[35] The War Department's action in commissioning men to a foreign government was not only a flagrant discourtesy to the State Department, but a violation of Federal law. Moreover, Chino-Japanese relations were strained by the Formosan question; war was possible, and excited Chinese officials were already questioning American neutrality.[36] The presentation of arms to Japan at such a time was highly indiscreet. Fish spoke to Grant.[37] He pointed out that even delegates to scientific congresses or trade conferences were always commissioned by the Secretary of State; that the numerous gifts to foreign sovereigns in the past had all been made through the State Department. Apart from the question of law, "I cannot allow this to pass without remonstrance lest it be taken as a precedent."

The President hastily said that he was sure no disrespect had been intended, and that the action was mere thoughtlessness. "Well," rejoined Fish, "it is strange that the War Department and the military men who are so tenacious of etiquette and the respect due to themselves should be so heedless of what is due to others. I believe I understand the influence through which this was brought about"—he meant Babcock—"and I am tired of his interference with my Department." Grant made no recorded reply. There was no reply to make.

Fish's confidence in the President was not improved by an exhibition on September 15 of his capricious haste in Southern affairs. That day news came north of a sudden, spontaneous, and all but bloodless uprising in New Orleans against the Custom House clique which under Governor William Pitt Kellogg had been misgoverning the State. Kellogg's title rested on a disputed election, and was highly dubious. Fish went to the White House that afternoon to present a new Spanish Minister. As he ascended the stairs he was met by Grant's assistant-secretary,

[35] Fish to Davis, Garrison, September 28, 1874; Letterbooks.
[36] Porter, *Political History of Japan*, 273.   [37] Diary, September 14, 1874.

C. C. Sniffen, with a proclamation on Louisiana signed by the President, for which Fish's signature and the official seal were desired. The document was without heading, dated the 98th instead of 99th year of independence. Attorney-General Williams also came tumbling out, instructed to give the proclamation at once to the press. Inwardly wondering, Fish attached his signature and the seal. No Cabinet member save "Landaulet" Williams had been consulted about it.

That evening Bristow and Jewell called at Fish's house to obtain light on the matter. "They expressed surprise," he notes, "that a document of such importance and significance should be put forth without more of deliberation and without consultation with the Cabinet. (They are news members, otherwise they would not be surprised)." [38] Both men thought that Grant ought to defer his intended return to Long Branch. Fish earnestly concurred. The two visitors then hurried to Dr. Sharpe's residence, where Grant was staying, and where his luggage was already on a cart at the door. When they stated their views he decided to remain, and the trunks were brought back. He at once called a Cabinet meeting for 9:30 the next morning.

It quickly appeared that Grant's haste had been extremely unfortunate. The conservative majority in New Orleans, angered by the insolence of the Black League and by preëlection efforts of Federal officials to disarm all whites, had turned out in thousands, barricaded the streets, besieged the public buildings, and driven off the colored police. Within twenty-four hours they were victorious; their leaders proclaimed the deposition of Kellogg, kept in power for two years by Federal bayonets alone, and organized a new government under D. B. Penn. The situation required no immediate action in Washington, for violence had ceased at once. Fish records that this very evening of the 15th Grant received a telegram signed by many of the wealthiest and most prominent citizens of New Orleans, assuring him of peace and order.[39] What was needed was patient mediation between the Kellogg-Casey and Penn-McEnery factions. Grant soon shared the Cabinet's regret over the precipitancy with which his proclamation had committed the Administration to the maintenance of the wretched Kellogg Government. One or two Cabinet members even urged that the proclamation be revoked; Fish hoped that some compromise acceptable to the majority of white Louisianans might be found. But it was too late. With three

38 Diary, September 15, 1874.　　39 Diary, September 15, 1874.

warships and Federal troops hurrying to New Orleans, the State was quickly forced back under the Kellogg yoke.

v

On September 18, 1874, Fish went to Garrison. It was there that he received a letter from Grant's assistant-secretary, Sniffen, which he considered decisive.[40] "The President directs me to say," it began, "that he will be pleased to have a commission prepared for John E. Bowman of Kentucky to be Minister Resident to Ecuador in place of E. Rumsey Wing to be recalled."

The letter proved that the Babcock-Belknap cabal had again taken the President captive. Grant had been inveigled by what Fish in his diary terms "Babcock's ever-present and ever-interfering influence" to direct the appointment of a man of whose capacity he knew nothing, whose very name he mistook, as a family favor. It was too much. "I cannot run the State Department in connection with Casey and Murtagh and Babcock," wrote Fish.[41] He added that Babcock was the most dangerous of all, for he had brains, while beneath his suavity and gentlemanly manners he was designing, unscrupulous, and essentially arrogant. Fish did not know whether the current charges affecting his integrity were true or not; while they were confidently asserted, he had seen no real evidence for them. But he did know that Babcock's advice was often gravely injurious to the President. As for Casey and Murtagh, they were certainly knaves and probably fools. "I do not so much care that the trio get not only the honours but count the tricks, as that I do not like the association. I do not think that either law or propriety allows them or any set of men the control and influence which is accorded to them. I am tired of this sort of thing. I fear that the President has the 'third term' in his mind; it will be a grievous mistake for him or for the country—for both if it succeed. . . ." [42] He slept on the subject, and rose more determined than ever. The use of the venal and stupid *National Republican* to undermine his policies; the indecent appointment through the War Department of commissioners to a foreign state; the continual interference of a mere private secre-

---

[40] Sniffen to Fish, Washington, September 19, 1874; Fish Papers.
[41] September 21, 1874.   [42] *Ibid.*

tary with the Department of State—all this, he concluded, made it "unseemly" to remain. He wrote Grant: [43]

My dear General:

You are aware that for a long time it has been my desire to retire from official life. Nothing has retained me in the position which, unsolicited and unexpected, you urged upon me—which I accepted with diffidence and hesitancy, and have continued to hold at no small sacrifice—but my attachment to yourself, and the assurances often received from you of your desire that I remain.

The State Department, above all others, cannot be administered except with the most unreserved confidence given to its head by the Executive. When that confidence is shaken, or when the influence of the head of the Department in the administration of its affairs, or the formation of its policy, is overshadowed by others, a sensible or a sensitive man will appreciate that the time for his retirement has arrived.

A series of recent events leads me to the belief that my continuance in office is no longer useful. and to the apprehension that I have not the control, or the influence in matters relating to my own Department, which are necessary not only to a confident and satisfactory discharge of the delicate and complicated duties of the office, but also to the independence of feeling without which the high position which I have held in your Administration cannot be worthily occupied.

If I am not mistaken in this impression, my resignation and retirement to private life will bring me a relief which I have long desired. The only regret which will attend them, will be the less frequent opportunity of personal association and intercourse with yourself, and with the friends with whom I have been closely associated in connection with my official position during the past five and a half years. I therefore enclose herewith my resignation of the office of Secretary of State of the United States. To find a successor more competent than I have been will be no difficult task. You will, however, find none who will bring more of disinterested and loyal effort to promote the honour, dignity, and welfare of the nation, and of your Administration, or who will prove more anxious for your own personal and official welfare and success than

Yours very sincerely, Hamilton Fish.

Despite its positive tone, this resignation was not meant to be final. It was intended to bring Grant up with a jerk, and to teach him again, as he had been taught in the crisis of July, 1870, but had forgotten, that he must give Fish full control over foreign affairs or find a new Secretary of State. This time he must do it once and for all. Fish knew

[43] Fish to Grant, Garrison, September 22, 1874; Letterbooks.

that the President could ill afford his resignation at any time—that he could not possibly afford it just before the Congressional elections of 1874. The Secretary's fighting blood was aroused. Six months earlier, before these impositions, he had contemplated quietly stepping out about the time snow flew. But now he realized what a triumph his resignation, under the changed circumstances, would be for the Babcock-Belknap-Casey-Murtagh cabal, how fervent would be their rejoicings. He hoped, as his letters show, that Grant would reject it and let him dictate terms under which he would stay. He began for the first time to meditate serving as Secretary of State till the close of Grant's term, not because he loved office but because he could thus foil the backstairs gang which was trying to take control of the government, and drive the furrow of foreign policy straight to the end.

All this is implied in a single sentence of his explanatory letter to his new Assistant Secretary, John L. Cadwalader: "Either my resignation *must* be accepted, or some assurance [given] of the withdrawal of this Army influence—this backstairs, Kitchen-Cabinet control over the affairs of my Department." [44] Ten days passed without word from the President. On two of these days he was in New York City, but sent Fish no notification and intimated no wish to see him. While the Secretary surmised that Grant was preoccupied with the search for a successor, he felt that ordinary courtesy should have prompted some reply. Then on October 1 Grant curtly telegraphed: "Can you not come to Washington tonight and attend Cabinet meeting tomorrow?" Fish was busy attending a diocesan convention in New York, and could not leave. Nor did he intend to leave until Grant responded to his offer of resignation.

Finally, on October 3 he received a letter. Grant wrote that, knowing how long the Secretary had desired to retire to private life, "I do not see how I can again ask you to change your determination, as much as I regret your having taken it." He did not believe that it would be easy to find a successor. "I think that the public will agree with me in the statement that more ability, efficiency, and honest effort has [*sic*] not been in the place of Sec. of State for many Administrations back." But he asked a favor. "As New York will hold an election early in November, and change now might have some effect upon the result, I ask that all consideration of the question of your resignation be deferred

[44] Fish to Cadwalader, Garrison, September 23, 1874; Letterbooks.

until that time."

This was not unreasonable. Fish could have acceded to the request —had he really wished his resignation accepted; but he did not. He wished to bring Grant to a fair and square decision at once, *before the elections*. He had good arguments for asking immediate action; if he were to leave Washington he must soon advertise his house there, refurnish his Stuyvesant Square home, reclaim his stables, and hire new servants; and he could take none of these steps without letting the cat out of the bag. On October 22 he returned to Washington; two days later Grant, who had been in St. Louis and Chicago, also returned. Fish immediately called at the White House "to bring to a close the question of my retirement."

Grant began the conversation by saying how much he regretted the Secretary's resignation, and wished that he would withdraw it. When Fish replied that he had written the letter only after long deliberation and under a strong conviction of its necessity, the President continued his expostulations. It was very inconvenient to make a change just when the annual message was to be prepared, and papers presented to Congress; he had not been able to think of any satisfactory person for the State Department; Governor Morgan, Edwards Pierrepont, and Andrew D. White had occurred to him, but all were open to objections; he really did not know where to turn. And, he added plaintively, he was at a loss to know what Fish meant in saying that his resignation was a necessity. Why? This was precisely the opening Fish wanted, and he quickly remarked that he would explain his reasons. The diary continues:

He said that he wished I would state them.

I then entered into a very full statement of the various interferences to which I had been subjected, referring to the articles in the *Republican* last spring on Cuban independence; to Carpenter's resolution; to his own admission to me that he had encouraged Carpenter without any intimation to the head of the Department charged with foreign affairs; to Casey's connection with these Cuban publications in the *Republican;* to the War Department commissioning persons to the Emperor of Japan and his signing their commissions, and no intimation given to the State Department; to the attempt to put Ingalls in the quartermaster's bureau, and for that purpose to name Meigs as Minister to Russia . . . ; to Babcock's having written to Jones (Minister to Brussels) offering him the mission to Austria in the event of Jay's withdrawal; to Babcock having informed him of the Ecuadorian complaint of Rumsey Wing before I had an opportunity to state it officially, and when I did so, he expressed his determination to give the mission to a brother-in-law of General Belknap, and that on my asking his name he (the President) did not know it, evidently shewing that he had been forestalled by Babcock's interference to commit himself before he could be officially informed of the probable vacancy and before the officer charged by law and by usage and by propriety with the suggestion of names to fill such vacancy should have the opportunity of communicating with the President. . . .

I referred to the curt letter from his assistant-secretary instructing me to make the appointment to Ecuador, when in fact he was shown that an appointment was premature, and had verbally countermanded it afterward. I referred to the requisitions without consultation with me, or with my Department, for appointing two Missouri men to important Eastern consulates, adding that such things were continually recurring; that while I had great respect and very friendly feeling for General Babcock, I did not regard him as a safe counsellor to the President in matters pertaining to my Department, and that I could no longer submit to interference and meddling either by him or by the other Departments into the affairs of my Department, whether of policy or of appointment; that the War Department was allowed to override the State Department; that I was utterly tired of all this; that it indicated one or the other or perhaps both of two things: (1) That I had lost his confidence, or (2) That he was allowing my Department to be ruled and controlled by outside, irregular, and incompetent influences; that such being the logical . . . conclusion from all this series of events, in either alternative I could no longer remain.

All this was overwhelming. And yet only Grant's colossal and incredible carelessness was to blame; he never intended for a moment to place a slight upon Fish or to let Babcock do so. The Secretary had no sooner concluded than the President assured him of his fullest and most unreserved confidence; declared that these unfortunate events —which he now saw should not have been permitted—had in every instance been the result of thoughtlessness; and in short, made a profuse and sweeping apology. Fish thanked him. But, he said, "I cannot remain except with an understanding that in future there shall be more of reserve and of care, and that the interference by Babcock, or by other men working through Babcock, must cease. So, too, must the interference of other Departments, whether in matters of policy or in questions of appointment, unless regularly presented in Cabinet discussion."

"You may rely upon this understanding," said Grant. "Now that my attention has been directed to the matter, there will be no recurrence of any cause of complaint." And he reiterated his wish that the Secretary should continue in office.

"Very well, Mr. President," responded Fish with formal dignity. "Relying upon the assurances you give that I need apprehend no further cause of complaint, I will reconsider, and I now withdraw my resignation." He added that he had leased his house until May, 1875, and would not like to bind himself to any particular tenure of office after that date. But Grant always held that sufficient unto the day was the evil thereof. "Well," he said, closing the subject, "I am glad that you will remain until next summer and hope that you may be able to continue beyond that time. But I see that must remain an open question to be determined hereafter." With all their old friendliness, the two then took up some routine matters of foreign business.

Fish had won his victory. Had his resignation been accepted, Babcock would have stood triumphant, the latest and greatest of his intrigues against the principal members of the Cabinet a complete success. With none but Bristow and Jewell to oppose him, he would doubtless have completed the ruin of the Administration within a short time. Fish had used the threat of resignation to teach Grant a severe lesson, which even he would not soon forget, and to establish the rights of all Cabinet members—not merely himself—within their respective spheres. His moral authority was now greater than ever, and men like Belknap and Babcock would think twice before they again provoked him to anger.

FISH's diary has already given us several glimpses of the Administration's anxieties in the South; and as domestic affairs claimed more of his attention, he made fuller and more frequent entries upon the subject. The Congressional elections of 1874 were heralded by the usual Southern disturbances, exaggerated by the press; Republican journals making the most of Ku Klux outrages, and Democratic newspapers of Negro violence. The native Southern whites had been steadily regaining control. In State after State corrupt carpetbag governments had been overthrown by responsible property-holders, who erected "conservative" administrations to stop the plundering and restore order. By the close of 1870 four States—Tennessee, Virginia, North Carolina, Georgia—had been redeemed, and Texas and Alabama shortly followed. In the autumn of 1874 Arkansas was about to join the list. The States with "conservative" governments showed the least rioting, fighting, and intimidation; those in which the native white victory was still to be won offered the least security to life and property. The bloodiest outbreak in the fall of 1874, for example, was at Vicksburg, Miss., where Negroes marching upon the city were driven off with scores of fatalities; and Mississippi still groaned under the Carpetbag rule of Ben Butler's son-in-law, Adelbert Ames. The conservative reaction, inevitable, irresistible, and followed by less oppression of the Negro than might have been expected, was a great pacifying force. When Mississippi and Louisiana, Florida and South Carolina were again governed by their own whites, the whole South would enjoy order and a fair degree of racial concord—and not until then.

Fish had consistently felt that while Grant's Southern policy had the great merit of firmness, it lacked insight, generosity, and imagination. When the President took office many still hoped that the South would tolerate the carpetbag governments born from military reconstruction. In that hope Grant had made in 1869 his one generous gesture, asking that Virginia and Mississippi be allowed to adopt Constitutions without disfranchisement and test-oath clauses. But when the South revolted against the Carpetbaggers, when the Ku Klux Klan made violence epidemic, Grant fell back upon his fixed military idea of the restoration of order. To him the South seemed in rebellion against the results of the war; by the three Enforcement Acts of 1870–71, by proclamations, martial law, suspension of the writ of habeas corpus, and vigorous Federal prosecutions, by use of troops, Federal marshals, and deputies, he moved to quell this rebellion. The third Enforcement Act of 1871 had a double purpose. Its avowed object was to secure life, liberty, and property in disordered Southern States. The real object of many Republican leaders was to maintain their grip upon the South by giving the Federal Administration complete police powers, and the Federal courts complete jurisdiction over all offences. The Army and the Department of Justice were clothed with paramount authority. Years later this law and the first Enforcement Act were declared unconstitutional by the Supreme Court—but meanwhile they had served their purpose.

By the fall of 1874 the bankruptcy of Grant's Southern policy was admitted by all fairminded Republicans. E. L. Godkin pointed out that in the States under native white government, order was now comparatively safe, and "the Negro enjoys as much protection from the laws as the whites"; in States still under Negro control "the blacks have themselves become, in the hands of white knaves, oppressors of the worst sort." In States still hanging in the balance Federal marshals and Federal attorneys had risen to be autocratic political chieftains. They invoked the formidable powers of the Attorney-General and courts; they controlled the soldiers, and were always ready to call in overwhelming Federal forces; they gave orders to Carpetbaggers and Scalawags. The Attorney-General threatened to become a satrap lording it over one-third of the South. Sometimes the plainest mandates of the Constitution were overridden. In Arkansas during one crisis Federal troops were temporarily employed by the President not to defend the State against insurrection, but to prevent the *de facto,* and as it later proved, the *de jure* governor, from using State forces to expel a usurper from the State House. This was the Brooks-Baxter War of the spring of 1874, waged between two rival Republican factions, both unprincipled.

Yet with no constructive achievements outside finance and foreign affairs to present to the electorate, the Republicans in 1874 naturally emphasized the Southern question. Speeches and platforms dealt with the "outrages." The Indiana Chairman telegraphed editors in his State to play up "the horrible scenes of violence and bloodshed transpiring throughout the South." Financial questions being too dangerous to touch, the party demanded retention in office primarily that it might continue using the Army against the "rebels."

Back of the factional clashes and the efforts to bring about Federal intervention often lay the most sordid of motives. Thus Fish's diary for May 5, 1874, records a Cabinet discussion of the Arkansas difficulties. "The Attorney-General says there can be no possible doubt that Baxter is legally entitled to the office; his right having been decided by the legislature, which by the Constitution of the State is made the exclusive judge of the returns of the elections; both he and the President express the opinion that Brooks had received an actual majority of the votes, but that the President could not go behind the count and decision of the Legislature." And it continues:

> From some things said it appears that there is a railroad job at the bottom of this contest for the Governorship; that Baxter had peremptorily refused to sign subsidy bonds in favor of the road which had been authorized by the legislature, and the two Senators from that State, who had been friends of Baxter, are now opposing him. Williams said that Senator Dorsey with a good deal of feeling told him that everything he had was involved in this decision, and had become much excited, and threatened [trouble] when told that the President would be obliged to recognize Baxter.

At first Fish, while laboring constantly for moderation, in his few public utterances defended the Administration. But events in 1874 opened his eyes to the perils of the President's policy. On every hand he heard of its unpopularity. Elihu Washburne, in distant France, wrote him early in March that the Republicans would lose the next House unless a change occurred.[1] "That Louisiana business is very unfortunate. It will take a strong party to carry Pitt Kellogg and Judge Durell, to say nothing of Pinchback. The sooner the whole gang is thrown overboard the better. . . ." Southern correspondents expatiated upon the confusion and bitterness in their section. In offering General Henry C. Wayne of Savannah, a Southern Republican, the mission to Japan, Fish remarked that the Administration had been embarrassed by the "want of confidence and apparent opposition to the inevitable consequences of late events on the part of so many of those at the South

[1] Washburne to Fish, Arcachon, France, March 4, 1874; Washburne Papers, Vol. 90.

in whom it would have desired to manifest confidence." [2] This elicited from Wayne a notable indictment of the bad character of most of Grant's Southern appointments. He wrote: [3]

What you say of the reticence of Southern men is undoubtedly true, but . . . how can it well be otherwise when the public confidence and influence is bestowed upon men foreign to the community, not respectable in their education, manners, habits, and associations, who openly represent the lowest political sentiments, and who to further the extreme radical purposes use the confidence and influence they have to stir up the animosities of the negro against the white race? Take this city as a common instance. Gentlemen can have nothing to do with low class men controlling the Revenue Internal, the Custom House, and the Postoffice—all aliens to our community, and who if removed from office would only have to pack their carpetbags and squat somewhere else. I am not writing from prejudice, for as a citizen and as a U. S. Commissioner I have ever maintained the civil and political rights of the colored men. . . . Pass along our bay, and daily see the crowds of idle negroes crowding and loafing on the Custom House steps, like buzzards on a church steeple, filthing them with tobacco juice and impeding ingress and egress. In consequence no merchant goes to the Custom House if it can be avoided, sending a clerk. . . .

Now is this necessary? Is it just, in view of an ardent desire to reconstruct the Union? Is it wise to take men from Maine, Massachusetts, New Hampshire, Ohio, Tennessee, and Upper Georgia, to fill these important and responsible positions, when respectable gentlemen friendly disposed to the Administration and who only need proper encouragement, and whose stake is all in the community, can be had on the spot? The white vote in Georgia exceeds the colored by about 19,000. In Savannah the white vote is as 15 to 13. . . . All that Wilson, Atkins, Clark, Seeley, and the rest of the carpetbaggers can do is to stir up the negro ignorance, and get up a show of bloodshed alarming to all good citizens, and disturbing the public tranquillity. . . . The election for governor, and for the President last year speak a telling lesson. Smith was elected governor, on local issues, by over 60,000. . . . Greeley's majority on the contrary over General Grant was only a little over 9,000 though backed by Joe Brown. Here is a declaration that has not been profited by in Washington.

[2] Fish to Wayne, November 16, 1873; Letterbooks. Fish, like many others, had hoped early in 1873 that Grant would carry out a long-discussed plan for travelling in the South and informing himself at first hand of conditions there. An announcement in February that he would go pleased a multitude of Southerners, who believed the trip would enable the President to formulate a more liberal policy. But he received threatening letters from a few cranks, while the plan was attacked by men who had an interest in seeing him kept in the dark. He resolved instead to go to St. Louis, to look after some fire-damaged property. *Nation*, March 27, 1873.

[3] Wayne to Fish, Savannah, November 24, 1873; Fish Papers.

This protest was well taken. The nation was subjecting the Southern States by force to the perils and hardships of Negro suffrage, an experiment unprecedented in modern history. Common decency required it to see that the Federal officials in the South during this tremendous trial were true representatives of the ability, honesty, and public spirit of the North, who would have no partisan aims, but exert themselves to maintain harmony, prevent excesses and corruption, and lead the Negroes in an intelligent participation in government. Instead, by bad appointments and systematic encouragement of machines, the Administration fastened a crew of incompetent rogues upon the section.

I

It was the before-mentioned revolt in New Orleans in September, 1874, against the Kellogg régime which first produced marked Cabinet dissension. The political history of Louisiana had been the most tragic in the South. Lincoln had begun its reconstruction earlier than any other State. But the first moderate government had quickly fallen under Radical onslaughts; carpetbaggers and Negroes had taken possession of the State; and H. C. Warmoth, an Illinois adventurer who had been on Banks's staff, became governor. The State debt rose from less than $15,000,000 in 1868 to nearly $50,000,000 in 1871, while taxes more than quintupled. Before the war a session of the legislature had cost $100,000 to $200,000; in 1871 it cost more than $900,000. On taking office Grant had named as Customs Collector in New Orleans his brother-in-law James F. Casey, another adventurer, and as Federal marshal a Maine carpetbagger, S. B. Packard. They first acted in alliance with Warmoth, but shortly quarreled with him. In a contest over the organization of the legislature in 1872 Casey actually used a revenue-cutter to carry sufficient members out of reach for ten or twelve days to prevent Warmoth's party from achieving a quorum. In March, 1872, Grant reinforced Casey by appointing Ben Butler's brother-in-law Parker as Surveyor of the Port.

The elections for governor and legislature that fall resulted in a true South American melée. The three Administration musketeers, Casey, Packard, and Parker, sided with the Radical Republican party headed by William Pitt Kellogg. Defeated by John McEnery, who headed a coalition of Democrats and Warmoth Republicans, Kellogg trumped up a case under the Enforcement Act, went to a hard-drinking Federal judge named Durell, and obtained a "midnight order"—not sealed by the court, not signed officially, and not directed in the name of the President, as it should have been—under which the marshal used Federal troops to seize the State House, and to install as members of the legislature such persons as Kellogg and Casey designated. Washington immediately recognized the government thus set up.

Under this government Louisiana was still suffering in the autumn of 1874. The Senate Judiciary Committee had made an inquiry, and its majority had reported that Durell's order was illegal and void, and that Louisiana possessed no legal government; five of its seven members had declared that the rival or McEnery legislature possessed the better title. The best citizens of Louisiana had made an impressive appeal to Congress and the Northern public. Various journals had pointed out that corruption had grown deeper, contempt for public opinion more open, and lawmaking more reckless. But nothing had been done. The Grant Administration seemed adamant; Northern opinion was indifferent. Then, as the elections of 1874 approached, the Kellogg legislature passed a law placing the registry of all voters in the hands of the governor's appointees, without appeal to the courts. Under this law Kellogg could hold office until death. Forthwith, citizens of New Orleans began to arm and organize for resistance. Kellogg's police responded by raiding gunsmiths' shops and seizing fowling-pieces in private houses. The result was an indignation meeting, called by substantial New Orleans merchants, and the temporarily successful attack upon the government already described. "We say frankly," wrote E. L. Godkin, "that we know of no case of armed resistance to an established government in modern times in which the insurgents had more plainly the right on their side." [4]

Fish deplored Grant's haste in issuing his proclamation against the uprising. While he believed it impossible to recognize the revolutionary government, thus encouraging lawlessness and usurpation, he also believed that concessions should be made to Louisiana feeling. Bristow told the Cabinet that much sentiment existed even among the Federal troops against the Kellogg government and in favor of the Citizens' Party. Fish urged that conferences be arranged in New Orleans; that both factions be induced to withdraw; and that the coming election be

[4] *Nation*, September 24, 1874.

held under Federal control or joint control of the two parties. Bristow suggested that Fish himself go to New Orleans to effect an understanding and prevent further violence, but the Secretary replied that no Cabinet-member could travel many miles before news of his errand was telegraphed over the country and his usefulness destroyed.[5] Other names were suggested—Admiral Rodgers, and General Cowan of the Interior Department. But Grant, to Fish's regret, took a sterner course. He issued orders to military commanders in Louisiana that under no circumstances would the new government be recognized, and began moving troops and warships on New Orleans; McEnery yielded, and Kellogg was reinstated.

The elections of 1874 were a heavy blow to the Republican Party. Tilden rolled up more than 50,000 majority in New York. Democratic victories in Indiana, Illinois, and Missouri made certain the departure of Morton, Logan, and Schurz from the Senate. In Pennsylvania the Democrats gained a dozen Congressmen. Democratic control of the next House was assured, and able new men, like Hewitt of New York, promised aggressive leadership there. A conservative triumph brought Alabama into the redeemed list. The only consolation Republicans found was in the defeat of Ben Butler in his Lowell district. "What a sweep the Democrats have made!" John L. Cadwalader wrote Fish. "We deserve *some* of it. . . . Someone advised that troops should be sent to Butler's district to prevent intimidation." [6] But Fish feared that the lesson would be lost upon Grant. He wrote in his diary on November 8:

Postmaster-General Jewell called in evening to see me. Says he dined on Friday at the President's, who he thinks has no appreciation of the results of the late election, which have been overwhelmingly adverse to the Republican Party; that among the company at the President's were Babcock and

[5] Diary, September 16, 1874, recording two Cabinet meetings. Grant's attitude was described to Elihu Washburne by Marshall Jewell under date of September 19, 1874. "Grant means business in this thing. He is not mad about it, nor does he use any hard language, and he doesn't . . . say much, but his eyes are *sot in his head,* and he will never make it up as long as there's an insurgent pretender in the chair, and does not hesitate to call out all the force in the United States. He is cool and collected and thoroughly determined, and grows a little black in the face when talking about it, but that's all." Washburne Papers. Vol. 90.

[6] Cadwalader to Fish, Washington, November 5, 1874; Fish Papers. Marshall Jewell wrote Washburne on December 5, 1874: "The President does not feel that he is responsible for these little defeats, but I differ with him somewhat, because I think that with a better set of appointments we might have succeeded better at the polls." Jewell added: "Everybody does rejoice at the defeat of Butler. Bailey telegraphed on the night of the election, 'Butler Defeated, Everything Else Lost.'" Washburne Papers, Vol. 90.

his wife, and Tiffany (President's Methodist priest) and his wife; that at the dinner Mrs. Tiffany said she was glad of Dix's defeat in New York because he had gone back upon the President [Dix had rejected the third-term idea] to which Jewell says he took exception, but no others dissented.

Jewell added that this is the sort of talk with which the President is always surrounded. Jewell added that he did not think the President really appreciated the importance of the Republican Party.

Certainly the President's Southern policy continued unchanged. In Arkansas, where the Democrats and conservative Republicans had just adopted a new Constitution and elected A. H. Garland as governor, the former lieutenant-governor, one Smith, tried by some queer constitutional law to work up a case before Attorney-General Williams and thereby obtain control of the State. His plea was preposterous. Yet the Cabinet seriously considered it. Fortunately, Congressional investigators found that he had no support, while Williams laid down the opinion, according to the diary, that the validity of the new Constitution could not be denied because, several other States having adopted instruments in similar fashion, it would "not be safe." [7] A few days later, reading a rough draft of part of his annual message, Grant indulged in an outburst of spleen. He showed the Cabinet several loose sheets, which he said represented his real opinion of Reconstruction and the condition of the South. Fish characterizes them as "very strong and very just." They "might be well for a heated Congressional debate or a rough newspaper article," but they were "wholly beneath the dignity of his official position or of an official document." After reading them, the President remarked: "This is just what I want to say, but I don't think I can." [8] Whenever possible Fish urged caution; for example, he wrote on December 3:

President read draft of his message, excepting that part relating to currency and finance, which he had read on Tuesday; in the main a very good document, better written than some former ones, subjected to more criticism in a friendly spirit, and more discussion than on any previous occasion.

The part relating to reorganization of Southern States, especially Arkansas, was modified after considerable discussion, Bristow, Jewell, and myself urging modifications, Delano, Williams, and Robeson partly opposing them. Assertions of questionable powers on the part of the Executive and the expression conceding certain powers to Congress were those objected to on constitutional principles. . . .

[7] Diary, November 17, 20, 1874.   [8] Diary, December 1, 1874.

II

At this point the Louisiana pot again commenced to boil furiously. The election on November 2, with Federal troops and gunboats policing the State, had ended in a violent dispute. The face of the returns gave the Conservatives a heavy majority of the next House and a decisive majority of the Legislature upon a joint ballot; and the Citizens' Committee petitioned Grant to withdraw the military. But Grant refused and the Kellogg-Packard-Casey machine prepared to hold the State at all costs. The Returning Board, controlled by Kellogg, met November 11 to canvass the ballots. In six weeks of secret labor it so manipulated the vote as to give the House 54 Republicans and 52 Conservatives, with five seats undetermined and left to the decision of the Legislature. It had thrown out many local returns, acted with gross unfairness, and produced a list of members which impartial Northern judges unhesitantly pronounced fraudulent. Protests by the aghast Conservatives went unheeded. The legislature was to meet January 4, and they must move rapidly or be overwhelmed. They did move. On December 29 McEnery announced that he hoped to control the organization of the House unless prevented by Federal troops. On January 3 press reports stated that the non-appearance of three members (two sending word that "not having been elected they would decline to appear") and the arrest of a fourth, had dashed the Radical hopes of a majority.

But having acted with arbitrary haste in September, President Grant was prepared to do so again. The Cabinet meeting of December 29 showed that most members favored caution. When Grant stated that it might be necessary to place Louisiana under martial law, Attorney-General Williams even expressed doubt as to his authority to do so.[9] Nevertheless, rumors that the President had decided on "heroic treatment"[10] soon proved correct. Going over the head of General Sherman, to the latter's anger, he ordered General Sheridan—an officer hated next to Ben Butler in Louisiana, where he had behaved with great harshness as military commander—to New Orleans. Sheridan arrived January 1, 1875, but did not take formal charge till the night of the 4th.

[9] Diary, December 29, 1874. For the situation in New Orleans, see Lonn, *Reconstruction in Louisiana*, 270 ff. On details, especially the exact complexion of the House, authorities (like parties and newspapers of the time) differ widely.
[10] *Nation*, January 7, 1875.

Early on the 4th, 1,800 Federal troops were marshalled near the State House. At noon the House met, and amid great confusion elected a Conservative as temporary chairman. Though different witnesses gave different accounts, the Conservatives held an apparent majority, and they prepared to fill the five undecided seats. As they did so the Radicals began withdrawing. Organization of the House continued, and the temporary chairman was elected Speaker. Then suddenly the sound of marching men came from the corridors; with clattering scabbards General de Trobriand and his staff appeared at the door; and striding down the aisle, he produced two papers from Governor Kellogg, one denouncing the House as an illegal body, and another authorizing him to expel all members not certified by the Returning Board. A number were hustled out at the point of the bayonet. With the aid of a file of soldiers who kept order, and a former clerk who called the roll, de Trobriand reorganized the House. As he did so the last protesting Conservative withdrew, and left the chamber to the troops and the Kellogg party.

The news of this arbitrary interference created intense indignation all over the country. Garfield wrote in his diary: "The darkest day for the Republican party and its hopes I have seen since the war." [11] E. L. Godkin called in "the most outrageous subversion of parliamentary government by military force yet attempted in this country." [12] Great mass-meetings, addressed by prominent Republicans as well as Democrats, were at once held in Cooper Union and Faneuil Hall. This time the facts of the episode could not possibly be distorted; the legislature of a sovereign American State, the complete and final judge of the qualifications of its own members, with a legal quorum present, and acting in the orderly discharge of its duties, had been turned into the street by Federal soldiery. Nothing more destructive of the principles of American government could be imagined; and that it was done to aid such a crew of plunderers as Casey, Packard, and Kellogg added to the disgrace. Kellogg's order of course had no validity; no Governor or President in America has any authority whatever over the organization or proceedings of a legislative body. Nor was there any law, Federal or State, under which de Trobriand's intervention could be justified.

The general indignation was shared by Fish. At the Cabinet meeting on January 5 Secretary Belknap read a remarkably moderate report

[11] Smith, *Garfield*, I, 519.   [12] *Nation*, January 7, 1875.

from Lieutenant-Colonel Henry A. Morrow, an officer whose work had taken him all over the State, on Louisiana affairs, emphasizing the popular loyalty, to the Federal Government. It struck Fish as able, discerning, and truthful, and he said so. But in "other quarters" it was less acceptable. Attorney-General Williams pronounced the expressions of loyalty insincere. Grant concurred. When one member asked Williams his opinion of the proper policy to be followed he replied, "I would fight it out to the bloody end," a remark from which Fish warmly dissented.[13] Telegrams were read from Sheridan and Packard. The newspapers that day published reports that Grant was about to send Congress a message on Louisiana, and in the evening Bristow came to Fish's house with news that Senators Conkling and Edmunds were much worried as to its nature. They understood that the Attorney-General was drafting it, and expressed an earnest hope that Fish and Bristow would take careful precautions as to its tone and purport. Neither of them had the slightest respect for "Landaulet" Williams, whose influence over Grant seemed so peculiar. Fish was nonplused. Bristow had no plan of action, and it was obviously difficult to give Grant advice until it was asked.

Their discussion led, writes Fish in his diary, "to an expression by both of us of regret and dissatisfaction on the absence of serious consultation in Cabinet meetings of questions of interest instead of the consumption of time in the discussion relating to the filling of unimportant offices and in general conversation." They both deplored "the indifferent way in which Col. Morrow's very remarkable report had been received." Fish was grieved because Bristow had apparently agreed with Grant and Williams upon the insincerity of Southern professions of loyalty, and Bristow excused himself on the ground that his bitter struggle with the Ku Klux Klan in Kentucky had made him distrustful of Southerners. Fish pointed to the plain evidences of loyalty in Louisiana. "I refer," he writes, "to the readiness with which in September last the Penn Government in New Orleans had yielded the moment the General Government presented itself."

Before the Cabinet met again on January 9th ominous events had taken place in Louisiana. General Sheridan, arriving to take charge on the 1st, had formed his own views of the situation with such prodigi-

[13] Diary, January 5, 1875. The Morrow report was endorsed by General Emory, in command in New Orleans, and General Sherman, head of the Army. See Senate Ex. Doc. 43d Cong., 2d Sess., No. 17.

ous rapidity (though for three years its complexity had puzzled the government and country) that on the 4th he telegraphed a plan to the War Department. "I think," he stated, "that the terrorization now existing in Louisiana, Mississippi, and Arkansas could be entirely removed and confidence and fair dealing established by the arrest and trial of the ringleaders of the armed White League. If Congress would pass a bill declaring them banditti they could be tried by a military commission. . . . It is possible that if the President would issue a proclamation declaring them banditti, no further action need be taken except that which would devolve upon me." This plan for a general act of attainder or proclamation of outlawry, to be followed by the summary court-martialing of all citizens that Sheridan chose to arrest, momentarily stunned intelligent observers. Then the best leaders of the North rose as one man in protest. William Cullen Bryant and William M. Evarts uttered eloquent condemnations. Carl Schurz asked if these things were done in Louisiana, how long before they would be done in Massachusetts and Ohio?—how long before soldiers would stalk into the Federal House and pointing to the Speaker's mace, say "Take away that bauble?" Samuel Bowles declared in the Springfield *Republican* that the acts in Louisiana were "revolutionary, treasonable." The *Nation* asserted that to find precedents for Sheridan, students must go back to the loosing of Claverhouse's dragoons on the Covenanters, and of Louis XIV's soldiery on the Huguenots.[14]

Yet while the public disapproval grew to a hurricane, Secretary Belknap telegraphed Sheridan: "The President and all of us have full confidence and thoroughly approve your course. . . . Be assured that the President and Cabinet confide in your wisdom and rest in the belief that all acts of yours have been and will be judicious."

The Cabinet meeting on the 9th was one of the stormiest the White House has ever seen. Williams opened it by trying to justify the interference with the Louisiana legislature on the ground that the Federal troops were a *posse comitatus* called in to maintain the peace. Robeson enlarged upon this argument. President Grant, writes Fish, then "adopted the idea that the military having been there in pursuance

---

[14] For the text of Sheridan's dispatch see Senate Miscellaneous Docs., 43d Congress, 2d Session, No. 45. For Grant's approval of Sheridan's work see Senate Ex. Doc., 43d Cong., 2d. Sess., No. 13. For editorial opinion see Merriam's *Samuel Bowles*, II, 275, 276; *Nation*, January 14, 1875. A good treatment of the whole subject is to be found in the *American Annual Cyclopaedia*, 1874, article "Louisiana."

of a call made in accordance with the Constitution of the United States, it was to be regarded as a *posse comitatus.*" At once Fish interrupted with an emotion which he transferred later to his diary: [15]

I dissent from these ideas—[I] admit that the military were in New Orleans in pursuance of a call made in accordance with the Constitution, but [assert] that the army of the United States never can be regarded or used as a *posse comitatus.* The two ideas are inconsistent. [I] dissent from Robeson's argument as to the extent of the duty of the governor of a State to attend to the organization of the legislature; he has no duty to interfere forcibly unless there be an attempt by force to prevent the organization. The legislature is the judge of the returns of its own members; that the governor cannot interfere until called upon; unless there be a violent interference with the organization.

There is no allegation of forcible (Democratic) interference with the organization of the legislature in New Orleans. The returns exhibited a nearly equal number of each party as elected (neither party having sufficient to form a quorum) and a small number of contested seats. These contested seats would determine the majority of one or the other political party in the Assembly. A trick or snap judgment was attempted, under which a number of Democratic contestants were declared admitted, etc., thus giving the Democrats a majority of the House and a quorum. This may have been a fraud upon the people of the State, but was not a violation or breach of the peace. That thereupon . . . the United States troops came in and forcibly removed the persons who had been admitted to the contested seats. This was a wholly inexcusable interference, and an outrage upon the independence of the State legislature; that the governor could not authorize nor request such intrusion, and that his request to an officer of the army to use his troops either to prevent or to aid in the dispersion or even in the organization of a legislature was no justification of the military officer.

Attorney-General Williams interrupted to ask if Fish, when governor of New York, would not have used troops to resist any attempt to prevent the organization of the legislature, or to force into it persons not elected. Fish smiled pityingly. He replied that while he would certainly have used the militia to quell a violent attempt to prevent legislative organization, he would have had no right whatever to use it to control the decision of the legislature as to its own membership. After this crushing rejoinder he turned to Belknap's unwarranted telegram:

I then said that another point was presented by the telegrams which had appeared in the public papers as having passed between General Sheridan

[15] Diary, January 9, 1875.

and the Secretary of War. I had seen two telegrams from Sheridan which I regarded as unwise and very objectionable. One dated January 4th charged the whole community with indifference to defiance of laws and of murder, the other denounces persons as "banditti"; the connection of the two seems to include the community, or controlling element of these States, in the denunciation as "banditti"; that he proposes that Congress so declare them, in which case they could be tried by a military commission; that this conclusion is not justified by any law and arises either from an ignorance or a disregard of civil law. He then proceeds to say that if the President would issue a proclamation declaring them "banditti" no further action need be taken, except that which would devolve upon him, the inference being that he would try them by court martial. To these telegrams the Secretary of War replied that "the President and all of us have full confidence and thoroughly approve your course." If "all of us" is intended to mean the Cabinet, I say that I have not been correctly represented inasmuch as . . . General Sheridan's telegrams . . . did not allow me to have confidence in him in his present position, or to approve his course, and I am unwilling to appear before the public as having such confidence or as approving Sheridan's course.

He proceeded to condemn the entire course followed in Louisiana. He said:

That I think it is the duty of the Administration to disclaim and denounce the action of General de Trobriand in intruding upon the legislature, and to withdraw from the expression of confidence as made by the Secretary of War in behalf of the Cabinet.

That I believe that the masses of the people in Louisiana are like the masses elsewhere, honest, sincere, and moral, and would look upon crime and murder with the same abhorrence. That they wish to be engaged in their own vocations, but that the disorganization of society in that State and the lawlessness which has prevailed there since the war have made them timid and disinclined to interfere actively to repress or punish the outrages which occur. That the charge of indifference to murders against a community is unjust and very unwise.

Belknap made the lame explanation that his telegram had been submitted to the President, and that he had supposed no Cabinet-member would dissent from it. He also read the President's instruction ordering Sheridan to Louisiana; it was dated the day before Christmas, and Fish had never heard of it before—nor apparently had any other Cabinet officer, save Williams. "I think," Fish writes, "that when made public it will be severely criticized." [16] Both Bristow and Jewell ener-

16 *Ibid.*

getically sustained Fish. The former, though reiterating his distrust of Southern whites, strongly dissented from Belknap's telegram. Jewell declared the term "banditti" unfortunate, disapproved of Sheridan's recommendations, sharply condemned the invasion of the legislative hall by Federal troops, and asserted that he was opposed to any endorsement of Sheridan's acts.

In this heated discussion, which lasted until three in the afternoon, Grant was palpably embarrassed and took little part. When Fish suggested a public disclaimer of the action of de Trobriand and a withdrawal of Belknap's hasty telegram, he merely interrupted to say: "I will certainly not denounce the military action or censure Sheridan's proposals." But the debate had its effect on him. "As it advanced," records Fish, "he seemed to be somewhat impressed with doubt as to the entire correctness of what had been done." He might well have been!

That evening Robeson told Fish confidentially that Belknap had suppressed several indiscreet telegrams from Sheridan, one beginning: "The dog is dead." Blaine, Garfield, and Eugene Hale called at the Secretary's house. All were worried, and all much dissatisfied with Grant's military intervention and with the position in which Belknap's telegram had left the Administration. Next day a Republican Congressional caucus discussed the subject, but with little result; its chief feature being a temperate speech by Butler—"that is, temperate for Butler," Blaine told Fish—recommending a new election in Louisiana.[17]

But on Sunday the 10th Fish called at Bristow's rooms and found Jewell there with some interesting news. A Congressional sub-committee of two Republicans and one Democrat, Phelps, Foster, and Clarkson Potter, had been hurried to Louisiana to investigate. They had prepared an unanimous report. It would state, said Jewell, that no intimidation had been exercised in the recent election; that the returning board had been thoroughly corrupt and its decisions fraudulent; and that it had seated Republicans from districts in which Democrats had unquestionably been elected. They would also report that the White League included a large body of highly respected citizens, who would tolerate no rowdyism, and that the five legislators ejected by de Trobriand had been honestly elected. This news proved correct. Within a few days the report was published and produced a tremendous impression. The high standing of the three men, the thoroughness of their

[17] Diary, January 10, 1875.

investigation, based upon 1,500 printed pages of testimony, and their unanimity, rendered it conclusive.[18] It left Grant's course and Sheridan's harsh outburst more indefensible than ever.

III

Fish was now anxious that the Administration should find an honest path of retreat. Congress had passed a resolution calling upon Grant for information. Still hopeful that he would disavow the recent military acts, and in close touch with distressed Congressional leaders, Fish prepared the rough draft of a message which would have committed him to a clear abandonment of intervention. It asserted that the request of Governor Kellogg for armed assistance "was an unjustifiable call upon the military, and is well calculated to excite alarm as tending to the subversion of constitutional law and the independence of the legislature of a State." It also laid down a general rule: "The army of the United States should not be employed to control or to effect the organization of the legislature of a State, either on the order of a Governor or at the request of a claimant to the Speaker's chair." While it partially defended de Trobriand by saying that in view of previous lawlessness in Louisiana, "the military officer may . . . be excused for not assuming to disobey" Kellogg's order, it concluded that this action "cannot be made a precedent for any future intervention."

Fish never wrote a bolder or more statesmanlike paper. Showing it to Bristow, he tried to enlist his support. But Bristow had just been talking with Oliver P. Morton, a notorious die-hard in Southern affairs, and hesitated. The Secretary then, a few minutes before Cabinet meeting, read it to Grant. He made no comment or reply—a token that his stubborn temper had rejected it.

Nevertheless, this Cabinet meeting of January 11th showed that adroit manoeuvring could bring the President—half-unconsciously, all-reluctantly—to the strategic retirement now unescapable. He began in the worst possible way. Before the meeting he told Fish that he would under no circumstances apologize for anything that had been done; and in opening the discussion he said that he intended in his message "to recapitulate the events which he thought would show the necessity of what had occurred." [19] But Robeson shrewdly preceived an opening.

[18] *Nation,* January 21, 1875.   [19] Diary, January 11, 1875.

He suggested that in recapitulating events Grant should justify the presence of the troops under the governor's request in September; should say that the military officers had acted on January 4th without consulting Washington; and should thus lead up to a disclaimer of their action, or at least a refusal to approve it.

This was adroit, and most Cabinet members approved the suggestion. Belknap then read a telegram which Grant had sent to Kellogg on December 9 refusing the employment of the troops for certain purposes, and limiting distinctly the uses to which they might be put. Everyone agreed that this telegram should go to Congress to help relieve the Administration from the charge of assenting to the conduct of the troops on January 4. Attorney-General Williams was entrusted with the preparation of Grant's message to Congress, and it was agreed that certain Senators should be called in to examine it. Fish had by now learned how to deal with the "plain, blunt" soldier-President, and he records: [20]

After the meeting Robeson and myself endeavor to impress upon Williams the necessity of some disavowal of the military interference with the legislature which, he said, he had already gotten into the message as he thought so as not to excite the President's susceptibilities. Robeson said that he would go immediately to the Senate and try and prepare the Senators for the interview tomorrow.

The retreat was then duly executed. Noon of January 12 found President Grant reading Williams's draft to a group of Senators—Morton, Carpenter, Conkling, Edmunds (who Grant complained was rather crotchety), Frelinghuysen, Howe, and Sargent. They doubtless offered suggestions. In the afternoon the Cabinet made several amendments. Fish found it "much better than I had anticipated from his conversation a day or two ago. It is not all that I should wish but contains much stronger expressions of disapproval of the military interruption than were expected, and possibly stronger than the President is himself aware of." [21] On the 13th it went to Congress. Its most striking statements (intermixed with apologies for Sheridan, indictments of Southern disorder, and the like) were two. "I am well aware that any military interference by the officers or troops of the United States with the organization of the State legislature or any of its proceedings

[20] *Ibid.*   [21] Diary, January 12, 1875.

. . . is repugnant to our ideas of government. I can conceive of no case, not involving rebellion or insurrection, where such interference by authority of the General Government ought to be permitted or can be justified." And again: "I have no desire to have United States troops interfere in the domestic concerns of Louisiana or any other State." Certainly this was emphatic enough; and the emphasis was due largely to Fish's assistance.

The practical solution found for the Louisiana question also satisfied Fish. A compromise proposed by Representative William A. Wheeler of New York gave the Democrats control of the House, and, though the Senate was Republican, of both chambers on joint ballot; but they promised not to impeach Kellogg. For the first time in years the State now had a government which the people cordially accepted and under which they could make steady progress toward prosperity.[22] The "banditti" promptly proved themselves hardworking, order-loving citizens. A picturesque incident of the final reorganization of the House was a Negro's surrender of his seat to his old master, with a felicitous declaration that he was honored to yield it to one who had always been kind to him.

But even yet Grant had not learned his lesson. The ink was hardly dry on his message, with its virtual apology for high-handed acts in Louisiana, when he turned with equal rashness toward Arkansas. During December and January a powerful lobby from Little Rock, directed by Senator Dorsey, Senator Clayton, and ex-Governor Brooks, had been toiling day and night in Washington. They detested the new Conservative Constitution and Garland's Conservative administration. Arkansas was by no means so rich as commercial Louisiana. But for a simple agricultural State, just emerging from backwoods crudity, with no mines, manufactories, or large towns, it had afforded the Carpetbaggers handsome pickings. Taking control in 1868, they had increased the bonded debt in six years from $3,252,401 to nearly $9,000,000; the floating debt from zero to $1,865,000; and the annual running-expense to more than $1,000,000, though $300,000 should have been ample. Their six years' rule had cost a poverty-stricken people more than $17,000,000; and now that the Conservatives had turned them out, they hurried to Washington with demands that the Federal Government reinstate them. The Republican House appointed a committee to

[22] *Nation*, May 13, 1875.

inquire if the new Constitution, adopted by overwhelming vote, had been lawfully submitted, and if Garland were legally the Governor.

Headed by Poland of Vermont, it was an able committee. Yet at the very moment it reported, Grant took arbitrary action without the slightest regard for it. After a thorough inquiry, the committee declared that the new Constitution was in many ways better than the old, and was approved by a great majority of the inhabitants; that the State had been as peaceful since its adoption as ever before; that the mass of people desired order and good government; and that no ground existed for Federal interference. It declared that the principle was well established that any technical defects in the submission of a new organic law were cured by popular ratification, and "the people of every State have the right to make their own Constitution to suit themselves," so long as it harmonizes with the Federal Constitution. But the next day Grant sent Congress a startling message. He declared that Brooks had been lawfully elected governor in 1872; that the Constitution under which he was elected had been overthrown by "violence, intimidation, and revolutionary proceedings"; that if this were permitted, other Southern States might also "change their Constitutions and violate their pledges"; and that in view of so dangerous a precedent, Congress should "take definite action in the matter." It was clear that the Dorsey-Clayton-Brooks lobby had dictated the message. The astounded Fish wrote in his diary for February 9:

The papers of this morning gave a copy of a message sent by the President yesterday to the Senate, on Arkansas affairs; it is a message on which there has been no discussion or consultation in Cabinet, and to which had I been consulted I should never have advised; it is dangerous in its tendencies and inconclusive in its argument. Too many of the States have changed their Constitutions by proceedings similar to those under which the new Constitution of Arkansas has been adopted, to question the rightfulness of the proceedings. . . .

No allusion was made directly or indirectly to the message during the Cabinet session [today]. I did not wish to introduce the subject but was prepared to express a dissent, had an opportunity of so doing been offered to me.

On inquiry, he learned that neither Bristow nor Jewell had seen the message before it was sent, or had known that it was in contemplation. Bristow understood that Boss Shepherd and Senator Dorsey had induced Grant to write it. Further inquiries led Fish, as he wrote in his diary, to conclude that an attempted theft lay behind their activities. Dorsey, Clayton, and their friends in 1872 had counted out Brooks, who was probably elected governor, and counted in Baxter. But when Baxter refused to sign two million dollars' worth of fraudulent railroad bonds, his adherents turned against him. President Grant on May 15, 1874, had declared Baxter to be governor, denouncing Brooks and his party; now on February 8, 1875, he declared that Brooks had been elected and denounced Baxter and his followers! Senator Dorsey, later a principal in the Star Route frauds, was a neighbor and close friend of Boss Shepherd's, living in a house owned by him. Shepherd was a bosom friend of Babcock's. "I believe," commented Fish, "that there is a large steal in the Arkansas matter, and fear that the President has been led into a grievous error." [23]

It shortly appeared that the steal had complicated ramifications in Washington. Secretary Bristow (as he later told Fish) called at the White House on February 20. The President, introducing the subject of Arkansas, said that the sole object of his message had been to urge Congress to furnish an expression of opinion! Taken aback, Bristow remarked that he had understood it as an assertion of Grant's own definite views, his "determination." Not at all, said the President. At this Bristow expressed great gratification. While he was doing so Babcock came in— "Just as he always does," Bristow told Fish; "he never allows me to be with the President without coming into the room." Bristow, after praising the President's disclaimer of any intent of definite action, or of doing more than lay the responsibility upon Congress, inquired whether he might inform others of what Grant had said. "To my knowledge," he told Grant, "many of your friends, including some of your most pronounced and outspoken adherents, have been very much distressed by what they thought the purport of the message, and they will be proportionately relieved to learn of your real views and wishes. So, I think, will the whole country." [24]

"I see no objection to your telling others," said Grant. But Babcock quickly interposed. He declared that in his opinion nothing should be said; that it was necessary to be bold and to take decided ground, and that the President should not enter upon explanations or disclaimers. At once Grant withdrew his assent, remarking: "I do not wish anything said about it."

[23] Diary, February 11, 1875.   [24] Diary, February 21, 1875.

Bristow's comment, as recorded by Fish, was enlightening: [25]

Bristow said his position in the Cabinet was not agreeable; that Delano is continually working against him, and Babcock works with Delano; thinks that Shepherd is with them and has much influence with the President; says that Shepherd is financially very hard pushed; that he owes some $20,000 of taxes in the District; that the property on which taxes are unpaid is advertised for sale at an early day, and Shepherd and Babcock are endeavoring to prevent the sale and induce Congress to assume or relieve the taxes. That one of the members of the Committee of the District had proposed to another a such measure, but that Dennison was strongly opposed to it.

But the plot to benefit Brooks, Dorsey, and Shepherd failed. Public sentiment had reared too grim a front against Grant's action. The Springfield *Republican,* misconstruing the message as Grant's act instead of that of his backstairs advisers, said that it could be translated into one sentence: "Authorize me to make war upon the government and people of Arkansas in the interest of my third term." [26] Congress stood valiantly by the House Committee. Immediately before adjournment it passed Chairman Poland's resolution in favor of non-interference, many leading Republicans joining the Democrats. Garland proclaimed a day of thanksgiving in Arkansas, and within a few months Charles Nordhoff was sending the New York *Herald* graphic accounts of the contentment and orderliness of the people there.[27]

IV

But in the closing hours of Congress, Babcock treated the Cabinet to another display of audacity. Both houses had passed Henry Wilson's bill for the equalization of war bounties, a rather dangerous piece of political buncombe. On the excuse that the three-year recruits, who had enlisted earliest in the Civil War and done the most fighting, had been paid bounties of only $100 while later recruits had been given $300, it provided a sum estimated by the Second Auditor at $59,000,000 and the Paymaster-General at $100,000,000, to remedy the "injustice." Actually no such sum was due, for payments of some $60,000,000, considered final, had already been made. Moreover, with reduced receipts the Treasury could not bear such a burden. A powerful lobby backed it, with money for many hands. Grant courageously resolved

[25] *Ibid.*   [26] Merriam, *Samuel Bowles,* II, 238.   [27] N. Y. *Herald,* April 7–12, 1875.

to veto the bill. On March 4 he and the Cabinet gathered in the President's room in the Capitol. Adjournment was to take place at twelve. At eleven-thirty the measure, duly engrossed, was brought in; he called the members about him—the room being full of other people—and read his veto message; and after Fish had suggested a minor amendment, the Cabinet endorsed it. Grant then signed it, and called to Babcock to take it to the House.[28]

Babcock earnestly protested. "General," he said, "you are making a terrible mistake." The President quietly replied, "I have signed this and wish it to go to the House." Babcock left, but took with him only the last sheet of the message; and on his return, it was found that he had carried it to the Senate instead of the House. Noon had now struck, the House had adjourned, and it was too late to remedy the error.[29] It was clear that Babcock had resorted to this impudent manoeuvre in order to suppress the message. Next day certain gross misstatements upon the failure of the bill appeared in the Washington *Chronicle,* arousing the indignation of Fish and Bristow. Their purport was that the Senate, and not the President, was responsible for this failure. And though the President intimated that he would make the text of his lost veto message public, it was too late to gain any attention for it.[30]

[28] Diary, March 4, 1875.   [29] *Ibid.*
[30] Diary, March 5, 6, 1875; text of message is in Richardson, VII, 320.

MONTH by month in 1874–75 the front of battle against the evil influences surrounding Grant widened, and the conflict became more
desperate. In the autumn of 1874 Fish had grappled with Babcock,
Casey, and others of the Kitchen Cabinet, and repelled their assault
upon the State Department; in the spring and summer of 1875 the
conflict shifted to the Treasury and it came the turn of the tall, lean
Kentuckian, Bristow, to wrestle with them. By the centennial year all
the world knew that Bristow was the David who had slain that pano-
plied Goliath, the Whiskey Ring. But the spectacular struggle against
the Ring was only one part of the never-ceasing battle against the
forces of corruption in the outer rooms of the White House and the
Federal Departments.

The existence of a Whiskey Ring, though not its personnel or exact
character, had long been known. Men suspected in Lincoln's time that
dishonest distillers and rectifiers were conspiring with internal revenue
officers to evade the high Federal taxes; they knew in Johnson's time
that the evasion had become widespread. But not until midway in
Grant's first Administration was it fully organized under astute leaders
in St. Louis and Washington—the "Ring." The grand initiator of this
organization was General John A. McDonald, a rough-and-ready Missouri colonel, cotton-speculator, and claim agent whom Grant had made
supervisor of internal revenue, with a jurisdiction ultimately including
Kansas, Arkansas, Indian Territory, New Mexico, and Texas. As we
now know, the Ring was originally formed to raise funds for political
purposes in 1870, the year in which the Grant Republicans lost control
of Missouri through a party schism. It was continued for private profit
with McDonald as head and a steadily increasing list of aides. They
included the President's secretary, Babcock; the chief clerk in the Internal Revenue Office, William Avery, with other Treasury officials;
various revenue collectors, especially John A. Joyce of St. Louis; and
numerous politicians in Missouri, Illinois, and Wisconsin. In St. Louis
the Ring had the assistance of William McKee, owner and editor first
of the *Democrat*, and after its sale of the *Globe*. Many distillers and
rectifiers, from Milwaukee to New Orleans, were forced into the combi-

nation by an ingenious system of blackmail. That is, they were entrapped in some technical violation of the law, and threatened with
bankruptcy if they did not join the Ring. Others entered voluntarily.
In 1874, the distillers in St. Louis alone defrauded the Government of
about $1,200,000 in revenue, and Milwaukee, Chicago, Peoria, Indian-
apolis, and other cities added heavily to the amount.[1]

Profits by the Ring, and especially by the large distillers, were huge.
About two-fifths of the sums fraudulently withheld, it was later estimated, went to the higher government officials involved. Many gaugers
and other petty officials were paid by the distillers themselves. But the
Ring had heavy expenses. McKee at one time required nearly $1,000 a
week for the use of his newspaper. McDonald, whose salary was $3,000
a year, paid the bill of the President and his party at the Lindell Hotel
during a ten-day stay in St. Louis in 1874; and he received only partial reimbursement. His story that he bought Grant a pair of fast
horses, a road-wagon, silver-mounted harness, and whip as a gift was
false; Grant paid for them in full. But he and Joyce did purchase a
diamond shirt-stud for Babcock at a cost of $2,400, and when Babcock
subsequently grumbled that the stone was flawed, they replaced it with
a better one. The Ring footed heavy bills for protecting itself. In different cities and States large contributions were demanded of it, with
no questions asked, by agents of Republican campaign committees.

The Ring was safe so long as the political-minded Boutwell and the
careless Richardson of Sanborn-Contract fame were at the head of the
Treasury Department. But in 1874 Bristow's reformative zeal began
to fill its members with fear. He was at once listed with Secretary Fish
and Postmaster-General Jewell as a dangerous member of the Cabinet.
Before he had been in office six months he was marked for destruction.
By December, 1874, though as yet he had no suspicion of Babcock's
questionable activities and knew little of the Ring itself, he realized
that a formidable combination was afoot to shake Grant's confidence
in him and force him out of the Cabinet, and that Babcock and Delano
were its principal directors.

[1] The best sources on the Whiskey Ring are two excellent articles by H. V. Boynton in
the *North American Review,* October, 1876, and *American Law Review,* April, 1877; House
Misc. Docs., 44th Congress, 1st Sess., No. 186, being testimony given in the Congressional
inquiry; and John McDonald, *Secrets of the Great Whiskey Ring* (1877), a work full of
bias, and inaccurate in many particulars, but valuable if carefully used. I have sifted the
Logan, Jeremiah S. Black, and William E. Chandler Papers in the Library of Congress with
the aid of Mr. Jacob Weissfeldt, but found little of value. Access to the Bristow Papers,
still in private hands, has been denied me.

Fish knew that Ben Butler had also enlisted in the movement. Just before Christmas, 1874, Butler, now a lame-duck but as self-assertive as ever, called at the Secretary's house. His purpose was to apprise Fish that Bristow and Jewell were aspirants for the Presidential nomination, and hence not indefeasibly loyal to Grant—who was believed by many to desire a third term. He poured out a characteristic stream of mendacious detraction. Jewell, he said, had made an improper departmental report; Bristow's adoption of safety locks for transporting bonded goods was a "job," and "if the thing is pressed it will be found that an autograph letter of the President's was written urging issuance of a contract for them"; both men were lusty self-advertisers. Obviously he had been giving Grant the same malicious views. "It looks as though Butler means mischief," commented Fish.[2] Bristow did have ambitions for the Presidency—for which he was well qualified. But both he and Jewell were perfectly loyal to Grant, and of stainless integrity. Butler's real objection to them was that they were reformers. Jewell in these days was writing Elihu Washburne admiringly of Grant —"He is so honest and outspoken." He was writing also of his own high purposes. "I am afraid there is a growing feeling of distrust of our Administration. . . . We can only hold our ground by deserving it. I am very anxious to have a strong effort made in the direction of a pure Administration, so that we may regain what we have lost. I think we can carry the country next year, though I am not by any means certain of it. I wish some of our friends could see the importance of the cleaning-out process, but I am afraid they cannot. Meantime a few of us are pegging away as best we can." [3]

Still another man was eager to get Bristow out of the Administration—Secretary Delano of the Interior Department. General Cowan, his Assistant-Secretary, told Jewell in December, 1874, of Delano's activities, and frankly described his motive—if reformers like Bristow commenced inquiring into the Department, they would find it "rotten from top to bottom." [4] Indeed, men on the inside of government affairs had long wagged their heads over Delano. Fish had once received a letter from a Chicagoan named Van Doren, making grave charges against him, and offering to supply proofs. Boutwell had been suspi-

[2] Diary, December 2, 1874.
[3] Jewell to Washburne, December 5, 1874, April 23, 1875; Washburne Papers, Volume 90.
[4] Diary, December 19, 1874.

cious of his son's activities. He had told Fish in 1873, to quote the diary, "that John Delano, who was always accompanying his father, was not to be trusted, that he was notoriously in many discreditable schemes, that he had followed up to the Treasury Department some very unworthy Indian claims, urging their allowance; . . . that while he regarded Delano as an able man and thoroughly honest, he had in the Internal Revenue Department exhibited a want of administrative capacity. . . ." Fish had warned Grant, but without result. John Sherman also had said mysteriously in 1873, "Some things will shortly come out with reference to Delano." The sympathy of the sly Secretary of the Interior with the group arrayed against the aggressively honest Bristow could well be understood.[5]

Immediately after New Year's Day, 1875, Bristow himself called on Fish and poured out a new tale of woe—and of scandal: [6]

He says that his position in the Cabinet is not satisfactory, that he has a high regard for the President but that he is the object of a plot to have him removed. That Delano is determined to undermine him and is working to that end; that General Cowan called upon him saying that he felt it his duty to let him know of Delano's intrigues; that he, Cowan, was dissatisfied with Delano's course and felt that it was unjust and unfair towards him, Bristow.
That there were things in the administration of the Interior Department that compelled him (Cowan) to withdraw from it and that he intended shortly to do so; that the Department was thoroughly corrupt and that exposure must soon come and he wished to be out of it in time.

Bristow had curtly asked Cowan why he did not inform Grant of the abuses, and Cowan had replied that tale-bearing would be "disloyal" to Delano as his chief! But he professed willingness to tell all that he knew if Grant formally requested it. Bristow continued:

He says that Babcock is engaged with Delano in the efforts against him [Bristow]. He refers to a conversation in Cabinet on Tuesday about the "Colorado Land Thieves" and asks if I remember Delano's proposition to change all the Territorial officers, including Mr. Cook. He says that Mr. Cook and John Delano were engaged in the land frauds, and have quarrelled about the division; that Cowan tells him that Delano (the Secretary) was also interested deeply with them in their fraudulent practices.

From this Bristow turned to other members of the Kitchen-Cabinet:

[5] Diary, March 16, 1873, October 12, 1873.   [6] Diary, January 5, 1875.

In the course of the conversation Casey is mentioned, and I refer to the delicacy arising from his relations to the President, but express a want of confidence in him. Bristow says that in a recent case Casey had obtained $4,000 for his interference in a revenue case pending in one of the Northern cities.

I ask him if it be the case of Pratt & Boyd in New York. He replies in the affirmative and expresses surprise that I had heard of it; says that he had been informed by Pierrepont within the last day by letter, and wishes to know how I obtained the information. I decline telling him further than that I heard of it nearly a fortnight since from a young Republican, and ask whether he knew that Ingalls was engaged with Casey in the matter; he had not heard that. I tell him that such was my information.

He refers to a conversation with the President a few days since at which I was present, when the President told him that he must remove Taylor, the First Comptroller of the Treasury, saying that he had been behaving badly, and was disgracing himself in public places.

Bristow says that the ground for objection to Taylor is that he is one of the Auditing Board of Claims against the District Government, and that he has refused to pass some claims, which is the reason for the influence brought on the President to remove him.

He suggests the name of Babcock in connection with this.

The eternal cabal—with Babcock always its centre! During a Cabinet meeting on January 15, which dealt with such routine matters as reciprocity with Hawaii and a postal convention with Canada, Fish left the room to obtain a book. In the secretaries' office he found Casey and Babcock in close conversation. "I may look out for some development," he wrote in his diary. And sure enough, three days later the White House organ, the *National Republican,* printed an article upon pending financial legislation which Fish regarded as a palpable stock-jobbing manoeuvre to affect the markets.[7]

All winter the half-covert attacks upon Bristow continued. The still-powerful Alexander H. Shepherd shortly joined hands with Delano, Babcock, and Butler. He was no longer municipal dictator in Washington. Congress in 1874 had set up a new government of three commissioners for the Federal District. When Grant had taken the extraordinary step of naming Shepherd as provisional commissioner, Senator Edmunds had bluntly declared the nomination an insult to the country; Senators Thurman and Allison had described in frank language what knaveries the District investigation had revealed; and the

7 Diary, January 15, 18, 1875.

Senate rejected him with only six votes in his favor.

But he was still often at the White House, and a curious episode had just shown how potent his influence over Grant remained. Washington was greatly diverted during the latter half of 1874 by the so-called Safe Burglary affair, for implication in which Harrington, Assistant Federal Attorney, and Whitley, chief of the Treasury secret service, with others, were finally brought to trial. The accusation against them was not burglarizing a safe at all. It was conspiracy to injure an active Washington reformer, Columbus Alexander, by trumping up a burglary charge against him.[8] Alexander had been a leading figure in demanding investigation of Boss Shepherd and the District Ring; and his enemies had tried to discredit him by this charge of committing burglary to obtain evidence. There is little doubt that Harrington and Whitley were conspirators against Alexander.[9] They were connected with Boss Shepherd's organization, the motive was clear, and the evidence against them strong. Yet late in November, 1874, while Harrington was still under criminal indictment—the jury shortly afterward disagreed on his guilt—Grant invited him to a White House reception! [10] This courtesy (performed the same week that he appointed his brother Orvil Grant to the most lucrative Indian post-tradership in the West) was a defiant advertisement of the President's faith in Shepherd.

Poor Bristow might well feel in a perilous position, and Fish might well agree that the situation was growing intolerable. The two again bitterly discussed the situation on February 21. Fish's record ends with some grim words: "He talks of resigning, and thinks that he may feel compelled to do so. He refers to the frequent newspaper paragraphs of probable changes in the Cabinet on or after the 4th of March and to the rumours of my going out. I tell him that I am more than willing to go, and have within a day or two so written to a friend (Gov. Clifford). . . ."[11]

I

But by March, 1875, Bristow was at last accumulating the evidence needed to break up the Whiskey Ring and jail its leaders, and realized that he must at all costs cling to office until he had slain the octopus. He had lighted upon authoritative statistics, issued by the St. Louis Mer-

[8] Best account in N. Y. *Evening Post,* November, 1874.
[9] *Nation,* December 3, 1874.   [10] *Ibid.*   [11] Diary, February 21, 1875.

chants' Exchange to glorify the city, showing the amount of liquor shipped from it. Comparing these figures with the tax-receipts, he found that only about one-third of the whiskey had paid taxes.[12] George W. Fishback, who had bought the St. Louis *Democrat* from McKee, helped him devise a method of discovering the culprits. Elaborate precautions were taken to keep all steps secret from the Internal Revenue Service, plainly honeycombed with corruption. A new cipher was devised; no departmental officer save the Solicitor of the Treasury, Major Bluford Wilson, was informed of the relentless investigation under way. Bristow borrowed from the *Democrat* its efficient commercial editor, Myron Coloney, an expert in collecting data upon shipments. He corresponded with him only through a private citizen in Washington, for the postoffice had its spies. Coloney and a trusted Treasury agent, Yaryan, who went to St. Louis ostensibly to investigate delinquent railroad taxes, checked all railway and steamboat bills of lading to obtain accurate figures upon the shipments of liquor. The data they collected revealed the precise place, time, and scope of tax evasions. They also posted secret operatives near distilleries to check the movements of grain and whiskey; although these men were ultimately discovered and driven off, they obtained conclusive evidence of extensive night-shipments, an act illegal in itself.[13] During March and April evidence was gathered by similar methods in Chicago, Peoria, Milwaukee, Indianapolis, and New Orleans.

At last, on May 10, his preparations completed, Bristow ordered sudden and concerted raids upon all suspected houses to seize books and papers. Despite his pains, news of his intention somehow leaked out in Washington. Ring members had telegraphed to St. Louis: "The plague is advancing west. Advise our friends to leave the city." But it was too late. On the day named, the trap was sprung simultaneously in St. Louis, Milwaukee, and Chicago. Sixteen distilleries and sixteen rectifying establishments were seized. Their ledgers and files revealed a mass of fresh evidence, arrests were made, and in half a dozen cities the grand juries were shortly returning indictments. Many culprits fled to Canada. The facts unearthed were truly staggering. In fourteen months five members of the Ring in St. Louis had divided $250,000. The Commissioner of Internal Revenue found that in ten months

---

[12] Woodward, *Meet General Grant*, 420.
[13] Bowers, *Tragic Era*, 465 ff.; H. V. Boynton, *North American Review*, October, 1876.

(July 1, 1874–May 1, 1875) the government had lost $1,650,000 in taxes on merely the transactions which were brought to his notice. In two years it was conservatively estimated to have lost $4,000,000—some figures went much higher.

Immediately after the raids Fish, as a diary entry for May 22 reveals, learned for the first time that Babcock was involved—no overwhelming surprise to him:

> Bristow tells me that Babcock is as deep as any in the Whiskey Ring; that he has most positive evidence, he will not say of actual fraud, but of intimate relations and confidential correspondence with the very worst of them.
>
> That a man . . . appointed at St. Louis on Babcock's recommendation (McDonald) was the centre pin of the plot. . . .

There follows in the diary another of those reports of Grant's words which would seem incredible had they not been put in black and white at the time. "Well, Mr. Bristow," he said just after the raids, "there is at least one honest man in St. Louis on whom we can rely—John McDonald. I know that because he is an intimate acquaintance and confidential friend of Babcock's." "Mr. President," replied Bristow, "McDonald is the head and centre of all the frauds. He is at this very time in New York ready to take a steamer on the first indication of any effort to arrest him." [14]

Was the Machiavellian secretary to the President at last squarely in the net, floundering in the toils? It might be; but his audacity knew no bounds, his hold upon the President was too strong to be easily loosened, and unless positive proofs were assembled against him the outcome of the struggle which lay ahead would be dubious.

II

The struggle was complicated by the necessity, by now clear even to Grant, of replacing Attorney-General Williams and Secretary Delano with men of greater ability and probity. Since the cabal surrounding the President valued Williams for his pliability and Delano as an active ally against Bristow, it fought their dismissal to the last ditch. When defeat became certain it endeavored to control Grant's new appointments. Babcock apparently resolved, in desperation, that if these men went he would attempt to make Ben Butler Attorney-General, and his

[14] Diary, May 22, 1875.

own uncle, J. Russell Jones, Secretary of the Interior. This also sounds incredible; but Fish's diary contains much evidence of it. If he could succeed in this, and in averting the civil trial whose threat he perceived as soon as Bristow raided the distilleries, he might yet maintain his sway. He was playing for great stakes against desperate odds.

In getting rid of Williams the better element in the Cabinet were aided by the unexpected intervention of Mrs. Grant. Just before Christmas, 1874, a White House reception was tendered the King of Hawaii, at which Fish, as Secretary of State, presented a large company to the visiting monarch. When Mrs. Williams entered the East Room she was received by Mrs. Grant with icy frigidity, of which she subsequently complained to Babcock and others.[15] As it appeared later, her gossiping tongue had given offence. A few days afterward Mrs. Grant, dining at Postmaster-General Jewell's, told him that the Cabinet ladies were not expected at the President's reception on New Year's Day—an astonishing announcement. Meeting Mrs. Fish later that evening at a ball, she said she wished her to be present, but not all the Cabinet wives. When Mrs. Fish remonstrated against any discrimination, Mrs. Grant persisted that the presence of some of them—she meant one— would not be desired. Fish wrote two days later: [16]

I spoke to General Babcock on the subject, who told me that he felt that no discrimination should be made, and had already talked to the President on this subject, and inquired whether he might not refer to the conversation with me in again talking with the President.

I authorized him to do so.

Today a written invitation was sent by General Babcock in the name of Mrs. Grant asking Mrs. Fish to be present with the ladies of her family. I presume therefore that this difficulty has already been overcome, and that similar invitations have been extended to all the ladies of the Cabinet.

But it was significant that the President immediately suggested appointing Williams to the Russian mission. Fish successfully blocked this move, showing that the nomination would be very repugnant to Senate and public, and would excite unpleasant criticism.[17] Within a few weeks new charges against Williams were being confidentially discussed. Postmaster-General Jewell reported one day that he had lately asked Grant whether he objected to plain-speaking even if it affected a

---

[15] Diary, December 24, 1874.   [16] Diary, December 30, 1874.
[17] Diary, January 2, 1875.

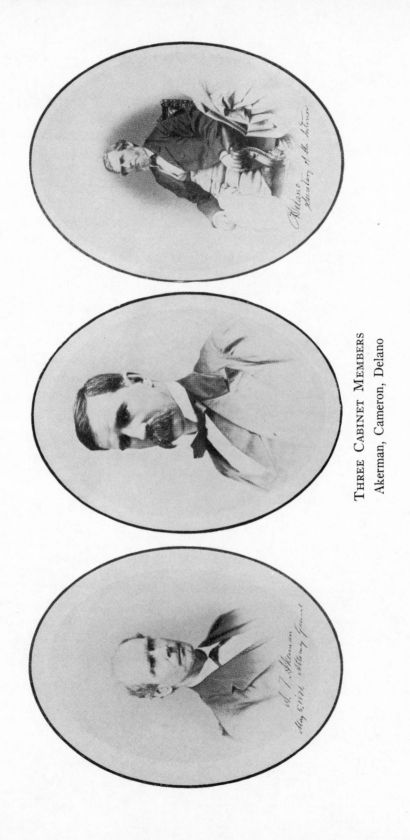

THREE CABINET MEMBERS
Akerman, Cameron, Delano

member of the Cabinet. "Certainly not," said Grant, "I always wish the Cabinet to feel entirely free to make confidential communications to me." Thereupon Jewell stated that he had learned from Senators Edmunds, Carpenter, Sherman and others that an investigation by the Judiciary Committee had developed facts which, if Williams remained in the Cabinet, would result in exposures very damaging to the Administration.[18]

The laxity with which Williams had long conducted his office had lately, in fact, crossed the line of corruption. From what Fish learned, Mrs. Williams was largely responsible. Expensively dressed, living fashionably on Rhode Island Avenue, keeping a fine equipage, entertaining well, she had exceeded their means. Queer rumors were now afloat. Men whispered that the Department of Justice had brought suit against the New York mercantile firm of Pratt & Boyd to recover large sums for fraudulent custom house entries; that a certain lady had asked $30,000 for stopping the suit; that—after the intervention of Grant's brother-in-law Casey and Babcock's close friend Rufus Ingalls, as mentioned above—large sums had been paid her and others; and that the suit had suddenly been dropped. Secretary Bristow, who had gathered most of the evidence against Pratt & Boyd, knew of these stories, as did Jewell. On hearing them Fish felt that the President needed his counsel. Jewell, indeed, had reported Grant as saying something about the Secretary's reticence and reserve, and about missing his advice. The night of April 12 found the Secretary writing:

I therefore took occasion today to speak to the President, referring to this statement of Jewell's and saying that it might possibly be that I had not had the opportunity of late of communicating as frequently or confidentially as formerly, but it was because the opportunity had not been presented, that there was no diminution of friendship or kind feeling. He expressed surprise and had no recollection of a conversation with Jewell of the nature referred to.

He then said he would say to me in confidence what he had proposed to delay saying to any of the Cabinet, but that he supposed that I was aware of what had taken place in connection with certain matters relating to the Attorney-General.

That he was expecting and thought he should have received his resignation; that Falls, the chief clerk in the Department of Justice, appeared to be giving information to the Manhattan Club in New York [a Democratic organization] of transactions involving the Attorney-General of a very serious

18 Diary, March 12, 1875.

nature; that he had a high respect for Williams but feared that he had been entrapped, or that transactions had passed through his hands without his notice, for which he could not fail to be held officially responsible, of a very disreputable nature; that Conkling had brought these things to his notice; and he had suggested to Williams that his resignation would be accepted.

Williams had offered it, either to take effect immediately or to send it in at the close of the term of the Supreme Court. He had therefore requested him to give him the resignation at present, to take effect at the end of the term.

Grant and Fish then discussed the possible appointment of Edwards Pierrepont to the vacancy. From his own point of view, Fish remarked, it would be "a very agreeable selection." It would give New York two Cabinet members, and perhaps displease Conkling, but Grant inclined toward it. Pierrepont was a lawyer of long experience and high position at the bar. His character and ability would go far to protect the Department of Justice from Democratic investigations, which Grant said he wished to avoid at all costs. Indeed, Grant appeared distinctly apprehensive, for he had heard from Bristow of "very alarming" acts of Williams's and wished them kept under cover. Fish learned with surprise that he had known nothing of the payment of $30,000 to a "certain lady," but the President spoke of anonymous and scurrilous letters that had been traced to her by peculiarities of phrasing and handwriting.[19] Mrs. Williams, in fact, had been engaged in nothing less than attempted blackmail in an effort to keep her husband—who should have been dismissed long before—in office.

Grant decided to call a special Cabinet meeting upon the Attorney-Generalship for Monday, April 26. On that date four members, Fish, Robeson, Belknap, and Jewell, were suddenly summoned to a White House conference. They had known nothing of the matter in advance —but the sleepless Babcock had. Realizing that Pierrepont's appointment was imminent, the private secretary notified Horace Porter, Judge Carter, and other New York friends. Bristow happening to be in New York, Carter paid him a Sunday afternoon call. After suggesting that Ben Butler would make an admirable Attorney-General, he declared that Butler, if given the office, would engage to support Bristow for the Presidency! Porter also saw Bristow, and mentioned that a special meeting of the Cabinet, or part of it, would be held next day to consider departmental changes. The vigilant Secretary of the Treasury instantly

[19] Diary, April 12, 1875.

grasped what was afoot. Sitting down, he wrote Grant a letter strongly urging Pierrepont for the Attorney-Generalship, and hastened out to post it.[20]

But on the 26th all obstacles melted away. It transpired that Conkling quite approved of Pierrepont. Fish, urging his nomination, was supported by Robeson, Belknap, and Jewell. Grant therefore decided to send it in at once. When asked whether it would not be better to ask Pierrepont's acceptance first, he characteristically decided to send him the commission and take the acceptance for granted! But this particular Barkis had been notoriously willing. Before the end of May, 1875, he was untangling the confused skein which Williams had left.

By this time Delano should also have been dismissed; but once more Grant demonstrated his reluctance to oust a subordinate "under fire." To do so conflicted with all his ideas of discipline, all the concepts of the long-friendless man upon loyalty to an adherent. Perhaps, too, Grant drew from a comprehension of his own blunders some sympathy for others who failed; and except when confronted with unescapable evidence, he was unwilling to believe that any associate had committed moral wrong. To the very last he tried to explain the delinquencies of Williams and Delano in terms of bad judgment, acts of bad associates, or newspaper lies. It appears that both should have been impeached; certainly Williams deserved it. Yet as late as April 29 Grant, according to Fish's diary, "spoke very kindly of Williams personally but lamented the influences surrounding him, [saying] that they had been brought by those in whom he had a right to have confided." He behaved in precisely the same way with Delano.

On April 9 the President had revealed that he knew well enough what was going on in the Interior Department, for the diary contains the significant entry: [21]

At Cabinet, Cowan represented Delano. The President told Cowan not to allow any more land warrants to be issued on pension claims.

He says that there is at least one firm in this city which has possessed itself, possibly through collusion with some persons in the office, of the names of those soldiers of the Revolution and of the War of 1812 who have not drawn their land warrants, and that fraudulent claims are presented in the names of these persons and warrants immediately issued; that these warrants are worth from $160 to $200 each.

[20] See what Bristow told Fish, Diary, May 17, 1875.   [21] April 9, 1875.

He was very peremptory in the direction to Cowan, using the expression, "Not another one from this moment." Cowan assented to the correctness of the fact stated by the President, and said he had been endeavoring to ferret out the parties.

I thought that there was a reserved thought on the part of the President in his reference to persons in the office supposed to be implicated.

There have been rumours current for several days affecting the head of the department.

We have seen how long the inner circles of the capital had been buzzing with sinister reports about Delano. The *Tribune's* Washington correspondent in April, 1875, published them in detail, asserting categorically that "corruption has at last been traced within the bosom of the Secretary's family"—by which it meant John Delano, the son.[22] Other newspapers made similar charges. Yet on the 29th Grant, in a confidential talk with Fish, told him that Delano would not yet resign, nor did he wish him to. "I think he has managed the department elegantly," he added, "and whatever wrongs may have been done were without his knowledge." He admitted that John Delano had been caught red-handed in corrupt transactions in Wyoming, but asserted that the Secretary was not involved and possessed no knowledge of the acts. Doubtless Delano had defended himself volubly—Rutherford B. Hayes tells us that he was "a good specimen of the lively earnest style of Western talkers"—and Babcock had of course stood up for him. But Grant's statement was too much for Fish, who interrupted:

I tell him that while I have personally liked Delano and have no knowledge of my own on the subject, I feel it right to tell him what may have been represented on the subject which I suppose to be worthy of credit; that I had been informed that the same party who transmitted the charges also asserts that he had seen a letter from Delano to Silas Reed (a surveyor) thanking him for what he had done and for the payments made to John Delano; that I was also told that General Cowan, when these charges were mentioned to him, had remarked that it was but a small thing when compared to others that were continually occurring. He replied that he must then allude to other transactions of John Delano, of which the father knew nothing; as I was only re-

---

[22] N. Y. *Tribune,* April, 1875. For a mass of material upon Delano's misconduct of Indian affairs, see House Report No. 98, 42d Cong., 3rd Sess., No. 778; House Report No. 778, 43d Cong., 1st Sess.; House Misc. Doc. No. 167, 44th. Cong., 1st Sess. A charitable historian declares that while he was "probably personally honest" he was "woefully lacking in high ideals of public service or an appreciation of the responsibility of a department chief." E. J. Benton, *Dictionary of American Biography.* It is perhaps not without significance that the whiskey frauds had developed greatly while Delano was Commissioner of Internal Revenue; Oberholtzer, *United States,* III, 167.

peating what I had heard, I expressed the hope that this might be so.

I inquired whether any Senator had spoken to him on the subject; he replied Morrill of Vermont had, but neither Conkling, Edmunds, or Anthony had. I told him I understood they all, as did also Frelinghuysen, express much concern. He said that Edmunds and Morrill, while both very good men, were always inclined to [credit] whatever the *Tribune* or the Springfield *Republican* said, and that whenever these sheets made charges against an officer of the government, accept them.

Grant concluded the conversation by saying, "If Delano were now to resign, it would be retreating under fire and be accepted as an admission of the charges." Fish did not tell him what he knew without being told, that it was the duty of the President to order an inquiry; for it was obvious that Grant's whole desire was to avoid investigation.

In June, it appeared later, Delano did go to Grant and offer his resignation, which Grant refused on the ground that he disliked the nature of the current attacks and the men making them.[23] No one else knew this at the time. So far as the other Cabinet members could guess, Delano might remain until March 4, 1877. As criticism of his record grew more serious, he merely struck out at Bristow more savagely. Feeling between the two became intensely bitter. On June 16 Attorney-General Pierrepont came to Fish in great anxiety. He said that Bristow was again so much distressed by the retention of Delano that he might resign at any moment, a step which would be a capital misfortune to the Republican Party and the nation. He urged Fish to go with him to Long Branch and try to persuade Grant to replace Delano before June 30, the end of the fiscal year. On June 21, they made the long trip. They besought Grant earnestly to take action. But he had just rejected Delano's resignation, and the interview was so discouraging that Fish did not even describe it in his diary.[24]

A few weeks later Fish's antagonism toward Delano was increased by an episode which, though trivial in itself, was distinctly irritating. In July the Cabinet discussed certain troubles with Venezuela which threatened to necessitate the recall of our Minister. Next day the press carried a full account of the conversation. Noticing it, Grant sent Fish a note emphasizing the rule that all Cabinet deliberations should be confidential unless publicity were explicitly authorized. "I write to you, my dear Governor," he concluded, "as the head of the

[23] Grant to Fish, Long Branch, September 10, 1875; Fish Papers.
[24] Diary, June 18–23, 1875.

Cabinet . . . to lay this matter before your associates in such manner as you may deem most proper. If there is eavesdropping, it should be corrected. If the result of pumping by correspondents, they (the correspondents) should be avoided." [25] At first Fish suspected Jewell, who was fond of having reporters about him and sometimes talked incautiously. But he denied that he had said a word; and Pierrepont then learned that Delano had communicated the proceedings to Gobright, the representative of the Associated Press, who had told all Newspaper Row.[26]

During the summer of 1875 the duel between Delano and Bristow threatened, like that between Jefferson and Hamilton in Washington's Cabinet, to involve a large part of the press. Delano tried to inspire articles showing that the attacks upon him sprang from men eager for political advancement, or balked in efforts to control the Interior Department. Bristow learned that a Washington dispatch in the New York *Herald* for July 24, levelling an accusatory finger at him, had actually been written in the Interior Department. "I will not submit to Delano's insinuations," he told Fish,[27] and immediately penned a counter-attack which appeared in the *Tribune* for the 26th. In a long talk with Fish that day he expressed great dejection, and again threatened to resign. Of course Fish remonstrated. But Bristow declared that the enormous influence, both moneyed and political, which his exposure of the Whiskey Ring had arrayed against him, had made his position almost intolerable.[28]

Meanwhile Delano found a new critic in Professor O. C. Marsh of Yale, a paleontologist who on the basis of personal observations among the abused Sioux in the Northwest published grave charges of graft and mismanagement in Indian affairs. Addressing Grant directly because, as he wrote, he distrusted Delano, he intimated that the Secretary was protecting a corrupt "Indian Ring." Delano met Marsh at breakfast in a Washington hotel this summer and poured out a flood of abuse, calling him "liar" and "poltroon." But Marsh kept his temper until the Secretary, exhausting his vocabulary, departed.[29]

At last, in the middle of August, Grant did secretly accept Delano's resignation; but it was not to take effect until October 1 and was to be kept quiet until the Secretary selected his own time and method of

[25] Grant to Fish, Long Branch, July 14, 1875; Fish Papers.
[26] Diary, July 13, 14, 20, 1875.   [27] Diary, July 25, 1875.
[28] Diary, July 26, 1875.   [29] *Nation*, August 19, September 16, 1875.

announcing it. Fish did not learn of it until September 11, when Grant notified him that he intended to leave for St. Louis in about ten days, and wished to have the question of Delano's successor laid before the Cabinet "as soon as you know I have passed Columbus, Ohio." [30] The President suggested that the Cabinet consider ex-Senator Scott, Wayne MacVeagh, and G. Dawson Coleman, all of Pennsylvania, ex-Senator Pratt of Iowa, and L. S. Felt of Illinois. He was making preparations for a sale of stock from his farm near St. Louis, and as he would not leave that city until about the 28th, asked to be informed of the decision by mail. Fish conferred with the only Cabinet members in Washington, Bristow, and Jewell. They were the three most upright and independent members of the Administration, and they resolved to tell Grant bluntly that several of the men proposed would not do. Fish wrote the President: [31]

The members of the Cabinet present were entirely agreed upon each of the following points:

I. That in view of the near approach of the Presidential election and the great importance of the immediately impending elections, it would be of doubtful expediency, if not a dangerous experiment, to bring at this time into the Cabinet any gentlemen not sufficiently known to the public, [so] that they would have to learn his competence after he takes office.

II. That the great financial question is at this time predominant, and that it seems essential that anyone now to be brought into the Cabinet should be not only sound on the financial question, and fully in accord with the hard money doctrine on which you have planted the Administration, but that his record on this paramount question should be such as to preclude criticism.

III. That although all of the gentlemen named in your letter of the 10th were not personally known to all three of us, we are satisfied that an association with either would be personally agreeable—Governor Jewell desired it to be stated that he personally knows Mr. Felt and has entire confidence in his ability and integrity—but he adheres to the *first* point stated.

The view taken in the *first* point, if accepted, would reduce the names suggested to three.

The controlling importance attached to the *second* point, and the fact that two of these three names had recently been in the Senate, led to an examination of some of the debates and proceedings in the Senate on April 28, 1874. On the passage of the bill over your veto which gave hope and laid the foundation of a restored credit and a sounder currency, one of these Senators (Pratt) voted to override the veto, the other (Scott) voted to sustain it. Should this reduce the number to two gentlemen from Pennsylvania (Mac-

[30] Grant to Fish, Long Branch, September 10, 1875; Fish Papers.
[31] Fish to Grant, Washington, September 24, 1875; Letterbooks.

Veagh and Scott), we are not prepared to entertain any preference between them. . . .

It was with great hesitancy that we approached your request that other names . . . should be canvassed, but the confidence implied in the request, and the importance of the appointment to be made and its effect on the public mind, led us to a consultation, from which we almost withdrew in hesitancy, not knowing how far the suggestion of John B. Henderson's name might fail to be personally acceptable to you. My own acquaintance with him is comparatively slight, but General Bristow and Governor Jewell know him more intimately, and unite in attributing to him high character and very eminent qualifications. My own slight acquaintance with him leads me to concur in their estimate.

John B. Henderson of Missouri, who as Senator seven years earlier had courageously stood with Fessenden, Lyman Trumbull, and four other Republicans in acquitting Andrew Johnson, would have been an ideal addition to the Cabinet. But would Grant's hatred of Johnson permit his appointment? The President lingered in the West, making an address to the Army of the Tennessee which attracted much attention. Declaring that the next civil contest would not be between North and South, but between "patriotism and intelligence on the one side, and superstition, ambition, and ignorance on the other," he denounced sectarian encroachments upon the common school system and sectarian meddling with politics. This ill-veiled attack on Catholicism puzzled observers.[32] By October 14 he was on his way back.

That day Fish, travelling to the wedding of Bancroft Davis's son in Newark, heard from Robeson an astounding piece of news.[33] The President had offered the Interior Department to Babcock's uncle, J. Russell Jones—an act in which Babcock's fine Italian hand was plainly evident. Happily Jones had declined. But with only less dismay Fish learned that Zachariah Chandler had accepted the place. Gone were the dreams of Henderson or Wayne MacVeagh strengthening the Cabinet! The President had obviously been prompted by his bad advisers to act with haste. Fish shortly entered in his diary: [34]

Returning yesterday from New York, Secretary Bristow got on the train at Philadelphia, and in speaking of Chandler's appointment as Secretary of the Interior Department, he said that he had dined the night before with

[32] *Nation*, October 7, 1875.
[33] Diary, October 14; Robeson had the news from Horace Porter, who had it well in advance of any of the Cabinet—from Babcock.
[34] October 26, 1875.

Mr. Borie, who, as he says, "sometimes tells things without meaning to do so," who told him that being with the President on his tour to Colorado, when they reached Pittsburgh on their return, Chandler entered the car, having arrived at Pittsburgh from Detroit some hours previously by a train which he left at Pittsburgh to wait for the President; that on entering the car he remarked to the President that he had received his letter and was much gratified to him for the offer made, and that he had concluded to accept it.

Bristow further stated that when Chandler was in Washington (later) he positively declared that he had no idea of the offer until after he had reached Washington.

The appointment of Chandler, in fact, had been managed by Babcock in a fashion positively insulting to several Cabinet members. A definite offer had been made Chandler by the 14th. Yet when Grant presided over a Cabinet meeting on the 15th he treated the subject as still open. He said that he believed Chandler's appointment, if made, would be well received by the country; and when Bristow and Pierrepont protested that they held an entirely different opinion, it was decided that the matter should be taken up again on the 19th, when Fish might be back from New York. Marshall Jewell and Bristow at once sent Fish word to hurry back, and John L. Cadwalader mailed him a warning letter. He reported that Bristow thought this "a move on the part of the Kitchen Cabinet at the White House to cover up something." His own opinion was that the plot possibly went deeper; that the Kitchen Cabinet had planned to place Chandler and Bristow at loggerheads, and thus get rid of the latter as "too troublesome." As the above entries show, Chandler had come to Washington with Grant, and actually the President had fully resolved on the appointment. On the morning of the 19th the commission was signed, Chandler was sworn in, and when the Cabinet meeting opened there he sat in Delano's chair!

What Bristow thought of this we may easily guess. What Fish thought is made clear by a scorching letter of October 20 (he had been detained at Garrison) to Cadwalader. He believed the appointment a grave mistake; Chandler, though incorruptible and generous, was violent of temper, hasty in judgment, fond of excitement, averse to labor, and surrounded by the worst type of politicians. But it was the manner of the appointment which chiefly outraged him. After asking the confidential advice of his Cabinet, Grant had completely ignored—had not even acknowledged —their suggestions. Without a word to them, he had offered the place to a man whom he had recently told Fish he would not think of appointing.

While the Cabinet remained in ignorance, Horace Porter had known instantly of the offer to J. Russell Jones and its rejection. Porter had also known of the definite offer to Chandler at least two days before the Cabinet was told that the matter was still open! "All this," Fish wrote Cadwalader, "shows an intimacy [as] illegitimate and unknown to the Constitution as it is derogatory and evincing want of confidence and of decent respect toward the members of the Cabinet."

Few Administration newspapers defended the appointment of so arrant a spoilsman. The best praise of the New York *Times* was that Chandler was a good man "to sit up nights and tell stories," the best praise of the Boston *Advertiser* that he was "a much more honest man than his enemies give him credit for being." The Michigan Legislature, amid the plaudits of reformers, had just declined to reëlect him to the Senate. His part in the expulsion of Jacob D. Cox was still remembered. A rich man, he was above financial temptation, but he represented a coarse political school, his personal habits were bad, and his associates were untrustworthy. Ill-tempered and noisy (in Civil War days he had been called "Xantippe in pants"), he had the reputation of a blusterer. His first important act, the dismissal of Chief Clerk Grinnell of the Patent Office, caused a sensation; for Grinnell had risen by patient endeavor, and was one of the ablest and most conscientious of all bureau officials.[35] He was kicked out (not even being allowed to resign) for the worst possible reason, his refusal to pay a political assessment that fall. E. L. Godkin commanded general agreement when he wrote that Chandler's appointment, "so close to the scandals which have just led to the retirement of his predecessor, cannot but be regarded as a fresh proof either of General Grant's contempt for the moral sense of the best portion of the community, or of his inability to comprehend it, and is of a piece with the renomination of Boss Shepherd."[36]

No one felt this more keenly than Fish. He had long disliked Chandler's influence over the President. That very summer he had received a letter from Grant which shocked him. Written apropos of a campaign circular which Chandler had just helped to draw up, and at a time (July 2, 1875) when Chandler was staying with the President at Long Branch, it read as follows:[37]

[35] *Nation*, November 25, 1875.   [36] *Nation*, October 28, 1875.
[37] Fish Papers; Cf. Diary, July 8, 1875.

I have just been shown a circular which it has been intended to distribute among Federal officials with the view of soliciting contributions (voluntary ones; for it does not contemplate that any one should be compelled to respond on pain of losing his position) for the laudable (*sic*) purpose of maintaining the organization of the republican party. Money is necessary for this purpose, to buy and distribute documents, print tickets, send speakers into the field, etc., and I do not see that any parties are more directly interested in this than the office holders whose places yield them a compensation of more than $1,000.00 pr. Annum. I understand it is to be distributed to none others.

You may say if you please to the balance of the Cabinet that my views on this subject are as here expressed.

This letter, a flat contradiction of Grant's statement in 1872 that "political assessments, as they are called, have been forbidden within the various departments," unmistakably expressed Chandler's code of ethics.

III

It was clear that Babcock was playing out his hand to the last card. His very audacity, as apparently he tried to thrust Butler and Jones into the Cabinet, and as he aided Zach Chandler to clamber there, commanded a certain respect. Throughout the summer, while Bristow assembled the evidence for his downfall, he displayed unshaken nerve. He continued to serve assiduously his old allies, Casey, Shepherd, Tom Murphy, and Rufus Ingalls, and trusted that in his hour of need they would serve him.

Babcock was no stolid, greedy plotter of the saloon back-room type; he was quick, alert, impetuous, daring, with the mien of a dashing soldier and the manners of a gentleman. Dressed expensively but quietly, looking with his imperial and moustache like a French staff officer, dexterous at turning a compliment or launching a sarcastic shaft, he was a formidable foeman. He was full of resource; defeated at one point, he would spring to another. In a different environment—under a Napoleon or Mussolini, who knew how to use an unscrupulous talent—he might have made a great name.

All spring Fish had fenced with him upon minor issues. One was an appointment for Tom Murphy's brother-in-law, Richard Gibbs, to some diplomatic post. Murphy urged it, Babcock supported him, and the President took their point of view. Gibbs had no visible qualification beyond a knowledge of Spanish; but while living in Cuba he had lost his property, and Murphy was tired of supporting him. Though Fish protested repeatedly, Grant was persistent, and early in April appointed Gibbs Minister to Peru at $10,000 a year.[38] Another issue was presented by Babcock's insistence on some post for a worthless New Yorker, Charles O. Shepard. Sent as consul to Kanagawa, Japan, he immediately quarreled with officers of the American navy. Fish wished to drop him entirely. But he was soon writing in the diary: "The President shows me a commission which Babcock had just laid on his table, of C. O. Shepard to Leeds, in place of Richards recalled. I made no comment, but handed him back the paper, which he signed. This is one of General Babcock's and General Meyer's appointments." [39]

A graver question was presented by Grant's effort, in which Babcock doubtless took a hand, to have wholly improper payments made to Tom Murphy. On January 27, 1875, Fish having gone to the Capitol to talk with various Senators on Canadian reciprocity, the expatriation bill, and other legislation, Grant followed him thither:

He sent for me to his room [writes Fish], and . . . refers to the amount due to St. Domingo for the lease of Samana Bay for the second year. He said that Murphy was nearly ruined, and had advanced some $40,000 or $50,000 on account of the rent, and that some others (without naming them) had also made advances; that the money ought to be paid; and that Conkling had spoken with him and suggested that I should bring the matter to the notice of the Committee on Foreign Relations.

I told him of the conversation which I had had, some months since, with Conkling, when he brought Murphy to my office, and when for the first time I heard or had any intimation or suspicion that any part of the money had been paid or that Murphy had any connection with it. I had told him that there was no fund out of which it could possibly be paid, and that Conkling at that time expressed himself to me as satisfied that nothing could be done without a specific appropriation of Congress, and had concurred in the opinion that the Administration could not afford to move in the matter.

He asked if it could not be paid out of the contingent fund of foreign intercourse. I explained to him that the appropriation only amounted to about $100,000, and with the strictest economy the expenditures could only be kept $2,000 below it. He suggested that an appropriation for $150,000 might be made without indicating its object.

[38] Diary, January 26, February 5, March 8, April 6, 1875.
[39] Diary, March 15, 19, 1875.

I thought that it would be impossible, and he asked whether I could not suggest such an appropriation, informing the Administration Senators of its object. I replied that I could not; that the present temper of Congress and the public was such that no appropriation of the kind could be expected, and that it would be very damaging to him and the Republican Party for the Administration to propose an appropriation for the St. Domingo Treaty.

The President admitted that he was precluded from asking but thought that I might.

I replied that that would be more injurious to him than a direct proposal from himself, as I should only do it, if at all, under his instructions and it would be regarded as an indirect evasion, on his part, of the responsibility.

I called his attention to the fact that St. Domingo had never made any demands directly or indirectly from the government for the second year's rent. He said that it had been paid, he supposed, by Murphy and others. I had never, however, heard any other than Murphy's allegation of its having been paid by himself.

He finally remarked that he supposed that the only thing would be for the party to make application to Congress, to which I replied that I could suggest nothing, but that the Administration should take no part in it.

Murphy needed $50,000; he alleged—Fish knew of no other evidence—that he had paid that much for a lease of Samaná Bay which Congress had never authorized; and the President of the United States asked that the money be secretly transferred out of some fund uncontrolled by Congress! On this comment would be superfluous.

Yet of a piece with it was the renewed effort of the White House cabal to place Rufus Ingalls in the quartermaster-generalship. The plan to create a vacancy by making Meigs Minister to Russia had failed. But in the spring of 1875 Meigs called disconsolately on Fish to exhibit an order from Secretary Belknap, written by direction of the President, detailing him to Europe for eighteen months to collect military information, especially upon quartermaster and staff appointments. The closing sentence stated that the object of his visit need not be made public. Though he ought to have been accredited by the State Department, as Naval Commissioners recently sent abroad had been, the order was a complete surprise to Fish. Taken in conjunction with the degrading suggestion of secrecy—for as Meigs said, no soldier would care to go as a spy—its object was plain. Meigs was to be gotten out of the way in order that Ingalls might seize upon his office. Bristow and Fish indignantly discussed this move. After remarking that Grant and Belknap had jointly asked him if he could not pay Meigs's salary while in Europe "in gold," Bristow gave the Secretary of State a piece of confidential information: [40]

> He says that he learns that Mr. Watson, who was formerly Assistant Secretary of the Treasury, last summer, when the effort was making to send Meigs to Russia in order to put Ingalls in his place, had stated that he had in his possession the history of a transaction which would expose Ingalls, and must prevent his confirmation and must show him unworthy of trust.
> He understood that the papers had been withdrawn from file in the War Department but that he (Watson) had secured copies which he would make public in case of Ingalls's appointment.

While we do not know to what offense this refers, we do know that the inner gossip of Washington implicated Ingalls in both the illegal sale of arms to France and the "safe-burglary" conspiracy to protect the District Ring. And Fish's diary contains other suspicious bits upon Ingalls.

In the spring of 1875 the President, to make a place for ex-Governor W. Madison Wells of Louisiana, whom even Sheridan had characterized in 1867 as "a political trickster and a dishonest man," asked Attorney-General Pierrepont to call for the resignation of Fisher, the Federal District Attorney in Washington. Pierrepont sent for Fisher, and communicated the request. Without complying, Fisher hurried to Long Branch—not to see the President, but to see Babcock. At about the same time Alexander H. Shepherd also posted to Long Branch, taking Ingalls with him. They spent a day with Babcock, Shepherd sticking so closely to the secretary that nobody else could come near him. Later Ingalls indiscreetly told Ben Halliday (through whom the information reached Fish) that the object of Shepherd's visit had been to plead for Fisher as a means of keeping the safe-burglary case hushed up. If the district attorney were not treated well, said Ingalls, "the God-damned fellow would kick the blanket off and expose the damned corpse." [41] Once more the machinations of the cabal were successful. On July 19 Shepherd himself carried to the Attorney-General's office a letter from Grant, too precious to entrust to the mails, stating that

---

[40] Diary, May 22, 1875. Though Meigs made this European trip, it is pleasant to record that he was not forced out, remaining quartermaster-general until 1882.
[41] Diary, May 20, 1875.

Pierrepont might suspend for the time being any action upon Fisher's case.

All this was sickening; and with a feeling of anxiety Fish confessed to his diary increasing doubts as to Babcock's financial honesty. Just after King Kalakua's visit Babcock handed the Secretary a bill for the printing and engraving of invitations to the White House reception. It came to $250, though Fish was confident that in New York he could have had the work done for $20.[42] Babcock held the office of Commissioner of Public Buildings in the District of Columbia, and Fish suspected that he was making it decidedly profitable to such men as Shepherd. Throughout 1875 the Secretary of State, much against his will, conducted an undignified struggle with Babcock to obtain funds for the completion of the south wing of the new State, War, and Navy building, in which his department hoped soon to find shelter. An error in the estimates of the supervising architect, Mullett, with other complicating factors, made necessary a re-allocation of funds between the different wings; and to this Babcock's consent was necessary. He showed an obstructive spirit from the outset. At one point Fish caught him in a direct falsehood to the President about the reasons for this obstructiveness.[43] A little later Fish compelled him to return to the appropriation for the State Department's quarters $2,370.73 which he had improperly used in work on the East Room of the White House and on the Scott Monument.[44] It was only after much vexation that he obtained the funds he needed.

And it was during this particular controversy that he became aware of Secretary Belknap's pitiable dependence on Babcock. The diary contains the two following significant entries:

Thursday, June 10, 1875.—I left this morning for New York. Last night I received a telegram from General Belknap, dated at West Point, saying that on the following day I would receive the paper which I had sent to him with his signature. He referred to the paper prepared by Taylor, the Comptroller, for the transfer of appropriation from the East Wing to that of the South Wing, of about $137,000. I left the matter to Mr. Cadwalader, to attend to the transfer when the papers should be received.

Mr. Cadwalader telegraphed me that it was not received Thursday, but arrived in Washington late on Friday, when it came postmarked "Long Branch" and bearing one of the President's postage stamps. It has been pre-

[42] Diary, February 9, 1875. In my opinion, the very able Babcock was avid of power rather than of money.   [43] Diary, April 12, 1875.   [44] Diary, May 22, 1875.

pared for Belknap's signature to precede that of the Secretary of State; he had transposed these and appears to have sent the paper to Babcock, without whom he can do nothing.

Monday, June 14, 1875.—I pay a visit to West Point, where General Belknap is staying, and he says that the transfer had been signed; I reply that I was glad to see he had sent it to the President for approval. He disclaimed, saying *"No."* He had sent it to Babcock to ascertain whether the amount stated was correct, as he professed to have no knowledge of the amount of the material.

I reminded him that the amounts had been stated in a previous correspondence and had been agreed upon before he left and that I had supposed that it was the President's approval, upon seeing the President's postage stamp. His private secretary, Mr. Barnard, was present and had been sent by Belknap to Babcock with the paper, and remarked that Babcock had put one of his own stamps upon it. The truth is, Babcock fancies himself President of the United States, and Belknap don't know better.

Fish added, with unwonted scorn: "Belknap referred to the transposition of the signatures and assigned as a reason deference to the State Department, which took precedence of the War Department. In fact, it is nothing but his moral cowardice, which wanted a name to precede his on the paper." [45]

IV

Meanwhile, Bristow had energetically prepared to prosecute the Whiskey Ring thieves. In the spring of 1875 the Federal Grand Jury in St. Louis indicted McDonald, Joyce, and a host of other men, and McDonald was immediately arrested there, posting $5,000 bail. Fish did not learn until later that Babcock's anxiety had been so aroused by the indictments that he asked Major E. B. Grimes, a St. Louis quartermaster, to call on Federal Attorney Dyer and ascertain his intentions. Grimes reported: "Colonel Dyer is as determined as Bristow, and tells me emphatically that if the President is in the Ring, he is going for him. I don't know what to make of it. But I have done all I can with him. Well, if he persists in covering the entire White House with disgrace, my suggestion would be to have him dismissed." Nor did Fish know that when Grant and Babcock made their September visit to St. Louis, Babcock repeatedly conferred with McDonald. According to McDonald's subsequent story, the two discussed their plight, the possibility of

[45] Diary, June 14, 1875.

blocking Bristow and Dyer, and even, if they should finally "hear the turn of the bolt," of obtaining a pardon. Grant himself met the indicted McDonald publicly, and expressed sympathy for him. When the President returned to Washington he manifested increased chilliness toward Bristow.[46]

The Government employed two special counsel to assist Federal Attorney Dyer in the St. Louis prosecutions—ex-Senator John B. Henderson and Major Lucien Eaton. It made an exhaustive search for evidence. In November the trials began. On the 14th Fish read with gratification that John A. Joyce, a subordinate revenue collector, had been convicted; his sentence was a fine of $2,000 and three and a half years in jail.

This first conviction had a touch of bouffe. Joyce obtained permission to make a speech from the dock. After denying his guilt, denouncing his enemies, and comparing the reform movement to a great miasmatic torrent which had wrenched many fair young oaks and tall sycamores from their roots, he remarked that "the flood even now is settling into its former bed, where the crystal waters shall again reflect the green foliage, the oak and the sycamore, and the gentle breezes and birds of spring shall make merry music in the aisles of a generous nation." [47] He also compared his fate with those of Galileo, Tasso, Columbus, and Napoleon. But as the trials proceeded the Ring found them no joke. Man after man was convicted. Judgments were obtained for large sums. On November 23 McDonald himself was found guilty and sentenced to three years in jail and a $5,000 fine. Next day the trial of a Washington official, William Avery, chief clerk of the Treasury, began; and in the background loomed up the arraignment of a more important figure— Babcock himself.

Thus far Grant had given full support to the investigation and prosecutions. The cases in St. Louis, where the grand jury had returned 253 indictments in all, were a shock to him; but if he had shown no enthusiasm, neither had he evinced antagonism.[48] Grant had never known McDonald well, though he had accepted the superintendent's attentions at the St. Louis fair in 1874, and in his careless way had taken his gifts of game and fruit for the White House table.[49] When McDonald went behind the bars Babcock winced, but Grant was pleased that a treach-

[46] McDonald, *Secrets of the Great Whiskey Ring*, 201 ff.
[47] *Nation*, November 25, 1875.
[48] Coolidge, *Grant*, 476; Grayson L. Kirk, *American Mercury*, July, 1934, p. 483.
[49] Bowers, *The Tragic Era*, 466; Hesseltine, *Grant*.

erous official had received justice. The President at first turned a deaf ear to men who told him that the Whiskey Ring exposures were a plot against his own fame and the safety of the Republican Party. W. D. W. Barnard, a St. Louis banker and distant relative, sent Grant a letter in July denouncing Dyer and Henderson, declaring that their enmity to the Administration made it important to appoint additional counsel to keep a watch on them, and giving the names of several accused revenue-officers who had said that Babcock's fate was involved with their own. Grant read this in Long Branch. He at once forwarded it to Bristow with an endorsement that the latter, his position barely tenable, made haste to publish in order to strengthen his own hand: [50]

". . . I forward this for information and to the end that if it throws any light upon new parties to summon as witnesses they may be brought out. *Let no guilty man escape if it can be avoided.* Be especially vigilant—or instruct those engaged in the prosecution of fraud to be—against all who insinuate that they have high influence to protect—or to protect them. No personal consideration should stand in the way of performing a public duty."

But when he wrote this Grant did not dream that Babcock might be guilty; he did not know how embarrassing some revelations would prove. McDonald's trial brought out the fact that Boutwell, in appointing him against protests by Carl Schurz and other leading Missourians, had said that it was too bad but he "could not help it"— the supporting influence was too strong.[51] That influence was Grant's. Avery's trial brought out the fact that when he, as Chief Clerk in the Treasury, had first been approached by McDonald and Joyce for improper information on revenue affairs, he had indignantly refused it. He had then received a letter from Grant himself assuring him that the two men were trustworthy, and should have what information they wanted.[52]

Moreover, Dyer, Henderson, and Bristow had found evidence indicating that the trail of corruption led to Babcock's door. In August they discovered a telegram from Babcock to McDonald signed "Sylph" and reading: "I have succeeded. They will not go. I will write you." This they interpreted as proof that Babcock had helped the Ring block certain investigations. Bristow, always direct and

[50] This endorsement was marked "confidential." Bristow had difficulty in obtaining Grant's permission to publish it, and there is some ground for believing that he issued it without permission; House Misc. Doc. 44th Cong., 1st Sess., No. 186, 349, 357 ff.
[51] *Nation*, November 18, 1875.   [52] Kirk, *op. cit.*

forcible, confronted Babcock with this telegram. He admitted writing it, but denied that it had any connection with the Ring, and gave an explanation which Bristow thought false. Bristow then showed it to Grant. The latter, forewarned by Babcock, gave the same explanation. "It doesn't refer to the whiskey business," he said. "It refers to an order for the transfer of a supervisor." "Unfortunately, Mr. President," rejoined Bristow, "that transfer order was not issued until February, 1875, whereas this telegram was sent in December, 1874!" [53]

The implacable Secretary of the Treasury had thereupon warned Babcock that he would be indicted when the grand jury reconvened in St. Louis in November. Bristow had heard that Babcock had been offered a position with the elevated railroad in New York; anxious not to involve the White House, he suggested to Horace Porter that he might well advise the colonel to resign. But Porter refused. "I think," Bristow told Fish, "that Babcock's friends consider him stronger in facing trial as the President's private secretary than otherwise." [54]

The implication was that Babcock's friends expected Grant to protect the adroit secretary. By December 1, 1875, it was clear that he would be on trial within a few weeks. Would the President still let justice take its course, or would he, as with Richardson, Williams, and Delano, be led by his sympathies for the culprit, and his fears for the reputation of his Administration, to obstruct it?

[53] Diary, September 17, 1875.   [54] *Ibid.*

As Fish uneasily observed, throughout the summer and fall of 1875 Babcock stuck like a burr to Grant's side. They remained at Long Branch until September 22 (C. C. Sniffen having secretarial charge at the White House), when both went to St. Louis, and they returned to Washington again in mid-October. Babcock had ample opportunity to furnish Grant with ingenious explanations of the evidence connecting him with the Whiskey Ring. It was significant that as deepening suspicion fell upon him, the President's hostility to the prosecutions grew. Within an hour after Bluford Wilson, Solicitor of the Treasury, informed Grant that he held evidence that $500 had been mailed from St. Louis to Babcock, Babcock knew about it; and he insolently told Wilson that anything said to the President was as good as said to him.[1] Fish was quick to note Grant's intense sympathy for his secretary, and his resentment of what he regarded as an attempt to besmear the White House.

During the trial of the Treasury official Avery, the prosecution introduced suspicious telegrams from Babcock to him and Joyce, which special prosecutor Henderson told the jury on November 29 showed Babcock's complicity. Babcock, forewarned of the telegrams, might have hurried west to explain them. Instead, waiting until it was too late to be heard in person, he telegraphed a denial. Then, adroitly taking advantage of the fact that he had retained his commission as major, he wrote Grant on December 2 demanding a military court of inquiry. This was an effort to create delay.[2] Such a court would take time, while if its verdict were adverse a court-martial would follow—Babcock meanwhile escaping civil trial. Grant submitted this demand to the Cabinet. Babcock's ally Belknap of course supported it, declaring it an "equitable right" when grave charges were made against an officer. As he gave plausible assurances that it would not interfere with a civil trial, the Cabinet assented. With a shock, however, Fish learned at the Cabinet meeting next day that Grant intended to place the inquiry under an officer who had shown marked friendliness to Babcock. He writes:

[1] House Misc. Docs., 44th Cong., 1st sess., No. 186; *Nation*, August 3, 1876.
[2] Grant Letterbooks, December 2, 1875.

December 3, 1875.— . . . Belknap reads some authorities on the organization and power of a court of inquiry, and it was decided that the court be ordered, and the President named Generals Sheridan, Hancock, and Terry, stating that he would have named Sherman but there was no precedent for assigning the Commander-in-Chief as judge of a court.

The Secretary of War reminded him that General Sherman while Commander-in-Chief had been detailed as presiding officer in the court of inquiry of General Howard. The President appeared to have forgotten this, but when it was brought to his attention he made no change, but left Sherman out and ordered it to convene in Chicago on the 9th instant. The Attorney-General was directed to inform the district attorney in St. Louis of the order, and to direct him to furnish the court with any documents and facts which they might require.

Sherman being excluded, Sheridan and Secretary Belknap might easily exert pressure on the court to bring in a whitewashing verdict. Attorney-General Pierrepont promised the uneasy Fish that he would not permit the civil prosecution to be suppressed. He said, as they left the meeting together, "that he would let the prosecuting attorney understand that this order would not suspend or interfere with the pending criminal proceedings at St. Louis, to interfere with which he said would be ruinous to Babcock, the President, and the Administration." Whatever this was worth, the St. Louis prosecutors kept their evidence under lock and key. When Sheridan's military court met in Chicago it found itself helpless without this evidence, as Hancock pointed out, and dropped the case.

On December 3, Avery was convicted. But Henderson, in closing the case, overstepped the bounds of discretion. Evidence had been presented that in 1874, when Commissioner Douglass of the internal revenue service was about to send two agents to make investigation in St. Louis, Babcock had gone to him and the President and blocked the inquiry. He had then sent the telegram signed "Sylph": "I have succeeded. They will not go." Henderson demanded of the jury; [3] "What right had Babcock to go to Douglass to induce him to withdraw his agents? . . . What right had the President to interfere with Commissioner Douglass in the proper discharge of his duties, or with the Secretary of the Treasury?" When Fish read the newspaper reports he instantly saw that this attack on the President could not be overlooked.[4] Pierrepont held the same opinion. Grant mentioned the occurrence to the

[3] N. Y. *Tribune, Herald,* December 4, 7, 1875.   [4] Diary, December 7, 1875.

Cabinet that day, and Fish records: "The President read an extract from the Cincinnati *Inquirer*, stating that it was a hostile paper and that possibly the remarks actually made might differ from the report; but that he was satisfied that Henderson was a personal enemy of his and was disposed to abuse him when opportunity offered. The indecency of a counsel, especially designated by the President, abusing him, was severely denounced by all the Cabinet."

Three days later, Pierrepont having sent for fuller information, Henderson's speech was read to the Cabinet from a sworn copy of the court stenographer's notes, together with an explanatory telegram from Dyer and a defiant one from Henderson. "Without dissenting opinion," writes Fish,[5] "it was agreed that the speech was an indecency and an outrage upon professional propriety." Pierrepont was instructed to dismiss Henderson, and wrote a telegram for that purpose in the Cabinet room. No President who felt a proper regard for the dignity of his office could have taken any other course; and the immediate appointment of J. O. Broadhead, a distinguished Democratic attorney, proved that the dismissal was not meant to cripple the prosecution of Babcock.

But Fish continued to be disturbed by the evident eagerness of men close to the President to shield Babcock. Indeed, Belknap was perfectly brazen in revealing his desire to save the Secretary by hook or crook. Just before Christmas he read the Cabinet a long report by Major Gardner, the judge advocate-general detailed to the military court. It harshly criticized Federal Attorney Dyer in St. Louis. Fish knew through Pierrepont that Dyer was able, honest, and impartial. His refusal to surrender his evidence against Babcock to the military court was quite proper. "The tone of this paper," writes Fish,[6] "made a very unpleasant impression on my mind at least as to the objects and expectations of results from that court." Belknap also read a sharp attack by Gardner upon the eminently correct behavior of Hancock in the military court. Fish writes that the Secretary of War seemed to lament "the loss of opportunity for some purpose I do not wish to speculate upon." Obviously, he and Babcock had planned to cripple or crush the civil trial by a military exculpation.

During December and January the hard-pressed cabal were laboring night and day to fill Grant's mind with distrust of the Whiskey Ring

[5] Diary, December 10, 1875.   [6] Diary, December 21, 1875.

prosecutions, now under way in Chicago, Milwaukee, and other cities as well as St. Louis. They were reinforced by Republican politicians worried by the effect of the scandal upon the impending campaign. These men told Grant that an effort was being made to destroy the party—worse still, to destroy *him*. They declared that Bristow was thirsting to win fame as a reformer, and to climb to the presidency on other men's ruin. Grant quickly imbibed the desired suspicions. The unhappiest feature of Henderson's indiscretion was that it strengthened them. Irresponsible journals and over-zealous Democrats likewise gave them color when they made sinister attacks upon the White House. Charges appeared in the Chicago *Times* of January 3 and New York *Herald* of January 5, 1876, that Orvil and Fred D. Grant, brother and son of the President, were implicated in the Whiskey Frauds. With set jaw, Grant mentioned these charges to the Cabinet, and ordered Attorney-General Pierrepont to summon the authors before grand juries; if they had any evidence he wanted it sifted, and if they did not he wanted their lies exposed.[7] He also asked that a detective, one Bell, be sent to St. Louis to watch for improper attacks upon the President, with orders to report directly to the Attorney-General.

But while this was proper enough, Grant unhappily went much further. As in all conspiracy cases, prosecutors of the Whiskey Ring were compelled to place heavy reliance on culprits who turned state's evidence; and it soon appeared that the cabal had filled Grant with a fierce prejudice against this type of evidence.

Late in January, 1876, William McKee, owner of the Ring newspaper, a man of wealth, family, and political power, was convicted. Some of the evidence in his trial had again reflected upon Babcock. Grant treated the next Cabinet meeting, as Fish writes, to an undignified outburst: [8]

The President speaks with a great deal of feeling about the conviction of McKee of St. Louis for conspiracy in connection with the Whiskey Frauds, and says he has read all the testimony published, and not a word is charged against him, McKee, by any person who is not himself confessedly a perjurer and a felon, while every respectable person who testified did so in his behalf. He said he had supposed there would have been a divided jury, inasmuch as whatever might be the evidence of his innocence, the state of feeling was such that there were sure to be some who would try to convict.

[7] Diary, January 7, 1876.   [8] Diary, February 1, 1875.

Pierrepont asked him where he had read the evidence, that he himself had only seen an abstract of it as published in the Eastern papers.

The President said it was that which he had read, and remarks that he thinks the conduct of our prosecuting officers in the Chicago cases was perfectly atrocious; that their stipulating to let clear the confessed rogues with the hope of being able to convict a few prominent persons he thinks outrageous.

Pierrepont disclaims any knowledge of any such proceedings. The President says he repeats what has been told him by Dutton (Supervisor of Internal Revenue). . . . The President seems to think that the Solicitor-General is responsible for the line of conduct pursued, which he condemns.

Solicitor Bluford Wilson, whom Fish knew to be ruggedly honest, was both feared and hated by Babcock and his allies. Early in the prosecution he resolved that if Babcock were guilty, he would prove it; if he were innocent, he would demonstrate that—but he would push the inquiry to the bitter end. He had written Henderson [9] urging him to neglect no precaution "to reach the bottom or top of the conspiracy." The cabal were assuring Grant that Bluford Wilson intended to release some of the worst members of the Ring if they would only incriminate men high in the government. On hearing Grant's outburst, Bristow courageously defended Wilson, saying that his letters to the prosecutors had authorized no such course as the President charged, and that he did not believe the attorneys were pursuing it. For a moment of tense silence the two men faced each other grimly. Then Grant, after instructing Pierrepont to telegraph the Federal Attorney in Chicago to ascertain the facts, dropped the subject.

I

Babcock's trial opened in St. Louis on February 8, 1876. What scenes occurred in the White House before he left it we do not know. But we do know some of the steps taken there to protect him.

On February 1 the Chicago *Times* published a circular letter which Attorney-General Pierrepont had written the Federal Attorneys in St. Louis, Chicago, and Milwaukee forbidding them to promise immunity to criminals who turned state's evidence. This letter, dated January 26, had obviously been extorted by Grant's pressure. Pierrepont later testified as much, saying that Grant had asked for it four or five times,

---

[9] Coolidge, *Grant*, 480.

and had wished it "even stronger." It was immediately republished throughout the land. Pierrepont wrote that he had read reports that immunity would be widely bestowed; and that the attorneys must not do "anything that might look like favoring or even protecting men who have defrauded the government." He ordered them to avoid "even the appearance of such favorable treatment," and ended by stating that he was determined to see "that no one has been maliciously persecuted; that no one has escaped through favoritism or partiality, and that no guilty person who has either been convicted or has confessed his guilt was left unpunished." As the House Judiciary Committee later pointed out, this was highly censurable. "The testimony of accomplices," the Committee stated, "has been used against their associates from the earliest ages of our jurisprudence." Indeed, it has often been the principal weapon of justice. We have seen that once before (page 592) Pierrepont had shown willingness to shield a criminal. Fish learned later that his promise not to let the proposed military court interfere with civil prosecution in St. Louis had meant nothing. After making it, he had telegraphed Attorney Dyer ordering him to furnish the military tribunal with all the evidence against Babcock. Dyer had read Pierrepont a stinging lesson. He replied that evidence procured by a Federal court in St. Louis could not be taken out of its jurisdiction and delivered in time of peace to military officers, especially when daily use was being made of it in grand jury work and the trial of cases. He would be held in contempt of court if he did this.

Pierrepont's circular would have been bad enough if never published. But Babcock—according to Pierrepont's subsequent testimony—filched a copy, which he sent his counsel, Emory Storrs, and Storrs saw that it was spread in the press. It appeared at a critical moment in the progress of the Chicago prosecutions. Some fifty distillers, rectifiers, gaugers, storekeepers, and others had been indicted in that city. A number of the distillers were rich men, of business and social standing. The Chicago correspondent of the New York *Herald* had predicted on January 5 that they would all plead guilty, and sentence would be suspended on motion of the government. This would be proper for three reasons. First, the conviction of the guiltiest men, the political originators of the Ring, could not be obtained without their evidence. In the second place, most of the distillers and rectifiers had been literally driven into fraud by competition, intimidation, and the general laxity of the revenue service. In the third place, the government meant to insist upon forfeiture of the seized property, and felt that it would be cruel to send these once-honored men to the penitentiary as well. They felt their disgrace keenly, while forfeiture would mean utter ruin to some. Much was expected from their evidence. Although no letters had been found signed by Babcock, a number had been discovered from an unidentified Washington official who had been the special informant of the Chicago Ring and whose papers disclosed him as "a person of great commanding influence." On January 14 thirteen distillers did plead guilty in Chicago. It was hoped that one man in especial, Hesing, would implicate Senator Logan and two Congressmen in approving the acceptance of political contributions from the Ring. But Pierrepont's circular smashed all such hopes.[10]

The circular had an immediate effect in St. Louis. Charles Nordhoff, one of the fairest journalists of the day, wrote: "About the time when this letter was sent . . . it became public that one Everest, concerned in the St. Louis Whiskey Frauds, was likely to give important testimony in General Babcock's trial." Everest, paymaster of the Ring, actually gave only minor evidence. In fact, all the conspirators who might have turned state's evidence became silence itself. Babcock could draw an easier breath as his trial opened.

It was unquestionably at Babcock's instigation that Grant thus crippled the prosecution. But no one can doubt that the President knew precisely what he was doing. Were it not for a significant entry in Fish's diary, it might be pleaded that he had acted in ignorance of court procedure and law. But Fish records that on March 17, 1876, Zach Chandler reported to the Cabinet that he had discovered extensive frauds in the Interior Department as Delano had been running it. Corrupt clerks had been padding the lists of persons entitled to quarter-section grants under some legislation of 1872, and about eight hundred fraudulent entries of land had thus been permitted. One minor official had confessed, while the Chief Clerk of the Bureau involved was obviously guilty either of dishonesty or gross neglect. "The President," writes Fish, "directs every effort to be made to obtain evidence, and protection for the Clerk from prosecution to the extent of the law if he can furnish evidence which will convict persons more guilty than himself." In other words, Grant was quick to order immunity promised to an officer in the Interior Depart-

10 See N. Y. *Herald,* January 5–15, for a mass of material on the Chicago Ring.

ment if he would incriminate other men; he was equally quick to stop the grant of immunity to far less censurable malefactors when to do so endangered his own secretary.

In still another way official interference had already been felt in St. Louis. Prompted by someone high in the government, George Bliss, Pierrepont's successor as Federal Attorney in New York, sent west a deputy, Roger Sherman, ostensibly to find evidence for the government. Bliss was what the *Nation* called a bouffe official; he always failed the government and let the rogues somehow win. Fish believed that the breakdown of the case against James Watson Webb was due to his inefficiency or worse. Informed observers were therefore not surprised when Sherman obtained evidence in disreputable quarters for the defendant, which he turned over to Babcock himself! "In bouffe prosecutions," wrote Godkin,[11] "the government always collects the evidence and hands it over to the defendant." It is perhaps significant that Bliss belonged to the Conkling-Arthur-Tom Murphy machine, and that Pierrepont had become a supporter of Conkling for the presidential nomination in 1876. Leaders of this machine were not averse to seeing Secretary Bristow, who was also mentioned for the nomination, checked and humiliated.

On the first day of Babcock's trial, the prosecution introduced telegrams to prove that he had been in constant communication with Ring members; it proved his clandestine intercourse with McDonald after the latter's indictment; and the Ring paymaster, Everest, went so far as to swear that he had seen $500 put into an envelope apparently for Babcock. The President that day called a special Cabinet meeting. Fish observed that he was worried and excited. He announced that he wished the Cabinet to discuss urgent messages from Babcock's counsel in St. Louis. Dubious of the outcome, they had implored Grant by telegram and letter to appear as witness. While the Cabinet sat another telegram arrived. It declared that the opening speech of the prosecution indicated an absolute necessity for Grant's testimony.

"The President," writes Fish,[12] "manifested a great deal of excitement, and complained that they had taken from him his secretaries and clerks, his messengers and doorkeepers; that the prosecution was aimed at himself, and they were putting him on trial; that he was as confident

[11] *Nation,* March 2, 1876; cf. N. Y. *Herald,* February 18, 1876.
[12] Diary, February 8, 1876.

as he lived of Babcock's innocence. (He referred to his long association with him, the entire confidence he had in him, and that he knew he was not guilty; that were he guilty, it would be an instance of the greatest ingratitude and trickery that ever was.)" Grant added that he had wished to give the Chief Justice a deposition in behalf of Babcock, but that the telegrams from Babcock's counsel indicated that this might not suffice. He therefore made an astounding proposal. "The President expressed his determination to go to St. Louis, to start either this evening or tomorrow morning, and said he should like to take at least two members of the Cabinet with him; and enquired of the Attorney-General whether he would accompany him."

For the President of the United States to rush halfway across the continent and enter a criminal court as witness would shock the nation. Fish protested indignantly. He brought out the fact that no subpoena can be served on the President. "I then remarked," he writes, "that should the President go, it would be a voluntary offering of himself as a witness for the defense in a criminal prosecution instituted by the government, of which the President is the representative and embodiment; that it would therefore place him in the attitude of volunteering as a witness to defeat the prosecution, which the law made it his duty to enforce."

Pierrepont and Butler supported Fish's view. The former called attention to the impending national election, which brought every act of the Administration under sharp scrutiny. So unprecedented a step by the Chief Magistrate would encounter acid criticism. Bristow frankly said that he thought the proposed action undignified and improper. Belknap was silent. Robeson alone favored Grant's plan. He even suggested that the Attorney-General might request the court to subpoena the President; to which Pierrepont tartly replied that as by law he was the prosecuting officer, it was not for him to have special witnesses summoned for the defence. Nevertheless, Grant was still eager to take the stand. He suggested that Robeson might take steps to have the court postpone the case, with a view to the President's subsequent appearance. But Pierrepont and Bristow again objected, while Fish attacked the President's idea in sweeping terms: [13]

I objected to the form of suggestion proposed, inasmuch as it intimated that the President might at a future time attend in case the case was post-

[13] *Ibid.*

poned to another time; that I did not think the President of the United States should in any case allow himself to be brought into court as a witness, and put on the stand to testify. I refer to the trial of Aaron Burr, when an effort was made to bring Mr. Jefferson into court as a witness.

The Cabinet was unanimous in the opinion that the President ought not to leave Washington during the session to be made a witness of, and there was no dissent expressed to the position which I took, that he ought not, under any circumstances, to consent to appear in court as a witness.

Various suggestions were made as to the mode of conveying the conclusion that the President would not appear as a witness. . . . While the discussion was going on, the President wrote in pencil what he suggested as an answer at first, with a view of sending it to the counsel for the defense, but this was objected to, on the ground that the government could not advise the line of the defense; some of the expressions were excepted to, and a part of it was rewritten by him.

During the talk Grant sheepishly admitted that he had told Babcock's lawyers, before they went to St. Louis, that he would appear in the trial! Babcock had doubtless extracted this promise. The Cabinet finally agreed that Pierrepont should inform the defense that it was "impossible and unseemly" for the President to attend, but that if the court requested it he would make a deposition. The defense attorneys (upon whom Babcock was said to have spent $25,000, at first retaining Ben Butler) acted on this suggestion. Grant made his deposition in the White House on February 12, the process occupying about five hours. Chief Justice Waite served as notary, and Bristow and Pierrepont were present. The President made a good witness, answering questions without hesitation, and giving emphatic testimony for Babcock's good character.

II

As the case against Babcock proceeded, additional evidence of a damaging character was produced. It was proved that when on several occasions the Ring was trying to prevent Federal investigations, he had furnished the members material assistance. In the spring of 1874 Joyce had telegraphed him from St. Louis to "Make D[ouglass] call off his scandal hounds." Early in 1875, when the Ring was opposing a Presidential order transferring supervisors and revenue agents, Babcock was again active and Joyce telegraphed him: "We have official information that the enemy weakens. Push things." It was proved that Babcock had helped to obtain a Collectorship for a leading Ring member, Maguire. As these facts came out, his counsel fought to have every possible scrap of evidence kept from the jury. It was shown that he had tried to delay the trial. He neither produced nor explained his side of the correspondence with McDonald and Joyce in 1874–75. His lawyers failed to offer any rational explanation of his numerous suspicious messages to Ring members.[14] At one point Judge Dillon intervened on his behalf. Some strange cipher dispatches had passed between Luckey (another of Grant's secretaries) in St. Louis and Babcock in Washington just before the trial began. The prosecution was prepared to submit them. But the court ruled that this correspondence was tantamount to that between counsel and client, and was inadmissible.

Yet even as the injurious new evidence came out Grant's suspicion and resentment increased. Talking with Fish on February 15, he indulged in a new outburst.[15] The prosecution was aimed at himself, he said, not at Babcock. Bristow, possessed by the idea of his complicity in the frauds, was using every means in his power to destroy him. He had been watched by detectives while in St. Louis; these detectives were still trying to collect evidence that Ring members had paid his travelling expenses. All sorts of small devices were being employed to hold him up to public condemnation. He did not blame Bristow personally so much as a pack of flatterers who hoped to see the Secretary become President, and who were egging him on in his schemes. Grant spoke with equal resentment of Bluford Wilson. His hand was helping to control these intrigues against the President. Though the law gave the Attorney-General exclusive authority over Federal prosecutions, Bristow and Wilson in the Treasury had taken charge of these trials.

"I understand," said Fish, "that the law vests the control of suits for the violation of internal revenue laws in the Treasury Department."

"No," said Grant, "the Attorney-General and I have examined the law, and the Attorney-General has full control over suits. The Babcock trial will soon be over, and as soon as it is, Secretary Bristow will leave the Cabinet."

Fish knew that an attack along a broad front was now being made upon the prosecuting officers. Washington was full of outraged politicians growling, "It is time to stop this thing"; "It is killing the party,

---

[14] See *Nation*, March 2, 1876, for a careful analysis.
[15] Special memorandum by Fish, dated March 6, 1876; Fish Papers.

sir"; "There is a higher kind of statesmanship than going about with spies and informers, sir." One sector of the attack lay in efforts to take any connection with the whiskey cases out of the hands of the inflexible Bristow and implacable Wilson, and put them entirely in the hands of the pliable Pierrepont. An Act of 1869 clearly vested the control of such prosecutions in the Secretary of the Treasury. But the President was urged to interfere in spite of this law, and to insist that Bristow keep his hand off. Pierrepont, as the above dialogue indicates, was willing to support this interference. As a result of these manoeuvres a marked coolness sprang up between Bristow and Pierrepont. Another sector of the attack concentrated its fire upon Bluford Wilson. A host of politicians were demanding his outright dismissal. They included Senators who were particularly close to Grant. In Illinois Logan was connected by rumor with the Whiskey Ring, and in Wisconsin Matt Carpenter—two Senators whom Fish disliked for their soft-money, pro-Cuban, bloody-shirt proclivities; much evidence existed that their political organizations had received contributions from Ring sources. They were doubtless keenly interested in getting rid of Bluford Wilson.

Still a third sector, the most alarming of all, was busily occupied with efforts to promote a general Cabinet overturn. If Bristow, Jewell, and Fish could be compelled to resign in a body, many politicians would be jubilant. Some, as Nordhoff wrote, would like to see such an overturn because it would defeat and humiliate the reformers; others, because it would give jobs to themselves or their friends. Why tolerate such men when the example of Hoar and Cox showed how easily they could be ousted?

Fish knew, too, how innocent Bristow was of any wrongful intent, and how keen was his sense of duty. Only a few days earlier the Secretary, who regarded Fish as a kindly mentor, had poured into his ear a confidential lament upon his relations with Grant.[16] He wished to be loyal to the President, he said, and keep his confidence. But Grant was more and more openly hostile. Bristow assured Fish that he had merely assisted with the whiskey prosecutions—he had not tried to control them. Despite his rights under the law of 1869, he had given no orders to Attorney Dyer, but had allowed Pierrepont to direct the cases. He observed with grief that the President's manner was cold, distrustful, and offensive. When Grant talked with him he indulged in cutting thrusts and

16 Diary, February 6, 1876.

insinuations. After referring dejectedly to the crippling effect of Pierre-pont's circular upon the prosecutions, Bristow went on to say that he was not an active candidate for the Presidency—that he did not see how he could afford financially to take the office so early in life. He spoke again, while Fish protested, of resigning:

He asks my advice. Remarking on the delicacy of advising in such matters, I expressed the hope that he will not resign; that assuming that his name is to go before the convention as a candidate for the nomination, his resigning at this time . . . would at once be accepted by the public as admission of disagreements between him and the President, and would make him the rallying-point for all those in the Republican Party hostile to the President, which would at once lead to the distraction of the party, and possibly to the nomination of himself on an independent ticket, but would, I thought, defeat his chances of nomination as the regular candidate of the party. . . .

He reminded me that last summer he had proposed to resign, and that in September he went to Long Branch, having his resignation in his pocket, and had handed it to the President, who had told him that he did not wish to accept it, that he was throwing away a great opportunity, that he was more likely than any one person to be named as his successor, and that there was no one whom he would prefer, and he begged him to take back his resignation, which he did; and that the President added that he would be in Washington about October 1, when they would consider the subject again, if necessary; that the President did not return until some weeks after the time named, and that nothing further had been done on the subject. . . .

I endeavored to soothe him, and suggested that the President at this moment was naturally sensitive with regard to the pending frauds, and that his friendship for Babcock was very sincere, and his confidence in him was very great; that he naturally disbelieved the charges against him, and possibly also felt that the prosecution of persons who were appointees of his reflected upon the Administration.

I advised him to wait and take no action. . . .

Babcock's trial ended February 24 in acquittal. A decisive influence had been produced upon the jury by Grant's deposition. The President swore that he had never noted anything in his secretary's conduct or talk which indicated a connection with the Ring, and that in view of their close relations he believed that if Babcock had been guilty he would have known it. After his emphatic statement, a vote to convict Babcock would have been a vote to accuse Grant of complicity or incredible blindness. But the evidence against him in any event lacked conclusive-ness. Most men who studied it were morally convinced of his guilt, but full legal proof was wanting. Organs like the *Tribune, Nation,* and

Springfield *Republican* were content to see him escape the penitentiary, but they were convinced that his resignation from the public service and the army ought to be instantly demanded.

Although Grant's eyes were at last partially unsealed to Babcock's true character, it was impossible for him ever to give up completely a prejudice either for or against a man. He now behaved with the most unworthy indecision. The day after the acquittal he announced that he intended to make his son, U. S. Grant, Jr., private secretary.[17] "He said it was hard on his son, as it would put him back a year, but he was compelled to have someone whom he could absolutely trust to open letters, and if he did that he could do nothing else." But two days later Babcock boldly returned—and Grant let him resume his desk in the executive office. On February 29 Fish called at the White House, stalked grimly past Babcock, and bearding Grant, protested in outspoken terms. "Yes," said the abashed Grant,[18] "but Babcock is there only temporarily. An article in the New York *Tribune* the other day stated that he was to be ejected. When I saw that I allowed him to take a message to the Senate; but it will not occur again." On March 1 Babcock was still in the office. Grant called that afternoon on Fish, who lifted his eyes inquiringly:

The President said [writes Fish] he would resign today, and that he had appointed his son as his private secretary, and there was no place for Babcock in the office; that he had promised his resignation today, and the President had waited a half hour before coming to see me for it, but it had not come.

I told him he had nothing to resign. After a moment's pause he smiled and said, "That's true, he's only got to stay away."

That was Babcock's last day in the White House. But he temporarily retained his place as Superintendent of Public Buildings and Grounds; Grant presently appointed him Inspector of Lighthouses; and he saw the President occasionally. In April he was indicted upon the safe-burglary charges, and Shepherd went bail for him. But there was no sign of a movement in the army to force his resignation.

Meanwhile, a campaign of vengeance was begun against Babcock's prosecutors. Of Secretary Bristow's fate we shall say something later; a Damoclean sword hung over his head. To the Cabinet the day after Bab-

---

[17] Diary, February 25, 1876.
[18] Diary, March 1, 1876; these passages explode the fictitious account in Coolidge, *Grant*, 485.

cock's acquittal Grant said: [19] "Now that the trial is over, the question
to be considered is whether Mr. Dyer is to be dismissed." No Federal
officer could have been more faithful to duty than Dyer. A pained silence ensued. No one said a word until Grant himself broke it. A few
minutes later, when Pierrepont remarked that Henderson had presented
a bill for $26,000, the President burst forth belligerently: "I will not
pay Henderson one cent. If he wants to collect anything he can go to the
Court of Claims. I leave it to you, Mr. Pierrepont, if you think Henderson rendered any service whatever to the government." Pierrepont
quietly replied that he had rendered good service, and had been instru-
mental in recovering a great deal of money. Dyer soon made himself
more obnoxious than ever by opposing the applications of various convicted men for pardons. In July Grant had him dismissed. Bluford
Wilson had already prudently resigned. Summary treatment was also
meted out to Yaryan, head of the special Treasury agents, who had
played a leading rôle in exposing the Whiskey Frauds. First an attempt
was made to ruin him by the production of one Moore, a Treasury employee, to swear that a detective named Bell had told him that a lawyer
named Woodward had told him that Yaryan and another revenue officer had brought two distillers to Woodward's office and in his presence
extorted money from them. When Bristow heard this silly tale he dismissed Moore. The President promptly ordered him restored, and subsequently promoted. Then as soon as Bristow was out of the way, Grant
sent another peremptory order directing Yaryan's dismissal, which the
Commissioner of Internal Revenue executed with earnest expressions
of regret.[20]

III

But in these years one scandal did not end before another began.
Corruption had for some time been suspected in the War Department.
On February 10, 1876, the New York *Herald* had called for an investigation. A House Committee under Chairman Hiester Clymer was soon
taking evidence. Early on March 2, while Fish was still abed, Bristow
called in great excitement.[21] Belknap had been exposed as accepting
large payments for an Indian post-tradership. The Committee held
incontrovertible evidence of his conviction, and was about to present a
report with a demand for impeachment. Fish urged Bristow to call

[19] Diary, February 25, 1876.   [20] *Nation*, July 6, 1876.   [21] Diary, March 2, 1876.

upon the President at once with the news.

Unfortunately for the ends of justice, Belknap had heard the report even more quickly than Bristow. Early that morning a friend on the Committee had notified him of its findings. Before ten o'clock he had reached the White House with a resignation on which the ink was hardly dry. It was a bold move to forestall impeachment—for the Committee could not report until afternoon. Grant immediately sat down and wrote: [22] "Your tender of resignation as Secretary of War, with the request to have it accepted immediately, is received and the same is hereby accepted with great regret." This was a rash act, and when he realized the fact he was apologetic if not truly contrite. Fish records that at the Cabinet meeting next day Grant, staring at Belknap's empty chair, made a lame explanation: [23]

The President spoke of Belknap's defection, saying that yesterday he had really, in the first part of the day, been unable to comprehend its magnitude and importance, the surprise was so great that it was really not until evening that he could realize the crime and its gravity. [!] He spoke of his long-continued acquaintance with Belknap in the army, of his having known his father as one of the finest officers of the old army, when he himself was a young lieutenant.

He directed the Attorney-General to consider the law with a view to consider what action could be taken against the late Secretary, either criminal or civil.

He said that he had accepted the resignation on its being tendered, and under the wrong impression, as he did not fully understand the statements of Belknap, who was very much overcome and could scarcely speak. He did not know that acceptance was not a matter of course.

There was little excuse for Grant in being taken by surprise. All officials of the War Department and all well-informed newspaper men knew that some very dubious operations had been countenanced by the Secretary. Only three weeks earlier the Washington columns of the *Herald*, conducted by the able Charles Nordhoff, had fully exposed the way in which Belknap was farming out the trading-posts in the Indian reservations. Its long story showed that in a considerable list of instances the licensed trader paid a share of the profits to some favorite of Belknap or of the Administration. Thus the trader at Camp Supply in Indian Territory paid an Administration favorite $10,000 a year; that at Fort Sill had paid $6,000 a year (as Belknap now confessed);

[22] Woodward, *Meet General Grant*, 426. [23] Diary, March 3, 1876.

that at Fort Dodge $2,000, and so on. The *Herald* stated that a relative of Mrs. Grant received part of the profits of a New Mexican tradership, and one of Babcock's relatives part of those from the Fort Wallace store. The total thus given away to Administration pets reached at least $100,000 a year. And Grant could have obtained information from a closer source—from Orvil Grant, himself a beneficiary. "Let the President," the *Herald* now caustically remarked, "send for his own brother and question him about the money that was made in the Sioux country by starving the squaws and children. The President will find it all printed in the *Herald* of last July, column after column, in great detail from a correspondent sent by us into that country to seek out the frauds."

Belknap, a pouchy-cheeked, beetle-browed, curly-haired man with a tremendous flowing beard and the air of an unctuous politician, had yielded to sheer greed for money. His wife when he came to Washington was a woman of social ambition. His salary was $8,000 a year; she liked to dress expensively, maintain a luxurious household, keep carriages, and give dinners with the best vintages. She knew an astute New York contractor, Caleb P. Marsh, and sometimes visited him and Mrs. Marsh. In the summer of 1870, in return for hospitality, she offered to obtain him a post-tradership. Marsh visited Washington and applied for the tradership at Fort Sill. He was told that the holder, John S. Evans, was also in Washington to ask for a reappointment; perhaps, said Belknap, Marsh and Evans could reach a partnership arrangement. They did. That is, Evans (who had made a large investment at Fort Sill) agreed to pay Marsh $12,000 a year in quarterly instalments for being let alone. Of this sum Marsh agreed to give half to Mrs. Belknap. In the fall of 1870 he sent her the first $1,500; a few weeks later she died. It is possible that Belknap did not know where the $1,500 came from—but the payments were continued.[24]

The Secretary, when the scandal broke, tried to hide behind the skirts of his dead wife. He said that while Marsh's evidence did not incriminate him, it did affect persons so closely "connected with him by domestic ties" as to "greatly afflict him, and make him desire to secure the suppression of that part of the evidence at any cost," and that he had therefore not tried to exculpate himself. A few facts indicate the value of this tale. After Mrs. Belknap died in December, 1870,

---

[24] For full evidence on Belknap's derelictions, see *Cong. Record*, 44th Cong., 1st sess., Vol. IV, which (records of impeachment trial) gives all the facts.

Marsh called on her sister, Mrs. Bowers, to see the baby she had left. He testified: "I said to her, 'This child will have money coming to it before a great while.' She said, 'Yes; the mother gave the child to me and told me that the money coming from you I must take and keep for it.' I said, 'All right'; and it seems to me that perhaps I said the father ought to be consulted. . . ." The baby died in June, 1871. Mrs. Bowers went to Europe. Belknap, unmarried and childless, continued to receive the quarterly payments from Marsh. If he happened to be in New York when they fell due, he accepted them in person; if not, they were mailed to him. After he married Mrs. Bowers, they received the payments together—now cut in half because Evans could not pay more. The total paid was about $20,000, equivalent to two and a half years' salary for Belknap.[25]

Though Grant required an entire day to comprehend the gravity of Belknap's offense, he never expressed to the Cabinet—so far as Fish's diary records—any sense of outrage; while journalists who visited the White House shortly reported that he felt great annoyance over the spirit behind the House investigations. They were being conducted for "partisan purposes." On March 9 the Committee on War Department Expenditures struck close to the President. Orvil Grant, his nomadic brother, frequently mentioned by the press as an adventurer, testified upon his own activities as an Indian post-trader. He said that, having been unsuccessful in other employments, he had applied to the President for a license as an Indian trader; that the President had informed him of four posts from which the traders were shortly to be removed; and that, applying for all four, he at once (1874) obtained them. He placed "partners" in them, who agreed to give him a large share of the profits. To no post did he give any real time or labor; in one only, and that not until a few weeks earlier, did he invest any capital—$2,000. In brief, he received a handsome income for his influence with his brother, as Marsh had received an income for his influence with Mrs. Belknap. Godkin caustically remarked that the essential difference between the President and Secretary lay in this, "that while Belknap allowed his wife to sell traderships and apply the money to his household expenses, the President allowed his brother to sell them and keep the money himself." [26]

[25] See the excellent account in *Harper's Weekly*, March 18, 1876.
[26] N. Y. *Tribune, World*, March 10, 1876, for Orvil Grant's testimony; *Nation*, March 16, 1876, and *Tribune*, March 11 and April 4, 1876, for comment.

But could Belknap be brought to justice? Fish believed that he should both be impeached and criminally prosecuted. Marsh, after first testifying, fled to Montreal, where reporters found him looking "haggard and anxious." But on March 22 he was induced to return to Washington, where he and his wife testified before the House Judiciary Committee and a grand jury. Attorney-General Pierrepont on March 31 called the Cabinet's attention to his availability, and asked its opinion upon a criminal prosecution. The President turned to Fish for advice. "I reply," writes the Secretary, "that under the circumstances I thought that the Administration would be held up to much criticism should it fail, after the announcement it had made of its intention to prosecute, to institute and press such proceedings; that if Marsh's testimony had been correctly reported and there was no other evidence against Belknap than such as had been made public before the Committee, I did not suppose he could be convicted, but that the Administration owed it to itself and the country to press the indictment." Robeson and others concurred, and Grant directed the Attorney-General to proceed. But as Fish feared, the evidence was insufficient for a criminal indictment. Hope for justice had to be pinned to the impeachment proceedings.

While these were pending several Cabinet members showed what Fish thought an improper sympathy for Belknap, and Mrs. Grant threatened to overstep all bounds of prudence. On March 26 she informed the Cabinet members, by messenger, that she wished to see them after their meeting that day. They duly filed into one of the private rooms of the White House. Mrs. Grant, shedding tears, her voice quavering, urged them to show some token of regard for the Belknaps.[27] She wished them and their wives to call at the Secretary's house. Mrs. Belknap, she explained, was overcome by her disgrace. She had asked permission to see Mrs. Grant at the White House, promising to manage the call so as not to be recognized; and Mrs. Grant, while refusing to let her come in secret, had permitted her to call openly the previous Sunday. The Cabinet discussed the subject. It appeared that three members, Robeson, Jewell, and Zach Chandler, had called on Belknap. Fish was shocked. He said with some sternness that he had not called because he felt it better for both the Administration and the Belknaps that he stay away. Robeson was apologetic, explaining that he had made his first call on Belknap as a fellow-Princetonian, and his second

[27] Diary, March 26, 1876.

because the disgraced man had specially requested him to come. He was perhaps excusable; the other two were not. Belknap was on trial for a grave offense against the government, and any indication that he was being given advice or moral support by the Administration would be most unfortunate. There had been more than enough of that in the Babcock case.

Fish and others impressed this fact upon Mrs. Grant. Robeson expressed regret that she had received Mrs. Belknap. He pointed out how important it was to the Belknaps themselves that they speak to no one except their counsel upon the charges against them. By this time Mrs. Grant was again in tears. "I suppose you are right," she said from her handkerchief, "but I do feel *so* sorry for them."

Belknap's counsel first tried to postpone his impeachment trial to December. They then fell back upon the technical plea that since the Constitution limits impeachment to "civil officers of the United States" the Senate has no jurisdiction over any person who has resigned office. This plea, if sustained, would have done much to render the process of impeachment nugatory forever. But late in May the Senate decided, 37 to 29, that it had jurisdiction, and on June 1 the proceedings against Belknap were resumed.

During June and July, 1876, much of the Senate's time was given to the Belknap trial, a happy mode of celebrating the centenary of American independence. The evidence against Belknap was conclusive. Marsh unwillingly but positively swore to all the facts—his application for the tradership, Belknap's request that he "see Evans," his bargain with Evans, and his direct payments to Belknap. Evidence was presented that outsiders had called Belknap's attention to the peculiar arrangement at Fort Sill long before the final exposure. Yet on August 1 Belknap was acquitted by almost a strict party vote. On the first article 37 stood for conviction and 25 against, the required two-thirds thus being unobtainable.[28] Of those who voted not guilty, 23 said they did so because they believed the Senate lacked jurisdiction—though the Senate had definitely decided that question. Conkling sprinkled the proceedings with bursts of rhetoric, declaring that the trial had been "forced by the order of a mere majority," and that this was the "first attempt in our history to stretch the political power of impeachment." He doubtless spoke for Grant, but emphatically not for Fish, who would

[28] Rhodes, *United States,* VII, 191.

have liked to see Belknap properly punished.

By this time the reputation of the Administration was gone. Other scandals, as we shall see, had come to light. In Fish's diary after the spring of 1876 we detect a tone of apathy, as of one who no longer felt either hope or fear for the credit of the government. It was too late for either. The Belknap and Babcock scandals were from one point of view mere episodes whose significance can easily be exaggerated. The petty thievery they represented was of minor import compared with the wholesale extortion that went on under unjust tariffs and tax laws, and the wholesale looting of the West by railroad and mining corporations. But they did have great importance as symptoms of the general laxity which permitted these larger offenses against the American people. Half-awakened to what was going on, the public was now far more nearly unanimous (as a host of journals declared) that Grant should not be permitted a third term than it had been eight years earlier that he should be chosen President. Fish was plainly dejected. He had only one desire, to conclude his custodianship of foreign affairs with credit, and to have done with public office forever. Since the international scene was calm, in the late summer of 1876, for the first time, he took a genuine vacation at Garrison. Most of September and the first half of October he spent on the Hudson, and though he transacted necessary business, for the most part he left affairs in the hands of the capable Assistant Secretary, John L. Cadwalader—a New York attorney who had succeeded Bancroft Davis in 1874. The Presidential campaign was under way; he and others could take comfort in the fact that whether Hayes or Tilden won, the Augean stables would receive a much-needed cleansing.

THE virtual collapse of the Grant Administration during 1876 in all departments save foreign affairs is so impressive a fact that its neglect by most writers upon the period is astonishing. Historians, like the people at the time, have fastened their eyes so completely upon the Hayes-Tilden contest as to ignore the breakdown of the national government. Yet breakdown is not too strong a word. Various Administrations have closed in gloom and weakness—those of the Adamses, Van Buren, Buchanan, Taft, Wilson, and Hoover. But no other has closed in such paralysis and discredit as (in all domestic fields) did Grant's. The President was without policies or popular support. He was compelled to remake his Cabinet under a gruelling fire from reformers and investigators; half its members were utterly inexperienced, several others discredited, one was even disgraced. The personnel of the departments was largely demoralized. The party that autumn appealed for votes on the implicit ground that the next Administration would be totally unlike the one in office. In its centennial year, a year of deepest economic depression, the nation drifted almost rudderless.

Grant's political bankruptcy could not have been better demonstrated than by his penultimate annual message, December 7, 1875. This document, filling twenty-four printed pages of Richardson's compilation, was given strength by just two elements, the twelve pages on foreign affairs by Fish, and the three pages on finance by Bristow. Both were admirable. But the President's contribution displayed a total lack of vision. After a veiled attack upon Catholicism, in which he spoke of the dangers of ignorance when played upon by priestcraft, he urged a constitutional amendment requiring the States to maintain sufficient free elementary schools for the education of all children; forbidding the teaching of religious tenets in schools; and prohibiting the use of school funds or taxes for the aid of any religious sect. He urged that all ecclesiastical property, save cemeteries and perhaps church edifices, should be taxed. Finally, he suggested the stoppage of the importation of Chinese women and the destruction of polygamy. This, with measures to give the nation a sound currency, was his centennial programme!

I

When Congress received this message it was acutely conscious of the impending Presidential campaign. Not a move was made in the Democratic House or Republican Senate without reference to the election. A swarm of House committees was soon investigating the executive departments. At first Fish hoped that little wrongdoing would appear. He wrote a friend [1] that the looseness and extravagance of the war period had doubtless created abuses and left habits of carelessness and waste; "but I think they will find less of intentional wrong than many even of those who have been, and of some who still are, friends of the Republican Party, apprehend." He was quickly disillusioned. The committees discovered gross corruption in the Interior, War, and Navy Departments; they did much to discredit the Department of Justice; they forced the resignation of the Minister to England; and they cast dark suspicion upon Blaine's conduct while Speaker. As the Grant Administration sank deeper into the mire, party captains cautiously detached themselves from it. Men closest to the President, notably Conkling and Oliver P. Morton, were seen to be unavailable for a Presidential nomination. The Republican rank-and-file demanded a reform candidate, like Bristow or Hayes. After the compulsory resignations of the spring and summer, but one man in the Administration retained high prestige and general respect—Secretary Fish.

The Administration did not, it could not, resist the investigations. But Fish's diary shows that they were accompanied by a great deal of friction between Department heads and House leaders. Even Bristow, despite his reformative tastes, resented some House demands. A committee asked him to show it the recommendations upon which a certain Treasury official had been appointed, and the papers bearing upon his subsequent removal.[2] Bristow did so. But the committee then demanded the names of all persons who had spoken to him upon this appointment and removal, with the purport of their statements! This was as indefensible as the demands the Senate later made upon Grover Cleveland under the Tenure of Office Act, which Cleveland so dramatically resisted. Bristow resentfully brought the request before the Cabinet, which decided that it should be ignored. Fish also writes: [3]

[1] To G. S. Orth, December 10, 1875; Letterbooks.   [2] Diary, March 24, 1876.
[3] *Ibid.*

Bristow has received a subpoena . . . signed by the Speaker of the House calling upon him to produce several original papers, some of which he has responded to, but the question is a grave one whether the House has the right to call for such papers. No decision is reached on the abstract question. As the question will probably come up again, I call attention to the fact that the Treasury stands in a different position to Congress from the other Departments; as it makes its report to Congress, while the others make theirs to the President.

Jewell mentions that the Committee on Postoffices and Postroads of the House had sometime since entered a subpoena . . . requiring the production of a large number of papers, including original vouchers to the amount of nearly half a million; that the clerk and messenger of this Committee are both persons discharged from the Postoffice for fraudulent proceedings, and that he is unable to obtain possession of these vouchers.

The House at one point showed distinct impertinence. It passed a resolution by Representative Blackburn calling upon the President to inform it whether he had performed any executive acts or duties at points distant from the seat of government, and if so, for what period and what reasons. This was a revival of the old charge that Grant spent too much time idling at Long Branch. The Cabinet discussed it with much irritation. In due time Grant made a spirited reply, pointing to the long absences of nearly every President since Washington from the capital, and to the efficiency with which public business could be transacted from other points. Meanwhile, the Cabinet had again discussed the "annoyance" of the repeated House resolutions for information, and the "extraordinary range" of its demands.[4]

Grant shortly laid down the sensible rule that no original document might be taken from Departmental files for the use of Congressional Committees. Sworn copies could be taken, and free access to the files was to be permitted; but books and papers which might be essential to executive work must not be removed.[5] Bristow had already acted on this principle, sending sworn copies only and keeping strict account of the cost of making them.

When the Cabinet discussed what course it should take if questioned upon conversations between the President and its members, Bristow again advised a defiant stand. "I shall say that conversations within the Cabinet are privileged and cannot be revealed," he declared. He recalled that when President Johnson's impeachment was about to be

[4] Diary, April 4, April 7, 1876.
[5] Memorandum by Assistant-Secretary Cadwalader in Fish Diary, April 18, 1876.

voted, Secretary Stanton had told Congressional leaders of what took place in several Cabinet meetings. But Bristow thought he had done this hastily or inadvertently. Indeed, James Speed, who had been Attorney-General 1864–66, had told Bristow that he remonstrated with Stanton, who confessed that he had acted thoughtlessly and mistakenly. The Cabinet agreed that all consultations between the President and its members, or between Cabinet members alone, were confidential and should never be disclosed. They agreed also that any member who was called before a Congressional Committee should state this position at the outset.

All this was entirely proper. But the Democratic investigators had ample evidence at hand and discovered a staggering mass of corruption without prying into Cabinet secrets.

Even the State Department, or rather the diplomatic service, did not wholly escape. Everybody knew that Fish's vigilance, industry, and stern integrity lifted his Departmental work in Washington above suspicion. But British victims still complained of Minister Schenck's activities in promoting the Emma Mine swindle. A House Committee under the brilliant Abram S. Hewitt examined Schenck's connection with it. It found what Fish himself should have discovered, and punished by dismissal, four years earlier. In Europe, Schenck's name had become a byword. As an American observer testified, it was seldom mentioned without a laugh, a sneer, or an explosion of wrath.

Schenck's pose as the frank, innocent investor in a reputable property was quickly exploded. It was shown that he had really known nothing of the Emma Mine, a Utah silver holding which bore a shady reputation. When the Emma Company was organized in England he had lent his name as Minister to its advertised list of directors in return for an annual salary of $2,500 and the offer to carry £10,000 worth of stock in his name one year free of charge, with guaranteed dividends. If the stock fell he could surrender his block without loss; if it rose he would profit handsomely. It was for these money payments that he had helped push the company—that even in withdrawing under Fish's orders, he had assured Britons that it was a good investment. When he received inside information that dividends would cease, he had not only disposed of his holdings at high prices but had tried to sell the stock short. Exposure of these manipulations brought Schenck home in disgrace in the spring of 1876, after pleading diplomatic immunity at the London station to avoid a court writ.[6] We may be sure that they gave Fish some self-reproachful hours.

The Hewitt Committee refrained from censuring Fish by the slightest word. It showed that he had acted quickly and properly when he heard of Schenck's directorship. It showed that he believed his order to resign had been promptly and fully obeyed. His error lay simply in his ready acceptance of Schenck's solemn word that he held no interest in the mine that he had not paid for. He knew Schenck as a brave soldier, an earnest member of Congress, a loyal subordinate on the High Commission, an effective Minister to England. He knew how heavy was the financial pressure on our grossly underpaid diplomats; he believed that under this pressure, Schenck had thoughtlessly made an improper connection but dropped it when reminded of his duties. Nevertheless, Fish's negligence in the matter was one of his most serious errors. It would have been much to his credit had he made the investigation which Louis Jennings' charges in 1872 demanded, and anticipated the Hewitt Committee's findings. Without judging either Fish or Schenck too harshly—for the latter was quite right when he wrote in resigning, "Don't send anybody here who is not rich"—we may say that the Ohio brigadier should have been ordered home four years earlier.

II

The investigation of the Navy Department was a far more disturbing matter. Secretary Robeson's conduct of it had long been regarded with suspicion; and now a House Committee brought out facts which to many seemed to require his resignation if not impeachment. It was proved that when he took office in 1869 he had been poor, with less than $20,000 worth of property and a slender law-practise. He had shortly formed business connections with the "grain, feed, and flour commission" firm of A. G. Cattell & Co. of Philadelphia, which did a small business on $30,000 capital and had never possessed any connection with the navy. As the Cattells testified, after Robeson entered office their commission business consisted almost entirely in levying heavy percentages upon contracts with the Navy Department; and it was evident that the contractors paid these sums simply because of their presumed influence with the Secretary. The Cattells grew rich.

[6] For full evidence on the Emma Mine see House Report 579, 44th Cong., 1st Sess.; Nevins, *Abram S. Hewitt*, 301 ff. For the accusation that Schenck was a heavy gambler, and his famous pamphlet on draw-poker, see the *Nation*, February 18, 1875.

So, *pari passu,* did Robeson, who had large money transactions of an ill-defined nature with the firm. Although his savings before he became head of the Navy Department had been meagre, they grew so rapidly thereafter that between April 4, 1872, and April 4, 1876, as the Committee proved through his bank-book, he deposited almost $320,000 with three separate banking houses. One member of the Cattell firm paid for Robeson's property at Long Branch. He likewise made Robeson a present of $3,000, which he listed in a "gratuity account." Of course the Cattells denied that Robeson had any share in their "commission business," but it was a suspicious fact that the firm's bookkeeping was too chaotic to be interpreted, that payments as large as $180,000 had been entered in a lump without itemization, and that important papers had been destroyed.[7]

In July, 1876, the House Committee reported that Robeson was guilty of carelessness, extravagance, and lawlessness, but declared that it found no direct evidence of corruption. The *Sun* and *Tribune* remarked that it was very exacting, and that it would have been surprising if so shrewd a lawyer as Robeson had left much direct evidence available. But his sudden wealth, his relations with the Cattells, who knew nothing of naval business and yet made hundreds of thousands by regular percentages on naval contracts, and the gaps in the Cattells' books, remained unexplained. "We believe that no man in his senses," wrote Godkin,[8] "can read the evidence taken and doubt that a secret partnership existed between the Secretary and the Cattells, by virtue of which they levied toll on contracts and he levied toll on them." The Committee asked the House to refer the question of impeachment to its Judiciary Committee, to report at the next session—which proved too busy with the disputed election to think of anything else. But it recommended the immediate court-martialling of two Paymaster-Generals, the Chief Naval Constructor, and the Engineer-in-Chief, and the commencement of criminal proceedings against two subordinate Naval Constructors. The inquiry revealed anew the lamentable weakness of the navy for aught save coast defence, and the atrocious waste of public funds year after year by the "repair" of worthless ships.

---

[7] See House Misc. Doc. 170, 44th Cong., 1st Sess.; of this enormous report Pt. 3 is most valuable for the Cattells. A. G. Cattell, E. G. Cattell, and Robeson all had cottages at Long Branch. For Robeson's the Cattells paid $13,072; Pt. 3, p. 153. See also House Report 784, 44th Cong., 1st Sess., for "Belknapism in the Navy."

[8] *Nation,* July 20, 1876.

Most painful of all to the country—more painful even than Belknap's downfall—was the House inquiry into the Whiskey Ring Trials. It was not merely that, as the *Nation* remarked,[9] the "revelations of intrigue, corruption, servility, and lying in 'Administration circles' at Washington make up such an exhibition as has never before been presented to the public." Sadder still was the light which the testimony threw upon Grant himself. Bluford Wilson, who had now resigned office, gave the most striking evidence. With convincing honesty, he brought out Grant's intense hostility to the trials and efforts to hamper them in every way possible. He swore that Grant had manifested open chagrin when the law officers of the government refused to surrender their evidence against Babcock to a military court, and had told Bluford Wilson that it was an "outrage." He showed that when Grant had been given confidential evidence against Babcock he had promptly imparted it to his secretary. Both he and Edwards Pierrepont substantiated Nordhoff's statement that Grant had ordered the unwilling Attorney-General to write his circular letter forbidding the use of accomplices' testimony. For the first time the public learned that Babcock had forged a passage in a letter by Bluford Wilson to excite Grant's prejudice; that government detectives had been active in crippling the prosecution in St. Louis; and that Grant had accused Bluford Wilson and Carl Schurz of promoting the trials as a conspiracy against him.

Especially curious was Bluford Wilson's testimony upon Babcock's "sylph" letter ("I have succeeded; they will not go.") Horace Porter, the President's former secretary, had told Wilson that the "sylph" was a disreputable St. Louis woman who had attempted to blackmail Grant; that Babcock and Porter had obtained McDonald's help in getting rid of her; and that later Babcock and McDonald playfully called each other "sylph." Grant denied this story with a contemptuous gesture. But he showed no resentment toward Porter, remaining on friendly terms with him. The "sylph," as a matter of fact, had been a young woman with whom Babcock and McDonald had associated in St. Louis, but whom Grant had never seen. The House investigation (at which Pierrepont, Henderson, Dyer, Broadhead, and many others testified) showed that Grant remained wholly loyal to Babcock so long as only

---

[9] The full evidence before this Committee, one of the most disturbing documents ever published by the government, is in House Misc. Doc. 186, 44th Cong., 1st Sess. Bluford Wilson's testimony, with many original documents, is given p. 353 ff.

the Ring frauds were in question. But when it was alleged that Babcock had been mysteriously involved in the Black Friday affair, and that he had assigned his property to Gardner, the judge-advocate of the proposed military court, Grant had lost confidence in his secretary. As the inquiry ended, Bluford Wilson's friends published documents which showed that the cause of Attorney-General Williams' resignation was the discovery that various blackmailing letters sent the President, his family, and Cabinet members had been written in part by H. C. Whitley, previously chief detective of the Treasury Department but later employed by Williams, and in part by an unnamed person closely related to Williams. Mrs. Grant's hostility to Mrs. Williams now became clear to Fish and others!

This was the more interesting because still another investigation struck near the President himself. A House Committee overhauled the expenditures of the Department of Justice with special reference to the use of the secret service funds. It found that under Williams some suspicious transactions had occurred with Grant's explicit approval. In particular, John I. Davenport, Federal Commissioner and Chief Supervisor of Elections in New York, had been paid more than $40,000 by Grant's order for "preventing frauds" in the metropolis, furnishing no sworn accounts and making out no vouchers. Davenport was called to the stand. He testified that he had been one of Ben Butler's crew during the war, serving on his staff in charge of "scouts and spies." After the war he had performed services for the Republican Party in New York. He had helped the Union League Club promote the two Federal Elections Acts of 1870 and 1871, which provided stringent penalties for fraudulent voting and strict oversight of the polling by Federal officers. Receiving his commissionership and supervisorship under these laws, he had gone to work to dig up evidence of fraud, and had spent $10,000—so he alleged—from his own pocket. Finding that he "was being impoverished," he had asked Grant to have him reimbursed from the so-called secret service fund provided by the second Elections Act. And Grant had obligingly issued the requisite orders.[10]

From a mass of confusing evidence just a few clear facts emerged. Davenport had obtained not only $10,000, but $34,000 additional—most of it on the eve of the election of 1872. For this he was able to prove no service save about $12,000 worth of work in compiling re-

[10] House Report 800, 44th Cong., 1st Sess.

cords of voters. Even as to this it was shown (a) that much of the work had been done by men paid from other sources for it, and (b) that it was begun as a private speculation of Davenport's, and the books remained his property! The whole affair appeared as much a "job" as the raid of another of Butler's protégés, Sanborn, on the Treasury. But while Sanborn's raid had been assisted by Secretary Richardson, Davenport's had been assisted by Grant. The House Committee asked why Grant had not ordered Davenport paid from the judiciary fund? It knew no explanation, "unless it be that every dollar of the judiciary fund has to be accounted for in the Treasury Department, by vouchers showing just how it is spent, and not a dollar of the other fund, which is under the direction of the Attorney-General, has ever been accounted for yet."

Fish had heard rumors of this scandal for some time. When the Senate refused to confirm Williams as Chief-Justice, Mrs. Williams had threatened to use it as a weapon against Conkling. Later, when he was about to be dismissed as Attorney-General, she had apparently used it against Grant himself. It is significant that the House inquiry now deeply alarmed Attorney-General Pierrepont. Fish writes under date of April 20, 1876: [11]

> The Attorney-General, Edwards Pierrepont, called at the Department and expressed great concern at some testimony which had been given before one of the investigating committees.
>
> He had previously told me that Judge Williams had paid about $185,000 to Whitley, the late chief of the detective service, for which no regular vouchers had been returned; that Whitley had been examined before the Committee, and testified that he had paid $40,000 to John I. Davenport of New York, by direction of Judge Williams; that Williams had been examined and had testified to the correctness of this statement, and that he had made the payment by the express order of the President, and that he, Pierrepont, felt very solicitous at this disclosure and feared that serious charges would be made against the President.
>
> In the evening he calls at my house, and says that he has seen the President, who was in company with Robeson.
>
> The President told him that the whole expenditure had been made in accordance with the law to prevent frauds in election. Robeson said it was all right, as there was another law besides this one which justified it; that subject had been discussed in full Cabinet and approved. Pierrepont enquires whether I have any recollection. I have not with regard to the authority of the expenditure of the money.

[11] Diary.

Fish and others had always found it difficult to understand why Grant retained Williams in his Cabinet after his proved dereliction in paying household bills from Department funds. Whitley, who had paid Davenport $40,000 under Grant's orders, was now revealed as Mrs. Williams' collaborator in blackmailing letters. Had Grant been entrapped into an illegal step? Was this the secret of Ben Butler's statement to Rockwood Hoar that he "had a hold" on Grant? Was it the secret of the blackmailing letters? Certainly the Federal Elections Acts did not authorize payments for "preventing" frauds; they merely authorized payments for exposing and punishing them. Pierrepont was evidently still alarmed despite Grant's and Robeson's assurances. At this same call on Fish he showed an impatient desire to get out of the Administration at once. What Fish thought of the matter we do not know. What knowledge he had, if any, of Grant's acts in connection with Williams and Davenport is equally a mystery. From the spring of 1876 his diary lapses into reticence on questions outside of State Department affairs; a reticence which reminds us of his statement to his daughter that, in deference to Grant's good name, he had excluded from this record the worst facts which came to his knowledge.

Still other inquiries reflected disastrously on the Administration. A Congressional investigation of the Freedmen's Bank, which had failed with cruel loss to thousands of poor Negroes, showed that it was a monstrous fraud under the guise of philanthropy.[12] It showed also that its connection with "Boss" Shepherd's District Ring had been very close, the bank lending money freely to Ring contractors on worthless security; and everyone remembered how intimate Shepherd had been with Babcock, and how warmly Grant had befriended the boss. An investigation of the New Orleans Custom House proved that Federal money had been drawn on fictitious payrolls and used for political purposes—and everyone knew that Grant's brother-in-law had controlled the Custom House. The summer of 1876 brought the news of Grant's vengefulness toward those who had pushed the Whiskey Ring trials—the dismissal of the efficient Federal Attorney Dyer in St. Louis; the summary decapitation of Yaryan, head of the special agents in the Treasury Department; and the ousting of John C. New, who as Treasurer had been one of Bristow's ablest assistants. The Commissioner of Internal Revenue, Pratt, was actually gotten rid of because he had

[12] House Report 502, 44th Cong., 1st Sess.

kindly given a letter of regret and recommendation to Yaryan on the latter's dismissal—a piece of *lèse-majesté*.

The summer also brought the news of a tragic event which, to those who knew its inner significance, threw another lurid ray upon the President's acts. One of the most effective witnesses before Hiester Clymer's Committee on War Department Expenditures had been General George A. Custer. He had testified courageously to waste and abuses in the War Department's management of Indian affairs, reflecting sharply on Belknap and others. For this the resentful President had removed him from his command on the eve of the expedition which Sheridan had planned against the Sioux in Dakota Territory. Only after loud public outcry and pronounced manifestations of protest from the army did Grant relent sufficiently to permit him to lead one regiment of 600 men, with the rank of major, in an expedition in which he had expected to be the chief figure. Chafing under the injustice and humiliation, Custer showed less caution than was requisite in approaching tremendously superior numbers of Indian warriors.[13] The night of June 25 found him and his 264 brave soldiers dead on the field of battle in the Little Big Horn Valley.

III

By midsummer the two strongest members of the Cabinet, next to Fish, had willingly left it—Bristow and Jewell. Both had long been under heavy fire. Bristow had acquired a very considerable popularity in the East: his bluff, hearty demeanor pleased the public, his policies as head of the Treasury were recognized as sound, and his destruction of the Whiskey Ring had been a spectacular feat. But the professional politicians detested him. They knew that he had become a veritable symbol of Reform. They knew also, from the first days of 1876, that he would muster a large following in the Republican National Convention. In April and May, when James G. Blaine was laboring under charges growing out of his railroad connections, Bristow's star seemed mounting toward the zenith. Such reform organs as *Harper's Weekly,* the *Evening Post,* and the Springfield *Republican* hoped for his nomination; the reform leaders who met at the Fifth Avenue Hotel in New York in May made it clear that he was their favorite. The natural

[13] See W. J. Ghent's article on Custer, *Dictionary of American Biography,* with citations.

result was that all the machine leaders, all the "stalwarts," all the adherents of the President, joined hands against him. And between Grant and Bristow the breach swiftly became deep and impassable. The President viewed him with open suspicion and dislike, as a traitor to the Administration of which he was a part.

As the antagonism between Grant and Bristow became intense, Fish did his utmost to mollify both and bring them to a mutual understanding. Between January and April, 1876, he talked repeatedly with them. Grant, whose mind had been "poisoned" (a now-familiar term in this connection) by corrupt officials or jealous politicians, was fierce in his prejudices. At first he had blamed Bristow's advisers and satellites; by the spring of 1876 he spoke of Bristow himself in the most scathing terms. He believed that the Secretary had plotted to ruin him by misrepresenting him as a member or ally of the Whiskey Ring. Fish besought Roscoe Conkling to use his influence with Grant against any abrupt break. He represented to other associates of the President the folly of any party schism at the opening of a hard-fought Presidential contest. But all this was in vain; Grant merely hardened his will, while the hue-and-cry against Bristow increased. Late in April dastardly attacks were made upon his official honor. The Secretary met these imputations of corruption with refreshing promptness: he demanded his accusers' evidence, insisted upon clearing up the question immediately, and covered his opponents with shame. Blaine, Oliver P. Morton, and other leaders were meanwhile allying themselves against Bristow as a candidate for the Presidential nomination. They believed that the attacks of reformers upon them were traceable to Bluford Wilson and other friends of Bristow. When General James H. Wilson, brother of Bluford Wilson, proposed Bristow as a member of the Union League Club of New York, the Secretary was ignominiously blackballed.

Early in May, Bristow resolved that he would endure his galling chains but a few weeks longer. On the 15th Fish, going to the White House, found him there. Their confidential talk was immediately interrupted by the arrival of Edwards Pierrepont. The two soon left together, and as they went Bristow poured out his anguish to Fish: [14]

He said he regretted Pierrepont's coming into the room, as he wished to have a conversation with the President in my presence; that his continuance in the Cabinet was exceedingly irksome and disagreeable to him; that the

[14] Diary, May 15, 1876.

President was again under the influence of the Whiskey Ring and accepts their statements, and was about to remove one of Commissioner Pratt's most trusted officers (Yaryan); that he had made up his mind to fix a day when he should retire from the Cabinet; that he was undecided whether to ask him to name the first of June, or the end of the present fiscal year (June 30), but he would not remain longer; that he was being charged with circulating reports against others, when in point of fact there was a band of detectives who were dismissed persons from the (Treasury) Department for fraud and improper conduct who were persecuting him in every possible way—visiting every part of the country where he had ever lived or practised law or done any business, hunting up every case in which he had been employed and every transaction in which he had ever been engaged, misrepresenting them and maligning him; that these persons were impecunious, had an office in Washington, and were supported by funds drawn from New York and directed by those hostile to himself; that he could and would no longer endure the annoyance of his position.

Fish by this time realized that Bristow's early departure was inevitable, and made no demur. He frankly said that the imprudence of several of Bristow's supporters, including Bluford Wilson, was partially responsible for some of the attacks on the head of the Treasury. Other candidates for the Presidential nomination (he meant Blaine, Morton, and Conkling) sincerely believed that the hostility they encountered among reformers had been instigated by the Bristow group, and had retaliated. Bristow at once disclaimed any sympathy with the recent assaults upon his Republican rivals. He was irritated and depressed, and spoke of the action of the Union League Club with evident pain.

For three weeks longer the situation dragged on without change. Grant and Bristow evinced a freezing coldness to each other at Cabinet meetings. Then on June 6, at the close of one such icy meeting, Grant asked Fish to remain. When the room was empty he said confidentially that he and Bristow had held a long conversation the previous day. Bristow had given his resignation, to take effect June 20, that being his forty-fourth birthday and also a date subsequent to the coming Republican Convention. "I wish nothing said of it," cautioned Grant,[15] "for I have not mentioned the fact and will probably not do so until after the Convention."

The announcement, made soon after, was received by the best part of the press and public with profound regret. Bristow was easily the best Secretary of the Treasury since McCulloch; next to Fish, he was

[15] Diary, June 6, 1876.

easily the ablest officer the Cabinet had known since the resignations of Cox and Hoar. He was loved for the enemies he had made. Under a happier star, he might have been Grant's successor in the Presidency, for he had shown strength, integrity, and unyielding courage. It was his misfortune to serve in such an Administration that his very display of courage and reformative zeal made an enemy of its head.

With him departed his fellow-adherent of reform, Postmaster-General Jewell. He had offended the politicians by his stern refusal to let spoilsmen and corrupt contractors play havoc with his department. One of his first acts had been to break up the practise of obtaining postal contracts by a felonious abstraction and examination of competing bids. He had discharged incompetent officers, punished participants in fraud, and made honesty and fidelity the basis of employment. He offended Zach Chandler by refusing to let the Postoffice be made an auxiliary of party politics.[16] A typical spoilsman was quoted as saying, in explanation of the fact that "the boys don't care much for Jewell": "Why, God damn him! he runs the Postoffice as though it was a factory!" It was easy for the politicians to "poison" Grant's mind against him also. As early as June 18 the President spoke to Fish of the urgent desirability of replacing him by another man. Fish protested. "I express my opinion that it is not desirable unless for good reason," he writes.[17] "He, however, seemed strongly inclined to make the change."

Thereafter Grant treated Jewell with brusque discourtesy. On June 18 the Cabinet discussed the fact that although the fiscal year was about to expire, Congress had not yet made appropriations to keep up the work of government. Jewell declared that he would continue to carry the mails, appropriation or no appropriation, a stand in which public sentiment would certainly have supported him. Grant remarked that he must conform to the law, and Jewell replied that he would maintain the mails unless the President gave orders to the contrary. For some reason this offended Grant.[18] Perhaps he thought that Jewell ought to be willing to stop the mails without placing the responsibility upon the Chief Executive! He also informed Fish that Jewell had misrepresented him in making public announcement that the entire Administration

16 These last are his own words; *Nation,* July 13, 20, 1876.
17 Diary, June 18, 1876.   18 Diary, June 27, 1876.

desired a large reduction in Western Union rates upon government telegrams. This announcement had offended the heads of the Western Union, who had evidently come to Grant! He had been brought to a thoroughly prejudiced view of Jewell—and he never abandoned a prejudice. The climax was a scene in which Grant treated his Postmaster-General with downright rudeness—a scene pictured with dry conciseness in Fish's diary:

Monday, July 10, 1876.—Returned yesterday from New York, and called on the President this morning, and found him talking with Jewell of some appointments.

The President manifested much impatience and to several questions which Jewel put answered he would attend to it himself.

He then requested Jewell to leave the room and wait, as he wished to speak to me. As he left the room, the President said he intended to ask him for his resignation, as he could stand his annoyance no longer, and asked me whether I knew Mr. Thompson of Indiana, who he thought had been in Congress while I was in the Senate.

I asked him if he meant Dick Thompson. He looked up his card and found it was Richard W. Thompson. I told him he was, I knew, an uncommonly eloquent man, but I was under the impression that there were some stories connecting his name with some land affairs which were not satisfactory.

He said he thought of appointing him or Tyner as Postmaster-General.

Jewell's resignation also was widely lamented. He was received in Connecticut with warm testimonials of sympathy and esteem. Independent editors amused themselves by compiling a list of heads that had fallen under the Presidential axe within a few weeks—a Secretary of the Treasury, a Postmaster-General, a Commissioner of Internal Revenue, a Chief of Special Agents, a District Attorney, a First Auditor and Fifth Auditor of the Treasury, a Treasurer, and a Solicitor of the Treasury. It would be easy to say that the Secretary of State should, by a prompt resignation, have joined the exodus. His great work was done. His departure would have been a salutary moral protest against Grant's recent acts. There was no longer aught but discredit in a connection with the Grant Administration; with a gesture of austere self-purification, he could have detached himself from it. But Fish still thought—and there can be little doubt that he was right—that his duty lay in driving his furrow to the end.

IV

Meanwhile, the Republican National Convention, meeting June 14 in Cincinnati, had faced a difficult problem. Throughout the early spring Blaine had held the strongest following and his nomination had seemed probable.[19] But on May 31st James Mulligan of Boston had appeared before one of the House investigating committees—and from that hour Blaine's chances sank. He was still an active aspirant, but his explanation of the "Mulligan letters" and of his railway transactions was far from satisfactory. A large field of candidates pressed him hard. One was Oliver P. Morton, who had the support of Indiana and had been diligent in obtaining Carpetbag delegates. Three others were Conkling, Hartranft, and Hayes, the favorite sons of New York, Pennsylvania, and Ohio respectively. Veteran calculators estimated that Blaine would receive nearly 300 votes on the first ballot, Morton about 130, Conkling about 100, and Hartranft and Hayes about sixty each.[20] Bristow's strength was difficult to measure, but it was believed that he controlled more than 100 delegates. If Blaine failed, it would be anybody's race.

Many astute men believed that Fish would be the best possible nominee. President Grant himself concluded shortly before the convention that a "dark horse" would win, and fixing upon Fish as the strongest man, wrote a letter to be used in his behalf if opportunity offered. George William Curtis declared in *Harper's Weekly* that if men were properly informed of the services Fish had rendered during the preceding seven years, they would realize that he stood preëminent among those to be considered for the nomination. Thomas Nast supported this statement by a cartoon in which he presented Fish for President and Hayes for Vice President as the ideal ticket. Kenneth Rayner of North Carolina published a letter in the New York *Times* urging Fish's nomination. But he would be sixty-eight years old before election day; he lacked the support of his State, controlled as it was by Conkling; and he did not want the nomination. He wrote Rayner that he was "not even an aspirant"; that he had been too long behind the scenes not to know how much of the apparent pomp and splendor of office was really

---

[19] Rhodes, *United States*, VII, 209 ff.
[20] Stanwood, *History of the Presidency*, 3rd ed., 313 ff.

but "pain and toil and vexation"; and he wished only to close "with credit the part assigned me in the present role." He was an impartial onlooker at the contest.

As such, the eager manoeuvring of some of the candidates disgusted him. He was displeased by the conduct of Bristow's aides. He was still more displeased by Conkling. That temperamental and imperious autocrat grew petulant when Grant preserved an outward neutrality between him and Morton. He indulged in peevish outbursts, and late in April went to Attorney-General Pierrepont, who had become his supporter, with a set of vehement complaints. Pierrepont reported them to Fish. Conkling grumbled that the Administration had given him no endorsement; that he had received no support from Chandler in the Interior Department, from Jewell in the Postoffice, or (looking Pierrepont full in the face) from the Department of Justice.[21] A little later Conkling came to Fish himself with the same reproaches. He declared that the Administration had never granted him any patronage—though it was notorious that Chester A. Arthur had been made Collector in New York, and Thomas James Postmaster, at his desire. He complained particularly that he had never been given the disposal of any foreign appointment. Fish did not quarrel with the crestfallen leader, whose reproaches sprang from the bitter disappointment of long-cherished hopes that Grant's mantle would fall on his shoulders. The Secretary did, however, compile a list [22] of thirteen or fourteen appointments, including two Ministers, one consul-general, and nine or ten consuls, which had been made on Conkling's written recommendation!

But Blaine's conduct was the most reprehensible. That adroit leader, forced to deal with the charges against him, had staged a *coup de théâtre* in the House on June 5, reading part of the Mulligan letters (nobody knows how much he suppressed) with his own comments. The next Sunday, June 11, he suffered a seizure which made further appearance before the House Committee impossible. This illness, on the very eve of the Convention, was convenient as making further inquiry into the letters impossible, but inconvenient as raising a question of Blaine's physical fitness for the Presidency. The day the Convention opened Blaine called upon Fish to play a part which he found exceedingly distasteful. The story is told in his diary:

[21] Diary, April 20, 1876.
[22] Diary, June 26, 27, 28, 1876; Memorandum, Fish to Grant, July 13, 1876; Fish Papers.

June 14, 1876.— . . . Returning home about 5:30 o'clock, and being engaged to dine at 7 with Mr. Cadwalader, who was sitting with Mrs. Fish and myself in the parlor, Mr. Blaine's son (Walker, I think) called, saying his father asked whether I could take him for a short drive this afternoon, at about 6:30 P. M., in an open carriage.

I told him I would be glad to place the carriage at his disposal, but being engaged to dine at 7, I might not be able to accompany him, but that possibly he might like to drive with Mrs. Blaine. He replied that his mother could not accompany him. I suggested Mrs. Fish, unless he had some other companion. He hesitated, but said he thought his father wished me to ride with him.

I then told him I would call. He thanked me, and remarked, as I thought incautiously, "That will have a right good effect in Cincinnati."

We took the drive, Mr. Blaine indicating the streets through which we should pass. When I returned from dinner, Governor Jewell walked with me to my door, and while standing there Dr. Verdi, one of Mr. Blaine's physicians, passed, apparently coming from Mr. Blaine's house. He stopped, as he said, to thank me for taking his patient out to drive.

I remarked that I hoped there had been no ill consequences from the drive. He replied, "Oh, no. He went to bed soon after, and is sleeping as quietly as a child. But the news has been telegraphed to Cincinnati, and has produced great enthusiasm among his friends."

Blaine had not only advertised his convalescence, but had made it appear that the Administration was solicitous for his early recovery, and that Fish, who actually had never admired him and now regarded him with distrust, was his demonstrative friend.

When the palm went to Rutherford B. Hayes, Fish was well content. He knew that the party could easily have made a far worse choice. Moreover, its unity was now assured. Had Bristow been nominated, the powerful body of politicians aligned with the Grant Administration would have been sulky or hostile. Had Blaine, Conkling, or Morton been named, an equally important body of reformers and independents would instantly have swung to Samuel J. Tilden. With good reason, Hayes was the one candidate who had gained strength on every ballot of the Convention.

The clamor and excitement of the most closely-fought Presidential battle in our history began. When Congress adjourned in mid-August all the activities and scandals of the Grant Administration fell into the background. Men were glad to forget it; glad to fasten their eyes on the promise of a fairer day offered by the Centennial Exhibition in Philadelphia, with its proofs of scientific and educational progress, its imposing exhibits of manufactures, its art-galleries, and its striking new inventions. Fish might now have retired gracefully. But as we have said, he chose the better part in remaining.

v

Why? Why not drop out with Bristow and Jewell, leaving the Administration to unrelieved discredit? For one reason, Fish had piloted the nation's foreign affairs through seven years of fair and stormy weather; was it not his duty to see the remaining eighth of the course well and truly completed? For another reason, Grant's Cabinet was practically re-made during six months of 1876; the steadying hand of its senior member was much needed. For a third, he could still restrain Grant himself from errors dangerous to the nation.

Fish had approved Grant's choice of Alphonso Taft, an Ohio lawyer and judge of high repute, as successor to Belknap in the War Department. We have seen that when Grant proposed to fill the Postmaster-Generalship with Richard W. Thompson, Fish prevented it on the ground that he had been engaged in land scandals. The place went to James N. Tyner, Second Assistant Postmaster-General, who at least represented the principle of promotion. It is related that Grant called him to the White House. "I have decided, Mr. Tyner, to ask for your resignation," he said. Tyner reddened and bowed his head submissively.—"And to appoint you Postmaster-General," said Grant.

Another change in the Cabinet grew out of Schenck's enforced resignation as Minister to England. At the beginning of March, 1876, the British mission was offered to Richard Henry Dana, Jr., an ideal appointment. Fish had been at great pains to bring it about, and to disabuse Grant of the fear that Dana, as a Bostonian and a Harvard graduate, was too heavily impregnated with Sumner's ideas. Though best known for his immortal *Two Years Before the Mast*, Dana was an expert on maritime law and usage, had written much on general legal topics, and in 1866 had brought out a revised edition of Wheaton's *International Law*. Fish hoped that the Senate would confirm him at once. But the nomination met vigorous opposition from three sources: from Ben Butler, who accused Dana of bolting the Republican ticket on several occasions and who especially resented the fact that Dana had contested Butler's Congressional district with him in 1868; from William Beach Lawrence, who charged that Dana had pirated the notes to Lawrence's own earlier edition of Wheaton's *International Law* (1855); and Simon Cameron, who wished to see his son Don made Minister. The intervention of so intellectual a figure as Lawrence was especially deplorable. Fish keenly resented the attempt of his old law-partner to defeat "one of the best nominations that could be made." [23] The Senate Foreign Relations Committee first requested Grant to withdraw the nomination. When, with Fish's backing, he refused to do so, the Committee made an unfavorable report. The question then, in April, 1876, came before the Senate for decision.

Fish knew that the charge of plagiarism against Dana had no real substance. The heirs of Henry Wheaton, who died in 1848, had found repeated editions of his *International Law* called for; they first employed Lawrence, whose well-annotated edition had high value; when some of his opinions gave offence to Northerners during the war, they turned to Dana; and Dana used Lawrence's work as freely as that of other authorities on international law, but not more so. Many of his notes resembled Lawrence's, his translations were almost identical, and he reproduced a quotation of Lawrence's from Blackstone which included a typographical error. But his borrowings were broadly legitimate; he added much original material of his own; and the work was not for his own profit, but that of the Wheaton family, which claimed the sole ownership of Lawrence's notes.[24] Lawrence's waspishness had long been notorious. But for Ben Butler any club sufficed to beat Dana. Cameron, hopeful of an important place for his son, brought Conkling over to the opposition by adroit overtures; he spoke highly of the latter's Presidential aspirations and gave out an interview in which he said that Conkling was steadily gaining strength. Oliver P. Morton joined the hostile alliance. The result was unescapable: to the chagrin of intellectual circles in both England and America, the Senate defeated Dana's confirmation by the emphatic vote of 31 to 17.

The upshot bore out the shrewd calculations of Simon Cameron Grant considered various names for the English post. His first proposal was almost incredible. When Fish and Hewitt discussed the latter's report on Schenck, Hewitt gave as his principal reason for wishing to include some words of censure for the Administration the fact that he had

---

[23] Diary, March 15, 1876; see C. F. Adams, Jr., *Richard Henry Dana*, II.
[24] See the careful examination of this question in the *Nation*, April 6, 1876.

strong ground for believing that Schenck would be allowed to return to London. He had heard that Schenck had gone to the White House and implored to be sent back! Grant now proved that there was truth in this extraordinary story, for Fish writes: [25]

I talk to the President of the action of the Senate in the rejection of the nomination of Mr. Dana. He suggests Schenck again. I tell him that with a sincere regard for Schenck, I do not think it would answer; that the criticism for retaining him has not been confined to the Democratic press, but has been equally strong in a large majority of the Republican papers.

Schenck again! Here alone is sufficient indication of the reasons why it was well for Fish to stay in the Cabinet. Great pressure was exerted for the appointment of a New York attorney named Stoughton. But Fish, who knew the details of a grave scandal connected with his name, protested vehemently. Then Attorney-General Pierrepont, with a suddenness which surprised everybody, decided that he would accept the English mission if it were offered—announcing this decision to Fish on the same day that he expressed fear that Grant would face grave charges over the secret-service expenditures. He would make a good Minister, and Fish assented. This left the Attorney-Generalship vacant, and Grant at once asked how it would do to appoint Stoughton to that office! "I told him," writes Fish,[26] "I feared it would give rise to a great deal of scandal, and I thought it very inadvisable at present to incite any more criticism of public men than possible." For a time Grant thought of appointing Wayne MacVeagh, a choice which Fish warmly approved. But after consulting with various Senators, and especially Cameron and Conkling, the President decided to move Alphonso Taft from the War Department to the Attorney-Generalship, and to select Don Cameron for the former position.

Don Cameron, as readers of *The Education of Henry Adams* know, was a man of character and ability, with a wife (the niece of John Sherman) of wit and beauty. Yet his appointment was astonishing. A man of forty-three, he had never held office, was known only as the head of a small railroad, the Northern Central, which had recently been absorbed by the Pennsylvania system, and had no claim to a Cabinet position save as the son of Simon Cameron. Political commentators

25 Diary, April 6, 1876.
26 Diary, April 25, 1876. Fish proposed Cortlandt Parker of New Jersey, a gifted man who refused diplomatic appointments under Hayes and Arthur, for the place.

surmised that he owed his appointment to a bargain between his father and Conkling, by which the Pennsylvania delegation was to be swung to Conkling in the Republican Convention, and Conkling was to furnish White House favors in return.[27] Though the event at Cincinnati did not bear out this surmise, this was perhaps because Conkling's chances were seen to be hopeless. At any rate, he was far better than Stoughton.

But Fish's chief service in connection with the Cabinet was in helping Grant select a fit successor to Bristow. The President's first impulse in filling the Treasury was not to find an able administrator of finance, but someone acceptable to leading politicians and ready to help eject Bristow's aides in the Whiskey Trials. Speaking with Fish in June, he suggested another Cabinet shake-up; moving Zach Chandler from the Interior Department or Don Cameron from the War Department to the Treasury! Of the two he preferred Cameron. Fish objected to these transpositions. He objected also to the men. "I ask," he writes,[28] "if he is sure of Cameron's being sound on the currency question, saying that his father is a little shaky, and that it is most important that he should not only be strong but aggressive." So it was; an unfriendly Secretary could easily cripple the Resumption Act of 1875. Don Cameron's views were uncertain, and he later became an outspoken silverite. When Fish suggested the name of Senator Lot M. Morrill, Grant caught at it "very cordially." Morrill had paid close attention to finance, opposed the Inflation Bill, and ardently supported the Resumption Act. The President at once made the appointment— and no better Secretary could have been found.

Thus between February and July, 1876, the Cabinet was virtually remade. New men were administering the Treasury, the War Department, the Department of Justice, and the Postoffice. Of the older members, Robeson was left without reputation and facing possible impeachment; Zach Chandler was being permitted—very improperly—to give most of his time to managing the Republican national campaign. Since the beginning of his term Grant had been served by twenty-five Cabinet ministers, with a longer list of resignations and replacements than any other President in our history can show.[29] Save for Fish, he had systematically gotten rid of the ablest and most upright of his Cabinet

---

[27] *Nation*, May 25, 1876.   [28] Diary, June 19, 1876.
[29] This includes Sherman in the War Department, and one other temporary incumbent. Theodore Roosevelt had 18 different men in the Departments represented in Grant's Cabinet.

officers within a short time after their appointment. Rockwood Hoar, taking office in 1869, had gone out in 1870. Jacob D. Cox had kept his place hardly longer. The able Bristow and faithful Marshall Jewell had been retained for only two years. Had Fish now resigned, the inexperienced and ill-assorted Cabinet would have lacked the one mentor and guide who gave an element of statesmanship to the Administration.

VI

To the very end Fish was resolved to permit no meddling with his Department by the political gangsters who infested the capital, and to repel every attack upon his prerogatives. In April, 1876, he crossed swords with Zach Chandler in a significant way, foiling his and Senator Conkling's effort to stultify the President in order to gain a petty political object. The scene was a Cabinet meeting on the 7th. Chandler remarked that one Parsons, a Federal office-holder in Albany, wished to accept a nomination for State office. Conkling had asked him to obtain from the President an exception to the Executive Order of 1873 which forbade Federal appointees to run for State office unless they first resigned. This was one of the most salutary orders Grant had ever issued, and Fish bristled resentfully. He writes in his diary: [30]

This Executive Order was issued through the Department of State. The head of that Department is from the State in which Albany is situated, and of which Conkling is Senator, but he (Conkling) selects the Secretary of the Interior to do such work.

The President without hesitation said, "Yes, if he is a Republican, and he must be, if Conkling wants it." I said, as quietly as possible, that "This revokes your Executive Order." The President said, "The order was intended to prevent a number of Federal officers filling the legislatures of Southern States."

I answered, "It went much further, and much correspondence took place, and a particular definition was made and published of local offices which could not be held by Federal officers, confining those which could be held principally to school offices and the like." The President said he had relaxed it with reference to several smaller towns and villages, to which I replied that the order had been officially proclaimed through the proper Department, and there had been no official or authorized public revocation in any case. Chandler said, "Then I will tell Conkling you authorize the acceptance of the place."

Sometime later, towards the close of the meeting, the President asked

[30] Diary, April 7, 1876.

Chandler where the place was that the office was to be held, adding that he had remitted the order in some small towns, etc. Chandler replied, "Albany." I added, "The capital of the State of New York." After a moment's pause the President said, "I do not think he ought to take the place." Chandler said, "Cannot I tell Conkling that you will allow it?" "No," said the President, "I must stand by the order." "Then," said Chandler, "must I tell Conkling that he cannot hold it?" The President answered, "Yes."

Early in the summer, again, he had stood like a rock in preventing the consumation of Tom Murphy's final attempt to raid the Treasury. We have noted that on January 27, 1875, Grant came to Fish with the strange story that Murphy had disbursed a large sum as the second year's rental for Samana Bay, and had asked if Fish could not repay it out of the funds of his Department. When Fish said no, he had asked if payment could not somehow be arranged without recourse to Congress.[31] Murphy offered no proof of disbursement. Even if he had, Congress had never authorized the payment of rental. The Jay Cooke Papers indicate that Murphy, Jay Cooke, Henry D. Cooke, and Spofford, Tileston had advanced the rental, but that Collector Murphy's share of the payment had been small, and that Spofford, Tileston had bargained for certain private advantages in return for their outlay.[32] Nevertheless, Murphy finally asked $150,000 for all concerned, and Grant had wished the Secretary to assist in obtaining it!

Now the claim was adroitly resurrected. On July 14, when Fish was with Grant at Deer Park, Md., Murphy unexpectedly called at the State Department. He had evidently chosen the moment of Fish's absence.[33] To Assistant-Secretary Cadwalader he explained that William Windom of Minnesota, chairman of the Senate Appropriations Committee, was about to send the Department a message asking what sum had been due to Santo Domingo for the lease of Samaná Bay. Conkling, he went on, had arranged to include Murphy's claim for $150,000 in the Sundry Civil Appropriations Bill, slipping it into the measure in Conference Committee, so that it would not be debated by the two houses. But Windom had asked for more information upon the item, and was hence sending a telegraphic inquiry. He wished Cadwalader to furnish the right answer. The amount which had been paid by him-

---

[31] Diary, January 27, 1875.
[32] Henry D. Cooke to Jay Cooke, July 13, 14, 1871; Jay Cooke Papers.
[33] Diary, July 14, 1876.

self and other patriotic men for the second year's rental, he explained, was $150,000; he was now to be repaid $50,000, and Spofford, Tileston were to get the remaining $100,000. If Cadwalader would simply send Windom a telegram to the effect that the State Department considered the item proper, the Senator would be satisfied and the appropriation would pass!

But Cadwalader was no simpleton. "Does Senator Windom understand the facts about your advancing the money?" he inquired. "No," admitted Murphy. Then, seeing that he had blundered, "Yes." Some further conversation ensued. "Well," Cadwalader finally said, "I do not believe in your claim. I will not stand in the way of getting the money out of Congress if Congress wants to give it. But I will certainly not send Windom a telegram which he will regard as the assent of the Department to the justice of the claim and the propriety of an appropriation. And you had better not have me answer any questions about it. If I do, I might hurt your scheme for an appropriation." Murphy waited for half an hour, and then left. He had barely gone when Windom's telegram to Fish arrived. It read: "Have the United States paid the amount due under lease of Samaná Bay? If not, how much is due and for what time?" Cadwalader telegraphed: "In the absence of Mr. Fish I cannot reply to your telegram just received." [34]

Fish did not return to his desk till four days later. The day before he came back Murphy sent a despairing telegram to Grant at Deer Park: [35] "Committees of both houses have agreed to the payment of one year's rent for Samana if the Secretary of State will telegraph Senator Windom today that such rent is past due and unpaid. Tomorrow will be too late. T. M." This message reached Fish's desk with the following White House endorsement: "Mr. Murphy says it is most important to have this matter attended to at once, and the President has directed me to send you a copy of the dispatch and ask you to consider it at once. Very respectfully, U. S. Grant, Jr., Secretary." Grant knew better than to *direct* Fish to take favorable action! He would instantly have had the Secretary's resignation had he done so. Fish at once sat down and wrote Windom the following note, a flat refusal to approve the claim: [36]

[34] Windom to Fish, Cadwalader to Windom, July 14, 1876; Fish Papers.
[35] Murphy to Grant, July 17, 1876; Fish Papers.
[36] Fish to Windom, July 16, 1876; Letterbooks.

For the purpose of explanation, I enclose a copy of the agreement respecting Samana Bay, entered into by General Babcock with the Dominican Government, the history of which agreement, so far as the action of the Senate is concerned, is known to you.

I am not aware of any payment made to the Dominican Government on account of the occupation of the Bay other than one year's rent paid in advance.

I also enclose herewith Executive Documents Nos. 17 and 34, 41st Congress, which give, I believe, all the information on the subject in the possession of the Department.

The following evening Grant requested Fish to call at the White House. He said in a rebuking tone that Murphy had complained that this letter to Windom would do him no good. Fish might have replied that he did not wish it to! He more tactfully contented himself with remarking that he had given Windom all the facts but had avoided any legal conclusions. "In the course of the conversation," he records,[37] "I told him that I had on several occasions advised Murphy that neither the President nor I could present the case to Congress unless a demand were made by the Dominican Government; that Murphy had said he would obtain such demand, but that I had learned the Dominican Government had been fully paid, and that the claim was now held by Murphy and Spofford & Tileston of New York. He remarked, 'That's true, it's a claim of our own citizens and should be treated as such.' "

This incident requires no comment. Murphy may have been entitled on moral though not legal grounds to a small payment. He was certainly not entitled to $50,000, for the papers of Jay Cooke show that he and Henry D. Cooke had advanced a lesser sum ($20,000 or $30,000 at most) to save the Samaná lease. Their motives may have been honorable.[38] But Spofford, Tileston had speculated in Santo Domingo affairs with dirty hands, and the attempt to give them $100,000 was indefensible. The methods used by Murphy, Conkling, and Grant himself in trying to slip the appropriation through without Congressional debate or notice were worse than indefensible. It is pleasant to record that they failed and that no payment was made. It is not so pleasant

[37] Diary, July 19, 1876.
[38] Henry D. Cooke wrote his brother Jay Cooke on July 13, 1871, that he was disgusted by the speculative activities of Spofford, Tileston & Co.; but "we agreed to advance part of the amount purely from patriotic motives—to save the credit of the government and to prevent the forfeiture of its lease from San Domingo." He added that "if the other parties back down, we may have to advance 20 or even 30,000 to make up the deficiency." Jay Cooke Papers.

to note that, though the Congressional inquiries should have placed the Administration on its mettle to avoid further criticism, this failure was received with chagrin in the White House.

It is in episodes such as this that Grant's moral obtuseness jars most painfully upon those who recognize the essential rectitude of the man. A strange myopia, a spiritual blindness, prevented him from seeing improprieties and delinquencies which shocked more sensitive people; and when his personal loyalty to associates was involved, his blindness seemed positively deliberate. It is only when we recall his long years of friendless hardship and misfortune that we can partially understand his inability to perceive wrongdoing in those who had gained his comradeship.

As Fish had played no part in the campaign of 1872, so he stood wholly aloof from that of 1876. He did not believe that a Cabinet officer should throw himself into a national election, and in his diary expressed emphatic disapproval of Zach Chandler's service as National Chairman. At first President Grant, for different reasons, also stood aloof. This quasi-neutrality of the two leading figures of the Administration proved a fact of cardinal importance for the future. When the campaign ended in a disputed election, they were in a position to take a reasonably impartial stand, and to resist the partisans who demanded drastic military action to hold the Southern electoral votes for Hayes. In the end Grant was to display a firmness and elevation which enabled him to close his eight years in the White House in a manner truly worthy of his reputation. Fully told, as at last it can be, the story is a dramatic one.

It was natural for Grant to view the campaign with mixed feelings. He had congratulated Hayes on his nomination and predicted his victory in November. But when he read the candidate's letter of acceptance, which warmly endorsed civil service reform, promised that the South would be allowed to govern itself without Federal interference, and declared against a second term, he was deeply offended. To an Ohioan who called at the White House, he said that the letter was in bad taste, for it reflected upon the policies of the Administration.[1] Hayes found it necessary to write the President a hasty explanation, declaring that his remarks had been intended to unite all factions of the party.[2] Nevertheless, Grant remained suspicious. Hoping that the Republicans would win, he felt little satisfaction in the thought that a reformer of Hayes' stripe would take his place. Most of the newspapers and former Liberal Republicans engaged in attacking "Grantism" swung into line behind Hayes, and confirmed the President in his feeling that his enemies had captured the party. There were moments when he thought that Tilden's victory might be the best result after all.

His uneasiness and resentment were not lessened by the treatment he received from Hayes' supporters as the campaign developed. Carl

[1] N. Y. *Tribune*, July 15, 1876; Hesseltine, *Grant*, 407.
[2] Hayes, *Diary and Letters*, III, 334.

Schurz did not hesitate to lard his speeches with sharp criticism of the Administration. Evarts, Bristow, and others implied it if they did not state it. As for the Republican press, half of it extolled Hayes as the very antithesis of Grant. Whitelaw Reid in the *Tribune,* Samuel Bowles in the Springfield *Republican,* and Curtis in *Harper's Weekly* sounded this note day after day. The *Nation* rejoiced [3] over "the break in the peculiar system of administration called Grantism which the election will in any case bring." Incensed by such statements, Grant tried to put an end to them. Washington soon rang with gossip upon the efforts of the National Committee to bridle some of its speakers. Grant's own organ, the *National Republican,* printed fierce denunciations. But men like Schurz, Bristow, and Jacob D. Cox could not pretend that the Republican régime had been a model of pure efficiency and that the talk of necessary reforms was iniquitous; they continued to speak their minds, and Grant continued to harbor resentment.

I

While the "Stalwart" politicians disliked Hayes as much as he did, they could not afford to sulk. Many of the Old Guard hoped for a political future, and they had to maintain a place in the party organization. Simon Cameron, Oliver P. Morton, Blaine, and Boutwell were soon strenuously engaged for Hayes, and even Conkling, after pleading ill health, took a tardy place on the stump. These men realized that Hayes' election would wipe off old scores, and serve as an Act of Indemnity and Oblivion for their misdeeds. They also comprehended that if they won votes and established a claim to gratitude, party usage would include them among the beneficiaries of the new Administration, and Hayes would disregard their pretensions at his peril.[4] Perhaps the most singular feature of the canvass was Zach Chandler's appearance as manager of a "reform" battle. The arch enemy of civil service reform, largely responsible for Jacob D. Cox's dismissal, the chief advocate of assessments upon Federal employees, strove to elect a candidate pledged to abolish all that he stood for. The campaign leader in New York, Alonzo B. Cornell, had just rebuked the Union League Club there for its "impudence" in passing resolutions in favor of pure government. Altogether, the Hayes canvass was an extraordinary spectacle.

[3] November 2, 1876.
[4] See the article by Charles Francis Adams, Jr., in *North American Review,* October, 1876.

Though Grant remained chilly, most of his Cabinet hurled themselves into the battle. While the Secretary of the Interior gave it all his time, the new head of the Treasury, Lot M. Morrill, made a speech in New York full of dire predictions of financial disaster if Tilden were elected. The Springfield *Republican* called it "a foolish and wanton attack on the public credit" which he had sworn to defend. All the Custom House forces were again marshalled in support of the party. The levies on Department clerks and letter-carriers were as relentless as if the practise had never been condemned. High officials assailed Tilden's record as an income-tax payer with statements professedly based on government documents. The new Attorney-General exerted his extensive influence in the South, where he controlled a host of employees.[5] When the struggle was over Godkin wrote (December 7): "The conduct of Chandler and Taft during the late campaign ought, as well as Morrill's, to be made illegal." That of Fish stood in sharp contrast with it.

One picturesque episode of the summer, which furnished Fish's only connection with the campaign, was the enforced return of William M. Tweed to American shores from Vigo, Spain. Various Republican leaders hoped that the boss, tracked down after a long search, could be used as a witness against Tilden. He might throw light on Tilden's early relations with Tammany and on his income tax payments. Grant himself took pleasure in the idea.[6] The story of Tweed's capture is interestingly related, with some new facts, in a letter by Fish to Thurlow Weed:[7]

The history of Tweed's arrest is briefly this. In June last our consul-general in Havana reported that two persons travelling with American passports had been clandestinely landed in Cuba, near Santiago de Cuba, whither they were conveyed by a fisherman and were arrested and placed on board one of the Spanish men-of-war.

The consul at Santiago was instructed to look after them and see that they were protected in all their rights. He intervened in their behalf and procured their release from close confinement on board the vessel, and obtained permission for them to come on shore, guaranteeing their presence, etc. Suspicion arose that one of them was Tweed, which was subsequently so far confirmed that the consul-general reported it to the Governor-General of Cuba, who

[5] Grant made some dismissals and appointments to strengthen the party. The choice of Tyner of Indiana as Postmaster-General was supposed to help Republican prospects in Indiana. Prompted by Illinois Republicans, Grant in August requested the resignation of J. Russell Jones as Minister to Belgium "for the good of the party." Grant Letterbooks, August 13, 1876.

[6] Grant to Fish, September 13, 1876; Fish Papers.

[7] Fish to Weed, October 20, 1876; Letterbooks.

agreed, with the assent of the government at Madrid, to surrender both persons to the U. S., and arrangements were making to that effect, when in violation of the understanding (as is reported to the Department), Tweed escaped, sailing in a Spanish vessel for Vigo. The Governor-General, learning his escape, dispatched a steam vessel of war to intercept the other, but it failed in the pursuit. The facts were telegraphed to Madrid, and the government then issued orders to various ports to watch the arrival of the vessel and arrest the two fugitives. . . . After a long voyage the vessel with the persons on board arrived at Vigo, and the two persons were immediately arrested, and our chargé at Madrid was notified of the fact, and that they would be sent back to Cuba, etc. Subsequently the Spanish Government *intimated* to our chargé that it would be more agreeable to them to deliver them in Spain, and as the *Franklin* was under orders to be at Gibraltar (on her return home, as I was informed) within a day or two, she was ordered to proceed to Vigo to receive the parties.

Immediately on the arrival and arrest at Vigo the fact was telegraphed to the N. Y. *Herald* and was published. The sheriff of New York, within a very few days, addressed the State Department, requesting the general government to obtain the return of Tweed to his custody . . .

Fish felt, as did Grant, that Governor Tilden and the New York sheriff had shown a plentiful lack of eagerness for the recapture of Tweed. They had left his pursuit entirely to the Federal Government. Tweed told interviewers that he had sought Spain because his advisers had told him it had no extradition treaty, and "good old sherry" was "very cheap." He impartially assailed Tilden, the Spanish Government, and Fish—but he did not reach home until after the election. It was too late for any damaging revelations.

To the end Grant maintained a correct course in the campaign. He was under great and constant pressure to use the mailed fist in the Southern States, but he made no really improper concessions to it. Many Republicans genuinely feared that Tilden, if elected, would be under the control of Southerners who would destroy the rights of the Negroes and demand compensation for their losses in the war. William A. Wheeler, candidate for Vice President, asserted that the Southern people regarded the 13th, 14th, and 15th Amendments "precisely as the French provinces did their cession to Prussia at the point of the bayonet." [8] So intelligent a man as Edwards Pierrepont, writing from the calm vantage-point of London, assured Elihu Washburne that he knew the "real sentiment" of the South—"it is that they have been impoverished by the North

[8] *Nation*, August 31, 1876.

and that if the chance comes they mean to be paid back what they have lost." But other Republicans, like Blaine, tried to revive the passions of the Civil War simply as a means of gaining votes. "We are dealing with a new rebellion," declared Senator Edmunds, who knew well the falsity of his words. The Republicans could obviously not carry a single State of the South but for the remnants of Federal control there, and Grant was besought to reinforce this control.

In one State the rash Democrats supplied genuine reasons for interference. On July 5–6 a riot at Hamburg, S. C., caused the brutal slaying of a number of inoffensive Negroes. The "massacre" was precisely what Grant with a quaint anti-climax called it: "cruel, bloodthirsty, wanton, unprovoked, and uncalled for." When Governor Chamberlain inquired by letter whether the President would supply Federal troops if further disorders made them necessary, Grant advised him to stand firm, "and I will give every aid for which I can find law or constitutional power." He added Mississippi was governed through officials chosen by fraud and violence, and that Louisiana had been the scene of equally deplorable violence. This warning, though extreme in its language, was not amiss.

The disorders in South Carolina continued. Determined to elect Wade Hampton as Governor if not Tilden as President, the whites formed "rifle clubs" and "sabre companies" and in some counties began a wholesale intimidation of voters. Chamberlain issued a proclamation early in October calling attention to the lawlessness of two counties, citing a long list of outrages, and ordering the clubs to disband. The Democrats still showed a defiant and turbulent spirit. On October 12 Grant and Fish met at the Fifth Avenue Hotel in New York to discuss the situation. The President expected a formal request for troops from Governor Chamberlain: [9]

He said he felt strongly inclined to grant it [military protection], but not yet having received official information or the facts in detail, he would await [them], but asked my opinion on the presentation, as stated by him, to be communicated by Chamberlain's letter, remarking that it was a grave measure. I thought that if the official presentation of facts should sustain the representations as stated by him, that it might be his duty to issue a proclamation.

I enquired whether the Attorney-General was in Washington, and advised that whatever communication he received from Chamberlain should be submitted to his careful consideration.

[9] Diary, October 12, 1876. For the situation in South Carolina, see F. B. Simkins and W. H. Moody, *South Carolina During Reconstruction.*

The President said that he should not act on so important a subject without most thorough consideration, but that if he did act, it would be efficiently and thoroughly, and would mean "work," as he should send all the available troops into the State to preserve peace. To my inquiry how many he could send, he replied several thousand.

Fish dwelt upon the importance of consideration and care. The request from Chamberlain soon came. On October 17 the President and Cabinet decided to comply with it, and Grant issued a proclamation declaring a state of insurrection and ordering all persons implicated to disperse within three days. Secretary Cameron the same day instructed Sherman to send all the available forces in the Atlantic Department to General Ruger at Columbia. Most independent editors supported the step. Bryant's *Evening Post,* which had long opposed military action at the South, declared the proclamation proper, for there was enough evidence of violence on both sides in South Carolina to make it dangerous to reject the governor's application. The whites received the troops good-humoredly, Ruger promised that they would maintain order fairly, and their presence relieved the tension.

II

Election day, November 7, raised the curtain upon one of the most striking dramas in American political history. Fish, after voting in New York, joined Grant in Philadelphia to attend the closing of the Centennial Exhibition. At dinner at George W. Childs' house on the 9th Grant and he discussed with the other guests the amazing result of the election: Tilden certain of 184 votes, Hayes certain of only 166 but claiming 185, and Louisiana, Florida, and South Carolina in dispute. As they sat talking, reports were brought the President of grave disorders in the South. Alarmed by them, Grant and Fish hurried to the Western Union offices in Philadelphia. Here, as Fish writes,[10] they "heard of the wrecking of trains, tearing up of telegraph wires, and general disturbances." Forces were already available in Louisiana and South Carolina, and Grant at once ordered General Ruger to Florida with troops. He gave him no specific directions. Fish, as they returned to Childs' house in their carriage, suggested that instructions were needed; and next morning the President telegraphed General Sherman asking him to order both Ruger in Florida and Augur in Louisiana to preserve order and to pro-

[10] Diary, November 10, 1876.

tect the legal boards of canvassers in their duties. Fish had written out a sentence: "Either political party can afford to be disappointed in the results of the election, but the country cannot afford to have the result tainted by the suspicion of illegal or false returns." Grant included this in his telegram, and it made a marked impression on the country.

Weeks of tense excitement followed. The first Cabinet meeting after the election, November 14, was largely given over to discussion of the possible necessity of precautions against violence and rioting. The President had been warned to take special measures against assassination. Wild tales were flying about. Fish met Colonel John S. Mosby, the Confederate cavalry leader, who by giving firm political support to Grant ever since 1872 had incurred much obloquy in the South; he was a resident of Warrenton, Va., where he practised law. It was he who had coined the reproachful phrase "the solid South," and he had labored for Hayes' election. "He told me," writes Fish,[11] "that the language of the Democrats now was more desperate and more threatening and violent than that of the Southern men on the election of Lincoln in 1860." A warrant for his arrest having been sworn out simply because he had prevented a Democrat from clubbing a Negro at the polls—so he said—he had fled from home. He feared that if Hayes were declared elected there would be bloodshed, and he had heard Democrats say that Grant must be the first man put out of the way. But Fish remained cool.

His coolness was particularly valuable when it became evident that several Cabinet members wished the Federal Government to go much further in interference at the South than he thought proper or constitutional. As he had stood against Belknap and Williams in the Louisiana troubles of 1874, so now he prepared to stand against their successors. For Don Cameron and Alphonso Taft, Secretary of War and Attorney-General respectively, joined hands with Zach Chandler and the discredited Robeson in an effort to commit the President to harsh military measures. It was natural for Zach Chandler, Republican Chairman, hater of the South, and lifelong exponent of rough-and-tumble politics, to take this stand. The tall, handsome Cameron, with his business background, lack of any marked insight, and long schooling in the Pennsylvania machine, also found it natural. But a better attitude might have been expected from Taft. This big, smooth-shaven jurist, so portly that chairs groaned under him, his broad brow speaking intellect and his

[11] Diary, November 14, 1876.

tight-pressed lips determination, unfortunately represented the essence of conservatism. Nearly as old as Fish, a graduate of Yale in 1833, he was a Republican of the hardshell school; and spending most of his life in the border-city of Cincinnati, he had learned to suspect and hate the Southern temper. Fortunately, the Grant of 1876 was not the Grant of 1874.

Fish's suspicions of a Cabinet intrigue were first aroused when on November 18 he learned by chance—through a casual word of gossip in the Washington *Star*—of a secret meeting of four members the previous day. When he made inquiries, Robeson and Taft gave him two materially different accounts of it. But he discovered that Zach Chandler, Cameron, Taft, and Robeson had met, apparently by preconcerted plan, in Taft's office just after the general Cabinet session. William E. Chandler of New Hampshire had just gone to Florida as an agent of the Republican National Committee. Here he was moving heaven and earth to turn a small Democratic majority into a Republican majority, and needed all the help he could get. He had written an imploring letter to Cameron, which the four Cabinet members discussed. Cameron had drafted a detailed reply; and at the end of the conference they had telegraphed Chandler that the views expressed in this reply would be given prompt execution. Taft did not tell Fish what these views were. The episode irritated the Secretary, who did not believe the Cabinet should be made an auxiliary of the Republican National Committee.[12]

But Grant had been taught a well-remembered lesson by the public condemnation of his acts in Louisiana and Arkansas in 1874-75, while he had no desire to pull Hayes' chestnuts out of the fire. He acted circumspectly. On November 26, a cold, stormy Sunday, rheumatism kept Fish home from church. Suddenly he was summoned by messenger to an emergency Cabinet meeting at the White House. Word had reached the President that the "rifle companies" in South Carolina intended to muster an army of 7,000 or 8,000 at Columbia two days later to overawe the Legislature which was to assemble at that time. Governor Chamberlain had appealed to Grant for protection against violence. The Cabinet decided that the call must be met; Grant directed Cameron to "sustain Governor Chamberlain in his authority against domestic violence"; and Cameron had troops concentrated at Columbia. This was proper enough. Violence was actually threatened, and the press reported that

[12] Diary, November 18, 1876.

the truculent rifle companies intended to install Wade Hampton in the Governor's Mansion by force. Troops should be at hand.

At first there was general confidence in the impartiality, moderation, and good sense of the Federal officers in Columbia. But unhappily, the troops acted under Chamberlain's orders to occupy the State House itself. On the 28th, contesting delegations of Republican and Democratic legislators arrived from two counties, Edgefield and Laurens. Sentries admitted the Republicans and excluded the Democrats. The former were thus enabled to claim a quorum—though they lacked a clear majority; the latter withdrew in a body to set up their own legislature, and awaited an opportunity to move back into the State House.

These events set the background for a stormy Cabinet discussion on Thanksgiving Day, November 30. Fish was seated with his family at a heavily-laden board when, just after one o'clock, Secretary Cameron called. He held telegrams from Governor Chamberlain and General Ruger. They announced that the Democrats had now obtained possession of the Assembly Hall in Columbia and organized their House there, with the Speaker and Clerk in their usual chairs. Chamberlain asked that Secretary Cameron order the troops to expel them; Ruger stated that he was waiting for directions. "Well?" inquired Fish. He had foreseen for several days that the more extreme Republicans would ask Grant to repeat in South Carolina, with slight differences, what he had done in Louisiana two years earlier. In 1874 troops had been used to drive Democratic claimants from the State House; now they would be used to exclude Democratic claimants.

Cameron admitted as much. "I propose," he said, "to instruct Ruger to remove the Democratic Speaker and Clerk, to put the Republicans in their places, and to expel and exclude from the State House the Democrats from Edgefield and Laurens Counties." At this Fish exploded: [13]

I object strenuously to any such orders or to any force being employed by the military other than in the repression of violence.

He urges that unless this be done the Republicans in Florida and Louisiana will lose heart and abandon their States.

I regret that if such should be the result, but earnestly insist that no wrong step should be taken on the part of the Federal Government, and that the military shall not be employed to control the organization of a State Legislature.

[13] Diary, November 30, 1876.

The discussion was transferred after dinner to the White House. Fish, Cameron, Taft, and Grant all assembled in the Cabinet room. Again Cameron, a rapid, impetuous speaker, proposed that troops take charge at the South Carolina State House. Taft in his heavy way supported him. With earnest solemnity, Fish objected. "I remonstrate and protest," he writes,[14] "against improper and unlawful employment of the military in any interference with the organization or any other purpose than to suppress violence and preserve the peace." He adds: "The President is of the same opinion." Grant had seen the light!

Taft and Fish argued the matter. The fat Ohioan asserted that the Republican House had been regularly organized on the 28th. True, some critics said that its 59 members, since the total House roster was ordinarily 124, did not make a quorum. Before the Civil War American legislatures had usually held that a majority of the whole number was requisite for a quorum. But, said Taft, during the war the Senate had frequently found itself without one-half the number of Senators from all States. It and the House of Representatives had therefore adopted the rule that a quorum should consist of a majority of the members returned and who had taken their seats. Since in South Carolina the Canvassing Board had returned 116 members, 59 would constitute a quorum. But Fish thought this bad law. He writes:

I objected to his argument and its conclusion. [I said] that the decisions of the Senate and House of Representatives to which he referred were made in a time of revolution, and like many things then done, were to be justified by the actual necessity for the preservation of the nation, and should not be appealed to as precedents; that on the formation of our government we had adopted the principle of representation and government by majorities, and that while in the British Parliament a small number, perhaps not exceeding a half dozen, constitute a quorum of the House of Lords, and some 20 or 30 a quorum of the House of Commons, although each house consists of several hundreds of members, our government was organized on the principle of the control by actual majorities, which I held to be fundamental and vital to the preservation of our institutions.

In reply to my remark as to the precedents cited by Taft during war and revolution, Cameron said, "This is war and revolution!" The President interrupted him by saying, "No, no! It is no such thing!"

Cameron proposed an order to Ruger to support Chamberlain and to exclude the Edgefield and Laurens members who were certified to by the Supreme Court.

[14] *Ibid.*

The President objected, saying that the troops were not there to act under the orders of Chamberlain, but were there to preserve peace and order, and he did not think that he (the President) had any right to say who should or should not be excluded from the Chamber.

Attorney-General Taft also hesitated to assent to anything so crude as the order proposed by Cameron. He suggested a telegram to Ruger and Chamberlain saying that the Administration thought that the Republican House was duly elected and organized. "No, I object to that also," said Fish firmly. "That is the very question involved. It is for the House itself to determine who are its members. The President and Cabinet are not competent to pass on the question; and even if we were legally competent, we have no evidence on which we should be justified in acting." Grant took the same view. He declared that the Executive of South Carolina occupied the same position in Columbia that the Executive did in Washington; and that the organization of the Legislature was a question for the State to settle, not the national government.

Obviously, this was a very different President from the man who had rejected Fish's advice upon Louisiana in 1874 and had acted in Arkansas in 1875 without consulting his Cabinet. An answer to Ruger and Chamberlain was deferred until the Cabinet meeting next day. When the members gathered they found a new telegram from Ruger which opened with the opinion that it would be best to let the two parties "worry it out." This supported Grant and Fish. But Chamberlain had meanwhile appealed direct to the President for assistance, and Cameron and Taft renewed their arguments. A spirited discussion ensued:

His [Chamberlain's] telegram to the President states that the object of the Democrats is to give the electoral vote of the State to Tilden.

The President has a telegram from Wade Hampton stating that the returns of the Presidential electors are not involved in the question.

Cameron also has a telegram from Bradley Johnson to the same effect, but stated that he would not believe them and that they intended to violate their pledges, and that as soon as Hampton should be inaugurated Governor a law would be passed changing the mode of appointment of electors and giving them to Tilden.

I asked how that could be done while there was a Republican Senate. The President remarked, "That's a fact, it can't be done." Cameron replied, "They will do it nevertheless; they will buy somebody." The discussion then turned on the organization of the House.

Cameron expressed a wish and Chandler silently nodded assent that the troops be authorized to eject the Edgefield and Laurens members. The President repelled the idea, saying that the Federal Government had no right to interfere in the organization of a State Legislature; that the country had been much excited with regard to what occurred in Louisiana, and that Republicans and Democrats both condemned such interference. That the authorities of South Carolina must settle the organization of their Legislature; that Chamberlain is the Governor of that State and must be so regarded until a successor is duly elected and inaugurated, and as the Executive of that State he has the same power there that he (the President) has in the general government; that the United States troops can only be used for the suppression of domestic violence.

Stubbornly, Cameron suggested that at least a telegram of encouragement be sent Chamberlain, and read a draft he had prepared. Still more stubbornly, Grant rejected it, but proposed a substitute which after some modification was written out: to the effect that while the situation did not call for any positive action on his part at the moment, he wished to be kept advised of later events.

Despite additional appeals from Chamberlain, despite renewed pressure from Chandler, Cameron, and Taft, the President—with Fish sturdily backing him—stood adamant against the use of Federal bayonets to impose a Republican House and Governor on South Carolina. On December 3 Wade Hampton sent Fish two excited telegrams,[15] asserting that the Republicans had planned "an attack on and possible murder of Democrats in the House," and asking that they be "restrained by orders from Washington." At the same time Ruger wired the President that he feared trouble. No notice was taken of Hampton's appeal, and Grant curtly informed Ruger that the military were not to interfere with either "pretended House." [16] Later that day Fish stopped at the White House. "I found Cameron and Chandler there," he records. "Each had telegrams from South Carolina, and each was urgent for authority for the troops to eject the Edgefield and Laurens members or in some other way to intervene forcibly. The President decidedly resisted this suggestion."

III

Grant's annual message, sent to a Congress seething with excitement, required careful consideration, and was taken up in a special Cabinet

---

[15] Hampton to Fish, December 3, 1876; Fish Papers.
[16] Diary, December 4, 1876; Grant Letterbooks, same date.

meeting on December 4. It was preceded by a calm general canvass of the situation. The President expressed a belief, founded upon the reports sent him, that at least part of the Tilden electors would be returned in Louisiana—and even one would make Tilden President. He spoke regretfully of the alternative possibility that Hayes might be seated by a canvassing board in Louisiana "whose past character has deprived it of any claims to confidence." Then at about two o'clock he began reading his long paper.[17]

At two points he discussed the Presidential contest, reviewing in very severe terms the conduct attributed to the Democrats, especially in the South. Fish at once suggested that it was impolitic to denounce in such harsh language a party comprising half of the people. And at once the two politicians in the Cabinet crossed swords with him. "I think the passages entirely right," said Cameron. "They may be accurate," replied Fish. "But such a state paper as the President's annual message is supposedly of elevated character and should be free from partisanship or imputations against a large body of citizens."

"As for me," ejaculated Chandler, "I think those passages the best part of the message, and believe they will do good."

"I differ from you," repeated Fish. "I think that they will do harm instead of good. The public is already sufficiently excited without such imputations from such a source, which will be resented by all of one party, and disapproved by a large part of the other."

Grant said nothing. But seeing him next day, and learning that the message was finished, Fish inquired whether he had retained the sections on the Southern elections.[18] He replied that he had not—he was satisfied that they would be useless and possibly pernicious. He had confined himself to a recommendation that measures be taken to guard all future Presidential elections against irregularities in counting the electoral votes. On the previous Sunday evening he had talked at length with Abram S. Hewitt, the able Democratic National Chairman, and assured him that he would not use troops to seat Hayes as President, or for any other purpose save the restoration of order if broken. The President, indeed, took a sensible attitude on nearly all aspects of the crisis. Cabinet members were being pelted with letters warning them of Democratic plots and impending violence, and suggesting precautions. One day the Cabinet meeting was interrupted by a deputation from the "Stars and

[17] Diary, December 4, 1876.   [18] Diary, December 5, 1876.

Stripes Association," whose leader proffered the armed services of that body. Grant told them that he apprehended no disturbance; and when one man asked him who would give orders if they were needed, he laughingly said that he had not yet thought about the question.[19]

Before Christmas steps had been taken by Congress to set up an Electoral Commission to decide the dispute over the Presidency. Though Fish's diary throws no light on the origin of the plan, it shows that the Administration cordially approved it. Meanwhile, affairs in South Carolina had settled into a grim deadlock, with Grant still holding himself strictly aloof. But immediately after New Year's the focus of interest in the Cabinet swung abruptly to Louisiana. The Kellogg machine was engaged in a desperate fight for its gubernatorial nominee, S. B. Packard, and the whole Custom House gang; and Chandler, Taft, and Cameron made one more effort to persuade Grant to use troops in the South.

The President informed the Cabinet on January 2, 1877, that Governor Kellogg had sent him a telegram which, though hazy, seemed intended to convey the statement that the Louisiana House had passed a resolution calling for Federal troops. Fish called attention to its suspicious vagueness, and Grant decided that it furnished no occasion for further orders.[20] But five days later a new application for troops came from Kellogg. Though it was Sunday, at one o'clock Fish was summoned through the midwinter cold to a special Cabinet meeting. He was the first to arrive. "It's the Louisiana trouble again," Grant informed him. He added impatiently: "They are always in trouble there and always wanting the United States to send troops." And he handed Fish, to the latter's gratification, a ready-written refusal to comply with Kellogg's request. The Secretary praised it warmly. When the President read it aloud to the full Cabinet, Fish suggested a slight emendation, which was made. Nobody ventured to attack it. But Cameron manifested "some impatience," and asked when the Federal Government *could* interfere. "Not until there is actual resistance or conflict," responded Grant. And Cameron remarked to Fish *sotto voce:* [21]

"I'm afraid that won't come, for our fellows down there won't fight."

But would the President stick to this wise position? When the Cabi-

---

[19] Diary, December 15, 1876.
[20] Diary, January 2, 1877. For the situation in Louisiana see Ella Lonn, *Reconstruction in Louisiana after 1868.*
[21] Diary, January 7, 1877.

net held its next regular session on January 9, it found that a large body
of telegrams had been pouring in from New Orleans. They described
threatening assemblages of armed men, expressed fears of violence, and
seconded the Governor's application for Federal assistance. Two rival
legislatures and two rival Governors-elect, the Republican Packard and
the Democratic Nichols, faced each other. But Grant was still resolved
not to interfere. He decided merely to telegraph General Augur the
purport of the warning messages, instruct him to caution the public
against unlawful acts, and ask him to report on the development of
the situation.[22] Fish was delighted, but Cameron and Chandler could
not repress their anger.

"Then we must wait until a shot is fired before we can act," grumbled
Cameron. And Chandler blurted out impulsively to the Secretary of
War, "If you telegraph General Augur, 'Consult Governor Kellogg and
place your troops as he shall direct,' wouldn't that settle it?" Fish commented sardonically, "Yes, that would settle it." And Grant said, with
a snap of his jaw, "We will not settle it yet that way at least." Chandler
and Cameron left moodily. Next day, as Fish read the news of growing
tension in New Orleans and thought over what they had said, the suspicion crossed his mind that they might secretly foment a disturbance in
New Orleans. But it was so ugly a suspicion that he merely hinted at it
in his diary.[23]

Telegrams continued to arrive from New Orleans; the Cabinet continued to discuss the question. At one meeting Cameron displayed unexpected moderation, agreeing to the inexpediency of "any present recognition" of either set of claimants. The President had pointed out that
while a Congressional Committee was examining the situation, it was
wise to defer any judgment on it. On hearing this, "Chandler for once
was quiet," remarks Fish.[24] But all the while the more radical party
leaders were active behind the arras. Men who had visited the South
beset the President. At length Grant made Fish his confidant. Calling
the Secretary to the White House on January 17, he remarked that
while he seldom lost sleep over public questions, lately he had been
much disturbed by Louisiana.[25] "Some of the rabid Republicans," as
he called them, had been importuning him to take extreme measures.
John Sherman and Eugene Hale, returning from New Orleans in an ex-

[22] Diary, January 9, 1877.
[23] But it continued to haunt him; Diary, January 11, 1877.
[24] Diary, January 12, 1877.　　　　　　　　　[25] Diary, January 17, 1877.

cited mood, had badgered him mercilessly.

"Perhaps," said Fish shrewdly, "Sherman and Hale committed themselves by hasty promises in Louisiana, and are trying to draw you after them." Time showed that Sherman had indeed promised almost everything in sight in an effort to make sure of Republican electors there. The President then launched into an interesting exposition of his views of the crisis:

He spoke with a good deal of warmth of the extreme incapacity of the men attempting to rule Louisiana, that they had no interests there, but had simply gone there to hold office and as soon as they should lose it, intended to come away.

He says he is opposed to the Fifteenth Amendment and thinks it was a mistake, that it had done the Negro no good, and had been a hindrance to the South, and by no means a political advantage to the North.

He read a letter of Longstreet, addressed to himself, which he said seemed to be proposing a political bargain, to which, of course, he could not be a party. The letter in substance stated that the Nichols Government would be content to recognize the "Hayes electors" if their government could be established, and invited a reply from the President; which he said he should not make.

After speaking again of his deep anxiety, the terrific pressure upon him, and his feeling that perhaps the Louisiana question should be laid before Congress, he mentioned Hayes' weak position there. Fish writes that he commented earnestly on the embarrassment of the Republicans from the admitted fact that the returning board had changed the majority of the Tilden electors, ranging from 6,000 to 9,000 votes, into a majority of 2,000 to 4,000 for the Hayes electors; while the board had failed to fill the vacancy in its membership. It is evident that Grant believed that Tilden had fairly carried Louisiana.

The President also commented upon his party's original plan for counting the electors. He felt sure that the Republican claim that the president of the Senate held the counting-power could not be sustained. "He named Conkling, Robertson, Conover, West, and others, including as he thought Edmunds and Frelinghuysen, who disavowed the right of the president of the Senate; and he felt sure that there was a sufficient number of Republican Senators of that opinion, with the Democrats, to make a majority in opposition. . . ." [26] Grant then turned to the future:

[26] Diary, January 17, 1877.

Throughout the conversation he expressed the greatest anxiety for a peaceful solution of the question, adding that while he most earnestly desired the declaration of Governor Hayes as President, he thought that should he come into power with his Administration embarrassed with the question of the votes of two or three States, he would be much crippled in power. On the other hand, if Tilden were elected, he would be unable to satisfy the expectations of the South, and with the commitments of his party against the use of the military for any purpose of the government, he would be unable to collect the internal revenue in the South; that already, since the doubts of the election, the whiskey distillers are running their stills, paying no tax, and that the running down of receipts has been very great. . . .

To the end the President's course remained admirable. He was redeeming the sorry record he had made in Louisiana two years earlier; he was demonstrating that he could not only learn a lesson, but show courage in reversing himself. The more vehement the demands for action in the South grew, the more sturdily he repelled them. He had become convinced that the day had ended for the use of Federal bayonets in deciding elections in the South, and against a whole cohort of extremists —against Morton, John Sherman, Conkling, Zach Chandler, Cameron— he was standing by his honest views. On the 27th he and Fish had another conversation.[27]

"He spoke with a great deal of feeling of the Louisiana troubles," Fish writes, "and of the importunity with which they were pressing him to recognize the Packard Government, inasmuch as it appeared that a majority of the members of the Legislature received the certificate of the Returning Board; that this Board was organized by a law of the State, but was in his judgment an outrageous contrivance, and had in its whole history been tainted with suspicion, if not with actual fraud; that he was convinced that it would be best for the people of Louisiana, both white and black, that the Nichols Government should be in power; that as a political question, he thought any action at this time looking to the recognition of either government would be injurious to the Republican Party, and to the ultimate success of Governor Hayes; that this whole question had given him a great deal of anxiety and trouble; that he had been importuned in season and out of season, to an extent which was indelicate if not indecent; that a recommendation from the city [Washington] had been made that Packard and his friends should force a collision so as to force the necessity of a recognition."

[27] Diary, January 27, 1877.

"I have abstained from bringing the question up for more Cabinet discussion," Grant concluded, "for I believed there would be about six members against me and one for me." Fish remarked that he thought Robeson would not be against his policy, nor perhaps Morrill. "Well," said Grant, "at best it would be one with me, one or two half-and-half, and four or five against me. But unless circumstances compel me I will not take any action at present, or until the full report of the Investigating Committee are before me and the Presidential issue decided." This was the old Grant, the Grant of Donelson, of Appomattox, and of the Inflation Bill veto—the Grant of whom Rockwood Hoar had just written to Fish: "He comes up to the mark so grandly on great occasions, that I wish he were more careful of appearances in smaller matters."

IV

And when late in January the fate of the Electoral Commission Bill hung in the balance, Grant threw his influence aggressively in its favor. He avoided discussing it with the Cabinet, where he feared fresh dissension. A majority of Republican Senators and Representatives were decidedly against it, holding that it would give Tilden the Presidency. Grant labored to convert them. He told Fish on the 20th that, believing such a tribunal necessary to prevent disorder and bloodshed, he had been actively buttonholing Congressmen and other leaders.[28] He had argued at length with Don Cameron, and believed that Cameron had abandoned his hostility to the bill. When the measure passed the House on the 26th the President commented with delight on the large majority it had received.[29] It then went to a close but victorious battle in the Senate. Edmunds and Frelinghuysen, two of its supporters, were anxious that Grant should accompany his approval of the bill with a special message to Congress, and they asked Fish to broach the proposal to him.[30] The Secretary agreed that a special message would allay uneasiness, augment the authority of the Electoral Commission, and incline the country to a readier acceptance of its verdict. He therefore drafted one, utilizing suggestions from the two Senators. On Sunday, January 28, on Grant's return from Baltimore, he spoke of the matter. "Knowing of your absence yesterday," he said, "I took the liberty of preparing a draft. It may be of assistance to you, but if you do not like it throw it in the fire-

[28] Diary, January 20, 1877.   [29] Diary, January 27, 1876.   [30] Ibid.

place." The President glanced through it. "I will adopt it as written," he said with his characteristic quiet smile.[31] "It is a great deal better than I would have done it—and somewhat longer." The message went to Congress next day.

The seating of Hayes as President, as everyone knows, was accompanied by a compact or "Bargain," by which a group of Democratic Representatives agreed not to filibuster against the completion of the count in return for a promise from friends of Hayes that he would permit all the Southern States to govern themselves. Though the "Bargain" was not consummated until just before March 4, negotiations were begun several weeks earlier. A humorous result was the sudden eagerness of Republican leaders, including some who had recently besought Grant for action, that there be no Federal interference with Louisiana and South Carolina. For example, Fish writes of the activities of a prominent Iowa Republican:

Sunday, February 18, 1876.—Mr. Kasson called this afternoon to see me, stating that there was a rumor that the Commission having decided in favor of Louisiana, the President was about to recognize the Packard Government, and that he thought the effect would be very bad, as the behavior of the Southern Democrats had been so good in attempting to defeat all filibustering attempts on the part of the Northern Democrats, and that they proposed to give the Administration a fair support, and he hoped no precipitate action would be taken.

I assured him that nothing but absolute necessity would induce him [the President] to recognize either government during his term of office. I promised to see the President tomorrow morning on the subject.

Next day Fish did see the President, finding him still embarrassed by radical importunities and not completely certain as to his course.[32] The Secretary pointed out that if the decision between the Packard and Nichols governments in New Orleans were not left to Hayes, Grant might impose on the new President a policy adverse to his views and jeopard the success of his Administration. Grant already inclined to this opinion, and a few days later told the Cabinet that he had definitely decided to leave the issue to Hayes.[33] Four days before he left office he sent Fish a succinct letter which he had written the Republican claimant, Packard. "In

---

[31] Diary, January 28, 1876; the message is in Richardson, VII, 422–424. An exceptionally well-written document, it praised the orderly adjudication guaranteed by the new law, and called for "peace and quiet and harmony between all parties and all sections."
[32] Diary, February 19, 1877.   [33] Diary, February 27, 1877.

answer to your dispatch of this date," it ran, "I feel it my duty to state frankly that I do not believe public opinion will support longer the maintenance of State Government in Louisiana by the use of the military, and that I must concur in this manifest feeling." While he held office the troops "will not be used to establish or pull down either claimant for the control of the State. It is not my purpose to recognize either government."

When Fish gave Grant his enthusiastic approval of this letter the Electoral Commission had practically completed its work. On Friday, March 2, Fish went—early, as usual—to a Cabinet meeting. As he entered the executive office Grant rose hastily to introduce a bearded gentleman of fine forehead and half-scholarly, half-soldierly demeanor, the President-elect. Next day Fish and Robeson called at the K Street residence of John Sherman, a massive gray stone pile, to see Hayes. Sentries, a sign of the disturbed time, paced before the door. The Cabinet had decided, on Fish's suggestion, that in view of the delay in deciding the election and the fact that March 4 fell on Sunday, they would resign not to Grant but to the new President. This would prevent any interregnum. Hayes approved the plan, and said that he hoped the whole Cabinet would remain for some days.[34] "Certainly," said the untactful Robeson, "but the sooner you can come to a conclusion as to our successors, the better." That evening, just before dinner at the White House, Hayes informally took the oath of office before the Chief Justice, to be repeated with ceremony the following Monday.

v

Hayes' inauguration was quiet and orderly. After he delivered his address from the east portico of the Capitol, he and Grant drove back together to the White House. At dinner Mrs. Grant presided for the last time as hostess. Before the evening grew late, the former President and his wife left for Secretary Fish's house, where they quietly spent the next few days.

For Fish was still Secretary. Not until the afternoon of March 12 did he surrender his office to William M. Evarts. In the interim he performed an important service to the new President. He was able to warn him against the machinations of Taft, Cameron, and Zach Chandler with

[34] Diary, March 2, 3, 1877.

regard to South Carolina and Louisiana, and to advise him earnestly to withdraw the Federal troops from those States.

It was a curious Cabinet meeting that took place March 6, with Hayes trying to gain from ex-President Grant's advisers some conception of his duties. All were present. The only business of importance transacted related to the South. Hayes incautiously spoke at the outset of the two Southern States which had rival governments, and Zach Chandler and Taft leaped at the opening. Taft instantly began reading a memorandum he had prepared, while Chandler sent for a volume of Grant's telegrams. Evidently there had been an understanding between the two men. Hayes passed to another topic, but a little later Taft again brought up Louisiana. "Has any consideration been given the question of the recognition of a *de facto* as distinguished from a *de jure* State government?" demanded Hayes. Cameron, Robeson, Taft, and Chandler at once opened like a pack in full cry.[35] They were all in favor of recognizing the Packard Government:

The three former (Fish writes) laid stress on the President's telegram of the 14th Jany. and Robeson spoke of the President's "vacillating" of late. The other two admitted what they called a "change of position" of the President.

I felt indignant that the three most subservient of the President's followers and flatterers while in power should so soon turn against him for a present purpose, and somewhat indignantly remarked that the circumstances under which the President had largely regarded the question in Louisiana were much changed from the representations made to him at the time of the telegram of Jany. 14th.

Chandler, with some indiscretion, remarked to the President that the Packard Government was chosen on the same vote on which he was declared elected President. Gov. Hayes rebuked him, and several of the members of the Cabinet simultaneously interposed, manifesting disapproval of this great indecency.

It was decided that copies of recent telegrams and orders should be laid before Hayes, with a brief by Attorney-General Taft. Fearful that political bias would color the brief, Fish called attention to the fact that none of the warnings of imminent violence in Louisiana had been realized, and that the alleged state of insurrection which the Packard Government had used as a pretext for asking Federal aid simply did not exist. "I did this," he writes, "in consequence of the stress which Robeson

[35] Diary, March 6, 1877.

and others were laying on what they called the 'Constitutional call' of the Packard Legislature." The idea that there was a Constitutional obligation to send troops simply because one claimant made a demand for them was absurd. And as he was leaving, Fish loosed a shaft at the Attorney-General.[36] Taft repeated that he was in favor of recognizing the Packard Government, and that Grant had changed front. "I replied somewhat angrily that he had not changed so long as there was any body of citizens represented by the Packard Government." Taft knew well that intelligent Louisianians were overwhelmingly against Packard.

Fish, indeed, used every opportunity to impress his moderate views upon Hayes. On March 7, by request, he called at the White House. The President, troubled by the discussion in the Cabinet, turned again to the question of the Southern States. "We had a short conversation on the condition of these States, and the attitude of General Grant toward them," writes Fish.[37] Hayes indicated that he had no intention of sustaining Chamberlain as Governor of South Carolina, for he asked what Fish would think of appointing him Marshal of the District of Columbia. "Very good, if the post is large enough," said Fish. "I understand it is worth from $6,000 to $9,000 a year," rejoined Hayes.

Valuing Fish's views, Hayes asked him to serve upon the investigative commission which he was sending to Louisiana. But the Secretary disapproved of any such commission. Since the essential facts of the situation were known in Washington, he thought it both unnecessary and unsettling. "It looks to me like a makeshift to gain time and occupy the public attention, or an expedient to find someone or something to share the responsibility of whatever the Administration may eventually decide, and on which to throw the odium of whatever is to be done that the public or the Republican Party may disapprove." When Evarts conveyed the President's invitation (not mentioning, Fish sardonically noted, that William A. Wheeler and Thurlow Weed had declined), he met a decided refusal. "I cannot see what the commission is to do," said Fish. Asked to take a day to consider the matter, on the morrow he said "No" more decidedly than ever, and at the same time gave Evarts some valuable information: [38]

Referring to the condition of things in South Carolina and Louisiana, I told him that had the Administration of General Grant continued . . . he

[36] *Ibid.*   [37] Diary, March 7, 1877.   [38] Diary, March 27, 1877.

would have removed the troops from the proximity of the Legislatures in both States; that he had become impressed with the necessity and propriety of no longer appearing to be sustaining a contested State Government by the military force of the United States, but that while troops had been placed in both capitals in pursuance of a regular demand . . . the facts subsequently developed had not justified the demand, or if they were such at the time as to justify it, had subsequently ceased to be cause for long-continued military interference; and that General Grant would have withdrawn them but for the effect such act might have had pending the electoral count, and because of a reluctance on his part, in the last days of his Administration, without knowing the views or wishes of his successor, to adopt a course which might affect . . . the policy of his successor's administration.

With warm approval, during the next few weeks, Fish watched the final steps taken by Hayes to carry out this wise policy of withdrawal in Louisiana and South Carolina. Before the end of April the Federal troops had been evacuated from their threatening positions in Columbia and New Orleans, the Administrations of Wade Hampton and Nichols had been installed in the two capitols, and the South was at last free.[39]

Meanwhile Fish, in his last days at the State Department, had collected, assorted, and filed all the diplomatic papers bearing upon his various foreign policies, leaving no confusion and no loose ends for his successor. To the story contained in the latest of these papers—an interesting and significant story, thus far neglected in following other threads in the history of the Grant Administration—we must now turn.

[39] Rhodes, *United States,* VII, 289.

DOWN the ringing grooves of change, while America was occupied with her industrial depression, her scandals, and her Southern problems, spun the world. Gladstone had given way in 1874 to Disraeli. With Lord Derby in the Foreign Office, the Disraeli Ministry was pursuing a vigorous policy abroad. The purchase in 1875 of the Khedive's shares in the Suez Canal gave Britain the keys of the East, and soon virtually brought Egypt into the Empire. The following year Victoria was crowned Empress of India. On the continent the dominant figure was Bismarck, a leader whom Fish greatly admired but never quite trusted. Germany, fast transforming herself into a great industrial nation, loomed up like a giant beside the French republic, as yet trembling with weakness, and sustained against the monarchist movement only by the genius of Gambetta. But there was still another giant on the continent— Russia, where Gortchakov was the astute master of foreign affairs. He, Bismarck, and the British statesmen were increasingly interested in the intolerable situation in the Turkish-ruled Balkans, which by 1876 made a Russo-Turkish conflict seemingly inevitable. Spain was still racked by civil war, but in the last days of 1874 the Bourbon dynasty was proclaimed again, Alfonso XII took the throne, and the hope for a restoration of peace grew brighter.

More than one observer traced a connection between the vigor of Disraeli's policy and the happy settlement of the *Alabama* Claims.[1] The Geneva decision had set England free to resume her leading rôle in European affairs. No longer haunted by the fear that in some sudden war a swarm of *Alabamas* would crush her ocean commerce, no longer troubled by American enmity, she could abandon Gladstone's narrow economic theories and the Cobdenite doctrine of non-intervention. It was impossible for so wealthy a nation, her power spread over so much of the earth, to be a mere passive spectator of history. Disraeli seized his opportunities brilliantly. With an imaginative stroke worthy of the author of *Lothair,* he mustered the millions of British pounds as Prussia had mustered her millions of armed men, and used them to plant British dominion squarely upon the Suez. It bulwarked India, and India,

---

[1] See Paris correspondence, N. Y. *Nation,* January 6, 1876.

with its Sepoys and Ghurkas, in turn secured Suez. The French were at first dismayed that the canal which their engineers and diplomats had built should fall into English hands, but they had no alternative except to consent. The crowning of the Empress of India was another brilliant stroke, a notice to the world that England would hold the Empire intact. After the limp years under Gladstone, Britain was again a great world figure. The fact did not displease Hamilton Fish. He had written in 1869 that the *Alabama* Claims made England less potent in a troubled world than the United States should desire; now he felt that she had her due influence, her right place in the balance of power.

While the world was changing, the tools with which Fish worked had changed also—and for the better. The second Grant Administration witnessed a distinct improvement in the diplomatic service, for which the Secretary was chiefly responsible. Two excellent men were held in office: the rugged Elihu B. Washburne in Paris, the learned George P. Marsh in Rome. When George Bancroft was replaced in Berlin by his nephew Bancroft Davis, the service lost nothing. Nor did it lose anything when that eccentric poet and old-school gentleman, George H. Boker, a rare and picturesque soul, succeeded Marshall Jewell as Minister to Russia. It was a clear improvement to have Caleb Cushing in Madrid in place of Sickles; to have Phillips Merrill in Brussels in place of J. Russell Jones; and to have Edwards Pierrepont in London in place of General Schenck. Fish would have liked R. H. Dana, Jr., a great deal better than Pierrepont, for he realized that the latter was mutable as water under pressure, and failed to keep his own counsel. He specially asked Grant to warn him to stick to his instructions and to rein his tongue in society. But at any rate Pierrepont would obey orders better than Motley had done, and keep himself above scandal as Schenck has failed to do. Another improvement lay in the selection of Edward F. Beale for Vienna in place of the quarrelsome and ill-controlled John Jay.[2]

To the end Fish did what he could to better the diplomatic service. The diary for November 26, 1875, for example, records that, driving to the funeral of Vice-President Wilson at the Capitol with Grant, he mentioned the recent death of Benjamin P. Avery, Minister to China. He suggested the appointment of George F. Seward, saying that he

[2] Jay's quarrel with Thomas Van Buren had continued, with acrimonious newspaper publications, while his controversy with his Vienna landlord produced scandal; Fish to Bancroft Davis, January 6, January 25, 1875, Letterbooks.

understood our interests in and relations with China better than any other man, and was a person of ability. A revision of Chino-American treaties must soon take place, and Fish would gladly entrust him with it. The President sharply replied: "I do not think I will appoint Secretary Seward's nephew. He is not much of a Republican, and I don't like any of the family." "Well," replied Fish, "I suggested the name in the public interest. Although I have no special reason for being fond of Governor Seward's family, I still think this the best appointment that could be made." They dropped the subject. But Grant thought the recommendation over, and early in the new year Seward's nomination was duly sent to the Senate. He made an admirable representative.

Fish remained exceptionally fortunate in the personnel of his Department. When Bancroft Davis became Agent in the Geneva Arbitration, his place as Assistant Secretary was taken by Charles Hale of Boston, who was green, inefficient, and irritatingly addicted to what Fish called "nasty cigarettes." Davis was reappointed to the State Department early in 1874, but that summer again resigned to go to Berlin. Fish chose as his successor John L. Cadwalader, a man of unusual gifts. At this time thirty-eight, Cadwalader was a graduate of Princeton and the Harvard Law School, a proficient lawyer, and full of brilliancy and energy. Fish's notes to him soon became almost as intimate as those he had written to Davis. Later in life he made a great name at the New York Bar. In William Hunter the Secretary of course had one of the really memorable civil servants of American history. Hunter had entered the State Department as a clerk in 1829; he had been made Second Assistant Secretary by special act of Congress in 1866. He had enjoyed the confidence of Van Buren, Livingston, Forsythe, McLane, Webster, Everett, Cass, Marcy, and their successors; he was laborious, faithful, and accomplished—the master of several languages; and his prodigious memory made him a veritable index to the Department. Fish records that once the Dutch Minister called to claim a right under an old treaty of 1782. This treaty stood on the books without any indication of obsolescence. But when Fish mentioned the interview to Hunter, the latter immediately replied, "Why, that Treaty was denounced by Mr. Adams while Secretary of State." Fish called for the correspondence, and a few minutes later Hunter brought in all the records, saying, "I was mistaken; it was not Mr. Adams but Mr. Monroe who denounced it." So it proved—the denunciation had occurred fifteen years before Hunter entered the Department, but it was familiar to him.

No Department could have run more smoothly than Fish's did by 1875, when it removed from the shabby orphan-asylum to Mullett's "grand Renaissance building" near the White House. He had increased his office force from about twenty-five to forty-five clerks. He had set up the new Bureau of Indexes and Archives, and perfected his central index for all departmental records. He had seen to the classifying and binding of huge piles of miscellaneous papers. The work of copying dispatches, which Seward had allowed to fall into disgraceful arrears, had been brought up to the minute and was kept there. Strict discipline ruled the office; one subordinate later wrote that he never opened a Legation mail without trepidation, for if a slip or oversight occurred the heavy hand of the Secretary was sure to fall. But it was a discipline controlled by fairness and moderated by kindness, and no Secretary ever had more confidence and loyalty from his assistants than Fish.

The *Virginius* affair was the last formidable storm on the sea of foreign relations that Fish had to confront. Thereafter, no important group of Americans were to become aroused over any international problem until, more than a decade later, Grover Cleveland threatened condign action against Canada in the fisheries dispute. Yet it was not a halcyon ocean over which Fish voyaged during his last three years in Washington. It was rather a choppy sea, with vexatious cross-currents, adverse gusts, and even two or three squalls. Not far to leeward always loomed up the grim rock of Cuban difficulties, on which an unskilful pilot might easily come to wreck. Nor was the log of his journey uninteresting. On the contrary, it contained, in the famous episode of Instruction No. 266, addressed to Cushing on Spanish-American relations, one of the most striking and puzzling of all Fish's diplomatic transactions. That story, and some others, have never yet been properly told.

I

When the world hailed the Geneva Award, two clauses of the Treaty of Washington remained to be executed. They proved singularly difficult to put into effect, and gave Fish and Sir Edward Thornton labor and trouble out of all proportion to their actual importance.

The first was the agreement that the two countries should not only observe the "Three Rules" of neutrality (Article VI) in their mutual relations, but bring them to the notice of other maritime Powers and invite other nations to accept them. At first blush this seemed simple. But unexpected difficulties soon arose. The British Foreign Office and the State Department disagreed upon the terms of presentation—that is, the interpretation of the Three Rules. It became evident that while the American Government was eager to urge them upon the world, the British Government was reluctant. The reason for this difference was simple: the Three Rules were essentially a statement of doctrines long held by the American Government, and no less a reversal of the position historically occupied until 1871 by the British Government. It is not strange that, as Thornton frankly told Fish in 1875, they were highly unpopular in England.[3]

Just what was new in the rules? The first required due diligence on the part of a neutral to prevent the equipping, fitting out, or arming within its jurisdiction, or the departure therefrom, of any vessel intended to cruise or carry on war with another Power. The second forbade the use of neutral ports or waters as a base of naval operations by any belligerent, and the augmentation of military supplies or arms therein. The third merely held the neutral government responsible for the exercise of due diligence in enforcing the first two. Now both nations had long imposed upon their citizens, under municipal law, the essential features of the Three Rules. The United States by its neutrality legislation of 1818, and Great Britain by that of 1819, had forbidden and punished the acts defined in the rules. But these enactments were addressed to individuals, and their language applied only to persons. They created personal obligations but did not assume to create national obligations; they fixed personal penalties, but did not establish national penalties or indemnities as for a breach of international law. What then? Did the Three Rules, now to be submitted to the world, provide any new national obligation which had not existed before? So far as the United States went, no; so far as Great Britain went, yes. In this fact lay the real basis of their inability to agree upon an interpretation.

Long before the Treaty of Washington the American courts had adopted, in a series of judgments, the principles of the Three Rules. They had treated these principles as parts of international law, which the government must observe just as its citizens must observe the Act

[3] Diary, October 28, 1875.

of 1818. The most celebrated case was that of the *Santissima Trinidad,* which is described in detail in the seventh volume of Wheaton.[4] This grew out of an augmentation of force that a South American warship, cruising against Spanish commerce, had received in Baltimore. Judge Story declared that "such illegal augmentation is a violation of the law of nations as well as of our municipal law," and awarded redress to the owners of property captured by the vessel. Several other cases, decided in similar fashion, made the national position of the United States precisely that asserted in the Three Rules. But the British courts, in the celebrated case of the *Alexandra* in 1863, had taken a very different position.[5] Moreover, in the discussion which preceded and followed this case Britain assumed two positions which it held until they were abandoned in the Treaty of Washington. The first was that England was not responsible to any foreign nation for the character of her purely municipal law, its gaps, or its defective administration. The second was that the statutes upon neutrality were not declaratory of international law, but supplementary thereto; and that Britain had never been under any international obligation to prevent the fitting out, equipping, or arming of the Confederate cruisers. The Three Rules cost the United States nothing, but England a vast deal.

It is not strange that while Fish urged action, the British Government held back. Into the details of the prolonged correspondence we need not go. Controversy raged chiefly over the Second Rule. The British Government interpreted it as not prohibiting the sale or exportation of military supplies in the ordinary course of commerce. The United States, however, interpreted it more narrowly—as not preventing the *open* sale (without mention of exportation) of military supplies in ordinary trade. The words "open" and "or exportation" provoked a wrangle almost worthy of Byzantine logothetes. Finally Granville consented to give up the latter term. Fish still insisted upon "open"; but Granville argued that it would make the two governments responsible to belligerent Powers for the clandestine sale of arms by their citizens.[6]

At the end of 1871 the correspondence lapsed for fifteen months. When it was resumed in the spring of 1873 the British Government declared that the question had become more complicated in the interim, and that recent Parliamentary debates had shown how impossible it

---

[4] Wheaton, *International Law* (Dana Edition), VII, 283.
[5] See *Case of the United States,* Geneva Arbitration, 161, 258 ff.
[6] Fish to Schenck, November 9, 1871; Granville to Thornton, December 23, 1871.

would be for England to lay the rules before other Powers without full explanatory comment. If they did, these Powers would at once ask: "Are you and the United States agreed upon the meaning of the rules to which you ask our assent?" Granville also thought it indispensable for Great Britain to guard herself against perilous inferences which might be drawn from some parts of the Geneva Award. He felt sure, he added, that the other Powers would reject the Three Rules anyway. Fish, in reply, expressed disappointment that Granville would not submit the rules even at the risk of their rejection, and denied that England and the United States differed in any essential respect as to their meaning. And in fact they did not. The word-chopping about "open," the other petty disputes, could have been cleared away in no time had both nations earnestly wished the rules submitted. But one did not— and delay favored its position. The *Virginius* crisis came on, the Ministry in England changed, and the subject substantially lapsed again from the fall of 1873 until the spring of 1875! [7]

It was resumed with an amusing exchange over responsibility, each side blaming the other for not answering its notes. But there was no question where the reluctance lay. Some plain talk was recorded in Fish's diary on October 28, 1875, when Thornton called on the Secretary. Fish brusquely asked if the British Government were ready to act on the rules.

"I hope," Thornton hesitatingly replied, "that the United States will not press them. The truth is that Mr. Disraeli and Lord Derby are afraid of the question. You must be aware that the Treaty has been very unpopular with the English public, and the Government shrink from bringing it into further notice."

"But *you* do not hesitate to press us on the Fisheries Commission," retorted Fish; "and though we do not think you have acted up to your agreement even there, we are proceeding in good faith on our part. We expect the same good faith on yours with regard to the Three Rules."

"Well, I beg that you will give us time. No harm can come by postponement."

Fish showed indignation. "We have waited now upwards of four years," he said. "If your Government wishes to abrogate the Three Rules, we expect you to say so honestly. If not, we expect you to urge

[7] See the excellent summary of negotiations in PRO, FO 115, 602, Derby to Thornton, July 10, 1876.

the rules upon other Powers. If Great Britain should become involved in war with Russia, she might expect us to observe them; but unless she carries out her part of the stipulation, the United States *may* be justified in considering the rules as no longer binding."

Fish might justly feel indignant. Great Britain, after making a solemn treaty engagement to submit the Three Rules, had haggled over the terms for four years and was now asking for further delay! He repeated his threat several times. In the spring of 1876 he told Thornton that if England desired to withhold the rules, "I should understand it as absolving both governments from their future compliance." He also repeatedly threatened that the United States would not assist in the creation of a Fisheries Commission until Great Britain acted. To this Lord Derby of course replied that the two subjects had no connection whatever. Finally the debate culminated in a sharp exchange of notes in the summer of 1876. In a communication of September 18,[8] Fish informed the British Government that Article VI of the Treaty stood as a unit, and "a failure to comply with one part thereof may, and probably will, be held to carry with it the avoidance and nullity of the other." But this could not have frightened Lord Derby. After collecting $15,500,000 from Great Britain under the principles of the Three Rules, the United States could hardly repudiate them in their application to British rights! The impasse continued, and the United States was balked in its hope of inducing the entire world to agree on strict rules of maritime neutrality. But as Granville had said, there was precious little chance of an agreement by the Powers anyway.

The other clause of the Treaty of Washington which proved difficult to execute was that providing for a Fisheries Commission: a body of three, one to be named by the President, one by the Queen, and one by the two jointly, to fix the compensation due to Canada for the greater value of the concessions which the British had made in the fisheries compromise. The erection of this Commission met various delays. The chief resulted from an attempt in 1874 to substitute a new Canadian-American reciprocity agreement for the plan of compensating the Dominion. Fish was favorable, as always, to the general idea of reciprocity. Canadian negotiators drew up a draft scheme. On June 18, 1874, Fish submitted it to the Senate for an expression of its views. Would the Senate accept a treaty in this form? If not, in some modified form?

[8] Sen. Exec. Doc. 26, 45th Cong., 3rd Sess., 76 ff.

With protectionists in the saddle, no reciprocity agreement whatever could be passed, and the Senate on February 3, 1875, resolved that it was not deemed expedient to recommend the negotiation of the treaty. Efforts to agree upon a Commission were then resumed. The difficulty lay in the choice of an impartial third member. Another long wrangle began. It may be briefly summarized in the following record of an extraordinary four-year journey around Robin Hood's barn: [9]

July 1, 1873.—Legislation having been passed by Congress and Parliament, the fisheries clauses of the Treaty of Washington go into full effect. American fishermen had already been given privileges in Canadian waters in the fishing seasons of both 1871 and 1872; the American Commissioners having pressed for this during the negotiation of the Treaty of Washington. It was now important to set up the Commission.

March-July, 1873.—Fish and Thornton discuss a third member; Thornton informally asks if Fish will accept M. Delfosse, Belgian Minister to the United States; Fish declines. His diary shows that his initial objection to Delfosse was that he had been discourteous to the American Government. Though accredited for many months, he had failed to present his credentials, and had not appeared in uniform, like his colleagues, at Grant's inauguration. Delfosse soon made amends. But Fish was also aware that Great Britain guaranteed the neutrality of Belgium.

July 17, 1873.—Fish writes proposing the choice of any member of the diplomatic corps in Washington who could speak English save M. Corti (Italy), M. Delfosse, and the Portuguese Minister. He explains that the two last are omitted because of the peculiar connection of their governments with England. Canadian sentiment meanwhile objects to any member of the diplomatic corps in Washington as likely to show bias.

August 19, 1873.—Under instructions, Thornton formally proposes Delfosse.

August 21, 1873.—Fish rejects Delfosse. Discussion renewed. Thornton explains the Canadian objections to any diplomat drafted from Washington. Fish invites some new proposal. Thornton under instructions proposes that the British and American Ministers at The Hague try to agree on a Commissioner. Fish declines this as a variation from

[9] Drawn from Fish's diary and dispatches, and Bancroft Davis's Memorandum to George F. Edmunds, March 30, 1878; Davis Papers.

the Treaty.

April 21, 1875.—After failure of the reciprocity efforts, Thornton under instructions renews a proposal that the Austrian Ambassador in London be asked to choose the third Commissioner.

May 8, 1876.—Following a long correspondence, Fish assents to negotiations upon an identic note to be addressed to the Austrian Ambassador. But he continues to press Great Britain for a direct understanding upon a third member. In this he is always foiled. England continues to insist that Count Beust, Austrian Ambassador, make the choice. Finally—

February, 1877.—Just before leaving office, Fish consents to Delfosse under the conviction that it is better to take a man he knows, in spite of the political connection between England and Belgium, than to trust to an unknown appointment made in London by a diplomat subjected to British influence. Fish had meanwhile been guided in his final appointment of the American Commissioner by the Senators from Massachusetts and Maine. All four, Boutwell, Dawes, Morrill, and Hamlin, concurred in recommending a fisheries expert named Kellogg, who was chosen.

Stubbornly tenacious of her own rights—Britain was always that. A host of Englishmen felt that they had yielded too much in the *Alabama* quarrel; they were averse to yielding more, and they had their way with both the Three Rules and the Fisheries Commission. The rules were forgotten. When the Fisheries Commission made its "Halifax Award" in 1877, Canada and Newfoundland received $5,500,000, considered an excessive sum in America—though actually it was a fair judgment on a case which the Canadian negotiator, Sir A. T. Galt, presented with exceptional ability.

Indeed, we may safely say that on one important subject only in these years did England yield to the United States. This was extradition, which occupied an almost incredible amount of Fish's and Derby's time, and was often discussed at length by the Cabinet. The Secretary's diary is full of it. Great Britain and the United States had signed in 1842 their first extradition treaty; in 1870 Parliament passed an Extradition Act which declared that no prisoner should be put on trial for any but the extradition crime; and in 1875 the British Government protested against the trial for a second offense of a criminal surrendered to the United States. Fish maintained that the principle of the Extradition Act did not apply to the Treaty of 1842, that this treaty could not be newly construed at the will of one of the parties, and that the British position, if persisted in, would make it impossible for the United States to ask or grant extradition. While continuing the discussion, England surrendered several fugitive criminals without insisting on her claim. The most famous was a large-scale smuggler and swindler named C. L. Lawrence, for whom Edwards Pierrepont, curiously enough, was counsel just before he became Attorney-General.[10] On this subject Fish maintained American rights and scored a victory. Soon after he left office England appointed a royal commission on the extradition laws.

II

Caleb Cushing had reached Madrid at the end of May, 1874, travelling by way of Lisbon, for northern Spain was held by the Carlist insurgents. He found that Don Antonio Cánovas was acting as Premier under the new sovereign, Alfonso XII, who had just assumed the throne at the age of seventeen. He found the country in hardly abated turmoil and confusion, though the army gave the Bourbon régime its wholehearted support. The government was still on the verge of bankruptcy; Don Carlos was supported by the ultramontane Catholics throughout Europe, and glittering balls given by titled ladies in Paris "for the benefit of the wounded" supplied him with funds; the republicans were grumbling and restive. The war in eastern Cuba dragged bloodily on. But it was generally agreed that when dictators like Prim and Serrano had not dared to give up the island, Alfonso's still-precarious government could not do so.[11] As a matter of fact, Cánovas throughout a long career was to prove a reactionary on colonial policy; still unconverted, he died under an assassin's hand just as (in 1897) Spain was about to eat the bitterest fruits of his acts.

Cushing was a curious compound of strength and weakness. Intellectually as able as any American in public life, a profound scholar, a gentleman, he was still in his prime. Fish wrote that he seemed as young and energetic as in 1860. Men who talked with him could hardly believe that he had graduated from Harvard in 1817 and been elected

---

[10] Diary, 1875–76, *passim;* a large number of entries.

[11] See despatches of H. S. Sanford, Brussels, to Fish, May 14, June 16, 1876, after talks with the Spanish Minister to Belgium: State Dept. MSS. The head of the conspiracy which had effected the restoration of the Bourbons was Count Valmaseda, the former irreconcilable Captain-General in Cuba.

to the Massachusetts Legislature in 1825—all but a half-century earlier. Loving Spain, enjoying the friendship of many Spaniards, he was naturally too optimistic as to Spanish policy. As time showed, the Madrid government was ready to do anything in reason to settle American claims, some of them very dubious; but it was not willing to go far in concessions to the Cuban insurgents. Reinforcements, armed action, a thorough conquest—these were still its real objects. The indulgent Cushing misjudged the situation. Moreover, Cushing dearly loved a long protracted correspondence, an intricate negotiation. It gave him the opportunity he craved to display his vast ingenuity, industry, and learning, and he seized upon unsatisfactory Spanish proposals and offers as if they were a solid foundation upon which to build.

During the summer and fall of 1875—the point at which the story begins to be worth telling—he bombarded Fish with private letters as well as official reports. Talking with both Cuban and Spanish representatives in Madrid, he had reached three grand conclusions.[12] One was that military action could not end the Cuban revolt. The royal armies could not subdue the Creoles in their forest fastnesses, nor could the rebels defeat the Spanish forces based upon Havana. Another conclusion was that emancipation could not be effected by an isolated act, but must be part of a complete scheme for the pacification of the island. The third conclusion was that this scheme of pacification would really require the assistance of some outside Power. The Cubans, if given less than full independence, would not trust the Spaniards save under strict outside guarantees; if given independence or full autonomy, they could not govern the island and furnish a proper degree of order without foreign support. Many cool-headed Cubans and Spaniards agreed with Cushing. Careful British observers also went far toward agreeing, as Lord Derby's speech to the British Anti-Slavery Society on May 26, 1875, indicated.

Obviously, the deduction from these conclusions was that friendly and peaceable American intervention offered the best road out. Cushing repeatedly urged it. He sent Fish two elaborate schemes for it, one drawn up by Cuban leaders in Madrid and one by an American there named Edward Belknap. "Every advocate of the independence of Cuba," he wrote, "or of its autonomy under the suzerainty of Spain, or

---

[12] See especially Cushing No. 154, Spanish Despatches, State Dept.; Cushing to Fish, Private, June 26, 1876, Fish Papers.

of the emancipation of the slaves, whether he be Spaniard or Cuban, turns his thoughts instinctively towards the intervention of our government." Belknap's plan involved British mediation as well. But Fish cut through such schemes with a single telegraphed question (July 21): Would Spain accept our good offices? Next day Cushing had to cable back the weak confession that "no manifestations of any such intention yet appear." Fish had no desire to burn his fingers again with an offer of mediation that Madrid would ultimately reject. He waited, asking Cushing to urge a prompt settlement of the long-standing grievances against Spain, particularly as to the embargoed estates.

Cushing, laboring valiantly at this, soon cherished hopes of a general settlement. Then in September the Cánovas Ministry fell and his work had to be begun over again. Already Fish had begun to show uneasiness regarding the delays of the new monarchy. Irritated by news that Burriel was receiving praise instead of punishment, he wrote on September 10: [13] "Spain seems to be false to the last." When details of the ministerial overturn arrived, they also proved disquieting; for Cushing wrote that another revolution seemed imminent, and might be unfavorable to the American demands. This drew from Fish a despairing complaint of the difficulty of treating with so unstable a government. "They are delaying a settlement," he wrote Cushing on October 6, "beyond the possible endurance or patience of either the government or people of the United States." Referring to the court-martial trials in Cuba, he observed ominously that the Spanish policy there was stamping the contest "with all the characteristics of a state of legal war." A general reconsideration of the American attitude, he wrote in closing, was under way in Washington.

"As between the Spaniards and the Cubans," he disgustedly informed Louis Jennings of the *Times*.[14] "I feel very much as my late friend Judge Kent said of two brothers: 'If there be anyone that I think less of than Judge D. it is his brother Professor D.; if there is anyone that I think less of than Professor D. it is Judge D." He rallied Cushing on his optimism and his unquenchable confidence in *mañana*. But during October even Cushing betrayed grave doubts. On the 5th, he wrote that if Spain gained some real successes in Cuba, the government would take a defiant attitude toward America. If both the Cuban and Carlist rev-

---

[13] Fish to William Hunter, September 10, 1875; Letterbooks.
[14] October 5, 1875; Letterbooks.

olutions were suppressed, a foreign war would be popular in Spain. The provocation of such a war seemed to Cushing by no means impossible. On October 16 he was hopeful again, writing that by patient insistence the United States might obtain redress for outrages against its citizens and see Burriel brought to book. But the 22d found him in fresh gloom. He doubted whether the Carlists could be overcome. The Treasury could not meet its current expenses. A dark prospect opened on all sides, and the state of the political factions was like the Biblical chaos before Genesis.[15] These weathercock turns of opinion interested Fish, but they gave him no encouragement.

Moreover, the Administration was once more under heavy pressure for action. Defeated in 1870 and 1873, the demand for intervention again reared its head. The *Sun* and *Herald* were bellicose; Fish wrote of "the wonderfully persuasive influence of Cuban bonds scattered broadcast among the noble army of newspaper reporters." Cuban refugees kept up their agitation. Indignation over the arrests, embargoes, military trials, custom house fines, and interruptions to trade was widespread. When the Cabinet met on October 26, Grant asked about affairs in Cuba. "This," Fish jotted down, "evidently comes from the inspiration of the Cuban bondholders who have been at work at Long Branch and at the office of the Washington *Republican* all summer." He gave the President a general explanation. Quoting consular reports, he asserted that Spanish officers were now really sustaining the insurrection for pecuniary purposes; that by a secret understanding with insurgent leaders, they furnished the rebel forces with arms and supplies. Grant remarked that he thought it would be necessary to send Spain a sharp message upon the heavy burden which the Cuban Government was imposing upon American property, and upon commerce by the heavy export duties; the United States buying enormously from Cuba and selling little there. His attitude was genuinely threatening. At heart, Grant always wanted to intervene in Cuba. He showed as much at the next Cabinet meeting, October 29th. With evident sternness, he asked about Cushing's work in Cuba. Fish made a worried entry in his diary.

I replied . . . that Cushing had been very earnest in pressing the settlement of the various questions with Spain; . . . that he had been instructed to intimate our impatience at the continuance of the war, and the possibility that we might find it necessary to assume a different attitude from that which we

[15] Cushing to Fish, Nos. 581, 588, 601, 620, 631: State Dept. MSS.

had already occupied.

That he had written a note referring to the recognition by Spain of the belligerency of the Southern States, and showing the justification which the United States would have, should they think fit to recognize belligerency of the Cuban insurgents.

The President inquired, Why not recognize independence?

I answer the difficulty was to find the government to which we might concede the existence of independence; that I could not ascertain that within the last five years there had been the semblance or pretext of a legislative assembly being convened; that in the early days of the insurrection an Assembly . . . had met from time to time, but that about five or six years since it had been suddenly disbanded, and so far as I have been able to ascertain, has not since been convened; that Mr. Lemus had admitted to me that the majority of the members of the body were wholly self-appointed . . . adding that "we do not know much about elections in Cuba."

But Grant was not convinced by these objections. During another Cabinet discussion of Cuban affairs on November 5, Fish asked his frank opinion as to the national policy. He promptly replied that we should recognize belligerency if not independence.

Congress, too, was about to sit—a Congress full of filibusters, the House controlled by Democrats intensely hostile to the Administration. The Cuban lobby was preparing to lay siege to it. Fish heard that Aldama, head of the Junta, was being besought to issue $20,000,000 additional Cuban bonds to be used wherever they would be effective. He heard also that such Cuban sympathizers as S. S. Cox among the Democrats and N. P. Banks among the Republicans planned to carry a stiff resolution recognizing either belligerency or independence—a move which Grant, if his mood did not change, would encourage. At this very moment the scandalous story of John A. Rawlins' bond-holdings was revealed to the Cabinet. Grant told the members that he, as executor of Rawlins' estate, had asked after the funeral for an inventory of all the property. The agent who made it out reported finding a number of Cuban bonds, which Grant asked him to destroy. However, having occasion within recent weeks to look into the safe, he had been surprised to find that they were still there. He seemed in doubt as to what should be done with the bonds. Robeson suggested that they be sold! Fish pointed out that it would not do for the President, even as executor, to be selling such bonds, and Grant agreed. The fact was later revealed that the bonds totalled $30,000. This was a painful episode, and recalled old apprehensions to Fish's mind.

What could he do? It would be possible to hold Congress in leash by a sternly argumentative message on the legal imbecility of recognition. But the President could not be induced to send in such a message unless a strong alternative course were adopted. Fish, moreover, himself now felt so nauseated by the unchecked bloodshed in Cuba, the selling of lives for a few dirty pesos, and so irritated by the delay in meeting our claims, that he was ready to offer a stern alternative policy. Early in November, 1875, the Secretary hammered out his plan. There should be an elaborate message to Congress pointing out the dishonesty and untenability of recognition—with nothing to recognize. There should be an emphatic note to Spain, warning the new régime that if it did not meet our demands at once our policy might be sharply changed. And as a third element, Fish resolved upon an appeal to the European Powers to support him by representations in Madrid for a stoppage of the Cuban war.

In short, his purpose was identical with that on several former occasions—to head off Congress and President and keep the situation in his own hands; but his means had to be new, and he tried to go further than before in pressure upon Spain. At the Cabinet meeting of November 5 he manoeuvred to bring Grant under control by obtaining approval of a stiff warning to Spain—a warning that unless the conflict were ended, the United States might feel it its duty to intervene. That same day he wrote Schenck outlining what he intended to put into the President's annual message to Congress.[16] Many Congressmen had been playing with the issue "in pure demagogism or sentimentality," and must be shown its true character. They must be brought to realize the grim responsibilities offered by the Cuban situation. He would show them that recognition, instead of being the *pacific* measure which holders of Cuban bonds pretended, was a measure of *war*. Dishonestly, indirectly, and without preparation, it would carry us into conflict. He would take steps to "compel Congress, with whom rests the war-making power, to decide whether it will have war. If we must have war, let us meet it honestly and advisedly, not by indirection and surprise."

Fish at once wrote his pages for the annual message. They constituted an exhaustive and unanswerable argument against recognition of the rebels in any form. That step would be legally and morally indefensible,

---

[16] Fish to Schenck, November 5, 1875; Letterbooks.

he proved, and would lead the nation into war on discreditable grounds. Fish then reaffirmed the readiness of the United States to mediate between Spain and the insurgents. He treated the American claims, the long Spanish delays in meeting them, and his hopes that they would yet be satisfied. He mentioned also the most recent Spanish gestures toward reform in Cuba. At the close he sounded a threatening note. He had Grant state that, since American interests and considerations of humanity demanded an early cessation of the war, he should feel it his duty, if hopes of a satisfactory adjustment and early peace were disappointed, "to make a further communication to Congress at some period not far remote." But the central argument was on the untenability of recognition.

At the last minute Grant flinched from sending this message. Fish learned in the Cabinet meeting of December 3, 1875, that "the President had altered and emasculated what I had submitted to him on the subject of Spain and Cuba." The Secretary "objected most strenuously," arguing that the watered-down version presented no argument against recognition, the real issue. And he went on: [17]

That it presented the question of intervention without any argument in its suggestion, which was of grave import, being practically a suggestion of a possibility of war.

That the people of the United States and the nations of the world would regard such bald presentation as insufficient, and unworthy of the grave consequences to which it pointed.

That with his approval I had sent an instruction to Cushing on the subject, which had been read in Madrid and in London, and which committed us to a certain line of policy which should be sustained and enforced by his message.

That the passages which he had read would make Mr. Cushing and myself unsustained, and render all our effort abortive.

Bristow and Pierrepont sustained my views, generally expressing the opinion that the subject should be treated more argumentatively. Jewell wished the same thing. . . .

Grant yielded to this pressure by the four ablest members of his Cabinet. He adopted Fish's long draft almost in toto, omitting only two short passages (one upon the increased Spanish military effort in Cuba, the other general in nature), and including the whole argument against a recognition of independence or belligerency. The paper, one of the

[17] Diary, December 3, 1875.

ablest Fish ever penned, gave the annual message a memorable distinction.

Its effect upon Congress and press was all that the Secretary had hoped. Upon the interventionists it fell like an icy douche. No man, after reading it, could continue to advocate recognition and pretend to intellectual honesty. A few days after it had been published Fish wrote Cushing that the "wild" war-fever had sensibly abated, and that as he had anticipated, the sentimentalists had been brought up short by realities.[18] He felt that his emphatic statement had come in the nick of time. There had been and still was a deep conviction that the brutality and turmoil at the nation's very doors had lasted long enough—after seven years, too long. Many individuals and some large economic interests were suffering. "It was necessary to speak decidedly, or Congress would have taken the control of the question out of the hands of the Administration."

So much for his successful measures to prevent an alliance of Grant and the Congressional extremists in behalf of recognition; but what of his effort to bring Spain to terms? This effort, embodied in Instruction No. 266 to Cushing and supplementary instructions to other Ministers in Europe, constitutes one of the most curious episodes in our diplomatic history. Fish hoped for a great success; his measure embodied sound common sense; but the result, alas! was total failure.

In No. 266, dated November 5, 1875, Fish recited the heavy list of American grievances against Spain. He declared that the continued failure to redress these wrongs raised the question whether "longer endurance ceases to be possible." He pointed out once more that while Madrid denied the existence of a state of war, her agents in Cuba made use of the rights and privileges of belligerency. Spanish-American relations were in such tension that even a minor incident might produce ungovernable excitement, and "force events which this government anxiously desires to avoid." It was plainly impossible for the situation to continue, and the United States expected prompt and spontaneous measures by Spain to ameliorate it. Failing of an immediate settlement of the questions at issue, the President "feels that the time is at hand when it may be the duty of other governments to intervene. . . . He will, therefore, feel it his duty to submit the subject in this light . . . for the consideration of Congress." Though the note did not say so explicitly, Fish desired a termina-

[18] Fish to Cushing, December 10, 1875; Letterbooks.

tion of the struggle on the basis of complete or nearly complete Cuban autonomy, and emancipation. This was the grand desideratum, and the only one in which other governments than the United States could be strongly interested.

Cushing was directed not to present No. 266 at once. He was to wait until Fish could learn whether Great Britain would not also press Spain for action. General Schenck was to read a copy of No. 266 to Derby, with the suggestion that if England exerted her influence at Madrid "to induce a settlement," a more speedy adjustment might result. The other principal European Governments were also to be approached in the same way. During this brief delay the United States took significant naval steps. The fleet was based for the winter on Port Royal, S. C.; warships were ordered to Key West for fleet exercises; and the commander of the European squadron was directed on November 13 to take two vessels to Lisbon as if on his own authority and if possible without attracting attention. On November 12 it was learned that Spain was sending two powerful ironclads, the *Vittoria* and *Saragossa,* to Cuba, with two more that were smaller but very speedy. Six other Spanish vessels were being fitted out, Cushing wrote, in great haste.[19] Evidently Spain also was afraid of Congress!

In asking for British representations in Madrid, Fish felt that he had ample justification both in precedent and in the general British attitude. The English were as hostile to Cuban slavery as the Americans. British citizens had been killed, British property embargoed, in Cuba. Layard and Sickles had repeatedly acted together in Madrid. They had made simultaneous representations in 1870 against slavery; they had protested simultaneously against customs exactions. Granville had instructed Layard to support certain other American positions. Following the *Virginius* outrage, the British Government had rejected Madrid's request for its good offices unless Spain agreed to comply with the American demands. In China the United States had similarly given support to British demands for commercial rights. Indeed, some evidence exists of a tacit understanding that American coöperation would be extended to England in the Far East, and British support to American policy in the Caribbean.[20] Fish had good reason to believe that London might now urge Madrid to end the war.

He hoped that Russia and Germany would take similar action, and

---

[19] Cushing to Fish, No. 652; Bemis, *op. cit.,* VII, 194.   [20] Bemis, *op. cit.,* VII, 196.

believed that Spain would then yield. How could she resist such general pressure?

IV

But these bright anticipations were all confounded when Spain, as several times before, parried the impending blow by a timely counter-stroke —and when Cushing lent her his best aid. On November 15 Madrid sent Fish a note, a summary of which reached him by cable. It met all the points which he had raised in his recent notes, and promised redress and reform in specific terms! Fish was naturally taken aback, while Cushing was pleased. The untoward results, as Fish saw them, are presented in a most illuminating letter he wrote Schenck a month later:[21]

I fear that Cushing's reluctance to present a positive message has induced him to find some expression in my instructions to avoid the full force and object of my No. 266. It contained no threat, but was intended (so far as Spain was concerned) to let her know that our patience was exhausted. So far as *home* matters were concerned it was intended to foreclose the questions of recognition of either belligerence or independence, to stop the mouths of blatant filibusters in a Democratic Congress, and to bring out the expression of what I never doubted to exist, *viz.*, the entire unwillingness of our people to risk a war for Cuba, and to show the insignificance of the loud-mouthed sympathy for the Cuban insurrectionists. The *home* effect has produced just what I expected. But Cushing had been conducting a long and able correspondence; he loves the controversy of negotiating on paper. He received a long, able, and very friendly but subtle and evasive note on 15th November. I doubt that it was what he had expected; he telegraphed me its general purport; it opened the door for long-protracted correspondence and negotiation . . . —a godsend to him, but nothing to us who want *something* to be settled. On receiving his telegram I telegraphed to you to delay presenting the instruction to Lord Derby, and in the meantime, by means of the cable, ascertained that the Spanish note would not, in any sense, change (in fact it does not touch the point of No. 266) the view or policy of the Administration, and requested the presentation of the instruction.

The delay had lost us the opportunity of learning from you the effect the note would produce on Lord Derby, and lost us the benefit of concurrent suggestion at Madrid, inasmuch as it was necessary to present the instructions in Madrid before the delivery of the President's annual message.

This was a disappointment. Next, Cushing, in presenting the instruction, seems to have told them what was very apparent, that my instruction bearing date November 5 was written before the receipt, and without knowledge of

[21] January 15, 1876; Letterbooks.

the contents or purport of their note . . . written on the 15th November, and seems to have intimated that nothing need be done on their part, until it be seen how far the Spanish note of [the] 15th might change the views, etc., of the President. On the receipt of my instruction, he says that Layard was prepared to back him up. But he seems to have held Layard back, who of course has reported something to London, and now what he is doing or will do remains to be seen. Russia and Germany were quite cordial, and prepared to say that the conflict ought to be brought to a close—this is all we wanted said.

He added that the United States had no desire to prescribe the terms of settlement; that he would regard annexation as an unmitigated calamity; and that, doubting the immediate fitness of the Cubans for independence, he believed the best possible arrangement would be a scheme of dominion government like Canada's. "It was something of this sort to which I hoped Spain would not be wholly disinclined, when she should have heard simultaneously from the principal European Powers their agreement that the time had come when the strife should be ended. . . . I shall yet hope, but I get no direct and *positive* information. Cushing's despatches are very able and exceedingly interesting, but inclining to be speculative and hypothetical." Fish was left groping half in the dark.

The conciliatory Cushing had not liked the tone of No. 266 at all. He did not believe that Spain had been so remiss as Fish alleged. The Legation files, he wrote on November 19, showed that no unfulfilled promises existed. Sr. Martos had met all his promises by signing the comprehensive agreement for a Claims Commission. Sr. Castelar had met his promise to release the embargoed property except in a single instance, that of Angarica, which hung fire on a question of citizenship later resolved by Serrano. "Much of the apparent misunderstanding for years," Cushing asserted, "has arisen from confounding *embargo* with *confiscation,* and from allowing the object of satisfying the clamors of property claimants (and mostly slave property of bogus citizens at that) to stand in the front-ground so as to push out of sight the transcendent question of death-sentences in violation either of our treaty-rights or of our rights of sovereignty." He thought that most of the claims by Americanized Cubans were presented in an effort to make Washington their tool for private objects. "Everybody here," he concluded, "Spaniards and foreigners alike, on looking back now on the last eighteen months, expresses astonishment in view of all the results which the United States have accomplished."

A few days later he wrote Fish more sharply still.[22] He defended his patience and his generous confidence in the Spaniards as the best means of winning diplomatic success. He was sure that Madrid would soon make all necessary concessions. And he pointed out that Spain was not the only nation with faulty institutions:

> . . . It pains me infinitely to have it confirmed that "hordes" of penny-a-liners, bribed with bonds of the Cuban Junta, are the masters of Congress, and so able to act on the foreign policy of the Government. That, it is true, is the universal belief in Spain, nay, in all Europe.
>
> It is a humiliating fact (or imputation) which Spaniards are continually throwing in my face. They frankly admit their own defects of ill-regulated ambition, of proclivity to insurrection and civil war, of indecision of opinion, and of occasional fits of savage cruelty. But they charge us with what they think is worse, corruption, public and private, financial frauds, a mercenary press, and the subordination of principle (including the highest interests of the country) to electoral demagogy.
>
> For these charges they have the authority, as they say, of our public journals, and above all, of Congress itself, which has, by its extra-constitutional investigations, so-called, dishonored beyond measure itself and the country in the estimation of Europe.

Fish, after hesitating for ten days over the Spanish note of November 15, had directed Cushing and Schenck on November 27 to present No. 266 at once. But he had made one concession to Madrid. Cushing was directed to say that No. 266 was "not intended as minatory in any sense but in the spirit of friendship."

The European response to the despatch was discouraging in the extreme. In Spain the Foreign Minister, Calderon, listened to No. 266 with an amiable face. He expressed his agreement with its general observations, and promised a detailed reply after full study; a promise which might mean much or nothing. Great Britain and most of the Continental Powers were chilly to the request for pressure in Madrid. London had of course been informed of the Spanish offer of November 15, while Layard knew Cushing's hostile views upon Fish's step and transmitted them to Lord Derby. Throughout Europe the Spanish Ministers besought the various foreign offices to rebuff the United States. Boker, for example, sent from St. Petersburg a vivid description of how the Spanish envoy hurried to anticipate him in an interview with Gortcha-

[22] Private, November 26, 1875; Fish Papers.

kov, and exerted all his powers of argument.[23]

Lord Derby told Schenck on December 2 that his government was willing to assist in any way that promised to promote peace in Cuba, "but is not prepared to put any pressure on the Spanish Government or to put forward proposals which he has reason to think it would not accede to." American efforts to induce him to alter this position all failed. Late in January he repeated his refusal. The French Government was even less helpful. Its Foreign Minister declared that Madrid could not yield without playing into the hands of the Carlists, which France did not desire. The Italian and German Governments contented themselves with vague expressions of approval of no practical value. The Italian Minister told Fish that relations between Rome and Madrid were delicate. The German Minister was more explicit. His country, he said, had suffered from the Cuban revolt, but it did not wish to take any decided step; it could not act except in concert with other European Governments; and Spain was so weak that other nations ought not to add to her troubles. Russia alone made representations of some vigor in Madrid.

And when early in 1876 the contents of No. 266 were revealed at home, the American response was also harshly critical. Part of the press at once condemned Fish's approach to the European Powers as violating the spirit of the Monroe Doctrine.[24] This was rather absurd. Fish summarized his real intention in a talk of December 30, 1875, with the Italian Minister: "That we desired the restoration of peace and good government, that we had no selfish or aggressive policy, did not invite or seek any forcible intervention by other governments, but simply asked an expression of their opinion as to the reasonableness of our attitude and demands on Spain. . . ." The Monroe Doctrine was not involved in this expression of a decent respect to the opinions of mankind.

As a matter of fact, Fish followed a precedent set by John Quincy Adams, who of all men might be supposed to know what the Monroe Doctrine meant. In 1824 Adams had formally asked the mediation of the Russian Government with Spain to bring about a cessation of Spanish hostilities with the new South American republics; and Fish had this action in mind in writing No. 266. As recently as June 17, 1870, the House of Representatives had passed a resolution authorizing the President to remonstrate against the barbarous conduct of the war in

---

[23] Boker to Fish, Private, February 11, 1876; Fish Papers.
[24] See, e. g., the *Nation*, February 3, 1876, "Mr. Fish's Facts."

Cuba, and to "solicit the coöperation of other governments in such measures as he may deem necessary to secure from both contending parties" an observance of the laws of war. Surely, an appeal for the moral support of Europe in calling for an end of the war was no more an infringement of the Monroe Doctrine than an appeal for its moral support in asking for reformation of the methods of war. No less a person than Admiral Polo had once, informally and casually, suggested to Fish that he might try to align Europe behind him in requesting a cessation of hostilities. The Secretary had acted with propriety and with logic. Nevertheless, most Americans seemed to disapprove his course; nor did he lighten their censure when he made a rather clumsy public statement on the question.

Altogether, No. 266 must be pronounced a failure at home and abroad. Fish had meant well; he might quote Addison, " 'Tis not in mortals to command success;" but he had miscalculated. The ground should have been more fully explored, the attitude of European Governments more carefully gauged, before he took so unusual a step. He should have realized the possibility, nay, the probability, of such a note as Spain sent on November 15 (for Madrid always tried to anticipate a session of Congress) and been prepared for it. With the cable at hand, he should have compelled closer harmony on Cushing's part. Nevertheless, when we call No. 266 a failure, we must not overlook one fact. It was the price paid for Grant's reluctant inclusion of Fish's powerful argument against recognition in his annual message, an argument that was a complete success.

Nor did No. 266 do any permanent harm to Spanish-American relations. Prince Gortchakov even thought that it had produced a healthy effect in Madrid. When Boker told him of the American criticism, Gortchakov said: [25] "What a mistake! I regard that affair as a complete triumph. You see that Spain is now eager to justify herself with all the Cabinets of Europe. Mr. Fish put her upon the defensive before the world." . . . There may have been some truth in this. On January 16, 1876, Calderon asked Cushing: "What is the precise thing Fish would like Spain to do under the circumstances?" There is no question that from that moment Madrid showed a wonderful complaisance to America —though not, unhappily, to Cuba.

Spanish-American affairs, indeed, rapidly entered upon a new era.

[25] Boker to Fish, February 11, 1876; Fish Papers.

Madrid undertook to treat Fish's formidable indictment as a subject for friendly negotiation, and Cushing gladly aided in the work. Early in February the Spanish Government sent the United States and the European Powers a careful reply to No. 266. It rebutted many of Fish's charges; asserted that reforms had been instituted in Cuba and that economic recovery was well under way there; and, declaring that the rebellion had become mere aimless brigandage, predicted its early extinguishment by increased Spanish forces. Much evidence was indeed at hand that the revolt was fast entering its final stages.

Before Fish left office most of the demands of the United States in behalf of its own citizens had been satisfied. In a new instruction of March 1, Fish answered Calderon's inquiry as to what he expected Spain to do. He laid down four general requirements: (1) a satisfactory understanding as to the rights of persons and property; (2) improved commercial facilities; (3) valid emancipation; and (4) a larger degree of self-government in Cuba, with a general amnesty. Replying in a note of April 16, the Spanish Government expressed almost complete agreement. The specific grievances of Americans were soon nearly all removed. Embargoes were lifted from practically all estates; trials by court-martial were abolished for American citizens, save when taken with arms in hand—and even then they were allowed counsel and the right of appeal; and American commerce was given fairer treatment.[26]

Cuba remained in chains. The collapse of the rebellion in 1878 by no means brought a disappearance of Creole discontent, for the Spanish promises of reform were inadequate and were badly executed. Not until 1880 did the Spanish Cortes pass an effective law of emancipation. With the spirit of revolt still smouldering, Spain and the United States had gained but a brief respite from the Cuban problem. Confronted at every turn, year after year from 1869 to 1877, by the heavy, irrational, irresponsible Spanish pride, Fish had been unable to effect a permanent solution of this problem. He had used every instrument at his command; he had outlined the elements of a lasting settlement again and again; he had extorted a few reforms. Had the Spanish sentiment of *pundonor* been qualified by only a little more wisdom, he might have succeeded. Once or twice he had seemed to hold victory almost in his hand. But in the end he could only say that he had done his best—and had kept the peace. He had kept it by preventing the main taproot of most wars—

[26] Protocol signed by Cushing and Calderon, February 4, 1877.

sentiment, excitement, public passion—from ever gaining strength.

To have kept the peace was in itself an achievement not without lustre. Throughout Grant's second Administration strong forces steadily continued to labor for war. That they took increased power from the industrial depression and presented a very real threat at the time of Fish's No. 266 is proved by many a document of the time. One pungent bit of evidence may be extracted, in closing, from the diary. On November 6, 1875, Ben Butler called on Fish. It was at a moment when the persistent border troubles with lawless Mexican elements were more worrisome than usual. He began by saying that he supposed the Secretary had some desire for Republican success in 1876:

He stated that at the close of the war, 1,400,000 soldiers had been disbanded, and that while many of them returned to peaceful pursuits, the others of them furnished the violent and idle element of society, the tramps and thieves at the North and the outlaws at the South.

That a war would furnish the best means of using up this population; that the business of the country was stagnant, and that a war would give stimulus to all enterprises; that history shows that in time of war even the peaceful classes were stimulated; that a war with Mexico would be popular at the South, and would put an end to all the questions arising out of Reconstruction; that the disorderly population would rush into the war and that "a larger part of them would be left in Mexico either under or above ground."

He thinks that by sending some colored troops, the fact of fighting side by side would relieve those who might survive and return home from all prejudice of color against the Negro.

At the same time, he considers a war with Spain would be good, and that it would be confined to the ocean, and would put an end to the troubles growing out of the Cuban question. That he was opposed to the granting of belligerent rights.

He thought that the two wars would greatly stimulate all the national industries of the country; give employment to what is now idle population, and would in its effect inure wholly to the benefit of the Republican Party.

I listened to him while he occupied more than half an hour in his statements and arguments; and made but little reply other than to suggest that one war was bad enough, but that two at once were more than I would have expected even him to have suggested.

v

He had kept the peace—he had kept the peace. The wheels of Fish's train as on March 27, 1877, he travelled from Washington homeward to New York, might have seemed to him to beat out that refrain. Under severe provocation and amid many perils, he had kept the peace with Spain. In spite of immense difficulties, he had not merely kept the peace with Great Britain, but had achieved a settlement with that Power which marked a great turning-point in Anglo-American relations, and a great precedent in the international arbitration of disputes. Against the advice of men who wished him to pursue a punitive and provocative policy toward Mexico, he had kept the peace with that troubled republic. His career as Secretary of State was perhaps less spectacular than that of his immediate predecessor, Seward, or than that of one or two men destined to follow him. But in substantial achievement, in its record of errors avoided and of triumphs won, it cannot suffer from comparison with that of any occupant of the office. He had held his high position during a difficult period of transition—transition from the unsettlement and excitement of the war years to the sobriety and steadiness of a new period of peaceful development. His labors during eight years had constituted one of the most important contributions to this process of transition and reconstruction. When he began filing away his papers in his Stuyvesant Square library, he could take pride in thinking that he had left our foreign relations almost clear of difficult problems, and on a footing of general amity and peace.

"Politics," John Morley says, "are a field where action is one long second-best, and where the choice lies constantly between two blunders." But Fish's calm sagacity had often been able to choose the very best, and to show that there were sensible alternatives to blunder.

IT is a bright kaleidoscope that the records of Fish's last fifteen years
bring before us. A spectator?—chiefly, but not wholly that. Spring days
of planning and planting in the four hundred acres of Glenclyffe; summer days of hospitable talk on the piazza, the Hudson a silver sheet
below; autumn days of driving amid the painted woods; winter days
again in Stuyvesant Square, the long table sparkling for the best of
New York's society, the fireplace ruddy for the children and grandchildren. A steady round of engagements: meetings of the trustees of
Columbia College, Fish at one end of the table in the old building on
Madison Avenue, solemn, long-bearded President Barnard with his ear-
telephone at the other; meetings of the Union League Club, Fish rap-
ping for order; meetings of the New York Historical Society amid its
wealth of paintings, busts, and books; meetings of the Astor and Lenox
Libraries; meetings of the Standing Committee of the Episcopal
Church; meetings of two vestries, St. Mark's-in-the-Bowery and St.
Philip's-in-the-Highlands; journeys to Washington for meetings of the
Peabody Fund trustees; meetings of the Society of the Cincinnati,
President-General Fish erect and dignified as befitted a son of Washington's old comrade. In the background, the slow procession of public life
moving by—the brilliant, erratic Garfield; debonair Chester A. Arthur;
sturdy Grover Cleveland; the coldly intellectual Harrison, with all that
these names connote. Then, before Fish turned the last page of his life,
bold Cleveland again.

To the last he moved in a spacious world and was busy with many
tasks; he kept a host of friends and conducted a wide correspondence.
For some years his interest in public questions was that of a warrior
who has just unbuckled his armor. He watched the limp administration
of the State Department by Evarts, a gifted man too far past his prime,
without enthusiasm, and the brief first Secretaryship of the adventurous
Blaine with alarm. He liked to have old comrades at his table—Sir Edward Thornton, to whom he wrote intimate notes and whose promotion
to be Ambassador to Russia pleased him; Senators Anthony, Howe,
and Edmunds; Rockwood Hoar. To the end of Grant's life his relations
with the ex-President were close and his loyalty was undiminished. He

was a shrewd commentator on passing events; a little conservative, a little limited, but independent and outspoken. He even engaged with zest in controversy, and when the "Boston Mutual Admiration Society" renewed its attack on him and Grant, returned shaft for shaft.

He was conscious that he had lived a rich life and often commented on the fact. He had known every governor of New York save George Clinton, he once wrote an old schoolmate.[1] "Of the Presidents of the United States, I have seen and shaken hands with all except the first four. I have dined (in the White House) with Tyler, Polk, Pierce, Buchanan, Grant, Hayes. Arthur, Taylor, and Garfield have dined with me, as also Pierce and Grant. My father, as I have been told, introduced Col. Monroe (afterwards President Monroe, and *entre nous*, excepting Hayes the weakest man ever occupying that position) to his wife." Though he could not remember any special meeting, he had known John Jay. "The Governor was President of the American Bible Society, and altho' he retired to Bedford on the close of his service as Governor, he occasionally visited New York, and on such occasions generally came to my father's house, where I feel confident that I must have seen him." He had known most of the parliamentary giants. "I agree to your judgment of Clay. He was superb—he *was* an *actor*, but of the grandest type; ambitious, arrogant, domineering, but full of generosity, and at times as susceptible to kindness and sympathy as a woman. . . . His acting was assumed, at times, for effect, and produced its effect; at times it was *real*, and then it surpassed all other acting." So he could comment upon American leaders from Albert Gallatin, whom he knew as an old man, to Theodore Roosevelt, whom he knew as a young leader (with Fish's own son Hamilton) in state politics.

In American foreign relations he continued to take the keenest interest. A little more than a year after he quit office the Halifax Award of $5,500,000 to Canada for American use of the fisheries fell upon the country as a sharp blow. Evarts wrote Fish that he was greatly chagrined by the judgment, that he had spared no pains or expense to present the American case well, and that he feared "we were overmatched in the Commission." Blaine also made a sharp attack on the Commission, and especially on Delfosse. Naturally Fish was at pains, in letters to Washington leaders, to defend his consent to Delfosse not as an ideal arbiter but at the best to be obtained. He at first blamed the

[1] To W. H. Bogart, July 16, 1884; Letterbooks.

Belgian. Writing to Thornton [2] upon Delfosse's impending marriage, he remarked that Sir John Macdonald ought to buy him a handsome gift. "Do you think that I ought to send Delfosse a present? How would a pair of scales do? Or a pair of spectacles? Or should it be an ear-trumpet for that ear which could not hear the evidence on one side?" But this was half-playful, and when Thornton remonstrated, Fish admitted that Delfosse might have acted with more justice than Americans supposed. He had, in fact, suffered the common fate of arbitrators. The British after the Geneva award had scourged Staempfli with scorpions. *Punch* once published an apt cartoon: "Arbitration! Ca' that arbitration? Why, they have given it against us!"

The controversy with Sumner's Boston friends was none of his seeking. Fish in the autumn of 1877 went to Boston to attend the triennial general convention of the Episcopal Church, remaining three weeks. At this moment the Edinburgh correspondent of the New York *Herald* reported an interview with Grant which was sharply critical of Sumner. The fiery Wendell Phillips responded with an address upon Sumner which was full of denunciation of Grant and denials of his statements. Thereupon Fish gave an interview to the Boston *Transcript* confirming what Grant had said of Sumner's neglect of certain treaties. When Henry L. Pierce, Sumner's literary executor, called for facts and dates, he promptly got them. "I addressed a letter to the *Transcript*," Fish wrote Grant,[3] "answering Mr. Pierce's 'enquiry' and giving, I think, a little more information than was expected. The public press has very generally noticed it, and without an exception so far as I have seen, has considered your statements as fully substantiated." Phillips repeated his lecture, with additional vituperation, in New York and Philadelphia. Fish then published a moderate letter in the *Herald*,[4] which, he informed Grant, "will be the last notice that I shall feel called upon to take of anything which that blackguard may say."

Such a quarrel could not be expected to generate much light; as Sumner's mind had been all egotism, so those of his followers Wendell Phillips and H. L. Pierce sometimes seemed nearly all fanaticism. Yet a few rays of illumination did reach the subject. Ben: Perley Poore, friend of both Sumner and Grant and substantially impartial, wrote Senator Anthony that the misunderstanding between them might easily

[2] September 21, 1878; Letterbooks.　　　[3] November 13, 1877; Letterbooks.
[4] N. Y. Herald, November 10, 12, 1877.

have been composed but for the meddlesome tale-bearing of John W. Forney and M. de Chambrun. Forney was an old woman, de Chambrun a too-impetuous admirer of Sumner, and their loose talk created bad blood. Poore also gave it as his opinion that Sumner had been subconsciously jealous of Grant. He felt a chronic hostility toward military power, dating back to his early oration on peace in Boston; Forney, Ashley, and other sycophants led him to believe in 1866–68 that he might win the nomination over Grant; and when a military upstart like Babcock showed him the Dominican treaty he felt an instant prejudice against it. Boutwell also made a contribution. His statement [5] that he had heard Sumner tell Grant, on that famous winter evening, "I expect, Mr. President, to support the measures of your Administration," was worth little after eight years. But he rightly observed that Sumner's great error lay in neglecting to return the President's call, and to inform him face-to-face that he could not support the treaty; thus leaving him under the wrong impression gained at Sumner's house. Boutwell had once told Sumner this, and the Senator had admitted his mistake.

In short, Boutwell and Poore seemed to agree that a little more frankness, more tact, and less heed to officious friends might easily have prevented the tragic quarrel. However this may be, the revival of the controversy had one happy result. It enabled Fish to place on record a frank and honest refutation of Sumner's story that the Secretary had tried to bribe him to drop his antagonism to the treaty. He wrote [6] that he most positively denied the imputation that at any time he had seriously tendered, or thought of tendering, the British mission to Sumner, "although some of his friends more than once urgently pressed it." Least of all would he have thought of doing so to gain Sumner's support for any measure. "If my respect at the time for Mr. Sumner would not have restrained me, I had too much self-respect to traffic with him or any other on such a subject." He continued:

. . . I called, as I was in the frequent habit of doing, late one evening at Mr. Sumner's, and found him much depressed and in tears. I vainly endeavored to rally him; and after his allusion to certain [matrimonial] troubles, which I need not indicate, contrasting his own relations in these regards with, as he said, my own more happy ones, and expressing the wish that some morning he might be found dead in his bed, I urged his leaving Washington

[5] Boutwell to Fish, November 12, 1877; Fish Papers.
[6] Letter to Boston *Transcript*, October 29, 1877.

to find relief from what, for some time, I had seen was becoming a morbid and disturbed condition of mind and of temper. I suggested his going to Europe. He presented difficulties, such as his engagement in the editing of his speeches, etc., and the cost, etc., when I incautiously asked if he would like to be Minister to England. He slowly said, "No, I would not like to interfere with Motley, who is my friend." This answer relieved me from an alarm into which a pause and apparent deliberation on his part had thrown me, and had presented the realization of the incaution into which I had fallen. I instantly availed of his reply, saying, you are right, you should go without any official cares or duties.

It was not until months after this conversation that the friendly and intimate relations which had existed for some twenty years between Mr. Sumner and myself became interrupted, to my great grief; and it was not until after such interruption that the suggestion was made that the incautious remark of mine, called out by sympathy with a lifelong friend, whom I found in deep distress and in tears, whom I feared to be in danger of falling into serious mental depression or worse, had been with any improper purpose, or to influence his action upon the San Domingo treaty. In fact, it was thoroughly well understood at the time, and had been for a considerable period before then, that there was no possibility of obtaining a sufficient number in the Senate to ratify the treaty, and that it was doubtful if a majority even of the Senators were in favor of it. Would Mr. Sumner, or any other hightoned honorable man, have continued on terms of personal intimacy for months with one who he thought had approached him with a dishonorable or a corrupt proposition?

The tendency of the reform press, in the first months of the Hayes Administration, to draw invidious comparisons between it and the Grant régime, irritated Fish. *Les absents ont toujours tort,* he wrote; now that nobody expected any favors of the Grant Administration, everybody abused it; its considerable achievements were forgotten. Except upon paper, he thought Hayes' reforms slender. The President and Cabinet talked much of the merit system, but like Grant, they found it hard to put into practise. Fish praised the Administration for its efforts to eradicate sectional antagonism and to govern the country honestly and economically. It had no Belknaps or Robesons. But he deplored the growing schism between Stalwarts and Half-Breeds, which threatened to deliver the country to the Democrats, and which he thought traceable largely to Hayes's clumsiness and partiality. "I wish we were assured," he also wrote Grant,[7] "of the same inflexible purpose

---

[7] August 4, 1877; Letterbooks. Fish wrote Grant in this same letter that the House leaders still threatened action against Robeson, and that Hayes's Secretary of the Navy, Thompson, spoke in harsh terms of Robeson's scandalous mismanagement.

of resumption and belief in solid hard money that marked your Administration; but John Sherman never, while a Senator, showed more than an Ohio man's policy on that question." This was unfair. John Sherman was a far stronger Secretary of the Treasury than Boutwell or Richardson had been; Hayes's veto of the Bland-Allison Bill in 1878 was much more resolute than Grant's initial attitude toward the Inflation Bill. But Fish was so deeply pained by the indiscriminate scorn now poured upon the Grant Administration, obliterating even its successes in the field of foreign relations, that he was unable to see Hayes or his official acts in a true light. No one knew better than he how weak some parts of Grant's record had been, but exaggerated criticism thrust him into an attitude of antagonism; his references to George William Curtis, for example, took on an acid tone of contempt.

I

As Grant slowly circled the globe, he wrote Fish letters which, never before published, throw a pleasing light upon his personality. He had first gone to St. Louis. *En route,* after stopping in Cincinnati, he informed Fish, "Com. Ammen and I visited the scenes and acquaintances of our boyhood [at Georgetown, O.] where we had not met for forty-one years before. The people seemed glad to see us, and realized no doubt more fully than we did the changes that had taken place with us. The change that I saw in others is so great that I felt no desire to tarry long." He added that his wife and he thought of making Washington their home. "Had you accepted the office of Chief Justice . . . I would have hoped to have you for a neighbor, as I now hope to have you always for a friend. Mrs. Grant was so affected at parting that she did not recover until exhausted to sleepiness." The ex-President, as Fish records in his papers, had made $25,000 from a fortunate mining investment, and resolved to exhaust it in travel. His next letter was dated London, June 22, 1877:

I have been intending for the last two weeks to drop you and Mrs. Fish a line to say how we have passed our time since arriving in England, but have been kept from doing so, until now, by constant engagements and a little by a disposition to procrastinate. The papers have kept the public very well acquainted with all the receptions and invitations I am offered so that it is not necessary that I should give any description. But my reception has been remarkable in two respects: first by invitations by all authorities connected with the Govt. from the Queen down to the Mayors and City Councils of almost every city in the United Kingdom; and second by the hearty responses of the citizens of all the cities I have visited, or at which trains upon which I have been travelling have stopped even for a few moments. It has been very much as it was in the United States in '65 directly after the war. I take this as indicative of a present very good feeling toward the U. S.

Many persons say to me quietly that they personally were our good friends in the day of our country's trial but they witness now many who were the reverse then that outdo their neighbors in respect and kindness of feeling for us now. Of course I know this is so, but I understand that the South was purely agricultural before the war, paid no attention to manufactories, and were free traders. Self-interest taught them that with separation they would reap large benefits from trade—almost exclusive—with the Southern Confederacy. I believe now the real feeling of the majority is that it is much better that the result should have been in favor of the Union.

Six weeks later, September 9, he was writing from Inverness:

During my tour it would have been a great comfort if you and Mrs. Fish could have been along. On this island the receptions have been a little too much like our departure from Philadelphia to constitute rest; but the welcome has been hearty and gratifying. But on the continent it was very pleasant. My receptions while quiet were hospitable and agreeable. The lack of English-speaking people was all that was required. In ascending and descending the beautiful mountain passes of Switzerland and Northern Italy Mrs. Grant always regretted she could not have some of her old friends like Mrs. Fish to help her enjoy the scenery. But, as you say in your letter, the papers have kept you fully advised of where we have been and what has been done so nothing further on the subject is necessary from me.

I note what you say about the working of Civil Service reform and the new Administration. I think Mr. Hayes is perfectly honest in his intentions; but, if so, I think he will find out that there are two great humbugs influencing him now; namely, reform and reformers. But I hope all will work out right and that three years hence, the Republican Party will be united and triumphant.

A communication nearly a year later from Vienna contains some items of military history: [8]

Your very welcome letter of the 12th of July reached me in St. Petersburg, where I enjoyed a visit of about two weeks, very much. While in Berlin Gortchakoff expressed a great desire to see me, but his physical condition

[8] August 22, 1878; Fish Papers.

was such at the time—from gout—that he could not walk. I went therefore
to see him, and had a long pleasant talk. He asked me about my proposed
visit to Russia, and seemed to regret that he would not be there when I arrived—I expected at that time to reach St. Petersburg some three weeks
earlier than I did—but said I would meet with a most hearty reception.
Whether felt or not the reception was most cordial in appearance. Our Minister was requested days before my arrival to notify the Prime Minister the
very moment I got there. He did so and in two hours after—although the
Minister, Gortchakoff, lived some twenty miles out by rail—an answer was
sent fixing the time for an audience with the Emperor. When I called the
Emperor approached me and taking me by the hand led me to a seat, after
which we had a talk of some twenty minutes or more. I know this is an uninteresting subject to write about, but I tell you because we both had serious
apprehensions that the case would be quite different. There is no doubt but
that the United States stands very high in the estimation of the Russians,
from the Emperor down. They fully expect some day to have their aid in
the settlement of European matters, which they think further from a satisfactory and peace-inspiring relation than before the Berlin Congress met.

I read all the New York papers regularly, and get slips from papers from
all parts of the U. States, good and bad, abusive and commendatory. I am
very sorry Young published what he calls our table talk. There is not one
word in it which was said with a view of its publication or even of its being
taken down. Mr. Young travelled with us up the Nile and on the Mediterranean and during so many weeks much was said upon war matters, etc.
He told me afterwards that he was so much interested in many things I said
that he had taken them down from time to time, with as much accuracy as
he could, for further reference though he did not know that he should ever
publish it. He handed me the manuscript—enough of it to fill two pages of
the *Herald*—to read, I put it in my trunk and forget all about it for several
months, until after Jesse had gone back to the United States. I then looked
for it but could not find it. I supposed it had been packed in Jesse's trunk.
But further search produced the documents, which I read over hurriedly and
struck off a large part relating more particularly to my civil administration.
The balance was substantially correct except in relation to losses in the campaign from the Rapidan to the James River. I said that Welles and Taylor
and other writers would soon have it pass into history that we had a 100,000
men killed in that campaign to reach a point which could easily have been
reached, by boat, without loss, and ignoring the fact that Lee sustained any
losses during this time; that 40,000—I thought about 39,000—would cover
such losses; but that Badeau's book would give the facts with the greatest
attainable accuracy. I said our reports from time to time of killed, wounded,
and missing would show a much greater loss. But of the missing reported
many would turn up in a day or two, many again would be found in the
hands of the enemy and would afterward be exchanged, and many again were
slightly wounded but not disabled from duty. . . .

Grant added that after a month's rest in the mountains he would pay a visit to the only countries he had not yet seen in Europe, Spain and Portugal. The next summer (1879) he hoped to be in Long Branch, and would probably make Galena his winter home. "I am quite ready," he concluded, "to believe that you have been working quite hard as a 'farm laborer' and that some days you may earn as much as 25 cts. by your labor, and that your hands are blistered, your face bronzed, etc., but it taxes my credulity too much when you say you would not *swop* your present position even for a place in Mr. Hayes' Cabinet. . . . Do you suppose either Schurz or Evarts would fully credit your statement? But I shall keep it as a profound secret. I too am entirely content with my present lot. But I do not know what the offer of such a position as you speak of might effect. The President declining to give me the Berlin position which Halsted of the Cincinnati *Commercial* urged so strongly upon him, might prevent me from accepting any other position under this Administration. Then too I should object to association with Schurz. I make up my mind the position will not be offered to either of us, and it is an easy matter to decline what we know we cannot have."

Not until September, 1879, did Grant return through the Golden Gate, to begin a journey eastward across the country which proved a triumphal progress. He found waiting for him a still-admiring people. He found waiting, too, the politicians—the Stalwart leaders, the Old Guard, who had adroitly engineered a third term movement. Three men, Conkling in New York, Don Cameron in Pennsylvania, and Logan in Illinois, each at the head of his machine, hoped to make Grant the next Republican nominee. It was not creditable to him that he lent himself to the movement. Nor was it creditable to Fish that, like Boutwell, he approved of the movement. He gave his reasons in various letters to his friends. The coming election would be hotly contested; during their long tenure the Republicans had made many enemies; it did not greatly matter which of several good men they nominated; but it was of the greatest importance that they choose someone who would be victorious. Only by a victory in 1880 could they break the unity of the "solid South" and restore a healthful division into parties in that section.

These reasons are far from impressive, and Rockwood Hoar refuted them in a sharp yet complimentary letter.[9] Confessing himself a

[9] Hoar to Fish, May 19, 1880; Fish Papers.

bit old-fashioned, Hoar remarked that he believed the popular aversion to a third term, save in some dire emergency, entirely sound. Moreover, with all respect and regard for Grant personally, he thought that the character, history, and relations of the politicians most prominent in pressing his nomination were such as to excite anxiety and distrust. It was important to find a candidate who would command wholehearted party support, and in whose ability and uprightness the country would have unquestioning reliance. "I do not quite see in any of the leading candidates all that wisdom and safety require—and hoping, therefore, that the convention at Chicago may make a more prudent choice, I will merely add that my own candidate, first, last, and all the time, is Hamilton Fish of New York, and that I have urged upon all the Massachusetts delegates whom I have seen the wisdom of working quietly in that direction. The credit of a large part of what was best in President Grant's Administration belongs to his Secretary of State—and in the private history of that debt what was prevented is perhaps as deserving of gratitude as what was done." Though Conkling would be antagonized by any New York nomination save his own, "your name would give us . . . a vigorous, united, harmonious, and successful campaign." This was handsome of Hoar. The New York *Herald*, and a few other newspapers, also advocated Fish's nomination. But he was seventy-two, and few could really think him available.

Grant's defeat in the Chicago Convention was a bitter mortification to the ex-President. But his friends hastened to make it possible for him to live in New York on a scale befitting his position. On November 10, 1880, Fish received a letter signed by George W. Childs, Thomas A. Scott, Anthony J. Drexel, and J. Pierpont Morgan, asking him to be one of twenty gentlemen to make up a fund of $100,000 to be invested for Grant's benefit. He cordially assented; but before arrangements could be perfected it was announced that another group, headed by George Jones of the *Times*, had raised $250,000 as a fund for the general. The $100,000 was then used to buy him a house on Sixty-sixth Street near Fifth Avenue.[10] Fish did not wholly like these gifts, writing that Congress ought in decency to give all ex-Presidents a pension of $25,000 a year. He was glad, however, to have Grant a neighbor again. The general was often at the Stuyvesant Square house; Fish's engagement book mentions him and members of his family dining there in

[10] Fish to Childs, November 13, 1880, March 12, 1881; Letterbooks.

1881 and 1882, as they doubtless did oftener. The two men met also as trustees of the Peabody Fund.

Fish was therefore a close witness of the sad decline of Grant's fame during 1881–84, when his attempts to meddle with the patronage under President Arthur, and the well-known fact that he was interested in Wall Street operations, dimmed the lustre of his name; and a close witness also of the swift transformation, blending tragedy and triumph, which followed in 1884–85. Few pictures of Grant are less pleasant than that of the affluent soldier living at ease in a fine house and giving his time to Mexican railway schemes and the vague financial transactions of Grant & Ward. No picture is more heroic than that of the doubly-stricken man, fortune and health irretrievably gone, battling against pain at Mount McGregor to finish his memoirs and leave his family a modest support. The country beheld again the Grant of Vicksburg and the Wilderness. Its faith that he was really a hero came back, this time forever. His errors were forgotten as men read how, dictating when he could not speak above a whisper, writing on a pad when the whisper was gone, he completed his book. His last and greatest victory had been safely won when, on July 23, 1885, he died.

Fish laid his own fervent tribute on Grant's coffin in an article in the *Independent* of July 30, 1885. He described instances of Grant's magnanimity. He told of his willingness to yield a preconceived opinion— as when he gave way to Fish's insistence upon Charles Francis Adams as Arbitrator at Geneva. He touched upon his frequent shrewdness of judgment. And, testified Fish, "I think he was the most scrupulously truthful man I ever met."

II

After the election of 1884 Fish's interest in politics rapidly diminished. In this particular campaign he came near bolting the Republican Party, and hardly concealed his belief that Cleveland deserved election. He knew Blaine for a fascinating leader. But he had not forgotten the Mulligan letters and the other suspicious events of 1876. Moreover, he had learned enough of Blaine's record as Secretary of State under Garfield to feel a profound distrust for him. Bancroft Davis, who became Assistant Secretary of State again under Arthur, had discovered evidence which satisfied him that Blaine had pushed certain Pe-

HAMILTON FISH IN HIS STUYVESANT SQUARE LIBRARY

ruvian claims in the most improper and dangerous way. "We were on the highway to war for the benefit of as nasty a set of people as ever gathered about a Washington Department," he wrote Fish.[11] He accused Blaine of desiring to suppress certain documents in the matter; and some papers were mysteriously "lost." The State Department, he added, had become "greatly demoralized." Fish, recalling all this, sent a sharp refusal to Evarts' invitation in 1884 to attend a "ratification meeting" in New York. He did not like the demagogic platform, he wrote.[12] He did not like the nominee. "My mistrust of the foreign policy which I fear will be introduced, and the apprehension of other alleged tendencies, bid me pause." He did admire the personality and acts of Cleveland. In the end, with a wry face, he voted the Republican ticket. But he was never sorry that Cleveland was the victor. "He is a *Man*," he wrote later in another connection.[13]

Having long looked forward to retirement, Fish now found his keenest pleasure in home employments.[14] The larger part of each year was spent in town. The Stuyvesant Square house, at the corner of 17th Street and Second Avenue, had a spaciousness which suited him and his household. It was half-surrounded by a large garden, well planted with trees, shrubs, and flower-beds, with a fountain in the middle. The first floor contained a large hall with marble floor and marble busts; a handsome dining-room; a drawing-room with a carved marble mantelpiece which Fish had bought in Europe; the so-called blue room, hung in blue silk; and an octagon room. The two latter were used as approaches to the dining room, but for little else except when a large reception or dance was given. In the dining-room, which overlooked the garden, stood cabinets with old Dresden china, and two large sideboards; the table could be extended to great length. On this floor also was Fish's library, with a small room beside it containing a safe for valuable papers. A broad walnut staircase, lighted halfway up by a stained-glass window, led to the second floor. All rooms, even on the third floor, were high-ceiled, and most of them were large.

Fish spent nearly all his daylight hours in his library—for he took singularly little exercise. He was constantly at his desk writing, or in his big armchair reading. But when late in the afternoon he joined Mrs.

[11] Davis to Fish, February 8, 1882; Fish Papers.   [12] July 10, 1884; Letterbooks.
[13] To Robert C. Winthrop, October 2, 1885; Letterbooks.
[14] I am indebted for much information to Fish's grandson, Mr. Hamilton Fish Webster, whose recollections of him go back to the Secretaryship of State.

Fish and the family in the drawing-room for tea, his work ended. After dinner the card-table was brought out, for he loved a game of Bezique. Fish's collection of books was large and catholic, with standard sets in fine binding, and a constant supply of new works. Besides the library proper, a large office-room on the ground-floor below was filled with books. He had at his elbow numerous works of reference, sets of state papers, and books on American history. Most of the novels were kept at Glenclyffe. He read little fiction, though his fondness for Walter Scott was inextinguishable, and less poetry, but much history and biography. He also kept up his acquaintance with the ancient classics. "Yes," we find him writing in 1879, "I have read Froude's *Caesar* and Forsyth's *Cicero,* and I am half-vexed with Froude for proving Cicero to have been such a mean, self-seeking, faithless politician—and unfortunately Forsyth cannot acquit his client."

The entertaining in Stuyvestant Square was varied—large and small, formal and informal parties. He kept a good cook, and the meals were always of high quality. After dessert, the ladies leaving the room, the old gentleman loved to entertain his friends over Madeira, nuts, and cigars, even to the second and third Havana. He served claret, sherry, and port, but above all took pride in his Madeira; he always personally decanted and rebottled his large stock, and liked to discuss the various vintages. His talk kept to the end the tolerance and geniality that had always made it captivating, while his reminiscences of men and events gave it weight. He seldom quoted books, though sometimes a couplet of verse; he often quoted great figures of the past whom he had known.

At Glenclyffe, where he had more leisure, he kept much outdoors. In 1877 his farmer and superintendent broke down, and not wishing to discharge the man, he assumed the work himself. Grant often chaffed him on his agriculture, and made amusing calculations of the cost of his hay and potatoes. But then, Fish would rejoin, consider the feeling of independence! He grew enough apples and small fruits to be a liberal dispenser to his neighbors; he cut enough hickory wood for the fireplaces in Stuyvesant Square. He was proud of his flowers, and especially of his roses. Some bushes which he imported from England in 1878 proved the most beautiful he had ever seen, and he was greatly gratified when his neighbor Osborn remarked, "Well, heretofore I have been ahead of you in roses, now you have beaten me." He walked, drove, blistered his hands with a pitchfork, and talked with the stream of visitors. When the day's work was done he delighted to sit on the south piazza, enjoying the resplendent view down the river in the rich sunset light and watching the *Mary Powell* as she throbbed northward to Albany. On the north piazza hung a thermometer which he made it a rule to examine thrice a day, the last time just before going to bed; and he neatly entered the temperatures in red and black ink in large volumes. While he delighted to have his family about him, he could do without them. In June, 1879, he wrote Dr. (later Bishop) Whipple that the two unmarried children being absent on visits, "Darby and Joan are alone. My wife and I sit down and read together, we drive out together, we walk together, and tiring of this, we talk together. I do not think that we weary either of the other; we realize that we are old and accept the fact, grateful for the very many blessings which we have enjoyed."

From 1877 to 1887 he kept a neat account-book of his principal dinner guests, with diagrams of their places at table. It shows many of the fashionable names of the city—Livingstons, Duers, Astors, Belmonts, and the like. But more frequent are the names of such men as Joseph H. Choate, Whitelaw Reid, Lloyd Bryce, Abram S. Hewitt, and William Evarts—names that represent intellectual distinction. After he left Washington there was no one with whom he liked to converse more than with his son-in-law Sidney Webster. With his two old departmental associates, Bancroft Davis and John Cadwalader, he was always intimate; and at Garrison he saw a great deal of Osborn and Pierrepont. Of his lifelong neighbor Samuel B. Ruggles, one of New York's most extraordinary figures, he once remarked: "Ruggles can throw off more brilliant and pregnant ideas in a given moment than any man I ever saw." Such men as George L. Rives, ex-Senator Conkling, and Bayard Tuckerman also helped to make his drawing-room, with its unassuming dignity, one of the best centres of talk in the city.

Religious leaders, Bishop Potter at their head, were often at his board. To the last he remained extremely devout. He read his Bible faithfully every night; he always held family prayers—the servants attending—in the library or drawing-room before breakfast. But he never attempted to force his religion upon others. He instructed his children, he set them an example, but he went no further. Mrs. Fish, on the other hand, tried to see that the whole household put religious precepts into practise. She expected her children, and any guests in the house, to go to morning service on Sundays. All Fish's children were confirmed in the Episcopal Church, and one, Stuyvesant, became a notable authority on American church history.

With absent friends he was an assiduous, cordial, and interesting correspondent even when the ailments of old age—neuralgia and rheumatism—sapped his strength. His letterbooks give many glimpses of his personality. We find flashes of humor. Irritated by the centennial celebrations which dragged out from 1875 to 1889, and the flow of oratory they inspired, he surmised that William M. Evarts would yet be heard pronouncing an eloquent discourse on the centennial of the death of John Hancock's tomcat or the birth of Joyce Heath's first child. We find bits of sharp criticism. He learned in 1877 that Jesse Grant had behaved in England "like a cub." Writing John Cadwalader, then consul-general in Cairo, he remarked: [15] "If you meet him on top of the Pyramids, do not, I beg of you, for his parents' sake, push him off; but if from the top you see him at the bottom, look down upon him with the indignation of 'forty centuries.'" John Jay having become abusive of Grant and Fish, the latter thought his appointment by Hayes as head of an investigating committee very proper. "No one is better fitted than he to perform a duty similar to that which on the Channel steamers is assigned to one of the stewards, of holding a bowl in which anyone may relieve himself of any uncomfortable matter on his stomach."

But in general he was kindliness itself. He loved to recall old intimacies. When William Hunter celebrated his fiftieth year of service with the State Department, he wrote an eloquent letter of appreciation. When Thornton left Washington, he assured him that no diplomat had ever quit our shores "carrying with him as much of the confidence, respect, and affection . . . of the American people." Their eight years of almost daily intercourse, "with many hearty tussles, and perhaps an occasional 'official' (but never a personal) tiff," were among his happiest recollections. He expressed feeling grief over the death of Nelly Grant Sartoris in 1879, "a very lovely child and woman." He was always a peacemaker. When in 1882 the arrest of Irish-American agitators in England threatened to becloud relations between the two countries,

[15] January 25, 1878; Letterbooks.

he asked Sir John Rose [16] to urge the government to pursue a milder policy. He did what he could for sectional harmony. In 1885, Grant's death having created a vacancy on the board of the Peabody Fund, he requested ex-Governor William Aiken of South Carolina to propose General Sherman. Such a generous gesture would have a happy effect upon both North and South, he wrote. "Here is an opportunity where one of the most prominent Southern men may shew to the country and to the world that the animosities of the war are forgotten." He always insisted, to the same end, that the trustees of the Fund should constitute a truly national group, and not be a mere Southern body.

Even in his last years he gave assiduous labor to the two institutions nearest his heart, Columbia College and the Episcopal Church. One of the principal creators of Columbia University, John W. Burgess, testifies [17] that on his arrival in 1876 he quickly saw that Chairman Fish, S. B. Ruggles, S. P. Nash, and Gouverneur M. Ogden were the Big Four of the board of trustees. They were "all men of very superior intelligence and organizing ability"; they were all "chafing to move forward." The support which these four gave to President Barnard, Dr. Burgess, Nicholas Murray Butler, and a few others made possible the rapid emergence of a true university. Fish was heartily in favor of every one of the successive steps—the founding of the Faculty of Political Science; the removal of the Law School to Forty-ninth Street, its closer integration with the other departments, and its transformation into a real School of Jurisprudence; the renovation of the library; the steady strengthening of the faculty; and the rapid enlargement of graduate work. These progressive steps, in fact, were measures to which he had looked forward since the fifties. While they were being taken, he insisted that the undergraduate work should receive closer attention and be steadily improved.

The trustees met monthly—much more frequently than most college boards—and the labors of the chairman were heavy. A mass of Fish's papers relating to Columbia shows that in 1878 he was unhappy over its position. "The results attained in the educational direction of the College," he wrote the Treasurer, Gouverneur M. Ogden,[18] "appear to me very disproportioned to the means and the endowments of the institution." For this he largely blamed Ogden, whose influence had been

[16] April 18, 1882; Letterbooks.   [17] *Reminiscences of an American Scholar,* 176 ff.
[18] March 15, 1878; Letterbooks.

paramount in the board while Fish was in Washington. Without mincing words, he stated that "the failure of the college to rise to its responsibilities and to its duties" was due to Ogden's excessive conservatism and bad stewardship. He demanded an immediate change. With his usual thoroughness, he set to work to bring it about. Letters from Burgess show that he expected Fish first to prepare the board for each new measure, and then to carry it through. "Were you able," we find Burgess writing on May 14, 1882, "to accomplish the establishment of the librarianship and prize lectureship in the Department of Political Science? Or have you succeeded in putting them upon the way of accomplishment? I most earnestly hope that you have." While the institution grew, Fish constantly insisted that the faculty work harder, and that no previous gain be surrendered.

By 1885 he was more content and hopeful. He liked the younger leaders of the faculty, and gladly lent them aid. President Barnard he always regarded as somewhat visionary. In a letter of 1884 he remarks [19] that "were he as wise as he is fertile in suggestions for expenditures, the College would have a valuable officer at its head." Ogden's control of the finances (he invested $350,000 in an unproductive tract in the northern part of Manhattan which depreciated in value) he sharply criticized; while he deemed it improper that the Treasurer should also be a trustee. But for men like Dr. Burgess and Dr. Butler, whom he admired and trusted, he could not do too much. The Board was strengthened in the eighties by the addition of George L. Rives, Seth Low, and George L. Peabody. Under Fish it was a harmonious and effective organization. Each year he headed the commencement procession, and one student destined to eminence, Benjamin L. Cardozo, has testified to the awe with which he watched his stately figure moving across the campus, "the incarnation of History."

Thus serenely, thus fruitfully, his life drew to its end. The death of Mrs. Fish on June 30, 1887, ten years after his retirement from office, was an indescribable blow to him. During their married life of more than half a century, she had given him wise and efficient aid in every phase of his public career. He often said that he had never made an important decision without consulting her. Those who understood his constant dependence on her unfailing tact and forethought, and the exceptional closeness of their association in all matters of the mind and

[19] January 14, 1884; Letterbooks.

spirit, trembled for the effect of the rupture. It did instantly carry him into a seclusion from which, even in a social way, he thenceforth emerged with great reluctance. Yet he was too wise to give up his ordinary labors.

His own end came suddenly. His birthday, August 8, 1893, brought him many pleasant tributes, public and private. As yet he seemed little enfeebled. Passing the summer at Glenclyffe, he drove and walked much as usual. On the evening of September 6, dining with good appetite, he played his game of Bezique with his daughter Julia, the widow of Colonel Samuel N. Benjamin. He read the thermometer, wrote down the temperature, and retired cheerfully. But next morning, soon after rising, he died suddenly in his chair. With a quiet funeral, he was buried in St. Philip's Churchyard on the eastern bank of the Hudson; the churchyard in which his wife and daughter Elizabeth already lay under one of the most striking of all St. Gaudens's monuments.

In intellectual powers Fish was inferior to some of his political contemporaries. His mind was not quick, original, or rich. He had no brilliancy or wit, and not the highest kind of cultivation. He was entirely without eloquence—he always shrunk from speechmaking—and boasted few accomplishments. The talents which he possessed were somewhat fettered by an excessive modesty. There was nothing of the comet or the torrent about him, nothing that dazzled or overpowered; he was to outward view merely a plain, courteous, substantial gentleman. But this can be said of several of the greatest Americans, and Fish possessed qualities which, impressive by reason of their balance, made him one of the most useful leaders of his generation.

He was preëminent for the clarity and soundness of his judgment, for his perfect moderation and self-control, and for his quiet dignity and indomitable firmness. Almost invariably judicious, he seldom wrote or spoke a rash word (the 'Moran letter' was his only prominent error of the sort), or committed a rash act. Beneath the surface he had keen sensibilities and strong emotions, but he held them in complete rein, and during a long lifetime never acted from personal caprice, selfish ambition, or resentment. He was never moved unworthily by desire for office and power; by resentment of the plots against him and the malicious attacks on his reputation; by flattery or wheedling. He was in the highest sense a gentleman and a man of principle. Principle, to be sure, he always espoused calmly. He never acted with an absorbing enthusiasm. But he had convictions, he clung sternly to them, and in an age of laxity and corruption, he carried into public life an antique standard of dignity, honor, and justice.

What were these convictions? He never troubled to formulate his political philosophy and probably never thought closely upon abstract political principles; but he nevertheless held a well-moulded set of doctrines. We must return to early republican days for terms in which to define them. They were the doctrines of the Hamilton-Marshall school as modified by Clay and Webster; they were not at all the dominant doctrines of the Republican Party in the later sixties and seventies. The circumstances of his Federalist environment at birth, his aristocratic upbringing, his Whig tutelage in politics, all united to make him a conservative nationalist. He feared the disintegrating forces of American society, and believed in a sovereign state strong enough to protect minority interests against tyrannical majorities. Though he had none of Hamilton's rough contempt of democracy, he trusted the people no further than Marshall or Webster did. He had a strong property-consciousness. Beginning his career as legal adviser to monied New Yorkers, serving as head of the chief endowed institutions of New York, he felt keenly the importance of protecting property rights. This fact appeared repeatedly in his life, from his opposition to the Anti-Rent leaders to his support of the repeal of the Civil War income tax. He believed he firmly as Clay in sectional amity. He believed that education and civic training should have a larger weight in American government. The celebration of log cabins, hard cider, and split rails as ideal antecedents to a political career pained him; he was most at home with such men as Caleb Cushing, Rockwood Hoar, and Robert C. Winthrop, and did what he could to give them larger opportunities in politics.

But while the old Federalist-Whig doctrines furnished his underlying political philosophy, on them he necessarily reared more pragmatic beliefs. In deploring the heated issues of sectional conflict, 1850–1880, he not only manifested the Federalist passion for national union; he displayed the preconceptions of a landed aristocrat. In tastes, manners, and sympathies this descendant of the land-owning Stuyvesants, this son of a great up-State landholder, this resident of Glenclyffe, showed the conservatism and moderation of a country gentleman. He could understand the planter aristocracy of the South. He had little in common with the men who scrambled to exploit mills, banks, and mines—the masters of capital. He believed in a conservatively-paced development of the country, attended by careful efforts to preserve the harmony of sections and classes. He believed also in a sane balance of agricultural and industrial interests, and subconsciously was pained by the ruthless energy with which the latter gained their victory before his death. Perhaps the feeling was conscious, for he unquestionably thought more highly of Cleveland's first Administration, with its attempts to restrain the excesses of capitalism, than of those which just preceded it. He was happier, and spiritually was more at home, in ante-bellum America than in post-bellum America.

He was fortunate in his career. His gifts were administrative, not political. In the party arena, without forensic power, without subtlety, without aggressiveness, without magnetism, he could never have gone far. He had little taste for the parliamentary hurly-burly. It was a happy fate which elevated him to the highest appointive office in the American system, and kept him there for eight crowded years. For that office his equipment was superb. He had precisely the cast of mind required. A reader of his diary is at once struck and impressed by the stubborn skepticism, the instinct toward doubt and denial, with which he faced all proposals. When Polo, Thornton, or Bartholdi presented some claim, some request, Fish's characteristic response was a no, supported by all the objections he could muster. When politicians entered with demands, suggestions, or entreaties, again he was always skeptical, and often hostile. If his objections could be answered, well and good— but that required forcible argument. Always he was stern of temper, always tough of mind. The great need of the Grant Administration was somebody who could say "No!"—and in eight years Fish said it thousands of times. While in large matters of policy he was conciliatory, he always insisted upon American rights within the framework of international law, and always maintained them. Thornton in one of his letters to Granville has a phrase which pregnantly describes Fish as "encasing himself in an impenetrable armor of Dutch obstinacy."

His knowledge of French, German, and Italian was invaluable in consultation with diplomats. He was singularly free from international prejudices or dislikes. For France he had, as we have said, a strong affection. For England his feeling was rather of respect and admira-

tion; he knew how resolute Englishmen were in defending their interests, and in the relations of the two countries he trie ī to be equally
resolute in defending America's. But he had many British friends, his
daughter married an Englishman, and his liking for Great Britain increased steadily. In dealing with Spain, he preserved always a compas-
sionate feeling for the Spanish people as distinguished from their government. Never once did he fail to show consummate urbanity. His
cosmopolitan training in New York, his two years of European residence, and his high social position helped to make his intercourse with
foreign representatives remarkably frank and cordial.

His chief disability in office, arising from his sense of political inex-
pertness, was a certain self-distrust in dealing with politicians and the
electorate behind them. He knew that he was ill-equipped to make any
appeal to public sentiment; that he was not a Jefferson or Clay or Webster. He was hence never capable of the bold imaginative strokes of a
Clay or a Seward. He might at times even be accused of timidity, as in
his fears of the Senate in handling the indirect claims, and of both Senate
and House in Cuban affairs. But in general he manifested merely a wise
caution. He could be courageous enough when occasion demanded it;
and if he executed none of Seward's bold strokes, he was guilty of none
of Seward's occasional rash and ill-balanced acts. He moved one step
at a time, he was plodding rather than brilliant, but he reached his
goal.

While never political-minded, he could be very politic. He managed
some Senators adroitly. And in what has been said of his rectitude, it
is not implied that he was too good for human nature's daily food—
or for directing foreign affairs in a selfish world. He sometimes chipped
the cube of truth to make it roll. His diary reveals the fact that soon
after he took office Grant asked his advice in a very minor dispute
between Britain and Portugal, in which the President was arbiter. Fish
reported that Portugal had the better side of the argument, and that
Grant should so determine unless he believed that our relations with
England made a verdict in her favor advisable! Sir John Macdonald
was much amused by one of the closing scenes in making the Treaty
of Washington. The protocol or journal of proceedings was read over
and agreed upon. The British Commissioners confined themselves to
a strict report of what they had said. The American Commissioners
inserted numerous statements which they had never made—simply

for their effect upon the Senate! Fish was always practical-minded. But his realism was in general strictly subordinated to principles and ideals. A great political writer has said: "A man is always so much more than his words, as we feel every day of our lives, and what, he says has its momentum indefinitely multiplied, or reduced to nullity, by the impression the hearer for good reasons or bad happens to have formed of the spirit and moral size of the speaker." No associate of Hamilton Fish was ever in doubt as to his moral weight.

He rapidly gained a mastery of the technical side of his office. The Department had never been so efficiently managed as under him. His reforms of procedure not only economized time and labor, but assisted in the wise management of foreign relations. His subordinates trusted him as few Secretaries are trusted. Punctual, methodical, and accurate in the highest degree, he inspired those qualities in his office-staff. His capacity for labor was enormous. Only a reading of the diary can give a real conception of it. Year in and year out, he worked from dawn to dark reading dispatches, seeing diplomats, attending Cabinet meetings, consulting leaders of Congress, and writing instructions. In 1869-73 crisis followed crisis. And after labors that would have exhausted most younger men, amid social demands of the most exacting kind, he somehow found time and strength to set down an exact record of the day's occurrences, frequently reaching 2,000 words or more.

What did he accomplish? He must often have asked himself the question, and we can perhaps give it a better answer than he. Playing his part in two eras, one of sectional conflict and one of reconstruction, he strove for distinct goals in both. In his efforts to help avert the Civil War he utterly failed. Much was involved in that conflict besides slavery; it was essentially a collision between two distinct civilizations. The economy founded upon free labor and large-scale capitalism was too powerful to be checked by such men as Fish. Perhaps he exaggerated the rôle of the mere fire-eaters in precipitating the conflict. Late in life he wrote that about 1850 he had often thought that if the most intemperate politicians on both sides the Mason and Dixon line could be collected into a single omnibus and plunged beneath the Potomac, peace might be preserved. By 1860 it would have taken several omnibuses to effect the result, but he still believed it could have been attained. Doubtless this view of the causes of the Civil War underestimates the influence of the large underlying forces, and it perhaps indicates why men like Fish accomplished so little. They strove valiantly—but they proved to be puny straws in an overmastering torrent.

Yet after the war, raised to a place of real power, he decisively succeeded in his second great endeavor. He helped to prevent a reckless realization of the doctrine of Manifest Destiny. The thoughtless masses were ripe for another movement of national expansion, or if not ready, could quickly have been made so. Seward had been an expansionist. Grant was one. Sumner was one. It would have been easy to launch the nation in 1869 upon the imperialist path which it finally took in 1899. The conquest of Cuba and the annexation of Santo Domingo would have come first. Expansion into Canada would have followed. Had Elihu Washburne remained Secretary of State, such a course would have been probable; had Grant appointed Morton or Zach Chandler, almost inevitable. While the forces of economic imperialism were much weaker than in 1898, those of sentimental imperialism were stronger. The clock of American policy might have been set ahead by twenty years. In the papers of Elihu Washburne is a letter from James G. Blaine just after Grant's first election, asking Washburne to use his influence to have some man hostile to Great Britain and favorable to expansion named Secretary of State. What if someone of Blaine's own temperament had assumed the office? Fortunately, the State Department fell to the strong hands of a man who was resolutely opposed to imperialism, and opposed, above all, to the wars which must be fought to achieve it.

That Fish did the nation a great service in thus combating an expansion which would have added to the national confusion, strained the national finances, saddled a weak Administration with crushing burdens, and altered the temper and ideals of the American people for the worse, few will doubt. But this was not his only service. To the most erratic of our national Administrations he furnished an indispensable balance-wheel; in a time of national disgrace, he illustrated the validity of older ideals of rectitude and honor.

The literature of many peoples presents some variant of the old Teutonic legend of a sleeping hero, a Barbarossa who rests in his magic mountain, to come forth full-panoplied in time of direst national crisis and inspire the land anew. These are but legends; there is no way to awaken Charlemagne or Alfred or Washington. And yet there may be a core of truth in these folk-myths. The *spirit* of a past age may sometimes be reëmbodied in a national figure, and again move in its councils and help shape its policies. The career of Hamilton Fish illustrates that possibility. By a happy stroke of fate, at the moment when the American Government sank to the very nadir of disrepute, when greed and corruption seemed to sway most departments of American activity, there was reincarnated in the second officer of the republic the high integrity, the selfless patriotism, the regard for principle, the far-sighted judgment, which recalled the days when Fish's idols, Hamilton and Jay, walked the earth. The reappearance of these virtues was at once a reminder of a nobler past, and a promise that when the turbid confusion of the war years disappeared, and the deeper currents of national life reasserted themselves, the republic would ride forward into a brighter future.

1.—*Mexico.*

Secretary Fish was called upon to deal with chronic and serious border depredations by bands of Mexican outlaws and adventurers, and with troublesome smuggling from the Mexican Zona Libre, a belt six miles wide on the northern frontier. His policy was lenient and patient. Extended accounts of the subject may be found in J. M. Callahan, *American Foreign Policy in Mexican Relations,* and J. Fred Rippy, *The United States and Mexico,* supplemented by documents in *Foreign Relations.* Here I shall merely cite some of the new material in the Fish Papers.

The keynote of Fish's Mexican policy is to be found in two letters of 1875. On April 2 he wrote John L. Cadwalader: "There seems to be an apprehension of some coming difficulties with Mexico. . . . I have no doubt of the desire of a class of persons in Texas to get up a war with Mexico; the speculating contractors all over the country sympathize in such object, and there is at present a very large class of unemployed who would see adventure and excitement and chances in a war. Some may think that a war may secure the elevation to power of the political party which inaugurates it. It would, however, be very disastrous, and moreover, there is no cause for it. They are the lawless people of *both* nations who are committing the outrages, alternately on either side of the boundary." And on September 10 he wrote E. L. Plumb: "There is always a floating, speculating, unsettled class in the community, restless in all quiet, and ever seeking commotion and turbulence. I fear that the excitement of the late war has not quite left some of our military men, who long for the chances of distinction and of advancement which attended some other of their fellows. There is no doubt a strong feeling in Texas in favor of a war with Mexico; the border population (on both sides) is one of loose regard for laws, and with little appreciation of the blessings of peace, order, and good government. A war with Mexico would bring troops and circulate money in Texas, contracts would be tempting; in fact, our Eastern States have this 'noble army' of contractors, quite as numerous, quite as rapacious, and quite as patriotic as that blessed band of sharks in any part of the world. All these would look with complacency, at least, on a fight with Mexico." He added that the suggestion of war was absurd.

While Fish strove earnestly to protect our rights, his diary shows that he resolutely set his face against any course likely to lead to war. Cattle thefts and other border outrages by Mexican raiders aroused increasing indignation. On December 12, 1870, he instructed the American Minister, Nelson, to ask that the Chihuahua government permit the crossing of pursuit troops from the United States. President Juarez replied that Chihuahua would coöperate by the use of its own troops, but that the approval of his Congress would be necessary to permit the entry of American forces, and he could not ask it. Fish showed patience. He merely had Nelson say unofficially that if Mexico did not adopt measures to check the robberies, "it may become our duty at least to weigh the expediency of pursuing the hostile Indians into Mexico without the consent of the Government." Beyond strong warnings of this sort he did not go. On January 16, 1873, he wrote Nelson that the Mexican Government seemed so apethetic or powerless "that sooner or later this Government will have no other alternative than to endeavor to secure quiet on the frontier by seeking the marauders and punishing them in their haunts wherever these may be." But, he added. Nelson should not for at least the present "make a formal representation to this effect." In dealing with Indian trouble be was equally patient. The Kickapoos, who had migrated to northern Mexico during the Civil War, liked to make thievish raids into American territory. Early in 1873 Fish sounded the Mexican Minister, Mariscal, on measures to return the Kickapoos to their American reservation. Mariscal promised that his government would aid in the transfer by appointing a Commissioner to act with a similar American officer. But when Fish asked him pointblank whether Mexico would use "pressure" on the Indians, Mariscal said no; Mexico would try "to persuade them, but will use no pressure." (Diary, February 13, 1873.) Fish did not pursue the matter.

Late in the Grant Administration the rise of Porfirio Diaz to power presented a new situation. In February, 1877, Fish authorized John W. Foster, the very able Minister to Mexico, to recognize the new government if it would engage to repeal the Zona Libre and institute effective measures to prevent border raids. But he intimated that these conditions would not be pressed too hard. Early in the Hayes Administration a Congressional report (House Report 701, 45th Cong., 2nd Sess.) censured the "temporizing" policy of Fish, and Evarts adopted a stronger line. But it was the strength of the Diaz Government which finally brought a fair measure of border security—and meanwhile Fish's policy had kept America and Mexico on amicable terms.

2.—*The Isthmian Canal.*

Grant was deeply interested, as Seward had been, in an isthmian canal. One of Fish's first endeavors was to come to an agreement with Colombia for use of the Panama route. General Stephen A. Hurlbut, a military friend of Grant's, was sent to Bogota in 1869 with instructions to negotiate a new agreement like the unratified Cushing convention, under which the United States was to have the sole right to construct and own a canal, to be completed within fifteen years. Because of difficulties of communication Hurlbut was given a fairly free hand. On January 26, 1870, he signed a treaty. The United States acquired the exclusive right to construct and operate a canal; it was to guarantee it against attack, but other nations were to participate in this guarantee. Parts of the agreement were unsatisfactory to the Colombian Senate, which amended it; the changes were unsatisfactory to Fish;

and the treaty failed. (See Bemis, VII, 206 ff.; J. C. Rodrigues, *The Panama Canal*, 186 ff.)

Negotiations with Colombia were transferred in 1873 to Washington. The Colombian envoy, Martin, outlined the terms on which his country would negotiate a new agreement. He asked for a loan of $6,000,000 to Colombia, to be ultimately repaid from Colombia's share of the canal revenues; 25 per cent of the gross revenues of the canal; and an American guarantee of the defense of parts of Colombia lying outside the canal zone. Fish thought these terms absurd. He told Martin that the loan was "wholly inadmissible"; that 7 per cent of the gross revenues was as much as Colombia would be entitled to; and that the proposed engagement for the defense of Colombia was "vague, dangerous, and cannot be assumed." (Diary, March 11, 1873.) He also informed the Colombian Minister that his country must not suppose it was conferring a favor upon those who might undertake the canal, "and should be liberal in their terms in order to allure capital to the undertaking and to treat it as an object from which they were to derive pecuniary benefit." Further conversations between Fish and Martin came to nothing.

Meanwhile, Grant had appointed an Interoceanic Canal Commission to study the data gathered by exploring groups sent out by the Navy Department, with other material, and report on the best route for a canal. In February, 1876, it recommended the Nicaraguan route, with termini at Greytown on the Atlantic and Brito on the Pacific. This made further negotiations with Colombia useless and cast on Fish the burden of obtaining, if possible, definite rights from Nicaragua. Late in 1876 a new Minister from that little republic, Dr. Cárdenas, arrived in Washington. Admiral Ammen, who constantly urged an isthmian canal upon Grant, entertained him. "I can assure you," Ammen wrote Fish on November 11, "that he is well disposed on every proposal that you will probably make. I consider an armed police as necessary alike to the successful prosecution of the work, and to guard Nicaragua against filibusters, and I think he has now the same idea." (Fish Papers.) Fish accordingly prepared a draft treaty, which looked toward construction by an American company, but safeguarded the rights of Great Britain and other maritime nations. The principal maritime powers of the globe were to furnish a guarantee of the neutrality of the canal; it was to be open to ships of all nations at all times; and the neutral zone was to extend over waters within a radius of 150 marine miles from each entrance, and over a strip of land ten marine miles wide along the course of the canal. A board of control appointed by the guarantor governments should prescribe regulations for the use of the waterway. Fish showed the draft to Thornton, who agreed that it did not violate the Clayton-Bulwer Treaty in any way. (Diary, January 18, 1877.) Indeed, Fish never at any time intended to repudiate or whittle down the Clayton-Bulwer Treaty. The diary shows that he regularly and harmoniously consulted Thornton on isthmian matters. At one time he sharply reminded England of her duties under the treaty. (Bemis, VII, 207.)

But the draft treaty which Fish laid before the Nicaraguan Minister did not suit the latter. It seemed to contain impairments of Nicaraguan sovereignty; while Cárdenas wished the United States to furnish "material assistance" for the canal. He put forward counter-proposals which the Secretary did not like. Moreover, a month before the Administration ended, Fish heard that the Nicaraguan Government had granted a canal concession to a Peruvian company. "That is the way Nicaragua always does," commented the Costa Rican Minister. With the approval of the Cabinet, Fish therefore terminated the discussions with Nicaragua. (Diary, February 1, 2, 1877.) Like Seward before him, he had failed to obtain a solution of the diplomatic difficulties in the path of an isthmian waterway. But he left his successor, Evarts, a valuable legacy in plans and policy.

3.—The Orient.

Fish's Far Eastern policy, which was based on the doctrine of coöperation with the chief European powers, had decided vigor. In dealing with two problems particularly, the Audience Question and the Tientsin Massacre, he tried to bring about concerted action in China.

Since 1860 diplomatic representatives of Western Powers, on arriving in Peking, had sent their credentials to the regency which controlled affairs during the minority of the Emperor. But on February 23, 1873, the young monarch came of age and assumed charge of the government. The question of audience, a difficult one since the first American Minister had been refused an interview with the Emperor, was revived. Fish instructed our Minister that it "should now be demanded. You will accordingly make such a demand, not separately, however, but in concert with the representatives of the other Powers." (Fish to Frederick F. Low, December 21, 1872; Instructions, China.) He added, however, that it might be best not to make an imperative demand, but to proceed by degrees "and with due tenderness for the inveterate prejudices" of China. From time to time the audience question was revived. After the untimely death of the Emperor in January, 1875, the American Minister reported that advisers of the new monarch were disinclined to grant audiences to diplomats. Again Fish decided to act in concert with the European nations and so informed the American Ministers in London, Paris, Berlin, Copenhagen, and St. Petersburg.

The Tientsin Massacre grew out of the intense hatred of the Chinese in that area for the French, whose troops had behaved badly and whose authorities had sanctioned the erection of a Catholic edifice in the city over the ruins of a sacred temple. On June 21, 1870, an outbreak resulted in the destruction of the French consulate and a French orphanage; a score of foreigners, chiefly French, lost their lives. Disorders spread to other parts of the Chinese Empire. France, preoccupied with her European troubles, was helpless. Fish first sanctioned efforts by Minister Low in Peking to act in concert with other Western diplomats there in supporting the French chargé when the latter made formal demands for reparation. He also took cognizance of the danger that the Franco-Prussian War would imperil the united front of the Western Powers in China. "It appears to the President," he shortly wrote Minister Bancroft in Berlin, "that the hostilities between France and Germany, if conducted in Chinese waters, will operate on the minds of the Chinese to put in peril the lives of Europeans and Americans in that Empire." Bancroft was instructed to sound the government of North Germany to ascertain if it would not agree to a suspension of hostilities, and coöperative action between the French and German squadrons in Chinese waters, "as far as the protection of lives and property of Americans and Europeans may require." This advice was followed. (Fish to Bancroft, November 1, 1870.) The place of the United States in the closed front was reaffirmed by Fish a few weeks later, when he informed the Minister to China that his language in protesting against certain threats to American missionaries had been too moderate. Minister Low was instructed to speak not of American rights alone, but to say that "any violation of the rights of our citizens and any flagrant violation of treaty stipulations of other Powers may cause a change" in American policy. (Fish to Low, November 29, 1870.) The united front continued in China until the great rupture in 1914, when Germany's proposals for neutralizing the Far East were rejected by the Allies.

4.—*Fish's Descendants and Cuba.*

It is interesting to note that one of Secretary Fish's grandsons, Sergeant Hamilton Fish, serving with the Rough Riders, was the first American soldier killed in the Spanish-American War in 1898. Another grandson, Representative Hamilton Fish, Jr., as a member of the House Foreign Affairs Committee, led the campaign in Congress in 1933 against the Machado Dictatorship, and received from President Mendietta the highest Cuban decoration for distinguished services to the Cuban people.

PRIME MINISTER MACDONALD's letters to Tupper, Cartier, and other Cabinet associates during the Washington negotiations of 1871 (Canadian Archives) offer a shrewd commentary upon events, and tell a melancholy tale. He begins by relating how he was met at the Washington station by Thornton's carriage; took rooms at the Arlington; dined at Fish's house with the Commissioners "and a number of other swells"; and was pleased to find that the private instructions of the Foreign Office were broad enough to cover the Fenian claims. Schenck showed the British Commissioners over the Capitol. At the Senate door the Ohioan sent for Zach Chandler, "telling him that the British lion was waiting him and he must come out and confront him." Chandler showed extreme politeness.

But Macdonald was soon a very unhappy man. He learned that Fish insisted upon inshore fishery rights for the United States, but did not believe that Congress would renew the reciprocity treaty, and suggested a pecuniary equivalent. At this Macdonald tried to take a firm stand. "I told Lord de Grey that we had not even taken into consideration any other equivalent but that of enlarged commercial intercourse in the direction of reciprocity, and as nearly approaching the old Reciprocity Treaty as the exigencies of the U.S. Revenue would permit. That I did not at all know how a money payment would be received; but that my impression was that it would be out of the question for Canada to surrender for all time to come her fishery rights for any compensation however great." Granville authorized the British Commission to discuss a sale, at the same time expressing his preference for one in perpetuity. But the Colonial Secretary, Kimberley, supported Macdonald and Tupper in opposing a sale in perpetuity. When Fish offered $1,000,000 in perpetuity, the Prime Minister was indignant. He wrote Tupper that Fish during the discussion had mixed up and garbled some Canadian returns "in the most disingenuous manner." As March closed his British colleagues were pressing Macdonald for concessions. "I consented that we should accept free coal, salt, fish, lumber, and the coasting trade in exchange for the fisheries. I had ascertained almost beyond a doubt that the coasting trade would be refused. If, however, it had been accepted, I think . . . we would very soon have absorbed all the coasting trade on the lakes, and that portion of the Atlantic that they would have given us; probably to the 38th or 39th parallel." (To Tupper, March 29, 1871).

As the negotiations progressed, British pressure on Macdonald increased. The Americans offered free coal, salt, fish, and free lumber after July 1, 1876. The Canadian Cabinet demanded additions, telegraphing Macdonald that it would accept $150,000 a year, with $50,000 additional until lumber was free. Fish had meanwhile learned that there would be greater difficulty in getting free salt and lumber through the Senate than he had anticipated, and made this clear to the British. De Grey and Stafford Northcote kept urging the Prime Minister to be more reasonable. It was generally believed in England, said de Grey, that the danger from the fishery question was great and pressing; Granville had told him that if it alone were settled, the mission would not be a failure. But Macdonald minimized its dangers, and when reminded of Grant's last annual message, said that he understood that Ben Butler and not Fish was the author of the passages on Canada. A dispute fast ripened between Macdonald and his British associates.

By mid-April Macdonald was protesting vigorously against the British demand that the fishery question be settled along with the other disputes—that all the subjects be mingled. He urged "that Canada was not fairly dealt with in so intermingling them without her knowledge or consent, as they were all separate and distinct in their nature, and that if I had been aware that it was the intention of H. M. Govt. so to intermingle them it would have been a matter of grave consideration with me and with my colleagues . . . whether I should accept the position of Commissioner or not." He declared again that Canada did not wish to sell the fisheries, or lease them, but to exchange them for a fair tariff arrangement. He held "that the United States Government could not object, or raise any question, if we declined to sell or to lease, and that the present attitude of the American Commissioners was simply an attempt to bully us into a surrender of our rights by speaking of probable collisions involving the shedding of blood and consequent irritations, etc." Would the United States really countenance lawless acts by its fishermen, he demanded? But by mid-April de Grey took the view that the United States had made two offers that were both reasonable, and that Canada should accept one. The Americans had offered the free entry of coal, salt, fish, and (after 1875 or 1876) lumber; they had also offered to arbitrate the money-compensation payable for ten years' free fishing. De Grey told Macdonald on April 16 that a failure on the fishery question "would involve a complete disruption of the negotiations, and would leave matters in a much worse position than we found them." (Macdonald to Cartier, April 16, 1871).

Matters came to a crisis with a stormy meeting of the British Commissioners on April 17. For some days feeling between Macdonald and his colleagues ran high. On April 26 the Prime Minister showed de Grey a telegram to Cartier declaring that if England forced Canada to give up the fisheries for a sum to be fixed by arbitration, with free fish, it would be "a breach of faith and an indignity never before offered to a great British possession." De Grey sent Macdonald a stern letter of protest and denial. Macdonald reiterated, in a letter to de Grey, his statement that Canada was virtually being coerced. We find Macdonald writing Cartier on May 6 of a long talk he had had with de Grey. "I told him that . . . I must repeat my opinion that the arrangements with respect to the fisheries were decidedly injurious to Canada, whose interests had been sacrificed, or made altogether of secondary consideration, for the sake of getting a settlement of the *Alabama* and San Juan matters.

That I concurred entirely in the opinion expressed by the Canadian Government in your telegram which stated that the Canadian Parliament would not sanction the arrangement, and I said that the time must come when I must decide what course I would take. . . ."

To the end Macdonald believed that Canada had been treated unfairly by both the United States and Great Britain; he long hesitated to sign the Treaty, saying that it would be hard to make the Canadian people understand that he disapproved it; and his mental distress on the final day, as pictured by Fish, was thoroughly genuine and deeply felt.

The question of a reciprocity treaty between Canada and the United States again became important early in 1874. On March 28th of that year Thornton and George Brown of the Canadian Government called on Fish to discuss the subject. "Mr. Brown does most of the talking," writes Fish in his diary, "and wishes the Treaty, not for any material advantages, but to promote amicable relations and close intercourse between the two peoples." He inquired as to the wishes of the United States. Fish told him "that we have nothing to propose at all, the suggestion comes from them, and I doubt if any proposition could be made which would be accepted by the Senate and House, but am willing to see and consider any proposal which they have to make." They talked of reviving the arrangement of 1854, but Fish refused to accept any such proposal, recalling that it had been rejected again and again. Brown then remarked "that they may well be willing to stipulate to enlarge their canals to a capacity of fourteen feet; that they contemplate including copyright and patent rights reciprocity; they wish free introduction of their natural products, and might concede the manufactures of wood, iron, and leather, and possibly heavy cotton goods; would like also that the treaty should provide for the preservation of peace among the Indians . . ." Fish was non-committal.

As a matter of fact, Fish never had any real hope that the Canadian Government and the Congressional leaders could be brought together. His cautious handling of the situation appears in the following diary entries:

April 27, 1874.—Sir Edward Thornton and Mr. Brown call. . . . They read a memorandum dated this day. Their memorandum contains a proposition for a reciprocity of trade for a period of twenty-one years, and the relinquishment of the claim of Canada for compensation for the inshore fisheries under Article XXII, etc., of the Treaty of Washington. They also propose various other mutual engagements, including the extension of the patent laws and coasting trade, and the establishment of joint commissions for maintaining lighthouses, etc. They asked whether I would cause the memorandum to be printed for limited distribution. I decline giving any assurance to that effect and express disappointment at the nature of their proposal; that I can scarcely see in it the basis of any arrangement to which the United States can be brought to be a party.

May 25, 1874.—Sir Edward Thornton and Mr. Brown call . . . ; they were told that I would not submit in any form to the Senate the proposition which they had made. . . . In the course of the conversation I expressed a doubt whether it would be possible at this session to obtain any action from either branch of Congress, partly on account of the lateness of the session, but mainly on account of the revenue question. . . . They then stated that they had prepared a modified proposition omitting the coasting trade and had reduced it to the form of a Convention. They read this Convention and I cautioned them that my silence was not to be construed one way or the other.

May 27, 1874.—Mr. George Brown calls; has had an interview with Mr. Boutwell; submits a long list of manufactured articles and agricultural implements which he contemplates adding to the free list, also a synopsis of the proposed treaty; and confers with me as to persons with whom he may converse on the subject.

May 29, 1874.—Cabinet. . . . I also read the draft of the Reciprocity Treaty as proposed by Sir Edward Thornton and Mr. Brown; after consideration the President authorizes its submission, without expression of opinion, to the Senate.

May 30, 1874.—Mr. Brown called to say that he shall leave for Ottawa this evening. I impress upon him the danger of withdrawing any of the manufactured articles proposed for exemption, and refer to the tolls on the Welland Canal. . . .

June 6, 1874.—Mr. Brown has returned from Canada and says that he finds it necessary to make some modification in the schedule of free articles, proposing among others to limit flannels, blankets, etc., to those costing less than forty cents a pound, saying that we do not make the highest class of flannels and blankets in this country. I reply that the best blankets in the world are made in California. . . . He suggested some other modifications. . . . I told him that if the treaty were made, it would be necessary to provide that no higher duty should be imposed in Canada upon articles not free, the growth, produce, or manufacture of the United States, than upon like articles the growth, produce, or manufacture of Great Britain or any other country. . . . Brown left me to see Senator Boutwell and Benj. F. Butler and others relative to the free list of manufactured articles.

On June 11–17 Fish, Thornton, and Brown held protracted discussions of the treaty, arranging many details to suit Fish. Then on June 24, the morning after the adjournment of Congress, Fish's diary records the anti-climax: "Sir Edward Thornton and Mr. Brown call and inquire as to the present condition of the treaty. I tell them there has been no action, and the matter lies over until another session." But the ensuing session was hostile to any treaty. Fish talked with Brown on January 23, 1875, and writes that he "appears himself satisfied that there is no possibility of its being ratified." The Senate shortly thereafter signified its refusal.

The question of Rawlins' ownership of Cuban bonds is so important that I subjoin the entries in Fish's Diary which bear upon it:

July 26, 1875.— . . . [Bristow] . . . refers of his own accord to the President's allusion to the Cuban question at the Cabinet meeting, and asked if I knew that when General Rawlins died, $28,000 in Cuban bonds were found among his securities; that the President, who was his executor, had refused to put them on the inventory, and he believed had destroyed them. I told him that Rawlins' name for either $20,000 or $25,000 had been in a list shown me at the time by the Spanish Minister, whose detectives had the names of many parties to whom distribution of these bonds had been made.

Bristow says that he obtained this information in New York from a gentleman who knew the facts and whom I knew well, but who did not wish his name to appear.

November 5, 1875.— . . . While Secretary Robeson and myself were with the President, he (the President) referred to General Rawlins, stating that he was executor of his estate, and that at the time of his death, he requested General Smith to collect and make an inventory of all his property; that Smith has reported to him that he found a number of Cuban bonds, which he (General Grant) requested Smith to destroy, but some short time since, having occasion to look in the safe, he was surprised to find that instead of being destroyed, they had been kept.

To Robeson's inquiry "whether he had filed an inventory of the property," he said no, that with the exception of these bonds there was nothing except a house which Rawlins had purchased, but had not then paid for; that he himself had endorsed a note of Rawlins', in part payment of the house, but had never been called upon to pay it; whereupon Robeson remarked that the note by this time had been outlawed. . . .

The President seemed in doubt as to what should be done with the bonds. Robeson suggested that they be sold. I thought it would not do for the President, even as executor, to be selling such bonds, in which opinion he agreed. I then informed him that prior to Rawlins' death I had been told he had the bonds. . . . I further stated that Mr. Roberts had, more than once, produced a list of persons holding Cuban bonds; that they had been distributed very largely in this city, especially to representatives of the press and to some Senators and members of Congress, and others supposed to have influence. I said that I had been shown names in the list, but had never been shown the whole list. . . .

It is shown in a preceding chapter that the Cuban Junta contributed $20,000 in Cuban bonds to a fund for Rawlins' family. It would be pleasant to believe that this accounts for the bonds mentioned in these entries. But surely Grant would have known it had this been so; surely the fund for the family was not included in the estate delivered to Grant as executor; and surely the Spanish Minister's list refers to a time before the fund was raised.

The list of printed books and pamphlets used in preparing this work is too long for citation. A convenient general bibliography is published in pp. 453–460 of William B. Hesseltine's life of Grant; for diplomatic affairs it is supplanted by Samuel Flagg Bemis's thorough bibliographical volume on American foreign relations. The annual volumes of *Foreign Relations* (none exists for 1869) are indispensable. Fish lived long enough to help revise the proofs of Bancroft Davis's *Mr. Fish and the Alabama Claims* (1893) which therefore has special usefulness; he also helped pay for its publication. A fact little known even by students is that the annual volumes of the official Register of the State Department during Fish's service contain a thorough and careful list of all Executive and Congressional documents embodying material upon foreign relations. They are invaluable.

Fish's own papers offer the main foundation for this work. They include the voluminous diary 1869–1877, of perhaps 1,000,000 words; his letter-books 1839–1893, in number 48, filled with copies or impressions of his letters; a great mass of letters received, which had been carefully indexed under the direction of Mr. John Bassett Moore before they were turned over to me; two European diaries by Mrs. Fish and two by Mr. Fish; nine pocket memorandum-books 1883–1891; engagement-books, scrapbooks, and loose clippings. In addition, Mr. Fish preserved volumes containing copies of all his manuscript instructions to our envoys abroad, copies of his correspondence with foreign legations in Washington, and miscellaneous material bearing on his work as Secretary of State. His papers also contain all the printed books and reports issued by the Department of State during his eight years; manuscript volumes of materials on such erring diplomats as James Watson Webb and John Jay; and copies of the important papers of Bancroft Davis and others.

In addition to these materials, I have used the archives of the Department of State; the Dominion Archives in Ottawa; and the Foreign Office papers in the Public Record Office in London. Among collections of manuscripts which I have used during the five years spent on this book are the N. P. Banks Papers in Salem, Massachusetts; the Sumner Papers in Harvard University; the John V. L. Pruyn Papers in Albany; the Daniel Sickles Papers in the New York Public Library; the Fabens Papers, privately owned, through copies lent me by Mr. Graham C. Lovejoy; the Jay Cooke Papers in Philadelphia through copies lent me by Mr. Reinhard H. Luthin; and in the Library of Congress, the Bancroft Davis Papers; the Elihu B. Washburne Papers; the Grant Papers and Letterbooks; the Moran Diary; the Logan Papers; the William E. Chandler Papers; and the Jeremiah S. Black Papers. My efforts to obtain manuscript materials from the grandchildren of John Lothrop Motley and the son of Benjamin H. Bristow were unavailing.

Index